# PREFACE TO THE SECOND EDITION.

THE rapid sale of the first edition of this work, as well as its republication in America, is a satisfactory proof of the interest felt by the Christian public in the character and labours of Robert and James Haldane. The attempt to blend their lives together was not without its difficulties; but those who have travelled over their remarkable career, will easily perceive, that with the exception of the elder brother's mission to the Continent, there is scarcely any part of it, in which the history of the one is not associated with the history of the other. "Very fitly," says an able writer in the "Edinburgh Witness,"— "very fitly are their lives and labours recorded in one volume; for they were so beautiful in their unity, and indeed so much the complement of one another, that even in their Memoirs they could not be separated."

In regard to their earlier efforts for the extension of the Gospel in Scotland, the obliterating hand of time and the baneful influence of denominational prejudices, had perhaps, in some degree, effaced the record. "I thought," says a gifted and highly-venerated minister of Edinburgh, "that I knew the history, and could appreciate the character of both the brothers. But I find I had much to learn both of the men and of their work. Such an example as they were enabled to exhibit of simplicity of mind, godly sincerity of purpose, unreserved devotedness to the Saviour, and unwearied perseverance in his service, is indeed very rare, and is fitted to suggest very solemn reflections." To the same effect observes a minister at Birmingham, alike distinguished as a writer and an orator. "I was generally, and but generally, acquainted with the history and excellences of both, and of both I had formed an exalted opinion. But I knew not how excellent they were, and I have been led to glorify God in *them*. I have risen from the perusal of the work not only gratified but deeply humbled. What have any of us done for Christ, or are doing, compared with these servants of the Lord? They above us all could say, "For me to live is Christ." Another preacher, also remarkable for his genius and popular talents, expresses the same sentiments, in different words: "Certain I am that all true members of the Church Catholic will bend over the pages of their history with an interest approaching unto awe; for they so portray the self-sacrifice of two of Christ's disciples that a religious heart will not be able to ponder over them without much deep self-reproach." Similar feelings have been expressed by many eminent servants of Christ, both in this country and on the Continent. The following sentences are quoted from the letter of a well-known layman of the Church of England, himself a renowned champion of Protestant truth, who, like the Haldanes, commenced his career upon the ocean:—"To both indeed," says Mr. J. E. Gordon, "I had assigned a very honourable standing in the front rank of Christian enterprise, but I find I was very ignorant of their actual position. They present a very remarkable illustration of the wisdom of God in the adaptation of instruments to the work which they are destined to perform. At no period in the history of Scotland since the Reformation, had the spiritual vitality of her Church stagnated into a more apathetic and impracticable condition than it had

# The Lives of
# Robert and James Haldane

Painted by Colvin Smith, S.A.                    Engraved by G. Zobel.

*J. A. Haldane*

ÆT. 77.

From the Original in the possession of Alexander Haldane of the Inner Temple, Barrister at Law.

# The Lives of
# Robert and James
# Haldane

ALEXANDER HALDANE

The Banner of Truth Trust

THE BANNER OF TRUTH TRUST
3 Murrayfield Road, Edinburgh EH12 6EL
PO Box 621, Carlisle, Pennsylvania 17013, USA

\*

First published 1852
First Banner of Truth edition 1990
ISBN 0 85151 567 3

\*

Printed in Great Britain at
The Alden Press, Oxford

# THE LIVES

OF

# ROBERT HALDANE OF AIRTHREY,

AND OF HIS BROTHER,

# JAMES ALEXANDER HALDANE.

BY ALEXANDER HALDANE, ESQ.,

OF THE INNER TEMPLE, BARRISTER-AT-LAW.

---

" There is no man that hath left house, or lands, for my sake, and the Gospel's, but he shall receive an hundredfold now in this time, with persecutions, . . . and in the world to come eternal life." MARK x. 29, 30.—*See Address to the Public in* 1800, *by R. Haldane.*

" This is the last day of the year, and the last letter I shall write this year. My life has been wonderfully preserved, much beyond the usual course of nature. Goodness and mercy have followed me all the days of my life; and without the shadow of boasting, I can add, I shall dwell in the house of the Lord for ever."—*Extract from a letter of J. A. Haldane, December* 31, 1850.

---

THIRD EDITION.

LONDON:

HAMILTON, ADAMS, AND CO., PATERNOSTER-ROW;

AND W. WHYTE AND CO., EDINBURGH.

1853.

ALEXANDER MACINTOSH,
PRINTER,
GREAT NEW-STREET, LONDON.

at the period when the two Haldanes were summoned forth, and it required the blast and the wedge to *rive* asunder and drive asunder the granitic resistance which it opposed to the introduction of truth. But He who had measured the depth and intensity of that resistance was at no loss for instruments fitted to overcome it. Like those iron-headed steamers which are now employed in polar navigation, to plough their way through field-floe and pack-ice, these two gallant, stately, and formidable vessels, with their prows sheathed in heaven-proof armour, and the fire of the Spirit in their bosoms, not merely cut a passage for the long-imprisoned ark of the Gospel, but, moreover, towed her into clear water. Or, to use a different illustration, two men of family, fortune, influence, high character, indomitable courage, deep piety, and disinterested patriotism, are selected for the performance of a work which seemed to bid defiance to the power of human agency. They are hardened in carnage and storm, until, like the highly-tempered springs of a chronometer, they are qualified to become the *primum mobile* of a machinery, whose movements should vibrate through all Scotland, and set to her benighted and bewildered Christianity the right hour of the day."

Since the publication of the first edition, the Author has had the opportunity of visiting Geneva, Montauban, and Toulouse, and of witnessing the unabated affection and even increasing reverence which attach to the memory and the name of Robert Haldane. In conversing with MM. Gaussen, Merle D'Aubigné, Guers, Marzials, Chabrand, and Courtois, he has gleaned several interesting additional facts, whilst M. Frederic Monod, of Paris, has also most kindly furnished a few personal soüvenirs of the work of God begun at Geneva during the winter of 1816-17.

Some new testimonies to the extent and the results of Mr.

James Haldane's itinerating labours in Scotland will be found scattered through the volume, still further illustrating the statements of the former edition.

It was not the object of this work to exalt the men, but rather to exhibit the singleness of their aim and their stedfast adherence to the Word of God, as an example to others. It is, therefore, only needful to repeat, that if it shall in any measure present the two brothers such as they were, in faith and love and self-devoted zeal, it will have answered its design, and may, it is hoped, tend to promote the glory of God, by stimulating others to follow them, even as they followed Christ.

*18th November,* 1852.
    *Westbourne-terrace, London.*

---

Much regret has been expressed that the volume contains no print of Robert Haldane, but it was mentioned in the first edition that there is not a portrait from which one could be made. He would never sit for his picture, and two or three caricatures or likenesses, done from memory, at an immense disadvantage, and especially one of the latter by Dr. Malan, although they recal the original to those who knew him, are inaccurate in details and convey to a stranger a very erroneous impression. James Haldane, during the period of his greatest popularity, resisted all overtures made to him, both in London and Edinburgh, to allow his picture to be taken; but after his brother's death, he yielded to the importunity of his family, but not till he was approaching the great age of fourscore. The portrait by Colvin Smith, from which the print prefixed to this volume is taken, is much admired, both as a likeness and a work of art. Of him, too, there was a likeness, taken in the pulpit, about the beginning of the century, which has been republished in the collection of Kaye's caricatures of celebrated characters.

# CONTENTS.

## CHAPTER I.

## CHAPTER II.

### [1780—1794.]

## CHAPTER III.

### [1785—1795.]

# CHAPTER VII.

## [1797.]

# CHAPTER VIII.

## [1797—8.]

# CHAPTER IX.

## [1798.]

# CHAPTER X.

## [1799.]

## CHAPTER XIV.

### [1802—3.]

## CHAPTER XV.

### [1804—5.]

## CHAPTER XVI.

### [1799—1810.]

Progressive changes the result of circumstances—Mr. Ewing's zeal

## CHAPTER XVII.

### [1810—1819.]

## CHAPTER XVIII.

### [1816—17.]

# CHAPTER XXII.

## [1826—1833.]

# CHAPTER XXIII.

## [1828—1833.]

# CHAPTER XXIV.

## [1824—1833.]

## CHAPTER XXVIII.

[1848—1851.]

# THE LIVES

OF

## ROBERT HALDANE OF AIRTHREY;

AND OF HIS BROTHER,

## JAMES ALEXANDER HALDANE.

## CHAPTER I.

THEIR BIRTH AND ANCESTRY—GLENEAGLES—ANECDOTES—
THEIR PARENTS—THEIR GUARDIANS—EARLY CHARAC-
TERISTICS.

ROBERT HALDANE was born on the 28th of February, 1764, in his father's house, on the north side of Queen Ann-street, Cavendish-square, London. His younger brother, James Alexander Haldane, was born at Dundee, on the 14th of July, 1768, within a fortnight after his father's death.

Both on their father's and their mother's side, they were descended from an ancient Perthshire family, for many centuries possessors of the free barony of Gleneagles, a valley in the Ochil hills, opening upon the moor of Tullibardine, and the fertile plains of Strathearn, towards the distant Grampians, whose towering summits bound the prospect. In old charters, in the rolls of Parliament, and in other public documents, by the caprice of orthography, the family name is variously written Halden, Haldane, Hadden, or Hauden. Of Norse origin, it is still common in Denmark, and from Haldan Hill, near Exeter, to Halden Rig, near Kelso, the Danish chiefs, who were driven beyond the Humber by King Alfred, have indented many local

B

and unmistakeable traces of their leader's name, as mentioned by the Saxon chroniclers. There is no doubt that the lands of Halden Rig were called after the Northern warrior. But, passing by the mist-enveloped legends of a barbarous age, and approaching the light of modern records, when surnames became hereditary, it is on record that, three centuries later, a younger son of the border family of Halden, near Kelso, migrated into Perthshire, and married the heiress of Gleneagles, adopting the armorial bearings of that family, instead of his own, but retaining his surname, as derived from his paternal lands. In Scotland, oral tradition runs into the deep and far recesses of legendary antiquity. Its written documents are of comparatively modern date. "Nowhere," says a great Scotch antiquarian, Mr. Riddell,—"nowhere is ancestry more prized or paraded than with us, and yet in no country are the means of elucidating it so scanty." In proof of this, a charter of the lands of Frandie, forming part of the Gleneagles estate, granted in the twelfth century to Roger de Halden, by King William the Lyon, and still in possession of the family, is noticed by Sir James Dalrymple, in his Collections (page 392), as amongst the earliest extant.

Rather more than a hundred years later, Aylmer de Haldane, of Gleneagles, in Strathearn, is found amongst the barons, who, in 1296, swore fealty to Edward the First of England; and Nisbet, in his "Critical and Historical Remarks" upon the Ragman Roll, observes that the Haldanes were "even then barons of considerable consequence," adding, "the house of Gleneagles have vouchers for instructing their antiquity beyond most families in Perthshire." It would be alike tedious and unprofitable to trace their descent, from that period to the beginning of last century, through seventeen successive marriages, with the noble or baronial families of Graham, Arnott, Mar, Seton, Menteith, Montrose, Lawson, Mar (2), Perth, Glencairn, Hume, Tullibardine, Wemyss, Lovat, Grant, Strathallan, and Erskine of Alva. In fact, there would be nothing very remarkable to arrest attention, for they have left behind them little more than the record of their names, their knighthood, or their offices; and in this, as in most other genealogies, we are reminded of what Sir Thomas Brown quaintly observes : " There is no antidote against the oblivion of time; generations pass while some trees stand, and old families last not three oaks. The greater part of men must be content to be as though they had not been, to be found in the register of God, not in the record of men."

The most eminent of the mediæval Barons of Gleneagles was Sir John Haldane, who held, in very troublous times, several of the highest offices in the kingdom, and became successively Ambassador of James the Third to the Court of Denmark, Master of the King's Household, Sheriff Principal of Edinburgh, until, finally, as " Lord Justice-General of Scotland beyond the Forth," he attained a dignity next to that of the Lord Chancellor. In 1460 he married Agnes Menteith, of Ruskie, a descendant of the old Earls of Menteith, and one of the two co-heiresses of the half of the lands and honours of her maternal great-grandsire, Duncan, last of the ancient Saxon Earls of Levenax or Lennox, who was beheaded on Stirling Castle, in 1424, with his son-in-law, the late Regent Albany, and his own three sons.

This marriage entailed upon the Gleneagles family long and arduous litigation with Lord Darnley, who finally established his claim to the peerage and one-half of the lands, in right of his grandmother, the Duchess of Albany, whose priority in age, as the eldest daughter of the Earl of Lennox, had been disputed by Sir John Haldane.*

In 1482, when the Duke of Gloucester, afterwards Richard the Third, invaded Scotland, Sir John Haldane was appointed, with George Lord Seton, Alexander Ramsay of Dalhousie, ancestor of the Marquis, and Robert Logan of Restalrig, " joint Captains, Chieftains, Keepers, and Governors of the

---

* See the History of the Partition of the Lennox, by Mark Napier, Esq., a descendant of the celebrated inventor of Logarithms, and as such from the second co-heiress of Menteith, who divided with Agnes Haldane the other half of the Lennox. See also the learned Reply of John Riddell, Esq., the eminent Scottish legal antiquary.

town of Berwick, and to defend it against the invasion of our old enemies of England." The campaign was speedily decided by the defection of Douglas (Bell the Cat) Earl of Angus, and the other rebellious Barons, at the Bridge of Lauder; and Berwick, left unprotected, was forced to capitulate to the Plantagenet, never more to be retaken or restored. Sir John died in 1493, and was succeeded by his son, Sir James, who, shortly before his death in 1505, was, at a time of national alarm, nominated by King James the Fourth to be keeper of the King's Castle of Dunbar. His successor, another Sir John, had scarcely won his gilded spurs when he fell, in early manhood, on the fatal field of Flodden, along with a great part of the chivalry of Scotland, rallying round their rash but gallant monarch.

It was soon after these times of turbulence and war that the translation of the Scriptures into the vulgar tongue, was preparing, both for Scotland and England, a moral and religious revolution more complete and decisive than any which had yet occurred. On the 4th February, 1526, the first copy of the New Testament, translated and printed abroad in English, arrived in Britain. From that day may be traced the increasing progress of the Protestant Reformation, and in no country did it take a deeper or firmer root than in Scotland. In the vain attempt of Rome to arrest the circulation of the Bible, to stop the preaching and crush the truths of the Gospel, the whole nation was convulsed. In that long and arduous struggle the Haldanes seem to have taken a consistent part, on the side of religious freedom. The name of Gleneagles appears amongst the Lords of the Congregation, and during the reign of James the Sixth they stood by the Protestant cause, both in its prosperity and adversity. In 1585, when the Earl of Angus and the other banished Lords returned from England, to take advantage of the popular indignation roused by the persecuting acts of the Earl of Arran, the Laird of Gleneagles is mentioned by Calderwood as prominent in what was called "the raid of Stirling." He was a prisoner in the town when it was attacked, but was enabled to join the assailants, and assisted in the armed remonstrance with the King, which brought back the exiled ministers and drove Arran and his abettors into disgrace and banishment. It is mentioned, that when Sir William Stewart, Colonel of the Royal Guard, and brother of the obnoxious Earl, was driven back towards the Castle from the west port of Stirling, he was so hotly followed, " that Mr. James Haldane, brother-german to the Laird of Gleneagles, overtook him; and as he was laying hands on him, was shot by the Colonel's servant, Joshua Henderson." *

In the following century another Knight of the family was, in 1650, a leader in the Presbyterian army of the congregation opposed to Cromwell, and fell in the rout at Dunbar. His lady received from one who alleged that he was his messenger his own ring (which is still preserved), with an assurance that he was safe, but detained with other prisoners of rank in the castle of a nobleman near the battle-field. The chiefs said to be his companions in captivity were found as described, but Sir John had not been amongst them, and returned no more.

He was succeeded by Sir John Haldane, the last of the Knights of Gleneagles in the male line. In truth, the country was becoming more civilized and less turbulent, so that war ceased to be the chief occupation of those not compelled to till the soil. The change in the times was also manifested in the family arrangements, by which he transgressed the feudal notions of the exclusive rights of primogeniture, and in order to favour a mother's partiality for a younger son, occasioned the separation of a large section of the Menteith or Lanrick estates from those of Gleneagles.†

His successor, Mungo Haldane, who derived his not very euphonious Christian name from the ducal house of Murray, was a Member of the Scottish Parliament; obtained a charter

---

* 4 Calderwood, 390.

† This offshoot of the Gleneagles stock only remained at Lanrick for two generations. Patrick, the first proprietor, died young, having married Miss Dundas, of Newliston, who was, through her mother, one of the younger co-heiresses of the original stock of Halden of Haldenrig, in the South. The eldest co-heiress of that family was married to John, first

of his lands from Charles the Second, reciting his own services to the Crown and those of his progenitors; and is mentioned by Nisbet, in his account of the gorgeous procession of the Lord Chancellor the Duke of Rothes' public funeral in 1681, as bearing the banner of his relative, the Earl of Tullibardine and first Marquis of Athol.

He died in 1685. His son, John Haldane, served in the Scottish and British Parliaments for nearly forty years, and occupied a conspicuous place in public affairs, both at the Revolution and at the Union.

From the time of Cromwell the change in the history of Scotland becomes more decided. The Reformation had been the grand crisis of the nation, but, during its glorious progress, there was a long and deadly struggle between the despotic tendencies of the Crown, the turbulence of the old feudal Barons, and the civilizing influences of advancing Christianity. The strong bond of Protestantism, with its common dangers and common blessings, had been gradually drawing together the great mass of the Christianity, the intelligence, and the respectability of the English and Scottish nations, for more than a century before its consummation in the Act of Union of 1707.

Earl of Stair, who in her right acquired the lands of Newliston. Patrick of Lanrick left two younger sons, one of whom was a Professor at St. Andrew's, and was burned to death whilst reading in bed. John, his eldest, took part in the rebellion of 1745, but contrived to escape forfeiture, and returned, after many years of exile, to die at Lanrick, in 1765, at the age of 85. He survived his two sons, but left six daughters, of whom five were married and have numerous descendants. James Oswald, Esq., of Auchencruive, is the male representative of the eldest daughter of John Haldane of Lanrick. The Rev. James Haldane Stewart, Vicar of Limpsfield, is descended from the Lanrick family, his grandfather, Stewart of Ardshiel, who commanded the right wing of the rebel army at Culloden, having married a grand-daughter of Patrick. Mr. Stewart of Ardshiel on one occasion fought with and disarmed Rob Roy. Sir Walter Scott has borrowed the incidents of this adventure, giving the catastrophe a turn more suited to the dignity of his hero. It is the scene at the clachan of Aberfoyle. The warlike ancestry of the Vicar of Limpsfield strikingly contrasts with the gentleness of his own beautiful Christian character.

At this period, John Haldane, of Gleneagles, sat as one of the four Barons for the county of Perth in the last Scottish Parliament. He had been previously representative for Dumbartonshire, and, in 1688, sat in the Convention Parliament. He was also the first Member for the county of Perth in the first British House of Commons, and one of the Commissioners for settling the equivalents at the Union. He was a man of great energy and ability, a good speaker,* and much occupied with public affairs. One of his sisters was married to Sir William Murray, of Ochtertyre, and another to Mr. Smythe, of Methven. He was himself twice married, first to Mary, third daughter of David Drummond Lord Maderty, elder brother of the first Viscount Strathallan; secondly, to Helen, only daughter of Sir Charles Erskine, of Alva, ancestor of the Earls of Rosslyn, and grandson of John, Earl of Mar. He had a numerous family by both marriages. His eldest son, Mungo Haldane, was successively M.P. for the counties of Perth and Stirling, and died in 1757, at the age of seventy-three, unmarried. He was well remembered by a tenant of the Gleneagles estate, who lived to be more than a hundred years old, and who was known to many of the present generation. He used to tell how the Laird put an end to Sunday trading in the neighbourhood, by means not very consonant with the modern voluntary principle. It seems that Sunday trafficking was then prevalent in Scotland, in consequence of the packmen, or itinerant hawkers, bringing their goods for sale to the church-doors on the Lord's-day. As

* In "Wodrow's Correspondence" we find the following anecdote:— "The Septennial Bill is passed the Commons by a vast plurality. There is a story here of Mr. Haldane, of Gleneagles, and one Snell, an English gentleman. Mr. Haldane had a very handsome speech in favour of the Bill. Mr. Snell said he did not much wonder to hear that gentleman and others of his nation speak after that fashion, for their nation was sold and enslaved,—they would have their neighbours so dealt with; whereon were great heats. Sir David Dalrymple (of Hailes, and grandfather of the celebrated Sir D. Dalrymple, Lord Hailes) said the gentleman who spoke (Mr. Snell) knew well where he spoke, and that the House was his sanctuary. Others said, more plainly, that he durst not speak so without doors. Mr. Snell was brought to the bar, and to crave pardon, May 1st, 1716."—Vol. ii., p. 165.

chief magistrate in the neighbourhood, the Baron of Gleneagles issued an order prohibiting the practice. On the following Sunday he did not happen himself to go to Blackford Church, but, meeting his servants returning, he inquired whether the packmen had obeyed his mandate. Being informed that they had not, the old tenant used to tell, with great emphasis, how " the Laird clapped his hand on his sword," and declared that if he lived over another Sabbath, he would make the packmen repent of their perverseness. Accordingly, on the following Sunday, he himself went to the church, and, finding the packmen assembled as usual and spreading out their goods for sale, he drew out his sword and scattered them in an instant. Having pursued them down the hill as they fled in trepidation before him, the irate and portly Baron returned to the church-gates and tossed their wares into the adjoining lake. This exercise of a "rigour beyond the law," which in those days was not very nicely weighed, had the desired effect, and Sunday trading has never been again attempted near Gleneagles, from that day to the present. Mungo Haldane was succeeded by his next brother, Patrick, an able, active, and bustling politician, who, in his youth, was Professor of History at St. Andrew's; then M.P. for the St. Andrew's Burghs; then Solicitor-General; a Royal Commissioner for selling the forfeited estates; and at one time appointed a Lord of Session.* He survived for ten

---

* This appointment was made in 1721, during his father's life-time, and gave rise to a curious lawsuit as to the right of the Crown to appoint a Judge or Senator of the College of Justice, " without the concurrence of the College itself." The matter was carried by appeal to the House of Lords (See " Robertson's Appeal Cases," 422), and decided in favour of the Crown; but Patrick Haldane's right was not insisted on, and he received another appointment. He was objected to as not being a practising advocate, but the pamphlets which appeared on the occasion, one of them attributed to the celebrated Duncan Forbes, of Culloden, indicate strong political and personal rancour. Mr. Patrick Haldane is, amongst other things, not only charged with bribery at his elections, but with having induced his younger brother, James Haldane, then under age, the grandfather of the subjects of this Memoir, to assist in carrying off and imprisoning hostile voters, on pretended charges of high treason and Jacobitism.

years his only son, Brigadier-General George Haldane, of the Coldstream Guards, who was also Member of Parliament for the Dundee and Forfar Burghs, and died, in 1759, Governor of Jamaica.

Many ancient Scottish families were ruined by the change in their style of living and expenditure, consequent on being called to attend a Parliament, sitting in London instead of Edinburgh. Patrick Haldane's electioneering expenses, and those of his son, had not been compensated by their public appointments. When, in the same year, he succeeded his elder brother and survived his son, he found himself encumbered with debt and unable to retain his estates with comfort. Under these circumstances Gleneagles, being then unentailed, might have passed, like Lanrick, entirely out of the family, had it not been purchased by a younger brother of the half-blood, who had just returned from India with a large fortune, being the first Scotchman who ever commanded an East India Company's ship. This Captain Robert Haldane married a daughter of Sir John Oglander, of Nunwells, in the Isle of Wight, and becoming himself M.P. for the Stirling Burghs, is referred to in the Letters of Junius as the patron of Bradshaw. He died at Airthrey, on the 1st of January, 1768, without leaving any surviving issue, and was buried at Gleneagles, by his own desire, under the shade of four majestic spruce-firs, which he had himself planted in front of the old chapel near the ruins of the castle.

His elder brother was still living at his death, as well as his nephew, Captain James Haldane, the only son of another brother. But Captain Robert having acquired both the estates of Airthrey and Gleneagles by purchase, unfettered by any entail, they were entirely at his own disposal, and he determined to divide them. To Captain James Haldane, who had a good fortune of his own, and was averse to a residence on the northern side of the Ochils, he left the estate of Airthrey, with its southern exposure, beautifully sloping down into the Carse of Stirling, charged with a debt of 14,000*l.*; whilst the lands of Gleneagles and of Trinity Gask, charged with the remainder of his debts, were, in the first instance, entailed on the male descendants of his two sisters of the full blood, with remainder " to my nephew, Captain James Haldane, of the Duke of Albany East Indiaman." It was thus upon condition of merging his own name and arms, and assuming those of Haldane, that George Cockburn, only son of Mrs. Margaret Cockburn, of the family of Ormistown, in East Lothian, succeeded to Gleneagles, but on his death and the failure of his male issue, in 1799, it devolved on the celebrated Admiral Viscount Duncan, as being then the eldest surviving son of the entailer's other sister of the full blood, Helen Haldane, wife of Alexander Duncan, of Lundie, and also the maternal grandmother of the subjects of these Memoirs.

Their father was the only son of Colonel James Haldane, who married Margaret Pye, a lady belonging to a well-connected family then resident in the county of Durham, some of whom held considerable preferment in the Church of England.

Colonel James Haldane, like the rest of his generation, was a man of great stature and physical strength, and served from 1715 to 1741 in that squadron of the Royal Horse now known as the 2d Regiment of Life Guards. He embarked from Portsmouth on the Carthagena expedition, in command of General Guise's regiment of Infantry, but was obliged to resign on account of bad health, and died at sea on the 9th December, 1742, near Jamaica.

On the 15th December, 1762, their only son, Captain James Haldane, married his first cousin, Katherine, daughter of Alexander Duncan, of Lundie, and Helen Haldane, commonly called Lady Lundie, by the courtesy of Scotland then allowed to the wife of a minor baron. Of this marriage there were three children; namely—1, Robert, who succeeded his father in the estate of Airthrey; 2, Helen, born in 1765, who died in childhood; and, 3, James Alexander Haldane, his youngest and posthumous son.

FROM THEIR BIRTH TO THE DEATH OF THEIR MOTHER.

[1764—1774.]

A FAMILY history of six centuries and more than twenty generations, has been compressed into a very narrow space. Such
matters have in them more of private curiosity than public
interest. The quality or exploits of a remote ancestry belong
to the passing things of time, and are but bubbles on its rapid
stream, rolling down into the gulphs of oblivion. But the
character, the instructions, the example, and the prayers of
Christian parents belong to the things that are immortal, on
which God himself has been often pleased to suspend the
destinies of children. The means as well as the end are under
the control of Him who gives no account of his matters, but
determines all things by the council of his own will. Occasionally He sees fit, in a wonderful and unexpected manner, to
assert the sovereignty of his electing grace; yet for the most
part it will be found, that He works by instruments, and puts
especial honour on the use of his own appointed ordinances.
It was the privilege of the two brothers to be enabled, practically
to sympathize with the sentiments expressed in the noble lines
of Cowper, when he exclaims—

> " My boast is not, that I deduce my birth
> From loins enthroned, or rulers of the earth,
> But higher far my proud pretensions rise,
> The son of parents passed into the skies !"

Of their father, Captain James Haldane, his elder son knew but
little, and the younger nothing, except from the testimony of
others. He is reported to have been a man of much worth,
of popular manners, good sense, and ability, very generally
respected and beloved. It is related of him, that at sea he was
remarkable for his attention to moral discipline, and particularly
for putting down profane swearing. The late Mr. Scrimgeour,
of Tealing, and a son of Mr. Callender, of Craigforth, who
both sailed with him, used to tell how he cured his midshipmen of this profane and, as it has been justly termed,
" profitless vice," by compelling any one who thus transgressed

to carry a clog fastened round his ancle, for the remainder of the watch. He was also more particular than was then common at sea, in accustoming the young men to act like gentlemen, and when inculcating the duty of politeness, would jocularly remark, that he had himself spoiled a laced hat in taking it off to two French officers, whom he had brought home as prisoners from India, during Lord Clive's wars. He completed his last voyage at the close of 1767, and was on the eve of being elected an East India Director, when an inflammatory sore-throat, said to have been improperly treated, and ending in violent fever, carried him off, after a few days' illness, on the 30th June, 1768. He died whilst on a visit to his father-in-law, at the old house of Lundie (now Camperdown), near Dundee, where he had arrived a few days before. When asked, shortly before his death, as to his hopes for eternity, his reply, "I have full confidence in Jesus," indicated the simplicity as well as the sincerity of his faith. His attached and afflicted widow was not, therefore, left to sorrow as those without hope, but it was a severe shock to her health, and brought on her confinement nearly two months before it was expected. It took place at Dundee, on the 14th of July, just a fortnight after her bereavement, and, combining the name of the husband whom she had lost, with that of her father, who survived, she called her infant son James Alexander.

In order to be near her parents, Mrs. Haldane took up her residence at Dundee, in a house which belonged to the celebrated George Dempster, so well known as a leading Member of Parliament, and a friend of Mr. Fox, who had named him as one of the Commissioners of his famous India Bill. It was a large, old baronial mansion, now pulled down, pleasantly situated in a garden sloping down to the Tay. An ancient and well-remembered pear-tree, which still remains, was visited by her younger son not many years before his death.

Mrs. Haldane belonged to a family in which there had been much true religion.* Her father was distinguished as a strenu-

* An ancestor of the Lundie family, William Duncan, of Sea Side, left in his own handwriting a narrative of a remarkable preservation in his youth from shipwreck in the North Seas, in 1631, after being tossed about

ous supporter of the Protestant succession, and, as Provost of Dundee, did good service to the Government during the rebellion in 1745. Towards the close of his life he left the fine old family residence at Lundie Castle, to reside nearer the town, at Gourdie House, a name for which his eldest son substituted that of Lundie, but which was destined to be again changed to Camperdown upon the erection of a new and splendid edifice by his grandson. His second daughter, Mrs. Haldane, was herself a decided Christian. " She lived," said her eldest son, " very near to God, and much grace was given to her." When left a widow, it became her chief concern to bring up her children in " the nurture and admonition of the Lord." From their infancy she laboured to instil into their minds a sense of the importance of eternity, particularly impressing upon them the necessity of prayer, and teaching them to commit to memory and understand psalms, portions of the Shorter Catechism, and of Scripture.

" Her instructions," says her youngest son, in a memorandum found amongst his papers, were so far useful, that even when she was not present I made a conscience of prayer. What she said concerning sin and punishment also produced a considerable impression on my mind. I was desirous of avoiding sin, yet frequently committed those sins to which children are particularly exposed. I well knew that this was wrong, and

for forty days in a small boat. He thus begins : " My Lord God has put it into my heart to leave a record, how that he has been so extraordinarily merciful to me by sea and land,—how in many dangers, and from many perils, he did work my deliverance, and particularly in that miraculous one hereafter described ; that my successors may think on it, and, with God's assistance, it may be a mean to teach them to be humble and thankful to God for having so protected and preserved me, and made his fatherly love in so many ways known to me." At the conclusion of the narrative he mentions his first meeting with his grandfather after his escape, and then with his mother, and adds, " Who was very glad to see me, and thanked my Lord God for my preservation, who has been ever since very gracious to me. Blessed be his name, and the praises which I give are due unto him, desiring all those who shall succeed me not to be unthankful to God for his great mercies."

having been told that infants would go to heaven, I regretted that I had not died before I had sense to discern what was wrong."

He proceeds: " My mother died when I was vèry young, I believe under six, yet I am convinced that the early impression made on my mind by her care was never entirely effaced ; and to this, as an eminent means in the hand of God, I impute any serious thoughts which, in the midst of my folly, would sometimes intrude upon my mind, as well as that still small voice of conscience, which afterwards led me to see that all below was vanity without an interest in that inheritance which can never fade away."   He adds : " I mention this more particularly, because it may lead Christian parents to sow in hope the seed of Divine truth in the minds of their children, and may prevent their considering their efforts unavailing even where the things which they have taught seem to have been uttered in vain.   No means of grace is, I apprehend, more, perhaps none is so much, countenanced of God as early religious instruction."

The instructions of this devoted mother were not weakened or counteracted, as often happens, by apparent inconsistency.   Her life was a life of practical godliness and of cheerful trust in the Saviour.   Often when she had seen her children in bed, and supposed that they were asleep, she was overheard by them, and particularly by her elder son, on her knees by their bed-side, earnestly praying that the Lord would be pleased to guide them through that world which she felt that she was herself soon to leave ; that their lives might be devoted to His service upon earth ; and, finally, that they might be brought to His everlasting kingdom.

She died in 1774, of an attack of illness commencing with a cold which she caught when on a visit at Ferntower, near Crieff. Her medical attendant, Dr. Willison, although himself an avowed unbeliever, emphatically declared that such a death-bed was enough to make one in love with death.   It was another observation of the same physician, himself the son of the celebrated divine, and a melancholy example of his own remark, that grace was a very extraordinary moral phenomenon; that there was no doubt either of its existence or of its influence, or of the fact that it ran in families; but that it resembled certain constitutional diseases which are hereditary, and yet overleap particular generations. He was thus, in effect, bearing an unconscious testimony to the degenerating tendencies of our fallen and corrupt nature, as well as to the unfettered sovereignty and electing love of God. Shortly before she expired she was asked if she would like once more to see her children, but she declined, saying that it would only agitate her; that she had been enabled implicitly to surrender them into the hands of God, and she would rather leave them there. Her faith was strong, not only for herself, but for them; and that faith was not disappointed.

She was laid in her husband's grave, at Lundie, in the burial-place of the Duncans, near the spot where the ashes of her brother, the great Admiral, now also repose. The church-yard is situated in a retired and romantic spot on the slope of one extremity of the Sidlaw range, just below the Hill of Lundie, from whose commanding summit the eye wanders over one of the most extensive and picturesque prospects of varied magnificence and beauty. The Carse of Gowrie on the one side, and Strathmore on the other, with an array of castles, towns, churches, plantations, lakes, and streams, are bounded to the east by the ocean, to the south by the Lowland hills, and to the north-west by the wooded rocks of Dunkeld and the rugged mountains of Athol, and Braemar.

FROM THEIR MOTHER'S DEATH, IN 1774, TO THEIR GOING
TO SEA.

[1774—1785.]

WHEN death, which had previously robbed them of the guardianship of a father, now deprived them of the tender solicitude of their mother, the three children were scarcely old enough fully to appreciate the extent of their loss. The elder brother was ten years old, his younger scarcely six, whilst their only sister was eight. The union of parent and child is a bond, of which it has been finely said, by a celebrated orator, that it strengthens with life, acquires vigour from the understanding, and is sealed and rendered perfect in the community of love. Once severed, it is a tie too sacred and holy to be renewed. But, in the present bereavement, there were several compensations to be found in the watchful solicitude, the unremitting affection, and the superior qualifications of the relatives who undertook the guardianship of the youthful orphans.

Their grandmother, Lady Lundie, had, after her husband's death, resided with her daughter on the banks of the Tay, at Dundee. She had been, in her younger years, famed for her beauty, not only in Scotland, but in the gay circles of Bath, at the period of its greatest renown. From these scenes of pleasurable excitement, she had, however, long retired, and at the time of her daughter's death the care of her grandchildren became her chief occupation during the peaceful retirement of her remaining years. Her eldest son, John, a young man of great promise, died early, in China, in the service of the East India Company. Her next son, Colonel Alexander Duncan, married his second cousin, Miss Smythe, of Methven, but had no family, and was now a war-worn veteran, retired from the army, after having earned considerable distinction by his good and gallant service in the rebellion in 1745, in the campaigns in Flanders, and in Canada. The youngest son, Adam, the first Viscount Duncan, had also served for more than a quarter of a century in different parts of the world. At this time, and until the breaking out of a new war, he was enjoying the repose of peace, and, with his mother, resided in Mrs. Haldane's house and managed all their affairs.

Both uncles had seen much of the world, and therefore knew more of the value of a good education than most of the Scottish gentry of that period. The learning of the two boys was well attended to. At home they had a superior resident tutor, the Reverend Dr. Fleming, who afterwards became one of the ministers of Edinburgh; and they were also sent to the grammar-school at Dundee, that they might at the same time mingle with other boys, and profit by the stimulus of competition. James was destined for the sea, and it was judged important to push him rapidly forward in his education; but his progress was speedily arrested by a dangerous fever, which long confined him to the house, and of which he nearly died. An anecdote concerning him, which relates to this period, used to be told by his aunt, Lady Duncan. He was a boy of great spirit, and recited poetry with sentiment and animation. The Admiral had taught him, amongst other things, to repeat the celebrated speech of Cassius, in Addison's "Cato," beginning:—

> "My voice is still for war!
> What! can a Roman Senate long debate
> Which of the two to choose,—slavery or death?"

To enable him to give due effect to this piece of declamation, which certainly does not altogether accord with the views of the Peace Society, his uncle was accustomed to place him on a side-table, and after his task had been accomplished, make him jump down. During the delirium of his fever, whenever his uncle came to see him he immediately started up, and began, with great emphasis,

> "My voice is still for war!"

In the year 1776 his sister's health, which had never been strong, finally gave way. It was then customary in Scotland, as it is still in Switzerland, to resort to places in the country "for the goat's whey." Mrs. Haldane had for one summer occupied the house of Kinnaird, in Strathtay, near Dunkeld,* and Lady Lundie now took her grand-daughter to the Kallender of Crieff, in Strathearn, where she hired a house, near Ochter-tyre, the residence of Sir William Murray, to whom she was

---

* Her elder son had here a narrow escape from being kicked to death. One of the carriage horses was rather violent in the stable, and, knowing this, in a sportive mood he put down a stick from the loft and touched it on the back. The animal was so much excited, that he plunged and kicked till the loose flooring of the loft, being very low, was shaken to pieces, and the youthful author of this piece of mischief was himself knocked about like a ball, and expected every moment to fall down amongst the horses. Providentially he was unhurt.

doubly related, both as a Haldane and a Duncan. Whilst residing there the two boys were much at Ochtertyre, and found great enjoyment, in riding about on their ponies, or, attended by their tutor, in fishing for perch in the lovely lake of Monivaird, embosomed amidst the hanging woods and romantic hills which embellish those beautiful pleasure-grounds. The renowned General, Sir George Murray, was then a boy, under five years of age, probably dreaming as little of those fields of blood in which he was hereafter to be engaged, as did his young cousins of the more peaceful warfare they were to accomplish.

The brothers were much attached to their drooping sister, and it was long afterwards remembered how James, whose warm, affectionate disposition was remarked from his boyhood, never took his ride without dismounting to gather for her the blue-bells and the cotton-flowers, growing on the wild heaths and moors of Strathearn. A little while before Helen's death, she was taken to Edinburgh by her aunt, Miss Duncan, for medical advice, but it was of no avail. She died on the 11th of July, 1776. The Admiral was with them at the time, and Colonel Duncan was sent for, so that once more, at their early age, the orphan boys stood beside their two uncles at another funeral, when their only sister was committed to the dust, in the vault of the Murrays, in the ancient and romantic church-yard of Monivaird, which is now included in the park of Ochtertyre, and, with its little chapel, exclusively used as the mausoleum of the family.*

There is a story concerning their boyhood which belongs to this period. They were spending a day at Ferntower with their uncle and tutor, who were together, when the Admiral, turning towards the window, suddenly started up with an exclamation of mingled alarm and indignation. It happened that his carriage was standing before the door, although the horses had been taken out. Dr. Fleming had been instructing his pupils in the mysteries of the ancient battering-ram and catapulta. There

---

* The modern church of Monivaird is now at a considerable distance from the old churchyard.

was a steep bank in front, and a stone-wall below, which presented a most inviting object on which to try an experiment. With considerable exertion the two boys had turned the carriage round, and having given to the pole a suitable direction for a point blank charge, were just in the act of launching it down the precipitous declivity, when their uncle descried their danger and that of the carriage. It was too late to prevent the catastrophe; the chariot rolled down the bank with all the majesty of an engine of war, acquiring increased velocity at every step, and did the work of a battering-ram with so much effect, as to dash through the wall in an instant. Happily a broken pole was the total amount of the actual damage, besides the displacement of some masonry.

In the following year they lost their kind grandmother, Lady Lundie, who was rather suddenly taken from them, at an advanced age, in May 1777. In the same year Lord Duncan married the second daughter of the Lord President Dundas, the remembrance of whose charming vivacity, warm-hearted kindness, and many admirable qualities, the two brothers cherished with the grateful feelings of almost filial affection. Her friendship they enjoyed to the close of her long and happy life in December, 1832, and during many of her later years, it was the privilege, especially of her younger nephew, to minister to her spiritual comfort. After the marriage, it was necessary to make new arrangements, and the house in Dundee having been relinquished, it was determined that the two boys should go to the High School of Edinburgh. Accordingly, in September, 1777, they were boarded with the Rector of the High School, the celebrated Dr. Adam, the author of the "Roman Antiquities," and other valuable works. His house was in Charles-street, fronting the entrance into George-square, and overlooking the large mansion with the court in front, afterwards Lord Duncan's, but then occupied by the Lord Advocate, the Right Hon. Henry Dundas, first Viscount Melville. In a letter written many years afterwards, by Mr. James Haldane to his son, he says, " I have told you of Lord Melville, how, in winter, Dr. Adam, when he called your uncle and myself in the morning, used to point to his candle, burning in the room, where he had been labouring for a couple of hours before we were awake." There were along with them at Dr. Adam's several other boarders, also attending the High School, some of whom became publicly known, such as the Earl of Rossmore, General Sir William Erskine, who commanded the cavalry in Spain; two Vandeleurs, one of whom became a titled General, and the other an Irish Judge; also the eldest son of Lord Decies, then Archbishop of Tuam, George Ramsay of Barnton, &c.

Robert, then nearly fourteen, at once joined the fifth or Rector's class in the High School. James (although little more than nine) was placed in the third, then taught by Mr. French, a pious and estimable man, with whom he remained till August, 1779, when he, too, reached the fifth or highest class.

There were at the High School several contemporaries, who afterwards became distinguished in the fields of literature, law, or politics. Boys of all ranks, from the sons of the noble to the sons of the tradesman, were there associated. There were also two with whom both the brothers were afterwards to be connected in the religious movement in Scotland, but with neither of them had they at the time any personal acquaintance. The one was the well-known John Campbell, the African Missionary, who used graphically to describe the time when he first saw his future friend and fellow-labourer, James Haldane, an energetic and high-spirited boy, ever foremost in the race of fun and frolic. The other was Mr. Greville Ewing, the son of a respectable teacher of mathematics in Edinburgh. Mr. Campbell, who was born in 1766, was in the class of Nichol, the friend of Burns, and a partaker both of Burns' genius and vices; Mr. Ewing, although fifteen months older, was in the same class with James Haldane, consisting of more than a hundred boys, placed in order, according to their respective merits. Mr. Ewing, in spite of an interrupted education, was afterwards esteemed for his critical skill, but at that time he occupied a place about the middle of Mr. French's class. James Haldane was near the head, a position which does not always guarantee the same superiority in after life, although it is no doubt indicative of natural quickness. In noticing their course of study, it would be unjust to omit the name of their French master, Mr. Cauvin, more usually named Mr. Gavin, who died some years ago, leaving a large sum of money to found an hospital at Duddingstone, where he resided. With him they were favourite pupils, and after they left the High School were accustomed to go to his residence, and make very agreeable excursions with him, when nothing but French was spoken.

On the Saturdays, Sundays, and other casual holidays, the two brothers had a happy home at Nellfield, near Edinburgh, where their uncle then resided, until the war again summoned him to sea. Their long vacation was spent at Lundie House.

In connexion with their visits to Nellfield, there is a little anecdote indicative of the manners of the times, which used to furnish some amusement. When James Haldane happened to be walking out to his uncle's, he was overtaken by a young minister on horseback, who asked him where he was going. With great simplicity, the boy replied, "To Nellfield," which sounding very much like Melville, the minister supposed, from the nearness of their age, that the young gentleman was the son of the great dispenser of Scottish patronage, both lay and ecclesiastical, and was going to Melville Castle, near Lasswade. He was immediately invited to mount behind the saddle, according to the fashion of the day, when there were few wheeled vehicles, and was thus very pleasantly conveyed along the road. Arriving at the gate of Nellfield, James informed his conductor that they must now part. The disappointment manifested was inexplicable to the unsophisticated mind of a boy, but the story amused his friends, and was probably enjoyed by none more than by that busy statesman, from whom both of the brothers received much kind notice, and who had himself so deeply studied human nature and so well understood the springs of influence.

In his boyhood it was for a time the desire of Robert Haldane to fit himself for the ministry in the Church of Scotland, and at Lundie House he used regularly every Sunday to exhibit this inclination by addressing, or, as it might be called,

preaching to the domestics in the servants' hall.  This might be
considered, perhaps, as rather savouring of boyish sport, but he
himself spoke of it far otherwise near the close of his life, and
stated, that from the time when he was nine years old, he had
more or less of serious convictions as to the things of God.
It was also a frequent custom of the two boys, after they had
retired to bed, to converse together about the things to which
their departed mother had attached so much importance, and
this habit was, no doubt, in itself beneficial to both, tending to
cherish in their hearts a hidden spark of love to Jesus Christ
and the things of heaven.   But whatever were Robert's inclina-
tions as to the ministry, it was then deemed quite contrary to
ordinary usage in Scotland, that one of his fortune and position
should become a minister.   He himself was probably easily
persuaded on the point, more especially as the exploits of his
uncle kindled in his breast a desire to follow him into the navy
and share in the glories of the ocean.   At all events, his decision
was finally made early in 1780, when rather abruptly leaving
his studies at the College of Edinburgh, he joined the Monarch
at Portsmouth.

In 1779-80 and 1780-1 James passed through the Rector's
class, remaining there two years.   He was reckoned a clever,
shrewd boy, observant, and of quick perception, possessing a
retentive memory and the capacity of application, although his
love of adventurous sport strongly preponderated.   He was
nearly two years younger than the generality of the boys of his
standing in the school, but his usual place during his last year
at the Rector's class was about third, but on the final adjust-
ment of places, the industry of some of those usually below him,
and his own indifference on the subject, made him only seventh.
When Dr. Adam, before the public examination, went through
his customary plan of asking the upper boys if they were satisfied with their places, he put the same question to James
Haldane, and being answered in the affirmative, the Rector very
significantly shook his head, and intimated, that if his industry
had been equal to his abilities he might have occupied a higher
position.   Two or three years before, when he was under Mr.

French, Dr. Adam went to meet him as he was returning from school, intending to accompany him to some show or exhibition. But observing that his clothes had been soiled in the boisterous amusements of the High School yards, the Rector reproved his little pupil, and said that he did not himself choose to be seen in such company. Before dismissing the boy, he asked, however, what was his place in his class, and being told that he was Dux, or first, the enthusiasm of the learned Rector was kindled, and affectionately grasping the hand of his scholar, he exclaimed, " I would walk with you although you were clothed in rags ! "

In 1781 James matriculated in the University of Edinburgh, and for three sessions continued, under the observation of Dr. Adam, to attend the different professors of Greek, Latin, mathematics, logic, metaphysics, and natural philosophy, in their usual order.

In 1783 Colonel Duncan took him to London, on a visit to Gosport, where the future Admiral resided for five years with his family, during the peace, in command of the Edgar guardship. The interest of the journey, which in those days was a formidable affair, with the novelty of a new country and new places, became enhanced by the spectacle of a remarkable meteor which then passed over England. Whilst examining the wonders of the great metropolis, they resided on Clapham-common, in the house of the two Messrs. Webster, the great West India merchants, and thence proceeded to Gosport, where an acquaintance was begun with the great and good Dr. Bogue, which ripened into Christian friendship, only terminating with death.

It was the wish of both his uncles that he should enjoy the advantage of seeing as much as possible of his own country before going to sea. Accordingly it was arranged, that in August, 1784, Dr. Adam should accompany him and his schoolfellow, the late George Ramsay, of Barnton, on a tour through the north of England. They travelled on horseback, and the commencement of their journey was rather auspicious, for, stopping at Haddington, they accidentally made acquaintance with a gentleman of the name of Haldane, who, although an entire stranger, was so much pleased with his young namesake, that he presented him with a very handsome and well-bred horse, in order that he might not be worse mounted than young Ramsay, who had been furnished by his uncle, who was then the Tattersall of Scotland.

They travelled by Berwick, Newcastle, York, and Hull, into Derbyshire, returning by Lancashire and Cumberland to Edinburgh. They were accompanied on this tour by the Rev. Dr. Macknight, the well-known commentator, whose practical disregard of the Lord's-day made a deep impression on James Haldane. Although Dr. Adam was not an enlightened man in spiritual things, and then attended the very *moderate* teaching of the minister of St. Cuthbert's Chapel-of-Ease, yet he had been accustomed to reverence the outward symbols of religion. But when they had crossed the border, and arrived in an Episcopalian country, Dr. Macknight persuaded his learned friend that, being out of the bounds of Presbytery, and under no obligation to countenance Prelatical worship, it would be very absurd to allow their journeying plans to be deranged by the intervention of the Sabbath. This convenient doctrine at first surprised, but at last proved very palatable to the young travellers. For a time, Dr. Adam felt very much ashamed when they entered a town or village when the church-going bells were calling the people to the services of the sanctuary. But these scruples were soon overcome by the doughty commentator, who was thus in effect giving a practical warning against that frigid scheme of rationalistic Arminianism which pervades his writings. There was no theologian whom the two brothers in after-life regarded as a more dangerous corruptor of the truths of the Gospel.

On their return to Edinburgh, James Haldane bade farewell to Dr. Adam and the house in Charles-street, where he had now spent nearly seven years of his life. The months during which he remained in Scotland before going to sea were chiefly passed at Lundie House, and the Colonel's unvarying kindness was always cherished by him with grateful recollection.

He was now in his seventeenth year, and before noticing the

chief incidents in his life at sea, it may be natural to ask, What was his spiritual condition, and what were his prospects as to an eternal existence ?

Long after their mother's death, both the brothers were much solemnized by a sense of the importance of those things which she had so earnestly inculcated. Their sister's death had doubtless tended to deepen the impression. When they came to Edinburgh they used to be remarked, and even laughed at, for their reverence for sacred things. Robert Haldane's inclination for the ministry has been already noticed; and two elderly ladies from Durham, who then lived in Edinburgh, the cousins of their deceased grandmother, the widow of Colonel Haldane, often lamented that young James should be destined for so rough a profession as that of a sailor. They did not desire him to be a Presbyterian minister, but said that it would be much better were he to enter the English Church, to which they themselves belonged, in which he might possibly become a Bishop, and added, as interfering with this airy castle, the expression of their regret at the death of their brother, who had in his gift excellent preferment. But whatever appearances of seriousness continued for some years, they were not enduring, as will be seen from the following extract from the manuscript already quoted :—

" Till I was twelve years old I continued to pray, go to church, and read my Bible or other good books on the Sabbath, but it was only from a principle of duty, and was indeed only that kind of bodily exercise which profiteth little. I had no pleasure in any religious duty, but conscience retained a certain influence, and made me afraid to give them up. I was well pleased if any slight illness, or anything occurred which seemed a sufficient excuse to myself for staying at home on the Lord's-day. Indeed, I hardly attended to one word I heard when at church, but only made a form of joining in the different parts of the worship. Sometimes, however, I had serious thoughts; occasionally, on a Sabbath evening, after reading the Scriptures or other books, I felt a kind of flow of the natural passions, and had a good deal of pleasure in prayer. This always puffed me up with thoughts that I was very good. But to show how much I considered prayer as a task, if I had bowed my knee in such a frame as this before supper, I considered it unnecessary to pray again when I went to bed. About that time, the text of Proverbs xxvi. 12, ' Seest thou a man wise in his own conceit,' &c., struck me a good deal. I had just been thinking that I was in the right road to heaven, but that text rather cast a damp upon my hopes, for it seemed to describe my character. I generally used a form of prayer, but when I felt such emotions, I prayed in such words as occurred. From about thirteen to sixteen, I became more careless, often spending the Sabbath evenings in idle conversation with my companions, and I was pleased to find my conscience become less and less scrupulous. I also began to swear, because, according to the fashion of the times, it seemed to be manly, and except a form of prayer, which I still kept up, every serious idea seemed to have fled. Some things, however, occurred, which led me back to a kind of decency. Some vexation I met with from a quarrel with some companions, caused me to pray to God, and I began again to read my Bible on the Sabbath, and completely gave up swearing for a season. They laughed, and I endured some ridicule for thus spending the Sabbath, but the opposition rather confirmed than altered my determination. I do not mention this as anything praiseworthy; it certainly proceeded more from pride than principle."

Are we, then, to suppose that the instructions of his sainted mother had not fallen like the good seed into good ground? Had it been scattered by the wayside, or on stony ground, or amongst thorns, and so perished without yielding fruit? Had her prayers been offered up in vain? Had the confidence of that faith, which burned so bright in the hour of her departure, been on behalf of her children a vain trust in the promises of the Gospel? Had she miscalculated the meaning of these declarations made on behalf of the offspring of believing, prayerful, and persevering parents? It will be seen that the blossoms of youthful piety had indeed nearly disappeared,—that they had proved like the early cloud and the morning dew. But yet the pious labours of the trustful mother had not been in vain. Her prayers had ascended before the mercy-seat, " perfumed with much incense," and were registered in heaven. The good seed was only buried, not lost; and by and by, after a long winter, it was destined to spring up in " the power of an endless life," instinct with blessings for her children and her children's children, nay, for thousands who were to receive the Gospel from their voice or from their writings.

# CHAPTER II.

[1780—1794.]

THE current of this narrative has conducted the reader down to
1785, when, in his seventeenth year, James Haldane went to
sea. It is now time to notice the career of his elder brother,
from the period when he rather unexpectedly quitted his studies
in Edinburgh, and in the spring of 1780, being then also in his
seventeenth year, entered the Royal Navy.

The revolt of the American Colonies was the first great public
event which excited the interest of the two brothers, and even
the younger used to mention his boyish recollections of the
excitement, produced by the sudden arrival of the declaration of
independence, and the prospect of the war with France. It was
in 1779 that the establishment at Nellfield was broken up, and
their uncle once more engaged in active service. It may easily
be supposed with what interest his two youthful and affectionate nephews followed the history of his exploits; how their
ardent spirits exulted in the renown he obtained in Rodney's
action off Cape St. Vincent, where the Monarch, outsailing all
the fleet, bore the brunt of the engagement, disabling two line-
of-battle ships and capturing a third; how they sympathized
with the burning indignation expressed by him, when the
Channel fleet was afterwards compelled to retreat before the

French, and he himself could only "stand looking over the stern gallery of the Monarch," sea-sick as well as heart-sick through contending emotions of shame and vexation. It was shortly after this, that Robert Haldane himself joined the Monarch, and remained in that ship until the spring of 1781, when it was ordered to the West Indies, and Lord Duncan's health having previously severely suffered from the climate of the Havannah, he was persuaded to relinquish a tropical expedition for active service nearer home.

Before he was enabled to commission the Blenheim, of 90 guns, in order to prevent loss of time, he transferred his nephew to the Foudroyant, of 80 guns, commanded by his friend and contemporary, Captain Jervis, the future Earl St. Vincent.

Of the Foudroyant, Mr. Haldane was accustomed, even in old age, to speak with something of youthful enthusiasm. It had been captured from the French, and was the finest ship in the British Navy. It was not only a model of naval architecture, but was gilt to the water's edge; whilst its height between decks was greater than that of the Britannia of 100 guns, which carried the flag of the renowned Admiral Barrington, to whose squadron it belonged. He used to mention that on visiting that Admiral, whose younger brother was the well-known Bishop of Durham, and whose elder brother had been one of his father's guardians, he found himself obliged to stoop between decks of the flag-ship, whilst in the Foudroyant, although standing nearly six feet high, he was able to walk upright.

But a short time after he joined the Foudroyant he was called to take part in the celebrated action with the Pegáse, which was the foundation of all Lord St. Vincent's great fame. It was a night engagement. A French fleet of six sail-of-the-line was retreating before Admiral Barrington with twelve. The chase began at noon on the 19th of April, and the Foudroyant, out-sailing all the rest, and leaving them as if at anchor, singled out the Pegáse at 10 at night, and at 47 minutes past 12, having run at the rate of eleven knots an hour, brought her to close quarters. The respective forces of the two ships were nearly equal; for although the British had six guns more than the enemy, yet the latter had sixty more men, with a greater weight of metal, carrying forty-pounders on the lower decks, and a crew of seven hundred seamen.  These particulars Mr. Haldane used to say had been omitted in narratives of the action, although Admiral Barrington's despatch mentions, in general terms, that the two combatants were in point of force nearly equal.  He often referred with pleasure to an instance of his gallant Commander's magnanimity.  Just as the ships were about to open their fire, the officer on the forecastle called out that the enemy had "put her helm up to rake."  Captain Jervis instantly exclaimed, "Then put the helm a-starboard," meaning to deliver his broadside from the starboard guns.  At that critical moment one of his midshipmen,—a friend of Robert Haldane's, the gallant Bowen, who fell by the side of Nelson at Teneriffe,— perceived that an opposite manœuvre would give to the Foudroyant the advantage of the first fire, and enable her to rake, instead of being raked.  On the moment, this gallant young man, standing by the wheel, called out, " Port, port; if we put our helm to port, we shall rake her."  His eagerness admitted of no denial.  The helm was brought to port; the broadside of the Foudroyant was poured into the Pegáse; and when the smoke cleared off, Captain Jervis, in the enthusiàsm of the moment, pulled off his hat on the quarter-deck, and turning to the young officer, exclaimed,—" Thanks, Bowen: you were right."

The battle lasted three-quarters of an hour, and the skill as well as the zeal which directed the guns under Robert Haldane's charge, attracted the notice of his observant Commander.  During the heat of the action, holding a lantern in his hand, he was seen directing the elevation of a gun.  An old sailor warned him that he was making himself a mark for the enemy; but he indignantly repelled the admonition, telling his well-meaning and sensible adviser that, in the discharge of duty, he should disdain to think of personal danger.  At one time the ships almost touched each other, and a gunner being asked why he did not withdraw the rammer, replied that he could not on account of the Frenchman. The gun was discharged with the rammer undrawn.

After the Pegáse was laid on board, and had struck, the ships separated; and it blew so fresh, and there was so much sea, that it was with great difficulty and the loss of two boats, that an officer and eighty men could be sent into the prize to bring off forty prisoners. During the action, the watchful eye of the hero of St. Vincent had marked the zeal and gallantry of Robert Haldane, and he indicated his approval by appointing him to accompany one of the lieutenants to take possession of the Pegáse, with orders to bring back its commander, Le Chevalier Cillart. There was another reason which prompted the selection. He had very soon discovered both the attainments and the force of character of Robert Haldane, who was the only officer on board who understood French. The duty assigned to him was discharged with his usual courtesy, determination, and zeal. On boarding the Pegáse, he found the decks floated with blood, seven men lying dead at one gun. Having been conducted through this scene of slaughter to the Chevalier, he explained the nature of his orders, but the Frenchman protested that it was out of the question to get into an open boat in such a sea and at such an hour. The necessity of the case was explained, the weakness of the captors in point of numbers as compared with the vanquished. Still the captain demurred, when the lieutenant, who had charge of the prize, by drawing his sword, added a very significant argument, which fully compensated for his inability to express himself in French. The Chevalier then submitted, and was conducted safely by Mr. Haldane to the Foudroyant, amidst murmurs which promised to bear in mind this treatment when he returned to France.

After the action Sir John Jervis wrote to Captain Duncan, congratulating him on the determined spirit and ability of his nephew, and predicting that Robert Haldane would one day be an ornament to his country. This prediction was to be fulfilled in a manner far different from that which the hero of St. Vincent then imagined. His renown was not to be won on the quarter-deck of a British man-of-war, or amidst such scenes of blood as those which had, for the first time, somewhat solemnized the exulting joy of the young warrior. But even then, amidst the satisfaction derived from the applause of the great officer under whom he served, there was one circumstance, the recollection of which interested his mind during the very last days of his mortal career, although sixty long years had elapsed. He mentioned that, on that night, on going into action with the Pegáse, when his heart beat high with ardent zeal, he breathed out an earnest prayer to God, that he might now be strengthened to discharge his duty as became a British sailor, in defence of his country. It was not that he then made any open profession of religion, or had any settled or abiding principle of godliness in his heart. On the contrary, pride, ambition, the love of distinction, and other forms of worldliness, were all in the ascendant. But, beneath this heap of rubbish, there was still germinating in the hidden recesses of his inmost soul the incorruptible seed, implanted by a mother's hand, and watered by a mother's prayers. Invisible to mortal eye it there existed, and, on such an occasion as that of his going for the first time into battle, seemed like a spark of life ready to burst out, and make the gallant youth act not as a reckless unbeliever, but as a Christian hero.

After the return of the Foudroyant to Spithead, and during the period which elapsed before the relief of Gibraltar, he had frequent opportunities of spending much of his time at Gosport, and attending the ministry of the late David Bogue, whose influence on his own mind and that of his brother, both intellectually and spiritually, was greatly blessed. Dr. Bogue was a Scotch Presbyterian minister, educated for the Established Church, who ultimately settled, in 1778, at Gosport, where he continued until his death, in 1825, the pastor of an Independent congregation, but still foremost, throughout the land, in all those great objects of Christian philanthropy, which marked the close of the eighteenth century.

Between 1779 and 1787 Gosport was the head-quarters of Lord Duncan. Till the peace of 1783 he was attached to the

Channel Fleet, successively commanding the Monarch of 74, and the Blenheim of 90 guns, and chiefly cruizing between Spithead and Gibraltar. After the peace, he commanded the Edgar guard-ship until he obtained his flag, in 1787. These circumstances are to be numbered amongst the providential links in the history of both the brothers, for it was thus that they were both brought much into contact with Dr. Bogue, to whom they became warmly attached. They attended his ministry, and by him they were directed in their course of reading and in their choice of books, both on shore and at sea. Thus is it that the Lord is pleased to work out his designs of mercy and of love, in a way which we cannot comprehend, subordinating all the changes and chances of life to the purposes which he has foreordained, leading his dependent creatures by a way which they know not, until the mystery of God shall be accomplished, and the events which seemed only accidental, shall be seen to have been guided by the unerring hand of Infinite Wisdom.

During the summer of 1782, Admiral Barrington's squadron was placed under the orders of Earl HOWE, whose duty it was to protect our shores and commerce, menaced, as they were, on the one hand by the Dutch, and on the other by the French and Spanish fleets. Towards the end of the summer preparations were made for a great expedition to relieve Gibraltar. At this period, when the grand fleet lay at Spithead, Robert Haldane witnessed the loss of the Royal George, which happened on the 29th of August, 1782. On the morning of that memorable day, soon after breakfast, he was looking through a telescope, watching the operation of heeling over of the ship, when, on a sudden, it capsized, filled, and sunk. There were at least twelve hundred souls on board, including women and children, and, in charge of a boat from the Foudroyant, he was one of the most active in picking up and saving the drowning crew. Of those who went down not more than three hundred were rescued; and at Portsea and on the beach at Ryde, in the Isle of Wight, so many dead bodies were interred, that it is calculated that nine hundred must have perished.

The state of public affairs at this juncture may be inferred from the fact, that the catastrophe of the Royal George was regarded as a national calamity, not merely involving the loss of an admiral and a gallant crew, but diminishing the strength of the grand fleet, then under orders for Gibraltar, and expecting to encounter a greatly superior force, combining the navies of France and Spain. On the 11th of September, Lord Howe sailed with thirty-four ships-of-the-line, besides frigates, and a great convoy of one hundred and forty transports, carrying troops, stores, and provisions. The relief of Gibraltar forms one of the most striking incidents in the memorable siege, when the united resources of the Bourbons of France and Spain were vainly lavished, for the recovery of that celebrated fortress. It was a great crisis, and it was generally believed that its reconquest would have ruined the influence of Britain to the eastward of the Pillars of Hercules, and given to her rivals the command of the Mediterranean. Lord Howe's fleet was much inferior to the enemy. But Mr. Haldane, in after-life, used often to dwell on the remarkable interposition of Providence, by which he believed that the disparity of force was, in some degree, neutralized, and the convoy enabled to land their supplies. On the 10th of October, a look-out frigate returned to Lord Howe, with the formidable intelligence that the combined fleets, anchored in Algesiras Bay, consisted of fifty sail of the line, besides frigates. On that night a sudden and violent tempest scattered and disabled the French and Spanish fleet, whilst the British rode secure under the lee of the African mountains. Several of the enemy, including some three-deckers, were driven ashore, others were compelled to run to the eastward, and all were, more or less, damaged; so that, when Captain Curtis arrived from General Elliott on the 12th, he was enabled to inform the Admiral, that there then remained in the bay only forty sail-of-the-line, and three of 56 guns. But this was not all. On the 13th the enemy put to sea, partly to protect his scattered ships, and partly to intercept the British convoy. He cleared Europa point, and passed the night *perfectly becalmed;* whilst Lord Howe being to the eastward of the rock, taking advantage of an easterly wind which sprung up, carried the convoy safe into Gibraltar, amidst the cheers and acclamations of the garrison. In the performance of this manœuvre the Foudroyant was the leading ship, and bore the chief part in the affair. The gallant Earl's movement was no doubt masterly, but the storm which burst with fury on the combined fleets on the 10th, and the calm which paralyzed them on the 12th, together with the sudden change of the wind, were all contingencies enabling the British to effect the grand object of the expedition. To those who would banish the remembrance of an all-seeing God from their own hearts, and exclude the Omniscient and Almighty from the government of His own creation, such incidents will appear the result of accident, and a reference to an overruling Providence will provoke the smile of ridicule. But to those who delight to trace the finger of God in the smallest as well as the greatest of human affairs, such facts will furnish, as they did in after-life to Mr. Haldane, fresh matter of grateful meditation on the character of Him, all whose ways are wonderful, who "holds the winds in his fist, and the waters in the hollow of his hands," and who does amongst the inhabitants of the earth according to His own good pleasure. "Whoso is *wise*, and will observe these things, even they shall understand the loving-kindness of the Lord."

After the relief of Gibraltar, Lord Howe gave orders to return from the Straits, but so intent on action were the crew of the Victory that they refused to put round the wheel, and their murmurs almost amounted to open mutiny, until the Noble Admiral assured them that they should fight in the open seas. An action did take place, in which the British loss amounted to 276 in killed and wounded. Sir John Jervis was much dissatisfied, and pacing the quarter-deck of the Foudroyant in great excitement, with his hat in his hand, continued to exclaim, "For shame! Lord Howe." But the enemy had ten sail-of-the-line more than the British, with friendly ports in case of a defeat, whilst Lord Howe was not only inferior in force, but had no shelter for damaged or disabled ships. Mr. Haldane used also to state, that in passing Lord Howe's orders for closer action from ship to ship, some mistake occurred, which caused them to haul their wind, and so separated the fleets. In the morning the enemy did not choose to renew the combat.

After this affair the fleet sailed for England, and an incident occurred which again discovered the young sailor's force of character. The Leocadia, a Spanish sixty-gun ship, was chased by the fleet, and the Foudroyant, as usual, far outsailing the rest, was rapidly coming up with her, when a signal from Lord Howe induced Sir John Jervis at once to abandon the chase.* It was, however, when the Foudroyant was carrying a press of canvas in pursuit, that Robert Haldane was ordered to take his post on the fore-top-gallant mast, and remain on the look-out till recalled. The mast sprung, and as there was no order to descend, he expected at every blast to be hurled into the deep. Another midshipman thought himself justified, under the circumstances, in retiring to a safer position. Not so his companion, who remembered his commander's maxim, "never to make a difficulty" in carrying out an order. He therefore heroically remained, as did an old seaman, who advised him to lay hold of the lower parts of the ropes, so that, in the event of the anticipated plunge, there might be a better chance of keeping hold of the mast with their heads uppermost. At this moment there arose a cry of "A man overboard!" Sir John Jervis instantly gave an order to shorten sail, and then for the first time discovering the perilous situation of those on the look-out, they were commanded to come down. Those who remember the character of Lord St. Vincent will easily imagine the impression produced by the determination with which his orders had been obeyed at all hazards.

On its arrival at Spithead the Foudroyant was paid off, and Sir John Jervis was appointed to commission the Salisbury, of fifty guns, and to hoist his broad pennant as Commodore of a squadron, bound on an expedition, intended to combine a voyage round the world for purposes of discovery, with an attack on the Spanish settlements in South America. Robert Haldane was

* Sir George Collyer, less attentive to orders, followed and captured the Leocadia, but not till the next day.

one of those expressly selected to accompany him, as a young
man of whom he entertained high expectations, whom he
constantly employed as an amanuensis, and whose services he
valued both on the deck and in his cabin. Long before this
Sir John Jervis had won his regard, and when the fleet sailed for
Gibraltar he had declined his uncle's kind proposal to remove to
the Blenheim, justly considering that the comforts of being with
a relation were counterbalanced by its necessary disadvantages.

The peace put an end to the South American expedition.
The Salisbury went to Newfoundland, but not under Sir John
Jervis, who, for a time, retired into private life. Mr. Haldane
made this voyage, but having no longer the prospect of immediate promotion, returned in the Æolus frigate to Lisbon, and
thence rejoined his uncle at Gosport.

All incitement to enterprise being thus withdrawn, he bade
adieu to a service to which he was enthusiastically attached to
the very last. Even to the end of his career, nearly sixty years
after his retirement, it was interesting to observe how easily his
youthful predilections seemed to revive when the British navy
was the topic of conversation. To everything which concerned
its efficiency, as an arm of national defence, or the moral welfare
and comforts of sailors, his sympathies were always alive. He
was never an egotist, and talked little of his own exploits, even
to his nearest relations. But there were occasions when, in the
confidence of friendly intercourse, he might be drawn on to
speak of his adventures at sea ;—how he had been on one occasion reproved by a lieutenant for taking the wheel from the
helmsman, and how Sir John Jervis, ascertaining that it was in
order to learn to steer, applauded his zeal, and issued orders
that all the midshipmen should take their turn at the wheel;
or how, in his uncle's ship, when pursuing some French men-
of-war, the Monarch, outsailing the rest of the fleet, got into
the midst of a convoy, but the discipline of the ship was such,
that boats were let down on each side without swamping, filled
with armed crews to take possession of the prizes, whilst the
Monarch never slackened her speed, but, with studding sails set,
bore down on the flying ships of war.

When the subject of manning the navy was in 1840 so prominently brought before the public by Admiral Hawker, writing under the signature of " A Flag Officer," he read and made notes on his pamphlets, and used to say that under-manning was the worst possible economy, and that Lord Duncan always denounced the system.  He would also tell how, in his own time, an economical order had been sent down from the Admiralty, to the effect that the line-of-battle ships should carry water-casks on deck to supply other vessels at sea; and how Lord Duncan had indignantly declared, that whilst he obeyed the order as in duty bound, yet it was his intention to avail himself of his own discretion, as soon as he got to the back of the Isle of Wight, by staving every cask on the deck of the Monarch the moment he descried a strange sail.  But there was nothing of this kind on which latterly he talked with greater interest than on the care which Lord Duncan took of the health and comfort of his men, and of his efforts to prevent the necessity of their being subjected to the constant wear and tear of keeping " watch and watch."  One of the chief evils of under-manning consisted, he thought, in the necessity thus imposed on the commander of constantly requiring his men to keep " watch and watch," even when drenched with wet, instead of allowing them alternately the opportunity of eight hours of repose.  On this subject he spoke with much earnestness not long before his death.

In fact, his natural bent towards the navy was remarkable; and considering his energy and force of character, his foresight and powers of combination, together with that faculty of inspiring confidence which he eminently possessed, it is no matter of sur-prise that two of the greatest British Admirals under whom he served, should have concurred in the prediction that he would himself rise to renown.  His career was to be distinguished, but not in the way which attracts the admiration of the world. The blood-stained laurels of the conquering hero were not to encircle his brow, nor was he to merit and achieve stars, coronets, or ribbons.  But as a good soldier of Jesus Christ, he was to fight the good fight of faith,—to wrestle with princi-

palities and powers and spiritual wickedness in high places,—
and finally, finishing his course with joy, to lay hold of the
palm of victory and the crown of righteousness, but only to cast
them all before the throne of God and the Lamb.

Robert Haldane was in his twentieth year when the peace of
1783 brought his short but active and eventful career in the
navy to a close.  The real business of his useful life did not
begin for twelve years afterwards, when his brother also quitted
the sea, with a mind impressed with the littleness of time and
the magnitude of eternity.

Robert remained for some months at Gosport, enjoying the
advantage of Dr. Bogue's society and tuition, and then proceeded to Edinburgh, where, during the ensuing session, he
resumed his studies at the University.  The summer of 1784
was passed partly at Lundie House, and partly in a short tour
to Paris and the Netherlands, accompanied by Dr. Bogue.  In
that eminent minister's private journal, as published in his Life,
which has been so ably written by Dr. Bennett, he says, " We
spent a month in wandering through France and Flanders.  It
was not good for my soul."  On his return home, Dr. Bogue
adds, " I bless God that my lot is cast in a land of Gospel light,
and adore him for the care of his providence over me in this
expedition, and desire to live to his glory."

The winter of 1784-5 was again spent in attending the
professors at Edinburgh, and in the spring he set out upon
what used to be called " the grand tour."  Embarking at Har-
wich, accompanied by a naval officer who had been with him
in the Foudroyant, and soon afterwards became Admiral of the
Turkish fleet, he passed through the principal cities of Holland
and Germany to Vienna, where he remained for some time.
Thence, crossing the Tyrolese Alps, he visited Venice and the
chief cities in Northern Italy, Rome and Naples, returning home
by Florence, Marseilles, Nismes, Lyons, Switzerland, and Paris.
He was naturally an acute and penetrating observer, a great
admirer of scenery, particularly of mountains ; and the interest
which he took in his travels was always manifest, whether he
spoke of the Alps, the Pyrenees, or the Appennines, or discoursed

of the antiquities which he had examined at Nismes, at Lisbon, at Herculaneum, or at Rome.

On the 28th February, 1785, whilst he was abroad, he had attained his majority, and in the month of April in the next year, shortly after his return home, he married Katherine Cochrane Oswald, then only in her eighteenth year, second daughter of the late George Oswald, Esq., of Scotstown, by his wife, the daughter of Mr. Smythe, of Methven, in Perthshire. Mrs. Haldane was the younger sister of the present Miss Oswald, of Scotstown, as well as of the late Richard Oswald, Esq., of Auchincruive, long M.P. for Ayrshire. The union was destined to prove long and happy. It lasted nearly fifty-seven years, and Mrs. Haldane was singularly adapted to be a true helpmeet in all his future plans, participating in his designs of usefulness, aiding him by her prudent counsel and sympathy, and never interposing her own personal wishes or comfort as an obstacle to their accomplishment.

In September, 1786, they settled at the old House of Airthrey, near Stirling, and in the month of April, 1787, their daughter and only child was born.

For nearly ten years after his marriage, his time was, in a great measure, occupied with country pursuits, partly in improving his estates, and partly in ornamenting his pleasure-grounds, at a time when landscape-gardening was less common in Scotland, than it has become during the last fifty or sixty years. In these, as in other things to which he turned his energies, he was eminently successful, and those most acquainted with the subject were, in after-years, often glad to consult him on the best method of laying out grounds, overcoming natural difficulties, or transplanting trees. At Airthrey there were many fine old trees, chiefly beeches, elms, and limes, but in some places they had been planted at the beginning of the last century with too much formality. This he undertook to remedy, at a period when the practice of transplanting full-grown trees had scarcely been attempted in Scotland. His experiments in this way were generally successful, and at the time attracted so much wonder as to give rise to the absurd report amongst the people, that he was contemplating the removal of the old house to a preferable situation.*

The situation of Airthrey, on the last slope of the Ochil range of hills, is singularly picturesque. Water was the one thing wanting to complete its beauty. This Mr. Haldane determined to remedy. Before he had been settled there six months he commenced the excavation of an artificial lake, covering thirty acres of old pasture land in the park, into which he conducted an abundant supply of water from the hills. He also erected, in 1791, a new house, in a castellated form, which was designed by Adam, father of the late Lord Chief Commissioner, and the grandfather of Sir Charles and Sir Frederick Adam. Mr. Adam was the architect of the day, but his mansions do not impress us with a high opinion of his taste or skill. Mr. Haldane also built a stone wall, extending four miles round the park, enlarged the gardens, conducted walks through the woods which cover the overhanging rocks and hills, and erected summer-houses on such elevated and commanding positions, as overlook the most picturesque views of the surrounding scenery. Eastward, the silver Forth, winding through one of the richest agricultural valleys in the world, seeks the far-off German Ocean, lingering in its progress through woods and rocks, villages, towers, and towns, whilst westward its source is hidden amidst the grandeur of the lofty Grampians. Stirling Castle, Craig Forth, the Abbey Craig, and other striking objects, with the ruins of Cambuskenneth, all so rich in historical recollections, lend a deeper moral interest to the magnificence of the scene, more especially when the glow of the setting sun gilds the purple mountains with its changing hues, and diffuses a softer radiance over the varied realms of natural beauty.

Amongst the erections in the woods of Airthrey, was the

* When the site of the Botanical Gardens of Edinburgh was changed, more than twenty years ago, Dr. Robert Graham, the Professor of Botany, was indebted to Mr. Haldane, for much useful advice and assistance as to the transport of a large number of forest trees, of various kinds and considerable dimensions, some of them from thirty to forty feet in height, which were removed from the old ground to the new, a distance of two miles or upwards.

hermitage, which existed for many years after Mr. Haldane left
the place, but which has long since tumbled into ruins.  It was
constructed after the model of the woodland retreat to which
Goldsmith's Angelina is led by the "taper's hospitable ray,"
and discovers the slighted Edwin, who had sought for consolation in a hermit's life away from the haunts of men.  " The
wicket opening with a latch," " the rushy couch," "the scrip
with herbs and fruits supplied," all the other sylvan articles
of furniture described by the poet, were there, whilst on the
sides of the adjacent rock, or within the hut itself, were painted
at proper intervals,—the invitation to "the houseless child of want
to accept the guiltless feast, the blessing and repose," concluding
the last with the sentimental moral,—

> " Then, pilgrim, turn, thy cares forego,—
> All earth-born cares are wrong,—
> Man wants but little here below,
> Nor wants that little long."

The erection of this hermitage had nearly cost Mr. Haldane
his life, for, standing too near the edge of the rock, giving
directions to the workmen, his foot slipped, and but for a post
which he was enabled to grasp, he would have been precipitated
to the bottom.  The celebrated Henry Erskine, with his usual
ready wit, exclaimed, " It was a post for life !"  But not
content with the erection of this ideal hermitage, Mr. Haldane,
who in his younger days always delighted in a practical joke,
advertised for a real hermit, specifying the conditions, which
were to be in accordance with the beau-ideal of Goldsmith's
ballad, including the prohibition of animal food.  But the
restrictions did not prevent the author of the jest from being
obliged to deal seriously with applications for the place, and one
man, in particular, professed himself ready to comply with
all the conditions except one, which was that he should never
leave the wood.  To the doom of perpetual seclusion the would-
be hermit could not make up his mind to submit, and the
advertisement was not repeated.

Shortly after the construction of his beautiful lake, Mr.
Haldane was again placed in imminent danger.  It was winter,

and, during the frost, there was a large party of visitors and others on the ice, enjoying the amusement of skating and curling. He was himself standing beside a chair on which a lady had been seated, when the ice suddenly broke, and he was nearly carried under the surface. With his usual presence of mind he seized on the chair which supported him, and quietly gave directions to send for ropes, as a rash attempt to extricate him might have only involved others in the impending catastrophe. Providentially there was help at hand, and by laying hold of the ropes brought by a gamekeeper and an old servant, he was happily extricated from his perilous position.

It is said, that before the time of Charles the Second, there was not one inclosed park in Scotland, and this fact may assist us in estimating the amount of improvement which has since been accomplished. By those who remember how many of the principal mansions and parks in Scotland are of modern date, or who consider what must have been their state at the period when Sir Walter Scott describes the old château of the Baron of Bradwardine, and down to the time of Dr. Johnson's tour to the Hebrides, it may easily be supposed that Mr. Haldane's doings at Airthrey excited a great deal of interest in the country, and stirred up a disposition both to embellish and improve.*

* Since the publication of the first edition of this work, a letter has been placed in the hands of the biographer by Lady Henrietta Allan, which serves to illustrate the occupations with which Robert Haldane was engaged at the age of twenty-four. It is the reply to a letter addressed to him by the proprietor of Erroll Park, who had heard of what was going on at Airthrey, and desired information as to the transplantation of full-grown trees :—

"*Edinburgh, June* 8, 1788.

" Sir,—I have just received your letter, and shall be extremely happy if I can be of the least use to you in transplanting your trees.

" The trees I transported are full grown ones, of about eighty years old; this is their second year, and they are doing as well as I could wish. Indeed, from the manner in which I transplanted them, I had little fear of their doing well from the first, as the whole root was always taken along with them, which, from its weight, kept them perfectly steady, and afforded the same nourishment as before. I measured one of the roots, which is about forty-five feet in circumference. As to the

It was, moreover, impossible to be in his society without admiring his great abilities, his originality of thought, his vivacity, and general information.  His superiority was never disputed, and, as a young man of rising character and great promise, he attracted somewhat of admiration and envy.  The probability of his coming into Parliament for the county was commonly spoken of, not only because of his own merits, but because, in those days of oligarchy in Scotland, his abilities and force of character seemed to be appreciated by the most influential men in the county, and particularly by the late Duke of Montrose, the Lord-Lieutenant, at whose residence both the brothers had been accustomed to visit from their boyhood, and who was himself an occasional guest at Airthrey.  His near

method of lifting them, it is attended with more trouble than expense, as very few people are required, and very cheap machinery.  I am very sorry that, owing to your letter going first to Airthrey, and then coming here before it found me, I will not have an opportunity of sending my carpenter, Croall, to you, as he is gone already to Arbroath, and will return about this time by the way of Fife.  He could, however, have been of very little use to you, as he was no ways more employed than the other servants, and I am afraid does not so perfectly understand it yet as to be able to direct the doing of it himself.  I intend to be in Angus just about the time you would probably transplant your trees, and shall call upon you, in passing, myself, and acquaint you of every particular of the method I took, so that you can prepare everything for the operation ; and I shall with pleasure ride down to you from Lundie House, when you are all prepared, and give any assistance in my power, and have not the least doubt of transplanting the largest tree at Erroll, if you choose, to any place you will.  I would be very happy if you would take a ride to Airthrey, as it would be a satisfaction to see the trees doing so well, and I would describe to you the whole method I adopted, and show you all the apparatus I used.  I shall be extremely happy if you will spend a few days with me.  I am to go home on Thursday, the 10th, and shall be there about eight days.

" I am, Sir,

" Your most obedient servant,

" ROBERT HALDANE.

" *John Allan, Esq., Erroll House, Perth.*"

Such is a picture of the operations in which Mr. Haldane was then employed.  They were at all times characterized by originality.  He had not yet entered on the important business of his existence.

neighbour, the celebrated Sir Ralph Abercromby, who was always remarkable for his sagacity and quick discernment of character, used often to say, that he never was in Mr. Haldane's company without hearing something worth remembering.

In the winter of 1792-3, both Sir Ralph and Mr. Haldane being in Edinburgh, agreed to attend Dr. Hardy's lectures on Church History, and as Mr. Haldane's house was then in Frederick-street, and Sir Ralph's at the west-end of Queen-street,* the General used every day for several months to call for Mr. Haldane, and walk with him across the bridges to and from the College, conversing much on the topics suggested by the Lecturer, and on matters of general interest.

It may be easily supposed that these daily meetings were long remembered. It was to enter on a course of foreign service, which continued with little intermission till his death, near Alexandria, that Sir Ralph Abercromby was suddenly called away from these peaceful and instructive occupations.

But a new career was also about to open on Mr. Haldane,— a career in which he was not to command the applause of listening senates, or, like his gallant friend, " to close a life of honour by a death of glory," but a career in which all his talents, all his energies, regenerated, renewed, and sanctified, were to be consecrated to the service of God, and the promotion of that kingdom for whose coming we are taught to pray.

* Connected with Sir Ralph Abercromby's house, in Queen-street, there is a recollection which marked the simplicity and benevolence of that great man's character. The Commander-in-chief in Scotland usually had two soldiers as sentinels before his door, but Sir Ralph declared that it was a " custom more honoured in the breach than in the observance," and, considering it to be a useless parade, he would not allow the men to be thus fatigued. The sentry-boxes therefore stood untenanted at his door during all the time he held his command. His boundless popularity as a general was due as much to his consideration for his men in their quarters as to his own conspicuous gallantry in the field.

# CHAPTER III.

[1785—1795.]

HAVING sketched the history of Robert Haldane down to the
year 1794, it next becomes necessary to trace that of his brother
to the same period.

James Haldane was in his seventeenth year when he entered
the service for which he had been intended from infancy. For
three generations the family had possessed the chief interest in
one of the East India Company's " regular chartered ships," the
property of which was shared with other connexions or friends
of the Gleneagles and Lundie families, including Mr. Coutts,
the banker, and the Dundases of Arniston. At the time he
went as midshipman in the Duke of Montrose, the command
of the Melville Castle was held by Captain Philip Dundas,
half-brother of the late Viscountess Duncan, and father of the
Right Honourable Robert Adam Christopher, M.P., now Chancellor of the Duchy of Lancaster. But an arrangement provided, that as soon as James Haldane attained the age which
qualified him for the command, Captain Dundas should retire.
Before he sailed, an offer was made to his uncles, which, had it

been accepted, would, humanly speaking, not only have insured a splendid fortune, but turned the current of his life. Mr. Coutts had been on terms of much intimacy with his father, to whom it is said that the great banker reckoned himself to have been indebted, at a time when he was a junior in a house in St. Mary Axe, near Leadenhall-street, before he migrated westward to the Strand. Mr. Coutts, therefore, offered to take him into his bank, with a view to a share in the business, but added that he scarcely liked to recommend the experiment, as there would probably be more of drudgery than would suit a high-spirited young man with such good prospects of his own. The tempting proposal was declined, and the circumstance is now only noticed as one of the incidents in a life, in which the guiding hand of an overruling Providence was uniformly conspicuous. Mr. Coutts always continued to evince the same friendly feeling, and not long before his death told Mr. James Haldane that few things would confer on him more pleasure than to be of use to any of the family of his old friend.

The Duke of Montrose, East Indiaman, was bound on a voyage to Bombay and China. The commander, Captain Gray, a well-known officer, perished, many years afterwards, near Madagascar in the Blenheim, along with Sir Thomas Troubridge and a crew of six hundred men. The third officer, Mr. Patrick Gardner, was the son of one of the tenants of Gleneagles, and had gone to sea under the patronage of the family. He was reckoned a first-rate navigator and practical seaman, so that on every account it was a great advantage for the young midshipman to be under the care of one whose own personal interests were likely to conspire with kind feeling in his favour. This expectation was not disappointed; and the opportunity of quietly studying in Gardner's cabin, as well as of receiving his practical instructions, not only contributed to James Haldane's future skill in seamanship, but also to his proficiency in general knowledge.

The voyage was tedious, even in those days, when a great monopoly prevailed, and economy in time was of little consequence. The charge for freight in an East Indiaman then ranged as high as forty pounds sterling per ton, and upwards.

The same freight now ranges as low even as forty shillings. In like manner, the crew of an Indiaman varied from a minimum of 126 up to 180 men. The Duke of Montrose carried 145 ; whilst little more than a third of that number would now be deemed adequate. The armament of the Company's ships used to be on the same scale, each carrying from twenty-six to thirty-six guns, and sometimes successfully beating off, or even capturing ships of war. Many of the captains, such as the Elphinstones, Lindsays, Ramsays, Dalrymples, Drummonds, and Trenches, were the younger sons of the nobility. Some of them were baronets ; most of them were either connected with the landed aristocracy or the great merchants, and frequently indulged in expensive habits, which rendered them rather objects of jealousy to the juniors in the Royal Navy, who had not the same means of acquiring fortune. These matters are all so much changed since the alteration of the Company's charter in 1814, and the complete overthrow of the monopoly in 1834, that this notice of a splendid service now extinct may not be wholly superfluous.

In many respects, it might be said that James Haldane's conduct on board the Montrose was highly exemplary. He resolutely set himself to master the details of his profession ; his attention to his duties attracted the approbation of his superiors ; and his zeal and energy were always combined with good sense, intelligence, and skill. He had also been furnished with a valuable store of books, consisting of the most useful histories of ancient and modern times, besides a good selection of the poets, dramatists, and writers on general literature. These books, which filled a large sea-chest, and afterwards occupied a considerable space in his library, were chosen by the discriminating taste of Dr. Bogue, of Gosport, who also took care to add a few well-selected useful religious works, amongst which was Doddridge's "Rise and Progress." It was often in after-life matter of surprise, that a sailor should have been so well-read and well-informed. The fact was, that not only did he go to sea at a later period than usual, but he was always fond of reading, so that, whilst ploughing the ocean or visiting distant regions, he was also deep in history, biography, voyages, and travels, diversifying these pursuits with the best of our poets, not omitting some of the French authors, and the most distinguished writers on Philosophy, Rhetoric, and Metaphysics.

It is on the 12th January, 1785, that the log of the Montrose begins. In one of his letters towards the close of his life, which recals early scenes, he observes that the ship came round to Portsmouth in March, when he spent a short time at Gosport, and sailed on the day after his cousin, the present Earl of Camperdown, was there born.

In the course of this voyage several incidents occurred, calculated to make a deep impression on his mind. On the 2d of June it was blowing very hard, and it became necessary to take in sail. For this purpose James Haldane was ordered to go aloft, with a party of men. Just as he was beginning to mount the rigging, Captain Gray called out to him to stop, and ordered an able seaman to go *first*. The log notices that, in taking in the main top-sail, "James Duncan fell from the yard, and was unfortunately drowned." He was struck on the head, and knocked overboard. Had young Haldane been first, he would doubtless have found a watery grave. He saw the drowning seaman amidst the billows, and never forgot the anxious look which eagerly sought, but sought in vain, for succour. He used also to mention that this sailor was the only man, in the whole course of his experience at sea, of whom he ever heard or knew anything which indicated the possession of a vital acquaintance with true Christianity. It was the general remark that it would be well if all on board were as fully prepared for death as James Duncan. On the 6th August the ship arrived at Bombay, where it remained more than two months, and James Haldane was much on shore with the late Mr. Crawford Bruce, who had come out in the Montrose, as well as with the Hon. William Fullarton Elphinstone, then the captain of an Indiaman, but afterwards a director and chairman of the Company, from whom, on different occasions, he afterwards experienced much kindness.

Exactly a year from the date of their arrival at Bombay, they

E

reached Macao, in China; and after remaining there four months, the Montrose proceeded homewards, and arrived at Deptford on the 16th June, 1787.

The continuation of the manuscript already quoted, intituled, "Dealings of God with my Soul," enables us to trace the progress of James Haldane's spiritual history:—

"After going to sea, I went on much in the same way for about a twelvemonth, having no more fear of God than others around me, excepting that I abstained from taking His name in vain, and that I read my Bible on the Sabbath, and still used a form of prayer. During that voyage, which lasted above two years, I just recollect one occasion on which my prayers deserved the name. A man had been murdered, another severely wounded, by some savages on an island (North Island, near Bantam), and as I had been the last who had been with them, before it happened, I considered my preservation as an instance of God's care of me, and with some gratitude I gave Him thanks. Indeed, I had cause. A few hours before it happened, attracted by curiosity, I went alone into the woods, on purpose to converse with the same people who soon afterwards committed the murder. They had been all day about us, while getting water for the ship. I came to their fire, but they were not there, or probably I had returned no more. During the same voyage I fell overboard from a boat. As I could not swim, I thought I should have been drowned, but was so hardened, that, although I recollect what passed in my mind while in the water, I never considered the consequences of death. Providentially I had an oar in my hand when I fell from the boat, but remembering that an old sailor had told me that no one need be drowned who could keep hold of an oar, this proved the means of my preservation. Some other things occurred, which might have struck me, but my conscience was becoming seared, as with a hot iron. On my return I never thought of going to church in London, because they had not the same form of worship there as in Scotland. This shows how easily the mind finds an excuse for a neglect of duty. My conscience, even at that time, would have testified against me, had I stayed away from public worship in Scotland, yet the difference of form in England easily silenced its rebuke. I now began more fully to surrender myself to what is called a life of pleasure, yet however inconsistent, I still had sometimes a form of prayer, but this became gradually less frequent. Indeed, it was wholly given up in the morning, and often at night I fell asleep in the midst of this duty, while pleasing myself with the thought, that such prayers might be of some avail. When I felt any check of conscience, I satisfied myself with thinking, that I was at least as good as any in the ship in which I sailed; that probably no one else even made a form of prayer, and thus that the balance was in my favour, and I thought, Surely God would never cast so many into misery. On my first voyage I was brought under more than common concern, by 'Doddridge's Rise and Progress,' which I read, like some other religious books, as a task. I found I was not right, and resolved to begin to amend, but my resolution was like the morning cloud and early dew. I now quieted my conscience with the consideration that I wronged no one, and therefore could not be very criminal. The Lord laid his hand on me during one voyage, and I was supposed by all to be dying. I thought so myself, but was at that time perfectly hardened, and sometimes considered how I should talk to those around me, when dying, determined, although I might feel it, I would show no unmanly signs of fear. The Lord however restored me, and preserved me from other dangers in which I had plunged myself by my folly, and all the return I made was to harden myself in my rebellion."

The allusions in the above memorandum to his further departures from God, have particular reference to his future voyages, and to the life of pleasure which he afterwards led both in Calcutta and in London. His second voyage was in the Phœnix, also commanded by Captain Gray, his friend Gardner being chief officer, and himself fifth. During its continuance he spent nearly six months on shore at Calcutta, at a time when the state of society in that great city was such that it would have required the power of the highest principle to have escaped its seductions. There were also peculiar circumstances which rendered his position in this respect more difficult. He had at Calcutta a friend and relation high in the service, and expending a great income, who welcomed him with the most affectionate hospitality, and loaded him with kindness. Mr. John Haldane, with his younger brother, the late General Robert Haldane, were the sons of a deceased relative, who held an office in the Excise in London, and had been originally nominated one of the executors of Captain James Haldane's will. Mr. John Haldane lived in splendour, having a great establishment in Calcutta, and another at Garden Reach, which, from its luxurious magnificence and the number of lustres with which it was adorned, used to be jocularly called "the *illustrious* house of Haldane." Living with him and introduced to all the gaiety of Calcutta, James Haldane's life was at this time one constant round of excitement and fashionable dissipation. His society was much sought after, and he derived some advantage from the attentions he received from the Marquis of Cornwallis, at whose residence he was a frequent visitor, and by whom he was noticed as a well-informed, agreeable, and superior young man. On his leaving Calcutta, a splendid entertainment was given to him by his friends, which was attended by the principal civil and military officers, and his return as Captain of the Melville Castle was anticipated as an accession to their social gaiety. The convivial habits of the times were at that period sufficiently bad in England. In the climate of India they were hardly tolerable, and instead of wondering at the mortality which then prevailed, it is only marvellous that it was not greater. As an example of the state of society, it is said that a little time before, Mr. John Haldane being persuaded that he had amassed a sufficient fortune, had resolved to return home, but the ship in which he had taken his passage having been wrecked at the mouth of the Ganges, he was received with some other passengers into the house of a gentleman in the neighbourhood. After supper they sat down to cards and played so high, that, before morning, Mr. John Haldane, being a great loser, determined to return to Calcutta, which he never left, except in the discharge of his public duties, till his death in 1803. After James Haldane's eyes were opened to the folly of that giddy round of pleasure, in which he had been himself involved, he wrote repeatedly and most affectionately to his friend, at Calcutta, setting the truth before him, and earnestly intreating him to remember that life was too short even for such follies as the world deems innocent. The celebrated Dr. Carey, in a letter, dated 27th of September, 1804, thus writes :—

" I am favoured with yours of January 4th, of the present year, for which I return you my hearty thanks. I trust that every expression of that regard which is borne to the cause in which I am embarked, has an effect upon my spirit of a salutary nature.

" I am sorry to say, that John Haldane, Esq., departed this life about two months before I received yours. I delivered the letter and parcel to Rev. Claudius Buchanan, who undertook to communicate the same to the gentleman who has the disposal of Mr. H.'s affairs, who, I understand, is — Forsyth, Esq.

" Your intention of coming to this country engaged my heart in love to you, though I am now convinced that the Lord has abounded in goodness to you by preventing your taking that step."

Mr. James Haldane made in all four voyages to India and China, and in the fourth, which lasted fifteen months, as second officer in his old ship, the Duke of Montrose. A circumstance occurred in connexion with his third voyage, which, for the time, made an impression on his mind, and led him to think of an overruling Providence. Through the late Sir Robert Preston, a contemporary of his father's, who had himself laid the foundation of his great fortune as an East India captain, he unexpectedly received an appointment as third officer of the Foulis Indiaman. Owing to inevitable circumstances he was detained in Scotland, and not having been fully informed of the urgency of the case, he found to his surprise and mortification, on his arrival in London, that the Foulis had sailed, and his place had been filled up. He was immediately nominated third officer of the Hillsborough, under Captain Coxwell ; but the loss of the first appointment was, on several accounts, very mortifying, and occasioned at the time much vexation. He little thought of the guardian arm that was around the child of many prayers. The Foulis was never again heard of, and is supposed to have foundered or been burned at sea.

There was another occasion on which he ran some voluntary risk of a different kind, in consequence of the shortness of the time which had been allowed for his outfit. The ship was in the Downs, and having stayed in London till what he considered the last safe moment, he posted down to Deal with great rapidity, and arrived in the middle of the night. There was a gale of wind, interposing much difficulty and no little danger in the way of getting on board, but a high bribe soon tempted the daring boatmen of Deal to take him alongside his ship. It was his object to announce himself as present to the Company's officer, specially appointed for that purpose, but the report had been already sent off, notifying Mr. Haldane's absence. The official was called up, and requested to despatch another letter intimating the arrival. By no means in good humour at the untimely disturbance, he peremptorily refused, but at last, after some altercation, admitted that it might be proper to make the announcement, if there were any means of doing so. In those days there were no electric telegraphs, the mail was gone, and the night most tempestuous. The young officer urged that he would himself be responsible for the safe conveyance of the despatch, and in the sequel carried it on shore, and posting up to London delivered it at the India House before the post-office delivery of letters, and again returned with equal rapidity to the Downs. It may be noted as characteristic of the India service in its palmy days, that it was then unusual for an officer of any East India ship to travel with less than four horses.

When he sailed, in 1792, he was in his twenty-fourth year. A skilful navigator, a good seaman, and as an officer distinguished alike for his firmness and suavity, he was looked up to by his companions as a fortunate young man, of superior talents, attainments, and prospects. The chief officer, Mr. Charles Dundas, was in bad health, and the Captain, although a man of worth and respectability, had not much confidence in himself, so that, in a certain sense, the command of the ship substantially depended on Mr. J. A. Haldane. In every emergency of difficulty or of danger, it was to his dauntless resolution and experienced seamanship that all eyes were turned. The Captain himself acknowledged that, when it blew hard at night, or the navigation was difficult, he never slept with comfort unless he knew that James Haldane was on deck, and when the voyage terminated he testified his sense of these services by the presentation of a costly collection of charts, as a grateful acknowledgment. On one occasion it happened, as appears by the log, that on the 12th of June, 1792, the ship had nearly struck on the rocks in the Mozambique Channel, under circumstances similar to those which, about the same time and in the same seas, occasioned the loss of the Winterton, with a number of the crew, including its commander, Captain Dundas of Dundas.* The promptitude and decision of James Haldane saved the Montrose from a like catastrophe. It was soon after midnight, or very early in the morning, when a passenger, walking upon deck, became alarmed at some conversation amongst the older seamen, which he overheard. He instantly went to Mr. Haldane's cabin, and rousing him from sleep, told him of his fears, and brought him immediately upon deck. The officer of the watch had previously apprehended no danger, but the Captain having been called, and the lead heaved, it appeared that, instead of being out of soundings, the depth was only nine fathoms. The Captain was undecided, when Mr. Haldane, considering that there was no time for further parley, put a speaking trumpet to his lips, and the cry, " Every soul upon deck this instant," sent alarm through the whole ship, and in a moment brought the men from their hammocks. To put the ship about was the work of a few minutes, and this was scarcely accomplished, before the shout, from the main-top, " Breakers ahead," warned them of the imminence of their danger, and discovered that half an hour's sailing in the same direction, would have probably left the Montrose a wreck on " the Barren Islands."

* An interesting account of the loss of the Winterton was some years ago published by George Buchan, Esq., of Kelloe, who was one of the passengers, and an attaché to Sir George Staunton's embassy.

The Montrose arrived at Deptford on the 19th June, 1793. The commencement of the war with France had been announced before the ship reached St. Helena, and from that island a large fleet of Indiamen were in company under convoy. This circumstance occasioned a frequent interchange of hospitality between the officers of the different ships, and in those days of convivial excess the result was anything but favourable to habits of sobriety. Happily James Haldane was never, even in his early days, inclined to exceed the bounds of temperance. He was, on the contrary, naturally rather abstemious : but, for a young man fond of society, full of life and spirit, it was almost impossible to escape without sometimes being carried away by the stream. In fact, it was considered a reproach to the hospitality of any ship which sent a party away sober. When the Duke of Wellington went to India, as Colonel *Wesley*, the same practices prevailed. But we have lived to see the time when such degrading scenes are deemed low and immoral, when a young man is not inevitably shut up to insobriety, unless he chooses to make himself peculiar, when swearing is deemed as vulgar as it is profane, and when religion and virtue are no longer treated only as objects of ridicule.

It was, however, after dining on board another ship that James Haldane, on returning to his own, very narrowly escaped falling down the hatchway, which must have proved certain death. He was only slightly injured, and his preservation was almost miraculous, but the circumstance awakened serious thoughts, and made a lasting impression on his mind. To him it was at the time the more mortifying, as the captain, who was himself reckoned rather an austere man, had previously been kindly cautioning him against these convivial meetings, telling him that the inebriety to which they were sure to lead might be well enough for some others, but in one of his superior mind, and with his resources, was altogether unworthy.

It might seem, perhaps, scarcely needful to allude to such things, except to show the greatness of the change afterwards wrought on his moral character by the grace of God. But, for the same reason, it may be right to mention a duel in which he was involved on his voyage from India in the Hillsborough. The facts are chiefly derived from the information of his own second and that of two of his brother officers. The ship was crowded with passengers; amongst these there was a captain of Dragoons, who was returning home,—a notorious shot, a successful duellist, and much of a bully. It afterwards appeared that he had been forced to leave the King's service, in consequence of his quarrelsome temper and aptitude for such brawls. In the course of the voyage he made himself very disagreeable, and was rather an object of dread. On one occasion some high words between him and Mr. James Haldane arose out of a proposal to make the latter a party to a paltry trick, designed to provoke an irritable invalid as he lay in his cot with his door open, and, as it turned out, actually in his last illness. An indignant refusal issued in this captain's taking an opportunity deliberately and publicly to insult Mr. James Haldane at the mess-table. In return the aggressor was very plainly told of the opinion entertained of his conduct, at which he became so much irritated as to throw a glass of wine in Mr. Haldane's face. He little knew the spirit which he evoked. To rise from his seat and dash at the head of his assailant a heavy ship's tumbler was the work of an instant. Providentially the missile was pitched too high, pulverized against the beam of the cabin, and descended in a liquid shower upon the offending dragoon. A challenge ensued, and Mr. J. Haldane consulted with a friend as to the propriety of accepting it. That the challenger was under a cloud with his own regiment was certain, although the particulars were unknown, and it was decided that it was optional to accept or decline the cartel. But, as the matter was then doubtful, it was ruled that, in obedience to the code of honour, it was safer to give the captain the benefit of the doubt; and the more so, as the reputation of the challenger as a shot might probably be regarded as having influenced a refusal.

The preliminaries being arranged, it was agreed that they should meet at the Cape of Good Hope; but the captain of the ship suspecting mischief, refused leave to land. The meeting was accordingly postponed till they arrived at St. Helena, when they all went ashore, unobserved, very early in the morning. The night before James Haldane made his will, wrote a letter of farewell to his brother, and then went to bed, and slept so soundly that he did not awake till he was called. It happened that, owing to the apprehension of being observed and detained, the duellists had only one case of pistols, which belonged to James Haldane's second, a naval officer of some distinction, afterwards better known, during the war, as Admiral Donald Campbell, who commanded the Portuguese fleet, and also enjoyed a pension for services rendered to Lord St. Vincent and Lord Nelson. The two antagonists were placed at twelve paces distant, and were to fire together by a signal. Before the pistol was delivered into Mr. J. Haldane's hand, his second, in a low tone, repeated what he had before told him, that this was a case in which he must have no scruple about shooting his challenger; that it was not a common duel, but a case of self-preservation, and that one or the other must fall. The signal was given, and, as Mr. J. Haldane raised his pistol, with strange inconsistency he breathed, as he himself related, the secret prayer,—" Father, into thy hands I commend my spirit;" thus verifying the observation of Tertullian, that in moments of imminent danger men involuntarily call upon God, acknowledging his presence and his providence, even when they seem practically to forget his existence and trample on his laws. With this prayer in his heart, and, as Admiral Campbell testified, with his eye fixed on his antagonist, without a symptom of trepidation, he calmly drew the trigger, when his pistol burst, the contents flying upwards and a fragment of the barrel inflicting a wound on his face. The other pistol missed fire, and the challenger immediately intimated, through his second, that he was so well satisfied with the honourable conduct of Mr. Haldane, that he was willing that the affair should terminate. This message was accepted as sufficient. Bowing to each other, they parted with civility, but, as might be anticipated, without reconciliation. To such matters he scarcely ever alluded, but the facts were known to his brother and by him repeated not long before his death.

As a contrast to the spirit manifested at this time, it may be mentioned that, about ten years after the duel, Mr. James Haldane happened to be at Buxton, in the public room of one of the great hotels. There was a window open near the place where Mrs. J. Haldane was seated, and fearing, on her account, the effects of a draught, he shut it. A swaggering young man, more intent to display his self-consequence than his gallantry, with great rudeness immediately reopened it. Mr. J. Haldane said, " There was a time, Sir, when I should have resented this impertinence, but I have since learned to forgive injuries and to overlook insults."

At the period of which we write, " affairs of honour," as they are miscalled, were of such common occurrence, that those who chose to live under the tyranny of the world felt it frequently impossible to escape. Indeed, from his ardent temperament and almost prodigal courage, it is perhaps matter of surprise, considering the spirit of the times, that such a young man was not oftener thus involved. It has been said by his contemporaries, that this was partly owing to the fact that his known determination usually shielded him from insult, and partly that his natural disposition being amiable, the spirit which would not brook an insult was equally averse to offer provocation. In themselves, duelling and personal quarrels were abhorrent to his nature, and, more than once, when his co-operation as a second was requested, he was the means of effecting reconciliation without bloodshed. In one of these cases, both of the intended belligerents had requested to be allowed to place their honour in his hands, and refusing to act against either as an antagonist he was enabled to arrange the matter to their mutual satisfaction.

There was, indeed, one occasion, some years afterwards, which attracted much attention at the time, when he prevented a duel between a friend of his and a very notorious and highly connected colonel, who, not many years ago, wrote his own memoirs, under the title of a Baronetcy, which he had assumed, without legal authority, on the ground of collateral descent. This colonel had fought more duels than most men, and was equally expert at his pistol or his rapier. He had frequently wounded, and, at least, in one affair, killed his antagonist. Sitting in a large party at a dinner-table, after the ladies had withdrawn, at the house of his brother-in-law, in the neighbourhood of Stirling, the belligerent colonel engaged in a trifling dispute with an elderly and much respected gentleman, at whose head he finally levelled a decanter. This act of violence had been preceded by a torrent of abuse which moved the indignation of the whole company, although every one, including their host himself, seemed paralyzed. Scarcely had the decanter sped its way, when, at the same moment, the colonel's own collar was seized by the muscular arm of a young man sitting by his side, and he himself and his chair were suddenly projected into the middle of the room. Rising from the ground, his paroxysm of rage now sought another object of attack, but he was so calmly confronted by the steady eye and determined bearing of James Haldane, whose character was well known to him, that he involuntarily and obviously cooled. He contented himself by hastily demanding the meaning of this uncalled-for interference in a quarrel that was not his, and being briefly but emphatically told that every gentleman was bound to prevent violence in his company, the irate duellist once more turned his reproaches on the original object of his ungovernable fury, and with great skill adopting the words of the unwelcome pacificator as a satisfactory explanation, walked out of the room, exclaiming, "As for my friend, Captain Haldane, his object was only to prevent violence." Colonel B——, of I——, who had been so rudely insulted, was himself a well-known Perthshire gentleman, and at first considered that he was obliged " to demand satisfaction," but the two brothers went to his house the next day, and succeeded in convincing him that even according to the wretched code of honour then prevalent, he was absolved by the subsequent rencontre from any such obligation. So far as the aggressor was himself concerned, it seemed as if a spell had been broken ; the terror which was connected with his name was dissipated. He shortly afterwards went abroad, and during the occupation of Egypt, joined the British army after its landing. But Sir

Ralph Abercromby, as Commander-in-chief, sent him a peremptory order instantly to depart, with an intimation that it would be at his own peril if again found within the British lines. He retired to France during the war, and never again returned to reside in Scotland.

It will be seen in a future part of these Memoirs, with what power and effect Mr. J. A. Haldane assailed the practice of duelling. There is no doubt that the attention he then excited, and the crowds who came to hear him when, in 1804, he preached on the death of Lord Camelford, were partly due to the knowledge of the fact, that he himself had been a votary of the so-called laws of honour, and had been seen to brave the wrath of one of the most notorious duellists of his time.

A little before the occurrence just related, there was another, which had attracted some notice in the county. It happened that a warrant had been issued for the apprehension of a tenant on the Airthrey estate, who was a very desperate character, and had committed an act of swindling, accompanied by forgery. When the officers went to apprehend him they were severely beaten, and came to the house of Airthrey in the evening to report the result and solicit additional aid, as well as the authority of Mr. Haldane's presence. Both he and his younger brother accordingly went, taking with them some of the servants. On arriving at the house of the culprit, at the mill near the Bridge of Allan, or the modern village of Airthrey Wells, they found the doors and windows barricaded, and the man, with his dogs and some of his sons and servants, armed with guns and bludgeons, threatening death to any one who dared to break in. The officers were themselves alarmed, but neither of the two gentlemen whose aid they had claimed chose to be thus ignominiously repulsed. Whilst considering how to proceed, Mr. Haldane, with characteristic generalship, walked round the premises, and suddenly called out to his brother that there was an unguarded window, which had been overlooked by the besieged in their plans of defence. James Haldane, with determination equally characteristic, no sooner heard the announcement than he sprung through the window, which dropped behind him, just as the defenders, attracted by the noise, were hurrying to the point of attack. Pausing for a moment to produce his pistols, looking his intended assailants steadily in the face, warning them as to the consequences of assailing him in discharge of his duty, he coolly walked to the front door, which he unlocked, and then left the peace officers to remove their prisoner. The culprit, although ably defended by Mr. Maconochie, was convicted, and banished.

The change of social habits since the last generation passed away, is a fit subject of congratulation and thankfulness. In the higher ranks of society the vices of drinking, swearing, and duelling, are now nearly as vulgar as they were once fashionable. Three centuries ago swearing was so common, that a chaplain, preaching the funeral sermon of a titled lady of the noble house of Berkeley, belonging to the Court of Queen Elizabeth, mentions it as a proof of her virtue, that she was never heard to use a profane oath. Within a much shorter period than sixty years ago it was difficult for any young man who did not affect singularity to escape from the contamination of that convivial intemperance which disgraced the age. It was not every one who could act like Dr. Johnson, who, unable to resist the temptation, at last substituted lemonade for wine, so as to enjoy social intercourse and yet avoid excess. Even Mr. Pitt could enter the House of Commons so much intoxicated, that Mr. Fox, who could well sympathize with the indiscretion, moved an adjournment; and, as connected with these Memoirs, it is rather a curious circumstance that this historical fact occurred after the great Premier, in company with his friend and colleague Mr. Dundas, had been dining at Deptford, on board the Melville Castle, with Captain Philip Dundas, shortly before Captain Haldane assumed the command. It is not wonderful that profane swearing and duelling should be connected with deep potations, and that vices should have been fashionable in the last generation which would now be reckoned vulgar and discreditable. The pious Colonel Blackadder, in his remarkable diary, which includes the wars of Marlborough, bewails an occasion of nuptial festivity when, in the neighbourhood of Stirling, he had himself, in his old age, been betrayed into intemperance, and even persons having a reputation for religion were known to be not wholly exempt from the habit of infringing on the third commandment.

If such topics have been glanced at in connexion with Captain Haldane's early life, it is for the purpose of furnishing a just representation of his natural character before it was changed by grace. In reading these incidents, who would believe that this is the same person of whom Mr. Simeon not four years afterwards writes: " The Lord has favoured you with a meek and spiritual mind?" The gentleness and benevolence of his character increased as he advanced in age, even to the last, although its force and energy were never broken.

His elder brother, a short time before his own death, during a well-remembered walk at Auchingray, was relating to the biographer some of the facts which have been just recorded, and finished his interesting details by saying, " See, then, the power of grace."

There was a time when, to use the emphatic words of James Haldane, few seemed to be more " stout-hearted and far from righteousness,"—when the dread of the world was the only fear which influenced his actions, and God was not in all his thoughts. But neither the world, the flesh, nor the devil, were destined long to retain their prey. He was " a chosen vessel," ordained to be himself a monument of Divine mercy, and an instrument to convey that mercy to others. His whole nature was to undergo renovation. The good seed, still lodged in his breast, was soon to burst forth and produce its glorious fruits. The proud heart which would not bend before his fellows, or before the world itself, was to become broken under a melting sense of the Saviour's love. That lofty spirit which would not quail even at the approach of death, and which could not brook a word or a look that menaced it with insult, was to abandon its stubborn rebellion and become lowly, humble, and contrite before the Lord. His energies, his courage, his determination, were indeed to remain, but these energies, that courage, that determination, were to be directed into a nobler channel.

They were to be consecrated to the service of another and a better
Master. They were to be no longer the attributes of a haughty
rebel, but a part of the glorious panoply of the Christian hero,
the devoted, self-denying, faithful champion of the cross.

---

James Haldane's fourth voyage in the Duke of Montrose
ended on the 19th June, 1793. In less than a month he
attained the age of twenty-five, and having passed the necessary examinations, he was nominated to the Melville Castle,
bound to Madras and Calcutta. The ship was ordered to be in
the Downs at the beginning of the following January, but
before the time arrived he had taken another step, which exerted
an important influence on his future life.

Soon after he went down to Scotland, he met at Airthrey a
young lady, to whom he was married on the 18th of September
following. She was the only child of Major Alexander Joass,
of Culleonard, in the county of Banff, by Elizabeth Abercromby,
daughter of George Abercromby, of Tulliebody in the county of
Clackmannan. In early life Major Joass had served in the
Royals, with his brother-in-law, Colonel Edmonstone, of Newton,
but having been disabled for active service by rheumatic fever,
he accepted the appointment of Fort Major and Acting Deputy-
Governor of Stirling Castle, which was conferred by the
Governor, his uncle, General James Abercromby, of Glassaugh.
This office placed him with very easy duties, in an agreeable
residence, in the centre of his own friends and his wife's, where
for thirty years, although much of an invalid, he made the old
palace at Stirling Castle famed for its hospitality. Major
Joass, having no male issue, had sold his paternal estate of
Culleonard, near Banff, to the Earl of Findlater and Seafield,
and unfortunately some years before the great rise which took
place in the value of land in Scotland. His only daughter was
a general favourite, and such was the charm of her vivacity and
the sweetness of her disposition, that it was naturally expected
she should make what is called "a good marriage." It is not,

therefore, matter of surprise that there should have been some hesitation as to the proposed union of an only child with a younger son, whose prospects were, indeed, excellent, but whose fortune was still to come from the ocean and from foreign climes. Difficulties, however, gave way before strong attachment, aided by the affectionate zeal of Mr. Robert Haldane, who was anxious that there should be a new attraction to help on the arrangement by which he hoped to detain his brother at home.

The following letter from Sir Ralph Abercromby, then on service with the Duke of York in France, written in the heat of a busy campaign, is at once interesting as coming from so distinguished a General, and as indicating the good sense of his manly character.

" *Lieut.-General Ralph Abercromby to Major Joass.*
" *Camp before Dunkirk, August* 27, 1793.

"MY DEAR MAJOR,—You may easily conceive that, in a matter in which your family is so nearly concerned, an old friend and near relation cannot but be interested. If your daughter likes Mr. Haldane, which is the case, there is no difficulty. They have and will have abundance. He is a young man in a profession which will command fortune; and allow me to say, it is a better match for real happiness than if ' Miss Joass' had married an idle country gentleman, let his character be what it may. I warmly congratulate you on this event; and from the good principles of the family into which your daughter goes, I have no doubt of her happiness.

" We are now preparing for the siege of Dunkirk. I hope it will be of shorter duration than that of Valenciennes. That of Bergens will follow, so that we shall have no idleness. I keep my health wonderfully well. Sir Robert Laurie is here with us. He begs his compliments. I am sorry it has not been in my power to pay as much attention to several young gentlemen from our country as I could wish. Young Duff is a fine lad; so is young Shawfield. My love to you all.

" Ever yours, affectionately,
" Rʜ. Aʏ."

Shortly after their marriage, Captain and Mrs. James Haldane proceeded to London, where, for some months, they resided in Sackville-street, Piccadilly. Between the bustle of preparing for the voyage and the gaieties of the metropolis, there was not much opportunity for serious thought. Mrs. James Haldane had been carefully brought up, and accustomed to

F

the ministry of Mr. Simeon's friend, Dr. Walter Buchanan, and more recently to that of Dr. Innes. She was, therefore, a good deal shocked at the disregard of the Lord's-day, and the abandonment of public worship. It is a striking thought, that her husband was then borrowing the arguments he had learned from Dr. Macknight on his tour with Dr. Adam, as to the difference between neglecting these duties in Scotland and in England, adding, at the same time, that it was much easier to get to heaven than she imagined. Such arguments are not, it is to be feared, out of date, in the present age, but they were formerly much more common. In illustration of this, Mr. James Haldane used himself to tell of a scene to which he was witness, at the castle of a noble Earl in the county of Forfar. It happened that a celebrated and somewhat eccentric Duchess arrived rather unexpectedly on a Sunday. Out of compliment to her Grace and her London habits, she was offered in the evening the amusement of cards. This improper compliance was contrary to the usages of the family; and her instant and emphatic reply, "Not on this side of the Tweed, my Lord," whilst it rebuked the complaisance of her noble host, implied that she felt ashamed of the proposal.

The preparations for the voyage were completed before the end of December, including the arrangements for Mrs. J. Haldane's return and safe convoy to Scotland. Their separation was the only dark spot in the horizon, as all things seemed to smile on a bright future. They had met with kindness from all their family connexions and friends in London, including Mr. Secretary and Lady Jane Dundas. Captain Haldane also visited that distinguished Minister at Walmer Castle, and received from him the hearty and unsolicited assurance of his support and interest. Mr. Hobart, afterwards Earl of Buckinghamshire, was then going out as Governor of Madras, and he informed Mr. Coutts, the banker, that he had been requested by the President of the Board of Control to remember that Captain Haldane was one in whom he took a personal interest. The fact of his wife's uncle, Sir Robert Abercromby, having been Governor and Commander-in-chief at Bombay, and being then at the head of the whole Indian army, was another circumstance in his favour, whilst above all, his own reputation was sure to give full effect to all his family and personal influence. As the value of a command then greatly depended upon the number and quality of the passengers returning home, it may be easily supposed that few of his contemporaries took leave of the East India House with brighter prospects.

The Melville Castle had been manned with unusual rapidity, the popularity of the captain rendering employment in that ship an object of competition with seamen. It arrived at Portsmouth on the 31st of December, 1793, and it was expected that the East India fleet, consisting of no less than twenty-five ships, would shortly sail under a strong convoy. But after all was ready, there were various circumstances which combined for their detention. In the first place, the Government then entertained a plan for availing themselves of the Indiamen to reduce the Mauritius; and in the next place, there was a continuance of westerly winds for such an unusual period, that the fleet, which should have sailed in January, did not weigh anchor till the month of May. Upon these contingencies was suspended the future history of Captain Haldane's life.

It was during this interval that a circumstance occurred, strongly illustrating the same force of character and indomitable courage which always marked his career. The part he took in quelling the mutiny on board the Dutton has now become " a history little known," but for many years it was often spoken of by those connected with the great East India fleet, finally amounting to thirty-six ships, which were then collected at Portsmouth. The following account was kindly furnished by the Rev. Christopher Anderson, not long before he rested from his useful labours. His brother was a surgeon on board the Dutton, and kept a journal, in which the facts were noted. There are a few other incidents which were gleaned from Mr. James Haldane's own conversation, but they were in full accordance with Dr. Anderson's narrative, and add but slightly to his vivid description of the scene.

At the close of 1793, a large East India fleet was detained,

by various causes, in the Downs and at Spithead, from
Christmas to April following.  A mutinous disposition was in
December detected and subdued, in the case of three or four
men, on board the Dutton, Captain Samson.  On the 31st,
the Melville Castle and two other East Indiamen anchored at
Spithead.  The Carnatic and many others followed, till they
came to be styled "the grand fleet."  By the 19th March,
however, in paying off certain men at Portsmouth from the
Dutton, such a spirit was evinced as induced the Captain to
apply for assistance to His Majesty's ship the Regulus.  The
men complained that, owing to their detention, their stores
were exhausted, and they demanded an additional advance of
pay to purchase tea and other comforts.  The crew of the
Melville Castle had received this indulgence, as a boon which
it was reasonable to grant.  It was refused by the Captain of
the Dutton, and hence the mutiny.  On the evening of the
19th, Lieutenant Lucas, of the Regulus, with his boat's crew,
came on board, to demand four of the ringleaders, the *same
men* formerly mentioned, when the greatest part of the crew
hastily got up the round shot on deck, threatening that they
would sink the first boat that came alongside.  The crew
emboldened and increasing in fury, the Lieutenant thought it
prudent to leave the ship, as did also the Captain, under the
impression that their absence might assist in restoring peace
and quietness.  The crew, however, becoming outrageous, were
going to hoist out the boats.  The Carnatic Indiaman, hearing
the confusion, fired several alarm guns, and armed boats from
the other ships were now advancing.  By this time the crew
of the Dutton, being in a most serious state of mutiny, had
begun to arm themselves with shot, iron bars, &c., and at last
made a determined attack on the quarter-deck.  The officers,
having lost their command, were firing pistol-shots overhead,
when one seaman, getting over the booms, received a wound,
of which he died six days after.

It has been said that the mutineers threatened to carry the
ship into a French port, but at this moment, far more serious
apprehension was felt lest the men should gain access to the

powder magazine, and madly end the strife by their own death, and that of all on board. One of the two medical men had serious thoughts of throwing himself into the water to escape the risk. It was at this critical moment that Captain Haldane, of the Melville Castle, appeared at the side of the vessel. His approach was the signal for renewed and angry tumults. The shouts of the officers, " Come on board; come on board," were drowned by the cries of the mutineers, " Keep off, or we'll sink you." The scene was appalling, and to venture into the midst of the angry crew seemed to be an act of daring almost amounting to rashness. Ordering his men to veer round by the stern, in a few moments Captain Haldane was on the quarter-deck. His first object was to restore to the officers composure and presence of mind. He peremptorily refused to head an immediate attack on the mutineers, but very calmly reasoning with the men, sword in hand, telling them that they had no business there, and asking what they hoped to effect in the presence of twenty sail-of-the-line, the quarter-deck was soon cleared. But, observing that there was still much confusion, and inquiring where the chief danger lay, he was down immediately at the very point of alarm. Two of the crew, intoxicated with spirits, and more hardy than the rest, were at the door of the powder magazine, threatening with horrid oaths that whether it should prove Heaven or Hell they would blow up the ship. One of them was in the act of wrenching off the iron bars from the doors, whilst the other had a shovel full of *live coals* ready to throw in ! Captain Haldane, instantly putting a pistol to the breast of the man with the iron bar, told him that if he stirred he was a dead man. Calling at the same time for the irons of the ship, as if disobedience were out of the question, he saw them placed, first on this man and then on the other. The rest of the ringleaders were also secured, when the crew, finding that they were overpowered, and receiving the assurance that none should be removed that night, became quiet, and the Captain returned to the Melville Castle. Next day, the chief mutineers were put on board the Regulus, and the rest of the crew went to their duty peaceably.

" Had any one," said the venerable narrator, " then foretold that this daring captain of the Melville Castle would ere long become a minister of Christ, the pastor of a large Christian Church, and of a larger congregation, and that this surgeon on board the Dutton now bound for India, and well known afterwards as Dr. James Anderson of Edinburgh—would, after returning home, one day join that Church, where he remained for years until his dissolution, nothing would have appeared so incredible."

This was the last of the perils of James Haldane's life at sea, in which his bold and adventurous spirit seemed to take pleasure. The time had now come when he was to enter on a holier calling, and to be engaged in occupations of more enduring importance. The change was not, however, sudden, but gradual; not the result of enthusiastic excitement, but of calm reflection. " Marriage," it has been said, " sobers even the soberest." It operated on his moral feelings with a most beneficial influence. He had been thoroughly disgusted with the bacchanalian joviality of his last voyage from St. Helena; he also felt the responsibility of his new position, as Commander of a ship with a numerous crew of officers and men, besides passengers and soldiers. He resolved that his influence should be exerted for good, and that he would set an example befitting his station, by having Divine worship on board. To all this it may be added, that the idea of parting so soon and for so long a time from his young wife, to whom he was tenderly attached, was justly assigned by some of his friends as one circumstance that made him for the time at least more thoughtful and reflective. A remarkable letter which he wrote some years afterwards to his old friend, Captain Patrick Gardner, furnishes an interesting account of the gradual development of the change which was begun in the Melville Castle during the four months he lived on board ship at Portsmouth.

" *Dumfries, June* 29, 1801.
. . . " My giving up the sea at the time I did was, I believe, thought strange by many; but I have never repented it, nor do I find my time hang heavy on my hands. We are all apt to imagine ourselves of great consequence, and I believe we often think we are occupying the attention of others when they hardly think of us. Perhaps this is the reason of my

supposing you have heard of a considerable change in my views since we met. If I can judge by what I feel towards you, you would inquire about me : and I could smile at the answer you might probably receive, and the surprise it might excite in you. Perhaps you might figure me gloomy and melancholy, incapable of enjoying the comforts of life, from fear of hell : or I might be represented as a wild enthusiast, considering myself inspired or favoured with particular revelations. On either of these suppositions, I could not blame you for not renewing our correspondence; but neither the one nor the other is the case. I never was acquainted with solid, rational happiness till my attention was turned to religion. My former merriment was really like the crackling of thorns under a pot. I was governed by passion, and under such a guide no wonder if I missed my road. Although I believe I had as few qualms of conscience as any one, being completely unconcerned about religion and eternity, my own mind was not altogether satisfied. I knew I must die, yet it was a subject I banished from my thoughts. The peace of mind I enjoyed did not arise from any good reason. I had to hope either that I should be happy or be annihilated after death, but from total inconsideration, like a person who should stop his ears and shut his eyes when danger was approaching, and then fancy himself safe. My present peace of mind does not arise from any vision or supposed new revelation I have received. I had a book by me which, from prejudice of education, and not from any rational conviction, I called the Word of God. I never so far surmounted the prejudice of education as to profess infidelity, but I was a more inconsistent character. I said I believed a book to be a revelation from God, and treated it with the greatest neglect, living in direct contradiction to all its precepts, and seldom taking the trouble to look into it, or if I did, it was to perform a task,—a kind of atonement for my sins. I went on thus till, having much time on my hands when the Melville Castle lay at the Mother Bank, I began to think I would pay a little more attention to this book. The more I read the more worthy it appeared of God ; and after examining the evidences with which Christianity is supported, I became fully persuaded of its truth. There is no man who considers the evidences with the smallest impartiality but must come to the same conviction. Even Rousseau admits the strength of the evidence, but he says he remains in suspense, because there are many doctrines which he thinks unworthy of God. In other words, he will not submit his pride of understanding to a book which himself allows is supported by the strongest evidence as coming from God. This suspense is now over, and neither he nor any other man shall be able to complain they have been hardly dealt with. The Infidel, whether by profession or practice, shall be convinced they meet with no more than they deserve. The error lies in their heart, not in their understanding; they choose the darkness : they determine to live in sin, and they persuade themselves while here, being blinded

by passion, they shall escape punishment. My paper, and I fear your
patience, is done, but the subject is important. I beg you would seriously
consider it. I hope to hear immediately from you, and am,

"Very sincerely yours,

"J. A. HALDANE.

"*Patrick Gardner, Esq., Commander of the Scaleby Castle.*"

In another document he thus details the results of his study
of the Bible:—

"At length some impressions seemed to be made on my mind, that all
was not right, and knowing that the Lord's Supper was to be dispensed, I
was desirous of being admitted, and went and spoke with Dr. Bogue on
the subject. He put some books into my hand on the nature of the
ordinance, which I read, and was more regular in prayer and attending
public worship. An idea of quitting the sea at this time was suggested
apparently by accident, and literally so, except in so far as ordered of
God. The thought sunk into my mind, and, although there were many
obstacles, my inclination rather increased than abated. Being now in the
habit of prayer, I asked of God to order matters so that it might be
brought about, and formed resolutions of amendment, in case my prayer
should be heard. Several circumstances occurred which seemed to cut
off every hope of my being able to get away before the fleet sailed; yet
the Lord overruled all to farther the business, and I quitted the ship
about two days before she left England. . . However dark my mind
still was, I have no doubt but that God began a work of grace on my
soul living on board the Melville Castle. His voice was indeed still and
small, but I would not despise the day of small things, nor undervalue
the least of His gracious dealings towards me. There is no doubt that I
had sinned against more light than many of my companions who have
been cut off in their iniquities, and that I might justly have been made a
monument of His wrath."

The chief obstacles to his leaving the sea, arose from the
opposition of his own uncles, and from his wife's relatives.
They naturally considered it an act of folly to relinquish
prospects of fortune such as he had before him, and the idea of
a young man sitting down as "an idle country gentleman" was
one which Sir Ralph Abercromby had in his letter particularly
singled out as unfavourable for happiness. Mr. Robert
Haldane had previously, although without success, made some
disinterested and generous proposals to induce him to settle
at home, and in the neighbourhood of Airthrey. But

when he heard that an offer of 9000*l*. had been made for the command, being at the rate of 3000*l*. a voyage, exclusive of the Captain's share in the property of the ship and stores, which amounted in all to 6000*l*. additional, he wrote strongly recommending that it should be accepted, as he considered that his brother's present means and future expectations were ample. His letter decided the matter, and Captain Haldane, quitting the Melville Castle,* rejoined his wife in Scotland early in the summer of 1794.

During that summer they resided chiefly at Stirling Castle and at Airthrey. On the 6th October, their first child, Elizabeth, was born, and in less than a month afterwards the death of Major Joass dissolved their connexion with Stirling Castle, and all its agreeable associations. A letter from Sir Ralph Abercromby on the marriage of his niece has been already given. The following, addressed to his sister on the removal of her husband, was written during the bustle of the disastrous campaign in Holland, and a few days after his wound in the successful sally made upon the French at Nimmegen:—

" *Elst, November* 16*th*, 1794.

" MY DEAR SISTER,—From my not writing, I trust you will not accuse me of unkindness. With Mrs. Abercromby alone I correspond, and it sometimes happens that I have not an opportunity. She has regularly informed me of everything that related to your family. I cannot but feel severely a change that has lately taken place in it. I have lost an old and a most worthy friend. It would have given me the greatest satisfaction had Providence so ordered it, that we should have met once more after the end of all these troubles. He is gone to a better world, and is relieved from the pains of this. It is an event which you and all his family foresaw. Still that does not diminish the severity of the stroke. I am told Mr. Haldane is an excellent young man, with a great share of humanity,

---

* The Melville Castle was afterwards sold to the Dutch, and, being fitted out as a troop-ship, was wrecked on the 23d November, 1802, on Dymchurch-wall, near Hythe. Out of 472 persons who a few days before left the coast of Holland not more than eighteen escaped the raging billows. The Dutton was also lost in 1796, near Plymouth, but in consequence of the energetic skill of Sir Edward Pellew (Lord Exmouth), the crew were saved.

and that his conduct at this trying time has been most praiseworthy. I hope it will always be so, and that he and his wife will be a comfort and consolation to you. Knowing your sensibility I much fear your health must have suffered. You must endeavour to support yourself from such motives as reason and religion will suggest. I have a distant hope that I may see you this winter. I shall probably find you near us all. I beg to be kindly remembered to Mr. and Mrs. Haldane. Believe me to be, my dear Sister,

"Yours, ever most affectionately,

"RA. ABERCROMBY."

On leaving Stirling Castle, Mr. and Mrs. James Haldane at first took a house in George-square, Edinburgh, and were led to attend the ministry of the excellent Dr. Walter Buchanan, who, as already remarked, had formerly been minister of Stirling, and of whom it is said by Mr. Simeon, that he was "a Scotch minister, whom I think it one of the greatest blessings of my life ever to have known." They were also introduced about the same time to the Reverend David Black, the minister of Lady Yester's Church, who was eminently a man of God and a promoter of all good works. These excellent men found them earnest inquirers into the things of God, and were no doubt useful in directing their spiritual studies. But their progress was gradual, as will be seen hereafter.

The history of James Haldane's life has now been conducted to the end of 1795. In the summer of that year he had made a visit of some length to his uncle, on board the Venerable, when the North Sea fleet was in the Downs. His frequent reference, more than fifty years afterwards, to the incidents which then occurred, indicated the pleasurable excitement he enjoyed as a guest under the flag of his distinguished relative. It was at the time when Admiral Cornwallis made his celebrated and successful retreat with only five sail of the line, which repulsed·and kept at bay twelve of the French with as many frigates. He used to relate how Admiral Duncan, on a visit to Walmer Castle, found Mr. Pitt in deep despondency, considering the capture of Cornwallis and his little fleet inevitable; and how the Premier was reassured, although still half-sceptical, when his gallant visitor scouted his apprehensions and forbade him to think so meanly of five British men-of-war. "What," said Mr. Pitt, "do you think that, against such odds, they have a chance?" "A chance, Sir!" exclaimed the veteran chief, "Frenchmen do not yet know how to take a British ship." Mr. Pitt was cheered, though incredulous, and soon afterwards invited the Admiral to dinner. On the morning of that day the news of the repulse of the French, and the safe arrival of the intrepid Cornwallis, reached the Downs, but, by some mistake, the welcome intelligence had not been forwarded to Mr. Pitt. On going in the afternoon to dinner, the Admiral, on entering the reception-room and shaking hands with Mr. Pitt, exclaimed, " Give you joy, Sir!" Mr. Pitt, oppressed with anxieties, had relapsed into his former despondency, and observed, "Joy! Admiral—what joy? Nothing is yet known of the fate of Cornwallis." An explanation soon put Mr. Pitt in possession of the agreeable tidings, that Frenchmen did not yet know the art of taking British ships, and British seamen did not know when they ought to consider themselves beaten. He declared that the Admiral had taken a load from off his mind, and that he never sat down to dinner with a lighter heart. It was at Walmer Castle that the celebrated Marquis of Wellesley used to meet Lord Duncan, at the time when he describes the Premier's admiration of the joyous and gallant bearing of the hero of Camperdown.

Mr. J. A. Haldane used also to tell how it happened, about the time of his visit to the Venerable, that Admiral Duncan had been the means of pressing the services of Sir John Jervis on the notice of the Premier, and overcoming his prejudices against an officer who had joined in characterizing the war as "unnecessary, impolitic, and lamentable." On Sir Charles Hotham's recal, the appointment of Commander-in-chief in the Mediterranean was first offered to Lord Duncan. But he was so well persuaded of the importance of the command in the North Seas, that he the more easily allowed other earnest and effectual persuasion to influence his determination to decline the proposed change to a more distant scene of action. He was next consulted by Mr. Pitt, Lord Melville, and Lord Spencer, as to the fittest officer for that post, and he told them that, beyond all doubt, it was Sir John Jervis.   It was objected that the latter had too much mixed himself up with politics, and too strongly reprobated the war, to render it expedient to nominate so decided an opponent of the Government.   But Lord Duncan still insisted that his friend's qualifications were paramount to all party considerations, and Mr. Pitt was at length convinced.   To this circumstance Lord St. Vincent's career of distinction may probably be traced. The fact is not mentioned in any of the Lives of Lord St. Vincent; but it rests on the undoubted evidence of Lord Duncan's nephew, who was with him at the time, and heard all the details of these discussions after the appointment had been confirmed.   Lord Duncan was himself so unostentatious, and so little disposed to boast, that even his own early services at the Havannah, Goree, Belleisle, St. Vincent, and Gibraltar, would have been comparatively unnoticed, had it not been that Lord Spencer, without a prompter, remembered "Keppell's Captain."   His Lordship's choice was rewarded by the undaunted firmness which maintained the blockade of the Dutch fleet during the mutiny of the Nore, and by the splendour of his victory off Camperdown, which at once crushed the naval power of republican Holland, and effectually warded off the intended invasion of Ireland.

When Mr. J. A. Haldane returned to Edinburgh, his mind became more and more occupied with religious investigations, and a reference to his own recollections will enable us to trace its progress.

"On my return to Scotland, I continued to inquire about religion more from a conviction of its importance than any deep conviction of sin.   I was, however, sensible I had been a great sinner, but my views of God's mercy were such that I was under no great alarm.   A Socinian minister with whom I met was of use to me (a Mr. Edwards), not from conversation, but because his opinions brought the great mystery of godliness under my consideration.   When I heard of the controversy respecting the person of Christ, it did not seem to me of very great importance. I had what the world calls charity for both parties, thinking both were Christians. When the matter was discussed I took the side to which I had been accustomed, but I had hardly any opinion on the subject. A conversation I heard between a person who was arguing, if not in favour of Socinianism, at least taking from them any degree of guilt or danger for their opinions, and an eminently pious man, now in glory, struck me much. The latter was not disputing for victory, but maintaining that truth which was sweeter to his soul than the honeycomb. Christ was precious to him, and he justly considered that those could not be his friends who degraded his character. I shall never forget the earnestness with which he said, 'If I did not know my Saviour to be God, I should this night lie down in despair; the Scriptures could, in this case, convey no comfort to my mind.' The expression struck me much, and led me to compare my views of Christ with his. I compared the Scriptures which he and others quoted, and the result was a conviction that Jesus was indeed the Son of the living God. I took some opportunities of conversing with the person to whom I have alluded, and, being desirous of having my mind satisfied and of submitting to the truth, I soon became more established in this fundamental and most important of all truths. Conversations I had with two pious ministers* were also very useful to me. They saw I was inquiring, that I was indeed desirous to know the truth, and bore with much self-confidence, which I displayed in argument, of which, at that time, I was particularly fond. Fuller's ' Comparison of Calvinism and Socinianism' was peculiarly useful to me, not so much from the general argument, which is admirably conducted, as that it brought into my view that text in Job where he expresses self-loathing and abhorrence. I saw that my views of sin must be very inadequate, and I asked of God to teach me all He would have me to know. I shall here remark, that the principal benefit I received from reading other books than the Bible was, that they explained to me more fully those doctrines of which I was before satisfied, for I was too fond of my own opinions to read those books which opposed them. I did, however, consider the Scripture as a certain authority. As

* Probably Dr. Innes and Mr. Shireff.

soon as I found it against any of my opinions, I readily gave them up. My thoughts began now to be particularly turned to election, a doctrine which, indeed, was foolishness unto me; it seemed so irrational, that I thought I should never embrace it. A good minister, with whom I frequently conversed on the subject, told me, I should by and by change my opinion. I thought it impossible: and so much attached was I to my own way of thinking, that I could hardly suppose that sensible, good men, did really believe the contrary. I always thought that I had the better in argument on this subject. I was well pleased to enter upon it, and although every conversation left me more established in my own opinion, yet they were afterwards of use. Once in particular that minister read to me the first chapter of the Ephesians, and said, if the doctrine was not clearly established by that passage, any meaning whatever might be affixed to Scripture. This passage made some impression on my mind. But however erroneous my views were, my whole thoughts were engrossed about religion. Having nothing particular to occupy my attention, I meditated on these things, and gave myself wholly to them. I hardly read any but religious books, and it was my chief concern to know the will of God. This, however, afforded food for pride,—I thought my attainments were great, and had much self-righteousness. Although I professed that my hope was fixed in Jesus Christ, yet my doings were not wholly forgotten. I gradually, moreover, got clearer views of the Gospel; and, in reading the Acts of the Apostles, xvii. 4—8, ' As many as were ordained to eternal life believed,' my whole system, as to free will, was overturned. I saw that being ordained to eternal life was not the consequence of faith, but that the children of God believed because they were thus ordained. This gave a considerable blow to my self-righteousness, and henceforth I read the Scriptures more in a childlike spirit, for hitherto I was often obliged to search for some interpretation of Scripture which would agree with my system. I now saw more of the freeness of the grace of the Gospel and the necessity of being born again, and was daily looking for satisfactory evidence of this change. My desire was now set upon frames and feelings, instead of building on the sure foundation. I got no comfort in this way. Gradually becoming more dissatisfied with myself, being convinced especially of the sin of unbelief, I wearied myself with looking for some wonderful change to take place,—some inward feeling, by which I might know that I was born again. The method of resting simply on the promises of God, which are yea and amen in Jesus Christ, was too plain and easy, and like Naaman, the Syrian, instead of bathing in Jordan and being clean, I would have some great work in my mind to substitute in place of Jesus Christ. The Lord gradually opened my eyes; He always dealt with me in the tenderest manner, and kept me from those horrors of mind which, in my ignorance and pride, I had often desired as a proof of my conversion. The dispensations of his providence towards me much favoured the teaching which He has vouchsafed to afford. The conversations of some of the Lord's people with whom I was acquainted were helpful to my soul; and, in particular, I may here add, that the knowledge of Scripture which I acquired in early life was very useful to me when my views were directed to the great concerns of eternity. Many things were then brought to my remembrance which I had learned when young, although they seemed wholly to have escaped while I was living in forgetfulness of God. Instead of those deep convictions which are experienced by some with much horror of mind, the Lord has rather shown me the evil of sin in the sufferings of his dear Son, and in the manifestation of that love which, whilst it condemns the past ingratitude, seals the pardon of the believing sinner. In short, I now desire to feel, and hope, in some measure, that I do feel, as a sinner who looks for salvation freely by grace; who prefers this method of salvation to every other, because thereby God is glorified through Jesus Christ, and the pride of human glory stained. I desire daily to see more of my own unworthiness, and that Jesus Christ may be more precious to my soul. I depend on him for sanctification as well as for deliverance from wrath, and am in some measure (would it were more!) convinced of my own weakness and his all-sufficiency. When I have most comfort, then does sin appear most hateful; and I am in some measure made to rejoice in the hope of being completely delivered from it by seeing, in all his beauty, Him who was dead and is alive, and liveth for evermore.   Amen."

These were the notes of Mr. J. A. Haldane's confession of faith on the occasion of his ordination.   He held fast the beginning of his confidence stedfast to the end, and with unswerving consistency maintained the same doctrines down to the very close of life.

# CHAPTER IV.

[1794—5.]

THE ten years which immediately followed Robert Haldane's
abandonment of the naval profession, after the peace of 1783,
was a period of much activity and interest. But, like the first
twenty years of his early life, it was one of peculiar training for
loftier and more enduring objects. For two years he had chiefly
devoted himself to a voluntary course of study at Gosport and
at Edinburgh. He had next made the tour of Europe, and
after his marriage, he turned, with characteristic intensity, to
country pursuits, determined to master agriculture, both practically and as a science, in this respect setting an example to his
neighbours, and acquiring the reputation of being a better
farmer than many, with whom it had been the business of their
lives. His skill in landscape-gardening, and in planting was
displayed at Airthrey, and was afterwards still more conspicuous
at Auchingray, where the resources of art were not so much
favoured by the beauties of nature.

But the spell by which his mind had been bound to the world
and the passing things of time was now to be broken, and the
same process of spiritual renewal which, during the winter of
1794, had been at work in the heart of his younger brother,
soon afterwards began to operate on his own. It is a singular
but a remarkable fact, which he has himself left on record, that

G

he was aroused from the sleep of spiritual death by the excitement of the French Revolution.

That great moral and political convulsion was not unforeseen. Its approach had been discerned in the demoralization of a profligate Court, a corrupt aristocracy, an infidel priesthood, and an overburdened people. The social disruption of France had been foretold by Lord Chesterfield, and other keen political observers. Yet it came upon Europe like an earthquake, casting down thrones, coronets, mitres, and altars, mingling in one heap of ruins the trophies of feudal grandeur and the monuments of sacerdotal tyranny. Like most young men of ardent, generous, and energetic minds, Robert Haldane was roused as from a lethargy by the events passing around him. He saw, or imagined he saw, looming through the mist, the prospect of a new and better order of things, when oppression and immorality would cease, and Governments would be regulated by a paramount regard for the welfare of the people. He admitted that good and evil were wildly contending for the mastery, but he was sanguine as to the result, and dropped out of his calculations the corruption of human nature, and the hopelessness of any solid reformation apart from the influence of a Divine agency. But he was neither discontented himself, nor impatient of any real or fancied grievances, and was therefore practically little disposed to disturb the order of society in his own country, or to countenance levelling principles, either in regard to rank or property. He stood aloof from all political societies, and steadily refused every invitation to countenance, either by his name, his presence, or his purse, the meetings or the plans of the "friends of the people." So far as property was concerned, he had everything to lose, and little to hope for, in the event of change. In regard to social rank, he was himself satisfied with his own position, and by no means ambitious of distinction. Whilst he did not envy those above him, as little was he disposed to favour the encroachments of democrats. He appreciated ancient descent and old nobility, not as things possessing any intrinsic value in themselves, but as links in the chain which help to secure stability to the State, or, in the words of Burke, "protect it against the levity of Courts, and the greater levity of the multitude."

His alleged democratic tendencies were afterwards studiously exaggerated and misrepresented by those, who wished to cast discredit on his designs for the propagation of Christianity. Beyond all doubt, however, he was for a time somewhat dazzled with the delusive prospect of a new order of things. It is remarked by Sir Archibald Alison, in speaking of the French Revolution: "The young, the ardent, the philosophical were sanguine in their expectations of its success; a new era seemed to have dawned upon the world, from the rise of freedom in that great empire; the fetters of slavery and the bonds of superstition appeared to be dropping from the hands of the human race. It was not merely the factious, the restless, and the ambitious who entertained these opinions; they were shared by many of the best and wisest of men; and in England it might with truth be said, what an eloquent historian has observed of Europe in general, that the friends of the French Revolution comprised at that period the most enlightened and generous of the community." *

But if the bold, the ardent, the enlightened, the generous, and the speculative, who had life before them, looked with pleasurable interest on these revolutionary changes, and "hoped even against hope" in the midst of sanguinary violence, another and still more influential portion of the community regarded these movements with unmixed horror. For the most part, those who had passed through life and had property to lose, as well as the timid and the peaceful, trembled lest the political contagion should spread; whilst the adherents of the Established Churches, both in England and Scotland, and a great majority of the landed aristocracy, were united with the holders of office in deprecating all political discussion.

Society was thus divided, and in no part of the empire did the divisions rise to such a pitch of violence as in Scotland. Had Mr. Haldane been generally met by men of large and

* Vol. i., p. 321.

enlightened minds, his ardent wishes for the amelioration of mankind, as expressed in private, would have been more candidly judged, and he would not have been tempted occasionally to defend measures or principles tending to excess. The most eminently pious ministers within a wide circuit round Airthrey eagerly sought his society, and discerned in his impatience of " all the oppressions done under the sun," and in his repugnance to follow the beaten track, the hope of a blessed change, when, with a ripened understanding and a renewed heart, the same generous impulses would direct his steps into the paths of Christianized philanthropy. They rightly judged that even then he was nearer the kingdom of God than many of the alarmists, who were most shocked at the freedom of his sentiments, and his aversion to a war with France, which, like his old commander, Lord St. Vincent, he regarded as "unnecessary, impolitic, and lamentable." With secular men of enlarged views, whom he valued and respected, there was indeed no serious collision of sentiment. With Sir Ralph Abercromby, who belonged to Mr. Pitt's party, his intercourse up to the year 1793 had been intimate and mutually satisfactory. At a still later period it is evident, from the letter already quoted, that he had not lost the confidence of that great man, when he alluded to "the good principles of the family" into which his niece was about to marry. There are other circumstances from which it is clear that Robert Haldane's sanguine hopes of the French Revolution had not interrupted his intercourse even with some of the chief members of the Government. With Mr. Pitt's bosom friend, Mr. Secretary Dundas, he continued to be on excellent terms, as may be proved by the fact that he was a visitor at Dunira after party spirit had begun to run high. Even after his brother's return home, so late as the summer of 1794, the Duke of Montrose, then Lord-Lieutenant of the county, and an active member of Mr. Pitt's Government, was himself a guest at Airthrey. These facts are scarcely necessary to refute the exaggerations afterwards industriously circulated, concerning his extreme political opinions, and anything so ridiculous would not now have been referred to, had it not been for the revival, hereafter to be noticed, of old and forgotten misrepresentations in the Life of Mr. Wilberforce, by his sons.

But Mr. Haldane was fond of argument, and often took pleasure in startling the prejudices of narrow-minded lairds, for whom prospects of social amelioration had no charms. Impatient of any semblance of sympathy with the changes in progress, they were yet eager to engage him in debate, and, conscious of his superiority, they would invite some man of ability or skill, generally a lawyer on circuit, such as Mr. Graham of Meiklewood, or Allan Maconochie, afterwards Lord Meadowbank, whom Lord Cockburn describes, in his "Life of Jeffrey" as a man "of singular ingenuity, restless mental activity, full of varied knowledge, and ready at all times for an argument with any body upon any thing." On Mr. Haldane's death-bed, in 1842, when reviewing his past history, and extolling that watchful providence which had preserved him whilst living at a distance from God, he referred to a circumstance which occurred about this time. He had been dining at Ardoch, then the residence of a well-known Baronet, about nine miles to the north-west of Airthrey. According to one of the evil customs of the times the gentlemen had sat long after the ladies had left the dinner-table. Mr. Haldane had argued much. It was late, and the night was dark. He had intended to ride across the Sheriff Muir, but Mrs. Haldane, apprehensive of the danger, remained longer than she would otherwise have done, to convey him home in her carriage. He had, however, ordered his horse, and would not be persuaded to go by the circuitous highway road through Dumblane and the Bridge of Allan. Heated with wine, and excited by argument, he mounted and galloped off, crossing the upland moor, and dashing through the broken ground and woods of Pendrich and Airthrey, regardless of the imminent risk to which he was exposed. He reached home more speedily, and in safety, but it may indicate the impression which this recollection made upon the mind of a man not much disposed to talk of dangers, that in the weakness and exhaustion of ebbing life, he mentioned this preservation as one of the leading events in his history, on the review of which he was filled with mingled emotions of humble penitence and adoring gratitude. He said, that on this and other occasions, he felt that he must have perished had he not been held in the grasp of Omnipotence.

It will at once be understood, from what has been said of his political opinions, how easy it was, at a time of such party violence, to exaggerate and pervert them, especially after his religious movements had provoked opposition. But his own account of the matter, published in 1800, has completely disposed of what he himself termed the " gross misrepresentations of his conduct and views." * The narrative is the more interesting, as it, in fact, contains the history of that spiritual change of heart through which he was enabled to discover the only true source of happiness, whether personal, social, or political.

After stating that there could be no vanity in asserting that he was amongst the foremost of those whose political opinions were, at that period of religious excitement, misrepresented, he proceeds :—" Until the commencement of the French Revolution I had never particularly turned my attention to political discussion. I had read Delolme's Treatise and Blackstone's ' Commentaries on the Laws of England,' and was a sincere admirer of the British Constitution. I had also perused with much satisfaction Smith's ' Inquiries into the Nature and Causes of the Wealth of Nations.' The first books I read upon the subject of government, after the change that took place in France, were Mr. Burke's ' Reflections,' Mackintosh's ' Vindiciæ Gallicæ,' and afterwards several of the pamphlets by Christie, Paine, Barlow, Priestly, and others, which appeared in such great numbers about that time. Although I did not exactly agree with these writers, nor, indeed, with any that I happened to meet with, a scene of melioration and improvement in the affairs of mankind seemed to open itself to my mind, which, I trusted, would speedily take place in the world, such as the universal abolition of slavery, of war, and of many other miseries

* " Address on Politics." 1800.

that mankind were exposed to, which appeared to me wholly to result from the false principles upon which the ancient governments have been constructed. I exulted in this prospect from motives of benevolence, and, as far as I know, without any allowed mixture of selfishness. I rejoiced in the experiment that was making in France of the construction of a Government at once from its foundation upon a regular plan, which Hume, in his Essays, speaks of as an event so much to be desired.

" In every company I delighted in discussing this favourite subject, and endeavoured to point out the vast advantages that I thought might be expected as the result. At this time I was in habits of intimacy with some very worthy clergymen, residing at and in the neighbourhood of Stirling. They were acquainted with a principle I did not then admit, and which, although a fundamental part of the creeds of the Established Churches both of England and Scotland, is not generally admitted,— I mean, the total corruption of human nature. Reasoning from their firm persuasion of this truth, they assured me that such effects as I expected, unquestionably so desirable in themselves, could not flow from any change from government, and that the cruelties in France, then beginning to be exercised, were the natural effect of certain circumstances in which the people of that country stood, and would, in a greater or less degree, take place in any country in a similar situation. I widely differed from them, and continued to manifest my own opinions, ascribing all, or most of the enormities of the French, solely to the state of degradation to which I thought their minds had been reduced during the ancient despotic Government.

" Numerous political Societies, about the same time, were established in England and Scotland, but of these I expressed my decided disapprobation, and never went near a single one of them. I always thought, that by them the minds of the people were much more likely to be inflamed than informed, and that they were calculated to produce confusion rather than reformation. Besides, as I saw so many well-informed men, who had at first approved of the French Revolution, beginning to set themselves directly against any change in this country, I was

persuaded it would ensure the most dreadful consequences were
any attempt to that purpose to be made by these Societies or
their leaders. The French were making the experiment upon
themselves; from them I wished to see its effects. I thought
that these would be so good as soon to convince other nations,
and make them willing to follow their example, and I hoped
that this might one day take place without either bloodshed or
loss of property.

" I am sure these were distinctly my sentiments at the time
my mind was most filled with political speculations; as I recollect, when the Societies were set on foot, that I wrote a letter to
a friend, expressing my strong disapprobation of them, containing also the other opinions I have just mentioned. This letter
he showed to several persons at the time, and, for aught I know,
it may remain to this day. I there took pains fully to declare
my sentiments, and kept a copy of it, and of another letter, in
which I expressed my abhorrence of all secret cabals or open
violence against the Government, and these, together with a
speech I delivered at Stirling in a County Meeting, which I had
accurately written, I should have been inclined to have inserted
here, had I not a considerable time ago committed them all to
the flames, as treating of a subject which I had renounced for
ever.

" Having mentioned that speech, it may be proper to say
something concerning it, as it made some noise at the time, and
being the only circumstance in my public conduct that could be
taken hold of, has been carefully kept in remembrance, much
mis-stated, and made a ground of accusation against me to this
very day.

" A meeting of the freeholders of the county of Stirling was
called on the 1st of July, 1794, to consider the propriety of
arming corps of volunteers throughout the county, at which his
Grace the Duke of Montrose was in the chair. I had never
before in public delivered my sentiments respecting any political subject; but, when called upon in my place, I thought it
proper to come forward and explicitly to avow them. The view
I took of the question before the meeting was, that all those who

disapproved of the present war must, to be consistent, oppose the measure of forming volunteer corps, as arming the men who should compose them would only enable Government to send more of the regular forces out of the kingdom, and so to persist in the war; but would add nothing to the internal security of the country, the professed object of the measure. Besides that, as it was said many were disaffected to Government, the measure itself must be dangerous, by putting arms into the hands of such; and, at any rate, that it seemed an attempt to govern the country by force, which, if the majority of the people were disaffected, would be impossible, if otherwise unnecessary. I then delivered my opinion upon what I conceived the impolicy and unjustness of the war. I afterwards described what I considered to be the true character of a person properly called a democrat, as a friend of his country, a lover of peace, and one who cherished the sentiments of general benevolence, and contrasted it with that of persons who held opposite sentiments, who were desirous of hugging their prejudices, and of adapting the maxims of Government belonging to the seventeenth to the end of the eighteenth century, a period so much more enlightened. I next endeavoured to describe the bad effects of prejudice and of undistinguishing resistance to everything new, although confessedly far the better, as exemplified in the history of all nations, and particularly in the history of the Reformation. I afterwards took a view of the advantages which I was confident the world would derive from the principles of freedom being better understood in the universal peace and security that would consequently prevail; although I observed that an attempt to strangle these principles in their birth, by the convulsed grasp of the expiring monster despotism, had caused the most dreadful disturbances in Europe. I then declared to the freeholders, that I thought they would have been much better employed had they been meeting to consider how all abuses that were generally allowed to be such might be reformed, than in following the example of those Societies, who had most improperly intended to arm, but who might easily be prevented from doing mischief by that power which Government already possessed. I added, that from their situation in life, they would assuredly have much more influence with their countrymen in any other way than as armed men. And I concluded the whole with a solemn declaration of my conviction of the propriety and truth of the sentiments I had stated.

" The above is an accurate account of the leading features of what I said that day, and I am persuaded those who were present will bear witness to the faithfulness of this report. The above speech created to me many enemies, and caused much misrepresentation, but the consequences of it, I reckon, were eventually very happy. It produced, indeed, a considerable coolness and distance on the part of some of the neighbouring country gentlemen; but this led me into the company of others, from whom I derived more advantage.

" I have mentioned above that I was frequently in company with several respectable clergymen, who lived in my neighbourhood. However much, from knowing more of the actual state of human nature, they might perceive the improbability of attaining universal peace and justice in the world, and of all human affairs being conducted upon these principles, they nevertheless thought me sincere; and instead of withdrawing from my company, constantly attempted to lead my mind to infinitely higher concerns than those I had hitherto pursued.

" With this view, they persevered, and often sat till a late hour at night, (when, perhaps, they had to rise early to depart to their parochial duty,) conversing after the period above alluded to, (viz., the meeting of freeholders of the county of Stirling,) not always on political arrangements, on the government of this world, as was commonly supposed, and falsely reported, although of these we also spake, but chiefly upon the concerns of our immortal souls, and the things that belonged to our everlasting peace. The effects have been profitable to them and to me, and such, I trust, as they and I shall mutually rejoice in when time shall be no more.

" Conversing with these gentlemen, and reading a good deal upon the subject of religion, I was brought gradually to perceive in some measure the glory of the doctrines held out in Scripture, and the consistency of the truth as it is in Jesus. I became anxious to be better informed, and daily gave myself more and more to the investigation of it. I happened to be at a friend's house two winters, in a situation where I had much leisure for such inquiries. I enjoyed great comfort in pursuing them, and think I can truly say, that under a deep sense of my own ignorance in the things that related to God, and considerable perplexity, amidst opposite opinions on the subject, I earnestly besought the Lord that he would enable me to distinguish between truth and falsehood.

" I know it has been said that at one period I was a Socinian. The report is not true. A Socinian clergyman, who accompanied a friend of mine (a Mr. Edwards, whose brother was an officer in the Foudroyant,) upon a visit to England, was some time in the year 1793 at my house; we often discussed his sentiments, I constantly endeavouring, with the little knowledge I had upon the subject, to maintain the Trinitarian views, in which, in the language of the pastoral admonition, I had been "bred up." I used often to retail his arguments, partly to learn from others better informed than I was, what could be urged against them, and also to dispute upon the subject as a matter of speculative inquiry, without any proper impression of its awful solemnity or importance. Indeed, the fact was, I neither understood the one side of the question nor the other. But I recollect, when I came seriously to consider the matter, I was three or four days really in doubt whether it much signified what I believed concerning this doctrine : but I did not long continue uncertain respecting its importance, although it was some time before my mind was settled, and I never did profess to be a Socinian.

" After I returned home, the same subjects chiefly occupied my attention; and whatever good or harm the study of politics may have done to others, they certainly led the way to much good to me.

" Before the French Revolution, having nothing to rouse my mind, I lived in the country, almost wholly engaged by country pursuits, little concerned about the general interests or happiness of mankind, but selfishly enjoying the blessings which God, in his providence, had so bountifully poured upon me. As to religion, I contented myself with that general profession which is so common and so worthless, and that form of godliness which completely denies its power. I endeavoured to be decent, and what is called moral, but was ignorant of my lost state by nature, as well as of the strictness, purity, and extent of the Divine law. While I spoke of a Saviour, I was little acquainted with his character, the value of his sufferings and death, the need I stood in of the atoning efficacy of his pardoning blood, or of the imputation of his perfect obedience and meritorious righteousness, and of the sanctifying influences of the Eternal Spirit to apply his salvation to my soul. When politics began to be talked of, I was led to consider everything anew. I eagerly catched at them as a pleasing speculation. As a fleeting phantom, they eluded my grasp; but missing the shadow, I caught the substance—and while obliged to abandon these confessedly empty and unsatisfactory pursuits, I obtained in some measure the solid consolations of the Gospel; so that I may say, as Paul, concerning the Gentiles of old, ' He was found of me who sought him not.' "

It will be seen from these extracts, that Mr. Haldane's conversion was neither sudden nor violent. It was the act of God, and, as such, mysterious in its origin, decisive in its character, and effectual in its results. The good seed had been deeply implanted in his own heart, and that of his brother, by the loving piety of an affectionate and God-fearing mother. To her latest breath it had been watered by the earnest and anxious prayers with which she devoted her orphan children to the Lord, and, strong in faith, called down upon their heads the blessing of God Almighty. For a time the impression made upon their hearts by her instruction and example seemed indelible. Their nightly prayers by their bed-side were followed by conversation about their Saviour, such as their mother had delighted to encourage. Both seemed to take pleasure in heavenly things, and the elder expressed an inclination for the ministry. But time wore on. Their mother was no longer near to warn, to admonish, to instruct. The world, with its amusements, its temptations, its attractions, seemed gradually to efface the impressions of early piety. By degrees all profession of religion was abandoned, and from an early period of their history till the time when the elder brother had attained the age of thirty, and the younger the age of twenty-five, there was nothing in their religious character to distinguish them from the great majority of their friends and associates, who were living in the discharge of what they regarded as their social duties. They were at least as moral and correct in their deportment as their neighbours, but in other respects without any concern about Christ or eternity.

But although the incorruptible seed was thus buried in the gaieties, the pleasures, the vanities, and the pursuits of the world, it was not destroyed. It was still destined to spring up through the life-giving influence of the Holy Spirit. It is remarkable that this change took place on both brothers, nearly at the same time, although it was in the younger first developed. From the day when in January, 1794, he began prayerfully to study his Bible on board the Melville Castle, his mind had become more and more intensely interested with Divine things. When he arrived at Airthrey four or five months afterwards, he found politics, rather than religion, the engrossing theme of conversation. With these subjects he could no longer exclusively occupy himself. A more glorious object had begun to engross his mind, and doubtless his change of character had its influence on his elder brother, who was yet engrossed with the world. Him he accompanied to the Freeholders' Meeting in the County Hall at Stirling, and heard him deliver that remarkable speech which was to be so much talked of, and to produce such results. It was chiefly distinguished for the boldness with which the speaker came forward, single-handed, in his place, in opposition to the Lord-Lieutenant and principal landholders, to express with equal force and eloquence sentiments which were admired by many of the lookers-on, but which were no doubt dangerous in their tendency, and eminently distasteful to the aristocracy of the county. The personal coldness which ensued was not likely to elicit concessions from Mr. Haldane, and he was not the man to quail before what was called the reign of terror in Scotland. But it threw him more into the society of pious and learned ministers, such as Dr. Campbell of Kippen, afterwards of Edinburgh, much famed for his solid piety and massive theology; Mr. Somerville of Stirling, and Mr. Shireff of St. Ninian's, each eminent for his masculine turn of thought and decision of character; and Dr. Innes, chaplain to the Castle, and second minister of Stirling, whose agreeable conversation, pleasing manners, and attractive style of preaching, added weight to the influence of his consistent character and genuine Christianity.

With these or others he often conversed, as he says, "till a late hour at night." It might rather be said till an early hour in the morning, for it was in the evening that he always most delighted to converse, and the lateness of the hours, both at night and in the morning, was one of the peculiarities for which Airthrey was in those day celebrated. His habits were in some degree the same till the close of his life; and if he had a friend or a visitor with whom he particularly desired conversation, he generally chose the evening, immediately after family prayers, and seemed to lighten up with fresh vivacity and earnestness when others had retired to rest.

No sooner was his mind directed to "the concerns of his immortal soul," than he pursued the momentous subject with characteristic intensity. His intellectual constitution did not suffer to take things for granted, or to adopt superficial views of any subject which interested his mind. When Christianity forced itself on his notice he determined to survey it in all its bearings. He began by reading much and deeply on the evidences of Christianity, including not only Butler, Paley, Watson, and other popular writers, but such learned repositories of information as the ponderous volumes of Lardner. The fruits of his studies were long afterwards given to the public in his work on the Evidences of Christianity. But at this time they were greatly blessed to his own soul, for they were pursued with deep humility, and with much prayer that the Lord would enable him "to distinguish between truth and falsehood." No wonder, then, that he should have proved another instance of the Lord's gracious declaration, "If any man will do his will, he shall know of the doctrine, whether it be of God."

There was a considerable similarity between the history of his spiritual illumination and that of his younger brother. In neither case was it to be attributed to any sudden impulse or external influence. It was not to be traced to the ministry or the instructions of any one in particular. From the conversation of several clergymen he derived help amidst the perplexities which impeded his inquiries. After he had made some progress in the Divine life, it was Dr. Innes who first induced him to commence family worship at Airthrey.* It indicated the sincerity of his prayers and confessions, when he said that it required some effort publicly to acknowledge one's self to be a vile sinner. But he added, that although he traced his turning to God instrumentally to the early instructions of his mother, and never had been entirely without convictions, from the time he was nine years old, and although he did not attribute his conversion to any other human agency, yet that, if he were to point out the individual from whom he had derived most spiritual light at the beginning of his career, he would mention a journeyman mason, of the name of Klam, or Clam, of Menstrie. This good man was employed on some of the works at Airthrey, and was, like many of his class, especially in former times, not only remarkably intelligent, but well read in his Bible, and in the writings of the best old Scotch Divines. With him Mr. Haldane once walked several miles through the woods of Airthrey to a distant part of the estate called Pendrich, and on the way the conversation turned from the subject of masonry to the glory of the great Architect of the universe. The views of Divine truth, and of faith in the finished work of Christ, which this humble

---

* Dr. Innes relates, that one evening, after discussing with Mr. Haldane till long past midnight, the former proposed, for the first time, that they should conclude with prayer. Mr. Haldane readily assented, and, on rising from their knees, he warmly shook Dr. Innes by the hand, and without another word of argument affectionately wished him good night. It was on the next evening that Mr. Haldane commenced family worship.

but intelligent and well-taught Christian unfolded, as they went along, were so plain and scriptural, and above all, so much divested of those balancing statements of truth by which Mr. Haldane had been perplexed, that he saw the Gospel to be indeed glad tidings, and ever afterwards looked back with thankfulness to that memorable walk, in which he began to discern more clearly that, in the matter of justification, faith must cast away all reliance on the shifting sands of frames or feelings, and fasten only upon the Rock of Ages. To recal the name of the almost forgotten stone-mason of Menstrie is a pleasing duty. It is one which will be found in the register of God, although lost in the records of man.

# CHAPTER V.

[1795—8.]

THE current of the narrative has now conducted us to the
end of 1795. In regard to each of the two brothers, the grand
crisis of his life was decided, and a change had come over both,
the results of which stretch into eternity. No longer engrossed
with the passing vanities of this transitory world, its pleasures,
its gains, or its glories, all their energies had become concentrated on a new and absorbing object. Each of them, by the
rich mercy of God, had now passed "from death unto life,"
and from the bondage of Satan into the kingdom of Jesus
Christ. Each was in Him "a new creature." "Old things
had passed away." The strength of their natural character was
now to be developed in relation to nobler and more enduring
ends.

Between the brothers there was much similarity in point
of talent and disposition, but there were also strong shades
of difference. Both were bold, ardent, and energetic. In the

H

younger there was greater quickness of perception and readiness
of utterance, whilst in the elder there was greater originality of
character as well as a larger infusion of habitual caution. In
both there was a deep, natural spring of genuine benevolence;
but in the younger brother it was more apparent, and his affectionate friendship was in its generosity and disregard of self, in
his earlier years, prone even to overleap the strict bounds of
prudence. This had often been remarked by their early associates, and whilst both were daring, James was more ready to
carry his object by a sudden dash, whilst Robert was more wary
and thoughtful. Yet such are the contradictions that meet us
in the analysis of character, that it sometimes happened in the
course of their lives that Robert Haldane seemed to act upon
impulse, when James hesitated and considered. This was in
some measure the case with the scheme for a foreign mission,
which Mr. Haldane adopted before his younger brother had yet
made up his mind as to any plan of active usefulness.

It was at the period when, to use his own words, he had
"obtained in some measure the consolations of the Gospel," that
his attention was called to the importance of more decidedly
attempting to promote that "kingdom," for whose coming we
are taught to pray. Dr. Innes has recorded the fact, that
"having received, when in Stirling, the first number of the
periodical accounts of the Baptist Mission in India," he sent it
to Mr. Haldane, then living at Airthrey. He was exceedingly
struck with this memorial of the first of those modern Missions
to the heathen, which shed a ray of light over the moral darkness of a century then closing upon Europe amidst political
and social convulsion. He was deeply impressed with the
grandeur of the enterprise, and with the purity of the motives
which had induced Dr. Carey to quit his native land to make
known the Gospel in foreign parts. His mind, enlightened by
a spark of heavenly fire, took a right estimate of the man whom
the Marquis of Wellesley afterwards promoted to a Professor-
ship in the College of Fort-William, but whom Sydney Smith,
in his spiritual blindness, could ridicule as a "consecrated
cobbler." The Serampore Mission made a deep and indelible

impression on Mr. Haldane's mind; but Dr. Innes is mistaken in supposing that it was now for the first time, that he entered on the investigation of the evidences of the Christian faith. Mr. Haldane's own words are conclusive on this point, if there were no other record on the subject: "Some time *after this* (namely, after he had obtained the solid consolations of the Gospel), when I trust that I had been led to choose the good part which cannot be taken from any one, and to adopt the views of religion I now hold, I first heard of the Baptist Missionary Society, and their Mission to Bengal." But the amiable and excellent Dr. Innes' recollections are quite accurate, when he goes on to state the manner in which his friend became impressed with a sense of the necessity of devoting himself—his life, his talents, his fortune—to the cause of God. "Christianity," he said, "is everything or nothing. If it be true, it warrants and commands every sacrifice to promote its influence. If it be not, then let us lay aside the hypocrisy of professing to believe it." "It immediately struck me," says Mr. Haldane, in his own narrative, "that I was spending my time in the country to little profit, whilst, from the command of property which, through the goodness of God, I possessed, I might be somewhere extensively useful." In another publication he says, that after his attention had been called to the salvation of Jesus Christ, "I had seen the accounts of the Baptist Mission in Bengal, which pointed out both the condition of the natives as destitute of the Gospel, and also the wide, promising field then opened for the exertions of Christians. A strong desire occupied my mind to engage in the honourable service. The object was of such magnitude, that, compared with it, the affairs of time appeared to sink into nothing, and no sacrifice seemed too great in order to its attainment."

Still, although pondering this great design, he came to no sudden determination. For nearly six months he considered the matter deliberately, and having proposed it to his wife, who had also been led to "choose the better part," and in whose prudence he placed much reliance, he obtained her cordial consent. About the end of 1795, the London Missionary

Society was instituted by several eminent Christians, some of them members of the Church of England, some Presbyterians, and some Independents. Amongst these was his old friend, David Bogue, of Gosport, whose thrilling appeal on behalf of the Heathen had before this time roused a missionary spirit throughout the country. Mr. Haldane was amongst the first in Scotland to enrol himself as a member of the Society, and in a brief summary of the chief incidents of his life, which he drew up in 1839, there is the following memorandum marking an era in his history :—

"1796. January.—Subscribed 50*l.* to the London Missionary Society. Attended it (General Meeting) in May. In winter, in George's-street, North-side."

His brother at the same time declared his adhesion to the good cause by a similar donation.

Whilst the London Missionary Society was exciting the attention of Scotland, Dr. Innes, whose ministry at Stirling attracted much attention, was a frequent guest at Airthrey, and his mind was much occupied with the cause of Missions. To him, therefore, after conversing on the subject, Mr. Haldane proposed that they should "go to Bengal, and spend the remainder of their lives in endeavouring to communicate the precious truths of the Gospel to the Hindoos who were living under the British Government." "To render the Mission as efficient as possible, I wished," says Mr. H., "to take others with me, others in whose devotedness to the service of God I had confidence, and who, by their knowledge and previous habits at home, might be useful in the undertaking. Mr. Innes, with whom I had then frequent intercourse, appeared to be well qualified for the work, and I had long been acquainted with Mr. Bogue, of Gosport, who also seemed qualified for it, whilst the warm recommendations of Mr. Ewing by (his brother-in-law) Mr. Innes, directed my attention to him as a third associate. After Mr. Innes agreed to form one of the Mission, I went to England on purpose to see Mr. Bogue. When formerly in habits of intimacy with him, I had been unacquainted with the Gospel, and although, from recollection, I believed his sentiments respecting it corresponded with mine, I thought it was necessary, in so important a matter, fully to ascertain that this was the case. I accordingly went to London, and saw him at a Meeting of the Missionary Society, and afterwards spent some time at his house at Gosport. . . . I never gave Mr. Bogue a hint of the business till having been some time with him, I was satisfied with his qualifications for the work, and it was late one night (22d May, 1796), when he and I were sitting together, after the rest of the family had retired, that I opened to him my design, and without either hesitation or delay, he gave his consent to accompany me, and expressed his fullest approbation of the plan."

It was, indeed, grand and comprehensive, whilst ample funds were to be provided by Mr. Haldane. The venerable name of David Bogue, then in his forty-seventh year, was in itself a tower of strength, and would have added weight to any Christian enterprise. A man of Johnsonian character, capacious intellect, unflinching courage, commanding stature, and dignified appearance, he added the reputation of a scholar and a philosopher to that of an experienced Christian and a great theologian. Mr. Innes, although twenty years younger, was respected and beloved by all who were capable of appreciating his devoted piety, his consistent practice, and his attractive preaching. His brother-in-law, Mr. Greville Ewing, also under thirty, was not yet ordained to a particular charge, but was assistant minister to the excellent Dr. Jones, of Lady Glenorchy's Church, and, at a time of great spiritual deadness, was in high repute for his ardent zeal in the cause of truth, as well as for his literary taste and his critical acquaintance with the Scriptures. Each was a regularly educated minister, the one ordained, the other licensed by the Church of Scotland, and both willing to devote their lives and talents to the Indian Mission.

But they were not to have gone without other aids. Mr. John Ritchie, a respectable and pious printer in Edinburgh, was to have superintended a well-equipped printing establishment, aided by catechists, city missionaries, and schoolmasters. In short, no expense was to have been spared in furnishing all that was needed to make the Mission useful, whether as the means of publishing translations of the Scriptures and tracts, educating native teachers, or instructing native children. For every one concerned Mr. Haldane was to supply the necessary outfit and passage money, and also to provide an independent competence for those whose co-operation involved the loss of their means of subsistence. For each of his three ministerial coadjutors the sum of 3,500l. was to have been appropriated, as compensation for the sacrifice of their incomes or prospects in a Church which did not promise great worldly emolument, and of which the first Viscount Melville once said, that it was "founded on the rock of poverty." In addition to this provision and the first outfit, and to secure the Mission from the consequences of his own death, a further sum of 25,000l. was to have been invested in the names of trustees. There was something almost lavish in Mr. Haldane's generosity towards his coadjutors, and in after-times he learned the necessity of more rigidly economizing the funds which he consecrated to the service of the Gospel.

Benares was the spot on which they were to have unfurled the banner of the cross,—Benares, the metropolis of Oriental Paganism, the holiest of the holy cities of the Hindoos,—Benares, with its glorious temples and gorgeous shrines, dedicated to the countless idols, worshipped beneath the burning sun, which sparkles in its crystal fountains, and gilds the glittering domes and minarets of its benighted population. It was a bold selection, characteristic of the founder of the Mission; but although the time was not yet come for such an aggression on the empire of the prince of darkness,—although a massacre which happened a few years afterwards might have immolated these missionaries,—although nearly thirty years later, Bishop Heber, in practical contradiction to the noble spirit which breathes through his Missionary hymn, pronounced a Mission to Benares "Utopian,"—yet have we lived to see that Pagan city occupied by Christian missionaries, who can tell of converts to the Gospel, rebuking the doubts of the accomplished Prelate, and fully justifying the determination of Robert Haldane.

The sacrifice of talents, of property, and of self, was to have been unreserved. Mr. Haldane was to sell his beautiful estate of Airthrey, much of which was ornamental, and productive of expense rather than of income, whilst India was to have been the scene of his future labours and earthly existence.

But man proposeth, God disposeth. To embark on such a mission without the consent of the East India Company and the Government, was an act of imprudence not likely to be committed by a man of foresight and caution. Mr. Haldane went to London in May, 1796, partly to consult Dr. Bogue and solicit the needful permission, and partly to attend the first General Meeting of the London Missionary Society. It was expected that his brother would also join in the Mission, although the health of his young wife and her increasing family added weight to the opposition of her relations, and determined James Haldane prudently to await the issue of his brother's application to the Indian Government.

Mr. Haldane remained in England during the summer, and in the following November Mrs. Haldane joined him with their only child, a girl then under ten years of age, having posted to London, under the escort of Mr. Ewing, who had been sent for to meet Dr. Bogue.

Dr. Bogue's diary for May 22, 1796, contains this entry: "Mr. Haldane spoke to me about going on a mission to Hindostan." From the meetings in London he accompanied his old friend to Gosport, but for some time cautiously abstained from mentioning his own plans. The feelings with which he once more visited that warlike seaport were very different from those by which he had been actuated on former occasions, when full of naval zeal he had sailed from the same harbour in pursuit of glory, in the Monarch or the Foudroyant, with Duncan or Jervis for his captains, and Barrington or Howe for his admirals. An anecdote is told of him, connected with an old Scotch lady, from whom he had before received much kindness, and whose husband long filled a naval station at Portsmouth. It is only worth referring to as calculated to illustrate what was the natural gaiety of his character. He called on her one evening soon after his arrival at Gosport in 1796, and was most kindly welcomed. Desirous to be useful to his old acquaintance, he asked Mrs. M——, before he rose to depart, whether she would allow him to conduct family worship. The old lady herself had a great deal of humour ; she had been accustomed to Robert Haldane from the time he was a boy, and knew the playfulness of his disposition, and how much he delighted in good-humoured, practical jokes. Ignorant of the change which had taken place in his feelings and pursuits, she imagined when she now heard him propose to conduct family worship that he was in jest, and gravely rebuked what she justly deemed the impropriety of trifling with sacred subjects. " Family worship!" she exclaimed, in broad Scotch accents; "none of your jokes, Mr. Haldane; that's o'er serious a subject." Mr. Haldane with some difficulty convinced the good lady of her mistake, and that he was in earnest. Great was her astonishment. Those who only knew Robert Haldane from the gravity of his writings and public character, could have no idea of the buoyancy of his spirit, and of his natural love of what was playful and jocose. At a late period of his life, many were the amusing anecdotes which his venerable aunt, Lady Duncan, used to tell of his own and his brother's youthful days at Nellfield and at Gosport; and he himself would smile at the recital of the jokes, of which he was reminded, quietly adding some new point of interest which had been forgotten.

The great objection to the evangelization of India, was to be found in the fears and the prejudices of the East India Company. That powerful commercial body had long ruled over India, without seeming to imagine that their mission extended beyond the material arrangements necessary for the acquisition of wealth, and the dispensation of patronage. They had then justly subjected themselves to the indignant eloquence of Burke, when, in his speech on the India Bill, he exclaimed, "With us no pride erects stately monuments which repair the mischiefs which pride has produced, and which adorn a country out of its own spoils. England has erected no churches, no hospitals, no palaces, no schools. England has built no bridges, made no high roads, cut no navigations, dug out no reservoirs. Every other conqueror, of every other description, has left some monument, either of state or beneficence, behind him. Were we to be driven out of India this day, nothing would remain to tell that it had been possessed during the inglorious period of our dominion by anything better than the ourang-outang, or the tiger."

Mr. Pitt's Board of Control had introduced the commencement of a better system, so far as concerned civilization, but against every attempt to christianize the people there had been arrayed a ghastly front of commercial opposition. In 1793, when a new charter was granted, Mr. Wilberforce had succeeded in persuading the House of Commons, in general terms, to pledge themselves to the duty of "promoting, by all just and lawful means, the religious improvement of the natives." Two days afterwards, he ventured on specific resolutions for establishing schoolmasters and chaplains throughout India, and he again succeeded. But the Court of Directors "met and strongly reprobated my clauses," and the result is told with bitter sarcasm in a letter to Mr. Gisborne:—"The East India Directors and proprietors have triumphed. All my clauses were last night struck out in the third reading of the Bill, (with Dundas' consent!! This is honour!) and our territories in Hindostan, twenty millions of people included, are left in the undisturbed and peaceful possession, and committed to the providential protection of Brama." (*Life*, vol. ii., 267.)

Under these circumstances, for Mr. Haldane to have gone to India, as some advised, without the consent of the Company, was a proposal which would have been at variance with the wise foresight which always marked his character, and was discerned in the successful management of his own worldly affairs. The result of such an imprudent step it is not difficult to imagine, but he was not disposed thus to peril his property, his time, or his character, on such a foolish errand. It was one thing for a few obscure but noble-hearted men, like him who was sneered at as "the consecrated cobbler," to steal into a Danish settlement at Serampore, and begin those translations of the Bible which have already shaken the superstition of India to its foundations. It was quite another for a man of position to devote a fortune to an object, which the House of Commons acknowledged as a duty, which they did not dare to perform. Was it likely that the spirit which crushed the humane efforts of the friend of Pitt, and tempted Dundas into a breach of promise, would have yielded to Robert Haldane, had he chosen to set at defiance the India House and Board of Control ?

With a prudence which marked through life all his boldest measures, he resolved to go to India if he could obtain the consent of its Government; but if that consent were withheld, not to go at all. To Mr. Dundas (Lord Melville), then at the head of the affairs of India, being President of the Board of Control, as well as Chief Secretary of State, he had been known from his childhood. He addressed him boldly, and with candour, explaining to him all his past or present views, political and religious, as he afterwards did to the public in his address on politics. Mr. Wilberforce thought that more of reserve, and what might be deemed *finesse*, would have been better; but such tactics did not suit the character of Mr. Haldane's mind, and had Mr. Wilberforce been aware of Lord Melville's ample means of knowing every thing concerning the intending missionary, and of Lord Duncan's aversion to his nephew's expatriation, he would have himself admitted that in honesty and frankness consisted the best policy.

In a letter addressed to the Right Honourable Secretary, dated Sept. 21, 1796, he solicits an interview, and at once tells the wily statesman that he is prepared to give him the fullest explanations of his political sentiments. "I mean not," he says, "to retract anything I have ever said, or deny what I now hold; but if, in consequence of the following communication, you should be desirous,—as, indeed, you will be entitled

—to know what my views are, I am happy I have it in my power completely to satisfy you by answering any questions you may please to propose to me on the subject." He adds, "that even if I be deemed mistaken, my stake in the country might be regarded as a guarantee for the sincerity of my attachment to the present order of things." He then reminds the Minister that he had never obtruded his opinions, whatever they were, on the public, "except *once*, when he considered himself called upon in his place," as one of the freeholders of the county,—at that time a very select body, consisting of the principal landed proprietors, whose numbers, it may be worth while to state, did not exceed sixty. "Whatever fear may be expressed, with regard to the political sentiments of any of us, as making it dangerous to send such persons to India, will not apply here. As citizens of this country we conceive that we have a right, and we esteem it a duty, to speak freely our sentiments about Government. As missionaries abroad we have no such business. Our mouths, on that subject, will be sealed for ever, when we devote ourselves to preach only the Gospel of Jesus Christ and what it contains in a foreign land. On all men it enjoins peaceable and quiet lives, which we shall uniformly inculcate. Indeed, I trust we shall be found useful in no common degree (should God grant us success) in promoting the peace and happiness of the country and the stability of the Government, which we believe to be the best, in India. We are fully convinced that nothing will tend to bind India so closely to England as the introduction of the Gospel among the natives. And, at the same time, we are confident that nothing will provoke God to deprive England of the Empire in the East and the benefits resulting from the possession of it, so much as neglecting to send the Gospel to them, and especially refusing to allow it to be sent, when you are humbly entreated to grant permission. Our business and our aim is to propagate the Gospel and save the souls of the miserable heathen, and we should think ourselves culpable in the highest degree were the rulers, or those who are intrusted with the direction of commerce, ever to have any just cause of complaint of us. Surely it can never be thought that we have any sinister views in this business, or any other than what we hold out. To it we dedicate our all; we leave very many comforts in this country (for I assure you that it is not discontent that carries us away), and we risk—nay, almost certainly incur—bad health and many inconveniences and disagreeable circumstances that natives of the opposite side of the globe must necessarily encounter. Indeed, considering everything, if we do not go with pure views and from good motives, in the language of the apostle, I have no hesitation to say, 'We must be of all men most miserable.' "

In another letter to Lord Melville, dated London, September 30th, 1796, it is further said, " Many thousands have gone to India to attain a decent competency or splendid affluence; we go with a direct view, not to enrich ourselves, but to save the souls of men. And, surely, Sir, it is no unreasonable request that at least we may be permitted to go out quietly and enjoy the protection of the Government of India while we demean ourselves well. If we do not act there as we propose, the Government can at any time send us home; we shall be sufficiently in their power. I am persuaded, however, they would never hear of us, but as inculcating quietness and peace."

In the above letters Mr. Haldane, with characteristic manliness, avowed his previous political opinions, and, without professing to retract them, only protested against those exaggerations which had falsely represented him as a democratical revolutionist, eager to overturn every monarchical Government. His own explanations, which have been just quoted, sufficiently refute this calumny. On his state of mind in regard to politics, in 1796, he says himself, in his "Address on Politics," published in 1800 :—

" I had not seen at that time, indeed, as I have since, that it was my privilege to abstain from all political interference in this country; nor was I so deeply and practically convinced of the corruption of human nature, as I trust I have since been, so as to expect less from it, under any political arrangement. Yet, as a missionary, I had determined to renounce the subject, thinking that, at least in that situation, I might with a good conscience give it up altogether." "This," he emphatically adds,—"this was expressly settled and agreed upon as an *essential condition* to be observed by all of us who joined in the intended Mission."

In reply to this letter the President of the Board of Control very politely invited him to his house, personally to explain his views and intentions in private. He had, in fact, several interviews, at one of which Mr. Pitt came into the room before their conference was ended. Mr. Pitt no doubt regarded the scheme as a well-meant Utopian ebullition of youthful zeal. In the "Life of Mr. Wilberforce," his sons have given a very erroneous and partial account of Mr. Haldane's designs for an Indian Mission and the part their father took in the matter. It is, perhaps, not to be wondered at, for they have themselves in so many instances misunderstood the character and ignored the objects of their illustrious parent, that it would have been singular had they been more successful in the case of a stranger. But, in the preface to a subsequent publication, they have expressed their regret in terms which must silence censure. "In particular," they observe, "they feel that, for want of full information, they have not done adequate justice to the designs of Mr. Haldane for the establishment of a Mission in the East Indies." So far as concerns their own motives or conduct in the affair, this acknowledgment is ample, but it is not an antidote to the misrepresentations for which it apologizes.

The allusions to these designs are brief and unsatisfactory. First comes a detached extract from their father's diary:— " 8th October, 1796.—Very busy seeing Pitt and Dundas about abolition convention plan and *East India Missions*. Pleased with Dundas's candour." Then some explanatory remarks:—

" Having failed three years before in his endeavours to obtain a national provision for christianizing India, he was eager to forward those individual efforts which, though a poor substitute for his proposal, were all that could at present be attempted. Mr. Haldane and some other Scotch gentlemen were at this time desirous of engaging in such a Mission, and he exerted

himself to obtain Mr. Dundas's assent to the undertaking."
This introduces the following extraordinary sentence:—"*In this
he would probably have succeeded if their extreme political
opinions* had not alarmed the Government." If Mr. Wilberforce, as a member of the Church of England, failed in his
modest efforts three years before to establish chaplains for our
own countrymen and schoolmasters in India, was it likely
that he should now succeed on behalf of a member of the
Church of Scotland, whose politics had been opposed to the
Government? But the narrative of the biographers is continued
by an extract from his diary of earlier date than the first which
they quoted. It runs thus:—"I am sorry to find that all
perfect democrats, believing that a new order of things is
dawning, &c. Haldane very open. I told him I thought that
he, by imprudence, had injured the cause with Dundas." This
entry, dated 4th October, if accurately copied, is glaringly
unjust. Even if it were conceded as fully as it is disproved,
that Mr. Haldane was a *democrat* in the proper sense of the
term, Mr. Wilberforce had at this time never seen two out of
the four heads of the proposed Mission. How, then, could Mr.
Wilberforce have spoken of *all?* Dr. Innes, in fact, never
came to London about the matter, and Mr. Ewing not till
November. Now, in regard to both of these gentlemen, the
tongue of calumny never charged them with interfering in
politics. Indeed, after commenting on his letters to Mr.
Secretary Dundas, it is remarked by Mr. Haldane that the
expressions, "'as citizens, &c., we deem it our duty, &c.,' did
not apply to my two associates in Scotland, who, as ministers
of the Gospel at home, *always* thought it their duty to act in
the same manner, in every respect, as they would have done
if missionaries abroad, and as having nothing to do with
politics." It may be added, that so much was this the case,
that Dr. Innes was appointed to the chaplaincy of the Castle
instead of the senior minister at Stirling, the excellent Mr.
Somerville, because some exception was taken to the politics of
the latter, in consequence of an unguarded and partly jocular
speech made at his own table, which had been reported and

misrepresented, after the manner of those evil times, by the wife of an officer of rank, who was his guest.

That Mr. Haldane had at first taken a favourable view of the French Revolution has been already stated, but he had at all times not only eschewed connexion with disaffected but even with violent Reformers. His own words are conclusive :—" My principles, at all times, were too well known for any one to solicit my attendance in the self-created political societies. I never had any private intimation of what was going on among them. At that time I often publicly declared, had I ever known of anything dangerous to Government, even if I had lived in Turkey, where they have one of the worst Governments, I should have accounted it my duty immediately to reveal it. The only solicitation of this kind ever made to me was a request, by letter, to subscribe money for those persons (Hardy, Horne Tooke, and Thelwall) who had been tried in England for sedition, and acquitted. Although acquitted, *I highly disapproved their conduct.* I wrote an answer to the person soliciting me, to the effect that he had wholly misunderstood what my political sentiments had always been, otherwise he would not have made such a proposal to me." . . . . " From these extracts," continues Mr. Haldane, " it may be seen what my views at that time were. Indeed, offering to go to Bengal, was certainly declaring in language sufficiently strong, that it was not politics I had in view, when I wished to place myself, my family, and property entirely under the power of a Government which is so strong as that in India."

Such was the refutation which Robert Haldane published of the calumnies by which his private opinions were misrepresented during the heat of the French Revolution. Mr. Wilberforce probably little imagined, that, after more than forty years had elapsed, the same calumnies would reappear under cover of his time-honoured name, by means of fragments of his diary, perhaps, as in some other cases, inaccurately copied, and by loose memoranda of private conversation containing statements inconsistent both with Mr. Haldane's sentiments, acts, and opinions, as well as those of his colleagues. " Much," say his biographers, "as he disliked their views, and earnestly as he argued against their *revolutionary* principles in a long talk about government, he yet, on every ground, regretted the decision of Mr. Dundas." "I could not persuade him, though, as I told him, it is on your own grounds the best thing you can do. In Scotland such a man is sure to create a ferment. Send him, therefore, to the back settlements, to let off his pistol *in vacuo.*"

Well may the Bishop of Oxford, and his brother, the Archdeacon of York, admit that, "for want of full information, they have not done full justice to the designs of Mr. Haldane." The most prejudiced reader has sufficient means to enable him to detect the misrepresentations, no doubt unintentional, of which they have been guilty. To transpose short isolated fragments from a diary without regard to the order of time, to take one fragment of the entry on the 8th of October, and then, after some interpolated and inaccurate statements of their own, to serve up another isolated fragment from an earlier entry on the 4th of October, and, finally, to wind up these unsatisfactory mutilated excerpts with a *mélange* of disparaging conversational recollections, reflecting on the chief of a Mission which their father, more than forty years before, strove to forward, is a method by which any design, however noble, might, together with its author, its origin, and its objects, be easily overwhelmed with obloquy and suspicion.

To suppose that Mr. Wilberforce laboured in common with Mr. Charles Grant and Mr. Pitt's brother-in-law, the Right Honourable Edward Eliot, to send men of "revolutionary principles" as missionaries to India, is a libel on their memory, while it throws an air of ridicule over the whole of the imputation. Certain it is, that Mr. Haldane's intercourse with Mr. Wilberforce produced, on the mind of the former, a far different impression from what his biographers would lead us to imagine, and we shall now give his own account of his first interview with the illustrious abolitionist.

When Mr. Haldane had secured the co-operation of his friend Dr. Bogue, he next proceeded to seek the best means of operating on the Directors and the Board of Control. He solicited the influence and support of the leaders both of the religious community and the political world, but Mr. Wilberforce was by no means the first nor the principal auxiliary, whose aid he sought. He was himself personally acquainted with several members of the Government, including not only Mr. Secretary Dundas and the Duke of Montrose, but the Lord Chancellor Rosslyn, who was a family connexion, and whose brother-in-law, Lord Alva, had been a trustee of the estate of Airthrey, and taken an active part in the management of his young relative's concerns. He was received with kindness and hospitality by Mr. Eliot, another member of the Administration, the father of the first Earl of St. Germans, and brother-in-law of Mr. Pitt, whose early death was a loss both to the State and to the Christian Church. He experienced much courtesy from Dr. Moore, the Archbishop of Canterbury, and was treated with more than courtesy by Dr. Porteus, the Bishop of London. Mr. Erskine, afterwards Lord Chancellor, also welcomed him with great kindness, although the value of his admiration for the humanity of the enterprise, was somewhat lessened by the appeal to his Maker's name as the guarantee of his support. It was not till nearly four months after his first arrival in London that he saw Mr. Wilberforce, who was during that time at Buxton, nor did a meeting with him take place until after Mr. Haldane had written to Mr. Secretary Dundas, and fully and repeatedly conversed with that distinguished Minister. On the 4th of October, 1796, when first introduced, along with Dr. Bogue, to Mr. Wilberforce, the latter apologized for not rising, as his feet were wrapped in flannels, and he was suffering under a severe fit of the gout. He strongly and cordially approved of the plan, and became so much animated and elated as Mr. Haldane unfolded the details of the scheme, that forgetting his gout in his admiration of the grandeur of the design, the philanthropist kindling into positive enthusiasm, jumped up, and, to the entertainment of his guests, skipped about the room entirely free from pain. When he came to talk over the difficulties that impeded their plan, and heard of the

I

frank and open manner in which Mr. Haldane had written and
talked to Mr. Dundas, Mr. Wilberforce, whose turn of mind
was inclined to a more insinuating diplomacy, expressed his
doubts whether greater reserve might not have been more
prudent; and this is probably the meaning of the little dis-
jointed extract, "Haldane very open.   I told him I thought that
he, by imprudence, had injured the cause with Dundas." But
Mr. Haldane maintained the superior wisdom of straightforward,
out-spoken honesty and frankness in such a matter, and urged
that suspicions are always excited by that unsuccessful *finesse*
which, in after-life, often brought on Mr. Wilberforce the taunts
of worldly politicians, such as Mr. Canning, who compared him
to a waterman looking one way and rowing the other.   But
nothing took place to damp the pleasure with which Mr.
Haldane always spoke of this interview, and of his subsequent
and repeated social intercourse with Mr. Wilberforce, and
still less to sanction the cold and disparaging tone of the
Biography, unless the monstrous supposition be assumed, that
Mr. Wilberforce was himself insincere in his professions.
Mr. Haldane's own remark upon the Biography was this, that
far from having to complain of any sharpness in debate with
Mr. Wilberforce, he had only been surprised at the marked
deference with which the sentiments of one who had not the
same advantages of age and Parliamentary position, had been
treated both by Mr. Wilberforce, Mr. Eliot, and the rest.
There are other extracts from the Diary, which cumulatively
prove how warm and true an interest Mr. Wilberforce took in
the East India Missions: *e.g.,* "23d Dec.   Breakfasted
early, with Dundas and Eliot, on Mission business; Dundas
complying, when Grant and David Scott also—sat long."
Again: "26.   Grant, Eliot, and Babington, at dinner.   Consultation on East India Missions, and discussing all evening."
Once more: "18th January, 1797.   To town and back, to
dine at Henry Thornton's, where Simeon and Grant, to talk
over Mission scheme."

Is it possible to believe that all the interest in Mr. Haldane's
Mission scheme expressed by Mr. Wilberforce, was nothing

better than shallow pretence, and that his communing with Eliot, Grant, Thornton, and the rest, was to issue in nothing more than the expression of a vague opinion,—that, on Mr. Dundas's own principles, it was better to " send him to the back-settlement, to let off his pistol *in vacuo ?"* Mr. Newton writes, " Assure Mr. Haldane I love, honour, and pray for them all." Both Mr. Wilberforce and Mr. Eliot, who was a member of the Government and Mr. Haldane's chief supporter, knew what his biographers overlook, that it was not in reality politics that " alarmed the Government." Politics did not stand in the way of Mr. Wilberforce's own scheme, and yet it too had signally failed. But politics furnished a good excuse. It was vain to tell Mr. Dundas that Mr. Haldane was a young man, that he had never publicly engaged in politics ; that he had now renounced them for ever, and was occupied with nobler objects. The shrewd, but worldly-minded Secretary of State had no sympathy with the things of heaven. He had no sympathy with Missions to the heathen abroad, or Missions to the unconverted at home. As the cousin of Mr. Haldane's grandfather, and uncle by marriage to Lord Duncan, he was a family connexion, and had known both the Haldanes from their boyhood. Whilst he disliked the scheme in itself, he also contended that its founder was no weak and simple enthusiast, but a man of shrewdness and good sense, a cool reasoner, of acute and vigorous intellect, backed by high courage and indomitable energy. He knew also one of Mr. Haldane's associates, as a minister of no ordinary character, to whom he himself had been induced, on the solicitation of his niece, when residing at Gosport, to offer the living of St. Cuthbert's, which, on Dr. Bogue's refusal, he conferred on the only baronet of the Scottish Church, the late Sir Henry Moncrieff, so long the leader of the Evangelical party. It is very likely that the wily Secretary, of whose duplicity Mr. Wilberforce so often and bitterly complains, did on this occasion also penetrate the philanthropist's reserve, but forbore to tell him that he knew more of Mr. Haldane's character than he chose to avow ; that he himself was moreover then in communication with one near and dear

relative of the Haldanes, who had watched over them with
paternal affection from childhood, and down whose manly cheeks
the tears had been known to flow at the idea of their expatriation. It is, however, not improbable that Mr. Wilberforce,
trying to parry the force of the Secretary's objections, observed,
that a man such as Mr. Dundas described, would surely be more
dangerous in Scotland than under a despotic and powerful
government like that of India. The esteem and respect which
Mr. Wilberforce expressed towards him, not only at that period,
but nearer the close of life, must be regarded as hollow, slippery,
and insincere, before we can believe that the conversational
memoranda of the biographers convey a true impression of
Mr. Wilberforce's sentiments. How little they understood their
father's impressions on this subject, may be gathered from the
following extract from a letter of Mr. Wilberforce's friend, the
late Dr. Porteus, Bishop of London. His Lordship, in writing
from London House to Hannah More, on the 16th of January,
1797, says :—

" What think you of the noble sacrifice Lord Cornwallis has made, of
domestic ease and happiness, and of every blessing the world can give, to
the interests of his country? This is genuine patriotism indeed! None
but he himself could quiet the military commotions in India, and he
himself made the offer of his services. I hardly ever heard of such an
instance of self-denial. He is past sixty, and has nothing to wish or hope
for from Government. Yet, on recollection, there is another instance of
*heroism* with respect to the same country not less honourable to the actors
in it than this. I lately saw three Scotchmen (Mr. Haldane, Dr. Bogue,
and Mr. Ewing), who are all going to India without support, and without
protection, to make converts to Christianity. When we hear of these,
and some other instances of disinterested feeling and benevolence that I
could mention, who will dare say that there is no religion or virtue in the
world ? " *

It was but a few days before the date of this letter that Mr.
Haldane received from the East India Directors the following
official answer, refusing the permission which had been solicited :—

" GENTLEMEN,—The Court of Directors of the East India Company

* Memoirs of Mrs. Hannah More, by Mr. Roberts, 3d vol.

have had under consideration your letter of the 29th ultimo, requesting permission to proceed to India, with your families, and reside in the Company's territories, for the purpose of instructing the natives of India in the knowledge of the Christian religion; and I have received the Court's commands to acquaint you, that however convinced they may be of the sincerity of your motives, and the zeal with which you appear to be actuated, in sacrificing your personal convenience to the religious and moral purposes described in your letter, yet the Court have weighty and substantial reasons which induce them to decline a compliance with your request.—I am, Gentlemen,

"Your most obedient, humble Servant,

"WILLIAM RAMSAY, Sec.

" To Robert Haldane, Esq.
" The Rev. David Bogue.
" The Rev. Greville Ewing."

But although thus baffled in their first attempt, they did not regard the matter as settled. The following letter, from Dr. Bogue to a clergyman at Bristol, exhibits his views of the Mission, and proves that it was neither lightly taken up nor lightly abandoned :—

" The plan of sending out young men unaccustomed to the task of religious instruction never appeared to me calculated to produce the end we had in view. I always thought it the duty of more experienced men to lead the way, and offer themselves for the service of the heathen; but, like you, I thought myself too old for the office of a missionary. But about eight months ago, I received an invitation from my friend, Mr. Haldane, to accompany him to Bengal, to assist him, along with two others, in carrying into execution a plan for the conversion of the heathen, which he had formed about a year before. After weighing the subject maturely, I accepted his call, and declared my readiness to go : the two others we had in view, Mr. Ewing and Mr. Innes (whom some of your Bristol people know), have likewise engaged to go with us. What you mention as to age, and the uncertainty of the climate agreeing with me, is just. But these things must be left in the hands of the great Head of the Church. I am a necessary link of the chain. As we are to live in the close union of brothers, it would not do unless we knew each other, and from what we know, could place some dependance on suitableness of disposition, &c. Though a more suitable and a younger person could be found, he wants the qualification of old friendship and acquaintance which I possess."

A few months afterwards, a long and very powerful memorial was drawn up and presented to the Board, urging them, by every motive of policy and of duty, to review their decision. It appeals to all the principles most likely to operate on the human mind,—to their justice, their interests, their humanity, their love of literature, their philanthropy, their religion, their hopes and fears for this world and the next. The advantages to be gained from a permission, the shame consequent on a refusal, are all powerfully set forth.

But the warning as well as persuasive voice of this memorial was as ineffectual as the first. The " extent of their petition," with their "plan and their designs," are set forth in the following words:—

" If we obtain leave from your Honourable Court, we propose to go out to Bengal, with our families; to take a few persons with us as catechists, and to settle in a part of the country which may be found most convenient, both on account of a healthful situation, and for furnishing opportunities of communicating instruction to the natives. When we have made ourselves masters of the language, we design to employ our time in conveying the knowledge of Christianity to the Hindoos and Mahommedans, by translating the Sacred Scriptures for their use, by conversation, and by erecting schools to be kept by the catechists for teaching the children the first principles of religion. Such is our object, and we have sufficient funds for its support.

" The favour we ask of you, Gentlemen, is leave to go out to Bengal, and protection there, while we demean ourselves as peaceable subjects of the Government, and good members of the community."

But this leave was denied. " It was," says Dr. Bennett, in his admirable Life of Dr. Bogue, " it was said at the time that one of the Directors declared he would rather see a band of devils in India than a band of missionaries." Whatever may be alleged of the impiety of this speech, there is no reason to doubt its sincerity. " The things which the Gentiles sacrifice," said the inspired apostle, " they sacrifice to devils and not to God;" and the interest of Paganism was warmly espoused by men who would have deemed themselves insulted if they had been denied the Christian name. The controversy which soon after arose on this subject, proved that nothing truly Christian could obtain the sanction of the majority of those who then ruled the affairs of India. In pamphlets and periodicals, the most embittered hostility to the propagation of Christianity was openly avowed by some of their civil and military officers. But it was all perfectly natural, for not only were many of those who fought so zealously for Juggernaut and the Suttees against Christ and his Cross a disgrace to the Christianity which they affected, but a leader in their ranks actually wiped off the very name as a foul blot from his dishonoured brow, and at an immense price purchased the privilege of becoming a worshipper of Bramah.

Happily, we have lived to see the day when restrictions on the propagation of the Gospel have been swept away; and great as is the glory which redounds to the name of Wilberforce for his labours in the cause of Africa, it may be said to have been eclipsed by the results of his zeal for Asia. The battle fought at the renewal of the charter in 1812 was fiercely contested, and even Warren Hastings came forward, in his old age, to lend the lustre of his genius to the enemies of the Gospel. In spite of his transcendant talents, his moral character was low, and his career of selfish ambition unhappy. As contrasted with that of Wilberforce, we are reminded of the declaration of the Almighty, "Him that honoureth me I will honour, but he that despiseth me shall be lightly esteemed." The progress of Christianity in India since 1812 has been more than commensurate to all the cost bestowed upon it, and has done much to blot out the reproach of Edmund Burke, when, in words that burn, he contrasted the conquests of England with the achievements of Tamerlane. Amongst those who have since governed India, the name of Lord William Bentinck ought never to be forgotten. He assumed his office under great disadvantages, and more especially as his appointment was the act of Mr. Canning, in opposition to the wish of the Court of Directors. He was, in consequence, compelled to carry into effect some of the most unpopular measures, which had been evaded by his predecessors, such as the reduction of the army allowances, and he was left to bear the odium it entailed, as if the act had been his own. But in the face of every difficulty, the influence of Christian principle was always paramount in the Government House at Calcutta whilst occupied by Lord and Lady William Bentinck. With one stroke of his pen, that upright and intrepid Governor abolished the inhuman practice of Suttees, and left an example to future rulers, demonstrating the folly of those who imagine that there can be danger in forbidding the violation of the plainest statutes of the Almighty. The success which attended this measure will for ever rebuke the enmity of his detractors, and immortalize the name of Lord William Bentinck. He went out to India, as he told Sir Fowell Buxton before he sailed, resolved to abolish Suttees; and without swerving from his purpose, it was carried into effect, in spite of all the sinister predictions of the enemies of the Gospel.

Before taking leave of the India Mission, it would be improper to omit the fact, that Mr. John Campbell was one of those whom Mr. Haldane desired to take with him as a catechist. In writing to the Countess of Leven, Mr. Campbell says: " I have never hinted, but to Mr. Newton, what I now mention. Mr. Haldane and his associates in the intended Mission to Bengal have applied to me to accompany them on their humane enterprise. . . . . After thinking upon it for a few nights and days, I told Mr. H. that my mind was reconciled to go, but that I had *voluntarily* promised Mr. Newton not to engage in any Mission without apprizing him. . . . . Should I go, I shall use all means to prevent my home plans from falling to the ground. I am not in the least dissatisfied with my present station, trade, or success. None have less cause to murmur." The Countess, as well as Mr. Newton, opposed the design, as taking away a most valuable labourer out of a field of usefulness at home for an uncertain benefit abroad. Mr. Newton wrote : " I have no doubt but Satan would be glad to see you shipped off to India, or anywhere, so that he might be *rid* of you, for you stand in his way where you are." This answer neither satisfied Mr. Campbell nor Mr. Haldane ; and at the desire of the latter, the question was referred to the deliberate and devotional judgment of the Eclectic Society, or, as Mr. Campbell was wont to call it, the " Newtonian tea party," which then met around Mr. Newton's chair, and was afterwards connected with St. John's Chapel, Bedford-row. The appeal

brought down an answer, too long for insertion here, which
Mr. Philip has, however, preserved in his Life of Mr. Campbell,
because he thinks "it throws light upon the spirit of that holy
but not heroic circle."

It seems that there were fifteen present at the Eclectic meeting,
that all were unanimous in admiring the generosity and disinte-
restedness of Mr. Haldane's offer and design, but that none of
them approved of the plan for carrying it into effect. They
considered that the difficulties in the way should be regarded
as a providential intimation against it, and that an attempt to
overcome those difficulties by endeavouring to make the Mission,
"a common cause with all serious people, was more likely to
excite public disturbance than to prevail on the Company."

Mr. Newton and his friends seemed also to think that in
determining on a mission to the heathen, it was not proper to
fix on Bengal, or to name a particular city, which they then
supposed to be Patna. The answer is obvious. The neglected
state of the millions of India was the object which had stirred
up Mr. Haldane, and he did not insist on going to a particular
city, excepting so far as it was necessary to name some spot for the
satisfaction of the Company; and finally, whilst he was prepared
to succumb to difficulties, if found to be insuperable, he did not
think it right, slothfully to take it for granted without a struggle
that the lion in the way could not be chained, or the obstacles
surmounted. Had Mr. Wilberforce and his friends yielded to
the argument derived from difficulties at the outset of the Church
Missionary Society, it would have been strangled in its cradle,
and never accomplished the great work by which it has been
distinguished.

With such arguments Mr. Haldane was not satisfied. His
power of influencing the wills of others was great, and the
following appeal which he addressed to Mr. Campbell, for a time
made the good man's mind "like a windmill:"—

"If you think, from what your friends have said, that you
ought to stay at home, I certainly have no title to desire you to
go to India. At the same time, I must say, that this is the
most important step you ever took in your life. The argument

of your friends cuts deep the other way.  They advise you not to go, because, they say, there are so many able friends at the head of the Mission.  Surely they have not considered that you, and another Christian under your direction, would have the entire oversight of an Indian city!  The men at the head of the Mission can assist but little.  Almost the whole will depend upon the person they send.  We think you eminently qualified for such a station.  The Lord has much people in Edinburgh to carry on all your plans.  An imprudent missionary in Bengal might injure the cause of Christianity for an age.  An individual leaving Edinburgh could not affect it materially.  I say all this, because you told me that you were easily impressed with a thing at first.  Be not therefore led away by the advice of your friends at once ; weigh the matter well yourself, with prayer to God, and a single eye to His glory.  Call no man on earth father, but decide for yourself this most eventful question that ever did, or probably ever will come before you."

No wonder that Mr. Campbell was shaken by this powerful and disinterested appeal ; but the advice of Mr. Newton and Lady Leven prevailed, and the simplicity of his motives were fully appreciated by Mr. Haldane, who soon afterwards found other work for him to superintend at home.  His biographer adds—" But how he managed to do it all, I cannot explain ; for at this time he was extending his business, and multiplying his correspondents at home and abroad, and originating Sabbath-schools, by letters and tracts all over Scotland.  Soldiers and sailors wrote to him for advice ; the needy and greedy for money ; the unclaimed outcasts for prayer and counsel ; dark villages for itinerants, and chapel-builders for help ; besides the hundreds, who ordered their Missionary Magazines, books, and Scott's Commentary, and paid their accounts through him. Mr. Newton knew all this, and would not hear of any other mission for him.  Mr. Haldane *saw* much of this, and as naturally thought him just the man for a city in Bengal."

But the abandonment of the scheme was accelerated by the operations of the younger brother, whose itinerancies in Scotland during the summers of 1797 and 1798 had already, as it has been truly said, " stirred to its depths the quiescent mind of Scotland." Robert Haldane was about to throw himself into this movement with his accustomed energy, and with reference to the Indian Mission thus writes :—

" For my own part, I am satisfied in having made the attempt, although it appeared by the event clearly the will of God that we should not go out. I have not a doubt that this was ordered for good, and our being prevented, whether from unworthiness, or from whatever other cause which we know not now, we shall know hereafter. I could not, however, help particularly observing the massacre of the Europeans that lately took place at Benares, where it is probable we should have been, had we obtained our desire. With the apostle, then, I would here thankfully exclaim, ' O the depth of the riches, both of the wisdom and knowledge of God ! how unsearchable are his judgments, and his ways past finding out.' "

Such was the termination of a design, —of which even the failure was calculated to excite additional interest on behalf of millions of our fellow-subjects, thus excluded from the sound of the Gospel by the self-interested policy of their commercial rulers. From this period Dr. Bogue co-operated with Mr. Haldane in several important plans ; and although in some things they did not always see " eye to eye," yet their mutual friendship and esteem remained unshaken and unabated to the end. In the year 1821, during his last visit to England, Mr. Haldane, after his return from the Continent, visited Dr. Bogue at Gosport, on purpose to converse with him on the great subjects connected with the kingdom of Christ, concerning which they were both so deeply interested ; and one of the very last letters written by the venerable Pastor of Gosport, a few days before his death in Oct., 1825, was addressed to his old friend, with whom, for the sake of Christ, he had once designed to spend his life in India. It was a letter introducing one of his pupils, to whom, in the note with which the introduction is accompanied, he says, " Robert Haldane's country residence is between Glasgow and Edinburgh. There is scarcely such a man in the world. You will find his counsels very useful."

# CHAPTER VI.

[1795—7.]

WHEN Captain James Haldane quitted the Melville Castle, he
would have been greatly startled had he been then informed that
within three years he was to become an itinerant preacher. So
far as he had any fixed plan, it was, after his father-in-law's
death, to become a landed proprietor, retire to the country, and
lead a quiet, useful, unambitious life. At one time he was in
treaty for the estate of Garnkirk, near Glasgow, which was
some years later sold for several times the amount for which it
could then have been purchased, had his wife approved of the
locality. Subsequently he had, with her consent, almost concluded a nearly equally advantageous treaty for the estate of
Chesterhall, about ten miles to the south of Edinburgh, a place
which has been since purchased by the Earl of Stair, who has
pulled down the house and included a large portion of the lands
within the splendid domains of Oxenford Castle. But circum-

stances interfered, and he was prevented from completing an arrangement which might have hampered his future plans of usefulness. A life of leisure was never to be his, and when he sketched out the prospect of settling as a country gentleman, he neither knew himself nor the mission he was destined to fulfil. But whilst residing in Edinburgh, and associating with such men as Dr. Walter Buchanan, Mr. Black, Dr. Erskine, and others, he soon became interested in their Christian objects, and still more in those of certain active and devoted laymen whom he met in their society.

Amongst the latter, the foremost place is due to Mr. John Aikman and Mr. John Campbell, two men who were afterwards his own coadjutors in the Gospel, and whose holy zeal and indefatigable labours were continued, although in different spheres, to the termination of their lives. It was with Mr. Campbell that the two brothers first became acquainted; and in a letter from Banff, dated 28th July, 1797, Mr. J. A. Haldane gratefully acknowledges the spiritual benefit received from that good man. "There is no one," he says, "more interested in our success than yourself, and none, I am persuaded, who remembers us more at a throne of grace. Therefore, be assured that when we are long in writing to you, it is not owing to forgetfulness. For I believe you are on each of our hearts. You ought to be on mine, for there is no one whose preaching, conversation, or writings have been so useful to me as the hours we have spent together." The man to whom this testimony is borne is entitled to peculiar notice in this Memoir, and his name has been already introduced in connexion with the Indian Mission. Mr. Campbell had enjoyed the benefit of a good education at the High School, but he afterwards engaged in trade, and had a large ironmonger's shop in the Grassmarket of Edinburgh, overlooking a spot which reminds the classical traveller of the ancient Roman Forum. He was a little man, active, with an intelligent, benevolent countenance, and a quick dark eye, of a very practical turn, and of a mind far superior to his position. Without pretending to commanding talent or much learning, he had a large stock of strong common sense and knowledge of

human nature, combined with impulsive zeal, and a heart overflowing with love to God and man.   Earnest, single-hearted,
prayerful, and devoted to his Heavenly Master, this indefatigable
and laborious man was enabled to achieve more for the kingdom
of Christ, and the welfare of his fellow-creatures, than many
other Christians of loftier station and superior abilities.   To
him belonged pre-eminently the character of a man of God, a
simple yet sublime title, and one which still lingers in the East,
even in countries where the knowledge of Jehovah has long since
disappeared.   He was in Edinburgh the living model of a City
Missionary, a district visitor, a Scripture-reader, a tract distribu-
tor, a Sabbath-school teacher, and a Sabbath-school originator,
long before Christians had learned to unite themselves together
in societies to promote these objects.   His warehouse was then
the only repository in Edinburgh for religious tracts and
periodicals, and became a sort of house of call, or point of
reunion, for all who took an interest in the kingdom of Christ.

Mr. Campbell was afterwards to become a preacher, an author,
a minister, and a missionary traveller, in the unexplored interior
of Africa.   But at the time of which we speak, he was occupying a post far more laborious, and, perhaps, as useful.   His
biographer, the Rev. Mr. Philip, has given a striking and
unexaggerated account of his labours at Edinburgh, when he
says, that "besides the care of his business, and of the sick and
orphans, he carried on a correspondence, enough of itself to
waste the health of any man who had only the night at his
command for writing.   The number of his letters is incredible;
and then they are all upon exciting subjects, and many of them
to persons whose rank or talents called for deliberation."   Once
in every week he wrote to the venerable Countess of Leven and
Melville, the friend of Whitfield, and the associate of the celebrated Countess of Huntingdon.   Mr. Campbell was her
almoner, and whilst her purse enabled him to cheer many a
lonely pilgrim in Edinburgh, "his reports of dying Christians
and of reclaimed wanderers, and of Evangelical movements,
cheered her Ladyship in Melville House."   With the venerable John Newton, the friend of Cowper, he maintained a close

personal intimacy for nearly twenty years, whilst with Thomas
Scott, the commentator, Charles of Bala, Andrew Fuller, and
Abraham Booth, he regularly corresponded, as well as with
many eminent laymen in London, such as Macaulay, Hardcastle, Grant, and Wilberforce.  His friendship and information
were rendered valuable by his knowledge of all the public
movements of truth and philanthropy in Scotland.  " He
had thus," continues his biographer, " to watch the public
mind in Edinburgh, and to consult with all who led it, and
to mingle in all the deliberations and efforts by which new
objects were brought before it.  And then he transcribed,
for private circulation, copies of whatever English or foreign
letters he received, which were likely to multiply or confirm
the friends of Evangelization, besides answering many a long
letter from the tried or tempted on Christian experience."
After this description, it may be understood how it was
that the good Countess of Leven, in writing to Mr. Grant,
the father of Lord Glenelg, playfully styled him " one of
the wonders of the world."

At the period at which this narrative has arrived Mr.
Campbell was rejoicing in the light of the Gospel with an
assured confidence, which till then he had not before experienced, but which never left him to the end of his protracted
and chequered course.  For many years he had known and
believed the truth, but his views of Christ had been rather
sought in the reflection of the inward work of the Holy
Spirit in his heart than in the contemplation of the finished
righteousness of Christ, and he had neither peace nor joy
in believing.  It was a subjective rather than an objective
faith.  Doubts, fears, and actual backslidings, had often
shaken his hope, and driven him almost to despair, even
at the time he was esteemed by other Christians and regarded
as a pattern.  At last, to use his own earnest words in a
remarkable letter published by Mr. Newton, " The cloud
which covered the mercy-seat fled away,—Jesus appeared as
he is!  My eyes were not turned *inward*, but *outward*.

The Gospel was the glass in which I beheld him.  In the time of my affliction, the doctrine of election appeared irritating and confounding; now it appears truly glorious and truly humbling. . . . I now stand upon a shore of comparative rest.  Believing, I rejoice.  When in search of comfort, I resort to the testimony of God; this is the field which contains the pearl of great price.  Frames and feelings are, like other created comforts, passing away.  What an unutterable source of consolation is it that the foundation of our faith and hope is ever immutably the same!—the sacrifice of Jesus as acceptable and pleasing to the Father as ever it was!  To this sacrifice I desire ever to direct my eye, especially at the first approach of any gloom or mental change."

One more extract from this striking document which so delighted Mr. Newton must suffice.

" After my deliverance," continues Mr. Campbell, " my ideas of many things were much altered, especially about faith. I perceive that this principle in the mind arises from no exertion in the man, but the constraint of evidence from without.  The Spirit takes the things of Christ, and discovers their reality and glory in such a manner to the mind of man, that it is not in his power to refuse his belief.  It is no mighty matter, nor is it any way meritorious, to believe the sun is shining when our eyes are dazzled with its beams.  The internal evidences of the truth of revelation had ten thousand times more effect upon my mind than all its external evidence.  There is a divineness, a glory, and excellence in the Scriptures, perceived by enlightened minds, which they cannot so describe as to make it intelligible to an unregenerate person.  Formerly the major part of my thoughts centred either upon the darkness I felt or the light I enjoyed.  Now they are mainly directed to Jesus, what he hath done, suffered, and promised."

It was when Mr. Campbell was thus exulting in the first joys of his spiritual emancipation that Mr. J. A. Haldane became acquainted with him, and after reading these extracts, it is more easy to understand how his experience was then made useful to the young disciple by exhibiting those refreshing views of the Gospel as glad tidings, proclaiming freedom from the condemnation of the law, and showing that our hopes are to be fixed only on the work which Christ has finished, although our conduct is to be regulated by what God has commanded. Mr. Campbell used in after-life to speak with pleasure of those communings with his new friend, and then modestly to add, " But very soon he got the start of me, and left me far behind."

It was in Mr. Campbell's shop that Mr. James Haldane was also first introduced to Mr. John Aikman. Mr. Campbell, with that good-humoured cordiality and attractive drollery which formed one of his characteristics, and to which he was indebted for much of his popularity, addressed the former somewhat to this effect : " You, Sir, are from the *East* Indies, and my friend here is from the *West*. You belong to the same prayer-meeting, and should be united." The introduction was mutually agreeable, and the commencement of a Christian friendship which no circumstances ever interrupted.

Mr. Aikman was a man of good talents and education, who was fond of reading, well acquainted with some of the modern languages, and so familiar with French that in after-years he was able to preach to the prisoners of war at Penicuick, near Edinburgh. He had been brought to the knowledge of Christ by reading Newton's " Cardiphonia; or Utterance of the Heart," which he purchased at a book-stall in London, under the supposition that it was a novel, and would do for a circulating library he was then establishing in Jamaica. He relinquished a lucrative business in that island from reluctance to be associated with traffic on the Lord's-day ; and having arranged with his partner, returned to Scotland with a moderate competence. At the time of which we are now speaking he was studying at the College, and attending the Divinity lectures, with a view to the ministry. He had neither the energy nor the physical strength of his new friend, for his health had suffered from residence in a tropical climate. But added to very agreeable social qualities, and general information, there was in him that warmth of piety, that constraining love to

K

Christ, that earnest zeal to advance his kingdom, which prompted him to efforts even beyond his power, and soon won the heart of James Haldane.

Amongst the anecdotes of which Mr. James Haldane had so large a store, was one connected with Mr. Aikman, which is worth preserving for the moral it inculcates. Mr. Aikman, when about to visit London, called upon Dr. John Erskine, at his house at Lauriston, in the suburbs of Edinburgh, to know if the learned divine had any commission to the great metropolis. " None whatever," replied the Doctor; "only if you see John Newton, commend me to him most kindly, and tell him how much I rejoice in all the good he is doing. But," added Dr. Erskine, " do you know, Mr. Aikman, there is one thing about Mr. Newton which surprises me exceedingly,—that he, being himself so faithful an Evangelist, should continue in a Church where the dogma of baptismal regeneration is admitted in any shape, whether direct or equivocal, into her formularies. That is a compliance which I could not sanction." When Mr. Aikman arrived in London, he repaired to the Church of St. Mary Woolnoth, Lombard-street, to hear the Word from the lips of the venerable Rector. After the service he went into the vestry, and delivered to Mr. Newton the kind compliments of Dr. Erskine, but of course without retailing the remarks by which they had been originally accompanied. Mr. Newton made answer, " Oh, my good old friend, Dr. Erskine ; I am always happy to hear of him. He is, indeed, a man of God. But do you know, Mr. Aikman, there is one thing surprises me very much about Dr. Erskine, more indeed than I can express ; and that is, that one so truly Evangelical in his doctrine can remain as the colleague of Dr. Robertson, who certainly preaches to his people another Gospel. That, Mr. Aikman, is a compliance which my conscience would not sanction."

The name of Principal Robertson recals that period which has been called " the midnight of the Church of Scotland." It was at its darkest at the period at which we are now arrived in the history of the two brothers. Here and there might be seen a burning and a shining light, as in Stirling and in its neighbourhood, yet it served only to make the gloom more visible.  It was a darkness that might be felt, and the infidelity of David Hume, Adam Smith, and their coadjutors, first infecting the Universities and seats of learning, had gradually insinuated its poison into the ministrations of the Church.  Some had altogether thrown off the mask, like the eminent and scientific Professor Playfair, to whose *moderate* preaching James Haldane himself had listened as a boy when living at Lundie House. He would sometimes smile at the recollection of the bow from the pulpit, which, according to the ancient usage of feudal times, was then directed at the close of the service to the pew of the chief heritor in the parish church, even when the youthful occupier happened to sit alone.  Other ministers, with more of inconsistency, exhibited the same infidelity as the amiable Professor Playfair, whilst they still ate the bread of orthodoxy, and in practice trampled on the doctrines and precepts of the Church. Dr. M'Gill, of Ayr, had published a Socinian work, of which the Rev. John Newton declared that it alarmed him "more than all the volumes of Priestly;" yet even he was absolved by the Assembly, and returned to Ayr the chief preacher in a district where the life and poems of the gifted but unhappy Burns have left a record of the low condition of clerical religion and morality.   Dr. Robertson, the friend of Hume and Adam Smith, was not without reason more than half suspected, whilst Dr. Blair's moral sermons had shown how, in Scotland, as well as in England, the professed ministers of Christ could become, in the words of Bishop Horsley, little better than "the apes of Epictetus."

The following extract may serve to show a state of things which modern historians sometimes try to ignore, although it proves the need that existed for a voice to rouse the people from the sleep of death.   It is taken from the "Autobiography of the Rev. Dr. Hamilton, of Strathblane," the father of the well-known and esteemed minister of the Scotch Church, Regent-square, London :—

"Principal Hill and Dr. Finlayson," says Dr. Hamilton, "ruled the Assemblies, and the parishes were occupied by the pupils of such divines as Simpson, Leechman, Baillie, and Wight. Many of them were genuine Socinians. Many of them were ignorant of theology as a system, and utterly careless about the merits of any creed or confession. They seemed miserable in the discharge of every ministerial duty. They eagerly seized on the services of any stray preacher who came within their reach. When they preached, their sermons generally turned on honesty, good neighbourhood, and kindness. To deliver a Gospel sermon or preach to the hearts and consciences of dying sinners, was as completely beyond their power as to speak in the language of angels. And while their discourses were destitute of everything which a dying sinner needs, they were at the same time the most feeble, empty, and insipid things that ever disgraced the venerated name of sermons. The coldness and indifference of the minister, while they proclaimed his own aversion to his employment, were seldom lost on the people. The congregations rarely amounted to a tenth of the parishioners, and the one-half of this small number were generally, during the half-hour's soporific harangue, fast asleep. They were free from hypocrisy. They had no more religion in private than in public. They were loud and obstreperous in declaiming against enthusiasm and fanaticism, faith and religious zeal. Their family worship was often confined to the Sabbath, or, if observed through the week, rarely extended to more than a prayer of five or three minutes. But though frightfully impatient of everything which bore the semblance of seriousness and sober reflection, the elevation of brow, the expansion of feature, the glistening of the eye, the fluency and warmth of speech at convivial parties, showed that their heart and soul were there, and that the pleasures of the table and the hilarity of the light-hearted and gay, constituted their paradise and furnished them with the perfection of their joy."

This is the testimony, not of a foe to the Church of Scotland, but of a friend; of a faithful minister, who lived and died in its communion. Dr. Hamilton also illustrates his melancholy description by a striking anecdote of a minister, who imagined that a sick man must have committed some awful crime, because, in the prospect of death, and under the convictions of an awakened conscience, he was bewailing his sins and earnestly inquiring—" What must I do to be saved ? " If we were disposed to add further corroborative evidence to the truth of his melancholy picture, it would be found in the graphic sketch which has been drawn of the dominant party by the brilliant pen of Mr. Hugh Miller, in his masterly review of the Infidel debate in the General Assembly, on the subject of Christian

Missions. The Assembly then met, as it had done since 1640, in one of the aisles of the grey and venerable cathedral of St. Giles, beneath whose shadows sleep the ashes of that great Reformer over whose grave it was said, by the Regent Morton, " There lies one who never feared the face of man." That aisle is described by Lord Cockburn, in his Life of Jeffrey, as a "plain, square galleried apartment, admirably suited for its purpose, the more so that it was not too large; and it was more interesting, from the men who had acted in it and the scenes it had witnessed, than any other existing room in Scotland." The debate in 1796, which Mr. Miller describes, furnishes a better illustration of the true character of Moderatism than the reader will be able to find for himself almost anywhere else. Dr. John Erskine, of Edinburgh, was for many years the revered leader of the evangelical party of the Church of Scotland, and is thus described by Bishop Hurd,—" Erskine, next to Warburton, is the deepest divine I have yet known." But Mr. Miller's noble portrait of this venerable man might have acquired some fresh touches of interest had the report from which he draws his materials enabled him to state the precise point in the speech of the minister of Gladsmuir which called forth the crushing reply of Dr. Erskine.

The overture under debate and the Resolution so vehemently opposed amounted to this, " That it is the duty of Christians to carry the Gospel to the heathen world." After describing the character of Dr. Erskine and some others, Mr. Miller thus proceeds :—" ' The *bruit* goeth shrewdly,' said De Bracy to his companion in arms, the Templar, ' that the most holy order of the Temple of Zion nurseth not a few Infidels within its bosom.' Hume, intending on one occasion to be very complimentary, said nearly the same thing of the Church of Scotland. Was the compliment deserved? And if so, what peculiar aspect did the Infidelity of the Scottish clergy assume? Was it gentlemanly and philosophic, like that of Hume himself? or highly seasoned with wit, like that of Voltaire? or dignified and pompous, like that of Gibbon? or romantic and chivalrous, like that of Lord Herbert, of Cherbury? or stupid in ruffianism,

like that of Paine? or redolent of nonsense, like that of Robert
Owen? or was it not rather of mark enough to have a character
of its own,—an Infidelity that purported to be Antichristian
on Bible authority,—that, at least, when it robed itself in the
habiliments of unbelief, took the liberty of lacing them with
Scripture edgings? May I crave the attention of the reader,
instead of directly answering any of these queries, to the facts
and reasonings employed by the Rev. Mr. Hamilton, of Gladsmuir."

Copious extracts are then given from the speech of him who was
rewarded for his services on this occasion with the office of Moderator! He argued, with a glozing affectation of reverence for the
Word of God, " that the gracious declarations of Scripture ought
to liberate from groundless anxiety the minds of those who stated
in such moving language the condition of the heathen." He
went further, and ventured even to borrow the Infidelity of
Rousseau, and more than insinuated that, in communicating
Christianity to the Indian or Otaheitan, we should only introduce the vices of European nations, whilst the influence of our
religion would not refine his morals or ensure his happiness.
The minister of Gladsmuir concluded, " Upon the whole, whilst
we pray for the propagation of the Gospel and patiently await
its period, let us unite in resolutely rejecting these overtures."
But there was one point which this " Moderate" had especially
laboured, and it was to show the *absurdity* of making revelation
precede civilization. " Men," he said, " must be polished and
refined in their manners before they can be properly enlightened
in religious truths." And, as he drew to the close of his
flowery harangue, he demanded, with an air of triumph, where
did we find the great Apostle of the Gentiles? Was it amongst
barbarians, such as those to whom it was now proposed to carry
the Gospel? or was it not rather in the polished cities of
Corinth, of Athens, and of Rome? It was when this orator
sat down that Dr. Erskine rose, with a dignity worthy of the
descendant of Lord Cardross,—a dignity to which his character,
his learning, and his age, added weight,—and, in a calm, firm,
energetic tone, uttered those crushing words which thrilled

through the Assembly,—"MODERATOR, RAX ME THAT BIBLE" (Reach me that Bible). There was something before which even his opponents quailed in the authoritative appeal thus made to the silent witness for God's truth, which still lay upon the table. The Bible was handed to him, and the Assembly seemed awed and electrified, and a death-like silence reigned through the vaulted aisle whilst the aged man of God turned up the sacred volume and read, in a distinct and audible voice, the account of Paul's reception at Melita, when "the barbarous people showed us no little kindness." "Think you," said Dr. Erskine, "that when Paul wrought his miracles at Malta, and was supposed to be a god, he did not also preach Christ to the barbarians, and explain whose Name it was through which such power was given unto men?" The rest of his speech was equally effective; but if the Moderates felt abashed by the discomfiture of their champion, they consoled themselves with the strength of the majority, by which they rejected the appeal on behalf of Missions to the Heathen.

It may be imagined with what feelings this debate was listened to, by him from whose lips these reminiscences were derived. But there was one favourite argument of the Moderates which sunk into his heart, and to which his future life returned a conclusive answer. They tauntingly asked, why not look at home? Why send missionaries to foreign parts, when there is so much ignorance, unbelief, and immorality, at your own doors? James Haldane felt the force of the appeal; he saw the difficulties interposed in the way of his going to India; and when he afterwards himself carried the Gospel into the parishes of Inveresk, or Gladsmuir, or Musselburgh, or preached at the cross of Ayr, in the presence of Dr. M'Gill himself, or in the College Close of Aberdeen, or in the town of Thurso, he could not forget the exhortations of the Moderate ministers in the General Assembly, when they resisted foreign missions by insincerely talking of the necessities of their own people.

Other, although less public proofs, of the degraded state of the dominant party in the Church might be mentioned, particularly a Presbytery dinner to which he was invited in Edinburgh, upon a special occasion, and to which he had gone, hoping for useful, perhaps spiritual, or, at least, rational conversation on those topics in which he was now chiefly interested. Instead of this the company were treated to Bacchanalian songs, the folly of which was aggravated into something approaching to wickedness by an admixture of ridiculous, if not profane, allusions to their own sacred calling and functions. The burden of one song was the prescription of "a bumper of Nottingham ale," in the pulpit at the different stages of a Presbyterian discourse. If, in the hey-day of youth and folly, while God was not in all his thoughts, he had been disposed to turn away from the convivial excesses of his comrades at sea, how was he likely now to appreciate boisterous merriment, combined with approaches to the same intemperance, in connexion with eternal realities, amongst the professed heralds of the Cross, whose duty it was to warn men to flee from the wrath to come?

Shortly after the debate on Missions and the exhibition of what Bishop Warburton, in writing to Dr. Erskine, termed, " Paganized Christianity," the visit of the Rev. Charles Simeon, of Cambridge, communicated to James Haldane another and holier impulse. At the close of the Assembly of 1796, Mr. Simeon, invited by Dr. Walter Buchanan, arrived in Edinburgh. It was his wish to make a short tour of pleasure in the Highlands, and it was arranged that he should meet Mr. James Haldane at Airthrey, and proceed by Balgonie, Melville House, Perth, Dunkeld, Blair Athol, to Glasgow. He went in the first instance to the house of Mr. Innes, in Stirling, and, as it was the sacramental week, he attended the preparatory services on the Saturday, and himself communicated on the Lord's-day. At Airthrey he found Mr. and Mrs. James Haldane expecting him, their brother being himself in London, privately and quietly engaged about his Indian Mission. Mr. Simeon's visit to Airthrey, although only for a few days, was not without fruit, as it was marked by the blessing which it brought to a young lady, to whom, after listening to her music, he spoke on the importance of consecrating this and every other gift to the glory of God.

It was on this occasion that Mr. Simeon took part, for the first time, in the Scotch Church, as a communicant at the Lord's-table, thus marking the Catholic spirit by which he was animated; but, after all, only following the example of the great Archbishop Usher and other distinguished ornaments of the English Church. There were, however, some rigid Presbyterians at Stirling, and particularly a ruling elder, who showed as great reluctance to communicate with a *Prelatic* clergyman as could have been exhibited by any High Church Episcopalian believing in apostolic succession. Neither bigotry nor its opposite is confined to a particular denomination. The celebrated Dr. Claudius Buchanan mentions in his diary, that he spent his last Lord's-day in England, with Dr. Bogue, and partook of the Lord's Supper with his Church at Gosport. The founder of our Indian bishoprics then little imagined that the son of his friend Mr. Wilberforce, the future Bishop of Oxford, would, as Rector of Alverstoke, so ignore the ministerial character of Dr. Bogue, as to rebaptize those who in infancy had received the rite at the hands of that apostolic man. Mr. Simeon was, however, fatigued, and bitterly complains of the preparatory service on Saturday, which lasted four hours and a-half. The first preacher, Mr. Robertson, discoursed for an hour and a-quarter. Then followed Dr. Campbell, whose " sermon was admirable," but lasted an hour and a-half. " But," says Mr. Simeon, " I had no ears to hear; the length of the service wearied me exceedingly. Nor was I singular : the whole congregation were much like myself. After Mr. C. had finished, Mr. Shireff, the minister of St. Ninian's, went up and added a word of exhortation." In talking of it at Airthrey, Mr. Simeon observed, that Dr. Campbell's and Mr. Shireff's sermon and exhortation seemed as if turtle and venison had been served after he had dined well on roast-beef and plum-pudding. Mr. Simeon's journal proceeds :—

" *Sunday, 19th.*—Went with Messrs. Innes and Campbell to St. Ninian's. Mr. Shireff began the service, and preached a useful sermon from Hebrews x. 10. After preaching above an hour, besides prayer and singing, he left the pulpit, and went to the head of the tables. There he gave an exhortation respecting the sacrament, which to me was more excellent than his sermon. I communicated at the second table, where Mr. Campbell exhorted. His exhortation was exceedingly precious to my soul. I was quite dissolved in tears. I made a full, free, and unreserved surrender of myself to God. Oh, that I may ever bear in mind His kindness to me, and my obligations to Him! After communicating I left them, and saw, as I came into the church-yard, one preaching there in a tent. I walked home (three miles to Airthrey) alone by choice, and met numbers coming to the sacrament, which, as I understood, lasted till about eight in the evening. They had about a thousand communicants, a fresh exhortation to each table, and a sermon to conclude. They who could stay there from beginning to end, with any profit to their souls, must be made of different materials from me."

It had been determined that the tourists should proceed on horseback, and Mr. Simeon, in an entry in his journal, soon after his arrival in Edinburgh, exclaims: "Everything that I could wish, and much more than I could have expected, has taken place. On Thursday, Sir John Stirling offered me his own mare for my northern tour, and this day Mr. (James) Haldane has offered to accompany me." It seems, however, that Sir John Stirling's offer, for some reason, was ultimately declined, for Mr. Simeon bought a horse at Stirling, which, from its colour and country, was playfully named *Dun Scotus*, but which did no great credit to his breeding, as appears from one of his letters, written some months after his return to Cambridge. "*Dun* Scotus," he says, "fell lame seventy miles from home, but brought me home safely. I kept him two months, with a farrier to attend him most of the time, and then sold him for nine guineas, so that I was not any great gainer by him." Mr. J. Haldane was better mounted; and, attended by one of his brother's servants, carrying the saddle-bags of both the travellers, after the fashion of the times, thus equipped, they left Airthrey on the 20th June. They proceeded down the valley of the Forth, by the road which beautifully winds along the southern base of the Ochil hills, through Alloa and Dollar, to Balgonie, in Fife, where they were hospitably received by

Lord Balgonie and his Lady, the daughter of that Mr. Thornton " about whose head," as the great Scottish missionary, Dr. Duff, has eloquently said, " the poet Cowper has woven a garland of imperishable renown." On the following day, Lord Balgonie himself rode with them to Melville House, the seat of his father, the Earl of Leven and Melville, under whose roof they found " something infinitely better than mere worldly pomp and grandeur." They then proceeded by St. Andrew's across the Tay to St. Madoes, and thence to Perth and Dunkeld. From this beautiful place, which Mr. Robert Haldane used, in the words of the Psalmist to call " the city of the wood," they proceeded on the Saturday to Blair Athol, returning the same evening to Moulin, where the Rev. Mr. Stewart, afterwards of Dingwall, and then of Edinburgh, at that time ministered. The results of this visit were very memorable. Mr. Stewart had been previously earnest about his work from a sense of duty, but in himself coldly orthodox; and like Luther, before he knew the *glad tidings* of the Gospel of justification by the finished work of Christ, groaning under a spirit of bondage and of fear. They reached Moulin on the Saturday morning preparatory to the Sacrament, and remained over the first service, which was by no means edifying. The next service was to be in Gaelic, and on this account they proceeded to Blair. At Blair there was no room in the Inn, so that they were glad to avail themselves of Mr. Stewart's kindness, and return in the evening to his hospitable manse. It was the occasion of revival to Mr. Stewart's soul; rather, as he himself says, "It was no revival; I never was *alive* till then." But his own letter to Mr. Black, written immediately afterwards, will best tell its interesting tale.

" What thanks do I not owe you for having directed my two late visitors to call at my cottage, as I have thus had the honour and blessing of entertaining angels unexpectedly. Messengers of grace I must reckon them, as their visit has been thus far blessed to me, more than any outward dispensation of Providence that I have met with. They were so kind as to put up with such accommodation as we could afford them, though our house was a good deal out of order on account of Mrs. Stewart's illness, and spent two nights with us. Mr. Simeon gave us his friendly assistance on occasion of dispensing the Lord's Supper, and frankly preached two discourses on the Sabbath, besides serving a table in English. This was the whole of the English service for that day. His sermons, and the conversation and prayers, I have no doubt, of *both* gentlemen, have indeed been eminently blessed to me. Since I first entered on my sacred office, I have not felt such a lively season as the last week has been. I had some private conversation, too, with my kind friend, Mr. Haldane, which proved not a little edifying to me. I shall not fail to return his visit when I go next to Edinburgh. When I have such friends as him and you to see, with the prospect of being introduced perhaps to Dr. Buchanan, possibly to Dr. Davidson and C., I shall think it will be incumbent on me to make my visits to Edinburgh more frequent than they have been hitherto. And I am sure I shall have vastly more enjoyment· in collecting spiritual knowledge, and deriving vigour and animation from the Fountain of life, through the conversation and counsel of the servants of the Lord, than ever I found, or can find, in the conversations of all the *literati* or metaphysicians that your University contains."

In another letter, addressed to Mr. Simeon, and dated November 25, 1796, Mr. Stewart begins : "Ever since the few happy hours in which I was blessed with your company, I have daily thought, with pleasure and gratitude, of the Lord's loving-kindness to me, in sending two of his chosen servants, so unexpectedly and so seasonably, to speak to me the words of life."

In another letter, he dwells on the impression produced by "the short interview" in Mr. Simeon's bed-room. This alludes to the manner in which his pious guest wished "good night" to his kind host, when the latter conducted him to his apartment. In doing so, Mr. Simeon briefly expressed his prayer that Mr. Stewart might be fitted for the important and responsible charge which he held as a minister of Christ. But the words were with power, and Mr. Stewart, under the influence of emotions produced by that memorable "good night," having next gone to Mr. James Haldane, and also conducted him to his room, they sat down together, and talked much and long concerning that Gospel which had been so recently revealed in all its glory and its grace to Mr. Simeon's fellow-traveller. The next morning was the Sacramental Sabbath, and Mr. Simeon himself not only communicated, but served one of the tables. The novelty of his position as an English clergyman made him, however, rather nervous, and occasioned some slight blunders.

In Mr. Simeon's interesting letter to Mr. Stewart, published

in his Life by Rev. W. Carus, there are one or two little matters
of detail which are inaccurate, but which are only worthy of
notice as showing how difficult it is to secure minute certainty
in the relation of facts. The reason of their leaving Moulin
upon the Saturday was their ignorance of Gaelic, and the reason
of their return was simply the want of accommodation at Blair.
Still, in any case, the circumstances were such as fully to warrant Mr. Simeon in saying, " It has often brought to my mind
that expression of the evangelist, ' He must needs go through
Samaria.' It is our privilege to expect those invisible interposi-
tions, if we commit our way to Him; and every instance that
comes to our notice should encourage us to acknowledge Him
in all our ways."

Mr. Stewart's conversion was followed by a remarkable revival
in his parish and neighbourhood, and he gave so much countenance to itinerant preaching that his biographer, the Rev. Dr.
Sievewright, with more of worldly policy than of Christian
simplicity, actually deemed it prudent, more than twenty years
afterward, to veil Mr. James Haldane's name under the initial
H., although the biographer was recording letters in which Mr.
Stewart himself expressly names this honoured servant of the
Lord as a "messenger of grace" to his soul.

On the following Monday they proceeded to Taymouth, a
place with which Mr. James Haldane was well acquainted,
having resided there as a guest at the Castle, and gathered
many interesting and fresh reminiscences of the pious Viscountess Glenorchy, whose husband did not live to attain the
Earldom. Whilst halting their horses at Killiecrankie, to view
that magnificent and rocky defile, where, amidst shouts of
victory, the Viscount Dundee terminated his dark career and
passed from the battle-field to the judgment-seat of God, Mr.
Simeon's horse was seized with a fit and came to the ground,
throwing his rider nearly to the edge of the precipice. On
recovering himself, and after a time remounting, instead of being
ruffled by the occurrence, he spoke in the most striking and
beautiful manner of the sudden transition he had nearly experienced. They had been conversing a little while before of the

things of heaven, and he remarked how wonderful it would have been to have been transported in a moment, beyond the bounds of time and space, to that place of which they had been discoursing, and so leaving this world of trouble and sin, to have joined the general assembly and church of the first-born, whose names are written in heaven.

From Taymouth they rode to Inverary, and thence to Arroquhar and Luss, whence, after three hours' walking, they reached the summit of the lofty Benlomond. "There," says Mr. Simeon, "amidst mountain scenery, inexpressibly majestic, we went to prayer together, and dedicated ourselves afresh to God." Nineteen years later, Mr. Simeon, for the third time, visited Scotland, and once more ascended Benlomond, although not with James Haldane, but with feelings of sacred and solemn delight, he recalled the fond recollection of that act of dedication in which his companion and himself, the one in his twenty-eighth, and the other in his thirty-eighth year, had devoted themselves to the service of the Lord.

On the following Lord's-day, Mr. Simeon preached twice at Glasgow ; and, after visiting Mr. Dale's establishment, at New Lanark, and the residence of Sir John Stirling, they arrived at Edinburgh on the following Saturday, "crowned with loving-kindness and mercy," and in time for the sacrament in the Canongate, at which he was next day a communicant. He preached in the evening at Lady Glenorchy's church to three thousand people. He adds, "Mr. Haldane gave me a parting prayer." Next day he says : "After sermon this morning, my dear friend, Mr. Haldane, left me, after having been my companion three weeks. We were mutually affected with fervent love to each other, and with thankfulness that we had been permitted so to meet together."

Mr. Simeon arrived at Cambridge on the 30th of July, but not without incurring the risk of another fall with *Dun* Scotus, such as he experienced at Killiecrankie. He was fond of riding on horseback, but in these days of railways and express trains, it is curious to look back to the customs of a period, little more than half a century ago, when a clergyman and a college-fellow reckoned the purchase of a saddle-horse at Stirling, to be the most satisfactory method not only of accomplishing a Highland tour, but of returning from Edinburgh to Cambridge.

Shortly after his arrival, he addressed the following letter to his friend :—

*" King's Coll., Cambridge,*
*" Aug.* 17*th,* 1796.

" MY DEAREST FRIEND AND BROTHER,—Though I have been arrived at home no less than ten days, I am far from having got through all the business which so long an absence has entailed upon me : I cannot, however, any longer delay the just expressions of my gratitude to you, lest I should appear to be unmindful of the many obligations which you have conferred upon me, and of the happiness I enjoyed in your company and conversation. I was called away from Edinburgh somewhat sooner than I had fixed for my departure from it; and excepting one more such little accident as I experienced in your presence, near Moulin, I was brought in safety and comfort to the end of my journey. But I greatly missed my fellow-traveller. Now and then my mind was enabled to soar a little; but having no opportunity of communicating its ideas, it grew torpid and dull. It was soon wearied in its flights, and distracted in its meditations. Even natural curiosity dozed, for want of some friend to whom one might express one's sense of the surrounding objects : nor did I find any occasional relief from conversation with any pious persons, for, except a Methodist preacher, whom I overtook on my road, about five miles south of Dunbar, I did not see so much as one person that feared God between Edinburgh and Leeds.

" And now what have I to do, but to devote myself more than ever unto God ? Surely this, my dear Brother, should be the effect which the Divine mercies should produce. I trust they have wrought thus on you, and I hope they will on me.

" I rejoiced greatly to see the amiable and spiritual dispositions of your dear partner, and ardently do I wish, for your sake, for her sake, for your family's sake, that she may increase in the knowledge of her God and Saviour. Bid her take courage, and press forward with more and more alacrity. She will have much to conflict with, no doubt : but she will find it an inexpressible advantage, that she has an husband that will go hand in hand with her, as a fellow-heir of the grace of life. Pray present my very affectionate respects to her, and tell her that my heart's desire and prayer to God, on her behalf, is, that she may come forth into the full light and liberty of the Gospel, enjoying a spirit of adoption, and an earnest of her eternal inheritance.

" I cannot conclude without begging you to accept my warmest acknow-ledgments for the kind attention which you showed me, during the whole of our continuance together. I trust that He who will not suffer a cup of cold water to go unrewarded, will one day recompense to you all the love which you showed towards the most unworthy of all his prophets, and I earnestly pray that He may be your Companion and Guide through life, and after death your everlasting portion.

"To hear of your welfare, and especially to hear of it from yourself, will be a rich gratification to

"Your very affectionate and most indebted friend,

"C. SIMEON.

"*James Haldane, Esq., Airthrey, Stirling.*"

Soon after the termination of the tour with Mr. Simeon, the two brothers were called to mourn the loss of their elder uncle and guardian, who died of gout, at Lundie House, at the beginning of August. He was a man of a very noble, gallant, and energetic character, whose services were so highly prized by the Government, that it was with difficulty he obtained leave to retire from the army. His name still lingers in America, in connexion with the campaigns in Canada, as appears from the fact, that it is prominently introduced in some of the historical romances of Cooper, the American novelist. It has often been said of Colonel Duncan, that had opportunity offered, he would, in all probability, have been as distinguished on land as was his brother at sea. To both of his nephews he well performed the part of a kinsman. In the management of the elder brother's property he showed peculiar judgment, and the estates of Lochton and Keithock, which he purchased for him out of their father's personalty and the savings of the minority, more than doubled in value. An anecdote, in connexion with a riot, which took place at Dundee, was often told by his nephews, as strongly indicative of his courage and military strategy. A violent mob had come out to burn down certain mills, which were unpopular. The civil power was quite unable to restrain their fury, and there were no soldiers at hand. The Colonel, in whose neighbourhood the mills were situated, mounted his horse, and skirting the line of the mob, rode briskly along, calling out as he passed his brother magistrates, in a determined tone, to offer

no obstruction to the advance of the people, but to allow the
soldiers to get between them and Dundee. The word passed
through the crowd, that soldiers had arrived, and the Colonel
was gone to intercept a retreat. A panic arose, and the rush
to regain Dundee soon left in tranquillity the scene of their
intended devastation.' In his county he was one of its most
influential aristocracy, and very shortly before his death turned
the election in favour of the late Sir David Carnegie, of
Southesk, in his contest with Sir David Scott. Having no
issue, Colonel Duncan was succeeded by his younger and only
brother, then Commander-in-Chief of the North Seas.

---

From Mr. Simeon's letters and the account of his tour, it is
not difficult to conclude, that James Haldane's progress in the
Divine life had been both rapid and decisive. With him
Christianity had become all in all, and his whole soul absorbed
in the love of Christ, went forth in an ardent desire to promote
his glory. For some time he had been a constant attendant
at a meeting, held at the Rev. David Black's house, in North
Richmond-street, where prayer was wont to be made by a few
earnest Christians, influenced by a desire for spreading the
Gospel, and promoting the glory of their Lord and Master.
One of these prayer-meetings was held on Friday evening, and
another on the Lord's-day morning. The former is described,
in November, 1795, as "now increased, and conducted on such
a plan as not to interfere with the duties of the family or the
closet. They assemble at seven o'clock on Sabbath mornings,
and continue about an hour and a half, during which time three
or four members usually pray, after having sung part of a psalm,
and read a portion of Scripture."

The Edinburgh Tract Society, which preceded the great
Society in London by several years, had been formed, chiefly
through the active zeal of the indefatigable Mr. John Campbell.
But the first *public* distribution of tracts in Scotland seems to
have been made by the Rev. Charles Simeon, who, during his

tour, scattered both in the streets and highways, "The Friendly Advice." Different opinions will be formed as to the wisdom of this practice. Much depends on time, place, and circumstances. But there is no doubt that, during the early part of his career, James Haldane witnessed much good fruit, in following the example of his Cambridge friend. The venerable Countess of Leven, who looked with alternate doubts and satisfaction on lay preaching, gave her unqualified approbation to this novelty, and offered Mr. Campbell ten or twenty pounds, to be laid out in tracts. She pleasantly reproves her faithful correspondent, for not reporting more concerning Mr. Simeon's tour, and asks, " Is it accident or design ? why, especially as your friend Captain Haldane was his travelling companion ? " He replies with his wonted drollery, " I am satisfied to be nailed to the Grass Market, till Providence draw the nail. When Captain Haldane was talking of the tour, I told him I *envied* him : but in a minute I saw my blunder, and checked myself."

About the same time Mr. Campbell began to institute Sabbath-schools in Edinburgh and its neighbourhood. To promote this object there was formed in Edinburgh, in 1797, a new Society, independent of clerical superintendence, for the establishment of Sabbath-schools in destitute localities. Connected with each teacher there was to be a committee, to aid him in the devotional exercises, and one of them was in rotation to deliver a short address to the children, parents, and any poor destitute persons that could be induced to attend. It was, in fact, a City Missionary and Sabbath-School Society combined. One of these schools was set up by Mr. Campbell at Loanhead, a collier village with a neglected population. Mr. James Haldane rode out with him to witness its commencement, but such was his reluctance to make himself conspicuous, that he could not be prevailed on to address a few words to the assembly of parents and children who crowded the Cameronian Meeting-house, which had been lent for the benevolent object. On the following Lord's-day evening, this was done by Mr. Aikman, and Mr. Campbell adds, " Oh ! how many precious addresses proceeded from the silken or silver lips of that man of God during the following forty years." Hitherto his plans had been confined to Edinburgh. Mr. James Haldane began to think that he might himself do something to extend such Sabbath-schools in the north of Scotland, although without any idea of preaching himself. But before making this attempt, which would have been incompatible with Mr. Campbell's occupations, he agreed to accompany that good man on a tour for a week to the west of Scotland. The following is the account of it extracted from Mr. Campbell's autobiography:—

" We set off on Monday morning, taking some thousands of tracts with us, in a one-horse chaise, distributing tracts to rich and poor as we proceeded. We obtained a meeting in Glasgow from a few friends of the cause of God, who were recommended to us as active and zealous. We laid before them the general neglect of giving religious instruction to the youth of our country, except in pious families—described the plan pursued in Edinburgh for educating the youth in the principles of the Gospel, by the formation of schools on the Sabbath evenings, and the countenance that was given to the plan, and the ease with which children were collected, with the trifling expense that attended its execution. After some conversation, those present were formed into a Society for establishing and conducting Sabbath-evening schools in Glasgow and the surrounding towns and villages. We acted in the same way and with the same success in Paisley and Greenock. We also called on ministers of different denominations in the towns through which we passed, and conversed with them on the subject of Sabbath-schools, all of whom, I think, approved of the plan. I remember all the persons to whom we offered tracts on the road, whether they were in carriages, or on horseback, or on foot, received them, except in two cases, the one a gentleman on horseback, who would not condescend to stretch forth his hand to receive the proffered tract, but rode sullenly on; the other was that of three gentlemen on horseback, to whom we held out tracts on both sides of the gig; two took no notice, the third partly held out his hand to receive them, but immediately drew it back, as if they had been infectious. We left them lying upon the road, which was then dry, that if they repented they might still have them. We afterwards looked back, when we saw them halting in a group at the top of a rise, and receiving them from a boy, whom they had sent back to bring them to them. I found afterwards that they were three Burgher ministers who were returning from the Synod; for the Rev. John Brown of Whitburn, eldest son of John Brown of Haddington, called upon me about three months afterwards to apologise for their rejecting our tracts. He said they heard who we were at the next town they came to (viz., Selkirk), and were sorry

that they so treated us, but they thought they were papers on politics, for
these were the sad days of Tom Paine, and the French Revolution, when
the nation was on the very verge of rebellion.  We arrived at home on
Saturday evening.  In three months afterwards we heard that the result
of this one week's exertion was the formation of *sixty* Sabbath-evening
schools!  The Christian zeal that had been excited in Scotland by the
lately-formed Missionary Society in London, greatly helped to the success
of our week's experimental journey."—*Life of Campbell*, p. 129.

This journey to the west of Scotland in the spring of 1797,
was the commencement of an active career of usefulness, which
was to continue for no less than fifty-four years.  But a reference
to his own notes will once more enable us to trace the steps by
which he was gradually led to become himself a preacher of the
Gospel :—

" For some time after I knew the truth, I had no thoughts towards the
ministry.  My attention was directed to the study of the Scriptures and
other religious books, for my own improvement, and because I found
much pleasure in them.  When I first lived in my own house, I began
family worship on Sabbath evenings.  I was unwilling to have it more
frequently, lest I should meet with ridicule from my acquaintance.  A
conviction of duty at length determined me to begin to have it every
morning, but I assembled the family in a back-room for some time, lest
any one should come in.  I gradually got over this fear of man, and
being desirous to instruct those who lived in my family, I began to
expound the Scriptures.  I found this pleasant and edifying to myself,
and it has been one chief means by which the Lord prepared me for
speaking in public.  About this time, some of my friends remarked that
I would by and by become a preacher.  A person asked me whether I did
not regret that I had not been a minister, which made a considerable
impression on my mind.  I began secretly to desire to be allowed to
preach the Gospel, which I considered as the most important as well as
honourable employment.  I began to ask of God to send me into his
vineyard, and to qualify me for the work.  This desire continued to
increase, although I had not the most distant prospect of its being gratified, and sometimes in prayer my unbelieving heart suggested that it
could not be.  I had no idea of going to the highways and hedges and
telling sinners of the Saviour.  However, I entertained some distant hope
that the Lord would direct.  Things which passed in conversation tended
to increase my expectation, and a tour I proposed to undertake to the
north with a view of establishing Sabbath-schools, at length opened a
prospect of being allowed to speak for Jesus.  The success of a journey
to the west country, increased my desire of going through the north, not

to preach, but to establish schools, while I was to be accompanied by a minister from England, who should preach in the towns and villages. Before we set out our plan was enlarged. Another Christian brother (Mr. Aikman), with whom I had become particularly intimate in a prayer meeting, who had studied for the ministry, agreed to accompany us, and both he and I began to preach in a neighbouring village about the same time. The journey to the north is pretty generally known, and ever since the Lord first allowed me to speak of him to others, I have found increasing pleasure in the work, and seen, I hope, more of the inward workings of my corrupt heart, while I have found His grace all sufficient."

Mr. Campbell's account of the "Origin of Lay Preaching at Gilmerton, near Edinburgh," is written in his own graphic matter-of-fact style,—

"I had," says Mr. Campbell, "an acquaintance in the large collier village of Gilmerton, and one who lived near it. They were frequently telling of the ignorance and irreligion of the inhabitants; and no wonder, for they had nothing like the Gospel in the Parish Church for at least forty years. These reports made me often feel compassion for them, and I remember calling on Dissenting ministers of different denominations, urging them to supply poor Gilmerton with a sermon now and then, which they were to mention to their presbyteries; but it came to nothing. Soon after this, a worthy friend of mine, a Mr. Buchan, one Monday morning introduced me to a Mr. Joseph Rate as a preacher from Dr. Bogue's academy at Gosport. On asking him what stay he intended to make in Edinburgh, he said for some weeks. I immediately related the circumstances of Gilmerton, and asked if he would preach to them, while he remained, on Sabbath evenings. He said he would, if I could get him a place to preach in and people to preach to. I said I had no doubt but I should procure both, for they had a kind of thatched town-house capable of containing at least two hundred persons; but Mr. Salmon comes to the Corn Market on Wednesday, and always calls upon me. I shall then be able to tell you positively about both the place and congregation. On mentioning the matter to Mr. S., he said, 'If you will assure me of a preacher on Sabbath evenings, I will insure you of a place and congregation,' which I cheerfully engaged to do. I mentioned the matter to Mr. James Haldane and Mr. Aikman, who were delighted with the circumstance, and as I was obliged to attend to my own bishopric at Loanhead that evening, they engaged to walk with Mr. Rate to Gilmerton, where they were glad to find a house full of people waiting for them. After sermon he intimated that he would preach there regularly on the Sabbath evening for some time, or until further notice. The next evening the congregation was increased, by persons coming from a greater distance.

During the succeeding week Mr. Rate was called to leave Edinburgh, as he expected only for a few days, of which the next Sabbath was one: but who was to supply Gilmerton for that Sabbath evening? There was no one, and yet a congregation would assemble. In our dilemma Mr. Haldane recommended to Mr. Aikman to do it; but he would not consent. However, he was afterwards gained upon to consent to preach, by Mr. Haldane telling him that if he would consent to preach the next Sabbath, and Mr. Rate did not return during the week, he would engage to supply the succeeding Sabbath. This offer, coming from a sailor, touched the right chord in Mr. Aikman's warm heart, and constrained him to comply with the solicitation to preach, and he did preach, greatly to the satisfaction of the judicious Christians who were present; and no Mr. Rate making his appearance the following week, Mr. Haldane was obliged to take his place on the Sabbath evening, much to the satisfaction of the congregation."

Mr. J. Haldane's first sermon thus alluded to was preached at Gilmerton, on the 6th May, 1797, and on the same day his third daughter was born. Amongst those who were present at the sermon was the well-known Dr. Charles Stuart of Dunearn, whom it may be proper here to introduce to the reader. Dr. Stuart was a lineal descendant of the good Regent Murray, and at one time stood third in prospective succession to that ancient Earldom. He was a man of deep piety, and induced to enter on the study of divinity, at a time when the ministry of the Church of Scotland presented few worldly temptations to a young man of birth and family. He was presented to the parish of Cramond, near Edinburgh, and married a daughter of the venerable Dr. John Erskine, who was himself partially disinherited by his father (the Blackstone of Scottish jurisprudence) because he had declined the profession of the law and assumed that of a minister, which, in the judgment of the Scottish aristocracy, was not then a choice worthy of a descendant of the noble houses of Buchan and Mar. Dr. Stuart did not, however, remain long satisfied with the Church of Scotland. In his thirst for general information, and the society of good men, Dr. Stuart had gone from the Divinity Hall in Edinburgh to one of the Dissenting Academies in London, and there imbibed notions unfavourable to the union between Church and State. For some time these opinions lay dormant, but at length he

became convinced that he ought not to baptize the children of
unbelievers, or admit to the Lord's table those who did not
make a consistent profession of Christianity. Acting on this
persuasion, he found, on examining his parishioners, that there
was hardly a family whose children he could baptize, or whose
adult members he could admit to the Lord's table. The pain
of his scruples was aggravated by his hypochondriacal constitution, and an alternation of high and low spirits, which made
him at one time as melancholy in his solitary hours as he was
at other times joyous as a companion. The result was that he
resigned his charge, quitted the Church of Scotland, studied
medicine, took his degree as a physician, and became a zealous
Baptist. Still it was his more peculiar honour to be "a lover
of good men" of every name, and a promoter of every enterprise
which had for its object the diffusion of the Gospel.

When James Haldane preached his first sermon, Dr. Stuart
was at once surprised and delighted with the power, the energy,
and the earnestness of the preacher. He pronounced him the
Boanerges of the new movement, and became from that moment
an admirer and friend. There is no doubt that Dr. Stuart's
influence on James Haldane was considerable, as it was also on
several other eminent men; and it would have been remarkable
if it had not been so, considering Dr. Stuart's active zeal,
affectionate friendship, as well as his elegant scholarship, critical
acuteness, general knowledge, polished manners, and attractive
qualities. In the preceding year the "Missionary Magazine"
had been commenced, under the auspices of Dr. Stuart, with
Mr. Ewing as the editor.

The preaching at Gilmerton was attended with a blessing.
The people flocked in crowds to hear Mr. Aikman and the Sea-
Captain. The parish minister, who had been at first quiescent,
now burned with an indignation quite inconsistent with his
professed *Moderation,* and took means to deprive them of the
school-house, in which they had hitherto preached, and which
had been filled to overflowing. But Mr. Falconer, a pious
baker, procured a spacious loft as a substitute, and when this
was found insufficient, a large barn, which continued to be filled

to excess by the people, who flocked from the neighbourhood, and listened with interest to these earnest and affectionate appeals. About this time an incident occurred, which Mr. James Haldane mentioned with emotion not long before his death, in conversing with the surviving sister of Mr. Aikman, who was one of the last persons he visited. He was crossing the High-street near the market, then held round the Tron Church, when a countryman, dressed like a miller, with a whip tied over his shoulder, rushed across the street, and eagerly holding out his hand, said, "Oh! Sir, I'm glad to see you." Mr. J. Haldane, surprised at this familiarity, replied, "I do not know you." "Ah! Sir," exclaimed the honest carter, as the big tear rolled down his manly cheek, "but I know you, for you preached the Gospel to me at Gilmerton."

Miss Aikman, who records this touching anecdote, goes on as follows :—"A considerable degree of general excitement arose out of the preaching at Gilmerton, and some even of the Evangelical ministers in Edinburgh became afraid of the consequences of lay preaching. But the two preachers increased in boldness, and hearing of the death-like state of the North of Scotland, and the carelessness and immorality of the ministers, resolved to make a tour, and examine personally into the state of religion, and preach the Gospel in the streets of the different towns and populous villages visited. They made this plan the subject of prayer and consultation, and when it was fixed that they should go, each of them wrote an address to the congregation at Gilmerton, and got a large impression printed for distribution on the road. In a letter I had from Miss Stuart (Dunearn), she says, 'My father has read both your brother's address and the Captain's with great delight.' They also reprinted a tract, written by the Rev. Charles Simeon, of Cambridge, entitled, 'An Advice to all whom it may concern,' and these tracts they gave away at every place where they preached, to all who would receive them, two years before the London Tract Society was formed in 1799. On the evening before their departure for the north, there was a special meeting for prayer held in the Rev. David Black's house, North Richmond-street, where they were recommended by the brethren to the grace of God for the work in which they were about to engage.

It was a memorable tour, the first of a series of successive itinerancies, in which Mr. James Haldane, at the beginning accompanied by Mr. Aikman, afterwards by Mr. Innes, or again by Mr. Campbell, during a period of nine years, preached in almost every town or populous village in Scotland,—from Berwick-upon-Tweed and the Solway Frith to John o' Groat's and the northern islands of Orkney and of Shetland. Good men may differ in their opinions as to the general question of the lawfulness of lay preaching, but no well-judging Christian will think it wise to condemn that on which the Lord himself has stamped the seal of his approbation. Upon the tour to the North in 1797, there was poured out a blessing which never can be mistaken, and whatever may be said of the regularity of their commission, it will be safer to adopt the sentiments so beautifully expressed in one of Mr. Simeon's letters to Mr. James Haldane, which will be hereafter given at large: "I think immortal souls of such value, that I should rejoice if all the Lord's people were prophets. If mercy and sacrifice stand in opposition to each other we may choose mercy; and if David and his men be perishing with hunger they may eat the forbidden bread."

# CHAPTER VII.

MR. JAMES HALDANE'S FIRST TOUR THROUGH THE
NORTHERN COUNTIES OF SCOTLAND AND THE ORKNEY
ISLANDS IN 1797—PRAYER MEETING AT REV. D.
BLACK'S —LAY PREACHING — LETTER TO THE " MISSIONARY
MAGAZINE "—MANNER OF TRAVELLING—LEAVE EDIN-
BURGH ON 12TH JULY—PERTH, SCONE, CUPAR, GLAMIS,
KIRRIEMUIR, MONTROSE, ABERDEEN — LETTER FROM
BANFF — ABERDEEN — MAGISTERIAL INTERFERENCE —
EFFECTS OF PREACHING AT BANFF—ELGIN—NAIRN—
FORRES—INVERNESS—PROCEED TO THE ORKNEYS—STATE
OF RELIGION THERE—CONVERSION OF AN OLD MAN OF
NINETY-TWO—PREACHING TO CROWDS AT KIRKWALL—
ACCIDENT TO MR. AIKMAN—BLESSING ON JAMES HAL-
DANE'S LABOURS IN CAITHNESS—LETTER OF MRS. M'NEIL
OF ELGIN—BATTLE OF CAMPERDOWN—STATE OF RELI-
GION AT INVERNESS—CONCLUSION.

[1797.]

WHEN Mr. James Haldane and Mr. Aikman commenced their
first preaching tour through the North of Scotland, they took
their commission from the obligation imposed on every believer
to proclaim to others the Gospel of salvation, and from the
prayers with which they were solemnly commended to the grace
of God in the house of their pastor, the much-honoured David
Black, the Minister of Lady Yester's Church. Disputes there
may be as to the lawfulness of what is called lay preaching, and
assuredly the great body of private Christians have neither the
opportunity, the ability, nor the leisure, to preach in public.
But the office of an Evangelist is, in some sense, imposed upon
every Christian in whatever sphere he moves. For surely it
cannot be denied that every believer is bound, in his family and

amongst his friends, to make known to others the glad tidings
of salvation. Accordingly we read (Acts viii. 1, 4), that when
" the Church were all scattered abroad, *except the apostles*,"—
" *therefore* they that were scattered went everywhere preaching
the word." " If," says an able divine,—" if the Gospel be true,
can there be any danger of sin in proclaiming its truths? If
the Gospel be salvation, and if God wills the salvation of men,
can it be sinful to tell them of that which saves from hell?"
But the question was fully and warmly debated at the time
Mr. J. Haldane entered on his itinerancies, and the arguments
which he has himself so ably drawn from Scripture in the
introduction to the Journal of his Tour in 1797, cannot now be
easily refuted. " We would not," he says, " here be understood to mean that every follower of Jesus should leave the
occupation by which he provides for his family to become a
*public* preacher. It is an indispensable Christian duty for every
man to provide for his family; but we consider every Christian
is bound, wherever he has opportunity, to warn sinners to flee
from the wrath to come, and to point out Jesus as the way, the
truth, and the life. Whether a man declare those important
truths to two, or two hundred, he is, in our opinion, a preacher
of the Gospel, or one who declares the glad tidings of salvation,
which is the precise meaning of the word *preach*."

Having very forcibly asserted the right of every man who
knows the Gospel to proclaim it, he next disclaims any design of
usurping or intruding into the Pastor's office, an office which
was quite distinct from that of an Evangelist, as evidenced by
the apostolic declaration that there were " some evangelists, and
some pastors and teachers." (Ephes. iv. 11.)

His reasoning is powerful, and its force was substantially
admitted by Mr. Simeon, Mr. Scott, the Commentator, as well
as the venerable John Newton, and others of his correspondents.
He winds up his able defence with the following words :—
" Such are some of the arguments which have satisfied our
minds that we have a right to preach the Gospel, founded both
on reason and on the Word of God. We formerly hinted that
our situation in life enabled us to undertake the journey without

interfering with necessary avocations, and we deemed the low state of religion a sufficient call for us to go to the highways and hedges, and endeavour to compel our fellow-sinners to lay hold on the hope set before them in the Gospel. The writings of laymen in defence of Christianity have always been considered peculiarly important, as there is less ground to suspect such men of interested motives, and the clergy are naturally led to refer to such writings when the enemies of the Gospel have ascribed their zeal to ambition and priestcraft. Strange, then, if we might not *speak* on subjects on which we might have written !"

Resting on these principles, actuated by these motives, encouraged by the prayers of their brethren, and stimulated by an earnest and affectionate zeal to promote the Gospel of their Lord and Saviour, Mr. J. A. Haldane, accompanied by Mr. Aikman and Mr. Joseph Rate, left Edinburgh on Wednesday, 12th July, 1797, having first drawn up the following manifesto of their designs :—

" *To the Editor of the ' Missionary Magazine,' from the Persons engaged in the Scotch Itinerancy.*

" The advantage of missionary schemes both in England and Scotland, has remarkably appeared, not only in exciting the zeal of Christians to send the Gospel of Jesus to the dark places of the earth, but to use means to extend its influence at home. With this view a missionary journey has been undertaken to the northern part of Scotland, not to disseminate matters of doubtful disputation, or to make converts to this or the other sect, but to endeavour to stir up their brethren to flee from the wrath to come, and not rest in an empty profession of religion. Accordingly, they are now employed in preaching the word of life, distributing pamphlets, and endeavouring to excite their Christian brethren to employ the talents committed to their charge, especially by erecting schools for the instruction of youth. As the Lord alone can crown their endeavours with success, and as He has declared, that for all the blessings He bestows on his Church and people He will be entreated, they earnestly request the prayers of the friends of Jesus. That their object may be misrepresented, they have no doubt. It has already been said, they are going with a design of making people dissatisfied with their ministers : but they can appeal to the great Searcher of hearts, that they are determined in their conversation or preaching, to know nothing but Jesus Christ and Him crucified. If they should meet with teachers who do not follow the apostolic rule, they will not bid them God speed, lest they become par-takers of their evil deeds; but they love no man more or less because he is of the Establishment or of the Secession. They would therefore request, that intercession should be made for them by the Church of Christ without ceasing, that they may have a prosperous journey; and that many who are now disobedient may be, by means of them, turned to the wisdom of the just, that God in all things may be glorified through Christ, to whom be praise and dominion for ever and ever. Amen."

They travelled in a light open carriage purchased for the occasion. They were largely provided with religious tracts, and pamphlets, which they had also printed at their own expense; and fresh supplies were forwarded to different stations on their route. Of Mr. Simeon's "Friendly Advice to all whom it may concern," they circulated 5,000; of Mr. J. A. Haldane's "Address," 4,000; of Mr. Aikman's, 3,000; besides 8,000 short sermons and other tracts. They were also accompanied by Mr. Joseph Rate as far as Inverness, where he was usefully occupied for more than two months, while his colleagues proceeded to the Orkney Islands and to Caithness. The account of this tour, as well as the Introduction and Appendix, were chiefly written by Mr. James Haldane. It is marked by the manly modesty which always characterized him, and is singularly devoid of egotism or self-seeking. Even the good done is scarcely noticed, and, in one of the few instances where it is just glanced at, it is said,—" To the name of Jesus we would desire to render all the glory of the undeserved honour and happiness of being instrumental in plucking any of our fellow-sinners as brands from the burning."

The Journal begins :—

"*July* 12.—Left Edinburgh (after frequent, earnest, and united prayer to God for direction and support), and arrived at Northfeery, where we immediately began our labours. Preached in a school-room to about fifty persons. Came forward to a village called Keltie Bridge about ten at night, where we preached next morning."

Having, on the 14th, preached at Perth, Scone, and Cupar Angus, they proceeded to Meigle, Glamis, and Kirriemuir, preaching in hospitals, at market-crosses, and in churchyards, attracting some attention, but not so much at first as afterwards.

In order to furnish an idea of their plan, and as this was the first occasion on which the false doctrines of the parish ministers were openly attacked, Mr. J. Haldane's own entry in the published Journal will probably be read with interest :—

" *Lord's-day, July 16th.—Kirriemuir.*—Preached in the morning, at eight o'clock, in the market-place, to upwards of 200 people. Went to church and heard sermon. The minister preached from 1 John iii. 8. The sermon did not appear to us glad tidings to sinners. The object of it was to show that the Son of God came into the world to instruct and enable men to destroy the works of the devil. He represented the Gospel as a contract between God and man, of which the equitable condition was repentance and sincere, although imperfect, obedience, ' which God,' he added, ' was too just and too good not to accept.' As he read the sermon, and repeated every passage of the smallest importance, it was impossible for us to mistake the meaning of any of them. The Lord's Supper was then dispensed; and it surely must affect the minds of all who know the importance of the Gospel and the value of men's souls, to learn that, immediately afterwards, upwards of 1,500 persons, daily acquiescing in such doctrine as has been mentioned, professed to commemorate the death of Christ. We heard one table served by a neighbouring minister. This person, to guard the communicants against the commission of sin, told them that, if they fell into any after that day, there remained no more sacrifice for them. . . . When the Church was dismissed in the evening, went to the top of a walled-stair in the market-place, which the congregation had to pass, and immediately began as usual by singing. There might probably be near 1,000 people who stopped. Preached to them from Mark xvi. 15, 16, ' Go ye into all the world, and preach the Gospel to every creature,' &c. Explained to them the Gospel, and the circumstances which rendered it glad tidings to every creature; showed that it was a dispensation wholly of grace, and that it was completely contradictory, both to Scripture and to fact, to represent a man as capable of doing anything in order to render himself acceptable to God. . . . Told the people, plainly, that what they heard was not the Gospel, and urged them to search the Scriptures for themselves, mentioning, at the same time, that our only motive in making these observations was love to their immortal souls, whose final state, we were convinced, depended upon their belief or rejection of the Gospel. As to their minister, we could have no ill-will towards him : but, on the contrary, sincerely prayed to God that he might give him repentance to the acknowledgment of the truth."

They again preached on the Monday morning, at Kirriemuir, to a large congregation, many of whom came in purposely from the country; and then proceeded to Forfar, where they preached in the street to a very attentive congregation, and took occasion to warn the people against Paine's "Age of Reason," which had been there extensively circulated and obtained some footing. At Brechin they preached to a crowded and attentive auditory, where, for the first time, they availed themselves of the town-drummer to announce the sermon. The Itinerants apologized for this mode of publishing their sermons, expressing a fear lest it might shock the feeling of some serious persons. "But," says Mr. H., "these emotions ought certainly to subside when we consider the vast importance of using every means to assemble careless sinners to hear the Word of God, and the impossibility of our adopting any other mode equally effectual for giving general notice in our limited time." Accordingly, the bellman or town-drummer, as the case might be, was generally charged with an intimation; and in the Orkney Islands the people, of their own accord, summoned their more distant neighbours by lighting beacon fires on the mountains.

At Montrose, where they preached twice, they observe, "We were sorry to learn that many of the children in Montrose were unable to read, in consequence of being sent to the cotton manufactory at a very early age. They are greatly neglected by their parents, and crowd the streets on the Lord's-day." This remark shows how soon the establishment of factories and the employment of young children began to corrupt and demoralize the people. With reference to the ignorance of the children there is the following note:—

"This is by no means to be considered as the unavoidable consequence of attending a cotton manufactory. In the cotton mills at Lanark, established by Mr. Dale, the greatest attention is paid, both in teaching the children to read and in instructing them in the principles of Christianity. It would be well if those who imitate that friend of his country in employing children in their manufactories, would imitate him also in his earnest care to communicate the blessings of religious knowledge to their tender minds."

Mr. Dale's establishment afterwards fell into the management of Mr. Owen, the Socialist, who for a time deluded the visitors of New Lanark by the exhibition of the practical fruits of Christian culture, as if they had been the result of his own wild and ungodly theories.

From Montrose the tourists proceeded to Bervie, and thence to Stonehaven, where, amidst the remnants of Popery and nonjuring Episcopacy, they " noticed the greatest indifference to the concerns of eternity that they had anywhere remarked," although there were two Episcopal chapels besides the parish church.

The following letter to Mr. Campbell, although hastily written, may be more interesting, and have in it more of freshness, than extracts from a journal prepared for the public. It is dated, Banff, July 28th, 1797 :—

" MY DEAR FRIEND,—It gave us much pleasure to hear of your welfare this morning, by your letter to Mr. Aikman. I received your other letter at Aberdeen, and it gave us cause to glorify God on your behalf when we heard he had so strengthened and countenanced you at Gilmerton. I hope and believe, that your labours there will not be in vain. But, while I am on this subject, I would say a few words as to your exerting yourself too much. You say you are sometimes at a loss what is duty, but I imagine all your friends see clearly that you ought to spare yourself. I do not mean to say what you ought to do and what not, but you ought to be guided by the state of your body, and not exhaust your strength. By following this plan you will, humanly speaking, do more in the Lord's service in the long run; and therefore here is a proper opening to exercise self-denial. Mr. Newton says, in one of his letters, that the devil would be glad to have you out of Edinburgh. I believe he would be glad to have you out of the world, although it were to remove you to a better. You will think it hard that I should first wish you to take more work and then find fault, but you know that nothing but unfeigned affection for you and desire to promote the Redeemer's glory can actuate me in this matter. I therefore think that you should endeavour to get some one to assist you at Lonehead, and you can give an exhortation at the end, and sometimes at Gilmerton. Perhaps you may get a *curate*. But you wish me to tell you what we are doing. I should have written to you before now, but I wrote to Mr. Ewing and told him to acquaint you of our progress, and really our time is so short that we cannot employ much of it in writing letters. I know there is no one more interested in our success than yourself, and none, I am persuaded, who remembers us more at a throne of grace. Therefore, be assured, when we are long in writing to you it is not owing to forgetfulness, for I believe you are in each of our hearts. You ought to be on mine, for there is no one whose preaching, conver-

sation, or writings, have been so useful to me as the hours we have spent
together. The letter to Mr. Ewing was from Stonehaven. We went on
next day to Aberdeen, and saw several brethren, who were very kind, but
seemed to think we were going rather too far in preaching in the streets,
&c. We spoke to them at supper about schools, &c., but there were so
many objections, that unless we had stayed and taught the schools ourselves, little good seemed likely to be done. But I hope what we said
will bring the matter under consideration, and that hereafter something
of that kind may be established. The parties are not much united, which
is a vast loss. We preached twice on Saturday at Old Aberdeen, once
there on Sabbath morning; twice on Sabbath, and once on Monday
morning, at Gilkomston, a small town in the neighbourhood. . . . So
that in two half-days we preached ten times in that town and neighbourhood. . . . I am to stay here all Sabbath. Intend preaching to-morrow
night at M'Duff Town, within about a mile from this place. To preach
on the Green Sabbath morning, at M'Duff Town afternoon, and here in
the evening. I have not found the least inconvenience from preaching,
although sometimes I have been obliged to raise my voice a good deal.
The people are really perishing for lack of knowledge. Pray, then, that
what we say may be blessed, and lead them to search the Scriptures for
themselves. We shall not have too many pamphlets. Indeed I suppose
we shall need to have sent us what we have left at Edinburgh. We shall
hope to hear from you by the time we get to Inverness. We were much
refreshed by your letter this morning, and some others which we received.
We need something to encourage us, although we have met with enough
of the Lord's goodness to put to shame our unbelief. He sometimes
brings us down that we may look to Him, but He has disposed the hearts
of all to behave to us with much civility and respect in every place.
It is a great comfort to know that so many of the Lord's people are
praying for us. We have, I am persuaded, experienced the benefit of
their prayers. It is now past five. You will soon, I suppose, meet at
Mr. Black's. May the Lord meet with you. I know you will remember
us. A. and R. will, I suppose, be preaching at the very time. I am
much obliged by your kindness to my wife. She is very sensible of it.
I expected to have heard from her to-day. Remember me to Mr. Ewing
kindly. I have got his letter. I shall write to him some time hence;
you can give him what information there is in this letter. It is written in
a very hurried manner, as you will see. I cease not to pray for you and
the people of Gilmerton and your colleague. May your labours be
crowned with abundant success. Remember us most kindly to Mr. and
Mrs. Black and all our friends. The brethren salute you much.

"I am, my dear Sir,

"Yours very affectionately,

"J. A. HALDANE."

M

At Aberdeen a circumstance occurred, which, many years afterwards, gave rise to a gross exaggeration, to the effect that they had been arrested at the instigation of some of the Professors, for preaching to the students in the College-close. When this idle tale was mentioned in a letter to Mr. J. Haldane, in the year 1842, as an old story still circulated on the authority of the widow of one of the Professors, then living at Brighton, he replied as follows:—

"The matter at Aberdeen was simply this. Intending to preach out of doors on the Lord's-day evening, I was told that the College-close would be an excellent place, so the town-drummer was sent round to give notice. On Sunday morning, before breakfast, I received a message from one of the Magistrates, who was also a Professor, that he wished to see me. On presenting myself, he inquired how I came to intimate preaching in a place which was not public. I replied that I had been informed that there would be no objection in any quarter. 'Who told you so?' I replied that I was told it and believed it, but would not say by whom. He pressed the matter very much, but saw I was firm. I had been so told by one highly respectable, who spoke in good faith, but whom I would not implicate. But I said, 'Since it appears that I was misinformed, I have no wish to persist, and I will preach elsewhere.' 'No,' said the Baillie, 'that will be worse; it will occasion a riot, and our windows will be broken.' 'Then,' said I, 'as you wish it, I will preach,' and accordingly I did so to a very great congregation. For this the place was well adapted. It is not impossible that the widow's story may be correct in regard to my telling the Professor that the Gospel was of more importance than the studies of the young men, though I do not recollect it. At all events, they were not engaged in their studies, at least within the College, on the Sabbath evening. There is, however, an episode to the story of the sermon. The Magistrates called their drummer to account, and fined him a guinea. He was obliged to pay, or would have lost his office. When I heard it, I sent him the money, with which he was very well pleased, as he had no expectation of it. Not long after my preaching, the

Magistrates of Aberdeen sent a complaint to the Admiralty of their trade not being duly protected. The Admiralty referred their letter to Lord Duncan (as Commander-in-chief of the North Seas), who told me that he wrote a very sharp letter to the Magistrates on the occasion. Of course, he knew nothing of any difference between them and me, but in those days they attributed the sharpness of his rebuke to their interference with me, and I met with no further interruption at Aberdeen."

The sermon in the College-close was the more remarkable on this account, that although Mr. J. Haldane had before preached to the colliers of Gilmerton, and also at various places between Edinburgh and Aberdeen, this was the first occasion on which he addressed a crowded audience, composed of persons of all conditions in life. It might be said that the whole population of Aberdeen turned out by thousands to hear an East India Captain. There was novelty in the fact; but his powers as a preacher were also beginning to be known, and the multitude was so great that even in the spacious court which they occupied they "almost trod upon each other." The people listened with deep attention as the speaker addressed them from Rom. i. 16, "I am not ashamed of the Gospel of Christ, for it is the power of God unto salvation to every one that believeth." He spoke with that earnest fervour of spirit which gives wings to thought, and inspires eloquence in those who are least solicitous about oratory. On a subsequent occasion he preached in the streets of Aberdeen on a Lord's-day evening, and next morning one of his hearers was found dead, but on his knees, in the attitude of prayer.

In the above letter Mr. James Haldane alludes to his intention to remain at Banff, to preach once on the Saturday at a village in the neighbourhood, as well as three times on the Lord's-day. These intentions were fulfilled, and his ministrations produced a deep sensation in the town and district. On the Sunday evening the Battery-green was usually crowded by multitudes, attracted by the military band which during the summer performed for two hours every evening. But on this occasion the commanding officer, in compliment to Mr. Haldane, very politely intermitted the parade, so as to leave the green undisturbed, and give the soldiers an opportunity of attending. But there is another circumstance connected with his sermon on the Saturday evening, which is still more interesting. It was unknown to him, and is one of the many instances which prove how little a preacher can be aware of the effect of the messages he delivers. It was communicated by the Rev. Dr. Morison, of Chelsea, after the death of Mr. James Haldane, of whom he said that a remarkable sermon of his, preached on a certain summer's evening in 1797, on the banks of the Dovern, near Banff, had been blessed to the conversion of his excellent and pious wife. The details are given in the following letter, written by Mrs. Morison :—

"*April* 29, 1851.

" MY DEAR SIR,—When the news reached us of your venerable and beloved father's removal from this vale of tears, I did indeed feel (though I never had the honour of a personal acquaintance with him) that I had lost a true friend, one to whom I shall owe much in eternity, where, through the mercy of ' God our Saviour,' I hope yet to meet him, and to converse on all the way in which the Lord hath led us, to prove us and to try us, in this wilderness. I do not know that the incident to which my husband referred, in a late note, is worthy of being formally recorded, yet to me it must always be so interesting that I cannot decline communicating it, as well as memory will permit at this distance of time.

" In the summer of 1797, Captain Haldane, as he was then called, visited my native town, in company with one or two other gentlemen whose names I do not remember. By the usual mode of advertisement, the tuck of drum, a sermon was announced, not at the usual place, the Battery-green, but at a neighbouring village, on the green banks of the gently-flowing Dovern. The reason for the selection of this spot was the fact, that the Battery-green had been previously engaged by a company of equestrians. I was then a very little child, and I well remember I had been invited by a school-fellow to accompany her to see the equestrians.

" We had actually set out to go to the place; but before reaching the spot, a worthy lady, who knew us both, met and accosted us, ' Where are you going, my young friends ? ' My companion replied, ' To the Battery-green, to see the horsemen.' ' Oh,' said she, ' you had better go with me to the green banks, and hear Captain Haldane; it will do you more good.' My companion said, ' No ; I can hear a sermon at any time, but I cannot see the horsemen.' She determined to execute her purpose, and went to the Battery-green; and so far as I have heard, she has never entered on the narrow path. Young as I was then, I was influenced by an unseen hand to accept the pressing invitation to go to the sermon on the green banks, and quitted my companion. Captain Haldane arrived on horseback at the place where the people were assembled to hear him. He dismounted, and gave his horse to the charge of another gentleman who stood by. He was then a young man, under thirty years of age, and had on a blue great-coat, braided in front, after the fashion of the times. He also wore powder, and his hair tied behind, as was then usual for gentlemen. And I can never forget the impressions which fell on my young heart, as your father, in a distinct, clear, and manly tone, began to address the thoughtless multitude that had been attracted to hear him. His powerful appeals to the conscience, couched in such simple phrase, at the distance of more than fifty years are still vividly remembered, and were so terrifying at the time, that I never closed an eye, nor even retired to rest that night. I cannot be quite sure what was your father's text; but from the frequent and pointed repetition of the words, ' *Except ye repent, ye shall all likewise perish,*' I have reason to believe that these must have been the subject of discourse. One thing I know, that the impression produced by what I heard was never effaced from my mind; for though I did not fully embrace the Gospel for years after I had listened to your honoured father, yet I never relapsed again into my former state of carelessness and indifference to eternal things.

> " ' And oft, amid the giddy throng,
> Did conscience whisper, Thou art wrong,
> Thou art not fit to die.'

" Thus, my dear Sir, very imperfectly, but truthfully, have I endeavoured to comply with your request; and praying that every blessing may rest on you and yours, I am," &c.

The sermon thus referred to produced a very general impression. The preacher pourtrayed the character of various classes of mankind,—the rich, the poor, the learned, the ignorant, the old, the young, the open sinner, and the self-righteous formalist,— exposing the various subterfuges under which the deceitfulness of the human heart shrouds itself, and concluding, in regard to each, " Except ye repent, ye shall all likewise perish."

In speaking of Banff and the neighbourhood, Mr. James Haldane observes, in the Journal:—

" Religion appears at all those places to be at a low ebb. A minister of this town published a Catechism, in which he openly avowed Socinian principles, and his opinions, we understood, had made considerable progress among the people. The Catholics here, as in some other parts of the north, are said to be upon the increase, partly owing to the zeal of their clergy, and the want of zeal in others. There is also here an Episcopal meeting.

" *July* 31.—Met at Cullen, and after preaching and distributing tracts, as usual, went on to Fochabers (a village in the neighbourhood of Gordon Castle). This place is notorious for its laxity of morals and indifference to religion. Of these we saw evident tokens in the carelessness and indifference of those to whom we preached.

"*August* 1.—Arrived at Elgin. The magistrates and ministers here prohibited the bellman from giving intimation of sermon; but though public notice was prevented, some friends of the truth were abundantly active, and at the appointed hour we had a congregation of about 600 persons, to whom we preached in the street from the steps of the church. Preached again in the morning. We found that the Socinian Catechism formerly mentioned had been introduced into the grammar school of Elgin. At a public examination, however, upon one of the ministers of the Presbytery, who *preaches the Gospel*, remonstrating against this innovation (in which he was opposed by the ministers of the town who were present), the Provost ordered this new Catechism to be discontinued, and the shorter one of the Westminster Assembly to be restored."

From Elgin they proceeded to Forres, and thence to Nairn, where they "met with a most affectionate reception from some friends of the Gospel, of the Anti-burgher congregation," amongst whom " the interests of the kingdom of Christ seemed to flourish," and where there were monthly prayer-meetings and Sabbath-evening schools. At Fort-George, the Governor declined permission to preach to the soldiers, on the ground that "he never heard of sermon in any fort on a week-day." Mr. Rate, therefore, remained behind, and his two friends, having preached at Campbelton on the way, arrived at Inverness on the 5th of August. Next day being a sacrament Lord's-day, both of them preached twice, at different hours, on a hill adjoining the town, and on the Monday they again addressed " very great multitudes," morning and evening. They also held a meeting to form a Society for establishing Sabbath Schools. Three were shortly after erected, and instantly met with great success.

On the 7th August, after once more preaching in the open air to a congregation of 500 anxious listeners, who stood all the time, although it rained, Mr. J. A. Haldane and Mr. Aikman left Inverness, with the design of visiting the Orkney Islands.

This plan was arranged under the following circumstances, thus detailed in the Journal:—

" Having heard whilst at Elgin that a fair was soon to be held at Kirkwall, at which there were usually great numbers of people from the different Isles of Orkney; and having also heard of the deplorable state of many of those Islands, from the want of religious instruction, we resolved that two of us should embrace the opportunity of going thither with the merchants from Elgin, and then return through Caithness, Sutherland, and Ross-shire, to Inverness, in which place and neighbourhood we thought it most advisable for one to stay and labour till the other two should return."

At Nairn they again preached to a numerous congregation, and were refreshed by the intelligence received from their Christian friends at that place, as to " tokens of the Divine presence" already manifested in connexion with this missionary tour. Having again preached at Nairn, Auldearn, and Forres, they arrived at Elgin, and again, morning and evening, addressed congregations varying from 700 to 1000 persons.

---

FIRST VISIT TO THE ORKNEY ISLANDS.

The visit to the Orkney Islands, in 1797, brought to the inhabitants a large outpouring of spiritual blessings. In the life of James Haldane, it demands peculiar notice.

In these days, when railroads, steam, and electricity have brought us into contact with almost every corner of the world, the Orkneys are still to a considerable extent separated from the rest of Britain. But fifty or sixty years ago, a tour to the northern islands of Scotland was an undertaking, so much more formidable than one to the Hebrides, that it was seldom attempted. The Pentland Frith, which connects the German Ocean with the Atlantic, from John o' Groat's House to Cape Wrath, was in itself a formidable barrier. It is the roughest and most dangerous of the Scottish seas, where the waves roll onwards, presenting a front, not sloping as in the ocean, but perpendicular as a wall, and where foaming whirlpools, powerful eddies, and startling waterspouts, produced by strong currents rushing in opposite directions, or by sunken rocks, have given occasion to descriptions in which poets and artists have vied with each other in painting the sublime and terrible. The impetuous tides of the Pentland run at a velocity varying from three to nine miles an hour, and the currents are often most dangerous in fogs or calms. These tides are, however, equalled by those in the intersecting friths or sounds,

> ————Where restless seas
> Howl round the storm-swept Orcades,—
> Where erst St. Clair bore princely sway
> O'er isle and islet, strait and bay;
> Still nods their palace to its fall,
> Thy pride and sorrow, fair Kirkwall!

The commencement of this missionary voyage is thus chronicled in James Haldane's Journal:—

" *August* 11.—Left Elgin and came to Brough-head, where a good many of our friends from Elgin and the people of the village assembled, to whom we preached. We then embarked for Kirkwall. Several of our brethren accompanied us to the boat, and bade us farewell, most affectionately commending us to the grace and care of the Lord Jesus. Sailed with a fair wind. It fell calm in the afternoon, and the wind seemed likely to become foul, but by the kindness of Providence a fair and brisk gale sprung up, which brought us safely into Scalpa Bay, about a mile from Kirkwall, by eight o'clock next morning. The merchants who freighted the boat, and the sailors in general, behaved to us with much kindness and respect. Preached in the boat on Friday evening. They listened with much attention, and frequently attended afterwards, during our stay at Kirkwall.

" *August* 12.—Arrived at Kirkwall. Were providentially directed to a friend of the truth (Baillie Jamieson), who received us with much kindness. Intimated sermon by the bell at half-past six in the evening, in the Palace Close, where we (Mr. Aikman) preached to a congregation of about eight hundred persons. This is a square, formed by a large and ancient edifice on the south, supposed to have been the palace of some of the Norwegian kings, and on the north by another, termed the Bishop's Palace. On the east is the church of St. Magnus, and on the west it is bounded by a wall. It is capable, probably, of containing ten or twelve thousand persons. Having heard that there had been only two or three sermons preached in the Island of Shapinshay (a few miles distant from Kirkwall), from the time of the last General Assembly, when their minister had left them, we resolved that one of us should spend the

Lord's-day in that island, while the other remained in Kirkwall. The minister of Shapinshay was at this time detained in Edinburgh, as an evidence in a trial; but it is well known to be the practice of ministers from that country, to take a considerable vacation at the time of the General Assembly.

" Before proceeding further in the account of our labours, we shall here offer a few remarks on the former and present religious state of Orkney. The islands of Orkney, according to our information, which is rendered strongly credible by what we actually witnessed, have been, for a period beyond the memory of any man living (except in one or two solitary instances), as much in need of the true Gospel of Jesus Christ, so far as respects the preaching of it, as any of the islands of the Pacific Ocean. Many of the parishes comprehend two or three different islands. In each of these the minister should preach occasionally; but owing to the want of churches, or rather to the churches being in want of repair, as well as to the occasional trouble and difficulty of crossing the Friths which intersect these islands, to say nothing of the want of zeal, many of the people see their pastor but seldom in the course of the year. It is a fact, that in some cases where there are two islands in a parish, or two parishes annexed in one island, and a church in repair only in one of them, the minister preaches in it on one Sabbath, but the next, when it falls to the turn of the other island or parish, he neither preaches there, nor in his other church, though it may adjoin his manse.

" It can occasion no surprise to those who know the Gospel and are acquainted with that enmity and opposition which the human mind naturally bears to its humiliating doctrines, to learn that the sermons of such pastors do not contain glad tidings to perishing sinners. At the same time, one would think that the most inconsiderate could scarcely fail to be struck with the strange inconsistency of teaching others that they will be saved by a diligent discharge of the duties of their station, while they themselves so openly neglect their own. The manners and conduct of the people, as in every other place, are corrupted in a due proportion to their ignorance of the Gospel, and to no part, in Orkney, as we learn, did this remark more justly apply, than it did about five or six years ago to Kirkwall, where, excepting two or three individuals, the great body of the people were utter strangers to the doctrine of justification by faith in the death and resurrection of Christ without works. It pleased God, however, in the riches of his grace, to look down with tender compassion upon the deplorable situation of this place, and to send them help out of his holy heaven. A native of Orkney, who had been apprentice to a pious tradesman in Kirkwall, went to Newcastle, where he attended with profit the ministry of Mr. Graham, the Anti-burgher. He returned to Kirkwall, and having experienced the benefit of religious society in the south, upon finding another person of views similar to his own, he proposed a weekly meeting for prayer and religious fellowship. This was immediately formed. One and another, whose minds it pleased God, by means of conversation or reading books, which were put into their hands, to bring under impressions of the infinite worth of their immortal souls, were added to their little meeting. Their numbers continued, from time to time, to increase. These persons now began seriously to feel their state of bondage, with regard to religious privileges. They found it was a yoke which they were not able to bear, and therefore determined, looking up to God for his countenance, to open a subscription for erecting a place of worship, where they might enjoy the blessing of the preaching of the Gospel. Their means were indeed but very slender, and appeared little likely to accomplish the end, especially in the view of that opposition, with which they knew they must contend. But he, whose glory it is to choose the weak things of this world to confound the mighty, appeared most eminently in their behalf, and they were enabled both to begin and to finish a house for the worship of God. They then applied to the Antiburgher Synod for a minister to preach to them. A minister was accordingly sent, and others successively since that time, all of whose labours appear to have been remarkably blessed. Many who were living altogether careless of Divine things, since the Gospel was preached in the new church, as it is called, have been brought under serious concern, and give good evidence, by their conduct, that they are passed from death unto life, and some who were avowed enemies have become the friends of the cause. The Lord appears evidently to have been preparing a people in this place for himself; and it is remarked, that since the time that this uncommon concern has been excited, a very considerable external reformation has taken place, even amongst those who do not appear to be under the influence of the truth. That the Lord's arm hath been made bare in behalf of these destitute isles in no common way, will appear from the fact, that two hundred persons were admitted to the Lord's Supper, upon the first celebration of that ordinance in the new church, in July last, after a strict and individual examination, in which the ministers enjoyed, as we are informed, much satisfaction. Several also were kept back, of whom good hopes are entertained. When the circumstance just stated is contrasted with the situation of Kirkwall but four or five years since, the friends of Christ may well exclaim with joy and gratitude, ' What hath God wrought!' ' The wilderness hath truly rejoiced; it hath blossomed as the rose. The Lord's hand is not yet shortened that it cannot save, neither is his ear heavy that it cannot hear.' "

On the next Lord's-day Mr. Aikman preached twice, to congregations of twelve hundred and three thousand persons, whilst Mr. J. A. Haldane, who was always the first to undertake the

more laborious duties, for which his physical health and energy
also better fitted him, crossed over to Shapinshay, in a boat
sent for the purpose by the people, and preached twice by the
sea-side, to congregations comprising the greatest part of the
population of the island. But this visit was rendered memorable by the conversion of an old man, of ninety-two, who had
been born in the reign of Queen Anne, and was now confined to
bed. Mr. J. A. Haldane visited him after sermon, and found
him hardly able to speak, although quite sensible. In the
Journal he says, " Asked him what was to become of him after
death ? He replied, he was very ignorant, could not read, but
had sometimes prayed to God. On being asked, whether he
knew anything of Christ, he acknowledged his entire ignorance." The old man stated, that he remembered how, when a
lad, herding cattle, under a sense of darkness as to his future
state, he once prayed to God that some teacher might be sent to
enlighten his ignorance. This prayer seems to have entered
into the ears of the Lord of Sabaoth, and, after being treasured
up for nearly eighty years, was answered almost at the last
hour of parting life. James Haldane was to the old man
as the messenger of peace, and preached to him the Gospel,
declaring that now the Lord was waiting to be gracious, and
that if he believed what the Word of God testified of his guilt
and misery, and of the person and work of Christ as that of an
Almighty Saviour, he should be saved. He " seemed much
affected, and grasped the speaker eagerly by the hand. He
cried to God for the pardon of his sins ; and being informed
that his prayers could only be heard through Jesus Christ,
who came to save the very chief of sinners, he called upon the
Saviour for mercy, and repeatedly exclaimed, *I believe, I believe.*
This recalled strongly to our mind the case of the blind man,
who, as soon as he knew the Son of God, worshipped him."

The same evening Mr. J. A. Haldane returned to Kirkwall,
but did not fail, as we shall presently see, once more to visit
Shapinshay, and the dying old man. It was a case to which he
often referred in after-life, and it was obviously near to his heart

at the time, as appears from his correspondence, and particularly from the following letter to Mr. Campbell :—

" *Kirkwall, August* 14*th*, 1797.

" MY DEAR FRIEND,—You did not expect to hear from me from this place when I left you, but the Lord does all things well. I have written to Mrs. Haldane to-day. You will hear from her some account of us since we came here. If, as there is reason to hope, our coming has been useful to the old man, there was a needs be for our coming. We intend to stay till Monday. There is a great fair here, which begins to-morrow. We intend to preach twice a-day, and visit some of the neighbouring islands. We go to-morrow to Stromness, which is the next largest town on this island, to preach, and visit Mr. and Mrs. Hamilton, with whom we intend to stay all night. I was much obliged to you for your letter. It increases my respect for Mr. Newton, that he should find so little difficulty in resolving the knotty point (as to lay preaching). If the Lord spares me to return, I shall write to him. We have left Rate at Inverness. I hope he may be the means of doing good there. The Lord has, I am persuaded, much people in that place. We received a supply of pamphlets there, which we needed, as we were quite run out. You were afraid we had too many, but this is not the case. I must request you to desire Mr. Ritchie to throw off two thousand more of my ' Address' immediately, and to forward one thousand of them to me at Aberdeen, first ship, together with all the other pamphlets he has belonging to me."

The letter here breaks off, and Mr. Aikman takes up his pen, and proceeds—

" Our dear friend having written thus far, was obliged to begin to prepare for preaching. He therefore handed me over the paper, that I might tell you a little of the goodness of the Lord, in his late dispensations towards us in this place, and in bringing us to it. Truly this has been the work of God, and not of man. We were led to think of coming here by hearing that a multitude of ' idle vagrants,' or busy vagrants rather, assembled here at these times, and that an easy opportunity was afforded us by the boats from Elgin. . . . Yesterday being Lord's-day, Mr. Haldane went to a neighbouring and desolate island, and preached two long sermons, and afterwards visited an old man of ninety-two, who knew nothing of Jesus, but appeared wonderfully affected. The Lord grant that the issue may be to the praise of his grace. I heard a shocking sermon in the Established Church in the forenoon, after preaching to about one thousand five hundred people, and was strengthened of God to bear an open and explicit testimony against it, from Pilate's question, John xviii. 38, before three thousand persons, I suppose. I told

them that I accounted it an unspeakable happiness to have stood upon
that place, and to have declared that there was no other name given under
heaven, by which men could be saved, but the name of Christ.

" We are just going to preach ; a great multitude is assembled. Our
dear friend, Mr. H., officiates. Remember us on Friday (at Mr. Black's
prayer-meeting).

" Ever yours affectionately,

" JOHN AIKMAN."

Mr. James Haldane adds a postscript—

" Thus far the *Company* letter. I preached to a large congregation,
who were much affected. Truly the concern among people here is
wonderful. Cease not to pray for us, and praise the Lord for his
goodness.

" Yours truly,

" J. A. H."

On the 15th August, they proceeded to Stromness, where
the minister, Mr. Hamilton, and his wife, the sister of Mr.
Zachary Macaulay, received them courteously. After preaching
they returned to Kirkwall, where, the fair having begun, multitudes both from the islands and mainland were assembled.
There, whilst the fair continued, their sermons from day to day
were an object of attraction, and were frequented by congregations amounting to 3,000 and 4,000, and, on the Lord's-day,
even to upwards of 6,000 persons.

" We have here," says Mr. J. A. Haldane, " much reason to remark the
goodness of God in disposing the people, the whole time the fair lasted,
to continue with regularity in their attendance. The fair was, in a
measure, *emptied* every evening. May He, whose blessing alone giveth
the increase, be pleased graciously to water the seed which hath been
sown with the dew of heaven, causing it to take root downward, and to
bring forth fruit upward, to the praise of the glory of his own rich and
sovereign grace !"

But amidst the excitement incident to addressing thousands
who hung upon the lips of the preacher, many of whom drank in
the words of eternal life, the poor, solitary, dying nonogenarian
at Shapinshay was not forgotten. Once more he visited him,
but found him unable to speak, although still sensible and
capable of expressing intense pleasure in once more seeing his
instructor. He was supported in his bed whilst Mr. J. A.

Haldane spoke, and showed that he understood what was said, by clasping his withered hands, and raising them to heaven as if in the attitude of thanksgiving.  Upon asking him whether he wished that prayer should be made, he evinced his desire, as far as possible, by attempting to speak.  " His wife said that he had wept much after our leaving him on the former day.  She had occasionally read to him parts of the Scriptures." He died on the next Lord's-day, and the joy with which he received the Gospel, the earnest delight with which he welcomed the second visit of his spiritual teacher, and the devout peace in which he departed, left no room to doubt that he slept in Jesus.

Rendal and Evie, forming one parish, were next visited.  It was found that in the latter island there had been no sermon for eight or nine years, and that at Rendal there was no Church service except on alternate Sabbaths.  Eggleshay and Rousay were in a situation as to spiritual things, nearly as destitute, although the proprietor, when at home, was accustomed to read a sermon to the people in church.  Kirkwall continued to be the head-quarters of the preachers until the 23d, when they separated, James Haldane taking the cluster of islands to the right, and Mr. Aikman the cluster of islands to the left.  The former embarking for Edie, was obliged, by the force of the tide, to land at Shapinshay, where, during the two hours he was detained, he went into a house and expounded the Scriptures and prayed.  After preaching at Edie, and visiting some sick persons, he crossed the Frith to Sanday, where he had some difficulty in procuring any lodging, but preached next day morning and evening to 750 persons, at two opposite sides of the island.  At North Ronaldshay he found that there was no school, and that there had only been a sermon five times since the year before.  He sent to the proprietor a proposal to erect one at his own expense, provided a site and grass for a cow should be supplied.  This disinterested proposal was, however, ultimately declined.  At Stronsay, whose mineral waters made it a place of resort in ancient times for the Danish chiefs, he met with a man who appeared to be a true Christian.  "Thus," he observes, "one and another of the sheep of Christ are occasionally found in places where they are least expected." After preaching to 800 people, or about three-fourths of the whole population, he took a boat for Shapinshay, and having walked across that island and taken another boat, he arrived before midnight on Saturday at Kirkwall. Next day, being Sunday, he preached in the Palace-close to 2,500 people, and on the Monday again preached at Kirkwall, and at Deerness and Tankerness, to large congregations. These services were exclusive of family prayer, with an exposition of Scripture, which was daily attended by as many as their room could hold whilst residing at Kirkwall.

After a stay of sixteen days they left Kirkwall on the 29th August, and having preached on that day and the following at different islands, they crossed the Pentland Frith in about two hours, being favoured with moderate weather. They had preached no less than fifty-five times in ten days, so that each must have preached nearly three times every day; but as the chief labour fell upon Mr. J. A. Haldane, the average of his sermons exceeded that number. The Journal adds—

"It becomes us here to remark the goodness of God to us, both in crossing the different Friths, and during the whole of our stay in Kirkwall, having never once been incommoded, while preaching, with rain, although sometimes the clouds had a lowering aspect. Walked two miles from the place of landing to Hoonah, to the great inconvenience of one of us (Mr. Aikman), who bruised his leg in coming from Eggleshay, a circumstance which, though apparently trivial at first, yet afterwards materially altered the plan of our journey, detaining us six weeks in the county of Caithness, instead of a fortnight, as we had at first intended."

---

JAMES HALDANE'S LABOURS IN CAITHNESS, AND THE BLESSING WHICH FOLLOWED THEM.

The number of inhabited islands in Orkney is now twenty-nine. The missionary tourists had preached in nearly all of them excepting Walls and Flota, which James Haldane took occasion to visit during his detention at Thurso. His detention, which arose from Mr. Aikman's accident, was providentially overruled for good, and probably there was no period of his life more distinguished by unmistakable marks of the Lord's favour than the six weeks during which he laboured in Caithness. In consequence of his excellent companion's confinement to the house, he was, in the public ministrations in Caithness, the sole preacher; and if any one wishes to estimate the force of his zeal, and the ardour of his desire to speak for Christ, let his labours in Caithness at this time be regarded. The state of religion in that county was then most deplorable. Thurso, that is, Thor's town, containing between 2,000 and 3,000 inhabitants, had not been catechised for forty years, a circumstance which then implied great neglect, and " in all the shire of Caithness, consisting of ten parishes," there was scarcely an instance of the Gospel being faithfully preached. At Thurso, a pious Anti-burgher minister laboured with some good results, and there were a few of those belonging to the Established Church who attended the Secession place of worship, without themselves joining its communion. But the good that was done by these Anti-burghers was on a very limited scale, and no effort was made to extend the Gospel beyond the bounds of their own chapels or the families of those by whom they were attended.

" It is," says the Journal, " a mournful fact, that it was the universal practice to commute for a sum of money the public profession of repent-ance enjoined by the Church of Scotland on those guilty of adultery or other open transgressions. When such persons have paid the fine they are admitted to the communion-table without scruple. When such practices as these take place to any extent, no wonder if the land mourn, and that the Lord threaten to visit us with his sore judgments. ' Shall I not visit for these things? saith the Lord.' Nor can it at all surprise those who know the Gospel to learn, that while the name and ordinances of God are thus profaned, men should in general be living without God and without Christ, and, consequently, without any well-grounded hope in the world. It gives us much pleasure, however, to remark, that the Lord hath not wholly left himself without a witness, even in those places which are most desolate. It is said that in this shire, about fifty or sixty years ago, the whole of the ministers were faithful preachers of Christ. Their testimony has been transmitted, and the instructions and example of humble individuals have been blessed of God for keeping alive a spirit of real religion in some of the interior parts of the country. It is remarked that those persons are, in general, such as live at the greatest distance from the churches, and who, in consequence, meet together by themselves for the purposes of religious conference and worship on the Lord's-day."

Such was the state of Caithness at the time when James Haldane preached in its chief town, on Thursday, the 31st August, 1797, his first sermon in the yard of the Anti-burgher Meeting-house to not more than 300 persons, " who seemed rather unconcerned." Thurso was crowded with strangers who had come up to the fair. On the following Monday he preached twice in a large yard, in the open air, to congregations "which seemed more attentive." Next day the congregation had increased to 800 persons in the morning, and about 1,500 in the evening. On the Lord's-day morning attention had become so much aroused, that before the usual church hours, he preached at half-past nine o'clock to 1,700 people, and although it began to rain, " no person moved." He then went to church, where a melancholy sermon was delivered, in which the minister cautioned the people against trusting for acceptance with God to the blood of Christ. " His peace-speaking blood," says the Journal, " was only for the holy and the good! " But against this false doctrine James Haldane testified in the evening to no less than 3,000 persons, assembled from places far and near, to whom he proclaimed the true Gospel of the grace of God. During the following week-days he preached morning and evening each day at different places in the county. The Journal contains the following entry on the next Lord's-day :—

" *Lord's-day, September* 10*th.*—Preached at ten o'clock to from 2,000 to 3,000 people, many of whom had come from the country. Preached again at two o'clock, to upwards of 3,000 persons, from the Second Epistle of John, verses 10 and 11."

Another letter to Mr. Campbell, dated 16th September, will give a short summary of his proceedings up to this date.

" *Thurso, Sept.* 16*th*, 1797.

" MY DEAR FRIEND,—This is Saturday night, and I am just returned from the Island of Walls, one of the Orkney Islands. It was the only one of any size we had not visited, and, being the nearest to this place, I thought it a duty to visit it, as we have been so long detained here by our dear brother's accident. After preaching, I left this place on Wednesday morning, preached at Walls and the Island of Flota on Thursday, returned at night to Walls, where I preached yesterday, and should have been here last night had not the wind been too strong. I desire to be thankful I am now arrived safe and may again set up my Ebenezer. I had this journey in contemplation when I wrote to Mrs. Haldane on Monday, but as I was not determined, and thought it might make her uneasy to hear of my crossing the Pentland Frith again, I said nothing about it. Indeed, I did not fully determine to go till it was time on Wednesday to set off. We have now preached in fifteen of the Orkney Islands, and in all of them the people have seemed affected under the preaching of the Gospel. I this evening received a letter from my wife without a date, but it seems, by the post-mark, to be about the 10th of August. It is directed to Inverness, and was written before our journey to Orkney was known in Edinburgh. Our dear brother's, Mr. Aikman's, leg, is not yet quite well, and, as we do not intend to run any risk of hurting it by early travelling, I cannot fix the day on which we are to leave this. There is much need of the Gospel here. I have been strengthened to preach twice a day here since we came, except two or three days, during which I have been in the country parishes. When we came here we could find no room in the inn, but the Lord directed us to a private house; both our host and hostess (Mr. and Mrs. George Millar) are most attentive. May the Lord grant our visit may be useful to them for one thing they lack. Remember me kindly to Mr. Newton when you write to him. Remember us affectionately to our dear friends with you. I am sure you do not cease to pray for us. I have, I am persuaded, felt the benefit of your prayers, especially on Friday evening. Give our love to Mr. and Mrs. Black and Mr. Balfour.

" I am, my dear friend,

" Yours, ever affectionately,

" J. A. H."

Mr. George Millar, of Thurso, is again noticed in the Journal, with this prayer attached,—" May the Lord recompense their kindness by bestowing on them blessings which perish not with the using." This prayer on behalf of their kind hosts was answered. They too were brought to Christ, and found that, in entertaining strangers, they had " entertained angels unawares."

On the 17th September, being the Lord's-day, he preached in the morning to about 1,500 people, and afterwards heard the parish minister preach from Titus iii. 8. He seemed much afraid of people abusing the doctrines of grace, and therefore told them that, though they were to be justified freely by grace, yet that afterwards they must be justified partly by faith and partly by works. He then intimated that there would be no sermon in the afternoon during the remainder of the season. It was the regular practice through this part of the country, as it was then, indeed, in other places farther south, to have only one discourse, of half an hour's length, during nearly nine months of the year.

On the evening of the same Lord's-day Mr. James Haldane preached to about 3,000 persons, from Eph. ii. 8—10 :—" For by grace are ye saved through faith ; and that not of yourselves : it is the gift of God. Not of works, lest any man should boast," &c. " Took particular notice of the sermon that had been preached." He then told them, that he had found it to be his duty, however unpleasant, to bear testimony against the doctrine which he had heard from their minister; but that, though he might be detained another Sabbath in Thurso, he would not again attend their church.

On the Lord's-day, September 24th, the weather being uncommonly fine, he preached in the yard to about 3,000 people in the morning. Mr. Aikman was still confined, but, as it appeared likely that he would be able to travel in the course of a few days, it was determined that his friend, on whom all the public labour had devolved, should spend the remainder of the time they might remain in Caithness in visiting the town of Wick and its neighbourhood. In the view, therefore, of leaving Thurso on the next day, Mr. James Haldane preached in the evening a farewell sermon to a congregation of 4,000 persons, of whom there were individuals from every parish in Caithness. It was a solemn occasion, and one calculated to stir the heart of the preacher. His text was from Acts xx. 32,—" And now, brethren, I commend you to God, and to the word of his grace, which is able to build you up, and to give you an inheritance among all them that are sanctified."

" The parish minister was present, and as it was generally understood that he had in view the doctrines we preached, when cautioning the people against their being taught to separate faith from works, occasion was taken briefly to recapitulate the apostle's doctrine, and plainly to show the absolute necessity of completely separating faith from works *in the important article of a sinner's justification before God*. At the same time the speaker appealed to those who had heard him, whether he had not uniformly insisted upon the absolute necessity of works, on the other hand, as the never-failing fruit and evidence of faith, without which the faith which any man *might say* he had would never save him. Took occasion also to refer particularly to the lives and conversations of many of those who were such strenuous advocates for the doctrine of works, and asked whether the total and open neglect, both of personal and family religion, afforded them any ground so greatly to glory in their pretended good works? Finally told them, that he was pure from their blood (referring to the discourse connected with his text), which could not have been had he not faithfully warned them against the false doctrines which he had heard preached to them."

The sermon thus referred to was one of great power and solemnity, which was long remembered in Caithness.

Having preached on his way to Wick, he arrived there on the 25th, and was most hospitably entertained by another Mr. A. Millar, the chief inhabitant, to whom he was a messenger of grace, under circumstances of deep interest. He preached during the week to large congregations, and on the market-day twice to 1,000 persons, morning and evening.

"*Lord's-day, October* 1st.—Preached in the morning to about 2,500 people. Heard the minister, in the forenoon, preach from Matt. xxii. 5, —'And they made light of it.' He represented that men, in becoming Christians, first began to work out their own salvation, and that then God wrought in them, &c. He spoke much of the criminality of such as found fault with ministers, 'who were,' he said, 'the successors of the apostles,—the ambassadors appointed to carry on the treaty of peace between God and man.' In the afternoon preached to about 4,000 people, and took notice of what appeared contrary to the Gospel in the minister's sermon, himself being present."

During the week days he continued as usual to preach at different places, sometimes once, and sometimes twice a day, in the country parishes, and again on the Lord's-day at Wick, to congregations which crowded together from all quarters, amounting in the morning to more than 2,000, and in the evening to upwards of 4,000 people. On the 5th October there is an entry where he notices having preached at Freswick, in the parish of Canisbay, where there was a small Society of Baptists, who had been formed into a Church by means of a pious Baronet, a Sir William Sinclair, who had preached amongst them for several years.

Mr. Aikman being now partially recovered, was enabled to join Mr. Haldane, although still rather feeble and worn out by his labours.

The results of this tour in Caithness will be again more particularly noticed, but perhaps it cannot at present be more fitly concluded than by the insertion of the following letter. It is written by the wife of a pious minister at Elgin, a venerable lady, who was one of those to whom Mr. J. A. Haldane was then the messenger of peace. She was the daughter of that Mr. A. Millar, of Staxigo, near Wick, whose hospitality is so gratefully acknowledged. Mrs. M'Neil's letter was written shortly after Mr. Haldane's death, and is dated 20th March, 1851. It is addressed to the excellent surviving sister of Mr. Aikman, whose own recollections have furnished some valuable incidents for this and the preceding chapter :—

" I now come to that part of your letter wherein you mention my dear and much loved and respected friend, Mr. James Haldane,—a name *very dear* to me. I have often thought that there was something of idolatry in my affection for that *good* man. If I have ever felt or known anything of the truth, he was the blessed instrument; and not to myself only, but he was the instrument used by God for the conversion of my dear brother and sister, in his first visit to Caithness. Both the latter died of typhus fever, in the hope of a glorious immortality, a few months after his visit to Caithness. I had a married sister, who died of fever about two years previous to your dear brother (Mr. Aikman's) and dear Mr. Haldane's visit to Caithness. At the time of her being seized with illness, I was young, thoughtless, and lively.

"The fever being deemed infectious, the doctor persuaded my parents not to allow either of my sisters or myself to see her. However, early in the morning on which she died, my eldest sister and myself were sent for to see her before her death. She had early in life been made a partaker of Divine grace, and was a most affectionate sister. We lived in the country. She lived in the town of Wick. Her husband brought us into the room where she lay; she was then in the agonies of death. I had never seen one in that state before, and being much attached to her, it made a very deep impression upon my mind, and I became much concerned about my soul. My health gave way, and I was wasted to a shadow. I concealed from every person the state of my mind, and always sought retirement, but did not know where to flee for deliverance from the guilt of sin. I had relations who lived within a few miles of Thurso. They wished me very much to visit them, in the hope the change might be useful to me, and my parents and their friends were equally anxious for this. But it was health to my soul which I needed and longed for. However, as they wished it, I went. Some days after I went there, my aunt had gone into Thurso, and when she returned she said the town seemed in an uproar, or something to that effect, 'about a remarkable preacher who had come there, and that he seemed very zealous, and was preaching in the open air.' I immediately set off, accompanied by one of my cousins. It was on a Saturday evening. I went with my cousin to the place. He was standing on the top of an outer stair, dressed in a grey coat, with tied hair, and powdered. But I think I shall never forget the fervour and divine unction with which he proclaimed the Gospel of mercy. It rained very heavily, and although very wet and miry where the congregation stood, no one, I think, moved to go away until sermon was over. I felt very unwell, but was rivetted to the place, and sorry I was when he finished his subject.

"On Sabbath, I went in the forenoon to the parish church. The minister's text was 4th and 5th verses of the sixth chapter of Galatians. In the evening Mr. Haldane preached in a yard, where it was thought there were 4,000 people assembled. He took occasion to show the fallacy of the doctrine preached in the forenoon. I was standing beside a number of the *genteel* people, but not religious people. Some of the gentlemen called out, 'Stone him!' others, 'Stop him!' However, no person obeyed their commands, and Mr. Haldane went on with his subject. At last these gentry all left the place, and I was very glad to be rid of them. This minister, of whose erroneous teaching Mr. Haldane had said so much, was a particular friend of my dear father. My mind was in distress lest my father should take any dislike to Mr. Haldane; and that if Mr. Haldane should go to Wick, I might not have the liberty to hear him. I next day wrote to my sister, giving an account of the whole matter, and said all I could in Mr. Haldane's favour. Your dear brother (Mr. Aikman) had hurt his leg in coming out of a boat. This confined him to his lodgings, in Mr. George Millar's house, for several weeks, so that I did not see him in Thurso. Owing to your brother being confined so long, they determined that Mr. Haldane should come to Wick until Mr. Aikman should get better. It seems they had previously no intention of stopping at Wick, but the Lord had purposes of mercy for some there. When Mr. James Haldane arrived, an express was sent to my father to let him know. When I heard this information given, my heart trembled between fear and joy. I was afraid my father would not allow my sisters and myself to go to hear him, because he had said so much about his favourite minister; and I was just saying to my eldest sister that I feared we would not be allowed, when my father came into my room, and said, ' Make yourselves ready to go and hear Mr. Haldane, and your mother and myself will also go.' I could not describe my joy. We went, and the people were assembling. It was in a large yard. Mr. Haldane, after singing and prayer, gave out the 7th verse of the first chapter of Haggai,—' Thus saith the Lord of hosts, Consider your ways.' My father heard with deep attention. As for myself, I was completely rivetted; my eyes could see nothing but Mr. Haldane, and my ears hear no sound but his voice. Well, that was the *text* and *sermon* which the Lord blessed for the conversion of my dear father. After sermon, my father said to my sister and me, ' Go in to Mr. Craig's, and give your mother's compliments and my own, and ask Mr. Haldane if he will kindly come out to Staxigo with you.' (Mr. Craig was my brother-in-law.) My joy was great, and I thought, surely the Lord has heard my prayers. Mr. Haldane very kindly consented at once, and he came, and for two weeks, if not more, he remained in my father's house,—indeed, as long as he was in the place, except when he went into the town to preach, which he did every day, and we always walked in and out again with him. My eldest sister then alive, and my youngest brother, were both at that time also brought to Christ, so that there were four of us who I trust were all brought out of darkness into God's marvellous light. Could I but love that worthy man ? He threw his whole soul into his subject, and commended the truth to every one's conscience, as in the sight of God. Your brother only came to Wick the day before they left the country, so that I only saw and heard him once at that time. Both of them, with Mr. Innes, came round again in 1799 ; but whenever they came, my father's house was *head quarters* with the whole of them.

" I recollect the last sermon Mr. Haldane preached in our chapel in Wick (some years afterwards, in 1805, on his fourth tour to Caithness) was on these words,—' Finally, brethren, farewell.' I thought, shall this be the last sermon he shall preach here ? and I felt my spirits sink within me.

" This was indeed *the* last. The last night he was in our house he read the 4th of Philippians, and made some remarks. He wrote me several letters, one of which I now inclose, and a very short one, mentioning that he had sent me some books for my Sabbath-schools.

" I may add that I believe there was not a district in Scotland where their labours were so much blessed as in Caithness. In Orkney, too, the Lord made them very useful. But the good done by those godly men was remarkable. Under God, they were the means of bringing the Gospel to Wick and Thurso.

" When Mr. Haldane came first to Wick in the year '97, it was in the harvest time, in the month of October. One gentleman, at that time a very careless man, gave liberty to the shearers to leave the field and go to hear Mr. Haldane, which they did, and reaped the field by moonlight. This I believe was only once. But from that time he paid more attention to religion, and, I believe, under Mr. Cleghorn's ministry, was savingly converted to the truth. Often did my dear brother Benjamin say to me upon his death-bed, that he blessed God he had ever known and heard dear Mr. Haldane. He died in February, '98, and my sister about three weeks after. My sister was twenty-four years of age, and my dear brother eighteen years. They were lovely and pleasant in their lives, and in death were not long divided. Both were beautiful and handsome, and both, if there were any favourites, were the favourites with my father, and were loved by all who knew them. I, too, was lying ill, and despaired of at the time. You may believe what a trial this was to our parents, but God wonderfully supported them.

" The deep distress of mind I was in when I first heard Mr. Haldane I could not describe; and when the Gospel was revealed to me in all its glory, my joy was great, so much so that I was sometimes so overcome with it, I thought I could contain no more. Often do I wish I now felt the same brokenness of heart, and the same lively hope which I had in the days of my youth. Often, when these good men were in Caithness, many would walk twenty miles to hear them, and return home in the evening.

" Worthy Dr. Innes has lived to see all those who then were fellow-helpers with him consigned to the house appointed for all living, while their emancipated spirits are now rejoicing before the throne of God. I trust he may be spared a long while yet, to labour for the good of souls. May he yet have many given him for his joy and crown! Mr. Campbell was only *once* in Caithness. He, too, was an excellent minister. Blessed are the dead who die in the Lord. May it be our happiness, my dear friend, to meet those holy men of God at His right hand, when we go hence and are no more!

" My letter is not fit for any eye but that of a friend; but though I write confusedly, perhaps Mr. Haldane may find some interesting things in it, to show how his worthy father was esteemed, and the good he was the means of doing in Caithness.

" All my blunders I hope he will kindly overlook. At my advanced age, on the borders of seventy-five, I cannot expect to be very free from blunders in my way of stating what I have, but I can vouch for all as facts which I have written."

Mr. James Haldane left Wick on the 11th of October, 1797, thus concluding his labours in Caithness, on a day memorable as that on which the great naval victory was gained off Camperdown. On that day he had preached twice, probably little thinking of the very different scenes, amidst which his gallant relative was engaged; although private memoranda, never intended for any other eye but his own, show how much that relative was habitually in his heart, and in his prayers before the throne of grace. He did not know of the victory for some time, although the booming of the guns was actually heard on that coast. On arriving at one of the towns, the public rejoicing announced the event. The place was in a great bustle, and the itinerants were shown into an inferior room. Having addressed a letter to his uncle, he desired the waiter to convey it to the post-office. The direction struck the man, and the letter was carried to the landlord, who, in a few minutes, entered, and apologizing for the mistake, begged the gentlemen to follow him to another room, as he was resolved that any friend of the Admiral's should have the best accommodation his house could supply.

It may now be hardly worth while to notice that amidst the many jibes and sneers, to which, as a matter of course, both the brothers were subjected, and which they bore with much good-humour, there was one relating to Lord Duncan's victory. It was reported that, instead of congratulating their uncle, they had both written to him a kind of expostulatory sermon on the horrors of war, and, instead of rejoicing in his success, had spoken of laurels stained with blood, and watered with tears. It is almost needless to state, that such ridiculous inventions could only receive credence amongst those who knew nothing of the Haldanes, or who, in their ignorance, imagined that too much religion had made them mad. So far from there being any foundation for the story, their letters of congratulation to the Admiral and Lady Duncan, expressed their genuine feelings of thankfulness to the God of battles, who had enabled him to triumph in the defence of his country, and by the destruction of the Dutch fleet to be an instrument in the hands of the Almighty, for saving the nation from the invading expedition with which Ireland was threatened.

In particular, Lord Duncan himself declared, that of all his letters of congratulation, none had gratified him more than that of his nephew, Robert Haldane. Mr. Haldane, in his letter, had not merely indulged in general topics, but with the critical eye of a sailor, who had been enthusiastically attached to the navy, and who possessed a mind equally penetrating and acute, entered on a review of the whole affair. He noticed the inferior and undisciplined state of a great part of the North Sea fleet, some of the ships being old Indiamen and undermanned, as well as the boldness of the manœuvre in braving the dangers of a lee shore, breaking through the enemy's line, and cutting off his retreat; and, above all, considering the superiority of the Dutch, as sailors, over the French and Spaniards, he gave the battle of Camperdown the preference over all the great naval actions which had then been fought. The imperfect results of the battles of the 1st of June, 1794, 23d of June, and 13th of July, 1795, were afterwards noticed by Lord Exmouth, whose remarks corroborated Mr. Haldane's opinion, that taking into account the difficulties of the position, and the energy with which the Admiral dashed at the hostile fleet, the completeness of the victory, and the numbers as well as the skill of the Dutch, when compared with the Spaniards or even the French, with whom Rodney, Howe, Hotham, and St. Vincent himself had been engaged, Camperdown was the greatest of all the naval victories up to that period of the war.* When Lord Duncan returned home, no one conversed with him more fully and familiarly, or with greater interest, than his nephews, on the details of the action, or of his proceedings during the previous more appalling Mutiny at the Nore, which Mr. Pitt always considered to be the brightest part of the Admiral's conduct, and, on account of which, a patent of nobility, as an

---

* Admiral Sir Charles Ekins, in his able Critical Dissertation on all the Naval Battles, has this remark. In the action off Camperdown " Eleven ships of war were captured by ten ships of the British squadron; as not more than that number were seriously engaged. More was accomplished, in proportion to the *means*, than in any naval engagement of modern times." Sir Charles Ekins adds, " Nelson, although not acquainted with Lord Duncan, after the Battle of the Nile wrote to tell him how he had profited by his example."—*Ekins' Battles*, 4to., pp. 234, 235.

Irish peer, was in preparation even before the victory of Camperdown. Mr. Pitt's sentiment was repeated in the speech of the Lord Chancellor, expressing the thanks of the House of Lords, and announcing that this was one reason why the " unprecedented honour," of summoning all the peers, had been adopted on that occasion.

---

## CONCLUSION OF THE TOUR.

Mr. James Haldane, once more accompanied by Mr. Aikman, having taken leave of Caithness, entered Sutherland, and came to Dornoch, the county town, where they received a melancholy account of the state of religion. But whilst the people were without the blessing of a preached Gospel, it was comforting to hear of the good done at " prayer-meetings," instituted about the time of the Revolution of 1688.

" Their origin is not very well known, but they began at a time when much of the power of godliness was experienced. They generally met at first in the minister's house, or in some private house in the parish. The parochial fellowship meetings are now all so numerous, that they meet in churches. The minister acts as moderator. He begins with singing, and then prays. In many places, especially if the meeting be thin, he reads a portion of Scripture, and explains it. He then asks if any person has a question, or case of conscience, to propose for the consideration of those who are to speak at the meeting. A passage of Scripture is then mentioned, and a question proposed from it, relative to experimental religion, by some person present. The moderator elucidates the passage, and states the question as intelligibly as possible. The speakers then deliver their sentiments with an earnestness suited to the importance of the subject, and the moderator collects their different ideas, corrects anything that may be improperly stated, and gives his own opinion. The man who proposes the question never speaks to it. In many places there is a prayer offered up about the middle of the service. One of the speakers prays after the service is over, and a psalm is sung. Occasions of this nature are highly and deservedly valued by the people. In many places, we understand they are the chief means of maintaining and carrying forward the work of Christ. It is here also worthy of particular remark, that until within these few years that some ministers have discountenanced them, it was the practice of a great part of the north country to hold public fellowship meetings on the Friday previous to the administration of the Lord's Supper. Experienced Christians here discoursed freely of the manner of the Lord's dealing with them, and were enabled often to speak much to the comfort and edification of their weaker brethren."

The above extract is inserted the rather, because it indicates that, even before the Haldanes, or Mr. Aikman, and Mr. Ewing, had left the Church of Scotland, the old " Fellowship meetings" had found much favour in their eyes. It will also show the origin of certain of the plans of social worship, which afterwards produced so much excitement amongst the Scottish Congregationalists.

Having left Dornoch, where the Gaelic was so generally spoken, that the people did not understand English, they came to Tain, where they found the people " highly favoured, being blessed with a zealous and faithful minister of the Established Church, who is the fifth of that character, in immediate succession." After preaching at Tain, Milton, Invergordon, and Drummond, they arrived at Dingwall, where they preached, both in the street and in the Town-hall, and then crossed the Ferry, " and, by the Lord's good hand upon us, arrived in safety at Inverness, in the afternoon of the 18th of October, where we had the happiness to meet, in good health, the brother (Mr. Rate) whom we had left. And here we joined in setting up an Ebenezer, saying, Hitherto God hath helped." Mr. Rate had been most usefully employed, during their separation, in preaching in the neighbourhood. In the following year he was again engaged in itinerating in the county of Fife, and ultimately became the minister of a Scotch Presbyterian congregation at Alnwick, where he laboured in the Gospel till his death, in 1844. He married a daughter of Mr. Macintosh, of Ragmore, near Inverness, and the sister of Lachlan Macintosh, Esquire, of Montague-square, London, long known as an eminent East India merchant, who has devoted his influence to the best objects.

The itinerants arrived at Huntly on the 26th of October, having preached at Auldearn, Forres, Elgin, Fochaber, and Keith, and met with a most affectionate reception from Mr. Cowie.

On the Lord's-day, 29th October, they preached five times at Aberdeen, and on the Monday proceeded by Stonehaven to Montrose, where they found Sabbath-schools established in the interval since their first visit, and that the Burgher minister had himself begun to itinerate his neighbourhood. At Brechin, after preaching, a minister of the Established Church, before unknown, came up to them and wished them God speed. From Forfar they went to Glamis, where they preached to a comparatively small, but very attentive audience. At Kirriemuir and Cupar Angus they had overflowing congregations, and on Monday, the 6th of November, arrived and preached at Perth, and on the following day at Auchterarder, near Gleneagles, whence they drove on to Airthrey, where the tour ended.

Mr. James Haldane, upon whom the labour had chiefly fallen during this long and memorable tour, began now to find that even his physical energies were unequal to his zeal. Of his voice, Mr. Rate said, that he had known one louder, but never one that combined such strength and compass; but powerful as it was, it had been over-laboured. In chapels, in town-halls, and covered places, or in the open air, on village-greens, at market-crosses, by the sea-shore, or by the river's side, he had preached to crowded audiences, and even when addressing multitudes, sometimes estimated at 6,000 and upwards, he had commanded silence and been heard with attention. He thus closes his narrative:—" Preached (at Auchterarder) in the School-house to about 300 persons, and then came forward to a friend's house in the neighbourhood of Stirling, one of us being much indisposed by a sore-throat, in consequence of the fatigue of much speaking. The condescension and goodness of God were also strikingly displayed in this, that though he had had frequent attacks of this complaint in the course of the journey, he had never been once disabled by its violence from preaching till he had fully completed the circuit."

In closing the Journal, Mr. James Haldane submits some striking observations to the consideration of those who love the Lord Jesus Christ in sincerity, with the view of exciting them to greater zeal for Home Missions. He describes the people,

with the Scriptures in their hands, as perishing for lack of
knowledge, as taught to put their trust in refuges of lies,
which the hail shall sweep away in the day of God's wrath.
" Surely," he exclaims, " their miserable circumstances are now
proclaiming in the ears of all who know the worth of a Saviour
and of immortal souls, ' Come over, and help us ! ' "

The details of this memorable tour in 1797 may be forgotten,
and even the recollection of the excitement it produced throughout Scotland may be ignored by ecclesiastical historians more
zealous for party than for truth. But the blossoms did not
" go up as dust," and the fruits cannot perish. Some accounts
will appear in this volume of the actual results, as seen after
time had tested their reality. But the extent of the blessing
will never be known till the number of the elect shall be accomplished, and the Lord shall hasten his coming. Multitudes
dated their turning to God from the period of this awakening.
Several years later, the Rev. John Cleghorn publicly named, as
within his own knowledge, in the small town of Wick alone,
forty cases in which there had been a solid work of conversion
by the preaching of James Haldane, which he compares to an
" electric shock." But it is not merely from such instances
that the good done must be estimated. It was far more visible
in the impulse given to the Established Church, and to the
seceder in Scotland. This very circumstance may have
tended to prevent the due acknowledgment of the services
of these labourers, but as they did not look for human
applause, or a crown of earthly glory, they were not
disappointed. Their ambition soared to a loftier height than
the approbation of their fellow-men. They were willing to
sacrifice all for Christ, and doubtless the labours and services
which, through grace, they were privileged and empowered to
render are recorded in the book of God, and will one day be
acknowledged in the presence of angels and of men.

# CHAPTER VIII.

[1797—8.]

AFTER James Haldane's return from his first northern tour
his position was completely changed. The idea of leading the
retired life of a country gentleman was at an end. He had
assumed a new character, incurred new responsibilities, and
attracted to himself the notice of all Scotland. He had " put
his hand to the plough" in the Gospel field, and to have drawn
back after such encouragement would have seemed an act of
spiritual rebellion and deep ingratitude. The slumbers of a
careless and worldly clergy had been broken,—the attention of
the people had been aroused; and whilst the Gospel had been
received by many, a still greater number began to inquire,
What must we do to be saved? There was great excitement,
and withal not a little irritation. Some derided his zeal as the
ebullition of a distempered brain, whilst by those who knew
that he spoke "the words of truth and soberness," the question
was eagerly canvassed, What confers authority to preach?
Various opinions were expressed even by good men, and by
enemies to the truth lay preaching was loudly and bitterly
denounced. In a qualified degree, it had been already sanctioned by the father of the Evangelical clergy, the learned and
pious Dr. Erskine, who, in the preface to one of his works,

bears testimony to the blessing which had attended the labours of a zealous layman in the Highlands, in convincing and converting many who would not otherwise have listened to the Gospel. Instances of remarkable revivals brought about by lay preaching were appealed to, and particularly those mentioned in the Appendix to the valuable "Historical Collections" of the late Dr. Gillies, of Glasgow.

But in regard to James Haldane, the blessing which had attended his labours was to himself, as to others, the best evidence of his call to the work. The celebrated Mr. Cowie, of Huntly, familiarly styled the Whitfield of the north, thus wrote:—"No honest pastor has anything to dread from the friendly visits of such men. They come not to shake his influence, but to place him higher in the affections of his people, by spreading the light of truth among them." And in a long letter, dated November, 1797, published in the "Missionary Magazine," the same experienced and able clergyman thus records his testimony:—"I and several other ministers heard Mr. James Haldane on his late tour; and I confess, though I have been little short of thirty years a minister, have heard many excellent preachers, and laid my hand on many heads, I have very seldom heard anything so much to my satisfaction, and nothing that could exceed Mr. Haldane's discourses. I could even say *more*, but I forbear. HE CARRIES HIS CREDEN-TIALS WITH HIM, AND NEEDS NOT RECOMMENDATORY LETTERS. (2 Cor. iii. 13.)"

Under all these circumstances, was it probable that James Haldane should falter in his course, and cease to repeat his practical answer to the question of Dr. Carlyle and the rest of the Moderates, when they opposed Foreign Missions by asking if we had not "enough of heathen at home?" He felt that he had been forgiven much, and knowing, in his own experience, the Lord Jesus as the only and Almighty Saviour, he spoke from the heart to the heart, and was honoured to become one of the chief instruments of that mighty movement by which all Scotland was stirred and the people roused from a state of spiritual death. But in carrying out these Home Missions it was needful to make some systematic effort to provide other preachers, and to continue and extend the work which he had himself begun in the summer of 1797. Dr. Bogue, always foremost in every attempt to promote the kingdom of Christ, had established an Association in Hampshire, the design of which was to make the Gospel known in the neighbouring towns and villages. Following in the wake of Dr. Bogue, a Society was established in Edinburgh by the Haldanes, consisting of Christians of different denominations, under the name of " The Society for Propagating the Gospel at Home." A preliminary Meeting was held on the 20th December, 1797, and the first General Meeting on the 11th January following, when a Committee of twelve Directors was appointed, all of whom were laymen, and nine of them engaged in secular pursuits. The following is the list as they appear in order :—

| | |
|---|---|
| " Mr. James Christie. | Mr. Robert Morris. |
| Mr. Robert Haldane. | Mr. Walter Russell. |
| Mr. A. Johnstone. | Mr. James Haldane. |
| Mr. John Campbell. | Mr. John Greig. |
| Mr. George Gibson. | Mr. George Peattie. |
| Mr. John Aikman. | Mr. Andrew Rochead. |

OFFICERS OF THE SOCIETY.

Mr. John Ritchie, *Secretary*.
Mr. Alexander Steel, *Treasurer*.
Mr. George Wilson, *Clerk*."

In their first address they declare,—" It is not our design to form or to extend the influence of any sect. Our sole intention is to make known the Evangelical Gospel of our Lord Jesus Christ. In employing itinerants, schoolmasters, or others, we do not consider ourselves as conferring ordination upon them, or appointing them to the pastoral office. We only propose by sending them out, to supply the means of grace wherever we perceive a deficiency." The labours of this Society were greatly blessed. It was one of its principles that its itinerants and catechists should make no public collections, and take no money privately from those amongst whom they preached, and it undertook to defray the expenses of stated ministers desirous of extending their sphere of labour. Public subscriptions for its support were received, but to a very limited extent, for by far the greater part of the funds were supplied by Mr. Haldane.

The principles and plans of this Society were materially aided and recommended by the pen of Mr. Cowie and other ministers, through the pages of the "Missionary Magazine." On the 24th December, 1797, its editor, Mr. Ewing, delivered a powerful and eloquent sermon in defence of field-preaching, which produced a great sensation, and served still more to alarm the Moderates. The occasion of this sermon was a request to preach on behalf of the Edinburgh Sabbath-evening Schools, which had been rapidly increasing under the influence of the new impulse. Mr. Ewing undertook to prove that the unfettered preaching of the Gospel was one of those characters of universality which distinguish the Christian from the Jewish dispensation, and he ably contended, that in the closing words of the Apocalypse, the whole system of revelation, and the whole mystery of God, seem to be resolved into the provision made for the universal propagation of the Gospel. " The Holy Spirit and the Church unite their voice, and continually cry to sinners, COME. This precious invitation is so necessary to be known, and known without a moment's delay, that every one that heareth is commanded to repeat it. Like a multiplying and never-dying echo, 'the joyful sound' must be on all sides transmitted from one to another, that in this accepted time, in this day of salvation, he that is athirst may come, and whosoever will, may take the water of life freely."

The publication of the "Journal of the Tour to the North," prepared and edited by Mr. J. A. Haldane, served still more to swell the mingled tumult of censure and approval which the new proceedings had called forth. The "Journal" went rapidly through three large editions, and thousands were eagerly bought up and read with interest. In the spring of 1798 Mr. Rate was commissioned by the new Society to itinerate as their agent in Fife, whilst Mr. John Cleghorn and Mr. Ballantyne, originally belonging to the Scotch Secession Church, who had also studied under Dr. Bogue, were dispatched to the north, to labour in those places where so great an awakening had followed the preaching of James Haldane during those memorable weeks, when the illness of Mr. Aikman had detained him in Caithness.

It was the privilege of the two latter to be able to preach the Gospel without charge, and their movements were therefore independent of any Society. They resolved, in the course of the approaching summer, to visit the south and west of Scotland upon the same errand of mercy as that which had previously conducted them to the north. Before setting out, they addressed the following letter to the "Missionary Magazine." It indicates the spirit in which their labours were undertaken :—

*"To the Editor of the ' Missionary Magazine.'*

" SIR,—We last year requested the prayers of our Christian brethren through the channel of your valuable publication. The favour we met with, and the many opportunities we enjoyed of preaching salvation, through Jesus Christ, to multitudes of our northern brethren, proved that their prayers were heard on our behalf. There has been, it would appear, in some places a shaking among the dry bones; and the anxiety which many have since expressed to hear the Word of God, we would hope is a token that the Spirit of life has entered into the hearts of some.

" Two of those who went out last year are about to set off for the western and southern parts of Scotland, with a view of calling upon the careless to consider their ways. While we take this opportunity of requesting a renewal of the prayers of our brethren for our direction and success, we would observe that it is our intention to adopt a different line of conduct from that which we formerly pursued, in animadverting upon the sermons of particular ministers. This afforded a handle to those who did not approve of our design, to represent us as actuated by party spirit and ill-will to individuals. While we can safely say our consciences bear us witness that our motives were very different, yet we now see the propriety of cutting off occasion from those who seek occasion, as well as of removing prejudice from some of our brethren who, in this particular, disapproved of our conduct. We accordingly take this opportunity to state, that we are resolved to confine ourselves in our intended journey to the declaration of what we consider as the truth of God, without making personal remarks on any individual.

" JAMES HALDANE.
" JOHN AIKMAN."

The itinerating system had become decidedly popular with
the multitude, and, during the winter and spring of 1797-8,
the preachers had not been idle.  There was a great awakening,
a general spirit of inquiry, and the *Moderates* were filled with
fear and indignation.  Most gladly would they have retracted
the exhortation to begin at home.  Most gladly would they
now have sent the Haldanes "to the back settlements."  Even
some of the friends of the Gospel began to tremble for the
whole fabric of the Establishment, and dreaded the approach of
a disruption.  " Our good clergy," writes Mr. Campbell to the
Countess of Leven, "have different opinions about it.  The
majority are in favour of it.  Dr. Erskine thinks that the
preachers should not take a text, but just give an exhortation.
The gentlemen say that they could not keep up variety in this
way.  Dr. Stuart thinks that they ought to have a formal commission from some Church.  As for myself, I did not give an
opinion at first; but now their plan vindicates itself to me, for
they are not preaching to the Church, but to the world."  The
venerable Countess closed her useful life just before the second
tour, in the summer of 1798.  Her Ladyship was one of those
who dreaded the consequences to the constitution of the Established Church which might result from so openly and plainly
exposing the faithless clergy.  In her younger days she had
encouraged Whitfield boldly to denounce and rebuke "hirelings,"
but age had rendered her more timid, although, amidst her
fears, she observes, that, " after all, anything is better than dust
gathering through drowsiness and indolence."

The boldness with which laymen had attacked the false
doctrines of unfaithful ministers, seemed to Dr. Erskine and
other fathers of the Church subversive of order.  To the judgment of such men they were willing to bow, and therefore,
in the foregoing letter, published at the outset of their tour in
1798, they announced that they did not intend in future to
pursue that plan, although there were those who considered
that the necessities of the times rendered the bolder course
preferable for its faithfulness, as well as its efficiency.  Violent
diseases require violent remedies, and the outcry which it pro-

duced was the best proof of its results, and from no tour were more abundant fruits gathered than from the first.

The following letters from Mr. Simeon contain his views at the mature age of forty, in regard to lay preaching and the recent tour. It will demonstrate that it was not merely whilst an inexperienced young man that such irregularities were countenanced by the patriarch of Evangelism at Cambridge. Between Mr. Simeon and Mr. James Haldane there long subsisted a close and affectionate correspondence.

" *King's College, Cambridge, April* 13, 1798.

" MY VERY DEAR FRIEND,—I have been long intending to write to you, and though my manifold engagements might, in a measure, plead my excuse for the delay, yet the true reason has been, that I have been in a state of utter uncertainty with respect to my projected journey, and was unwilling to write till I could speak something positively with respect to it. . . . If I can have my God to go before me in the pillar and the cloud, I long exceedingly to visit you once more; but if I cannot see my way clear, I am better where I am. Had my plan been finally settled, you would have heard from me long since; but I have dreaded any appearance of fickleness. A minister's word should never be yea and nay; he should plan with wisdom, and execute with firmness. O that God would direct my way. I hope I can truly say, 'Thy will be done.'

" With respect to your excursion, I am far from having entertained the opinion you suppose. I must acknowledge that I think immortal souls of such value, that I should rejoice if all the Lord's people were prophets. With respect to regularity, propriety, &c., the most godly men in all ages have differed in their judgment; and I find it so difficult precisely to draw the line in any case of my own, that I do not presume to judge for others. Some think they may eat meat, and others not; I neither judge nor despise, but leave all to their own Master. We certainly must not do MORAL evil, that good may come. But if mercy and sacrifice stand in opposition to each other, we may choose mercy; and if David and his men be fainting with hunger, they may eat the forbidden bread. I love all good men of all descriptions, and rejoice in the good they do, whether they do it in my way or not. I think for myself and act for myself, and leave others to do the same.

" As a minister who has a flock that is dear to him, I stand more aloof from those who might injure *them* than I should if I were a private individual. . . . But if I must err on one side, I wish it to be on the side of love and zeal.

" As for more union among the different parties of Christians, I do not much expect to see it. " Every man," said Luther, ' has a Pope in his own belly.' People of different sentiments may coalesce for a time, but there are few who will not be endeavouring to proselyte others. I have almost invariably found it so, especially among the different classes of Dissenters; but among the Moravians far less than any other sect. There is another bone of contention which at this time renders such a union more difficult than ever. A great multitude of men, whose piety we cannot reasonably doubt, have sadly hurt their own spirit by dabbling in politics. . . . You, my dear friend, I trust, have steered clear of this rock. The Lord has given you a meek and spiritual mind, and I earnestly pray that you may ever have it occupied with the best things. There is, indeed, danger, even to the best of men, lest their minds should be soured by opposition and disappointment. I hope your brother's disappointment (about India) and the opposition you may have met with in your itinerancies have not produced this effect. Let us look through second causes, and then we shall be prepared to say, at all times, ' It is the Lord, let Him do what seemeth Him good.' I promise myself much pleasure in the perusal of your ' Journal;' and, if we live to meet again, much delight in your conversation and prayers. Present my very affectionate respects to Mrs. Haldane, and believe me, yours, &c.,

" C. SIMEON."

A few days later the following letter was written, and indicates the substantial satisfaction, with which the patriarch of Evangelism at Cambridge viewed the proceedings of his younger and more unfettered friend. It shows, too, how Mr. Simeon was himself stimulated to follow in the very same track, with this difference, that he would restrict himself to Presbyterian Churches and Episcopalian Chapels.

*Rev. Charles Simeon to James Haldane, Esq.*

" MY DEAREST BROTHER,—My mind is now, with God's permission, fully made up to visit you, and to be at Edinburgh the 16th, or more probably 17th, of May. I have been reading your Journal, if not with *unqualified* approbation, I may truly say with *exceeding great joy and delight*. I bless and adore my God, who has stirred up your soul to seek the salvation of His people, and I earnestly pray that a blessing may attend your labour of love.

" Thus far I have no objection to have known. But what I am going to say must be kept secret from every living creature.* . . .

" I again request you," he says, " not to judge me before you know my reasons, but to believe that my heart is with all those who love our Lord Jesus Christ in sincerity. If I cannot do the good which you did, be thankful that I wish to glean your leavings, and to move in somewhat a more confined path, rather than do nothing.—With most fervent love, I remain, (with affectionate respects also to Mrs. H.,)

" Yours in the Lord,

" *April* 16, 1798."        " C. SIMEON.

Mr. Simeon did come to Scotland, and received from Mr. James Haldane affectionate aid and co-operation. The motives which actuated Mr. Simeon in withholding a more public approbation of lay preaching were fully appreciated, and did not for a moment cloud their friendship. It was, however, on this occasion that, preaching in the Tolbooth Church, Mr. Simeon prayed that the Assembly " might do no evil,"—a prayer which might have been most appropriate in private, considering the composition of the Assembly, but one which did not fail to produce irritation. Mr. James Haldane used frequently to remark that he generally observed that there was more of true wisdom in a simple and straightforward course, and that those who valued themselves on their own prudence often signally erred in this particular. In his opinion, Mr. Simeon's prayer did much to precipitate the exclusion from the Scottish pulpits of

* The secret which Mr. Simeon did not wish to be divulged, applied only to *that time*, and related to his plan of going northward, with Dr. Walter Buchanan, over the same ground as that which had been so lately traversed by Mr. James Haldane, yet not so as to appear altogether to be publicly identified with his lay friend. He therefore wished Mr. J. Haldane *privately* to prepare the way for him, by sending letters to his acquaintance in all the principal places where there were Churches belonging either to Presbyterians or Episcopalians, with the view of procuring pulpits where he might be allowed to preach. He adds, however, that he was not going to preach in the open air, or in opposition to false teachers. " It is not my plan to preach as you did, and therefore I wish nothing to be said to me upon that subject. If I were *alone*, or *with you*, I might act differently; but circumstanced as I shall be, my mind is made up."

the clergy of the Church of England and other non-Presbyterian bodies.

The venerable John Newton, of St. Mary Woolnoth, still more openly gave his countenance and blessing to the itinerants. " If," he writes to Mr. Campbell,—" if all were like-minded with Messrs. Haldane and Aikman, I would pray the Lord to increase their number a hundred-fold. Give my love to them, and tell them that I rejoice in their zeal, in their acceptance, and in their success. Why should not the Orkney and the Shetland Islands deserve attention as much as the Islands of the South Sea? I hope Gospel zeal will, in due time, sail northward to Shetland, and westward to St. Kilda, and all the intermediate islands."

Encouraged by past success, and by the prayers and good wishes of Christians of many denominations, Mr. James Haldane and Mr. Aikman set off on their second extensive tour on Thursday, the 14th June, 1798, travelling by Peebles, Biggar, Hamilton, Greenock, &c., into Ayrshire and Galloway, preaching the Gospel in all these districts, and finally completing their circuit home by way of Berwick. The attention which they excited was as great in the west and south of Scotland as it had been in the north. Multitudes flocked to hear the Gospel, and to the hearts of many it was brought home with power. In some places they encountered more opposition than before, and especially at Ayr, where James Haldane was interrupted in preaching at the market-cross, and summoned before the magistrates, who had been incited to interfere. But he had done nothing unlawful, and he was not a man to yield to intimidation. He was threatened with imprisonment if he should preach on the following day, as he had announced; but he assured the magistrates that menaces without lawful sanction were of no avail. He would not indeed preach at the cross, or at any place to which just exception might be taken, but in preaching out of doors he infringed no law, and, on the contrary, was protected by the Toleration Act. " Depend upon it," said one of them,—" depend upon it, that you will be arrested." The reply was characteristic, "And depend upon it, Sir, I shall be punctual to my appointment." He was on the ground at the appointed time, and preached to a great audience without molestation. One of the gentlemen most eager in opposition was a county magistrate, lately returned from India with a large fortune. In the course of this altercation, having discovered who the preacher was, and that they had mutual friends, he became more courteous, although still persisting in the determination to put down field-preaching. He appeared on the ground next day, with some other magistrates, as if intending to carry their threat into force. Mr. James Haldane proceeded, fearless of their menaces. They listened in silence to a powerful address, offered no interruption, and went away seemingly awed, conscience-stricken, and solemnized.

An account of his first sermon at the cross of Ayr has been written by a survivor, who himself owed his own soul to the blessed words which then for the first time reached his conscience. That good man, Mr. Watson, afterwards a minister in Dumfries, and long a valuable itinerant round Edinburgh, and forward in every good work, writes as follows:—

"15, *Calton-street, Edinburgh, April* 9, 1851.

"Although unwilling to put in writing the unpremeditated narration made by me two years ago, at a public meeting held in the Tabernacle, yet at your urgent and reiterated request I comply, rather than assume a position of refusal in a matter relating in some respects more to your father than to myself. The facts are simply these :—

"In the year 1798, your late venerated father, along with the late Mr. John Aikman, whose praise is in all the Churches, visited my native place, the ancient town of Ayr.

"On their arrival, one Saturday, intimation was publicly made by the town bellman that Mr. James Haldane was to preach at the cross the same evening, at seven o'clock. I received this information from a good old woman, who asked if I would go and hear. I replied, 'No, no; I never go to hear men who preach in the streets for bawbees.' In answer to which she assured me 'they were independent gentlemen, who did na' preach for siller.' This appeared to me so extraordinary that I at once resolved to go and hear for myself, which I accordingly did.

"His sermon was delivered with such fervour and earnestness as to produce a deep impression on the listening multitude.

"Intimation was also given that he would again preach, with the Lord's

permission, on the same spot on the following morning (Sabbath), at nine
o'clock.  I was at the cross, along with my father, before the hour, where
large numbers soon assembled.  The text was in John iii. 3, ' Except a
man be born again, he cannot see the kingdom of heaven.'

"About the middle of his sermon, the town-officers came from the
magistrates, and said, ' You must go with us to the Council-room,' where
the authorities were then assembled.  Mr. Haldane went, but requested
the people to remain, as he hoped he should not be long detained.  He
soon returned, and informed the people that he was commanded to preach
no more in that place, but he told them he would finish his discourse.
Before doing so, however, the officers were again sent to stop him ; but
when they came near, instead of putting their orders into execution, they
stood respectfully behind until he had finished, and they were heard to say
that they were ashamed to execute the orders against such a gentleman.

"I should explain that the cross stands, or rather stood, in a corner of
the street where there was an open space, which afforded accommodation
for the assemblage, and therefore the thoroughfare was little, if at all,
interrupted.

"On dismissing the people, Mr. Haldane intimated that he would
preach that evening on the other side of the river, on the Newton Green.

"The report of such treatment gave general offence to the inhabitants
of the place, and brought a still greater multitude to hear him in the
evening.  On Monday morning, Mr. Aikman preached to a large assemblage on the Town Green.  A private individual, who rented a part for
grazing cattle, had with generous indignation offered his portion of the
Green for the public accommodation.

"In the following year Mr. Haldane again visited Ayr, and the report
of his former visit and treatment having spread over the county, brought
together immense numbers to hear him.

"To the honour of my friend and then minister, the late Dr. Peebles,
let it be told, when sermon was announced on one of the evenings unfavourable to out-of-door preaching, he offered Mr. Haldane the use of his
church (the Newton parish church upon Ayr), where he accordingly
preached to a full house, from 1st Peter i. 18, 19, ' Forasmuch as ye know
that ye were not redeemed with corruptible things, as silver and gold, but
with the precious blood of Christ, as of a lamb without blemish and without spot.'  These were seasons of refreshing from the presence of the
Lord, and long remembered by many.

"Mr. Haldane's visits to the west of Scotland were the means of
awakening not a few out of their spiritual slumbers, and of infusing fresh
life into the languishing souls of many of God's own people connected
with other denominations.

"Although more than fifty years have run their course since these
things were done, the remembrance is as fresh on my memory as if they

were only the transactions of yesterday. In my imagination, I see Mr. James Haldane's manly form and commanding attitude, in youthful but dignified zeal, pouring out of the fulness of his soul a free, full, and ever-lasting salvation to the wondering multitude, who by the expression of their faces seemed to say, ' We have heard strange things to-day.'

" And I may well remember that first sermon of Mr. Haldane's, in 1798, standing as he did on the steps of the old cross of Ayr, as it may be said to have been the pivot on which the events of my after-existence all turned. It was that sermon that led me to Christ, and eventually to the relinquishment of my business and other engagements in Ayr. It was that sermon that led me to your uncle's academy at Dundee and Edin-burgh, from thence to the pastorate of the Congregational Church at Dumfries, which I voluntarily resigned after Mr. Robert Haldane's change to Baptist sentiments, a circumstance which more than forty years ago brought me again to Edinburgh, where I have since resided. It is far from my wish to convey the idea of any undue interference on the part of your late respected uncle, as proprietor of the Chapel. That gentleman ever acted towards me as a friend and a Christian.

"And now, my dear Sir, allow me to close this narration with my earnest prayer that the Lord God Almighty, who blessed Abraham and your father also, and made them blessings, may also bless you and yours, and all the house of your father, both small and great. And for his sake, I remain,

" Your most affectionate friend and well-wisher,

" WILLIAM WATSON.*

" A. Haldane, Esq."

There are many incidental evidences of the blessing which attended the tour of 1798, although no printed record of it has been published. In a letter from Annan, in the " Missionary Magazine," it is said : " Since Messrs. Haldane and Aikman visited our part of the country, a Sabbath-school has been erected at Annan, containing about eighty scholars, who appear to be doing well." Again, with reference to the same tour : " At Longtown there appears to be a spirit of inquiry after Divine things. At Canoby there have been five Sabbath-schools erected within these two months, containing about one hundred and thirty children." At Berwick they also preached

---

* It is due to Mr. Watson to state that, when circumstances had placed him in a position to repay the money expended on his ministerial educa-tion, he honourably proposed to return it to Mr. Haldane, who as frankly declined the offer, which he did not the less appreciate.

with great acceptance, and were hailed with joy by the friends of the Gospel. The people generally came out to hear in crowds, and numbers found, in these opportunities, a message of peace to their souls.

It was whilst prosecuting this second extensive tour, that a stranger appeared, whose arrival added fuel to the flame, which had already blazed up, both in the north and south of Scotland. The two preachers had repaired to Langholm, in the county of Dumfries, in the hope of doing some good to the multitude assembled at the annual fair. It was on a summer's evening, the 26th of July, when, walking on the romantic banks of the river Esk, they passed by an English clergyman, also enjoying the retirement of the scene, but engaged in close conversation with the minister of the parish. His person and errand were alike unknown to them. In such a place and at such a time, it was impossible not to be struck with his appearance. His tall, commanding figure, piercing eye, and aquiline nose, gave effect to a countenance beaming with intelligence, on which there was withal the indication of a natural drollery and irresistible vein of humour. It was the celebrated Rowland Hill, the brother of the well-known and pious Sir Richard Hill, of Hawkestone, M.P. for Shropshire, and uncle of that gallant peer, who, after having fought on almost every field, from Alexandria to Waterloo, was for so many years the Commander-in-Chief. Mr. Hill himself relates, in his own quaint style, the manner of his introduction to his new friends. The narrative is contained in his journal of his first tour in Scotland :—

" Having had no opportunity to appoint different stages at which to preach between Carlisle and Edinburgh, I spent the Thursday evening at Langholm. It happened to be the time of their public fair, and a sad example it exhibited, on my first night's lodging in Scotland, the opposite to what I expected to find of decency and good behaviour among the people in those parts. The fair was a downright revel; dancing, drunkenness, and lasciviousness, seemed to be the principal motives which had brought them together. In England I scarce ever saw a more disgraceful assemblage; and in some parts of Wales I have passed through large fairs, when it was pleasant to behold the innocent and well-ordered bustle of the day. After that traffic had ended, all returned at an early hour, with scarce an instance of a sober person being disgusted by a reprobate, or insulted by a drunkard.

"As the same horse, with a light vehicle, conveyed me and my servant from stage to stage, the next being a long one, I was under the necessity of spending the night in this temporary hell, but that I might enjoy a little respite from the wretched tumult, I took my evening's walk out of the town, by the side of a romantic river. Here I was very kindly accosted by a gentleman, who, I conceive, was the minister of the parish, and who, with much hospitality, offered me every accommodation his house could afford from the confusion of the town; but having already procured a private lodging, I declined his very friendly offer. While we were in conversation, Messrs. James Haldane and Aikman passed. These gentlemen were then unknown to me. I was told, but in very candid language, their errand and design; that it was a marvellous circumstance, quite a phenomenon, that an East India captain, a gentleman of good family and connexions, should turn out an itinerant preacher; that he should travel from town to town, and all against his own interest and character. This information was enough for me. I immediately sought out the itinerants. When I inquired for them of the landlady of the inn, she told me she supposed I meant the two *priests* who were at her house, but she could not satisfy me of *what religion they were*. The *two priests*, however, and myself soon met; and, to our mutual satisfaction, passed the evening together."

Mr. Hill next morning went forward towards Edinburgh, whilst his two friends remained to complete their itinerating labour of love.

---

Before Mr. Hill's visit to Scotland, and contemporaneous with the institution of the Circus as a place for preaching, there was another plan, which originated in the same ardent philanthropy and zeal for the glory of God, which marked the renewed character of Robert Haldane. It was a scheme for bringing over young Africans to Britain, with the view of educating them in this country in the principles of Christianity, and sending them back to their native land imbued with a knowledge of civilization, and, as far as human efforts could avail, with a knowledge of the Gospel.

The suggestion of the idea is due to Mr. John Campbell, and will be best told in the simple though somewhat quaint style of his own autobiography :—

"The formation of the London Missionary Society for extending the knowledge of the glorious Gospel to all ends of the earth, and the Society being composed of Christians of all denominations, had a most *electrifying* effect on the Christians of the North. ' We were like men who dreamed.' From the days of George Whitfield till then, the Christians on both sides of the Tweed had been fast asleep. . . .

"In a short time a similar Society was formed in Edinburgh, and I was chosen to be on the direction. The first field they fixed on for the theatre of their operations, was the Continent of Africa; to commence in the vicinity of Sierra Leone; to which some missionaries were sent, and several pious young men volunteered to the Sierra Leone Company to go to their settlement as clerks, &c., and one as chaplain. Death carried off the chaplain and some of the young men, and terminated the Mission. Musing on the unhealthiness of the climate to European constitutions one morning, this thought occurred: ' Might we not bring *over* Africa to England, educate her, when some, through grace and Gospel, might be converted, and sent back to Africa? If not converted, yet they might help to spread civilization, so all would not be lost!' The amount of which was to bring over twenty or thirty, or more, boys and girls, from the coast of Guinea, through the influence of Governor Macaulay; educate them in Edinburgh, and send them back to their own country, to spread knowledge, especially scriptural knowledge.

"I laid my proposed scheme before two or three judicious friends, who approved of it, as did also Henry Thornton, M.P., Treasurer of the Sierra Leone Company, and Mr. Wilberforce; but I entered more fully into the consideration of the matter with the late Charles Grant, Chairman of the East India Company, who had not been long returned from India, and had come with his family to Scotland on a visit to the Leven family. Having exchanged letters once a-week with the venerable Countess of Leven for a considerable time, she got Mr. Grant to promise to call upon me as he passed through Edinburgh on his way to London, which he condescended to do, and invited me to spend the only two evenings he was to be in Edinburgh at his hotel with him and family. This I considered to be a most favourable opportunity for consulting a wise, good, and experienced man, in regard to my then *favourite* plan. I was delighted to observe the interest he took in it, and the minuteness of his calculations regarding the expense of bringing them over from Africa and sending them back five years later."

Mr. Campbell's first efforts resulted in a correspondence with Mr. Wilberforce, Mr. Thornton, and others, of " the Clapham Sect," who highly approved of the plan, but hesitated as to the expense, and judged it better to postpone the scheme until at peace with France, when it might be hoped that the removal of the war-taxes would render it easier to obtain subscriptions.

About a year and a-half later, it happened in the month of March, 1798, that Mr. Campbell was invited to meet a few Christian friends at supper at Mr. Haldane's house, then in Prince's-street, Edinburgh. " At one time," says Mr. Campbell, " there was a pause in the conversation. Mr. Alexander Pitcairn, who sat opposite to me, said, ' Mr. Campbell, what has become of your African scheme ? I have not heard anything of it for a long time.' To which I replied, ' It is put off to the peace,' which created a general smile. Mr. Haldane asked from the head of the table, *what* scheme I had, never having heard of it." Mr. Campbell then relates how he explained his project, and how the conversation next turned upon the idea of having a place of worship built on the plan of Mr. Whitfield's tabernacles, and that, having mentioned that the Circus might then be obtained, as the Relief congregation had left it, Mr. Haldane looked to a lawyer who was present, and said, " Mr. Dymock, will you inquire about it to-morrow ? and if it be to let, take it for a year."

" It was believed," continued Mr. Campbell, " by many that this system of tabernacles was a scheme laid for overturning the Established Church. Now there was not one Dissenter present at that supper, where the matter was proposed and approved. All were members of the Establishment, and I believe the object of all, when they approved of the proposed scheme, was the collecting of sinners to the Saviour. When the meeting was concluded, every one returned to his own home, very prayerful.

" Next morning, I received a note from Mr. Haldane, wishing me to call on him as soon as I could. I went to him directly. He said that my African scheme had occupied his waking thoughts ever since I mentioned it last night, on which the following conversation took place :—' What is the real reason why you were advised to defer commencing the Institution ?' ' Entirely the dreaded difficulty of obtaining *funds* to defray the expense.' ' Have you calculated the probable amount of these expenses ?' ' Yes; the probable expense of bringing over thirty children, lodging, supporting, and educating them for five years, and their passage back to Africa, will cost from 6,000*l*. to 7,000*l*.' ' Supposing you were to write to the Governor of Sierra Leone, stating that you had *sufficient* funds for supporting such an Institution, and requesting him to collect thirty or forty of the sons and daughters of the African chiefs over whom he had influence, and send them over to you, do you think he would have sufficient confidence in you to fulfil your commission ?' ' I think he would.' ' On what do you ground that expectation ?' ' When the French destroyed the Settlement, or Freetown, Governor Macaulay came to London to lay the state of things before the Company. After finishing the business there, he visited Scotland, to see his relations. On coming to Edinburgh, he called upon me with a letter of introduction from the Rev. John Newton, which would be a sufficient passport to any Christian in Scotland, so highly were his works prized. The Governor had four sisters in Edinburgh living together, and as they had no particular friend to advise with, he requested me to engage to be their adviser; to which proposal I readily consented. In the course of a year after they came under my wing, I was bridegroom's man to three out of the four.' On hearing this statement Mr. Haldane was satisfied, and volunteered to be responsible for the whole expense, and gave me a letter to that effect. Accordingly, I wrote by that day's post to Governor Macaulay, Sierra Leone, requesting him to obtain thirty or thirty-five African boys and girls, and send them to Edinburgh, as I had obtained sufficient funds to defray all expenses. I sent it to the care of Henry Thornton, M.P., Treasurer to the Sierra Leone Company."

# CHAPTER IX.

MR. HALDANE SELLS HIS PATERNAL ESTATE—CORRESPOND-
ENCE WITH AND CHALLENGE OF PROFESSOR ROBISON
—MR. ROWLAND HILL COMES TO OPEN THE CIRCUS—
PREACHES TO IMMENSE MULTITUDES THERE, AND ON
THE CALTON HILL—MAKES SEVERAL TOURS, FIRST WITH
MR. HALDANE, AND THEN WITH HIS BROTHER—FINALLY
RETURNS TO ENGLAND WITH MR. HALDANE — CORRE-
SPONDENCE WITH MR. MACAULAY ABOUT THE AFRICAN
CHILDREN—MR. ROWLAND HILL'S JOURNAL.

[1798.]

"JUNE 16, 1798, was the last night I paid the labourers at
Airthrey." Such is the entry found in a short memorandum
of the dates of the principal events of Robert Haldane's life.
Dr. Innes, who was then minister of Stirling, relates, that
on that evening, in the prospect of quitting for ever his paternal
estate, Mr. Haldane assembled all his domestics, including the
gardeners and labourers, in the servants' hall, where supper
was provided for them and their families. On that occasion,
after attending himself to their comforts, he addressed them
personally, and took a kind farewell of them all, asked them to
forgive anything in which he had failed in his duties as a
master, and expressed his desire for their temporal and eternal
welfare. For some of those who were old or infirm, or had
been long on the estate, he secured small pensions. There was
one aged person who was much attached to the family, who
could not bear the disruption of the tie, whose forebodings were
dissipated by her own death on the very day when the family
left Airthrey. In the new proprietor they all found a most
benevolent and indulgent master, and more than twenty years
afterwards it was his pride to mention, that there was not one of

Mr. Haldane's people who had not been attended to as much as if their old master had remained.

It might seem rather improbable that Mr. Haldane's farewell to Airthrey should be associated with Mr. Rowland Hill's visit to Scotland. Yet such was the fact. It was on Mr. Haldane's invitation, and that of his brother, that Mr. Hill came, with a view to ulterior proceedings for the propagation of the Gospel at home. The field of his operation was changed, but the forces to be employed were the same.

Airthrey had been for nearly two years for sale, when it was purchased by an uncle of Mrs. James Haldane's, the late General Sir Robert Abercromby, G.C.B., then lately returned from India. The whole of the estate was not, indeed, at this time disposed of, but the sale included the house, park, woods, and principal farms, composing all that was either ornamental or useful to a place of residence. The lands retained, amounting to a third of the value of the whole property, were let on leases, like his other estates in Forfarshire, which gave little trouble as to management, and could only be regarded as an investment for money. He used himself to relate, that after he had resolved to sell Airthrey, he sent for Mr. Morison, of Alloa, to survey the estate and make an estimate. On the morning of the day when Mr. Morison arrived to begin his work, the chapter read in the usual course of family worship was the second of Ecclesiastes, containing the following verses:—" I made me great works; I builded me houses; I planted me vineyards; I made me gardens and orchards, and I planted trees in them of all kinds of fruits; I made me pools of water." It was impossible not to be struck with the coincidence.* His own account of

---

* Mr. Morison, whose judgment Mr. Haldane greatly valued, was the father of General Sir William Morison, K.C.B., who became M.P. for Clackmannan Kinross, after a brilliant course in India, where he attained the rank of Senior Member of Council, and was for some months Acting Governor-General. He owed his original appointment to Sir Ralph Abercromby, and the story is worth recording. Sir Ralph was going abroad, and a question having arisen as to the division of one of the farms on his father's estate of Tullybody, he consulted Mr. Morison, who undertook to procure a sketch of the fields in question. He did so, and

his leaving his estate, in the embellishment of which he had taken so much pleasure, runs thus :—

" For some time after this I did not lay aside my endeavours to get out to Bengal, and in the meanwhile was busied in selling my estate, that there might be no delay on my part if obstructions from without should be removed. I accordingly at length found a purchaser, and with great satisfaction left a place, in the beautifying and improving of which my mind had been once much engrossed. In that transaction I sincerely rejoice to this hour, although disappointed in getting out to India. I gave up a place and a situation, which continually presented objects calculated to excite and to gratify 'the lust of the eye and the pride of life.' Instead of being engaged in such poor matters, my time is more at my command, and I find my power of usefully applying property very considerably increased. I can truly say I experience the accomplishment of the gracious promise, that leaving house and lands (although in a very restricted sense), as I trust, for the Gospel's sake

Sir Ralph was much pleased with the plan; and on inquiry, discovered that it was done by the surveyor's son, then a youth of sixteen. Sir Ralph said he should like to have a portable plan of each farm on the estate executed in the same manner, so that, when on foreign service he might be able to correspond with confidence on any question that arose. The order was executed with equal precision and alacrity, and Sir Ralph, who was a quick discerner of character, discovering that the young man was ambitious of a military appointment, procured for him the cadetship which was the means of his attaining fortune and distinction. Shortly after Sir William Morison's return from India in 1840, the writer of these Memoirs met him both at his own house at Alloa and under the late Lord Abercromby's roof at Airthrey. It was pleasing to observe how little Sir William had been changed by prosperity. The man who had occupied the palace of the Governor-General of India had preserved the lowly mansion of his father unaltered, and was delighting himself with the early recollections of his honourable but comparatively humble origin. At Airthrey he remarked, that few things had struck him more than the reduced size of the rooms, which the vivid impressions of his youthful imagination had during absence magnified. He died in 1851, and in token of his gratitude to his early patron, left out of his ample fortune a legacy of 20,000l. to the grandson of Sir Ralph, the late possessor of Airthrey, the second Lord Abercromby.

alone, and what I esteem my duty, I have received manifold more, though, as it is added, 'with persecutions.'"

The "persecutions" here alluded to refer, first and chiefly, to the calumnious, and now ridiculous reports, which, in accordance with the evil spirit of the times, industriously attributed a democratic or revolutionary design to all his movements, whether Christian or philanthropic. One of these "calumnies" gave rise to a curious correspondence with a distinguished Professor of Natural Philosophy in Edinburgh. To insert the whole of it would be tedious. But as Professor Robison's reply to Mr. Haldane's first letter contained the offer of "satisfaction" in the usual way, it is proper to observe how he dealt with this challenge. The letters are to be found in Mr. Haldane's "Address on Politics," and are thus introduced :—

"While there remained any expectation of our going to Bengal I did not relinquish the object, but continued to use all proper means for that purpose. While I was thus engaged, a very unexpected and cruel attack was made upon me and my associates, in a well-known book, published by Professor Robison, although I had never been a Freemason, and knew nothing of the Illuminati. The first calumny was afterwards retracted by him in the newspapers. He introduced his accusation by calling me 'a very eminent friend and abettor of Dr. Priestly;' but he could not have been more unfortunate in his epithet, as there was no person to whom I stood more opposed in religious principles, nor did I ever agree with him in his political sentiments. I believe Dr. Priestly's religious system to be practical Atheism, and that it will lead its unhappy votaries to eternal destruction. If a man does not acknowledge the God of the Bible, in the emphatic language of Scripture, he has made God a liar; whilst the idea, set up in the mind, is a mere caricature of the imagination, and no God."

No. I.

"*Airthrey, September* 21*st*, 1797.

" Sir,—I have just been informed that a book, lately published by you, contains the following paragraph :—

" 'I grieve that he (Dr. Priestly) has left any of his friends and abettors among us. A very eminent one said in company a few days ago, " that he would willingly wade to the knees in blood to overturn the establishment of the Kirk of Scotland." I understand that he proposes to go to India, and there to preach Christianity to the natives. Let me beseech him to recollect, that among us Christianity is still considered as the Gospel of peace, and that it strongly dissuades us from bathing our feet in blood.'

" As it is supposed that I am the person alluded to in these sentences, I must request that you will inform me whether it is so or not.

" I am, Sir, &c., &c.,<br>" ROBERT HALDANE.

" *To Professor Robison.*"

No. II.

*From Professor Robison.*

" *Stirling*, 29th *Sept.*, 1797.

" SIR,—I received your favour of the 21st instant, on Wednesday, in the country, where I have been confined for some time by bad health. The moment I received it, I set off for this place to give you all the satisfaction in my power; and expected to find here ———, to whom I have the pleasure of being well known. His absence has disappointed my hopes of a friend, who might be a witness of what passed between us.

" I do not presume to judge why you suppose that you are the eminent disciple of Dr. Priestly alluded to in the passage which you have fairly quoted. I have not said that you are; but I cannot at present give you more satisfaction by answering your question, which I am sorry for, because it is required with politeness. Could I have found a proper friend to accompany me, I should have had an interview; but having had the honour of serving my King and country, as an officer in the Royal Navy, for several years, I have the stronger reasons for being cautious how I act, and must not yield to my wishes to give you more satisfaction at present.

" I can only say, that, if you still find yourself aggrieved, I am ready with my life to give you that *satisfaction* which one gentleman is entitled to require of another.

" Permit me to say, as an author, that inclination, as well as duty, makes me also wish to correct any mistakes that I have fallen into. I am therefore sparing no pains to come at the truth of several things which were repeated to me as the current talk of the country, both here and in England; and if I find that I have misrepresented anything, I will rectify it in the most public manner without loss of time. But this may require a few days, because my health is very indifferent, and I cannot bear the fatigue of travelling without a little interval of rest. This may retard, but shall not prevent my discharging, to the utmost of my power, the duty that I owe to the public. I am, with due regard, Sir,

"Your most humble servant,

"JOHN ROBISON.

"*To Robert Haldane, Esq., of Airthrey.*"

### No. III.

"*Airthrey, September 30th,* 1797.

"SIR,—I have this moment received your letter, dated from Stirling. You say you do not presume to judge why I suppose that I am the disciple of Priestly alluded to in the passage I quoted; by this seeming to insinuate that it may be some other person. I certainly could have no wish to apply to myself such a charge as your book brings against one who is desirous, you say, to go to India to teach Christianity there, were it possible for either me or my friends to suppose that you mean any other. It was upon this ground that my supposition was founded. If you, however, declare that I was not the person alluded to, that is quite sufficient; and, on this supposition, I am certainly entitled to require and expect, that you make this declaration (as you know that it is generally applied to me) upon every principle of candour and justice.

"I now beg leave to inform you, that I never made use of such an expression as the one referred to, nor ever said *anything at all like it ;* that the sentiment appears to me shocking in itself, and the most remote possible from every idea I entertain on the subject. No, Sir; I would not spill one drop of human blood to support or destroy all the religious establishments in the world. I should consider such a way of attempting to advance the interests of Christianity as infinitely mad and infinitely wicked. I have, over and over again, declared this, both in public and private; and it is well known by all my friends, and those who are intimate with me, to be my decided and fixed principle.

"I observe you say, that if you find you have misrepresented anything, you will rectify it in the most public manner, without loss of time. This is all that I require; and I have even no objection to your taking some days to gain all the information you desire. But then it must be done in the most explicit manner. No name should be mentioned, as there is none in your book; but it should be said, after quoting the sentence, that the author finds, upon inquiry, that it was totally void of foundation, and, therefore, that he takes the earliest opportunity of contradicting it. This, or something equivalent, must be put into the Scotch newspapers, and a note must also be written to the reviewers, lest they retail it.

"I feel that a regard to myself and associates, as standing, in some measure, on public ground, requires this. Had I not been in this situation I should very possibly have taken no notice of it, but should have let it pass, with many other unfounded calumnies that have been repeated against me.

" I should also imagine, that, as soon as you are satisfied of the assertion being unfounded, your own candour and feelings will dictate the very course here pointed out.

" As to your saying, that, if I feel myself aggrieved, you are ready with your life to give *that satisfaction which one gentleman is entitled to require of another*, it appears to me a very strange way of talking in this business. If you have publicly repeated a false calumny against one who never interfered with you, ought you not to desire, as soon as possible, even without being required, to make him reparation by as publicly contradicting it? which is the only rational satisfaction that can be obtained or given in such a business. If you mean the term, however, in any other acceptation, I must beg to inform you, that, whatever the maxims of the world in such a case might dictate, Christianity, which I consider as the gospel of peace, has taught me that it would be *no satisfaction* to bathe either my feet or my hands in your blood.

" I have only to add, that I think an interview would be very proper; and that it need not be prevented by your not having a friend to accompany you. I shall be happy to see you here this day if you find it convenient. I am persuaded the business might be amicably settled in a few minutes. It is not in my power to call upon you, as I am confined to-day by a cold and swelled face. I am, Sir,

" Your obedient servant,

" ROBERT HALDANE.

" *Professor Robison.*

" P.S.—I have not yet seen your book, but am happy to find the passage is fairly quoted."

The servant who carried the last letter brought it back, with the information that Professor Robison had left Stirling the day before. Mr. Haldane, therefore, inclosed it with a short note to the learned gentleman's country residence, near Glasgow.

In the meantime the Professor promised to insert in the newspapers an advertisement, containing a general acknowledgment of " a mistake of which he had been guilty in a work just published by him, entitled, ' Proofs of a Conspiracy.' "

To this Mr. Haldane replied, telling the Professor, that if he wished to make reparation, it would not do to insert such a modified retractation as would leave the impression that there was some foundation, however slight, for the calumny; but that he must add, that " nothing could be more *abhorrent* from the ideas or principles of the gentleman alluded to than the sentiments imputed to him." He concludes, " I am sorry that you have travelled about so quickly as to have injured your health. I would much rather have waited some days before the explanation had taken place."

To the handsome terms in which Mr. Haldane expressed himself as ready to save the Professor from the shame of an ignominious acknowledgment of his calumny, the Professor writes :—" Your letter most agreeably surprised me; and had I known what Mr. Haldane could do, I should have saved myself and him some trouble." What follows places the tyranny of the world and the immorality of duelling in a striking light. The Professor's reluctance to confess his error arose from the dread of being branded as a *coward*. When he found that Mr. Haldane had no intention of having recourse to pistols, the amiable but hasty Professor does not hesitate to make his apology : —

" I was sensible that I was the aggressor, and that your demand was most reasonable. The very demand made me suspect that I had misrepresented things. Yet I could not answer it without great risk, whatever might be my determination to do you justice. It was natural to expect that my refusal would draw on me expressions which, by the tyrannical rules of society, I could not bear with patience, and afterwards show my face in the world, and my wife and family would have been involved in my disgrace. I acknowledge that I could not bear that thought, and no way occurred to me for preventing this but the one I took, and *afterwards* to meet you, or correspond with you, in sight of a friend. You will, I dare say, allow, that when I could charge you with the sentiment expressed in my book, *these were natural fears*. But I would gladly hope that you did not misunderstand me when I said that I would give you what the world calls the *satisfaction* of a gentleman. I can only give you my solemn assurance that I never would have added the guilt of hurting you to that of slandering you, and that *I would have stood your passive mark*. I beg you to think of my situation, with all the extenuating circumstances that attend it. Even if I had had the courage to bear with opprobrious names, how could I remove the distress from the wife and children of a *coward* in the eye of the world? I did not know you, Sir, and my ignorance was innocent, for you were much misrepresented. Allow me to say, further, that you might do more service, perhaps, and have as great probability of success, if you would try to win over the infidels among ourselves. Also, one of these would, by his influence, be of more value than fifty Hindoos. Let me beseech you not to give up this thought. There are yet remains of religion among us, and I imagine there are still more obstacles in your way in India. The division into castes is next to insurmountable; for a religion which asserts the equality of all in the sight of God, will be called rebellion or sedition. But I ask your pardon. You have no doubt reflected deeply on it. I can only pray, May God be with you, and give you comfort. I am, with sincere wishes for your health and happiness, Sir,

"Your most obedient, humble servant,
"JOHN ROBISON.

"*Robt. Haldane, Esq., of Airthrey.*"

The Professor's public retractation of his error was not so handsome and complete as he had promised. He was ashamed to proclaim to the world the full extent of the error into which he had been betrayed, by collecting promiscuous gossip, and publishing it under the title of "Proofs of a Conspiracy." It may give some idea of the times, when it is remembered that the Professor's book was then actually held in high repute. But he was not the only person who urged the importance of encountering Infidelity at home rather than Paganism abroad. Whether all were as sincere in their exhortations as this learned and amiable but hot-tempered philosopher, may well be doubted. But, at all events, the advice was not thrown away either on Mr. Haldane or his younger brother; and like James Haldane's tour to the north, Rowland Hill's visit to Scotland had been one of its results. The express object of his coming was to open the Circus of Edinburgh as a place of preaching. It had been for some time used by a congregation belonging to the Relief Secession while their own chapel was rebuilding. During this interval the preaching of their minister, the Rev. Mr. Struthers, had attracted much attention, and the novelty of the place, as well as his eloquence, had drawn around him, out of all classes of the community, many who had not been previously accustomed to listen to the Gospel. Robert Haldane's own account of the opening of the Circus may be found in his "Address," so often cited. The following is an extract:—

"The next thing that took place among those plans which

seemed to have caused alarm, was the employment of the Circus as a place of worship, after it had been left by the Relief congregation, who first used it as such. A few persons, who wished to see the interests of religion more extended in Edinburgh, conversed together about forming a Tabernacle there,—a thought suggested by a minister from England (Mr. Simeon, it is believed), when on a visit to this place, not upon my invitation, but employed in preaching in the Established Churches. The general idea affixed to these houses called Tabernacles is that of large places of worship, where as great variety as possible is kept up in the preaching, by employing different ministers, in order to excite and maintain attention to the Gospel, especially in such as are living in open neglect of religion. Such are the different Tabernacles in London, to which, when they were erected about fifty years ago, very great opposition was made, and great alarm excited. Those of us who met to consult about this business were uncertain how such a plan might answer in Edinburgh. We therefore invited from England only three ministers at first. The Circus, as being a large and commodious place, was engaged for a few months, and Mr. Rowland Hill, so well and so long known in England as a successful and able preacher of the Gospel, opened the place. The multitudes that heard him, and the spirit of attention that seemed to be excited, encouraged us to go on."

It was on his way to open the Circus that Mr. Rowland Hill met Mr. J. A. Haldane and Mr. Aikman at Langholm. He left them on the morning of the 27th July, and on the day following his Journal announces his arrival. Mr. Haldane having then no residence in Edinburgh, Mr. Hill was received, as he says, " at the hospitable abode of Mr. James Haldane, in George-street,* where nothing was wanting but more gratitude and thankfulness on my part for such a kind and affectionate reception." Mrs. James Haldane fully appreciated the worth

* In the adjoining house, No. 14, George-street, there resided at that time Henry Brougham, the future Lord Chancellor of Britain. He was then in his twentieth year, having been born in 1778, in the house where David Hume died, in St. David-street, so named after the historian.

of the honoured guest, whom in her husband's absence she entertained, and always spoke with peculiar pleasure of this memorable visit.    Next morning Mr. Hill opened the Circus,— a fact which he thus announces in his Journal;—

" *Lord's-day, July* 29.—Preached for the first time in the Circus.   The building is large, and supposed to contain above 2,500 people.   It gave me pleasure to find that expounding, or *lecturing,* as it is there called, is the general practice in Scotland. The richness and glory that rest upon the language of inspiration are peculiar to itself; and I have always found that weighty, warm, applicatory remarks immediately therefrom come with a peculiar influence to the heart.   Surely, therefore, nothing less than a whole chapter, or at least a considerable portion, should be selected for these occasions.   We are never so assured that we make people wise unto salvation as when we lead them to the pure Word of God itself.

" My morning subject was the prayer of Moses, ' If thy presence go not with me, carry us not up hence.' (Exodus xxxiii. 15.)   I preached to the people the feelings of my heart. I felt the call to this city to be solemn and important.   Without our God we can do nothing.   A much larger congregation attended the evening service, and I took another subject just suited to the frame of my own mind, 1 Cor. i. 22—24 ; and I employed some time in showing Paul's method of treating his proud Corinthian hearers."

On the Thursday Mr. Hill preached to 2,000 people at Leith, in the open air.   His text was, " The Son of man is come to seek and to save that which was lost; " and he adds, " Plain language is the only profitable language for sinners like these." On Friday, he preached to 4,000 on the Calton Hill.   He observes, " The loveliness of the situation, the stillness of the evening, and the seriousness of the people, produced all that was desirable.   Oh, for more of the life and unction and power of the Spirit of God on my soul, that I may not disgrace the blessed cause I wish to uphold."

Such was the commencement of the preaching in the Circus, which produced so much excitement, but was so little intended to interfere with the stated places of worship that the early service at first began in the morning at seven o'clock, and another in the evening at six o'clock.

It was arranged, however, that Mr. Hill should not be idle during the week, and "Mr. (Robert) Haldane," says the Journal, "kindly commenced my companion in travel." Stirling was the first place to which Mr. Hill was conducted by his friend, who had then scarcely left his own place in the neighbourhood. Crieff, Dunkeld, and Perth were the next towns where Mr. Hill preached in this their first circuit. At Perth he met his old friend, the Rev. Mr. Garie, at one time the Chaplain to the excellent Lady Glenorchy, of whom Mr. Hill observes: "He is a man universally respected, not being less pure and holy in his life and conversation than evangelical and sacred in his views of the Gospel." He had been licensed as a probationer of the Church of Scotland, but was not permitted to enjoy its preferments. Through the recommendation of two noblemen, he was presented to the Crown living of Brechin, but his evangelical sentiments and holy life rebuked the levity and indifference of the Moderate ministers. His sentiments were therefore opposed, and he was ultimately rejected by the General Assembly, on the pretext that he had not passed through the seven years' academical attendance then required at the Scotch universities. This case produced a strong sensation. It was the means of inducing the purchase of the chapel for the use of Mr. Garie, which ultimately became the exclusive property of Mr. Haldane.

From Perth the itinerants proceeded to Kinross, where Lord and Lady Balgowny were amongst those who listened to Mr. Hill, as he preached to a large congregation under a rising ground on the banks of Lochleven. Having returned to Edinburgh on the Saturday after this rapid tour, he preached again in the Circus, and set off with Mr. Haldane on Monday morning, so as to be in time to preach in the evening in the churchyard of the old cathedral of Glasgow. "The scene," he remarks, "was solemn. The old cathedral stands *externally* in perfectly good repair ; and much it is to the honour of the city that it should so stand, as it is the only one left in a perfect state of preservation in that part of the kingdom." "Underneath," he adds, were the remains, I may venture to say, of millions waiting for the resurrection. Here I stood on a widely-extended space, covered, or nearly covered, with the living,— all immortals, 5,000 I should suppose, at least. What solemn work to address such multitudes! Who is sufficient for these things? I attempted to illustrate that passage, Isaiah lx. 19, 'Thy God thy glory.' Could we but explain to sinners, and make them feel that God, a God in Christ is their glory, and that it is their privilege to glorify God in return, we should have more than abundant recompense for all our little toil in a work so glorious."

The above passage discloses something of the secret of Mr. Hill's usefulness as a preacher. Those who have merely amused themselves with anecdotes illustrative of his humour and eccentricities knew nothing of the man, nor of the power that accompanied the word that he proclaimed. Near the spot on which that sermon was preached by Rowland Hill is the vault which now contains all that was mortal of Robert Haldane. His dust reposes within the walls of that cathedral which Rowland Hill then surveyed with admiration, whilst he spoke with so much feeling of the millions of the dead who were there awaiting the trump of the archangel.

He finally returned to Edinburgh, on Saturday evening, in time to preach at the Circus, at seven o'clock in the morning, again at eleven o'clock, and in the evening, under the canopy of heaven. "It was now," he says, "quite out of the question to preach within doors on the Lord's-day evenings. On the Calton Hill I addressed the most solemn congregation I have seen for many years—fifteen thousand, on the most moderate computation, were said to attend, some suppose a larger multitude. I know on these occasions one principal aim should be to alarm the sinners. This I attempted from Mark viii. 36, 37, from the consideration of the immortality of the soul, and the awfulness of eternity.

Mr. Hill had now officiated for three Lord's-days at the Circus, but he was disposed to make another tour through

Fife to Dundee, returning by St. Andrew's. " Hitherto I was
favoured with Mr. Haldane as my companion in travel. His
brother, Mr. James Haldane, was the kind friend who next
conducted me to other parts of the country. Our first visit was
to Melville House, the seat of the Earl of Leven, who scarcely
three months before had lost his venerable Countess. On the
Lord's-day he again preached in the Circus and on the Calton
Hill to great congregations, the latter supposed to amount to
15,000 or 20,000. On the following Tuesday he was, from
fatigue, unable to preach at Musselburgh. " Mr. James
Haldane," he says, " kindly undertook that office on my behalf."
His account of his last Lord's-day in Edinburgh is a picture of
Rowland Hill, his earnestness, his sincerity, and zeal, his quaint-
ness, and yet his realizing views of eternity, and his dedication
of himself to Christ :—

" *Lord's-day, September* 2d.—My last Sabbath in Edinburgh. The
Circus could scarcely contain the early or noon congregation. I conceived the most serious part of the hearers came together like those of
old, ' Early, my God, will I seek thee.' I therefore dealt with them from
that fine prayer of the Apostle Paul, Ephesians iii. 16—19. Reader,
mark that prayer; who can tell the worth of a Bible, if it were only for
the sake of those four verses—who can describe the blessedness of the
man who feels and enjoys its sacred contents?

" At the second service, I preached from Genesis xlviii. 22, 23, 24, on
Joseph's blessing. I thought the subject would well suit the lecture. It
is time that simple-hearted ministers should bestir themselves. Once was
I young, but now I begin to be old. I never had too much of the Seraph,
but always too much of the snail, having been shot at by many an angry
archer; though I fell so short, I was willing to encourage a young Society
to itinerate far and wide. May their zeal, guided by the Saviour's wisdom,
surprise the north : that many a dry formalist may blush for shame under
the humiliating reflection, how little has been done by them, while so
much has been accomplished by instruments they so completely despise !
May these be blessed with the boldness of the lion—the meekness of the
lamb—the wisdom of the serpent—and the harmlessness of the dove.

" On the evening of the day I preached my last sermon save one in this
vicinity on the Calton Hill (to 18,000). Shame forbade me a thousand
times to take a text, once the language of Paul, Acts xx. 24. I believe,
however, that a spark was felt of the same flame which he enjoyed, therefore I ventured. Had I a thousand lives, I trust they would be spent in
the Lord's blessed work. I dare not be fettered by human laws while I

am under a Divine command to preach the Gospel to every creature, and to spend and be spent for Jesus Christ.'

"I have been somewhat a sufferer by such a conduct, but laws like these appear to me not better than the statutes of Omri, and I dare not renounce the Lord's *standing* rule to all his ministers, while under the conjoined promise, 'I am with you always, even to the end of the world.'"

On the 3d of September he set off for England, "favoured with the company of Mr. Haldane." At Dunbar, after he had preached in the Methodist meeting-house, "Mrs. Cunningham," he proceeds, "came to meet us on that occasion, and took us home in her carriage. Mr. Cunningham, though a gentleman of fortune, dedicated himself to the work of the ministry, and for many years has laboured in connexion with the Antiburghers. We found the order of the house to be hospitality and friendship to the very utmost."

It was on this occasion and at this place, that a circumstance occurred, which, with many exaggerations and embellishments, has been related as an illustration of the eccentricities of Rowland Hill. The story shall be told as related by Robert Haldane, with his usual accuracy. On the Wednesday morning, after spending the preceding night at Mr. Cunningham's, they were about to proceed southward, when Mr. Hill's carriage being brought to the door, his horse was found to be dead lame. A farrier was sent for, who, after careful examination, reported that the seat of the mischief was in the shoulder; that the disease was incurable, and that they might shoot the poor animal as soon as they pleased. To this proposal Mr. Hill was by no means prepared to accede. Indeed, it seemed to Mr. Haldane as precipitate as the conduct of an Irish sailor on board the Monarch, who, on seeing another knocked down senseless by a splinter, and supposing his companion to be dead, went up to Captain Duncan, on the quarter-deck, in the midst of the action with Languara off St. Vincent, and exclaimed, "Shall we jerk him overboard, Sir?" On that occasion the sailor revived in a short time, and was even able to work at his gun. In the present instance the horse, too, recovered, and was able to carry his master on many a future errand of mercy. Meanwhile, however, the travellers availed themselves of Mr. Cunningham's hospitality, and remained for two days more at his place, near Dunbar. In the evening Mr. Hill conducted family worship, and after the supplications for the family, domestics, and friends, added a fervent prayer for the restoration of the valuable animal, which had carried him so many thousands of miles, preaching the everlasting Gospel to his fellow-sinners. Mr. Cunningham, who was remarkable for the staid and orderly, if not stiff, demeanour, which characterized the Anti-burghers, was not only surprised but grieved, and even scandalized at what he deemed so great an impropriety. He remonstrated with his guest. But Mr. Hill stoutly defended his conduct by an appeal to Scripture, and the superintending watchfulness of Him without whom a sparrow falls not to the ground. He persisted in his prayer during the two days he continued at Dunbar, and although he left the horse in a hopeless state, to follow in charge of his servant, by easy stages, he continued his prayer night and morning, till one day at an inn in Yorkshire, while the two travellers were sitting at breakfast, they heard a horse and chaise trot briskly into the yard, and looking out, saw that Mr. Hill's servant had arrived, bringing up the horse perfectly restored. Mr. Hill did not fail to return thanks, and begged his fellow-traveller to consider, whether the minuteness of his prayers had deserved the censure which had been directed against them.

At Berwick, Alnwick, Newcastle, Durham, Leeds, Rotherham, and Sheffield, Mr. Hill successively preached, sometimes in chapels, sometimes in churches, and sometimes in the open air, especially at Newcastle, where thousands congregated near the city walls. From Sheffield they travelled by Derby, Coventry, Warwick, Painswick, to Wotton-under-Edge, in Gloucestershire, which was Mr. Hill's home during the six months in the year that he spent out of London.

During his journey with Mr. Hill through Scotland and into Gloucestershire, Robert Haldane had been deeply pondering on all that he saw and heard with reference to Mr. Whitfield's plans for the revival of the Gospel in England. It became more and more his desire to attempt something of a decided character for Scotland. His younger brother's movement in the previous year, and the increasing success which was attending him as a preacher, still further stimulated his zeal, and passing through London, he therefore proceeded to Gosport, to consult his old friend, Dr. Bogue, as to the aspect of affairs in relation to the kingdom of Christ, and his own future operations. The Indian Mission was fully and finally abandoned, and plans for building a number of chapels throughout Scotland and educating preachers, were resolved on and discussed, as is shown by Mr. Haldane's correspondence, and the events which soon afterwards took place. Nor were the poor African children overlooked, as appears from the following letter to Mr. Campbell at this time, in consequence of a communication which that good man had received from Mr. Macaulay :—

*" Gosport, October 6th,* 1798.

" MY DEAR SIR,—I was favoured with your letter of the 24th September, which had lain some days here before I arrived, and it gives me great joy to be informed of its contents. I trust the Lord indeed intends to use us as instruments in this business; and, oh! that he may, by means of it, glorify Himself by giving these children the adoption of sons and daughters in his own family, and in making use of them to awaken and enlighten others who are sitting in great darkness and under the black shadow of death in their own country.

" Mr. Macaulay's letter is a very sensible one, and he seems cordially to enter into the plan, and also to think this time the fittest that could be chosen. Indeed, how could it be otherwise, if (as I trust) it has been fixed by Him who does all things well?

" I think it a favourable circumstance that he has most of the children with him, as he will be best able to judge of natural tempers and disposi- tions. I forget the age we fixed upon, but think about twelve years old the best; and he seems to say the same, towards the end of his letter. Were they to come much earlier they might forget their native tongue, which I should consider a great loss. It will be of the greatest conse- quence that most of them be the children of the chief people in the country, and who are most likely to succeed in the Governments, as they, in the course of Providence, will have much more in their power in diffusing the knowledge, both of Divine truth and of civilization, than a great number of any other rank. They may make as good smiths and carpenters at Sierra Leone as at Edinburgh, but the manners of civilized life, which are intimately connected with the diffusion of the Gospel, can be best learned here. I am persuaded Mr. M. must be very sensible of this. Tell him, by no means, if possible, to fall below the number fixed, but rather to exceed it. I do not think, however, that the number of girls should be much increased, as there are many temptations in their way, and it would increase the expenses, as the mode of their education must differ. . . . .

" If possible, there should be some provision for ten or twelve following every year, to make a regular rotation and keep it up; but all these things we must leave to Mr. M., and it is happy we are in so good hands. *At all events, I repeat it, he may exceed, but let him not come short of the number.* So much for Africa.

" You say that churches were provided in Glasgow. *It would be much better if you would provide fields.*

" Yours, &c.,

"ROBERT HALDANE."

Mr. Campbell, in his " Autobiography," states, that " for two long years he heard not a syllable from Africa." But this only shows how little reliance is to be placed on history depending on the memory of an individual writing after a long interval. The letter from Mr. Haldane, guaranteeing the payment of all the charges, still exists, and is dated 30th March, 1798. Within six months from that date Mr. Macaulay's reply to Mr. Campbell had arrived, and it will presently be seen that Mr. Campbell found the children in London in the month of June, 1799.

Soon afterwards a little volume containing a journal of Mr. Hill's tour was published by that zealous clergyman, and gave great offence. It consisted of two parts; the first of which contained the dedication to " Robert Haldane, Esq.," as the person at whose invitation he both ventured on his visit to Scotland and now printed his " Journal." It concludes thus :—

" I trust, my dear Sir, it is the prayer of my heart that you may be blessed with the most abundant success in all your attempts to promote the glory of God and the salvation of mankind. And may your brother and his worthy colleague, Mr. Aikman, in their disinterested zeal and the devotedness of their spirits, continue to preach Jesus among thousands in those parts where multitudes are perishing in complete ignorance, till they are crowned with all the success their hearts could wish.

" I am, with much affection,

" Yours, in the love and fellowship of the Gospel,

" ROWLAND HILL."

The second part, which contained his strictures, both on the Established and Secession Churches in Scotland, was that which gave most umbrage; and it was prefaced by the following characteristic dedication, which embodies so much of eccentric humour with solemn seriousness as to afford a better portraiture of the mind and character of Rowland Hill than many of the elaborate efforts of affectionate biographers. It is addressed,

*" To James Haldane, Esq.*

" MY DEAR SIR,—Or rather, my much respected brother and fellow-labourer in the Gospel of God our Saviour! Directed by my high esteem of your brother, I ventured on the publication of my ' Journal.' From my respect to your ministerial labours, I am now happy to address these remarks on my visit to Scotland to your more immediate attention. I am now *an old stager* in the itinerant's work, and I bless God for the line in which I have been called, being assured I have followed the will of God therein; and I am satisfied the salvation of many souls has been promoted thereby.

" In preaching through England, Scotland, Ireland, and Wales, I always conceived *I stuck close to my parish.* We are to ' preach the Gospel to every creature, even to the end of the world.' Go on, my dear Sir, be the maul of bigotry, and of every sectarian spirit among all denominations; declare vengeance against the unscriptural innovations of narrow-minded bigots, who, finding the Word of God uncompliant to designs like theirs, have combined together to support their dogmas, according to certain rules of their own creating; and all these as contrary to the sacred designs of God, that all Christians should be brethren and love as such, as the designs of Christianity can be to those of Mahomet, the Pope, or the devil.

" In the name of God, my beloved brother, with the sword of the Spirit in your hand and the life of God in your heart, pursue those hideous monsters even unto death.

" But you have given sufficient evidence how much you respect the Christian wheresoever you find him and however disfigured, not only by the wart, but by the wen of bigotry.

" I will not say that to a fraction all my observations on this subject may correctly comport with yours, though I flatter myself you and I are pretty near the mark, if we differ. I am sure we cannot disagree. Our hearts, I am persuaded, are congenial, though our original calling was completely different.

" You were educated for the maritime life, and from a situation creditable and lucrative, commenced a *peddling preacher*, crying your wares from town to town at a low rate, indeed ' without money and without price,' and scattering religious tracts as you travel from place to place; while it was my lot to be bred to the trade and to serve a regular apprenticeship for the purpose; but, being spoilt in the manufacturing, I never received but forty shillings—a story too trivial to relate—by my own occupation as a Churchman. Affluence is a snare; a decent independent competence is a blessing,—a blessing, indeed, if thereby we can preach Jesus freely, and prove to the poor of the flock that we can sacrifice our own profit if we can be profitable to them.

" Let it, then, be our glory to suffer shame and contempt for the sake of Him who 'hid not his face from shame and spitting' for our redemption; 'holding forth the Word of life amidst the dead in trespasses and sins;' meekly contented to suffer even 'the loss of all things,' should we meet with such a day of tribulation, provided we are but enabled 'to win Christ' and are blessed 'with souls for our hire.'

" With much sincerity of affection, I am, and ever hope to remain, your affectionate brother and fellow-labourer in the Gospel of our salvation,                  " ROWLAND HILL."

Mr. Hill was, by education and by principle, attached to an Established Church, and esteemed the Church of England, with its Articles, Liturgy, and Formularies, far beyond any other denomination; but it was such " a reduced Episcopacy" that he desired " as was recommended by the Archbishops Usher and Leighton." He greatly preferred it to Scottish Presbytery; and, referring to the Cameronians, denounced the old Solemn League and Covenant, as containing more of bigotry and persecution than the Act of Uniformity. He then glances at the Secession Church, founded by the two Erskines; afterwards divided amongst themselves into Burghers and Anti-burghers, with reference to the lawfulness or unlawfulness of the Burgess oath. The Relief Secession comes next under review; a body that arose out of the grievance of patronage, and which then contained 67 congregations, whilst the Burghers had 123, and the Anti-burghers 125.

Having dealt somewhat roughly with the peculiarities and " bigotry" of all the Presbyterian bodies, he devotes a passing note to the Scottish Episcopalians, which was, of course, at that time anything but complimentary. He describes them as allied to the *Moderates* in their evangelical doctrine, and adds, " As a proof of this, that good and truly spiritual and respectable man, Mr. Simeon, of Cambridge, being asked to preach but once in their chapels, after one sample given was asked no more, though he strictly adhered to a most regular conduct, so far as only preaching in the Established churches deserves that name. And, if the prevailing whisper be true, he is, on the next Meeting of the General Assembly, likely to meet with a very coarse compliment for his regularity. Not that the thunder-bolt of their high priestly indignation will be levelled directly against him,—a slant stroke will do the business the most effectually."

Having also lashed "the Moderates" in the Church of Scotland, describing them as "*moderate in religion*," "*moderate* in their notions of Christ," "*moderate* in their use of their Bibles," "*moderate* in their love to God," and practically teaching the people to be "*moderate* in their morality," he next assails the Baptists and Independents, concerning whom, as his "brethren," he expresses his thankfulness that they had never been, as yet, favoured with the "civil sword," and therefore never tempted to persecute. He considers Congregationalism to be a modern innovation, which took its first rise in the Church at the beginning of the seventeenth century, when good men, disgusted with the turbulent political preachers of the times, were induced to retire from the strife and congregate amongst themselves.

Scarcely has he done with the faults of his "Independent and Baptist brethren" than Mr. Hill turns round once more on the High Church Episcopalians, blames their unwarrantable pretensions to apostolic succession, and states the advantage of reviving the injunction : "Exhort one another daily while it is called to-day." "By this primitive mode of procedure," he adds, "a great number of very valuable ministers have been raised up, some from the army, others from the navy. We bless God for the names of a Captain Scott and a Captain Joss; for captains may have tongues and brains and grace as well as doctors; and men of inferior ranks in the same line, if not superior, have been equal to them in a wise conduct, a holy walk, and extended usefulness in the ministry of the word.

Others also shall I mention? Stonemasons, butchers, tailors, shopkeepers, and shoemakers, and a certain tinker, who lived a century and a-half ago (the Right Rev. Bishop Bunyan, the apostle of Cambridgeshire and Bedfordshire, and, though a Baptist, admitted all to communion with him whom he believed to be children of God),—all of whom gave evidence that grace, good sense, and knowledge of the Word of God, may so far possess the minds of plain mechanics, as to render them abundantly useful, at least *in their own sphere,*" &c.

Having thus launched out into a variety of animadversions on Episcopalians and Presbyterians, Baptists and Independents, all of whom he considers as having some shred of Popery, which he terms the "incurable abomination," Mr. Hill proceeds to give his advice as to what should be done for Scotland. "If," he says, in Edinburgh, "another place of worship should be built, what should be its glory? Let it embrace all who love the Lord Jesus, and be the centre of union among them who are now disunited. Let it, then, be called the Union Church, and let her prove she deserves the name. Let her pulpit be open to all ministers who preach and love the Gospel, and her communion equally open to all who love the Lord Jesus in sincerity. I would allot at least half the area of the church to the poor, that they may attend it with as much freedom as they attend a field preaching."

Other admonitions he gives as to an ideal Church, which was to be a kind of Evangelical Alliance of all the disciples of Christ. It was in journeying with Rowland Hill that Robert Haldane conceived the idea of opening other places of worship at Glasgow and Dundee as well as at Edinburgh. So far as these schemes were confined to the conversion of sinners, they were blessed in a way which commended them, in a greater or less degree, to the approbation of such men as Mr. Newton, Mr. Simeon, and Mr. Scott. But so far as they involved a new system of ecclesiastical polity, in the end they signally failed. To the poor the Gospel was preached; sinners were saved, and Christ was glorified. But when new Churches were established on the fancied model of primitive times, they only flourished for a time. In 1799, the Home Missionaries braved the artillery of the General Assembly's pastoral admonition, fulminated against them like a Bull from the Vatican, and they rose unscathed from the anathemas levelled at them by the Presbyterian seceders. It was when opposition from without died away that the internal instability appeared. The sequel of this narrative will exhibit the self-devoted zeal of men of God, and may stimulate others to multiply Home Missions and Scripture-readers. But probably it will rather tend to abate the ardour of those who, like Rowland Hill in 1798, think it as easy to reform wisely as to censure sharply, to apply the antidote as well as to indicate the disease, whether practical or theoretic, in any system of ecclesiastical polity.

One other observation shall close this chapter, and it comes from the pen of an able and distinguished writer, who has enjoyed the best opportunities of knowing the religious state of Scotland, at the end of the last century. It is contained in the following sentence borrowed from the " Quarterly Review."* It is as follows:—

" We should be sorry to malign either the living or the dead; but it is our deliberate opinion, that with the exception of France, there was not a more infidel country on the face of the earth than Scotland sixty or seventy years ago; and we further believe that she was mainly indebted for this bad distinction to the active exertion of her professors, and the indifference, disguised under the title of *moderation*, which generally distinguished the teaching of her more accomplished and influential clergy."

This opinion demands only one qualification. The infidelity of the professors and of the Moderates, although it had tainted the upper classes of society, had not penetrated to the masses, amongst whom there still remained the traces of that faith which characterized their forefathers. Whilst the field preachers were assailed by Synods and Presbyteries, " the common people heard them gladly."

* " Quarterly Review," vol. xci., p. 405.

# CHAPTER X.

[1799.]

THE plan for educating the children of African chiefs was but an episode in the midst of Mr. Haldane's efforts for the extension of the kingdom of Christ. His correspondence on his journey with Mr. Hill shows how his mind was directed towards the objects and welfare of the Circus and of the Society for Propagating the Gospel at Home. Mr. Bennett, of Rumsey, Mr. Parsons, of Leeds, Mr. Boden, of Sheffield, Mr. Burder, of Coventry, Mr. Slatterie, of Chatham, Mr. Simpson, of Hoxton, Mr. Taylor, of Ossett, Mr. Griffin, of Portsea, are amongst the names of those honoured men who were invited to preach in the Circus. Of these, the venerable Dr. Bennett alone survives, after a life of labour still devoted to the cause of the Gospel. The difficulty, however, of obtaining a regular supply of ministers was considerable, and for the Society suitable Evangelists could not easily be found. It was under these circumstances that, when in England in the year 1798, Mr. Haldane conceived the idea of educating a number of pious young men for the ministry, who might be selected, as in primitive times, from the various occupations of life, on account of their piety and promising talents, to receive instruction. Natural ability was to be one requisite, but evidences of a state of grace were to be the first and indispensable consideration. With the exception of his brother, the only person to whom he at first communicated his intention was Mr. Campbell ; and at the end of the letter, dated 6th October, 1798, already cited, relative to the African children, he thus writes :—" I intend to give one year's education to ten or twelve persons, of any age that may be fit for it, under Mr. Bogue, with a view to the ministry. Will you and my brother be looking out for suitable persons to be ready by the time I return ? " This marks the origin of those seminaries for preparing Evangelists, which he afterwards carried out on so large a scale.

But there was another circumstance connected with Mr. Haldane's visit to England which was contemporaneous and associated with the institution of the Seminary, namely, the erection of places of worship, after the manner of Whitfield's tabernacles, in different parts of Scotland. He reckoned that he might certainly calculate on his brother to supply the Edinburgh tabernacle, whilst possibly Mr. Ewing and Mr. Innes might occupy two other chapels, the one to be provided or erected in Glasgow, the other in Dundee.

The announcement of Mr. Haldane's determination to erect tabernacles, after the Whitfield model, in the great towns in Scotland, was followed by events which added to the prevailing excitement in the public mind. No sooner had he returned from Gosport, than, after fully conferring with his brother, he next proposed his plans to Mr. Ewing and Mr. Innes. On the 29th of November a sermon was preached by Mr. Ewing, in Lady Glenorchy's Chapel, Edinburgh, on the duty of implicit obedience to human authority in civil matters, although, in regard to religion, Christians ought only to obey God; and on the Saturday following, December 1st, Mr. Ewing relinquished his charge, and the communion of the Church of Scotland. Next Lord's-day that minister remained in retirement, but on the 14th of December he undertook a short tour to Dunkeld, from which Mr. James Haldane had just returned, bearing the tidings of a large spiritual harvest. Mr. Ewing's secession, although thus sudden at the last, was not wonderful; for no one can even now peruse his earliest contributions to the "Missionary Magazine" without seeing that his principles in regard to Ecclesiastical polity, like those of his Baptist friend, Dr. Stuart, strongly tended to Congregationalism. The storm that had been excited against Mr. Simeon, Mr. Hill, the Itinerants, and the Circus, probably quickened his movements, and his adhesion to Mr. Haldane's plan, in regard to Glasgow, was sealed by his resignation. A few days afterwards, about twelve of those principally interested in the Circus and the Society for Propagating the Gospel at Home, including the two brothers, Mr. Ewing, Mr. Aikman, Mr. Campbell, Mr. George Gibson, and Mr. John Ritchie, began to meet in private for consultation, when, after prayer and deliberation, they resolved to form themselves into a Congregational Church. Mr. Ewing, as most familiar with such matters, was requested to draw out a plan for its government, and, after repeated conferences, they with one voice invited Mr. J. A. Haldane to be their pastor. Hitherto he had aspired to no other office than that of an Evangelist, preaching in the villages round Edinburgh, when not engaged in distant and extensive tours, and more recently drawing around him crowds of attentive listeners on the Calton Hill. For the office of an Evangelist he had been, so to speak, consecrated or set apart, by the prayers of the Rev. David Black. But having given himself wholly to the study of the word, "meditating upon these things," he had become "mighty in the Scriptures;" "his profiting had appeared to all;" whilst his unction in prayer, the solemn and unpretending eloquence of his pointed, direct, and telling addresses, his persevering zeal and remarkable success, his unwearied attendance on the sick, and his spotless consistency of practice, seemed to mark him out as "a man full of faith and of the Holy Ghost," well qualified for the pastoral office. It was not, however, without deliberation that he accepted the call, nor until he had explained that he considered his own gifts to be better adapted for the duties of an Evangelist. But the call being persisted in, he yielded to what he deemed the voice of Providence, and assumed a post from the labours and responsibilities of which he never shrunk for the remaining fifty-two years of his active and useful life.

Mr. Aikman, who was one of the few who composed the original Circus Church, and was afterwards himself ordained co-pastor, has given the following account of its formation :—

"The chief principle which influenced the minds of the brethren who, I believe, constituted the majority of the small company first associated for observing Divine ordinances in the Circus, was the indispensable necessity of the people of God being separated in religious fellowship from all such societies as permitted visible unbelievers to continue in their communion. This was a yoke under which we had long groaned; and we hailed, with gratitude to God, the arrival of that happy day when we first enjoyed the so much wished for privilege of separating from an impure communion, and of uniting exclusively with those whom it was meet and fit that we should judge to be all the children of God. Some of our dearest brethren, however, did not unite with us on this principle. They were attached, indeed, to the fellowship of the saints, and would by no means consent to the admission of any amongst us, who did not appear to be such ; yet they were not then convinced of the absolute unlawfulness of their continuing in connexion with societies confessedly impure. Our brethren were well aware of our decided difference of sentiment, not only respecting the great inconsistency, but also unlawfulness, of any persons connected with us continuing to go back to the fellowship of those societies from which they had professed to separate, and they knew that our forbearance did not imply any approbation of this conduct. Persuaded, however, that they did not intend by this to countenance anything they judged to be contrary to the mind of Christ, we deemed it our duty to forbear, in the hope that that Saviour, whom we trusted it was their supreme desire to serve and to please, would grant us the happiness of being likeminded in this as in our other views of promoting the honour of His adored name."

The simplicity of the motives which influenced these holy men can never be disputed by those who marked their public course, or more narrowly watched their private walk with God. But whether the attempt succeeded,—whether it even secured that purity of communion after which they panted,—is a question which it might not be difficult to answer, but one which it is not the object of these pages to discuss.

Nearly three years subsequent to the opening of the Circus as a place of worship, Mr. Robert Haldane gives the following account of it in his "Address to the Public:"—

"After some time a Church was formed, of which, at first, we had no intention. The Gospel continues to be preached in the Circus to this day in an earnest and faithful manner. With respect to the doctrines taught, they are essentially the same as those contained in the Confession of Faith, and in the Articles of the Church of England, and preached by those in the Church of Scotland denominated Evangelical or Gospel ministers. The form of Church government is what has been called Congregational, a form long known and acted upon in England. A strict discipline is maintained. The characters of all persons admitted as Church members are particularly examined, and great numbers have been rejected, either from ignorance of the Gospel, or from not appearing to maintain a becoming walk and conversation. Disloyalty, as being one of those things which are contrary to the express precepts of Scripture and to the spirit of Christianity, would be a complete disqualification, and some have been rejected on this very ground. The Church members are exhorted to watch over each other in love; if any one be overtaken in a fault, he is reproved, but if convicted of departing from the faith of the Gospel, of deliberate immorality, or allowed and continued indulgence in sin, he is put away, and restored only upon credible proofs of repentance. Such regulations we believe to be according to Scripture, and calculated to promote edification.

"After a trial for a considerable time, I must say I rejoice in this Institution. Many advantages, I think, have attended it. At the Circus the seats are free to all; the ministers at present who officiate, either statedly, or occasionally, as those from England in summer, receive no pay for their labours, and all sorts of people are welcome, without either expense or inconvenience. By this means many in Edinburgh, I believe, have attended the worship of God, who, although they could afford it, would not have been at the trouble to procure a seat in any church where they are let. I have heard of several such people coming first from curiosity, or because they got a place without difficulty or expense, who afterwards have become sensible of the value of the preaching of the Gospel. I have heard of others who had been violent in their political sentiments, and abusive against the Government (not belonging to the Circus Church, for such would not be admitted there, but among the hearers), who, after attending there some time, have learned to respect lawful authority, 'to forbear speaking evil of dignities,' and to turn their attention from other men's faults to the corruptions of their own hearts. I have understood that ale-houses had been emptied and shut up, which used to be full on the Lord's-day, by the frequenters of them going to the Circus. There are, besides, many serious people who attend regularly, from deliberate preference of it to other places. In the evenings, also, a large place is thus open when most other churches are shut, and many stragglers occasionally drop in. Upon the other hand, I am often grieved when I think of the difficulty of procuring seats, almost to the total exclusion of the poor, in many churches of Edinburgh; and that so many of these, especially when they are collegiate charges, are shut up in the evenings, when they might be occupied, and the seats free. I am sure I shall be happy, as I often declare, to see the Circus thinned in the evenings, by more places of worship being opened. If good be done, and sinners converted to Jesus Christ, I care not where it may be."

The Tabernacle, or Circus Church, having been constituted in the month of January, 1799, no less than 310 persons almost immediately signified their desire to unite in its communion. Of these, however, thirty continued members of the Establishment, and only desired to be admitted occasionally to the Lord's table by their Circus brethren. Not a few of these 310 were persons who were first led to behold Christ as their Saviour by the preaching, in and around Edinburgh, of Mr. J. A. Haldane himself, or of Mr. Rowland Hill. But a very considerable number were old-established Christians, who had grown up under the admirable teaching of Dr. Erskine, Mr. Black, Dr. Colquhoun, Dr. Walter Buchanan, and other faithful ministers of the Established Church, who could not be expected to look with satisfaction on this secession.

Mr. J. A. Haldane's ordination took place on the 3d February, 1799, being the Lord's-day. It was an occasion memorable for its solemnizing influence, and the impression it produced upon crowds of spectators. A sketch, from the pen of Mr. Ewing, is given of this event in the " Missionary Magazine," from which the following extracts are taken :—

" On Sabbath, the 3d of February, Mr. James Haldane was ordained in the Circus of this city to be pastor of a Church which has been recently formed here on the Congregational plan, and in connexion with the institution of a Tabernacle. By desire of the Church, the service was conducted by Messrs. Taylor, of Osset, Yorkshire ; Garie, of Perth ; and Ewing of Edinburgh, ministers of the Gospel. Mr. Taylor began by giving out a part of Psalm cxxii. He then prayed, and read the following portions of Scripture, as suited to the peculiar occasion of the meeting, viz., Isaiah lxii., Ezek. xxxiii. 1—11, 1 Tim. iii.; after which he gave out the remainder of Psalm cxxii. He next introduced the solemn business of the day by preaching an appropriate sermon from John xviii. 36,— 'Jesus answered, My kingdom is not of this world; if my kingdom were of this world, then would my servants fight, that I should not be delivered to the Jews; but now is my kingdom not from hence.'

"After sermon, Mr. Ewing gave out the 64th hymn of the second book of Dr. Watts's hymns, entitled ' God the glory and the defence of Sion.'

"Mr. Garie, of Perth, next went into the pulpit, and after prayer and a short introduction, solemnly asked Mr. Haldane the following questions:—

"1st. As an unconverted ministry is allowed to be a great evil, will you, Sir, be pleased to favour us with some account of the dealing of God with your soul?

"2dly. Will you inform us what are the circumstances and motives which have led you to preach the Gospel, and to desire to engage in the work of the ministry?

"3dly. Will you favour us with your views of the leading truths of the Gospel?

"4thly. Will you explain your views and purposes respecting the duties and trials before you in the pastoral office?

" To these questions Mr. Haldane replied at considerable length, and in a manner that seemed to make a very deep and general impression. His account of the dealings of God with him contained a historical sketch of his whole life, in which there appears to have been many remarkable displays of providential mercy, as well as the most satisfying evidence of a saving change. His account of the circumstances and motives which concurred in leading him to preach the Gospel, were such as, in the unanimous opinion of the Church, and of many others, established a very clear call to the work of the ministry. The declaration of his faith was scriptural, explicit, and *uncommonly striking*. His views and purposes as to the work before him showed a strong sense of insufficiency, and a becoming dependance on promised Divine aid. Mr. Haldane here expressed his intention of endeavouring to procure a regular rotation of ministers to assist him in supplying the Tabernacle. He declared his willingness to open his pulpit for the occasional labours of every faithful preacher of the Gospel, of whatever denomination or country he might be. He signified his approbation of the plan of the Church which had chosen him for their pastor, as being simple and scriptural, but disavowed any confidence in it as a perfect model of a Church of Christ, to the exclusion of all others. He wished to remember himself, and ever to remind his hearers, that the kingdom of heaven was not meat and drink, but righteousness, and peace, and joy in the Holy Ghost. Finally, he declared that he meant not to confine his exertions to that Church, but to devote a portion of his time, every year, to the labours of itinerancy, to which he conceived himself, in the providence of God, to be especially called."

Thus far the " Missionary Magazine." Happily, the notes of Mr. James Haldane's answers to the ordination questions were found among his papers in a drawer, where they had lain undisturbed for nearly forty years. The substance of his reply to the first question concerning " God's dealings with his soul," has been already inserted in the account given of his early life and conversion to God, as well as the answer to the second question, as to his motives in engaging in the work of the ministry. He concludes : " The Church which has been lately formed were pleased to invite me to be their pastor. The charge I would accept, in dependance on the grace of Jesus Christ, not, however, relinquishing the idea of labouring as an itinerant, to which I think the Lord has especially called me."

Mr. Ewing states that the answers to the third question, in regard to views of doctrine, were uncommonly striking, but it is to be regretted that the notes are exceedingly scanty. Their brevity indicates how firmly the speaker already felt himself established in an acquaintance with the great truths of Scripture. The perfect inspiration and supreme authority of the Bible; the utter ruin and corruption of fallen man; his inability to save himself; the redemption of the sheep of Christ, his substitution and suretyship for the sheep given to him by his Father; the regenerating and sanctifying power and influence of the Holy Spirit—these and their kindred doctrines were then publicly avowed and held with unswerving consistency to the end.

The notes of his answer to the fourth question are as follows :—

" I consider the Christian life as a warfare. There is a constant struggle between the flesh and the Spirit, and renewed supplies of strength are constantly necessary from Jesus Christ. This is peculiarly the case in the ministerial work. No man is sufficient for these things. A minister, in an especial manner, should habitually cherish a spirit of humility and dependance on the Head of the Church. His situation and temptations are peculiar; he must not only keep his body under, and bring it into subjection, lest, preaching to others, he be himself cast away; but he must watch over the flock over which the Holy

Ghost has made him overseer, as one who would give an account. I do not expect my trials to be few, but to meet with many difficulties, especially if the Lord should honour me in the work. I should desire to give myself much to the Word of God and prayer, to study the Scriptures with attention, that my doctrine may ever be agreeable to the Word of God, and that I may rightly divide it, giving a portion to all who may attend my ministry. It should be my study to comfort the feeble-minded, and to lead the weak to the Rock of ages. I should endeavour to alarm the careless, reprove the backsliders, and to edify the body of Christ. To instruction, I should desire to add my example in every Christian grace, never rendering railing for railing, but in meekness, instructing those who oppose the truth. I should wish to act with tenderness to all who profess the faith of the Gospel, to possess much of that love, which thinketh no evil, and which covereth a multitude of sins. To bear with those who are weak in the faith, and may manifest an improper spirit on any occasion, to point out their error in love and meekness, and to be patient and gentle towards all men. To study to become acquainted with the cases of those amongst whom I minister, that I may speak to them a word in season, in public or private. To visit the sick and afflicted, and to sympathize with all, but especially with the friends of Jesus, as members of the same body. To study to maintain the ordinances of Christ pure. To study that discipline be maintained, without preferring one above another. To exhort or reprove, agreeably to the commands of Christ and his apostles, and especially to endeavour to cultivate a spirit of love, not only amongst our own members, but in myself and them towards every disciple of Jesus. I consider all Christians as members of one body, and that schisms and divisions consist in giving way to or cherishing a narrow party spirit. I consider the constitution of this Church to be plain and scriptural; but I dare not turn my back on those who, holding the Head, differ in lesser matters. I would desire to remember that the kingdom of God is not meat and drink, but righteousness; and that the Christian who is most spiritually-minded is acting most agreeably to the will of his Father in heaven. I value purity of communion as calculated to promote much spirituality; but can easily suppose, what often happens, that men, while gazing on, admiring, and adjusting the scaffolding, forget the building. I shall cheerfully bid every minister of Christ God speed, and hope our pulpits shall never be shut against any who teach the apostles' doctrine. Agreeably to our rules, I shall gladly receive, as an occasional communicant, every brother in Christ, whether he be of the Establishment, or of any other denomination of Christians. I shall endeavour to point out to parents, children, subjects, and others, their respective duties, and ever to maintain the necessary connexion of a knowledge and belief of the truth with purity and holiness. Finally, as it is proposed that a tabernacle should be united with the Church, I shall study to get supplies of such ministers as may be most calculated to rouse the careless, and edify believers. This will, of course, afford me time to preach the Gospel in the highways and hedges, which, I trust, I shall gladly embrace, testifying to all repentance towards God, and faith in our Lord Jesus Christ. I lay my account with trials and difficulties in the undertaking, but would desire to commit myself in well-doing to the God and Father of our Lord Jesus Christ, and to pray that, with all boldness, I may speak his word with success. Such are some of the important duties to which I think myself called. While I would consider myself bound to spend and be spent for Jesus, that I might win souls, I would remember that a special relation subsists between me and the Church now present. I would willingly account myself their servant, for Jesus' sake. I would crave their counsel, their love, and their prayer. I would put them in mind of the apostle's advice to the Church at Colosse, that they should say to their minister, in a spirit of love, Take heed to the ministry that thou hast received from the Lord, that thou fulfil it. After what I have said, I confess my unfitness for the work, and request the earnest prayers of my brethren in Christ, that I may find the grace of Jesus and his strength sufficient for me."

The narrative in the " Missionary Magazine" proceeds :—

" Having heard these full and edifying answers from Mr. Haldane, Mr. Garie turned to the Church, who were all seated round the pulpit, and asked an account of the steps they had taken in order to establish a pastoral relation between Mr. Haldane and themselves. Mr. Aikman, one of the members, having been appointed by the Church to answer this question, in the name of his brethren, rose, and stated, That it had long been the desire of several serious persons in this place to enjoy the benefit of Christian fellowship on a scriptural plan, and, at the same time to avoid that contracted spirit, which would exclude from the pulpit, or from occasional communion, any faithful preacher of the Gospel, or sincere lover of the Lord Jesus ; that some time ago, a number of the members present had, after frequent prayer and conference, agreed upon certain regulations, which appeared to them agreeable to the Word of God; and had thereupon formed themselves into a Church, by solemn prayer; giving themselves to the Lord, and to one another, to walk in Christian fellow-ship, and to observe all the ordinances appointed by Jesus Christ; that they then proceeded to the election of a pastor, and had unanimously chosen Mr. James Haldane, one of their number, to that office, and appointed his ordination to take place on that day, the 3d of February.

" Mr. Garie then addressed the Church again, and desired that if they still adhered to their choice of Mr. Haldane, and their desire that he should be their pastor, they should now signify that desire, by holding up their right hand. This being accordingly done by the members, Mr. Garie asked Mr. Haldane, after what he had heard and seen of the desire of his brethren respecting him, whether he would now finally declare his acceptance of their call ? This question being answered by Mr. Haldane in the affirmative, Mr. Ewing gave out Psalm cxxxii. 12, 17, while Mr. Garie descended from the pulpit, in order to engage in the ordination prayer. Mr. Haldane was then solemnly set apart to the work of the ministry, and to the pastoral office in that church, by prayer and imposi-tion of hands.

" After prayer, and giving Mr. Haldane the right hand of fellowship, Mr. Garie gave out the following hymn, entitled ' The People's Prayer for their Minister :'—

" With heavenly power, O Lord, defend
    Him whom we now to thee commend;
    His person bless, his soul secure,
    And make him to the end endure," &c.

" During the singing of this hymn, Mr. Ewing went to the pulpit, and, after prayer, preached a sermon from 1 Peter v. 1—4. At the conclusion of this sermon, he addressed himself particularly to the pastor, to the church, and to the congregation; and then closed the service in the usual manner. After the last prayer, he gave out three verses of the

fiftieth hymn of the second book of the Olney Hymns, entitled ' A Prayer
for Ministers.'

" The service lasted near five hours, during all which time a crowded
audience showed the deepest attention, and some seemed much affected.
We hope this was a token for good, and the beginning of many happy
days to this new-formed Church, while it may, perhaps, have been the
blessed occasion of awakening some who may yet be added to it."

Mr. James Haldane never aspired to be the leader of a sect.
His ambition was of a higher and holier order. But he was
the first minister of the first church formed among the new
Congregational Churches of Scotland. The biographer of Mr.
Ewing, who has written her Father's Life with filial affection,
bears the following pleasing and truthful testimony, derived
from contemporaries, as to " the state of things in Edinburgh,
particularly in connexion with the congregation and services of
the Circus :"—

" With many souls it was the season of first love; and even those who
had long known the grace of God in truth, looked back to it ever after, as
a time of life from the dead. There was a fervour of spirit; a love to
each other for the truth's sake; a delight in all the ordinances of the
Gospel, which makes it resemble more perhaps the Pentecostal period
in Jerusalem, than any that has succeeded it. The fear of singularity,
and the love of the world, seemed alike for the time to have lost their
power. The work of God in seeking the conversion of sinners, was made
the business of life." . . . " The multitudes, also, who crowded to the Circus,
the zeal and activity of those engaged in Sabbath-schools, and various
other useful institutions; the intelligence received from others, sent forth
to more distant labours : all these were animating in the highest degree.
They furnish in abundance topics for the most improving conversation,
while they become alike the source of thanksgiving and encouragement to
prayer." . . . " To warn, to beseech, or to exhort their fellow-sinners,
was a spontaneous, delightful employment; to describe the blessedness of
' peace with God, through our Lord Jesus Christ,' was but to express the
overflowing of their actual experience. And to crown all, they were at
peace among themselves."—*Life of Greville Ewing*, p. 186.

It would be delightful to linger over the memory of " those
times of refreshing," of which the recollection was so long
cherished by those associated with the Edinburgh Circus. As
yet there were no discussions about the order of primitive
churches, about their discipline, about modes of baptism, or

those other perplexing questions, which afterwards necessarily arose, and served to divert the force of that artillery, which was at first exclusively concentrated against the strongholds of Satan. There are now few survivors to speak from personal recollection of that memorable season. But there is only one testimony, borne both by the living and the dead, as to the fervour of devotion and the overflowing of Christian love, which marked the period. These were not the characteristics of a few fleeting weeks or months. They continued, more or less, for years, and the description of them will not soon be forgotten by those who were present at the commemoration of Mr. J. A. Haldane's Jubilee, in 1849, as given by the late Rev. Christopher Anderson. That venerable minister, who has now, too, gone to his rest, then stated that numbers were awakened or converted by almost every sermon, whilst even those who had themselves known the truth, looked back to the period as one of revival from spiritual deadness to a quickening life. The Circus first, and then the Tabernacle, were crowded by thronging multitudes, hanging upon the preacher's lips, joining with earnestness in the prayers, singing the praises of the Lord with their whole hearts, remaining during long services without wearying, and retiring in solemn silence, afraid, as it were, to desecrate the place where the Lord himself was present, and that presence was felt. Those tokens of a work of grace, extended far beyond the narrow limits of a sectarian inclosure. The impulse vibrated throughout Scotland, and served to reanimate the expiring flame of that noble Church, whose chosen emblem is still the bush that burns, but never is consumed.

Immediately Mr. James Haldane had agreed to officiate in Edinburgh, his brother proceeding on his original plan, next purchased the Circus in Jamaica-street, Glasgow, at a cost of 3000*l*., and converted it into a Tabernacle for a congregation, of which Mr. Ewing was to be the pastor. From Glasgow, Mr. Haldane, accompanied by Mr. Ewing, proceeded to Stirling, to propose to Mr. Innes the arrangement with regard to Dundee. Mr. Innes did not, at once, see it to be his duty to leave the Church of Scotland, but having been ordered, by a majority of the General Assembly to assist, personally, in the ordination of a minister, charged in open congregation as a profane swearer, he left the communion in which he could no longer continue with a good conscience, and availed himself of the offer made by Mr. Haldane.

"The Tabernacle of Glasgow," says Mr. Haldane, "was to be put into Mr. Ewing's hands during his incumbency. I promised to execute a deed for this purpose, and to fix his salary at 200*l.* a year, to arise out of the proceeds of the house. In order to make this salary the more secure, I was to become bound, in case of a short-coming, to pay the feu duty, or ground rent, the ordinary expenses, and the necessary repairs. On the 1st of December, after all the foregoing business was arranged, Mr. Ewing left Lady Glenorchy's Chapel, and began, January 2d, to teach the first class of students. In May, 1799, he removed to Glasgow, and, in the month of July following, I delivered to him the above-mentioned deed." It is necessary to add, that the surplus to arise from the Tabernacles at Glasgow and Dundee was not to belong to Mr. Haldane, but to be applied to the training and education of young men for the ministry of the Gospel in Scotland, under the superintendence of the two brothers, in unison with Mr. Innes and Mr. Ewing. As Mr. James Haldane declined to receive any salary, the whole of the income of the Edinburgh Tabernacle, after payment of expenses, was devoted to the Society for Propagating the Gospel.

It was Mr. Haldane's intention to have established his first seminary at Gosport; an intention which, had it been accomplished, would have been far more agreeable to his own feelings and conducive to Mr. Ewing's future usefulness and comfort. In the prospect of the Mission to India, Dr. Bogue, in his private correspondence, stated, that he considered his own long acquaintance and friendship with its chief, as indispensable to the stability of the plan. Mr. Haldane had, from boyhood, been familiar with Dr. Bogue, and regarded the veteran champion of the Gospel almost with filial affection. The friendship thus begun was cemented by Christian principle, and never was interrupted. Both were men of ardent mind, shrewd observation, deep sagacity, vigorous intellect, and determined will. Each was conscious of his own strength, remarkable for self-reliance, confidence in his own opinion, and a disposition rather to lead than to follow. But each was imbued with much, also, that was kind and gentle, as well as with a feeling of mutual respect, esteem, and forbearance. There was also on both sides great command of temper, and a tact which teaches a wise man how to maintain his independence, without showing jealousy lest it should be unintentionally assailed. Robert Haldane knew the points, in regard to which Dr. Bogue's scholastic theology and other attainments gave him an advantage. But Dr. Bogue also knew the strength of his younger friend, as well as Mr. Haldane's superior acquaintance with the world, and his advantages of position. There, consequently, was no jealousy between them, but, acting towards each other in the spirit of mutual esteem and Christian forbearance, they were enabled to journey on to the close of life, exhibiting, in relation to each other, how good men can even differ in opinion and still preserve, unbroken, the ties of friendship.

It was, however, ordered, that the young men should not go to Gosport. During the visit made to Glasgow and Stirling for the purpose of completing the arrangements about the Tabernacles, it was represented by Mr. Garie, and, with greater force, by Mr. Ewing, that if the students were sent to Hampshire, the friends of the new movement in Scotland would be exposed to that obloquy which attached to the exaggerated representations made of Dr. Bogue's liberal politics. Politics were the bugbear of the age; Mr. Haldane's had been attacked. Mr. Ewing was then without occupation, and the Glasgow circus could not be opened for six months. The objections to Dr. Bogue were plausible, and, with less than his usual caution, Mr. Haldane yielded a decided, though reluctant, consent to the remonstrances of his two fellow-travellers; and an immediate arrangement as to the students was deemed so urgent, that he agreed to place the first class under Mr. Ewing, even before he had the opportunity of consulting with his brother, according

to their uniform mutual practice.    It was unfortunate, both for
Mr. Haldane and Mr. Ewing, who were not at all calculated for
such mutual co-operation.    If anything were wanted to enhance
the character of Dr. Bogue, it is to be found in the fact, that,
although conscious of his own superior scholarship and experience, and by no means acquiescing in the wisdom of the
reasons which dictated this change of purpose, he nobly
merged all idea of personal advantage in the importance of
the sacred object which both had at heart.    Mr. Haldane
did, however, make compensation for the disappointment, by
procuring the institution of another class for students, to be
educated under his venerable friend, for the ministry in England.
Partly through his influence, and partly by his pecuniary aid,
ten young men were placed under the tuition of Dr. Bogue,
whose future character and usefulness, as the tutor of the
London Missionary Seminary, sufficiently refuted the objections
with which he was at first so often assailed.    When the name
of the Rev. John Angell James, of Birmingham, is mentioned
as one numbered amongst those whom Dr. Bogue always
termed "Mr. Haldane's students," at Gosport, it will be seen
that Dr. Bogue's political disqualifications were more imaginary
than real.    Of the Scotch students, the first class was placed
under Mr. Ewing's care, in Edinburgh.    It commenced with
twenty-four, all of these being Presbyterians, and none Congregationalists, in sentiment.    " Some of us," says Mr. Munro, of
Knockando, " belonged to the National Establishment, others
to the Relief, and not a few were Burghers and Anti-burghers.
The only qualifications for admission to the seminary were,
genuine piety, talents susceptible of cultivation, and a desire
to be useful to our fellow-sinners by preaching and teaching the
words of eternal life.    The grand object proposed by the zealous
originators * of the scheme was, to qualify pious young men
for going out literally to the highways and hedges to preach the

---

* The worthy writer of the above extracts, in using the word " *originators*," seems to imply that the origin of this benevolent scheme was to be
attributed to several.    Mr. Haldane never looked for human applause, or
for any earthly reward, and therefore was not disappointed when his

Gospel, unconnected with the peculiarities of any denomination." "Such," continues Mr. Munro, "were the materials placed under Mr. Ewing's tuition;" but he adds, with great *naiveté,* "before the termination of our prescribed course of study, we found ourselves decided and intelligent Congregationalists."

To this class the excellent Mr. Cowie, of Huntly, sent "four of his spiritual children." One of the first students was the Rev. Mr. Maclay, who went out as a missionary to America, and became a very useful and popular Baptist minister in New York. His eldest son is an eminent lawyer and Member of Congress in the United States.

The students were all maintained at Mr. Haldane's expense, according to a scale for each married and unmarried student, drawn up at the time by those well acquainted with such matters at Gosport and Rotherham. Before their admission they underwent a strict private examination as to their abilities and qualifications. But, next to the importance of engaging in the work on purely Christian principles, nothing was more strongly impressed upon their minds, than the assurance that there was no design to elevate them in their social position; that it was not intended to make gentlemen of such among them as were mechanics, but only catechists or preachers; and that, after their term of study was over, they must not look to their patron for support, but to their own exertions and the leadings of Providence. That this caution was needful must appear obvious to every observer of the ways of the world, and Mr. Haldane afterwards found that all his munificence was insufficient to protect him from the charge of covetousness. The Dundee Tabernacle was not opened till the 19th of October, 1800; but, during the interval, Mr. Haldane collected another class of

benevolence was either overlooked or unappreciated by those who experienced it. But it is due to his memory to state, that he was the *sole* originator of these academies. It was by him alone that the idea was first conceived, when away from Scotland. It was through his exclusive liberality that it was carried out. But for him years might have elapsed before it would have been attempted. And, when his bounty ceased to flow in this direction, it was long before anything systematic was done in the same way by the Congregational Churches.

missionary students and catechists, whom he placed under Dr. Innes, intending that these should also go to Glasgow to be instructed by Mr. Ewing for fifteen additional months. Their tutor, the venerable Dr. Innes, thus writes : " The second class was placed under my care for the first year at Dundee, in which the number was about *forty*. This class was transferred, in the second year of their studies, to Mr. Ewing, at Glasgow. The third class was also, for the first year, under my care. The number was twenty-two. This will give you some idea of the singularly *liberal*, I would say, *magnificent* scale, on which Mr. Haldane undertook to promote the preaching of the Gospel, as all of these students, in number more than sixty, were supported *entirely* at his own expense."

Dr. Innes adds, " In the Tabernacle at Dundee it was proposed that whilst the first part of the proceeds, to a certain amount, should go to the minister, yet the surplus, if any, should be devoted to the education of young men for the ministry. On one or two occasions the funds of the Tabernacle fell somewhat short of the amount specified, and I think it due to the memory of Mr. Haldane to say that that deficiency, though not a part of our agreement, he made up."

---

Whilst these arrangements were in progress Mr. Macaulay arrived in England, bringing with him twenty-four African children. The following is the narrative of Mr. Campbell :—

" At length," says Mr. Campbell, writing of the month of June, 1799, " a letter reached me one Monday morning, from Governor Macaulay, dated Portsmouth, informing me of his arrival there, and that he had twenty boys and four girls on board; and he expected that, by the time the vessel got round to London, I should be there to take them off his hands. I hastened with this intelligence to Mr. Haldane. In thirty hours after receiving the information of the children's arrival, I found myself seated in the London mail-coach, galloping to the south.

" I found that the African children had arrived a few days before me, and were lodging in a house behind a tavern at Clapham, where I soon visited them, and found there were twenty boys and four girls, all jet black, cheerful and happy. I walked with them across the Common to

Mr. Henry Thornton's. While going along, they scattered, chased and pushed each other, diverting themselves in the same way as a similar number of English boys would have done. On reaching Mr. Thornton's gate I counted their number, and found, as was uniformly the case afterwards on similar occasions, some were missing. It arose from companies dining in the neighbouring mansions, astonished to see a cloud of young Africans, sending out their men-servants to try and catch some of them, and bring them before them. When they observed me returning in search of the strayed, they always sent servants with them to meet me. People being pleased to look at them as curiosities, they fancied all were their friends, and most willingly went with any who asked them.

" I had a letter of introduction to the late Joseph Hardcastle, of whom I was to take counsel in anything relating to the Africans, and we almost settled for their passage to Edinburgh in a Leith smack. It was well we had not finished the bargain, for the next time I met Messrs. Thornton and Macaulay, I found they had learned that the small-pox was in Clapham, which rendered it indispensably necessary to have the children all inoculated, lest they should take it when on board of ship, and their lives be lost. Such a detention in London was very unexpected by me, but Mr. Hardcastle and I both saw the importance of the measure recommended ; wherefore I consented to wait till they should recover from the inoculation. They were soon all received into the Small-pox Hospital at St. Pancras."

It is to Mr. Macaulay's characteristic caution that the *inoculation* of the children is to be attributed. He had mentioned *inoculation* to their parents, and he preferred running a considerable risk, of which he had given notice, to a much smaller one, which he had not mentioned. But, in truth, the delay in sending down the children to Edinburgh had in it something more diplomatic than a dread of the small-pox. Mr. Macaulay had no doubt become alarmed at the ecclesiastical aspect of affairs in Edinburgh, and wished to detain the children at Clapham. He therefore objected to their education being under Mr. Haldane's sole management. The objection might, under the circumstances, have appeared to some equitable. Not so the attempt to fix Mr. Haldane with the sole expense. Mr. Macaulay evidently mistook the character of Robert Haldane, who was not simply an amiable philanthropist, but a cool reasoner and a shrewd man of business. On the first intimation of a design so unceremoniously to take the education of the children out of his hands, whilst he was expected to pay the entire cost, he wrote to Mr. Campbell, with his usual decision, declining to intrust the children to any but those acting under him. He concludes :—

"I consider this a very solemn and important charge, and hope the Lord will enable me to act to those children, while placed, in the course of His providence, under my care, with all the regard, solicitude, and affection which I could exercise towards my own."

Mr. Macaulay was too sagacious not to discover, very shortly, his mistake in trying to make Mr. Haldane a cypher in the management of the children, for whom, according to the new plan, he was to have the privilege of paying a sum estimated at 7,000*l*. A modified proposal was therefore made, both as to expense and management. But although Mr. Haldane distinctly stated that he had always intended to advise with others, and "especially with Mr. Macaulay," he peremptorily declined coming under any such engagement as a matter of bargain.

In a letter, dated June 18, 1799, he thus expresses his feelings :—

"I must say that this is a very extraordinary business. However, I am satisfied. The Lord seems to intend a different plan for the children. His will be done! I am sure my intentions were right. Conscientiously, and to the best of my power, it was my resolution, through His grace, to educate these children, and tenderly to have cared for them.

"As to Mr. Macaulay and the gentlemen of the Company, who knew the whole for nearly eighteen months, and never even hinted what they now desire, till after the children were in England and you in London, I think it would be much better for them to say, in plain terms, that they have altered their minds, than to make such proposals. That I should be at the whole or greatest part of the expense, and be allowed to be an overseer under a Committee, and this under another in London, or that I should act, according to Mr. Macaulay's undefined plan, 'in concert with other gentlemen, they adding to my subscription what was deficient, and I having my *due* weight in directing,' &c., are proposals singular in the extreme, which now come too late, and which, if they were in my circumstances, they would not themselves agree to. I distinctly meant, from the first, that I should have the *sole management*, and in consequence pledged myself to the *sole expense*.

"Mr. Thornton, Mr. Grant, and Mr. Hardcastle knew this, and there was time enough for Mr. Macaulay to have known it too, and I rather think he did know, from your letter to Sierra Leone, informing him that the children were to be educated at Edinburgh, from funds wholly provided there ; and if he had entertained any suspicion, he should have stated his objections before he left Africa, and inquired more minutely into it. . . . But it is needless to say more on the subject, except to put him right in one particular. Had I died, the burden of the children could not have fallen on the Company, but funds to complete their education would have been found amply provided by my will. Mr. Rowland Hill and Mr. Ewing, to whom I have communicated your letters, and also Mr. Macaulay's, coincide with me in my opinion of the whole."

In fact, there was little room for serious difference of opinion amongst candid men, and Mr. Macaulay found that Mr. Haldane's views were adopted even by some of the most influential Directors of the Sierra Leone Company, and very decidedly by Mr. Hardcastle, one of the leading Directors. Had it been otherwise, the attempt to restrict Mr. Haldane's powers to the privilege of continuing to pay, whilst he ceased to direct, would assuredly have failed. " We will not," he says, in writing to Mr. Macaulay, " we will not so mix the work. Either you or I shall have the whole charge." For fifteen months Mr. Haldane had been allowed to act, on the assumption that he was to be solely responsible. Under this impression, he had taken the lease of a house in the King's Park, Edinburgh, afterwards used for the Deaf and Dumb Asylum, which Sir Walter Scott has immortalized in his Heart of Mid-Lothian as that of "the Laird of Dumbiedykes." He had painted it, furnished it, and made all the other arrangements needful for the comfortable reception of the children, who were to be under the superintendence of Mr. Campbell, whose judgment and prudence were held in such esteem that Mr. Macaulay had himself intrusted to him the guardianship of his four unmarried sisters. If there had been a mistake at the beginning, it was too late to remedy it, except by a frank avowal of the error, and an offer to exonerate Mr. Haldane from all past or future charges. But funds were at last found by the Company, and the friends of Mr. Wilberforce and Mr. Thornton, for the education of the children ; and although they were not taught as Mr. Haldane had advised, and more attention was paid to their secular than religious training, yet some good was accomplished. They carried out with them to Africa many of the arts of civilized life. Whilst at Clapham, they convinced Mr. Pitt that the African race is not naturally inferior to the European. It may also be mentioned, to the credit of Mr. Macaulay, that in after-years, both in public and private, he expressed his respect for the character and talents of Mr. Haldane. One of his sisters was for many years a member of the Church, under Mr. J. A. Haldane's pastoral care, and was the occasion of frequent communication with Mr. Macaulay and her brother-in-law, Mr. Babington, of Rothley Temple. She was a woman of very superior mind, with an extraordinary memory, an amusing fund of anecdote, and a dramatic power of narrative, exhibiting somewhat of the family talent which has shone so brilliantly in her distinguished nephew. Mr. Campbell's biographer, in dismissing the subject of the African children, observes : " But although Mr. Campbell's African School, like Whitfield's Orphan School, came to nothing, it pledged his own heart to Africa, and revealed in his friend, Mr. Robert Haldane, a depth of benevolence which he never forgot nor ceased to imitate in his subsequent zeal for Africa."

# CHAPTER XI.

OPPOSITION TO THE NEW PLANS—PASTORAL ADMONITION—
OPPOSITION OF RELIEF CHURCH, AND OF THE ANTI-
BURGHERS—DEPOSITION OF THE REV. GEORGE COWIE,
OF HUNTLY, FOR ATTENDING PREACHING BY MR. J. A.
HALDANE AND MR. HILL—CHARACTER OF MR. COWIE—
HIS TESTIMONY TO MR. JAMES HALDANE—SECOND TOUR
TO THE NORTH; JOINED BY MR. INNES AND MR. AIKMAN
—VISITS THE ORKNEYS AND SHETLANDS—PREACHES AT
FULAH, THE ULTIMA THULE OF THE ROMANS—RETURNS
TO CAITHNESS, INVERNESS, EDINBURGH.

[1799.]

THE visit of the celebrated Charles Simeon, of Cambridge, had,
in 1796, been only intended as a tour of recreation. Its effects
at Moulin had, however, considerably discomposed the *Moderates*
of the Church of Scotland, many of whom were doing the work
and adopting the language of David Hume and his successors.
Their " death-like silence " and their " dread repose " had been
still more rudely disturbed in the following year, by the first
tour to the north by Mr. Simeon's companion in travel, Mr.
James Haldane, in company with Mr. Aikman and Mr. Rate.
But the tour through the south and west of Scotland in 1798,
at the period of Mr. Simeon's second visit to the north, followed
as these events were by the tour of Mr. Rowland Hill, and the
free strictures of his Journal, brought matters to a crisis.

For a long time the leaders of the *Moderates* had been meditating a blow at the itinerants. They had rejoiced to see Mr.
Simeon excluded from the Nonconformist Episcopalian Chapels,
and were determined that the Gospel which he preached should
no longer find a refuge in the pulpits of the Established Presbyterian Church of Scotland. The General Assembly holds its

annual sittings in May, and as its deliberations and decisions were to have an important influence on the future plans of the Haldanes, the following description is taken from Lord Cockburn's Life of Jeffrey:—

"The General Assembly is a sort of Presbyterian Convocation, which meets along with a Commissioner representing the Crown, for about twelve days yearly. It consists of about 200 clergymen and about 150 lay elders, presided over by a Reverend President, called the Moderator, who is elected by the Assembly annually, and very seldom more than once. Its jurisdiction is both judicial and legislative. As an Ecclesiastical Parliament it exercises, subject to very ill-defined limitations, a censorian and corrective authority over all the evils and all affairs of the Church. As a Court it deals out what appears to it to be justice upon all ecclesiastical delinquencies and disputes. Its substance survives, but in its air and tone it has every year been degrading more and more into the likeness of common things, till at last the primitive features, which half a century ago distinguished it from every other meeting of men in this country, have greatly faded. Yet how picturesque it still is! The Royal Commissioner and his attendants, all stiff, brilliant, and grotesque in Court attire. The members gathered from every part of the country,— from growing cities, lonely glens, distant islands, agricultural districts, Universities, and fallen burghs; the varieties of dialect and tone, uncorrupted fifty years ago by English; the kindly greetings; the social arrangements; the party plots; the strangeness of the subjects,—partly theological, partly judicial, partly political, often all mixed; the awkwardness of their forms, and the irregularity of their application; their ignorance of business; the conscientious intolerance of the rival sects; the helplessness, when the storm of disorder arises, of the poor short-lived inexperienced Moderator; the mixture of clergy and laity, of nobility and commoners, civilians and soldiers; the curious efforts of oratory; the ready laughter even among the grim, and consequently the easy jokes. Higher associations arise when we think of the venerable age of the institution, the noble struggles in which it has been engaged, the extensive usefulness of which it is capable, and the eminent men and the great eloquence it has frequently brought out. . . . Connecting every jurisdiction and every member of the Church (which then meant the people) into one body, it was calculated to secure the benefits, without the dangers, of an official superintendence of morals and religion; and to do in a more open and responsible way for the Church of Scotland, what is done—or not done— by the Bishops for the Church of England."

At the close of the eighteenth century the General Assembly was under the despotic influence of that Moderatism which, according to the graphic description of Hugh Miller, "purported to be Anti-christian on Bible authority;" so that when it robed itself in the habiliments of unbelief, it took "the liberty of lacing them with Scripture edgings." As its meeting approached the friends of the Gospel looked with well-founded alarm on its convention of 1799, whilst the muttering of the coming storm did not prevent James Haldane and his companions from setting out on a third tour, and one more extended than ever.

The "Edinburgh Advertiser" announces, under the head of Tuesday, May 28, 1799, "Overtures from the Synod of Aberdeen, and that of Angus and Mearns, respecting *vagrant teachers* and Sunday-schools, irreligion and anarchy." A strange medley is this announcement, and in our days ludicrous; but it is added: "The Assembly unanimously agreed to the overtures, and prohibited all persons from preaching in any place under their jurisdiction, who were not licensed as above; and also, *those who are from England*, or any other place, and who had not first been educated and licensed in Scotland. And resolved that a pastoral admonition be addressed by the Assembly to all the people under their charge."

The declaratory acts of the Assembly passed on this occasion, the one against "vagrant teachers," and the other against unauthorized teachers of Sabbath-schools, were, in May, 1842, rescinded by the unanimous act of the last General Assembly held before the Disruption in 1843. Dr. Cunningham, who moved the overture, spoke of it as "eminently discreditable to the Church of Scotland." He said, "It was passed for temporary purposes, and upon motives and grounds which, he believed, were now regarded by a great majority of the Church of Scotland as of the most erroneous and improper kind, and as amounting to nothing less than a hatred to the cause of evangelical truth." Another noble champion of the Gospel, the Rev. Dr. Guthrie, declared that he looked upon the Act of 1799 "as one of the blackest acts the Church of Scotland ever passed; and he rejoiced with all his heart that such an overture had been made as that introduced by Dr. Cunningham. The Act was passed not to exclude heresy from our pulpits, but to exclude truth." Dr. Candlish added the weight of his name and great talents to this condemnation, and remarked that it was notorious that that Act was framed for the very purpose of barring from the pulpits of the Church men whom it would have been an honour to any Church to employ in preaching the unsearchable riches of Christ. Such is the contrast between the spirit which animated the Blairs, the Carlyles, the Moodies, and the Hills of 1799, and that which characterized the majority which, in 1842, rallied round the illustrious Chalmers, the heavenly-minded Gordon, and their other distinguished compeers.

On the 3d of June, being the day after the passing of the Act of 1799, a Committee, appointed for the purpose, presented to the Assembly, a pastoral letter relative to missionary and itinerant preachers, which was carried, after a feeble resistance by a minority overborne by numbers and authority. Four thousand copies were ordered to be printed and circulated, and it was appointed to be read from the pulpit of every parish on the first Sunday after being received. The same Committee also presented a report hostile to *Sunday-schools*, which was adopted, but of it only 1,600 were ordered for the use of the Church, in its warfare against the disturbers of its death-like slumbers.

The whole of these proceedings were worthy of the period when David Hume said that the Scottish Church was more favourable to Deism than any other religion, a period which Dr. Cunningham has termed "one of the most deplorable of the Church's history." The pastoral letter was signed by Dr. Moodie, but was said to be the composition of Dr. Hugh Blair, whose intimacy with the unbelieving philosophers of his day, significantly contrasts with his aversion to enthusiasm in religion. A mutual admiration of genius and intellect was in his case, as in that of other Moderates, considered to be a bond of friendship sufficient to overbear all objections which sprung from any difference of sentiment in regard to God or to eternity. The admonition has no merits in point of composition, and

s

does as little credit to the intellectual as to the moral qualities of the Reverend Professor of Rhetoric and Belles Lettres.

The Procurator of the Church was, in the next place, empowered to proceed legally against unauthorized teachers of Sunday-schools, on the strength of certain obsolete Acts of the Scottish Parliament directed against " Papists and malignants." In short, itinerants and Sunday-school teachers were delivered over into the hands of the civil power, and it was not owing to any forbearance on the part of the Assembly, that the enmity of Moderatism was not exercised in the form of direct persecution, in the same manner that the kindred spirit of Arianism and Arminianism some years later burst out at Geneva and Lausanne.

In a letter written at the time by Miss Stuart, of Dunearn, to her friend, Miss Aikman, it is said : " You will probably have heard of the pastoral admonition which is to be read in all the churches, warning their congregations against the Circus preachers. Mr. Balfour (the late eminent Dr. Balfour, of Glasgow) was one of the Committee appointed to draw it up. I saw him for a few minutes after it was done. He appears in great distress about it. He says that he smoothed as many rough corners as possible, but that none of us will find out that when we see it. My grandfather (Dr. Erskine, of Carnock) and he agree that they are doing all they can to build up the cause they meant to destroy. I wonder what the ministers will do, who are known, like them, in the main to approve the design. It really brings them to the trial. Oh ! may God grant them to be faithful to light received, should, I think, be the prayer of all at present."

The pastoral admonition attacked by name the " Society for Propagating the Gospel at Home," and charged the *itinerant teachers* with " intruding into parishes without any call," " erecting in several places Sunday-schools," and " connecting these schools with certain secret meetings," " censuring the doctrine of the minister," as " opposed to the Ecclesiastical Establishment of the land," and acting " as if they alone were possessed of some secret and novel method of bringing men to heaven." The people are further warned not to follow up and down a set of men "whom you *know not whence they be.*" When Robert Haldane read their Bull, he quietly remarked that the dominant party in the venerable Assembly did not seem to be aware that, in using these words, they were appropriating to themselves the words, as well as the character of Nabal, when he sent his railing message to David in the wilderness.

The anticipations of Dr. Erskine and Dr. Balfour were, however, realized, and the bigotry of the Moderates only tended to the furtherance of the Gospel. Rowland Hill arrived at Edinburgh the following Friday, and found, as he says, "all the city quite thunderstruck at the fulminating *Bull* which had been issued." "But," he said, in his own quaint way, "we shall shine all the brighter for the scrubbing we have got from the General Assembly." He adds, in a note to his second Journal: "Three reasons alone can be assigned for their conduct; these are madness, malice, or an attempt to discover our treasonable plots; and the first of these reasons should seem the most probable, the pastoral admonition being dated on the day of the full moon!" Mr. Hill assailed the Assembly, both in print and in his sermons, with all the weapons of sarcasm and ridicule which so abundantly filled his quiver. But it too much engrossed his mind, and for the time marred his usefulness. It was often remarked by Mr. Campbell, that he never heard of any conversion as the fruit of this tour, and he attributed this to the effect of the Assembly's Bull, in distracting the good man's mind, disturbing the solemnity of his feelings, and leading him to launch out against the bigotry of the Moderates, to the exclusion of that Gospel which he so much loved to preach. This is a fact worthy of record, told as it is of a man whose whole career was so eminently useful. It was otherwise with James Haldane, Mr. Innes, and Mr. Aikman, who in the islands of the far north, thought little of the Bull fulminated against themselves, but much of the destitute people who hung upon their lips and drank in the words of eternal life.

But the Established Church of Scotland was not singular in

its efforts to crush the itinerant preachers.  In 1796, the Anti-
burghers in their General Synod, had passed a Resolution
against the constitution of Missionary Societies, and testified
against co-operating with persons in religious matters to whose
opinions they were opposed as a Church.  The Cameronians at
Glasgow declared of some of their body, who had attended a
missionary sermon preached by Dr. Balfour, that they were
guilty of conduct " sinful and offensive," and this censure not
being acquiesced in, they proceeded to actual excommunication.
The Relief Synod, at their Meeting in 1798, forgetting that
their founder, Gillespie, had finished his theological education
at Dr. Doddridge's academy, decreed, " that no minister shall
give, or allow his pulpit to be given, to any person who has not
attended a regular course of philosophy and divinity in some of
the Universities of the nation, and who has not been regularly
licensed to preach the Gospel."  This was levelled at the
English ministers and itinerants, who thinned their chapels.
" But," says Dr. Struthers,* " this liberal act was, in 1811,
allowed to drop out of their code of regulations, as something of
which they were ashamed."

To the same effect, in 1798, the Anti-burgher Synod passed
a decree against " attending upon, or giving countenance to,
public preaching, by any who are not of our communion;"
and in 1799, they went so far as to bring to their bar, and
finally to depose and excommunicate, one of the brightest ornaments that ever adorned their Church, the Rev. George Cowie,
of Huntly, of whom it has been eloquently said by the Rev. Dr.
Morison, who knew him well,—

" He had no competitor, no equal in the north of Scotland.  He was a
man of genius, bold and fearless in all his movements, and, in his feelings
of charity and liberality, half a century at least before the ecclesiastics of
his day.  In the pulpit Mr. Cowie was truly great.  His appearance was
that of dignified simplicity.  He could declaim, and he could be pathetic.
His discourses partook of the colloquial.  He had studied human nature,
and he knew how to approach it at every avenue.  The power he had
over an audience was great beyond description.  He could make them
smile or weep.  His appeal to the conscience was unceremonious and

* Struthers' "History of the Relief," p. 465.

direct. He never lost sight of the theme of the pulpit. All things were by him counted loss for the excellency of the knowledge of Christ Jesus his Lord. He was a stern reprover of sin ; but he melted with tenderness over the sinner, beseeching him to be reconciled unto God. I have seen hundreds dissolved in tears under his ministry, and I have wept from pure sympathy when I was too young to understand the message."

Such was the man whom, in September, 1799, the Associate Synod deposed "for countenancing the ministrations of what are called missionary preachers, by hearing them preach, and in various other ways." Mr. Cowie, on being asked whether he had heard the itinerant preachers, at first declined to answer ; but in a speech made on the occasion, he afterwards voluntarily acknowledged that he had heard both James Haldane and Rowland Hill, whom he regarded as highly-gifted Evangelists, and said that he considered the conduct of the Synod as a species of persecution, and as joining with the General Assembly in their opposition to a great work of God. Other proceedings were taken upon this confession, the result of which was that in April, 1800, he was deposed from the office of the ministry, and, with his whole Kirk Session, formally excommunicated. This intolerant and monstrous sentence, which now almost provokes a smile, was publicly intimated at Huntly, by the Rev. Mr. Mitchell, on the 18th May, 1800.

In relating this affair, Mr. Kinniburgh remarks :—" Mr. Cowie, when deposed and excommunicated, wrote thus to a friend : ' This is not the first time I have been excommunicated by men upon earth, and richly do I deserve to be for ever excommunicated by Him whom I have offended more than any other ; but instead of frowning on me when the world have, he meets me in love, as he did my brother the blind man of old.' His Church adhered to him almost like one man, and his popularity was not impaired."

The testimony of this holy, venerable, and eloquent minister to Mr. J. A. Haldane's preaching has been already noticed. It may be added, that although deposed for countenancing him, yet on the first occasion when James Haldane visited Huntly in 1797, Mr. Cowie would not go into the chapel, but sat at the windows of

the contiguous manse, where he could hear distinctly.  The sermon from John v. 28, 29, was solemn and striking, " Marvel not
at this : for the hour is coming, and now is," &c.   Mr. Cowie
was so overcome by the earnestness, the power, and the unction
with which the unlicensed Evangelist then spoke, that he felt
ashamed of his backwardness, and could no longer resist holding
out to him the right hand of fellowship.   He exclaimed, that
such a preacher " carried his credentials with him," accompanied
him into the chapel in the evening, and from that hour lent to
his preaching the sanction of his official character and influence.
In manuscripts which he left behind him, he records the impressions on different occasions made on him by James Haldane's
sermons, sometimes speaking of himself as at once " humbled
and inspired by the unction from the Holy One" by which they
were accompanied, and at another declaring that after such
a sermon he felt " as if he could never again ascend his own
pulpit-stairs."

## SECOND TOUR TO THE NORTH.

When Mr. J. A. Haldane undertook the pastoral care of the
Circus Church, in Edinburgh, he expressly stipulated that this
should not prevent his labouring as an evangelist in "the highways and hedges."   Before this event, the summer and autumn
of 1797 had been memorable for his tour, with Mr. Aikman, to
Caithness and the Orkney Islands.   In the summer of 1798 he
had traversed the west and the south of Scotland; and, after
his return, again visited Dunkeld and other places in Perthshire,
where his preaching had been greatly blessed.   In 1799 he
determined to make a second tour to the north with Mr.
Aikman.   Accordingly, Tuesday, the 7th of May, was appointed
for their departure from Edinburgh, a short time before the
Meeting of the General Assembly.   A sketch of this tour is
recorded in the " Missionary Magazine," from which it appears
that he set out alone, Mr. Aikman being at first detained at
home by severe indisposition.   Beginning at Dunfermline, and
proceeding by way of Kinross, to Perth, he preached twice in

each place at which he stopped, to large congregations, assembling in spite of unfavourable weather, and welcoming his visits with much cordiality. On the Saturday he arrived at Dundee, where, in his native town, he preached on the Lord's-day in the Relief Presbyterian chapel, to overflowing congregations. "Many," he says, "were obliged to go away." He adds, "The spirit of hearing in this place is remarkable. May they not be forgetful hearers, but doers of the Word." During the week-days intervening between the next Sunday, he preached at Kirriemuir, Forfar, Glamis, Brechin, and Montrose. On the Lord's-day he preached, by request, at Inchture, in the Carse of Gowrie, near Rosse Priory, the beautiful seat of Lord Kinnaird. There, in this country village, not less than a thousand people assembled in the afternoon to hear the Word; after which he returned to Dundee, and preached in the open air in the evening to a vast multitude. Thousands occupied the ground, listening in silence with solemnized feelings and deep attention.

Before Mr. J. A. Haldane left Edinburgh he had received a letter from Meigle, expressing *the determination* of the people to hear no more itinerants and accept of no more tracts. Thither he went on Monday, when " all the village turned out to hear, and the people expressed their strong disapprobation of the letter." It had been signed by several under the pressure of local influence, but they now declared their earnest desire to hear the Gospel and receive tracts.

On Tuesday, accompanied by Mr. Innes, who joined him at Dundee, he preached at Arbroath. After sermon they were overtaken by Mr. Aikman, who, having lost his place in the mail-coach on the Monday, did not arrive at Dundee. This accident is marked as providential, for, had he accomplished his purpose on the Monday, Mr. Innes would not have gone further; a circumstance which, as matters turned out, might have prevented the important tour to the Shetland Islands. It was now determined that they should all continue their route together, travelling in a post-chaise towards the north. At a small village, near Lawrencekirk, they were amused by the bellman's refusal to announce sermon. He assigned two reasons: the one, that he was himself a Jacobite; the other, that he understood the preachers to be Latitudinarians. Being asked the meaning of this long word, he said, that it was preaching gratuitously, or, as he expressed it, "for God's sake," of which he disapproved. They proceeded to Aberdeen and Banff, preaching as they journeyed, both in the open air and in chapels, to large congregations. But, on this occasion, to adopt the words of Robert Haldane, remonstrating, in a letter to his brother, against his excessive labours, the latter received a practical intimation that "his strength was not of iron, nor his bones of brass." Although he had been out only four weeks, he had preached more than sixty times, often in the open air to great multitudes; and continued exertion, as well as exposure to the rainy weather, brought on a sore-throat, which at last confined him to his inn, at Huntly. His fellow-labourers, waiting for his recovery, preached in some of the neighbouring towns and villages, where they spent the following Lord's-day. On their return to Huntly, they found Mr. J. A. Haldane quite unable to swallow, and so ill that he had determined to return home next morning. His portmanteau was packed, and a post-chaise bespoke for the next morning to carry him to Aberdeen. About ten o'clock the same evening the quinsy burst and gave instant relief. No sooner was the pressure of illness removed, than his plans were immediately changed. The post-chaise was counter-manded, or, rather, was employed to carry his friends the next day to Elgin and Forres. He himself remained quiet during the week; but on the following Sunday evening he actually preached in the open air, at Huntly, to a very large congrega-tion. At Forres he rejoined his party, and accompanied them to Inverness, preaching, as they went, to multitudes earnestly drinking in the words of eternal life.

At Inverness they heard, on the Lord's-day, "The Assembly's Bull" against *vagrant preachers* read in the church, and after-wards James Haldane preached on the hill to a large congrega-tion, from the words of a "*vagrant* preacher," formerly well known in Judea, Matt. iii. 10. On the 30th of June they arrived at Wick and Thurso, where they had satisfactory evidence of the enduring blessing that had accompanied the former tour. On the following Tuesday, 2d July, they crossed the Pentland Frith to Walls, and commenced their circuit of the Orkneys. Next day they went by sea to Kirkwall, where they found the Gospel flourishing. In the year 1798, after their first tour to Caithness, the Rev. Dr. M'Crie, the celebrated historian of John Knox, was sent to Kirkwall to ordain a minister. The impression made on his mind by the earnestness of the people and their interest in the Gospel never was effaced, and is said to have altered the tone of his preaching, and given to it more of that pointed simplicity and directness of personal appeal which from the first characterized the pointed addresses of Mr. James Haldane and Mr. Aikman. The following is an extract from a sermon preached to Dr. M'Crie's own people, in 1798; it is taken from his Life, as written by his son, who inherits the talents of his father:—

" In the country from which I have lately come," he said, " thank God, it is otherwise. *There* you will see persons hearing as those who have souls which must be saved or lost. *There* you may see the most lively concern depicted on every face, and hear the important question put from one to another, ' What must I do to be saved ? ' *Here* it is a miracle to see one in tears when hearing the Gospel ; and if, at any time, we witness the solitary instance, we are tempted to think the person weak or hypocritical. *There* it is no uncommon thing to see hundreds in tears, not from the relation of a pathetic story, nor by an address to the passions, but by the simple declaration of a few plain facts respecting sin and salvation. *Here* it is with difficulty that we can fix your attention on the sublimest truths during a short discourse. We must contrive to amuse you with some striking form of address. We must keep you awake by mingling amusement with instruction. *There*, in order to be heard with the most eager attention, one has only to open his mouth and speak of Christ, and, after he is done, they will follow him to his house and beseech him to tell them more about Christ. *Here* it is only certain preachers that can be patiently heard ; *there*, so far as we know, there has not been one from whom they have not received the Word gladly, nor one sermon preached that has not brought tears from the eyes of some."

Mr. Aikman stopped at Kirkwall, being invalided by inflammation in his eyes, and Mr. J. A. Haldane and Mr. Innes proceeded towards the Shetlands, preaching at several islands on their way. On the 10th of July they reached Fair Island, the first of the Shetlands, and the people heard, with thankfulness, the only sermon that had been preached there for six years. From the Fair Island they embarked in an open boat, and were out all night, "most of the time in heavy rain." On such occasions, and in all his tours, James Haldane's boat-cloak was through life a constant companion. He used to say that it had been with him three voyages to India, and often proved a friend in need, although, in his maritime career, he had then little dreamed of the nature of the services in which it was to be afterwards employed. They were hospitably received on the mainland of Shetland by a gentleman of the name of Ogilvy, and commenced their labours by preaching in a barn. Thence they proceeded to Lerwick, the principal town in the Shetlands, where they spent the Lord's-day. The people had then little connexion with Scotland, and a respectable woman inquired if Edinburgh was as large as Lerwick. Having next preached in Nesting, they visited the islands of Whalsay, Skerries, Tettar, Unst, and North Yell. The Rev. Mr. Mill, a venerable clergyman, of eighty-eight years of age, gave Mr. James Haldane his church to preach in; and after the service stood up and, in a commanding tone, warned the people to take heed to the words they had heard, more especially as this visit was a new and unheard-of occurrence in their history. At Unst they found that the minister had been captured on his voyage from Leith and carried to Bergen. Having next gone to Mid and South Yell, and crossed over to North-Maven, preaching especially to the fishermen, who were very eager to hear, Mr. J. A. Haldane and Mr. Innes separated, in order that they might take in a wider circuit. James Haldane himself went to Foulah, or Fulah, which is supposed by some to be the Ultima Thule of the Romans. It is twenty miles from the main land, contained about 200 inhabitants, and had no resident minister. On this island he preached four times, as well as in the parishes of Sandness and Walls; after which he joined his excellent colleague at Scalloway, and returned to Lerwick, where they spent five days, preaching each day, both in the town and neighbouring country. At Lerwick one of them heard the Gospel faithfully preached in the parish church. In the account of the tour they mentioned the great kindness they received from a gentleman to whom they had no introduction, and who insisted on their making his house their home. This was the more worthy of notice, as Mr. Hay was not himself, at that time, much interested in the truths of the Gospel, but he appreciated their motives and enjoyed their society. Mr. J. A. Haldane, speaking in his own name and that of Mr. Innes, says, "They (the itinerants) express the highest sense of gratitude for the hospitality they uniformly received from Shetland." "They laid their account," he adds, "with no other accommodation than the cottages afforded, instead of which they were kindly received, and frequently urged to accept the best accommodation in the gentlemen and ministers' houses. There was one, and but one exception, which, they believe, arose from misapprehension of their intentions, and which they would never have mentioned had they not imagined prejudiced persons might have misinterpreted their silence."

The exceptional case alluded to was one of which both the tourists were wont to speak with much good humour as a little incident in their travels which, so far as they were personally concerned, only afforded matter of mirthful recollection. They had landed one afternoon, weary and famished, at an island where there was but one respectable house, which was near the beach, and where they had hoped to have found a stranger's, if not a prophet's, welcome. Here they were very coldly received, with a strong intimation that the people had no need of more than the occasional preaching which was already provided. Leaving Mr. Innes in the house, Mr. James Haldane had gone down to disembark from their boat a large package of tracts for distribution, but, on returning and observing the same frozen, repulsive manner, he took Mr. Innes aside, told him that it was time to return, and, briefly apologizing to the inhospitable group for the intrusion, left the house with his friend. Soon after he preached on the sea-shore, when some of the party, who were themselves visitors, added to their incivility by sending for their own boatmen, who were listening to the sermon. When it was over, it was too late to think of again putting to sea, but, having obtained shelter in a fisherman's hut, they procured some salted-herrings and oat-cake for their supper and a dry floor for their bed. This affair occasioned great indignation amongst the upper, as well as the lower, classes in Shetland, and not only brought much reproach on the ungracious family, but induced others to redouble their kindness towards the missionaries, in order to wipe off the stain which had been, in their estimation, cast on the hospitality of the Shetlands.

James Haldane preached his last sermon at Lerwick, on the 7th of August, to "a large and attentive congregation," when the people expressed much gratitude and a strong desire for another visit. "It is to be hoped," he says, "that the seed sown here, as well as in more distant parts of the country, will not be in vain."

Having left Lerwick, they came to Dunrossness, preaching on the way at Coningsburgh, Sandwick, and Bigton, and were again received with much affection by their patriarchal friend, Mr. Mill. On Friday and Saturday they had large congregations, and on Sunday, the 11th, one went to Sandwick and the other remained at Dunrossness. The Bull of the General Assembly was powerless in this distant region, and the parish church, as well as the rocky beach, became temples both to the itinerants and the inhabitants of this district. They were now only waiting for a fair wind to return to the Orkneys, but were detained by thick and rainy weather until the Saturday, when they could not resist the invitation to spend the Lord's-day in a place where their preaching was so much prized. The 18th of August saw the conclusion of their labours in Shetland. They had spent nearly six weeks there, but still regretted that they could afford so little time to those who came in crowds to hear and were such earnest listeners. "The people were often much affected, and it is to be hoped," says Mr. J. A. Haldane, "that lasting impressions have, in some instances, been made. The Lord's word cannot return to Him void; and surely He did not send it in this unusual way to these distant islands, without having purposes of mercy to some." This hope was not to be disappointed. In going to the Shetlands, James Haldane had but fulfilled the wish expressed by his venerable friend, John Newton, that the Norsemen, belonging to these remote and neglected isles, might not be forgotten, whilst we were sending Missions to the South Seas. At that time the Shetlands contained a population of 26,000, occupying thirty scattered parishes, placed under the care of twelve ministers, of whom not more than two or three preached the Gospel. Soon after this tour and down to the close of his own life there were joyful tidings of the blessings that rested on these labours in Shetland. The religious state of the people had been previously deplorable, and much of the revival of religion which then took place may be distinctly traced to the Mission of himself and Mr. Innes. To adopt the words of a recent writer, " their earnest and rousing addresses broke in upon the dangerous repose of the people, exciting a spirit of inquiry there before unknown, when, by the blessing of God, not a few were turned to righteousness." *

Many years afterwards one of Mr. James A. Haldane's sons was travelling to Dundee on the outside of a stage-coach, when a respectable, but weather-beaten seaman, having heard his name, mentioned that he had been piloting a Greenlander from Shetland to Leith, and very respectfully inquired if his fellow-traveller was related to the celebrated Captain Haldane. On being told that he was addressing a son of that gentleman, the pilot said, with much feeling, " Then, Sir, it was from your father that I first heard the Gospel, more than thirty years ago, in the Shetlands." He added some interesting details as to the sensation produced amongst the people, the alarm felt by the Moderate ministers, and the good results that followed.

On the evening of the Lord's-day, after preaching at Sandwick and Dunrossness, the itinerants embarked in a six-oared fishing boat belonging to the Commissioners of the Northern Fisheries, hoping to reach the Fair Island before dark, and cross over to Orkney in the morning, so as to arrive in Kirkwall in time for

* "Kinniburgh's Historical Survey," p. 55.

the great fair. "They could not," says Mr. James Haldane,
"but feel regret in parting with their kind host and his family.
He took leave as one who was to meet us no more below, but
expressed his joy in the prospect of meeting in the presence of
Jesus, no more to part." Their voyage, although in fact prosperous, was not unattended with some anxiety, and was, at all
events, sufficient to try a landsman's courage; but Mr. Innes
felt he was in the path of duty, and did not hesitate to embark.
Although in his sketch of the tour, Mr. J. A. Haldane speaks of
the wind as fair and the weather fine, the swell of the ocean was
heavy, and the embarkation consequently so difficult that the
wives of the boatmen besought their husbands not to venture in
an open boat on a voyage to which it appeared they were not
accustomed, and which was so different from their usual fishing
excursions. The night overtook them before they reached the
Fair Island, and they missed it in the dark. The men became
themselves uneasy, but were encouraged to proceed, whilst
James Haldane took the helm, and, guided by the stars, steered
for North Ronaldshay. In the grey of the morning, one of the
boatmen, anxiously looking out, intimated in a doubtful tone
that he thought he saw the land. The welcome sound was at first
received with incredulity, when, as Dr. Innes relates, his friend,
quitting his post at the helm and going forward, looked for a
few moments with the practised eye of a seaman, and cheered
them with the words, "It is land." It was the height on
which stands the North Ronaldshay lighthouse, and soon afterwards, the boat being steered in that direction, they landed on
the Island of Sandy, after a run of fifty-four miles. The missionaries retired to bed, but the boatmen, having taken counsel
among themselves, determined to lose no time in returning to
Shetland. Mr. James Haldane was called up in order to pay
for their hire, and they then set out, contrary to his urgent
advice, as the weather was unfavourable, and the currents in
these seas are dangerous. The result was, that the boat being
no longer properly steered, they were carried out of their course,
away to the north-east of Scotland, where they were picked up
by a coasting vessel, at the mouth of the Moray Firth. Being

unaccustomed to any but fishing excursions, and doubtful as to their course, they lost all presence of mind, and such was their panic, that in their haste to get on board the friendly ship which picked them up, they forgot to make fast their boat, so that it drifted away and was lost. A futile claim was made by the Northern Fishery Commissioners, for compensation for the loss of their boat, but of course it could not be maintained, and was almost immediately abandoned.

On Monday evening, the 29th August, the itinerants arrived at Kirkwall, where they found Mr. Aikman at his post engaged in preaching. He had itinerated throughout a great part of the Orkneys, and everywhere had been kindly received. In the ensuing week they preached, morning and evening, during the fair, and visited several of the islands, as well as some of the parishes on the mainland. Mr. J. A. Haldane preached the last sermon on Sabbath, August 25, "to a very large congregation." On Monday they went to Stromness, on Tuesday to Walls, preaching twice or three times at each place, as well as at South Ronaldshay and Flota. On Wednesday they crossed the Pentland Frith in safety, and once more were gladly welcomed by their friends in Caithness. The Journal concludes as follows :—

" They also saw many pleasing fruits of their labours on a former tour. The desire of hearing is rather increased than diminished in Caithness; at the country places where they preached they always found large congregations. Those who have been already gathered in seem only to be a kind of first fruits of a more abundant harvest of souls in Caithness. What cause of thankfulness to Him who has raised up and placed in such a situation two ministers, whose desire for the increase of the kingdom of Jesus leads them not only to preach in their churches, but to go to the highways and hedges to compel sinners to come in.

" They preached at several country places during the week, as well as Thurso and Wick, and on Sabbath assisted at the dispensation of the Lord's Supper in Mr. Ballantyne's meeting-house. It is large and commodious, but not yet finished. The number of communicants was about 180, including upwards of eighty from Wick, most of whom have been brought to the knowledge of the truth since the itinerants first visited Caithness. They spent a most comfortable day; the multitude of people who attended obliged them to have sermon without as well as within, and in the evening the congregation was larger than any they had seen in

Caithness. By desire of the people, Mr. Haldane preached at eight next morning. He then set out for the south, leaving his brethren, Messrs. Aikman and Innes, who were to remain two or three weeks longer. On Wednesday he reached Inverness, preached there on Thursday, on Friday and Saturday at Nairn and Campbeltown, and spent the Sabbath at Inverness. The congregation in the evening was large, although the weather was threatening. On Monday he preached at Elgin, on Tuesday at Huntly, on Wednesday at Aberdeen, and on Friday, the 20th, returned to Edinburgh, after an absence of four months and a-half. His fellow-labourers arrived in town a few days ago, and confirm the account above detailed. They bear testimony to the remarkable work of grace evidently begun in Caithness, and give the pleasing intelligence, that at least thirty young people in Inverness appear to have been brought to the knowledge of the truth by attending the Sabbath-schools and itinerant preaching in that place."

Such was the conclusion of Mr. J. A. Haldane's third general tour, which was also his second to the north. He had now preached the Gospel in every part of Scotland, and abundantly distributed religious tracts from the Solway Firth in the south round about to the Tweed, and thence beyond Caithness and the clustering islands of the Orkneys and Shetlands. He had also skirted the fastnesses of the Highlands from Dunkeld to Sutherland, but had felt the difference of language an obstacle to his progress in these districts, an obstacle which often induced him to speak of the value of the miraculous gift of tongues which, in apostolic times, so wonderfully facilitated the diffusion of the Gospel. Much good was effected at the time, and down to the close of his life instances of the blessing that had attended his preaching were often unexpectedly brought under his notice. Amongst these it may be mentioned, that, in 1843, the late venerable and excellent Dr. Muir, of Glasgow, stated in conversation that he had met Mr. James Haldane in 1799 at Tain, where the Doctor was then tutor in a family related to the Oswalds, of Scotstown. A few kind but searching words addressed to the lady of the house, although not well received at the time, were afterwards blessed to her conversion. " She became," said Dr. Muir, " a pious and useful character."

During his absence from the Circus Church, Mr. J. A. Haldane's place had been supplied partly by the Rev. Rowland

Hill, partly by the Rev. George Burder, the author of the "Village Sermons," partly by Dr. Bennett, of Romsey, and partly by the Rev. George Collison, of Walthamstow, and other preachers.

This year was memorable for the institution of the London Religious Tract Society, of which the Rev. George Burder, after his return from Edinburgh, became one of the honoured founders. But in connexion with this great Institution, which has circulated so many millions of religious tracts, and whose usefulness daily increases, it should be mentioned, that before its establishment, the Edinburgh Tract Society had been formed, and that religious books and tracts had been circulated in myriads by the itinerants. Mr. Simeon, of Cambridge, first showed the example in 1796. In 1797, Mr. J. A. Haldane and Mr. Aikman, at their own cost, printed and circulated twenty thousand, and afterwards Mr. Robert Haldane, with his accustomed munificence, furnished an unlimited supply for all who had the will and the opportunity to avail themselves of his liberality in Scotland. But although the Haldanes, with Mr. Campbell and the other promoters of the Edinburgh Tract Society, were the precursors of the great Institution in Paternoster-row, they never claimed to be the originators of the system. At the Reformation, an immense collection of tracts was sold and distributed in Germany, of which a perfect set has been arranged by Dr. Bandinell, of Oxford, in the Bodleian Library. At the English Reformation much, too, was effected by religious tracts; and at a later period, the Puritans laboriously promulgated their opinions by the same efficient means. John Wesley also well understood the value of the press as a moral agent, and employed it accordingly. The publication of religious tracts was nearly contemporaneous with the invention of printing, and helped to shake the Papacy to its foundation. To combine for their gratuitous circulation was the idea of a later age.

# CHAPTER XII.

[1799—1800.]

THE pertinacity with which the adversaries of Evangelical
preaching continued to impute political motives to the originators
of the plans for propagating the Gospel at home, is characteristic of the angry spirit which disturbed the close of the
eighteenth century, and increased the panic produced by the
French Revolution. The proposal to put down field-preaching
by legislative interference, was not then an unmeaning threat,
and it was no fault of the leaders of the Moderate party, that
the pastoral admonition was not enforced by the power of
Government.

The letters of Professor Robison record his deep regret for
the error he had committed, and his promise to publish a full
apology. The editor of the "Anti-Jacobin Review," whilst
appearing to correct the Professor's unintentional calumny, was
still eager to foment excitement, by suggesting that Mr.
Haldane's conduct, in sacrificing his estate, was to be attributed
to the frenzy of revolutionary zeal.

" We have reason to be assured," says the editor, " that a sect is just
now forming in Scotland for the avowed purpose of sapping the foundation of the Presbyterian Church, as established by law. At the head of
that sect is a gentleman, who, in the first edition of Professor Robison's
' Proofs of a Conspiracy,' &c., was said to have expressed his readiness
' to wade to the knees in blood for the purpose of overturning every
establishment of religion.' From the postscript to the second edition of
the Professor's valuable work, we learn that Mr. H. disclaims all sanguinary proceedings; and we doubt not, but, before the breaking out of
the French Revolution, D'Alembert, Diderot, and Condorcet would have
said the same. The zeal, however, of Mr. Haldane against Establishments, must be very ardent; for it has prompted him to sell a beautiful
estate, and to apply part of the price to the endowment of a seminary in
Glasgow, for the express purpose of educating itinerant preachers, who
may propagate the Gospel in purity, wherever it is contaminated by the
baleful influence of Establishments."

To this disgraceful and injurious calumny, Mr. Haldane wrote
an indignant contradiction, which the "Anti-Jacobin" was
compelled to insert. A few extracts must suffice.

" You have asserted that there is a sect now forming in Scotland, at
the head of which I am, for the *avowed* purpose of sapping the foundation of the Presbyterian Church, as established by law. You have also
said that zeal against Establishments has prompted me to sell my estate.
These assertions, Sir, are both absolutely false. The public whom you
have misled, must therefore be undeceived, and, although you have no
title to any concession from me, I now inform you, that while I use the
liberty of every British subject, to judge for myself in matters of religion,
so far from avowing it, *I never entertained in my mind, the most distant
idea of sapping the foundations of the Established Church ;* and that it was
not for this purpose I sold my estate.

" I must request you to insert this letter in your *next* number; and
thus at least show yourself as ready to vindicate where you have injured,
and to retract where you have been misled, as to censure and make public
what you conceive to be reprehensible.

" I am, Sir, &c.,

" ROBERT HALDANE.

" *Edinburgh, June 26th,* 1799."

These reiterated, persevering, and malicious attacks at last
reluctantly determined Mr. Haldane to yield to the advice of
his friends, and publish a narrative of his proceedings, with a
statement of his opinions. He did so, in a widely circulated

pamphlet, alike remarkable for its clearness, its candour, and its force, intituled, " Addresses to the Public, by Robert Haldane, concerning Political Opinions, and Plans lately adopted to promote Religion in Scotland." The first edition was issued when the General Assembly, for 1800, was sitting, and produced a strong impression, greatly tending to put to shame the machinations of those, who had calumniated the Home Missionaries and their benevolent designs. It bears the stamp of truth on every page, whilst, with manly frankness, the author sketches his past history with as little of egotism as was compatible with its object, and traces to their source every one of the plans in which he was engaged. It is now chiefly interesting as the record of his early career, and a considerable part of the narrative has been introduced into the foregoing pages, as containing the most authentic account of his conversion to God, and the progress of his convictions.

" After I had fully, as I trust, desired to submit to the will of God, revealed in his Word, I had many conscientious scruples respecting my conduct, as it regarded politics. I saw that nothing external so much influenced human affairs as civil government, and that to it, in a great measure, might be traced the various opinions, situation, and character, of the different nations in the world, while these again had a reciprocal effect, and stamped the character of the other. I reflected that, becoming a Christian, I did not cease to be a citizen ; and I thought that, especially under the British Constitution, where public opinion is so much and so justly regarded, it was my duty to be well-informed in that science, which regulates and directs every public movement. I was persuaded that good general principles upon that subject were of great service to the world, and therefore thought it my duty to inform myself, as far as possible, concerning these, and carefully to store them up in my mind.

" I however began clearly to perceive that the Scriptures require the most conscientious and cheerful submission to the Government of the country, whatever it may be, stating it to be the ordinance or appointment of God himself to mankind for good.

" Soon afterwards it forcibly struck my mind, that the Lord Jesus himself, and his apostles, whose example we are called to imitate, though living in their own country of Judea, had not at all intermeddled with the subject : then why might not, or rather why ought not I, to follow them in this respect? This entirely satisfied my mind. I reflected further, that such conduct appeared in itself the best, as Christians could do much more good, by calling men's attention to the concerns of a future world, to their own depravity, and to the Gospel of salvation, than in being so much occupied with the arrangements of time, or turning their attention so often to the faults or defects of the kingdoms of this world. I immediately perceived the good effects that flowed from the Apostles' conduct in this respect. The doctrine which they preached wrought a rapid, and though gradual, yet a powerful change; and what philosophy, humanity, and political science had been unable to accomplish, the preaching of the Cross, and the noble moral principles connected therewith insensibly effected. The cruel treatment of prisoners, the shows of gladiators, the exposing of infants, domestic slavery, and many other glaring evils which disgraced society, but which the Apostles had never directly attacked, fell before the irresistible energy of their peaceful doctrine. The example of the Apostles, then, in this respect, I resolved to endeavour steadily to pursue. I have since done so, and of this resolution I do not repent. I was even much inclined to follow it a considerable time before the period above mentioned, and before I could fully satisfy my mind of the propriety of doing so, I perceived that, in this world Christians should beware, as much as possible, of adding to the ' offence of the Cross,' and this strongly inclined me to it. The humiliating method of salvation through a merciful Saviour, 'not by works of righteousness that we have done, but by the washing of regeneration, and renewing of the Holy Ghost,' will, of itself, be sufficiently offensive and irritating to the proud, unhumbled heart of an unconverted man."

Mr. Haldane next declares his views of the Scriptural doctrine of obedience, founded not on the Divine right of a particular dynasty, but on the character of the existing Government, as " the ordinance of God." The firmness and consistency of his opinions, when once formed, will be seen by reference to the last edition of his ' Commentary on the Romans,' which he published in 1842, shortly before his death, and in a letter to the " Edinburgh Christian Instructor," published in 1840. They are the same sentiments as those which Joseph Milner represents, as the opinions of the primitive Christians, and adopts as his own.

Mr. Haldane steadily adhered to his principle of imitating the early Christians, in not intermeddling with politics, till the year 1837, when, under an impression that the spirit of Reform, unsatisfied by the large concessions obtained in 1832, was at that crisis rather tending to revolution, he rode to Airdrie, from his house at Auchingray, and undeterred by popular excitement, after an interval of more than forty years, gave his vote as a freeholder. The Lanarkshire election turned upon a single vote, and, as Mr. Haldane not only voted himself, but by his example influenced the votes of other electors, there is no doubt that the decision was justly traced to him. It may be, that he carried his views of non-intervention too far, and he himself admitted that, as a magistrate, a legislator, or a freeholder, a Christian had political and social duties to perform. But, in reality, he only argued that to abstain from interference was a privilege, that every Christian is bound to remember that government is not the ordinance of man but of God, and therefore not to be lightly resisted or disturbed.

In the second edition of the " Address," Mr. Haldane states his views with regard to National Church Establishments. His sentiments on that subject indicate the ruling principle which guided all his movements, from the time that he was brought under the influence of the truth.

" In the first edition, I announced my intention of a second publication. At that time I had not a doubt that this would be rendered necessary by the proceedings of the General Assembly, then sitting. I meant in it to have stated more fully my sentiments respecting ecclesiastical establishments, but especially to have taken notice of the pastoral admonition, the conduct of the clergy in that business, and of any further steps they might have taken on the same subject in the last Assembly. I was happy, however, to find this unnecessary, a different line of conduct from what was expected having been adopted by the Assembly, and the charges formally advanced, I trust, finally abandoned. With regard to ecclesiastical establishments, it is sufficient in this place to declare, that whatever my sentiments respecting the good or evil attending them may be, I have no hostile designs (as has often been said) against the Established Church. I have avowed, in the strongest manner, my decided persuasion that all violence in religion is criminal and absurd. Besides, *I would much rather build up than pull down*, and, if possible, add to the means of instruction of my fellow-creatures, than in any way diminish them. While every man, in religious matters, ought conscientiously to abide by his opinions derived from Scripture, there is room enough in the world for all to exert themselves in doing good, without different parties devouring each other."

From these views Mr. Haldane never departed, and, on the

contrary, towards the close of life, became less and less disposed to pull down systems, differing from those of which he more particularly approved.  His "Address" for ever silenced the calumnies, which had been circulated with reference to the political designs of the Society for Propagating the Gospel at Home.  There is no doubt that the publication was very useful, as there was a most alarming project in contemplation for curtailing the right of preaching, and otherwise interfering with religious liberty.  Apart from other evidence, this intention appears from papers found in Mr. Wilberforce's repositories. and mentioned in his Diary.  Indeed it was twelve years afterwards openly stated in the House of Peers by the first Lord Redesdale, that Mr. Pitt's Bill was much stronger than the subsequent abortive measure of Lord Sidmouth.  In fact, it would have put an end to all unauthorized preaching, and rendered it difficult to obtain a license.  Mr. Haldane was not easily susceptible of fear, but in a letter, dated the 14th of April, 1800, he wrote to his friend, Mr. Hardcastle, urging that every effort should be made to avert the threatened blow. He offers to proceed himself to London, in order personally to put Mr. Wilberforce and Mr. Thornton in possession of all his views and plans.  He adds : " Should not an earnest address be circulated to all the Dissenters in every part of England, calling on them to join so many evenings every week for fervent prayer, to avert this catastrophe.  The Lord reigns, and can easily stop it.  This morning I read, in course, of the repentance of Nineveh, and of the Lord's averting judgment.  He may do the same on our behalf, for the sake of his own cause."

It was not, however, necessary to instruct Mr. Wilberforce as to the danger.  That good man himself declared that he was " never so much moved by any public measure," and that, if carried, it would have been " the most fatal blow, both to Church and State, which had been struck since the Restoration." Through the blessing of God, on the remonstrances addressed to the Premier, the menaced evil was averted, and the crisis passed over.

Mr. Pitt's threatened Bill for preventing unlicensed preaching put no arrest on Mr. James Haldane's itinerating plans. In a letter to Mr. Hardcastle, in the spring of 1800, Mr. Campbell remarks, " We are preparing in the course of next summer to make another attack on the kingdom of Satan." He was anticipating the campaign in which he was about to become the substitute of Mr. Aikman. Mr. Campbell had now altogether relinquished secular pursuits, and, at the solicitations of the two brothers, entirely devoted his time and energies to that cause to which his heart had long been consecrated. He had gone to Glasgow, where, in watching over the interests of the Seminary, he himself enjoyed the advantage of Mr. Ewing's tuition and the scientific lectures of Dr. Birkbeck. Mr. Campbell had not rashly adopted this step, but had consulted with such men as Newton, Scott, Booth, Fuller, Charles of Bala, Stewart of Moulin, Claudius Buchanan of India, and other Christians, both Churchmen and Dissenters.

It was on the 9th June, 1800, that, pursuant to the proposed plan, Mr. James Haldane set out on his fourth summer campaign, accompanied by Mr. Campbell. The usual request for the prayers of the Lord's people, which always preceded these excursions, is inserted in the " Missionary Magazine," " that the Lord of the harvest may render the important object of this journey effectual in the conversion of many sinners." The next number of the same magazine, dated 21st July, mentions that the journey appeared to be prosperous, " by the will of God ; " that, after leaving Edinburgh, they had preached that evening and next morning in Peebles, and proceeded by Biggar and Douglas to Ayr, preaching every day in the intervening towns and villages. In his Journal, Mr. Campbell, in his usual graphic style, writes : " I hope I shall bless God for ever for this journey. We are really a gazing-stock to men. Wherever we go in a town, doors and windows are everywhere thrown open to allow those within to examine our appearance as we pass along. When we enter a town we generally disperse a few pamphlets, to notify that the missionaries are arrived ; then, after putting up our horses, we take a walk through the town, to tell the people of the sermon. This, along with drum, horn, or bell (according to the custom of the place), makes our intention generally known. Last night I heard some of the hearers, after the sermon, expressing their surprise that there was no collection. ' They cannot be poor men,' said another. ' I cannot tell what they are,' said a third." The reader will remember the magisterial opposition which Mr. James Haldane had, two years before, encountered and surmounted at Ayr. There he now spent two Sundays, and instead of experiencing opposition, was recognised and welcomed by one of the magistrates, whilst the people flocked in crowds to hear, so that congregations in the open air, amounting to 3,000 and even 5,000 souls, " heard the word with much attention." On one of these occasions Dr. M'Gill, whose Socinianism had brought a scandal on the Church of Scotland and the General Assembly, was amongst Mr. Haldane's audience. It was of Dr. M'Gill that it is reported that he proposed to sign the Confession of Faith with the letters E. E. appended, meaning, errors excepted. At Ayr, on Sunday, 29th June, Mr. Campbell writes : " Mr. H. preached in the evening to about 4,000. Many of the gentry were present. His text was 1 Cor. i. 18. God gave him the opening of the mouth. He told them part of his own history. I sat at the outside. I believe not above forty people went away till after the blessing was pronounced, which was at nine o'clock. Afterwards a gentleman called on Mr. H., who had been much affected by the sermon. Understood that a good many had been brought under concern about the world to come by the last visit of Mr. Haldane and Mr. Aikman." At Ballintrae, " the Excise officer said, that since Mr. James Haldane's last visit the people had become much more orderly on the Sabbath." " At Portpatrick," says Mr. Campbell, " Mr. Haldane preached at the bottom of a stupendous rock at the north-west side of the town. The waves were rolling mountains high about a hundred yards below us. The scene was solemn. Mr. H. made many allusions to the troubled sea. The people were very attentive. About eight people belonging to the inn attended worship." At Stranraer he preached to about 1,000 people. At Stoneykirk, after he concluded, " I overheard a woman

telling her neighbour that she had heard him before at Mauch-
line, and never was so impressed with a sermon in her life."
"They are now," says the Magazine, citing a letter from these
Home Missionaries, "on their way to Dumfries, but their progress must be slow, as each of them preaches once, and very
often twice, *every day*. We have mentioned these circumstances
merely to remind our readers of the necessity of being instant
in prayer for the Divine blessing on the seed of the word."
Several instances "of the happy effects of the preaching of the
Gospel in the Circus" are then alluded to; and it is added, in
the spirit which always from first to last characterized their
labours, "The Lord works by whom he will; and we rejoice in
hearing of the conversion of sinners by whomsoever the Lord is
pleased to effect it."

There was little of egotism on the part of James Haldane.
He did his work as in the sight of God, and he has left few
written traces of his extensive labours in his own country. But
happily Mr. John Campbell kept a journal, and from his MSS.,
as well as from conversational memoranda and epistolary correspondence, many interesting details have been preserved of these
tours. Of every place to which they came, it might be said that
"the common people heard them gladly." Sometimes, however,
they met with fierce opposition instigated by bigotry or prejudice. At Sanquhar, in Dumfries-shire, a collier having directed
them in their route, begged that they would excuse his accompanying them, and earnestly entreated them not to mention the
countenance he had given to them, as it might bring himself into
trouble. Mr. Campbell relates how much this circumstance
entertained Mr. James Haldane, who mentioned, as they sat
together at supper, after a day of labour and opposition, that it
was the anniversary of an occasion on which he had dined at
Calcutta with the Governor-General at a very magnificent entertainment, and he added, "Had I been told in the midst of that
scene of splendour, which St. James's Palace could not have
surpassed, that in a few years I should be engaged in an occupation which would make my company shunned by a collier in

Sanquhar, I should have been indeed surprised." It was during the same summer of 1800, that, after visiting the little island of Cumbray, and the beautiful shores of Bute, they sailed over to Arran and preached in all its villages. The ignorance of the Celtic inhabitants was great, and as an instance of their rude manners, Mr. James Haldane mentioned, at his Jubilee Meeting, in 1849, that on a sacramental occasion he had been present in a parish church, where there was a pause, and none of the people seemed disposed to approach the tables. On a sudden he heard the crack of sticks, and looking round, saw one descend on the bald head of a Highlander behind him. It was the ruling elders driving the poor people forward to the tables, much in the same manner as they were accustomed to pen their cattle at a market. Had this happened in a remote corner of Popish Ireland it would have been less wonderful, but the Gaelic population of Presbyterian Arran seemed accustomed to submit to this rough discipline without a murmur.

Mr. Campbell's Journal supplies a continuation of the narrative of their tour. He says :—

" On reaching the west side of Arran we observed a long neck of land stretching towards the northern coast of Ireland. On inquiry we found it was Kintyre; towards the south end of which was Campbelton, the chief town, having a considerable population. As our parish extended to wherever there were *human* beings, and hearing that there was not one Gospel preacher in the whole range of seventy miles, except in the chief town, we determined to pay it a visit. We engaged a boat, and left Arran in the afternoon, making towards that part of the coast where there was a little inn, which we did not reach till about ten o'clock at night, and dark. After scrambling over the rocks on the beach, the seamen led us to the inn, where we found the inmates fast asleep; but the landlord was easily roused, struck a light, and soon cooked us a Highland supper, which is universally ham and eggs. He seemed to be quite exhilarated, being evidently willing to do his best to make us comfortable, so that it would have been cruel to have found fault with anything. He had been in the army, and readily joined us in our evening worship. He informed us that there were people living not far from him, who would come to sermon in the morning in front of his house. But only three persons came, with whom we had a little conversation. We then proceeded to Campbelton, where we stopped for several days, preaching mornings and evenings on the green slope of a hill, to about 1,000 people in the morning, and about 1,500 in the evening, and twice in the neighbouring villages during the day."

But their progress was not destined to be always so peaceful. By the advice of friends at Campbelton they had employed a messenger to go down to Kintyre, and intimate four sermons each day at the different villages. The clergy were all *Moderate*. They were, for the most part, deeply immersed in farming, fishing, or trading in sheep and cattle. Their official duties, if performed at all, were performed in the most careless manner, and many of them were Socinians.* At their instigation the Highland chiefs combined to put a stop to the itinerancies in their neighbourhood. One of the gentlemen, more zealous than the rest, a military man who afterwards succeeded to a baronetcy, encountered the missionaries at a place where he had intended to stop them, had he arrived in time. It was there that he first gave notice that the magistrates had resolved to allow of no more field-preaching. Mr. James Haldane plainly told the Gallant Major, as he had told the magistrates at Ayr, that the justices were exceeding their powers, that such an illegal mandate should not be obeyed, and that he would certainly preach at the places where sermons had been already intimated. The Major, although somewhat disconcerted by the calm determination with which he was met, repeated his prohibition, and said he should be at their next place of meeting before them. He was as good as his word, but ultimately faltered in his course. He sat on horseback during Mr. James Haldane's sermon, in a scarlet hunting-coat, witnessed tracts distributed amongst the people; but without mustering courage to offer any interruption, saw both of the itinerants mount their horses and depart. Soon after, the Major, attended by his groom, passed them at a hand gallop, and then pulling up, turned round once more, apparently resolved on putting in force the arrest which he contemplated. But as often as his eye encountered Mr. James Haldane's unflinching glance, his courage seemed to fail, and he again and again faltered and passed on. Arriving at White-

* Struther's History, p. 399.

house, which was the next preaching station, the Major was joined by the parish minister and several magistrates, all on horseback, and full of excitement. Field-preaching was one of those things which seemed beyond the reach of their philosophy, and to persist in it after their prohibition, appeared to these little chieftains like "bearding the lion in his den, the Douglas in his hall." It was evident that a great blow was meditated. Still James Haldane, in sight of the assembled magistrates, left the inn to preach in the middle of the town, and, strange to say, against him none of all the party mustered courage to execute the arrest. The people were, however, so much intimidated by the dread of their chiefs and of the magistrates, that, for the most part, they stood and listened at a distance. Mr. Campbell's duty was to preach at an adjoining village, and although his friend was left unmolested in the town, yet no sooner did he set out, than, to use his own words, he was " followed by the person in the red coat, and ordered by him, as a justice of the peace, to return to Whitehouse, which I did, and put my horse into the stable till Mr. Haldane returned from preaching." Mr. Campbell was a man of great faith and strong passive courage, but he was little of stature, and had not much of that bearing which, more especially on occasions of emergency, characterized his companion. On his return from preaching, Mr. James Haldane was surprised to find Mr. Campbell a prisoner at large. But to bring matters to an issue, he ordered their horses to be saddled, whilst he advised Mr. Campbell to go to the gentlemen, who were assembled in the adjoining room along with the parish minister, and inquire by what authority he was ordered to return to Whitehouse. They replied, pointing to a sealed paper, " There is a warrant to send you to the Sheriff of Argyll; and the volunteers who are to attend you will be ready in a few minutes." The parish minister had, on the previous Sunday, silenced their messenger, when announcing the preachings to the people as they were coming out of church. Standing with a heavy leaded whip in his hand, he exclaimed, " If you repeat that notice, with one stroke of my whip I'll send you into the eternal world!"

Mr. Campbell's Journal continues the narrative of their progress under arrest :—

"A sergeant, with a party of volunteers in their uniforms,
being arrived, we were told we might stop where we pleased;
that the soldiers had only directions to see that we went to the
Sheriff. As the soldiers had no horses, of course our progress
was slow. After dark, we arrived at the town where we should
have preached, and learned that a congregation had assembled,
and did not disperse till it was almost dark. We took up our
quarters at a good inn. As it was our custom to have worship
at all the inns where we halted, we had it there, and desired the
landlord to invite as many of his neighbours to attend as he
pleased. The room, which was of a good size, was well filled,
and our volunteers all attended. A chapter of the Bible was
read, and an address founded upon it being given, and prayer
offered, the company dispersed. Next morning, at seven o'clock,
we set off, and had about fifteen miles to march to Lochgilp-
head to breakfast. While at breakfast an old man called, who
said, ' We heard of your coming, and of your having arrived at
the inn; and though I have been a soldier in the German wars
of '56, and seen many prisoners, yet never having seen any
prisoners for preaching the Gospel, I thought it was my duty to
call upon you, and therefore am I come. But you will have
some things to converse about among yourselves, I therefore
wish you good morning.' On conversing a little with him, he
withdrew. After an interview with a Justice of Peace, to whose
care we had been committed, we went on to the Sheriff's, about
seven miles farther, under the care of the postmaster."

To the Sheriff they were very unwelcome visitors. He was an
old man, and having been apprised of their coming, was by no
means disposed to commit himself to the violent proceedings of
the anti-preaching chiefs. He put several questions, which were
satisfactorily answered, and after consulting with a gentleman
who sat with him as his adviser, he said, " But have you taken
the oaths to Government?" They replied that they had not,
but that they were most willing to do so instantly. The Sheriff
said that he had not a copy of the oaths, and that they must

therefore go to Inverary for the purpose. A merchant, from Glasgow, who had joined the itinerants, quoted the words of the Toleration Act to show that, " if *required* to take the oaths, they were to be administered before the *nearest* Magistrate." " Now," said Mr. J. A. Haldane, " you are the *nearest* Magistrate. We are peaceable, loyal subjects, transgressing no law, and prepared to do all that the law requires, but to Inverary we will not go, except as your prisoners and on your responsibility." The Sheriff had wished to make the affair a drawn battle, and to screen the Magistrates from blame, at the same time that he declined to act against the preachers. But Mr. James Haldane felt the importance of refusing all compromise, and of bringing the question to issue. The Sheriff was therefore obliged to give way, and after once more consulting with his friend, briefly said, " Gentlemen, you are at liberty."

The consequences were important. A great right had been vindicated, and the lawfulness of field-preaching admitted by the highest judicial authority of the county. The itinerants returned and preached at all the villages where they had been previously expected. The people who had been before intimidated from attending, now flocked in crowds to listen. " At Whitehouse," says Mr. Campbell, " when Mr. Haldane returned, the whole town seemed to have turned out." " He was," said another who was present, " in one of his finest keys," and spoke with an eloquence, a fervour, and animation, which seemed to have acquired redoubled force from the circumstances in which he had been placed. Mr. Campbell, too, preached with good effect in the neighbourhood; and in his Journal records the following anecdote, which serves to show the ignorance of the *Moderate* ministers of that day. He says : " I remember a curious intimation which a parish minister gave to his people on the preceding Sabbath. It was told me by a lady who was present. ' I have to inform you that those preachers who have been for some time disturbing the peace of the country are expected here also, but I hope you will give them no encouragement. It is possible they may preach and pray better than I do, but sure I am *they have not a better heart.*'"

The arrest was clearly illegal, and the Magistrates concerned in it might have been prosecuted, more especially the gentleman who, to use the words of a Scotch Judge concerning another affair of a similar kind, acted more like a constable than a Justice of the Peace. It is believed that they were informed of their mistake by the then Lord Justice Clerk, who had met the party on the road, and on inquiring the meaning of the formidable escort, was no doubt much surprised. But there was no desire to be litigious or revengeful. It was, however, a remarkable coincidence, and one which will not be overlooked by those who remember that nothing happens by chance, that when Mr. Campbell next met the fox-hunting Magistrate, who had acted towards him with so little chivalry, it was in the precincts of the Abbey of Holyrood at Edinburgh, where the Major was himself a prisoner at large within the bounds then allowed as an asylum for debtors. It may be added, as one of the little anecdotes which have escaped oblivion, and flit across the scene amidst the lights and shades of these bygone days, that on the morning when they left the Sheriff the whole party were drenched in a heavy shower of rain. Arriving at a small Highland inn, they called for breakfast and a fire, where they might dry their wet clothes. There was but one fire-place in the hut, and they were all crowding round it, with their coats off, some wrapped in tartan plaids or blankets, whilst ham and eggs were in preparation. Mr. James Haldane, whose naturally joyous spirit quickly caught the ludicrousness of the scene, exclaimed, " What a fine subject for a caricature : Field-preachers refreshing themselves after a shower ! "

The results of that tour to Kintyre were not evanescent, as will be seen from Mr. Campbell's account of a visit which he made to the same district two years after his arrest. On their return to Edinburgh, they prevailed on a worthy preacher, who was a native of the place, to go and labour in Kintyre. He had just finished his studies at Mr. Haldane's seminary at Glasgow, besides attending the College, and he keenly felt the spiritual destitution and ignorance of his countrymen. Before Mr. James Haldane's visit, Kintyre was, as Mr. Campbell says, a kind of *heathen* part of Scotland. But Mr. Macallum agreed to go and occupy the fallow ground, now for the first time broken up. His labours, although at the beginning attended with little effect, were after a few months crowned with signal success, as will be seen by Mr. Campbell's interesting narrative :—

" It was arranged that his head quarters should be at the very town where we were arrested, and that he should regularly visit out-stations in the region round about. I remember the first evening I preached there, that the sergeant of the party who guarded us to the Sheriff sat at my right hand in his regimentals, which he had previously put on for the occasion, and was now a converted man ; and on my left sat the minister's man, also converted, whose case was somewhat singular. When Mr. Macallum first went there, of course this man was prohibited from ever going to hear him, but one evening Mr. Macallum preached in a barn adjoining to the minister's stable, indeed only separated from it by an old gable. The man being in the stable when Mr. Macallum was preaching, and observing a hole in the gable, he naturally put his ear to it,—for stolen waters are sweet. The Gospel passed through this hole to his ear, up to his understanding, and down to his heart, so he became a new man, and his soul not being able to live without food, he was obliged to attend the ministry of Mr. Macallum, and consequently lost his situation at the manse or parsonage house.

" The people had been very anxious to build a place of worship, but no proprietor could be found willing to part with a piece of ground for that purpose; but in a singular way their work was accomplished. There happened to be a contested election, in which the minister took a different side from the landed proprietor in his immediate neighbourhood, which so incensed that gentleman, that, to be revenged on him, he gave to Mr. Macallum an acre of ground to build a chapel and a house for himself upon it, and assisted the people to erect them. There was also room on the ground for a garden. I have slept in the house. So thus God can make even the wrath of man to praise Him.

" I paid a visit with Mr. Macallum and a young man to the western side of the Island of Arran, in order to preach at a few places, and to return to a station of Mr. Macallum's to preach on the Sabbath. The case of the young man was not a common one. He had been, like his companions, very ignorant and careless. He heard Mr. Haldane preach after being freed from his arrest, and went home greatly alarmed about the state of his soul. He could neither sleep nor work; his poor friends did not know what to make him,—some recommending one medicine, others to make trial of another. All failing, they were recommended to

U

take him to the parish minister of a town a few miles off. His mother did so. He inquired of the mother what was the matter with him. She said she could not tell, but he could neither sleep nor work for fear of the day of judgment and hell. The minister informed her that a person had very lately come to the town to teach the people to *dance*, and was only to remain for a short time; he therefore advised her to put him for a month under *his* tuition; he had little doubt but he would be relieved. She took lodgings for her son, and placed him under the dancing-master for a month. Of course, he began to teach him how to make one foot point to the east, and another to the west, and so on. About the second day he got tired of the foolish work, jumped out of the window of the dancing-room, ran home to his mother, declaring it made him worse instead of better; so he gave up the dancing.

"Not long after this Mr. Macallum arrived, and commenced preaching in the neighbourhood. The young man went to hear him, and was greatly relieved under the first sermon. During our visit to Arran I had several conversations with him, and found his mind peaceful, and very desirous to be educated for the ministry.

"The Saturday being stormy, none of the sailors would venture to take us across the water to Kintyre. On rising early on the Sabbath morning, we found the wind very little abated, and the sailors determined not to venture. Hearing of a larger boat about two miles along the shore, we walked to it, and prevailed on the sailors to whom it belonged to attempt the passage, which turned out to be a very rough one. But the greatest difficulty was when we got within a hundred yards of the shore, which was strewed over with huge rocks, and foaming billows dashing over them. The sailors of course had taken down the sail, after which they paused for some time till a large wave had retired past us, when all immediately exerted their utmost strength at the oars, and the helmsman steered the boat in a serpentine course among rocks before the succeeding wave overtook us. It was the most skilful piece of seamanship I have ever witnessed. We preached near the spot where Mr. Haldane and I landed two years before, when only about three persons came to hear; now we had a congregation of upwards of 400, the effect of Mr. Macallum's labours among them. On leaving them, about a dozen of the people walked on each side of my horse, telling what miserable creatures they were when I first visited their country. One said he then acted as fiddler at all the dancing weddings round about, which he immediately gave up when his eyes were opened. 'The people said I had broken my fiddle to pieces, but that was not true.' An aged, grey-headed man then said, 'I was at that time chairman of a whisky-toddy meeting, that regularly met for the purpose of drinking whisky and water in the evenings. After Mr. Macallum came amongst us, one ceased to attend, then another and another did the same, till I was left alone in the chair. I began then to wonder what it could be that they liked better than good Highland whisky. This determined me to go and see; so I went and attended the ministry of our friend, and also found that which I liked better than whisky-toddy.' Thus the chair was vacated, and the meeting dissolved by the force of Gospel truth. Various others related their experience as we walked along, which I cannot now recollect, and have no written memorandum to help me. What was rather a novelty to me, was that I found the conversions as numerous among those who might be called the *aged* as among the young, which is seldom the case where the Gospel has long been preached. But in that part of the country I did not hear of any Gospel preacher having been there in that generation, or that of their fathers, consequently it was a kind of heathen part of Scotland. So it was, as among the heathens abroad, under our missionaries: conversions are as frequent among the old as the young; for if the Gospel does not soften it hardens; it is either the savour of life or death."

Not very long ago a gentleman travelling in Arran happened to call at a little cottage. He found the woman who resided in it deeply pious. On conversing with her he found that, many years before, she had received the truth by listening to a sermon preached in the island by Mr. James Haldane.

It is related, that one of the parish ministers having, after this itinerancy, vainly tried to oppose the preaching of the Gospel and to counteract its effects, became so miserable in witnessing its success, that, in a fit of despair, he threw up his living and emigrated to America. This was not a solitary case. Mr. J. A. Haldane, on another occasion, addressed a letter, containing a solemn warning to the minister of a parish south of Edinburgh, whose preaching was misleading the people. The letter so affected his conscience, that the minister resigned his charge and betook himself exclusively to farming.

Such were the direct or collateral results of Mr. James Haldane's first visit to Kintyre with his excellent friend, for whose earnest faith, practical usefulness, and amiable qualities, he always entertained much true regard. It was with reference to such scenes as that with the magistrates of Kintyre and the Sheriff of Argyll, that Dr. Lindsay Alexander thus spoke in his eloquent funeral sermon, preached in February, 1851:—

"Of all the influences which have been operating upon our people during the half-century just closed, none, perhaps, has

been more powerful and extensive in all its bearings than that
which commenced when God touched the heart of James Haldane with evangelic fire, and sent him from secular occupations
to the streets and highways of his native country to proclaim to
his fellow-men ' the unsearchable riches of Christ.'

" It needed such a man to accomplish such a work as he had
to undertake.  Men educated in the retirement of Colleges,
—men of timid, sensitive, or delicate tastes and temperament,
—men infirm of purpose or hesitating in action, would have
been bent and scattered before the storm which interest and
prejudice, and the old hatred of the human heart to all that
is earnest in religious life, everywhere stirred up against the
itinerant preachers.  It needed a man who had been trained
amid scenes of danger and of strife, and whose spirit was
accustomed to rise with opposition, to encounter and brave the
tempest.  Such a man was found in Mr. James Haldane.  The
habits he had acquired at sea, in battling with the elements and
with the untamed energy of rude and fearless men, stood him
in good stead when called to contend for liberty of speech and
worship in opposition to the bigoted and tyrannical measures of
those who would fain have swallowed up alive the authors of
the new system.  He was not a man to quail before priestly
intolerance or magisterial frowns.  Dignified in manner, commanding in speech, fearless in courage, unhesitating in action,
he everywhere met the rising storm with the boldness of a
British sailor and the courtesy of a British gentleman, as well
as with the uprightness and the unoffensiveness of a true Christian.  To the brethren who were associated with him, he was a
pillar of strength in the hour of trial; while, upon those who
sought to put down their efforts by force or ridicule, it is hard
to say whether the manly dignity of his bearing or the blame-
less purity of his conduct produced the more powerful effect in
paralyzing their opposition, when he did not succeed in winning
their applause."

# CHAPTER XIII.

[1799—1801.]

FROM the 6th of May, 1797, when Mr. James Haldane preached
his first sermon to the rude colliers of Gilmerton, down to the
autumn of the year 1800, the work which he accomplished
might have been sufficient for a life-time. Within that period
were included his four first itinerancies, which, taken together,
occupied more than twelve months of incessant exertion; during
which, for the most part, he preached at least once every day,
generally twice, often thrice, and occasionally four times. While
stationary in Edinburgh, before he was ordained, his labours in
the surrounding villages, and his occasional excursions to a
greater distance, were frequent and unwearied. After his
ordination, the Mission "to the highways and hedges," as he
called it, was not abandoned; and on the Calton Hill, of
Edinburgh, or beneath an overshadowing rock in the King's

Park, or on the links of Bruntsfield, Newhaven, Leith, Porto-bello, or Musselburgh, his voice was heard by thousands, interested, solemnized, or awed by his direct and earnest appeal to the heart and conscience. To his old friends and companions it was a marvel which they could not comprehend; whilst the masses, partly attracted by novelty, and partly touched by a sympathetic feeling of the powers of the world to come, were disposed to listen with delight to a sound which stirred their inmost soul and brought the Gospel of salvation to their door.

Whatever may be said of field-preaching, it was thus that Scotland was roused from its spiritual slumber. And when we think of the reluctance with which James Haldane at first en-gaged in the work, and how even his intrepid spirit then shrunk from addressing the people assembled at the Sabbath School at Loanhead, we are reminded of what Isaac Taylor has so eloquently said of Whitfield and Wesley: "The men who commenced and achieved this arduous service, and they were scholars and gentle-men, displayed a courage far surpassing that which carries the soldier through the hailstorm of the battle-field. Ten thousand might more easily be found who would confront a battery, than two who, with the sensitiveness of education about them, could mount a table by the roadside, give out a psalm, and gather a mob."

Amongst the many shorter tours which he undertook from time to time, there was one of some interest along the coast of Fife, in which he was accompanied by the late Mr. William Finlay, of Calton-street, Edinburgh, himself a native of the town of Anstruther, which has of late years acquired celebrity as the birthplace of Dr. Chalmers. Mr. Finlay was one of those excellent laymen, who at the end of the last and the beginning of the present century, were zealous in every good work, and, like Mr. Campbell, Mr. Ritchie, and other pious, intelligent, self-denying and noble-minded men in the middle ranks of Edinburgh, acted as Home Missionaries, and were forward in promoting within their own sphere, every useful work of Christian philanthropy. The inmates of the Magdalen Asylum, the prisoners in Bridewell, the destitute sick, with other objects of misery and compassion, were the peculiar care of William Finlay. He was delighted to obtain the occasional aid of Mr. James Haldane to preach in those places, where, as an Evangelist or Scripture-reader, he himself spent all his leisure. When Mr. James Haldane resolved to visit Anstruther, and itinerate through the villages on the east coast of Fife, Mr. Finlay himself acted as an *avant-courier*, going before to announce the sermons, and arrange as to time and place. On one occasion, having been asked if he were Mr. Haldane's servant, he replied, with beautiful humility, that he should be happy to fill that or any other office, so that he might assist in making known the Gospel of the grace of God. On arriving at St. Andrew's, the ancient seat of Scottish learning, and once the hotbed of Popish superstition and tyranny, they found it enveloped in the gloom of spiritual darkness, and oppressed by the leaden weight of Moderatism. Evangelical doctrine of any kind was a novelty, and the idea of field-preaching revolted all their prejudices. At the inn the itinerants were at first regarded with cold suspicion, and, amidst the chilling indifference which prevailed in that stronghold of Moderatism, it was impossible to find any church or building within which a sermon might be delivered. Going, therefore, to the outskirts of the town, so as to cause no interruption of thoroughfares, and taking his stand on a millstone lying near the shore, Mr. James Haldane, with his usual courage, self-possession, and tact, commenced the service by reading a portion of a psalm, whilst Mr. Finlay raised the tune. At first there were only a few gazing stragglers, but as the preacher's voice was heard in solemn prayer that Christ might be glorified by the word now to be spoken, the audience increased in number, and gradually drew nearer to the spot which he occupied. There was much in the historical recollections of St. Andrew's to awaken stirring emotions. The ruined Castle, washed by the surging billows of the German Ocean, told of the sanguinary acts of Cardinal Beaton and of his own miserable end; whilst, amidst broken arches and venerable towers, the echoes of the dying testimony of Hamilton, Wishart, and other noble Scottish martyrs, seemed still to linger, and sigh over the spiritual gloom of that depopulated place. It was under the influence of such recollections, that James Haldane announced as his text the pathetic words of the Evangelist, " When he beheld the city, he wept over it." It is easy to imagine the use he made of these memorable words, and how he was led to warn the people to bethink themselves of that Gospel which had been sealed with the blood of martyrs, but was now supplanted by the preaching of a hollow and heartless philosophy. The effects were striking. He was listened to with silent attention, but when he announced another sermon for the next morning, a soldier who was present advanced towards him, and respectfully said, that, if he would alter the hour, which interfered with the regimental parade, he would come himself, and also bring his comrades. Such a request could not be refused. The hour was changed. In the morning the soldiers crowded round the preacher, the chilling atmosphere of indifference seemed to have been penetrated by a beam of light, and the people of St. Andrew's, roused from their apathy, assembled in multitudes. His reception at the inn became cordial as well as civil, and although Professors and Moderates looked on with displeasure, the common people heard the word with gladness, and it is hoped in some cases with profit.

It would be easy to multiply other narratives of the shorter tours which he made in his zeal to proclaim the Gospel in the highways and hedges to all who were not blessed with a faithful ministry. But, in fact, it would be difficult to name any town or important village in Scotland, where, at one period or another, James Haldane did not, with all the energy of heavenly truth, give utterance to a full, free, and impressive invitation to " behold the Lamb of God, who taketh away the sin of the world." Filled with a deep and penetrating sense of the saving grace and power of Christ, it was from first to last his desire to make known that grace and power, with the assured confidence that the Gospel, whether it be received or whether it be rejected, never can be preached in vain.

But, if the younger brother was thus actively employed, the exertions of the elder were not less arduous, although in a

different way. The originality of his character had been
remarked from boyhood. He had made a noble effort to found
a Mission in India, and one which he did not abandon until
good men began to fear, lest the continued agitation of the
plan might be considered as an attempt to coerce the Government. Before he disposed of Airthrey, it was for several years
the centre of attraction to Christians of all denominations.
Clergymen and Dissenting ministers from England, and all parts
of Scotland, there found a cordial welcome. A kind of temporary
chapel was fitted up at the stables within the wood, where such
men as Dr. Bogue, Mr. Simpson, Mr. Ewing, and others, were
wont to preach on the week-days. The most animating and
interesting topics connected with the progress of Christianity
were discussed at Robert Haldane's table; and often did their
host sit up, with one or more of his guests, until the morning
sun, streaming through the shutters, put to shame the candles,
which had been once and again lighted to show them to their
apartments. In all his plans his wife became as much interested
as her husband; and when he sold his estate and reduced his
establishment, in order that his means of usefulness might be
increased, she voluntarily resigned her carriage, and would never
again allow of this expense. They had but one child, a much-
loved daughter, who was in her twelfth year when they left
Airthrey, and was married before she was eighteen to the late
J. F. Gordon, Esq., nephew of Dr. Stuart, of Dunearn. There were,
therefore, fewer domestic occupations to absorb Mrs. Haldane's
attention, and this enabled her to devote more of her time to
assisting her husband in the preparation of his works, by
copying his manuscripts, abridging letters of information, and
making extracts from other writers. The venerable Dr. Innes,
speaking of Mr. Robert Haldane's early life, thus writes:—

" In his latter days I had less of intercourse with your uncle. In early
life he was easy and pleasant, and could enjoy an innocent joke as much
as any one. Many a happy day did I spend at Airthrey. And when I
was engaged with your father, along with the late Mr. Aikman, in our
itinerancy to the north of Scotland, Orkney, and Shetland, in the summer
of 1799, Mrs. Innes remained with Mrs. Haldane three months. Often
did she speak of the pleasure she enjoyed in her and Mr. Haldane's

society, and of the advantage with which he appeared in the relations of domestic life."

Reckoning from the time he left Airthrey, in the summer of 1798, down to the summer of 1800, when he published his "Address on Politics," he had been the means of bringing over from Africa about thirty children of native chiefs, to be educated in the principles of Christianity. He had also opened the Circus, and made arrangements for large places of worship to be established, at his own expense, in Edinburgh, Glasgow, Dundee, Perth, Thurso, Wick, and Elgin. He had, even at that early period, selected about eighty students, and at his own expense placed them in a course of education, to continue for two or three years, under Dr. Bogue, Mr. Ewing, and Mr. Innes. He had printed for circulation myriads of religious tracts, and distributed Bibles and Testaments, when as yet there was no London Tract or British and Foreign Bible Society. He had formed, or assisted in forming, many Sabbath-schools ; and, finally, by bringing the well-known Andrew Fuller to Scotland, had given an impulse to the Serampore translations of the Scriptures, which were then languishing for want of funds, and were scoffed at as the abortive efforts of " a nest of consecrated cobblers."

It was on the 13th of October, 1799, that Mr. Fuller first preached in the Circus of Edinburgh. He was previously known by his able defence of the truth against Socinianism, in that work which Mr. Wilberforce lent and commended to the study of Mr. Pitt,—"The Gospel its own Witness." As an earnest of further aid and an inducement to visit Scotland, Mr. Haldane presented him with 100*l.* for the Serampore translations. The origin of this donation is thus told by Mr. Fuller's biographer :—" Mr. R. Haldane happening to inquire of Dr. Stuart what intelligence he had from the Baptist Missionary Society, the Doctor replied, ' Dismal intelligence ! The funds are low; and no success as yet.' ' As to funds,' said Mr. H., ' I always intended to give them something, but never did. Could you desire Mr. Fuller to draw on me for 100*l.*, and tell him, that if he would come down and preach, I am persuaded that my brother would welcome him, and so would Mr. Ewing.' The Doctor wrote by the next post. Mr. Fuller went down, and met with a kind reception." In reference to this visit Mr. Fuller used to say, that, till Mr. Haldane sent him his donation, he had not before known that it would be worth while to come to Scotland; but that he now saw, in his own case, the truth of Sir Robert Walpole's maxim, "That every man has his price."

Mr. Fuller's impressions are thus depicted in one of his first letters :—" I have been in company with Messrs. Robert and James Haldane, Aikman, Innes, Ritchie, and some other leading men in the Circus connexion. Certainly these appear to be excellent men, free from the extravagance and nonsense which infect some of the Calvinistic Methodists in England, and yet trying to imbibe their zeal and affection. Robert Haldane seems a very disinterested, godly man, and his wife as disinterested and amiable as himself. They have agreed to sell a large estate, and to live as retired as possible, in order to have the more to lay out for the furtherance of the Gospel." In another part of his journal Mr. Fuller observes :—" The characters principally engaged in this new denomination, as far as we can judge, seem to be some of the best in Scotland; excepting a few in other connexions, such as Dr. Erskine, Mr. Black, &c. The two Haldanes, with Messrs. Innes, Aikman, and Ewing, appear to us very intelligent, serious, and affectionate in their work; active, liberal, and, indeed, almost everything that we could wish. No drollery in their preaching, but very desirous to be and do everything that is right."

But, whilst busy in directing great plans and inducing others to make known the Gospel, Robert Haldane was not himself indisposed to assist in field-preaching. His first sermon was preached in the month of April, 1798. Dr. Innes was present, and gives the following account of it :—

" After becoming thoroughly acquainted with the leading doctrines of Divine truth, he felt a strong desire publicly to preach them to others. I was with him at his first attempt of this kind. We proceeded to Dunkeld on the Saturday evening; and next morning rode up to Weem, a few miles from Taymouth. After hearing sermon in the church, I requested the people, as they were dismissing, to remain, as a gentleman who was there wished to address them. This was something altogether new, especially as Mr. Haldane wore coloured clothes. We got the accommodation of a barn from a good woman in the neighbourhood, when he expounded the first eight or ten verses of the second chapter of the Epistle to the Ephesians with great clearness and force. This specimen showed how well he was qualified for public address. He, two years afterwards, took a house in one of the Straths (I think, Strath Bran) above Dunkeld, when he began to preach the Gospel to all around. But, with his characteristic vehemence and energy, he spoke so loud and so frequently, that he ruptured a blood-vessel, which made it necessary for him to desist."

Robert Haldane's voice was not naturally loud, but no doubt he preached too frequently, and to congregations which required more strength of lungs than it was safe for him to employ. His voice had neither the force nor the compass of his brother's, and he did not vary his notes in the way which often enabled the latter to arrest the attention of his hearers, and impart so much of solemnity and emphasis to his preaching. But it was calm, mellow, and peculiarly pleasing, its silver tones combining much both of power and pathos.

Mr. Robert Haldane himself used to relate an anecdote in reference to a sermon which he preached under a large shed, belonging to one of the principal inns on the Great North-road. He was posting from London to Edinburgh, probably in 1798, as he does not seem to have been in London for several years afterwards. Arriving on the Saturday evening at Stilton, in Huntingdonshire, he resolved there to spend the Lord's-day. He found that the Gospel was not preached in the church, and, in fact, that it was scarcely heard in any part of the county. He proposed to the landlord to preach in the evening, in the yard of the hotel. The landlord expressed himself much gratified at the suggestion, cleared out the carriages, which stood under a spacious and convenient covering, and desired intimation to be given of the sermon. Mr. Haldane then addressed a numerous and very attentive congregation. When he had concluded, the people remained as if rivetted to the spot, and intimated that they desired to hear more of these glad tidings. He began again, and spoke to an audience listening with fixed attention, for nearly an hour. The people were deeply moved, and expressed their thankfulness. Next morning he proceeded on his journey. A few years afterwards, probably in 1802, he again spent a Sunday at the same inn, but hearing that there was then a Methodist, or Wesleyan Chapel, he went there to worship. The Gospel was faithfully preached, and he was retiring, at the close of the service, when an old woman, looking at him with obvious surprise, exclaimed, " Here's the beginning of it all !" It turned out, on explanation with the minister and others, that the sermon he had preached some years before had been blessed to the awakening and conversion of some who heard ; that, in consequence, they were anxious to learn more of the truth and enjoy the blessing of a faithful ministry, and the chapel in which he had that morning worshipped had been erected.

In 1799 Mr. Haldane was so much occupied with the Edinburgh, Glasgow, and Dundee Tabernacles, as well as with the institution of his seminary and the selection of the students, that he does not appear to have been, for any lengthened period, absent from Edinburgh, where he had a house at the west end of Princes-street, although, with Dr. Bogue, he paid a visit to Lundie House, as is mentioned in that good man's biography. During the same summer he also accompanied Mr. Rowland Hill, during a part of his second tour in Scotland, along with the Rev. Mr. Slatterie, of Chatham. In 1800 he spent the summer in Strath Bran, at a place called Balaloan, and preached much there, and in Dunkeld and the vicinity. It was in the month of September, 1800, that he was obliged to desist from speaking in public, in consequence of the hœmorrhage in his throat, to which Dr. Innes alludes. This was not, however, of much consequence ; and, in after-years, he sometimes spoke for two or more hours continuously at public meetings ; and, at Auchingray, used to conduct a double service, lasting, according to the custom of the country places in Scotland, three hours, every Lord's-day. The year 1800 was one of great scarcity, and provisions were very dear. The supplies of food and clothing provided for the temporal wants of the people by Mr. and Mrs. Haldane caused their residence in the vicinity of Dunkeld to be long remembered, even by those who did not so much value the spiritual instruction which they were so desirous to impart.

---

No sooner had Mr. James Haldane accepted the office of stated minister of the Circus, than his brother proceeded to erect for him a spacious place of worship, on a site purchased at the head of Leith Walk, Edinburgh, which, after the fashion of Mr. Whitfield's chapels, was called the Tabernacle. It was built by Mr. Charles Black, a member of the Circus Church, and father of the eminent publisher, so long Lord-Provost of Edinburgh. It was larger than any of the city churches, and calculated to accommodate a greater congregation even than St. Cuthbert's. The entrance was by a descent of some steps, which conducted to three doorways, leading into the vestibule of a spacious area, rising like an amphitheatre, at a little distance from the pulpit. Above, there were two galleries, each capable of seating about eight hundred people. It was estimated that the whole place furnished sittings for three thousand two hundred persons, whilst, on special occasions, four thousand might be crowded within its walls.

The cost was entirely borne by Mr. Robert Haldane, and when the building was furnished, he offered to make it over in perpetuity to his brother. This Mr. James Haldane declined, alleging that, so long as it was devoted to religious purposes, it was as well in his brother's hands, who could, at his death, make what arrangements he pleased. But it was never contemplated by either of them that the property should become vested in trustees, so as to remove it beyond their own control, or expose it to the risks which have befallen so many orthodox Dissenting endowments.

In May, 1801, the Tabernacle was opened, and the congregation, which had for nearly three years occupied the Circus, took possession of this new and commodious building. Mr. James

Haldane's first sermon was from the words, "Ye are the temple of God." There, for nearly fifty years, he laboured and counted it his privilege, from first to last, to minister at his own charges in the Gospel of Christ. The accommodation which it supplied was at first partially, and in after-years entirely, free to the public, and whatever was produced by collections or otherwise, after paying the current expenses, was appropriated to the propagation of the Gospel. One of the last religious services performed in the Circus, was the ordination of Mr. Aikman, on the 17th of May. It was conducted by the late Rev. Mr. Moodie, of Warwick, and Mr. Ewing, of Glasgow, in concert with Mr. James Haldane, who preached the sermon from the words of our Lord's message to the Church of Philadelphia (Rev. iii. 2), " Hold fast that which thou hast, that no man take thy crown." The " Missionary Magazine" remarks : " The congregation assembled on this occasion was immense, the services of the day were solemn and interesting, much fitted to impress the minds of the audience with the incalculable value of the Gospel of peace.

Mr. Aikman, aided by ministers from England, had for some time generally supplied the Circus congregation in Mr. J. A. Haldane's absence. But the increasing number of Church members and the duties incident to such a vast congregation, rendered a plurality of elders almost indispensable. The two pastors laboured together most harmoniously; but it was not long before they saw the expediency or necessity of a second place of worship. As the Tabernacle was in the New Town, Mr. Aikman resolved to build for himself a chapel in the Old, adjoining the College. This was done entirely at his own expense, with the exception of two donations amounting to four hundred pounds from Mr. Haldane, which were designed as a recompense for Mr. Aikman's trouble in assisting to teach the students after the seminary was removed to Edinburgh. The "Missionary Magazine" for June 1802, thus notices the event :—

" On Lord's-day, the 30th of May, was opened a new chapel, lately erected in the street leading to Argyle-square, Edinburgh. This chapel has been built upon the same principles as the Tabernacle in this city, in the most perfect harmony with those connected in that important institution. The services of the day were in the following order :—Mr. Parsons, of Leeds, preached in the morning, from Matthew xvii. 20 ; Mr. Haldane in the afternoon, from Psalm cxlix. 2 ; and Mr. Aikman in the evening, from Psalm xxii. 30, 31. A Church has since been formed of persons in communion with the Church at the Tabernacle, for the observance of ordinances in this chapel, to be under the pastoral care of Mr. Aikman. Their formation was publicly recognised on Wednesday evening, the 2d of June, when, after an introductory discourse on the nature and order of a Christian Church, Mr. James Haldane commended the Church and pastor to the Divine blessing by prayer, and gave a very suitable and affectionate address to both. The service was extremely interesting. It presented a scene not frequently witnessed, a Church separating in love, in the hope of the extension of the Redeemer's kingdom. May the Lord realize their most enlarged desires !"

The first students who had finished their two years' course of preparation were now deemed fit for active service. Some went to Ireland, but for the most part they were scattered over Scotland. A letter to Mr. Robert Haldane, dated Sligo, January 21st, 1800, gives an interesting account of the labours of one of them, a Mr. Morrison, who had been sent to itinerate in the north of Ireland. Another of his correspondents thanks him for his liberality in furnishing the means for itinerating in Ireland, and prays that he may be "enriched with all the blessings of that joyful sound, which you are so blessedly instrumental in communicating to others." The success which attended this first Mission to the north of Ireland, was such as to stimulate further exertions in that quarter, against the strongholds of ignorance, error, and superstition.

In May, 1801, Mr. James Haldane once more proceeded to the south, but on this occasion took with him his wife and family, having established himself at Dumfries, as a centre from which he might radiate on preaching excursions. "For four months," it is said in the "Missionary Magazine," "he preached in Dumfries every Lord's-day, to large congregations, in the open air, or under a tent, and he also preached *once every day* in the neighbouring towns and villages, except in one week in the beginning of harvest." He was fond of riding, and had a powerful and excellent little grey horse, which seemed as patient of fatigue as its rider. Sometimes in his excursions from Dumfries, he would make a circuit of fifty miles in one day, and preach three times. To the good effects of these labours there was abundant evidence during his life, and since his death some pleasing testimonies have been added, as to permanent results in the district round Dumfries, of which he probably never heard.

At the close of his residence at Dumfries, he resolved to cross over to Ireland, and did so in the month of September, in company with the late Rev. George Hamilton, of Armagh. Almost on his first landing he was admitted into the parish church of Portadown, and on several occasions exhibited the remarkable spectacle of one not in episcopal orders, and not even belonging to the Episcopal Church, preaching to large audiences in an Episcopal diocese. The " Missionary Magazine" for the 19th of October, 1801, observes : " We have been informed, that he has preached to crowded congregations in different parts of the north of Ireland; and in a letter from himself of the 5th instant, dated Armagh, he says, 'I stayed a few days in Belfast, and preached in the neighbourhood. There is a great desire to hear in many places, and the people are uncommonly attentive. From all accounts, I hear that religion is at a low ebb.' Alluding to the young men prepared and sent over by his brother he adds, ' The Lord seems to have prepared the country for the young men, who will prove, I trust, eminently useful.' "

There is an interesting letter in the " Missionary Magazine" for December, 1801, signed " J. H.," in which he mentions "some displays of the power of God," in his late journey to Ireland, which appeared well calculated to excite gratitude and thanksgiving to the Lord. At that period Arianism, or some other form of infidelity prevailed, and a dead chill rested on the Presbyterian Churches of the north of Ireland, similar to that which prevailed in Scotland. A revival has since taken place, and Socinianism has taken refuge in a Remonstrant Synod. Mr. James Haldane notices in the letter just alluded to,

x

two families to whom the Gospel had been originally brought in a very remarkable manner by means of a maid-servant. He concludes : " The kindness met with in both families was great, and it was doubly pleasant as it was conferred for his sake, who is able to reward it, and who will not suffer a cup of cold water given in his name to pass unnoticed."

During his visit to the north of Ireland, Mr. James Haldane was kindly welcomed at the residence of his cousin, Colonel O'Hara, of O'Hara Brook, whose father, an Irish gentleman of family and of fortune, when quartered with his regiment at Dundee, had married a sister of Mr. James Haldane's mother. There were others of the family from whom also he experienced much kindness, particularly a sister of the Colonel, who resided at Coleraine, where one of her nephews, the Rev. James O'Hara, an excellent Evangelical clergyman, is now the Incumbent.

The details of the tour to Ulster must not delay the progress of the narrative, but some extracts from a curiously characteristic letter from Thomas Scott, the Commentator, just before Mr. James Haldane set out for Dumfries, will show the favourable light in which that judicious commentator regarded proceedings which so many would condemn as irregular. The letter is dated Chapel-street, May 1st, 1801 :—

" DEAR SIR,—I think you must have misunderstood my answer to your brother's invitation, in which I stated myself entirely incapable of accepting, consistently with my present situation and engagements in the Lock Hospital and the Asylum, which must be entirely suspended if I leave home, as I have no resource in this respect, and never can get any person to fill up my place. Indeed, I do not think it possible for me to procure any supplies in the chapel, and in my other places where I preach, which would satisfy the congregations, for all the ministers in our line are fully employed, and many more wanted. Add to this that my continuance in my present situation is very doubtful, and if I do continue, I shall obtain the whole service. This is now in agitation, and my presence here will be peculiarly needful through the summer, as all the usefulness of my future life as a preacher seems greatly to depend upon my success in this concern, which is too complicated to admit of explanation. At present I have more encouragement in my ministry here than formerly, but as absence from his work is one of the charges brought against Mr. De

Coetlogon, who preaches in the evening, which first gave occasion to the motion for dismissing him, has put matters on the present uncertain footing, so it would be extremely imprudent in me to give up my principal strong ground, that *I am always in my place at my work.* If I am enabled to stand my ground, my field of usefulness will be considerably enlarged, and my prospects improved, but if the opposite interest carry it against my friends, I shall have to begin anew in some other place, and at my time of life this appears to me very unpromising. It does not appear in the least likely, that if I continue at the Lock, it will even be practicable for me to leave home so long as a journey to Scotland implies; as I keep no curate, and no one can supply for me *but a regular Episcopal clergyman,* and the services *daily* required of me cannot be intermitted without violating my engagements, and acting contrary both to my conscience and credit. Should I be dismissed by the majority of the Governors, I should be set afloat, and I cannot tell whither the tides and currents might carry me.

"But besides this I am engaged in a new edition of the Family Bible, on my own account, and, contrary to what you suppose, it will cost me quite as much labour as at the first, and with this peculiar circumstance, that if I do not go on with it steadily, it will ruin, in all probability, me and my family, and injure my creditors. If I never leave it for a week, I shall not finish in less than four years from the beginning, perhaps from this time, and I deem myself bound to apply as much as possible, as health and other duties will permit, and to undertake nothing inconsistent with it. If I am enabled to bring it to a conclusion I shall consider it as the main business of my life; but while it is in hand I am decided against any journeys but what are absolutely needful. I shall not enter on the subject of *improvements,* but they will be as many as I am capable of making. The marginal references will be printed in the clearest manner I ever saw any. Many of other persons' will be left out, many original added. I do my best.

"I have no fear lest the circumstances of my not being able to come to Edinburgh should in the least prevent good in your line; you will find more acceptable and suitable preachers. Every man has his talent, and preaching a few sermons among strangers with effect is less my talent than some other things, and that of some other men.

"I rejoice to hear that you have encouragement in your work and design. I sometimes hear of you, and more frequently think of you. I pray God to direct, assist, and prosper you more and more. My Christian respects to your brother and all friends.

"I remain, dear Sir, your obliged friend and servant,

"THOS. SCOTT."

A few months earlier in the same year Mrs. James Haldane

lost her uncle, Sir Ralph Abercromby, who died on board the
Foudroyant, of the mortal wound received in the great battle of
Alexandria, which led to the conquest of Egypt. The letter of
condolence which her husband wrote to Lady Abercromby on
this event was striking and beautiful. Whilst in a tone of
becoming sympathy it did homage to the private virtues and
illustrious character of the departed hero, whose name would go
down with the history of his country, it displays the surpassing
importance of heavenly things, unfolds the doctrines, and presses
home the consolations of the Gospel in language alike distinguished for its directness, its simplicity, and its truth. This
letter was mentioned by Lady Abercromby with the interest of
one who valued the Gospel it set forth, when on an evening at
the house of Mr. James Haldane in George-street, nearly sixteen
years afterwards, the late Hon. and Rev. Gerard Noel had been,
at her request, invited to deliver one of those beautiful expositions which have made his visit to Edinburgh, in 1817, so
pleasantly remembered.

In October, 1801, Mr. and Mrs. James Haldane returned
from Dumfries. Their second child, a little girl, then rather
under six years old, was in a delicate state of health. She died
on the 6th of June following, but not before giving very
pleasing evidence of the grace of that Saviour, who said, "Suffer
little children, and forbid them not, to come unto me, for of
such is the kingdom of heaven." Her affectionate father published an interesting little memoir, intituled, "Early Instruction
recommended, in a Narrative of Catherine Haldane, with an
Address to Parents on the Importance of Religion." It is
remarkable for its truthful simplicity. There is no attempt to
embellish, and it is not possible to read it without discerning
the only motive which prompted the writer,—a desire to bring
glory to Christ and be useful to children. It ran through
eleven or twelve very large editions, and was widely circulated
by the venerable John Newton, who greatly admired it, and
considered it much calculated for usefulness. It was also translated into Danish by Dr. Henderson some years afterwards, and
was rather popular in Denmark, where the name, which is

common in that country, was an attraction. But the narrative
is here deserving of notice, because it in some measure discloses
a little of the domestic life of a man much before the public.
There are touches in it which indicate the tenderness of the
fond parent, and the confiding affection with which that tenderness was always reciprocated. A few extracts may be given :—

" From the time she could understand anything, Catherine was
informed that she was to give an account of her thoughts, words, and
actions, to God. She was early taught to listen to the reading of the
Scriptures, and to such little religious books as are adapted to the capacities of children. She soon began to attend to the parables and some of
the stories of the Old Testament. Her mother usually spent two hours
daily in reading, and talking on what she read, to Catherine and her
elder sister. They were never led to regard this as a task, and as they
found it entertaining, and were not desired to continue when they began
to tire, they always looked forward to it with pleasure, and were disappointed if anything occurred to prevent it. One or two of Mr. Newton's
hymns generally formed a part of this exercise. Catherine was fond of
them, and of her own accord, committed some of them to memory from
hearing them read. Accounts of pious children also early attracted her
attention.

" No particular impression appeared to be made on Catherine's mind
by the Word of God till she was five years of age. She had listened to
some parts of Scripture with seeming attention, but never appeared to
consider herself particularly interested in what she heard till one Sabbath
evening, when her younger sister was asking the meaning of being born
again ; Catherine immediately replied, ' To get a new heart from God.'
Her mother said she feared she did not know what a change of heart
meant, and spoke to her seriously. Catherine was much affected, and
after she went to bed, said to her maid, ' I have just been thinking on
that verse, " The soul that sinneth it shall die." ' From this time Catherine always seemed to be much more concerned about religion than
formerly. . . .

" In February, 1801, Catherine's health began to decline; but for a
considerable time her complaints appeared trifling, and hardly ever interrupted her play or her ordinary occupations. In May she went with us
to Dumfries, and whilst there became gradually worse. . . .

" She now spent more time at prayer than formerly, and took much
pleasure in hymns, and hearing of Jesus. She had long been accustomed
to hear a chapter of the Bible read to her after she was in bed. She
would never allow this to be neglected, either before or after she became
ill. . . .

" Instead of playing on the Lord's-day, the children were taught to repeat hymns to one another when alone. One Lord's-day, her mother, on going out, desired her to keep a Sabbath-school. When she returned she heard Catherine praying, along with the rest, that if it were the Lord's will, he would restore her to health; if not, to prepare her for death, and take her to himself. . . .

" She got food frequently as she was able to receive it, and we observed that she never took anything without silently asking a blessing from God. One day I noticed this to her mother, in Catherine's presence, and said she was a good child. She was vexed to have it spoken of, and cried, till I changed the subject. This showed a spirit very opposite to ostentation. A child may talk about religion to please its parents; but Catherine at this time had not spirits for anything of this kind, and, indeed, the truth of God had evidently before her illness made an impression on her heart.

" Although we had pleasing evidences of her mind being impressed about eternity, had noticed a remarkable change in her temper, and had observed that she never neglected prayer, yet we were anxious that she might be brought to speak freely, and tell us the present state of her mind. This was more desirable, as she did not show the same pleasure in hearing about religion as formerly, and seldom spoke on the subject. This led us to pray to our gracious Lord; he heard us, and gave us every satisfaction we could have desired. In April, her mother took her into a room by herself, and asked her if she could pray with her, told her she was dying, and spoke to her of the love of Christ. . . .

" After she went to bed, she desired her maid to read a hymn, which she had heard sung a little time before. When she read these lines—

" ' He takes young children to his arms,
And calls them heirs of heaven,'

she saw Catherine crying. Being asked why she cried, she said, she was sorry for her sins. She said, she would like to see papa. I went and spoke with her, and prayed. She told me she loved Jesus Christ. She ever afterwards enjoyed comfort of mind, and never expressed a fear of death.

" Thus was the Lord graciously instructing this dear little child, and, in some measure, perfecting praise from the mouth of a babe. Those who know their own hearts, and have been engaged in instructing children, will best judge whether mere human teaching could have so deeply impressed the truths of God on the mind of a child little more than five years of age. It is true the minds of children are tender and flexible, but the religion of Jesus Christ is not suited to their taste. They will not contradict you, tell them what you will on the subject; but unless they are taught of God, they will soon show the natural alienation of their hearts from him, by total indifference about religion.

" Two days afterwards, when she was much reduced, she desired to see her sister, of whom she was very fond. She put her arms round her neck and kissed her, saying, ' Love your Saviour : I am happy.'

" There were several hymns in which she particularly delighted, and which she would often desire to be read to her, such as that beautiful hymn of Cowper's,—

" ' There is a fountain filled with blood.'

She was particularly fond of the hymn,—

" ' In evil long I took delight,' &c.

And of the hymn,—

" ' Descend from heaven, immortal Dove,
Stoop down, and take us on thy wings ;
And mount, and bear us far above
The reach of these inferior things.'

" The Sabbath but one before her death, she asked for the hymn,—

" ' There is a house not made with hands.'

Before it was finished, she became too ill to listen to it.

" The last Lord's-day she was on earth her mother read to her several hymns of her own choosing. She desired Catherine to speak to her sisters, and sent for one younger than herself. Catherine put her arms round her neck, and bade her love Jesus.

" Though she was so ill, she came every morning, by her own desire, to family worship. She said little, but the remarks she afterwards made showed she was not inattentive. A short time before her death, she said to her maid, ' I have just been thinking how happy I shall be when papa, mamma, Elizabeth, and the rest, meet me in heaven.' She added, ' It was a pretty chapter and hymn that papa read this morning,—that there would be no need of candlelight there.' . . . She hardly spoke at all after this, but next day asked for the hymn,—

" ' There is a land of pure delight,
Where saints immortal reign.'

The last words she uttered were to ask for the hymn,—

" ' Jesus, I love thy charming name.'

On the 5th June, having for the last twelve hours been in a kind of slumber, she fell asleep in Jesus.

" Thus lived and died a child, whose story is an illustration of our Lord's words,—' I thank thee, O Father, Lord of heaven and earth, because thou hast hid these things from the wise and prudent, and hast revealed them unto babes ; even so, Father, for so it seemed good in thy sight.' She appeared indeed to have been taught of God. She had heard the Gospel, and had been made partaker of that precious faith, which is the gift of God. She had been affected with the weight of eternal things during the winter before she became ill. We observed a remarkable change in her before her disease arrived at a great height. For some time after she was taken ill, she said she would not be afraid to die if she got a new heart; but from the time she sent for me to pray with her, nearly two months before her death, she always expressed full confidence of going to Jesus. From that period I always went and prayed with her after she was in bed. If at any time I was later than usual, she kept awake, and frequently asked for me. She one day told her mother that she had not got a new heart at Dumfries, nor for a long time after; but that lately she knew that she had got one, although she could not tell on what day. Her confidence did not arise from thinking all children went to heaven. In order to ascertain this, I one day asked her if she thought her elder sister would go to heaven if she died immediately. Catherine replied she did not know. She suffered much with great patience. Her illness was tedious and uncommon; her head was much affected. Frequently when in bed she would repeat, ' My head, my head!' But the Lord gave her the victory over the fear of death, and graciously gave us satisfactory evidence, very uncommon at her age, that the instruction she had received was not in vain. My reason for writing an account of her is, that other little children may be led to love the Saviour. How happy will she and I both be in the day of God, if we shall meet some children at the right hand of Jesus, who were brought to him by reading the account of Catherine!"

The address to children and the address to parents which are subjoined to the account of Catherine are both earnest, practical, and striking. But the extracts from this little narrative are for present purposes, chiefly valuable as showing the character of the man. Occupied as he was with a numerous Church and a larger congregation, called upon, even when at home, to preach in the villages and towns within a wide circuit round Edinburgh, pre-eminently exemplary in visiting the sick and comforting the afflicted, he never forgot that his first duty was at home. There all his affections were centered, and there it was his study to win the confidence and love of his children by the most endearing sympathy, both with their amusements and studies, whilst it was his grand object to train them up in the nurture and admonition of the Lord. Every night did he pray beside the bed of his drooping child, and gently lead her to the feet of that Saviour whom he served. With this no public duty was ever suffered to interfere when within reach of home, and neither fatigue nor business were apologies for its omission. It was the same to the very close of his prolonged life, and he who had by nature the dauntless spirit of the lion, would evince the gentleness of the lamb, combined with all the tender affection of a sympathetic and loving heart. Great was the joy which reigned through the house whenever it was announced that, owing to any rare circumstance, he was to remain at home on a Lord's-day evening. His children gathered round his chair, whilst he examined them as to their knowledge of the Bible, listened to the hymns or portions of Scripture which they repeated, or interested them by the recital of stories after the manner of the parables, in which the imagination was gratified, whilst truth was imprinted on their hearts. But above all, it may be said that in nothing was the nearness of his habitual communion and walk with God more distinctly visible than in the surpassing value which, at all times and under all circumstances, he constantly attached to prayer. With prayer he parted with any of his family on going to a distance; with prayer and thanksgiving he welcomed them on their return; with prayer he taught them to ask the blessing of God in regard to everything that concerned them; whilst his own unclouded faith was that which imparted peace and joy to his heart, throwing the sunshine of cheerfulness around his path, so as to make his home happy and religion attractive.

# CHAPTER XIV.

[1802—1803.]

DURING five summers, beginning with that of 1797, Mr. James
Haldane had devoted himself to long and laborious itinerancies,
for the purpose of preaching the Gospel. In the summer of
1802 he sought no repose; but to recruit the health and spirits
of his wife, after the loss of their little daughter, they went,
with their eldest, to Buxton, in Derbyshire. The younger
children were left at the seaside, under the kind care of their
uncle and aunt; but wherever James Haldane went, it was
in the spirit of one whose lips had been touched as by a live
coal from the altar, and in whose breast there burned a flame of
love for Christ which could not be extinguished or concealed.
His visit to Derbyshire was a season of revival and awakening.
At the hotel at which he stayed there were many strangers,
to whom he had the opportunity of making known the Gospel.
He also preached in the ball-room, and was welcomed by a
pious Irish Bishop, whose son, a zealous clergyman of the
United Church, did not scruple to accompany him on many

preaching excursions in the neighbourhood. Amongst other places, they went to Macclesfield, in Cheshire, by invitation of the Rev. Melville Horne, who offered the use of his church and pulpit. But when the two friends arrived at Macclesfield, it turned out that some demur had been made on the part of one of the churchwardens to the irregularity of this proceeding. The sermon was therefore adjourned from the church to the churchyard, where the good Incumbent attended, along with the Bishop's son, and took part in the service by invoking the blessing of Almighty God on the word spoken by his Scottish friend. At Castleton-of-the-Peak they also met with clerical sanction, as the Vicar not only listened to the sermon, but after it was over, begged to offer his personal thanks to the preacher. At one place, near Buxton, there was a good but somewhat eccentric man, who, amidst surrounding darkness, for many years stood alone as a missionary to the poor. When he first heard Mr. James Haldane's faithful and energetic declarations of the Gospel of free salvation, he was so moved with surprise and delight that he could not contain his exultation. He afterwards introduced himself, and said that he had an "independency" of 20*l.* a-year, which enabled him to devote himself to the cause of Christ. There were several other interesting occurrences connected with the visit to Buxton, Matlock, and other places; and he did not leave the neighbourhood before he had proclaimed the message of salvation in many a hamlet, village, and town, as well as on the green hill-sides of the romantic county of Derby, and the neighbouring districts of Staffordshire. Everywhere his preaching was acceptable, and often it was made manifest that the word was with power.

In the summer of 1803 he prepared for another excursion into a part of Scotland from which he had hitherto considered himself excluded by his ignorance of the Gaelic language. But a very remarkable revival had taken place in Breadalbane, through the instrumentality of one of the Dundee students, who had been sent there by Mr. Haldane. In the neighbouring district of Blair Athol, Mr. Stewart, of Moulin, had been enabled to report that, since Mr. Simeon and Mr. James

Haldane visited his manse, about eighty people had been awakened by his own preaching to a deep and abiding sense of the Gospel of salvation. The account he published was very striking; but the revival in Breadalbane, although begun by a humbler instrument, was as plainly the work of God.

The blessing which followed the labours of Mr. Macallum in Kintyre was ushered in by the awakening begun by Mr. James Haldane and Mr. Campbell. That in Breadalbane was entirely begun by a devoted catechist, of lowly origin, a Mr. Farquharson, who had been recommended on account of his earnest zeal and godliness to Mr. Haldane's class at Dundee, but whose capacity of learning seemed, on trial, hardly to warrant his persevering in academical studies. He was therefore sent away to Breadalbane, at the end of his first six months, with the view of trying whether he might not be of use as a Scripture-reader amongst the poor and uneducated Highlanders. The district was at that time destitute of Evangelical preaching. There were actually no Bibles, scarcely any Testaments, and the people lived without prayer. So great was the opposition to the devoted catechist when he commenced his labours, that, in a circle of thirty-two miles round Loch Tay, every inn was shut against him, and there were only three families that would yield him hospitality. But it often pleases the Lord to work by the feeblest instruments, and " to choose the weak things of the world, and things which are despised, to confound the things that are mighty." Despite of opposition and neglect, he went from village to village during the winter, reading the Bible, and speaking the words of salvation to all who would listen. In the spring of 1801 there was some awakening, and early in 1802 so extraordinary a revival took place, that in a very short time there were about one hundred persons, previously ignorant of the Gospel, who seemed to be truly converted. These conversions occasioned a great sensation, and much opposition. It produced in these Highland glens a kind of religious persecution.

" Families," says Mr. Kinniburgh, in his " Historical Sketch," " were divided, false reports were raised and circulated for the purpose of bringing the new converts into disrepute.  Violent measures were devised and accomplished to deprive them of their houses and farms, and in not a few were their lives in jeopardy ; but they took joyfully the spoiling of their goods, knowing that in heaven they had a better and enduring substance. They thought less of their sufferings than of the happiness of suffering for Christ.  Here it deserves to be noticed, that then the work was going on in Breadalbane, there were instances in which, when the converts acted with decision, persecution gradually subsided, but when there was apparent wavering it increased."

Amongst the anecdotes of the new converts and of their altered conduct, the following is an example :—a number of young men had been addicted to poaching on the Earl of Breadalbane's estates, and were generally brought annually before his Lordship, who usually dismissed them, with a threatening rebuke.  One of these, who was also a smuggler, had his attention directed to the Gospel and was converted.  The next time the poachers were brought before the great Earl, he missed the smuggler, and asked what had become of him.  The gamekeeper replied, " My Lord, he has become a missionary, and will never trouble us again."  His Lordship observed, " I wish all these young men were missionaries."  The same young man had been in the habit of illegally making malt, but, after he embraced the Gospel, he had no peace of mind until he had informed upon himself and delivered to the Excise all the malt which he had on hand.

In 1802, the humble and holy man through whose instrumentality this revival took place was himself sent a prisoner to Aberdeen, for preaching the Gospel in Braemar.  Mr. Farquharson had not been many hours in gaol before a lawyer waited upon him and put a book into his hand, stating that a part of it was written in the very cell in which he was confined.  " Read it," said the gentleman, "and you will soon be liberated," and immediately retired.  To his no small surprise, Mr. Farquharson found it to be " Rutherford's Letters."  This led him to muse on the sufferings of the godly author, and he thought his own but light in comparison.  Mr. Farquharson was soon released, in consequence of the intervention of his friendly visitor, who was better acquainted with the Toleration Act than Mr. Farquharson's ignorant and bigoted persecutors.

The good work was not confined to Loch Tay. The pastor of the Tabernacle, at Dunkeld, in a letter, dated April 14th, 1803, reports that, exclusive of those who had been awakened under Mr. Stewart's ministry, at Moulin, he could himself speak of 145 who had experienced the power of Divine grace in and around Dunkeld since Dr. Bogue preached there as the first itinerant. By that sermon he knew of one who was converted. The rest were the fruits of the labours of the two Messrs. Haldane, Aikman, Ewing, Innes, Hey, Garie, and Campbell (of Dunkeld). From Aberfeldie Mr. Dewar, one of Mr. Haldane's students (but not the same who is now the Principal of Marischal College, Aberdeen), writes, in April, 1803, that no less than fifty-seven in that neighbourhood attributed their salvation to Mr. Haldane's missionaries. Two years before this time, Lady Glenorchy's chaplain, the good Mr. Garie, of Perth, had died, and, in a beautiful letter, written shortly before his death, he mentions having, within a few weeks back, received seventeen out of twenty-one applicants for Church membership, "most of them young persons, and lately awakened." He adds, " A young man, last week, received his first impressions under a sermon preached by Mr. James Haldane, in the mill at Inver; and a young woman, who had made considerable advancement under one he preached in the chapel here upon the jailor." The good man adds, "Although, in general, I feel a willingness to leave the world, whenever my Master shall call me, yet I have often, on a Saturday, felt a peculiar unwillingness to die till the Sabbath was over."

The accounts from Caithness were, if possible, still more delightful. At the same time that the missionaries in Breadalbane were writing home the intelligence just noticed, the excellent Mr. Cleghorn, the pastor of the Church at Wick, was detailing the blessings that had attended the previous itinerancies in Caithness. Whilst he reckoned at least forty cases of conversion which, at Wick alone, had come under his own knowledge, as the first-fruits of Mr. James Haldane's preaching in that place in 1797, he mentions, that now he reckons 120 as giving evidence of the power of Divine truth. He adds, that at Thurso the Gospel had been as successful, "if not more so."

It is not, then, to be wondered at, that Mr. James Haldane longed to visit, not only the scene of his own first itinerancy, but also Breadalbane and its vicinity. Accordingly, Mr. Campbell relates how he received an unexpected summons to return to Edinburgh from the west, where he was preaching, and that, on his arrival, he found the object was "to see if I would consent to go on a preaching tour of three or four months with Mr. James Haldane, to visit all the cities, towns, and large villages, in the north of Scotland, from Edinburgh to the Orkney Islands." Mr. Campbell adds, "Being the employment which, at that time, I loved, I instantly complied, and commenced making preparation for the journey."

On this occasion they travelled on horseback, attended by Mr. James Haldane's faithful servant, Daniel Macarthur, a pious Highlander, whose knowledge of Gaelic made him particularly serviceable in the Celtic districts. They left Edinburgh early in May, and Mr. James Haldane preached on the first Lord's-day a striking sermon in the Tabernacle of Perth, from a text appropriate to the errand of mercy on which he was bound, Jeremiah iii. 12, 13 : "Go and proclaim these words *unto the north*, and say, Return, thou backsliding Israel, saith the Lord; and I will not cause my anger to fall upon you : for I am merciful, saith the Lord, and I will not keep anger for ever." One of his hearers, and that for the first time, was Mr. Lachlan Macintosh, who was soon afterwards admitted into the seminary at Edinburgh, and has been long respected as the travelling agent of the Baptist Home Missionary Society. Mr. Macintosh relates how it happened that, after the sermon, whilst a group of ministers and others were gathered round the preacher, he was introduced to Mr. J. A. Haldane, who kindly spoke to him, and engaged him to announce the sermons as far north as Mr. M. had to go and twenty miles further, beginning at

Bankfoot, Dunkeld, up to Logierait, where they turned aside to Breadalbane.

" Though, at this distance of time," says Mr. Macintosh, " I cannot remember the sermons, I well remember their effects, both on myself and others. First our views were brightened and our hearts encouraged in the ways of the Lord. The sermons I had been used to hear were a complete jumble of grace and works,—our endeavours and the sufferings of the Son of God. Often nothing about Christ at all, but that God was merciful, so that I could not tell on what I was to trust for salvation. But in the sermons I heard from Mr. Haldane the distinction was made in the clearest and most solemn manner. The sinner was shown to be a guilty, helpless rebel, and all his righteousness as filthy rags. Then Christ was proclaimed as a glorious and sufficient Saviour, his righteousness free to all who believed, whilst all who believe would be constrained by love to obedience, not in order to save themselves, but because they were saved by his blood. The text which he quoted to me, on parting, I never can forget : ' Cleave to the Lord with purpose of heart.' It was a text which might have been the motto of both the brothers from the day when they knew the grace of God in truth."

On the occasion of the sermon at Perth there was one little incident annoying at the moment, but in after-years only remembered as ludicrous. Mrs. James Haldane, in her affectionate anxiety for her husband, had strictly charged his servant to watch over the comforts of his master, and, amongst other things, to be careful to make him take a glass of port wine immediately after preaching, to strengthen his throat. At the close of the sermon the faithful attendant, true to his orders, but interpreting them somewhat too literally, instantly walked from the vestry up the pulpit-stairs, carrying with him a glass of port, and very unseasonably interrupted his master, who had just sat down after concluding a very solemn appeal, by saying, " Here's the wine, Sir." The short reply was, " Go away, Daniel." Some years afterwards, when Daniel had left his master's service, he became a messenger in the house of the Edinburgh Commercial Banking Company, by whom his punctual attendance to orders and strict Christian fidelity were for many years greatly valued.

On arriving in Breadalbane they were enabled to report, that " there had been no exaggeration ; and that there really was a cloud of witnesses to the power of Divine truth, who were living by the faith of God, waiting for his second and glorious appearing." A pestilential fever was raging in the country, and prevented many from hearing the preachers, but it did not prevent either of the itinerants from visiting the sick and dying.

The venerable Mr. William Tulloch, pastor of the Highland Church, at the Bridge of Tilt, in Athol, thus writes:—

"Nearly fifty years ago, Mr. James Haldane made his first tour through the Highlands. He arrived in Breadalbane, where my wife's family resided. Her mother, who was a good woman, was at that time dangerously ill of fever, which was very prevalent in that part of the country. When Mr. Haldane arrived, he was made aware of this pestilence, and referred to it in preaching. When the sermon was ended, he entered the house and prayed at the bed-side of Mrs. Sinclair, who was so ill that not one of her neighbours would enter the door of her house for fear of infection. Before Mr. Haldane left that quarter he urged upon those that feared God to meet for prayer, that the Lord might remove the pestilence, and it was observed by all, that in a very short time the fever greatly abated, for many had died of it; and not long afterwards it disappeared altogether. And that visit was much blessed to many, both in soul and body.

"Mr. Sinclair was very much opposed to anything that had the appearance of dissent from the Established Church, but he was overcome by the kindness of Mr. Haldane, remarking, when he left, ' If that had not been a man of God, he would not have come into my house when there was so much danger.' From that time Mr. Sinclair showed the greatest kindness to Mr. Haldane ; and, after his death, his son, Donald Sinclair, opened his house to him and the other preachers, when they were in that part of the country. Upon Mr. J. H.'s second visit to Breadalbane (in 1805), many thousands heard from his lips the Gospel of peace, and many came from a great distance to hear.

"When he arrived in Blair Athol, he put up at the inn at Old Blair, and requested the landlord to allow him the use of the inn-hall, that he might preach the Gospel to the people. This was most pointedly refused. But Mr. Haldane was not to be discouraged. He went over all the village, but could not find a place. At last a man named Donaldson, a wright (carpenter) to the old Duke of Athol, offered him the use of his house and barn, where Mr. Haldane preached to multitudes, who came from all parts of the glens round about Blair. It is worthy of remark, that when the Duke turned out all the people from Old Blair, Donaldson was allowed to remain, which he did till his death, which took place only two years ago, at the advanced age of 102 years."

Y

Mr. Tulloch's letter closes by stating, that "the name of Haldane will long be remembered with veneration throughout the Highlands."

After being separated for some time, preaching and visiting in several districts, the itinerants met at Dalwhinnie, where, in the month of June, " the snow was deep on the hills, and falling thick; we had a great fire of peats, but it was so cold that great coats were put on. Yet, next day, at Baldeu, we preached to about four hundred people, at the side of a birch-wood, which kept off the cold wind. Mr. Haldane preached *in* the wood of Aviemore." They passed through Badenoch, Inverness, Dingwall, and Cromarty, preaching as they went. The north side of the frith was once called the Holy Land, "because of its faithful ministers." They could not then hear of " one who preached the Gospel." Such was the length of the days, that, from a very small New Testament, they could read on the mountain at eleven o'clock at night.

Onwards they proceeded, preaching as they went, till they arrived at John o'Groat's house, where they saw only the foundations of the old castle, and thence crossed in the mail-boat, by South Ronaldshay, to Kirkwall, the capital of the Orkneys, where large and listening congregations, in front of the Bishop's Palace, welcomed the return of itinerant preaching. One morning Mr. Campbell was surprised to find only a congregation of women at the place where he preached. But on returning to the town, the mystery was solved, by meeting Captain Gourly, R.N., who had come ashore, but not, as was supposed, with the intention of pressing the men. The Captain breakfasted with them. He was himself, for many years, a member of the Tabernacle Church, whilst flag-captain to the Admiral on the Leith station. " On a lovely morning," says Mr. Campbell, " Mr. James Haldane and I left Kirkwall in two boats, he to visit the western half, and I the eastern, of the group of islands." It would be easy to fill pages with a recital of hardships and privations experienced in these islands, of which Mr. J. A. Haldane however seldom spoke, and never, except as a subject of amusement. At one place, before they

separated, they were in the street of a small town, at ten o'clock
at night, seeking in vain a place of shelter. At last they were
directed to a farm-house, where they asked for shelter, and
were cordially received. Next day, as Mr. Campbell tells, that,
after preaching, they went into a house, hoping to be offered
refreshment, yet afraid to offend by tendering payment, but
got nothing but a cup of milk and water. "They then walked
about, intimating another sermon, until they were tired." At
length they called at the house of a slater, who hospitably
provided them with bread, milk, and cheese. Damp sheets,
hard beds, or none at all, and a scanty supply of food, were
amongst the luxuries of these remote itinerancies. But they had
both learned "to endure hardness, as good soldiers of Jesus
Christ," to sympathize with the far greater privations of the first
missionaries of the Gospel, and to regard these discomforts only
as trifles incidental to their campaigns in the service of the King
of kings.

Mr. Campbell was to have preached at an island between
Kirkwall and Stronsay, but a heavy gale of wind arose, which
prevented his arrival. However, he reached Kirkwall the day
after, when he found, says his biographer, that Mr. James
Haldane, who, like "an old sailor, had seen, from the state
of the weather, that it would be impossible to reach it," had,
with characteristic energy, not only discharged his own duties,
but procured a boat from Kirkwall, and having the gale blowing
in his favour reached the island, and preached himself to the
people. From Kirkwall they proceeded to Hoy, and then
crossed the Pentland Frith, of whose tumultuous waves, rushing
tides, gurgling whirlpools, and perpendicular rocks, Mr. Campbell gives a graphic description.

After leaving Thurso, they preached on their way to Edinburgh at all the principal towns in their route.

Shortly after their return in September, of the same year,
Mr. James Haldane undertook a short tour with Mr. Campbell
to the south of Scotland and north of England. On this
occasion Mrs. James Haldane accompanied her husband, and
with them Mr. Campbell posted to Berwick, where he remained

to preach on the Lord's-day, and Mr. and Mrs. J. A. Haldane next day proceeded to Alnwick, where they were hospitably entertained by Mr. and Mrs. Rate. On the following Wednesday, having been joined by Mr. Campbell, they journeyed to Carlisle, by Flamlingham and Chaullingford to Glenwhilt, where Mr. J. A. Haldane, as usual, gave an address, at the inn, to all who chose to attend at prayers. Passing through Gilsland, they arrived at Carlisle on the following day, when Mr. Campbell proceeded by the mail to Longtown, where, however, he was refused the chapel to preach in, "though Mr. J. Haldane's preaching, and mine, had been the means of its being built." It was now attached to the Establishment. Mr. and Mrs. James Haldane arrived at Longtown on the following day, and proceeded by Annan to Dumfries, where there was a Tabernacle, of which Mr. Robert Haldane became the sole proprietor, although it was originally erected at the joint expense of the two brothers. After a sermon, which Mr. James Haldane preached at Garlieston, when Lady Elizabeth Stewart was present, the Countess of Galloway invited them to her house, and the Earl announced his willingness to grant a site for a chapel in the village, as the church was three miles distant.

At Wigton the Provost supped with them at the inn. He had been previously in the habit of giving to Mr. James Haldane the use of the Town Hall. But, on the first occasion, when he asked permission to announce sermon by the bellman, the Provost replied, "No, no, Sir; you cannot preach here." Mr. J. A. Haldane answered, "I do not ask liberty to *preach*, but to ring." "Then you *will* preach." "Yes, certainly." "Very well, you may send out the bellman." At Sanquhar, the Antiburgher minister had inflicted Church discipline upon some of his people five years before, for hearing Mr. James Haldane, and it will be remembered that, in 1800, a collier begged that they would not mention that he had directed them on their road. "But to-day," says Mr. Campbell, "some Antiburghers broke through to hear me, and one of them told the minister yesterday that they *would* hear us."

They returned through Ayrshire, preaching as they went. On Saturday, the 24th of September, they arrived at Greenock, and on the following Lord's-day Mr. J. A. Haldane preached in the morning at Auldkirk, and in the evening at the Burgher meeting-house of Greenock. "The crowd," says Mr. C., "was great." On the 27th, Mr. Campbell having gone to Bishoptown, Mr. J. A. Haldane preached at Paisley, where a large congregation came to hear. On the following evening he also preached at the Tabernacle, at Glasgow, to a great audience. On the 30th they all breakfasted at Mr. Ewing's, and, having left at eleven o'clock, arrived in Edinburgh at half-past five in the afternoon. Mr. Campbell seems thus to announce the time, as indicating the rapidity of posting, as compared with the heavy coaches, to which he was accustomed in 1803. The same journey can now be performed within an hour by steam. Mr. Campbell used to mention it as a remarkable fact, that Mr. J. A. Haldane had told him, that the invention of coppering ships had brought India several months nearer to England. The discovery of steam has brought India within little more than a month from our shores. But great as is the power of steam, it is already, in one respect, eclipsed by the lightning speed of electricity. Mr. Campbell thus concludes his journal : —" During this tour we travelled about four hundred miles, had fine weather the whole way, excepting two days, preached in many dark corners, conversed with many disciples, I hope to their comfort and stirring up, and not one accident happened. Praise the Lord, O my soul."

Mr. Campbell did not long remain in Edinburgh, although this was not his last itinerancy with Mr. James Haldane. He was within a few weeks afterwards invited to occupy a chapel at Kingsland, near London, where he remained till his death, in 1840. He stipulated that his settlement in Kingsland should not interfere with his itinerating labours, and two years later he made another long tour with his old friend, whose popularity, as a preacher, continued unabated. The marvel had, indeed, in a great measure passed away; yet his unwearied labours, his solid attainments, and added experience, gave him a weight of

character, which was daily increasing. It is in speaking of him
at this period, that one who, to say the least, is by no means
too partial, makes the following remarks :*—

" At this time Mr. Haldane was a highly-gifted and deservedly *popular*
preacher, in the best sense of popularity. Mr. Campbell often says of his
sermons, ' they were solemn and striking, and the people all attention.'
It will both illustrate and verify this, to say, that the late Mr. Cowie,
of Huntley, himself the Whitfield of the north, in the estimation of
Rowland Hill, says, in manuscripts in my possession, that he was often
both humbled and inspired by Mr. Haldane's ' unction from the Holy
One.' This fact, I recollect well, although I was too young to understand
the sermons it refers to. Besides, he could not have been popular in Mr.
Cowie's circle, had he not been a powerful preacher."

The Rev. Andrew Fuller made a second visit to Scotland in
1802, and his letters contain an account of his progress, during
which he was accompanied by the now venerable and distinguished Dr. Wardlaw, then described as "a young man, of
promising character," brought up for the Burgher Secession,
which he had "left for the Tabernacle connexion." In the
same letter we find the following extract, given by Mr. Fuller's
biographer, under the date of Stirling, September, 1802 :—

" On Friday, the 17th, I rose early, and went to see the town and castle
before breakfast. This (Stirling) is a most romantic situation, the finest
spot I have seen in Scotland. Here the Scottish kings used occasionally
to reside. I suppose it was their summer-house. Near this is the late
seat of Robert Haldane, Esq., a seat, which a Scottish nobleman has pronounced to be ' a perfect heaven upon earth;' but which he sold, and
has ever since lived in a recluse style of life, laying out thousands every
year for the propagation of the Gospel, in Scotland and Ireland. ' Oh!
(say the gentry), he must have some deep scheme in his head.' Some
of the clergy cannot endure him; but he has great interest with the
common people. He is a great economist, in order to be generous.
He has saved 30,000*l.*, I am told, by the advance of the funds since he
bought in."

This statement with reference to Mr. Haldane's gains in the
funds was an idle piece of gossip, which a wise man might
possibly have written in the confidence of friendship, but which

* Philip's Life and Times of John Campbell, p. 356.

a judicious biographer should hardly have published without
inquiry, especially in the lifetime of a gentleman, the privacy of
whose personal affairs was thus unceremoniously invaded.
There was not even a foundation for the report, and in point of
fact, although Mr. Fuller was not aware of it, the rumour was
one of the many forms of calumny, by which an envious spirit
of detraction vainly tried to impeach motives which it could
not fathom, and disparage a liberality which it could not reach.
Mr. Campbell tells of a Highland Laird, who exhorted the
people not to hear the missionaries, adding, " Haldane is
making *ten* per cent. of his Tabernacles." The answer of the
poor Highlander was admirable. He did not contradict his
chief, but said, " Weel, Sir, if he were, he is doing *gude* to the
people." Probably neither the Laird nor his clansman were
aware, that the surplus, when there was any, never returned
to the proprietor, but was all appropriated to the preaching of
the Gospel.

The first outcry against Mr. Robert Haldane was raised on
the ground of politics. But no sooner was this silenced, than
another equally futile, but infinitely more absurd, was pressed
into the service of the opponents of Home Missions. Here was
a gentleman of acknowledged talents, the very reverse of an
enthusiast, and in all worldly matters distinguished for his calm
judgment, and shrewd, calculating turn of mind, who had sold
a fine estate, and was educating missionaries at a vast expense,
besides building or purchasing large places of worship in most
of the principal towns of Scotland. Everywhere, from Thurso
and Wick in the north, to Dumfries in the south, these chapels
were crowded, and as there were collections made at the door,
partly for the poor and partly for the spread of the Gospel, and
as rents were paid for some of the pews, the rumour went
abroad, that in these schemes the originator was, after all, by
no means neglecting his worldly interests. Seven years later,
the gossip of 1802, for a brief period, obtained renewed
currency, in consequence of expressions hastily used by Mr.
Ewing, writing unadvisedly with his pen, when he spoke of
Mr. Haldane as "adding thousand to thousand in the funds."

The actors in these busy scenes are now all removed from the haunts of living men, and the clamour of prejudice or of passion is silenced in death. Such statements are known to be ridiculous, and the bitterest opponent of Mr. Haldane's measures would no longer venture to impeach the sincerity of his loyalty, the extent of his sacrifices, or the purity of his motives. Such aspersions would now be unworthy of notice, were it not that future ecclesiastical historians might be disposed to mistake silence for admission. At the time of Mr. Fuller's journey to Scotland, in 1802, the portion of Airthrey which he retained unsold, exclusive of his lands in Forfarshire, exceeded in value the whole of his stock in the public funds. Mr. Haldane's liberality was, however, always under the control of a wise economy, and but for this and his calculating financial habits, it would have been impossible to effect what he did with the same means. But it is no matter of surprise that this very prudence sometimes proved distasteful to people not themselves accustomed to the management of property. Mr. L. Macintosh was on one occasion alluding to the fact, that Mr. Haldane's generosity was often regarded rather as a proof of his wealth than of his liberality, and he added, that there were those to whom Mr. Haldane had shown great kindness, who, instead of feeling gratitude, seemed to look upon his fortune " as a wreck cast upon the shore, to which all ought to be allowed to help themselves." The same excellent minister was, on another occasion, much grieved to hear one, who had been raised from the station of a mechanic, censuring his patron's economy. " You seem," said the new-made preacher, in a flippant tone, " to wince when anything is said against Mr. Haldane." " Yes," replied Mr. Macintosh, " I always feel ashamed to hear him found fault with by those whom he made gentlemen, and who, but for his purse, would still have been cobbling shoes."

In the year 1802 the studies of Mr. Ewing's second class ended, when the Glasgow seminary was closed, and another was immediately opened in Edinburgh on a larger scale, more under the control of Mr. Haldane and his brother. In theology the students had the advantage of the personal instructions of Mr. Aikman, aided by the practical good sense and Christian experience of Mr. John Campbell. To them was added, as Classical Tutor, Mr. Thomas Wemyss, " a gentleman," says Dr. Lindsay Alexander, " who has secured to himself a very respectable place amongst biblical scholars by his work on the ' Symbolical Language of Scripture,' and his translation of the Book of Job." Towards the end of their course, Mr. Campbell retired, but his place was supplied by Mr. Wm. Stephens, whose very striking history is detailed in the " Missionary Magazine." He was a man of good parts and fine elocution, who had been at one time on the stage, but was brought to the knowledge of the truth, and became a powerful and useful preacher. He was at first a minister at Aberdeen, and next came to assist in the Tabernacle at Edinburgh, where he remained until he adopted Baptist sentiments. He then proceeded to England, and settled at Rochdale, where he preached for many years until his death. In 1803, the Rev. Mr. Cowie, of Montrose, originally a licentiate of the Church of Scotland, took Mr. Aikman's place, and also assisted at the Tabernacle. He was a man of deep piety and of very amiable and agreeable manners, possessed of considerable talent, although his usefulness was somewhat impaired by unequal spirits and a tendency to morbid depression.

The following is the account given of the Seminaries by one who was indebted to them for his own education, and became not only an occasional preacher but the able instructor of the Edinburgh Deaf and Dumb Institution. It is extracted from the lamented Mr. Robert Kinniburgh's " Historical Survey of Congregationalism in Scotland," which contains the only accurate narrative that has yet appeared of the early proceedings of the originators of the Circus and Tabernacle system :—

" I. The *first* class began in January, 1799, under the tuition of Mr. Ewing. In December, 1800, this class completed their term of study, and were sent to different stations as preachers. In it were John Munro, George Robertson, &c.

" II. The *second* class commenced in January, 1800, at Dundee, under

Mr. Innes. In this class were a few who had been catechists, and who were found to possess talents capable of being trained for the ministry. In the early part of 1801, all of this class were removed to Glasgow, and were under Mr. Ewing for fifteen months. In it were Dr. Paterson, Alexander Thomson, &c.

" III. In 1801, the *third* class began in Dundee, under Mr. Innes, but its students met with a very serious interruption, being sent for a time to supply stations with preaching at the end of the first year. They, however, came to Edinburgh in 1804, and finished their term of study. In this class were Francis Dick, Alexander Kerr, &c.

" IV. The *fourth* class began in Edinburgh, in 1802, under Messrs. Aikman and Wemyss, with the addition of Mr. Stephens, towards the close of the second year. In it were William Newry, Peter M'Laren, &c.

" V. In 1803, a *fifth* class was organized under Messrs. Aikman, Wemyss, and Stephens, Mr. Cowie taking Mr. Aikman's place during the second year. In it were Dr. Russell (Dundee), John Watson (Musselburgh), &c.

" VI. The *sixth* class began in 1804, under Messrs. Wemyss, Stephens, and Cowie, for the first year, but were under Mr. Cowie alone during the second year. In this class were Alexander Knowles, John Black, &c.

" VII. The *seventh* class assembled in 1805. In it were William Orme, John Neave, &c. This and the next class were under Messrs. Cowie and Walker.

" VIII. The *eighth* class met in September, 1806. In it were Thomas Smith (Rotherham), Robert Aikenhead, &c. Mr. Cowie resigned the tutorship in the spring of 1808.

" IX. A *ninth* class was formed in the end of 1807, and was under the care of Mr. William Walker till December, 1808, when the Seminary was given up, after having sent out nearly 300 preachers.

" The course of study of these classes generally extended over two years, with a vacation of six weeks in each year, and embraced English grammar and rhetoric, the elements of Greek and Hebrew,—the last three classes had Latin in addition,—lectures on systematic theology, and essays upon prescribed subjects. Each student in rotation delivered sermons before the class, the tutor making his remarks. One day in each week all were required to speak in rotation from a passage of Scripture appointed for that purpose, the tutor making concluding observations. The students were supported, had medical attendance when needed, their education and class-books were given them, and they had access to a large and well-selected library,—all at the expense of Mr. Robert Haldane. Although, in consequence of the urgent demand for labourers, the young men were sent out with more meagre attainments than would have been proper in other circumstances, yet among them there were very many who would have done honour to any of the religious bodies of the day. Dr. Struthers, speaking of these seminaries, says, ' Among the 300 sent forth from these classes, before they were altogether given up, there were some *choice spirits* who, having got a start in learning, pushed on their private studies with vigour, and obtained success.' This is quite correct. There were ' *choice spirits*' among them, some of whom subsequently made attainments in actual scholarship equal to and beyond the attainments of many who boast of their University education ; while others of them, although they did not aspire to be erudite scholars, yet, by diligent application, rose to eminence as preachers and writers. Speaking generally, those sent out from the seminaries were men befitting the times in which they lived. They were raised up in mercy to a perishing world ; and if they did not succeed in drawing multitudes to their chapels, it must be ascribed, in a great measure, to the unbending principles which they ever maintained. Thus, a succession of efficient preachers was secured, on a plan adapted to the necessities of the times, and which provided for the supply of their wants, without presenting any temptation to those to embark in the cause whose avarice was greater than their zeal for doing good." *

In addition to the nine classes enumerated above, as conducted at Mr. Haldane's expense during ten years, there was another taught by the Rev. Mr. Hamilton, at Armagh, and at least two others in Scotland, of which Mr. Kinniburgh does not seem to have been aware. The one was at Elgin, under Mr. Ballantyne, and the other was at Granton, under Mr. L. Macintosh, in 1820 and several subsequent years. There was another on a smaller scale, instituted at Paris, under the care of the amiable and excellent ministers, MM. Francois, and Henri Olivier, of Lausanne, during the time when, in 1824, they were for three years banished from the Canton de Vaud. Both the brothers also contributed to the maintenance of theological students, at a later period, taught by Dr. Carson, in Ireland. The arrangements connected with the erection or management of the Tabernacles and Missionary Seminaries, in themselves involved a large amount of labour and responsibility. But Mr. Haldane

---

* Dr. Struthers, in his " History of the Relief Church," observes : " He (Mr. R. Haldane) set up academies in Glasgow, Dundee, and Edinburgh, under Messrs. Ewing, Innes, and Haldane." This is a mistake, excepting so far as Mr. James Haldane assisted his brother in watching over and superintending the progress and education of the students.

had also on his hands the chief direction of the " Society for Propagating the Gospel at Home," besides the labour of corresponding with many parts of Scotland, England, and Ireland.

Even at this early period, he was not indifferent to the claims of the continent of Europe. At one time he endeavoured to prevail on a pious and judicious merchant at Leith, William Alexander, Esq. (the father of the Rev. Dr. Lindsay Alexander), to proceed to Leghorn, which was a free port, with the view of trying what could be done in the way of introducing Bibles or tracts into Tuscany and other parts of Italy. A few years later, he also proposed to an able Irish clergyman, for whom he entertained a sincere regard, to settle at Hamburgh, with a view to establish a missionary station for promoting the Gospel in Germany. Both of these designs failed. But it was doubtless well that they were in his heart; and when in after-years we find him at Geneva and at Montauban, instructing the students of these Protestant Colleges in the knowledge of the truth as it is in Jesus, it will not be forgotten that at the outset of his career, and during the space of ten years, he had been accustomed to draw around him those young men whom he educated in Scotland, for the purpose of enlarging their views as to the glory of the person of Christ, and the great doctrines of the ever-blessed Gospel. From these details, it will be seen that his ardent and energetic mind was as much engaged in the missionary work as if he had accomplished his original plan, and as an evangelist had expatriated himself amongst the heathen at Patna or Benares.

# CHAPTER XV.

MR. JAMES HALDANE PREACHES ON THE DEATH OF LORD
CAMELFORD, KILLED IN A DUEL — CIRCUMSTANCES OF
THE DUEL, AND THE REV. MR. COCKBURN'S ACCOUNT OF
THE NOBLE LORD'S CHARACTER—MR. JAMES HALDANE
VISITS BUXTON—GOES TO DUBLIN—PREACHES IN THE
BETHESDA CHAPEL—MR. WALKER, FELLOW OF TRINITY
COLLEGE — MR. JAMES HALDANE GOES TO LONDON—
DEATH OF ADMIRAL LORD DUNCAN—TOUR TO BREAD-
ALBANE, INVERNESS, CAITHNESS, &c.

[1804—5.]

EARLY in the spring of 1804, Mr. James Haldane preached a
remarkable sermon on the death of Thomas Pitt, second Baron
Camelford, who was mortally wounded in a duel by Captain
Best, and died in great agony four days afterwards. This fatal
catastrophe had produced an extraordinary sensation, more
especially following as it did on another duel, in which Colonel
Montgomery, not many months before, fell by the hand of
Captain Macnamara, in a wretched quarrel in Hyde Park about
their dogs. These events were calculated to arouse attention to
the miserable fruits of the world's code of honour, in submission
to which a young nobleman, at the age of twenty-nine, nephew
to the great Earl of Chatham, and cousin to the Prime Minister,
had forfeited his own life, extinguished a peerage, and sacrificed
a great fortune, which chiefly fell to his sister, the wife of the
celebrated Lord Grenville. Lord Camelford was not one of the
common run of fashionable men, living upon town. He had
fine natural talents. His illustrious uncle had bestowed much
pains on his education, and addressed to him a series of letters
with a view to his improvement, which have been since published. He had been passionately fond of science, and in many

subjects connected with literature was no mean proficient.  But
in those unhappy days, when duelling was reckoned a mark of
spirit, he had acquired in the navy and in the world of fashion
the reputation of a first-rate shot.  He had provoked and been
concerned in many duels, and on one occasion, where the death
of a superior officer in the West Indies had left some doubt as
to the seniority of the next in succession, he brought the matter
to an issue by giving to his rival, a Lieutenant Peterson, certain
orders, on disobedience of which he shot him dead on the sea-
beach, although at the head of an armed boat's crew, ready to
uphold their commander.  For this rash act he was tried by a
court-martial, but being found in the right as to his seniority, and
consequent title to give the order, he was honourably acquitted.

The notoriety thus acquired was not diminished by the fact,
that he had returned Mr. Horne Tooke to Parliament for his
pocket borough, and threatened to substitute his own black
servant in case of his nominee being declared by the House of
Commons disqualified as a clergyman.  Lord Camelford and
Mr. Best were both in the navy, and intimate friends; but they
had at the time a bet of 200l. depending, as to which was the
better shot.  The meeting took place through the instigation
of an abandoned woman, then under the protection of Lord
Camelford, who falsely accused her former protector, Mr. Best,
of having spoken disrespectfully of his Lordship.  This greatly
incensed the irascible Peer, who went up to Mr. Best at the
Prince of Wales Hotel, in Conduit-street, where they usually
dined, and after some altercation, pronounced him "a scoundrel,
a liar, and a ruffian."  Mr. Best observed that these were expressions which admitted but of one answer, and a meeting was
arranged for the next morning.  But in the course of the
evening he conveyed to Lord Camelford the assurance, that the
information on which his Lordship spoke was unfounded, and
that a retractation of the words used under a wrong impression
would be perfectly satisfactory.  They again met in the morning
at a coffee-house in Oxford-street, and once more Mr. Best
pleaded for reconciliation, adding, "Do not persist in expressions under which one of us must fall."  At this very moment

Lord Camelford knew that he had been imposed on, and had written a declaration on his will that he was the "aggressor in the spirit as well as letter of the word." But false pride would not allow the haughty Peer to listen to a remonstrance, which might impeach his courage, and he replied : "Best, this is child's play; the affair must go on." On proceeding to the ground, behind Holland House, he reiterated to his second, the Hon. W. Devereux, the statement he had appended to his will, but said that he was fearful that his reputation would suffer if he made any concession to one whom he rather thought was the best shot in England. They were placed at fifteen paces from each other, fired together, and Lord Camelford fell, to all appearance dead. In an instant he recovered the shock, so far as to exclaim, "I am killed, but I acquit Best; I alone am to blame." Captain Best and his second instantly rode off; and Lord Camelford's friend, on pretence of going for a surgeon, did the same as soon as a countryman came up, who found his Lordship lying on his back, in the lower part of a field overflowed with water. His Lordship was unwilling to be moved, but was at last placed in a chair and conveyed to Little Holland House, where he lingered in great pain till the following Saturday, and then died. The ball had penetrated his right breast, passing through the lungs, and lodging in the back bone. He sent for his solicitor, and made a codicil to his will, in which he stated, that although most people desire that their remains might be conveyed to their native land to be interred, "I wish my body to be removed, as soon as may be convenient, to a country far distant, to a spot not near the haunts of men, but where the surrounding scenery may smile upon my remains." The place he chose was on the borders of the Lake of St. Lemprierre, in the Canton of Berne, where three trees stood on a particular spot. The centre tree he desired to be taken up, and after his body was there deposited, to be replanted. He added, "Let no monument or stone be placed on my grave." At the foot of this tree, his Lordship said he had passed many hours, meditating on the mutability of human affairs. He left 1000*l.* as compensation to the proprietors.

In the spirit evinced by Lord Camelford may be traced something resembling that unhappy, morbid tone of mind that characterized Lord Byron. But it was not merely the circumstances of this remarkable duel, nor yet the conduct of the unhappy nobleman, that determined Mr. James Haldane to call attention to it from the pulpit. What seemed far more to demand special notice and animadversion, was the style in which the event was published, and the character of the deceased drawn by his Lordship's intimate friend, a reverend gentleman, then a Fellow of St. John's College, Cambridge. That clergyman painted Lord Camelford as " a curious mixture of much that was virtuous and much that was vicious, all in extremes." He described him as irascible in temper, " which brought him into many broils," but " warm in his affections, and almost unexampled in his benevolence." He did not " distribute less than 4000*l.* a-year in the purchase of commissions for gallant young men, and in the relief of decayed seamen and soldiers." He was " a stern adversary, but the mildest and most generous of friends," often the dupe of the designing and crafty supplicant, but oftener " the soother of real sorrow and unmerited woe." He had read " *sceptical books* for the purpose of puzzling the chaplains on board the ships in which he served," and thus his mind had become tainted with infidelity; but yet he " was not without a proper sense of religion at the awful moment when the levities of imagination give way to the solemn convictions of the mind." There was thus a balance struck between vice and virtue, infidelity and faith, which was followed up by an assurance, that " in the worst moments of his pain, he cried out that he sincerely hoped the agonies he then endured might *expiate* the sins he had committed." Mr. Cockburn also informed the public, that he had enjoyed many conversations with his Lordship, who little more than a week before his death had said, " No sensible and well-informed man can presume to say that Christianity is false. I do not yet venture to assert that it is true, but I confess the probabilities are in its favour." It was thus that Mr. Cockburn, whilst unable to palliate the vices of Lord Camelford, down to the moment when he plunged into eternity, still endeavoured to paint what he termed "his counterbalancing virtues," and seemed to countenance the hope of the dying Peer, that the agonies of his death-bed might be an expiation for his sins.

No one who knew James Haldane can wonder that his spirit was stirred within him, when he saw such statements circulated and read with avidity, whilst the public mind was fixed with intense interest on the romantic character of Lord Camelford, as drawn by his reverend apologist. The opportunity seemed calculated to be useful to those who at other times might not be disposed to listen to the Gospel. He knew the censure to which it might expose him, but he publicly announced that, without the possibility of injuring the dead, and in the hope of doing good to the living, it was his intention to preach, on the next Lord's-day, with reference to the death of Lord Camelford. Of the multitude that thronged to hear that sermon there are now comparatively few survivors. Some have lately departed, and amongst these the venerable Christopher Anderson. Of this sermon, he wrote, not long before his own death : " It was understood that Mr. James Haldane meant to examine and expose this melancholy affair. Familiar as he had been for years with sea life, and once himself under tyranny of these miserable 'laws of honour,' there was no man better qualified. The fear of God was now his governing principle, yet it required no common fortitude to meet such a case before such an audience."

The spacious building in which he preached, then capable of seating more than 3,000 persons, was crowded to the doors. It was at the time of the threatened invasion, when the whole nation resounded with the clang of arms, and the most peaceful civilians were often arrayed in military costume. When he entered the pulpit, there rose before him, not only the usual congregation, but officers in full uniform from Piershill barracks and the Castle,—cavalry, infantry, artillery, and volunteers, officers on Lord Moira's staff, magistrates, men of letters and philosophers, men of business and retired gentlemen, all assembled to hear what was to be said in reprobation of duelling, and of the account circulating in print, from the pen of the

z

Rev. Fellow of St. John's, Cambridge, who attended the death-bed of Lord Camelford.

It was a great occasion, and Mr. James Haldane's MS. notes give a rough outline of the manner in which he treated the subject. He took for his text no passage of Scripture, but holding in his hand a page of the "Edinburgh Advertiser," which was found amongst his papers at his death, he began by stating, that in deviating from the usual practice of discoursing on a portion of Scripture, it was not his intention to lead his hearers away from the Word of God, but rather to call their attention to a subject which strikingly illustrated its truth. "Thus," he said, "we find the Lord taking for the subject of his discourse the fall of the tower of Siloam, and the apostles speaking to the people from events as they occurred. Lord Camelford," he continued, "was mortally wounded in a duel, and after languishing some days, expired. He was attended by a clergyman, who gives the following account." He then read the whole of the extract, with marked emphasis, adding, "Let us, by the help of God, attend to some considerations which this melancholy statement naturally suggests." The following MS. notes can furnish but a faint idea of the topics handled, and none at all of his impressive manner, or of that instinctive power by which he seemed to bring his audience into the imme-diate presence of God :—

" 1. The manner of his death.

" What a striking proof is there in the practice of duelling that duellists have not the fear of God ! Can anything more plainly show that they prefer the praise of men to the praise of God, and that in the most deliberate manner ?  It does not arise from a sudden gust of passion, but the great bulk of men in a certain rank of life live in the habitual determination in this way to set God at defiance. They even plead that it is necessary, or they would forfeit their honour. Now, every man holding such sentiments is habitually guilty of deliberate rebellion against God, and, according to the Lord's exposition of the law, is a murderer. Matt. v. 28. It has been observed, that perhaps there is no other sin which men habitually resolve to practise, whenever a temptation shall occur. In consequence of the great increase of the army, this is likely to become more frequent. Every one in the rank of an officer, or even of a private in some corps, considers himself as a man of honour, that is, a man who is bound by his character to trample on the laws of God; to set Him at defiance, and to risk rushing into His presence a murderer or a suicide.  Psalm x. 13."

The second topic discussed was "Lord Camelford's character," as drawn by his clerical friend, and the notes proceed:—

"His character.  Great vices counterbalanced by great virtues, especially benevolence.  Here notice the false views of benevolence.  There is a kind of instinct which leads us to pity distress.  Without this, society would be a Pandemonium, and could not exist.  But this is very different from true benevolence; for men pity others when in great distress, who would have been grieved to see them in great prosperity.  True benevolence is a universal principle, and necessarily connected with love to God, the greatest and best of beings.  False benevolence is confined to ourselves, and perhaps a few connected with us.  True benevolence is a steady principle, discovering itself in various ways, according as there is opportunity to do good to others.  False benevolence is partial, leading us, according to our caprice, to do some acts of seeming kindness, while we can at pleasure deliberately gratify our passions at the expense of the happiness of others and the good of society.  Here we see a man confessedly guilty of very great improprieties, who lived in habitual contempt of God, yet munificent in his charities, &c.

"3. The awful levity and contempt with which he treated revelation.  The Almighty God, in compassion to man, condescends to send a revelation of mercy, and a creature to whom it is addressed shall actually read books to find arguments for the sake of proving it to be false.  Thus the madman scatters arrows, firebrands, and death, and says, Am not I in sport?  Here is the mind capable of the most lively efforts of active benevolence, who would pour contempt on the Son of God, who would jest with his sufferings and death, and rob mankind, as far as his puny arm was able, of what sweetens life, and supports in death.

"4. But it seems, ' he was not, however, without a proper sense of religion at the awful moment,' &c.  There is a moment when reckless unbelief gives way to the solemn convictions of the mind.  These, although stifled, are not effaced.  All men hold the truth in unrighteousness; their own hearts condemn them, knowing the just judgment of God, that they who do such things are worthy of death.  By indulging in sin they drown, but do not satisfy, their conscience, which will, sooner or later, testify against them and stop every mouth.

"5. Here, in Lord Camelford's own words, we see the natural conviction in the mind of man that sin deserves punishment.  He knew he needed some expiation.  In wealth, and in the midst of his pleasures, he might have smiled at the idea that God would be so strict as to call him to account, or he might consider the money he lavished as a sufficient atonement for any improprieties of conduct; for such is the deceitfulness of the human heart, that men, amidst the commission of the grossest sins, seek to establish their own righteousness. It is said, he gave away thousands yearly, yet conscience demanded another expiation, and he found that, even in his own judgment, all these acts of benevolence were insufficient to entitle him to the favour of God.

" 6. Notice the blindness of the human heart here discovered,—he hoped that the pain produced by his own conduct, by perishing in a duel, although convinced he was completely wrong, that the immediate consequence of this crime would ' *expiate* ' his guilt. Alas! how do they mistake who imagine that a few hours of pain will satisfy the infinite demands of Divine justice.

" 7. This, however, could not give relief. It was but like a drowning man snatching at a straw. He was driven to appeal to the *mercy* of God, and to desire it might be sought for him by prayer. Here we see how in distress the stoutest heart fails, and the convinced sinner, feeling his need of God, would appeal to his mercy. But, ah! he had neglected the great salvation,—overlooked the only way of obtaining mercy; and, in this dreadful situation, with an awakened conscience, it appears he had none to inform him how God is just, yet justifies the ungodly. Without the knowledge of Christ, all is uncertainty,—groping in the dark. Without the knowledge of Christ, mercy can only be expected by overlooking the justice and truth of God. Men may vainly imagine that repeating prayers, or expressing sorrow for the past, will recommend them to the mercy of God; but a deceived heart turns them aside, nor have they understanding to say, ' Is there not a lie in my right hand ? '

" 8. How many methods do men employ to ruin themselves, sheltering themselves under the opinion of others! Mr. Cockburn says : ' I have heard it asserted, by those who would fain shelter their own follies under the authority of others, that Lord Camelford, after the most serious reflection and inquiry, doubted a life hereafter. I wish, with all my soul, that the unthinking votaries of dissipation and infidelity could all have been present at the death-bed of this poor man ; could have heard his expressions of contrition for past misconduct, and of reliance on the mercy of his Creator ; could have heard his dying exhortations to one of his intimate friends, to live in future a life of peace and virtue. I think it would have made impressions on their minds, as it did on mine, not easily to be effaced.' It is evident he doubted, when in health, and could then ridicule religion : but now, all this was over. The sceptic and the scoffer stood appalled in the presence of the King of terrors. Infidelity may harden the mind in prosperity, but is a miserable comforter in the hour of trial. It vanishes when its aid is most needed. Now he acknowledges a God, laments his own misconduct, and places his reliance on mercy. But what is the foundation of that confidence? Is it the death of Christ? Alas! his name is not once mentioned. Was it founded on the pain he endured or the prayers he offered? How awful if the conscience be thus lulled! It is like sleep produced by opium, which nowise diminishes the force of disease, and is only the forerunner of fresh pain and anguish.

" 9. Notice the excellence of that conduct which flows from religion, living soberly, righteously, and godly. It receives testimonies from friends and enemies. To it the dying servant of Jesus, finishing his career with joy, looks back with delight. (2 Tim. iv. 6.) To it the degraded courtier testifies, ' Had I but served my God as I have served my King, He would not have left me in my old age.' To it this man, who had no longer opportunity of indulging in sin, and, consequently, being able to judge impartially, condemns his own conduct and recommends a life of peace and virtue.

" Improvement. First, the cause of taking this subject. It is objected, that it is improper to notice the dead. Scripture does so. I have done so for the sake of the living. I have taken the account given of him by his friend. No wish to hurt his character, nor can what I or others say affect his eternal state.

" 1. The madness of treating Christianity with contempt, without giving it a serious hearing.

" 2. Folly of putting off thoughts of death to sick-bed, when racked with pain or stupified with medicine.

" 3. The amazing goodness of God in the gift of his Son, and the satisfaction which the knowledge of this imparts to the mind. No conjecture, but the word and oath of God."

In the following words the Rev. C. Anderson thus concludes his own personal recollections of the soul-stirring sermon preached on this striking occasion :—" In his address Mr. James Haldane took up the statement given in the public prints, paragraph by paragraph, exposing and reprobating it, as he went on, in a manner which such a man alone could do. The immense audience was still throughout, in awe before his earnest manner and thrilling language; and some then present, and yet alive, well remember that solemn scene even to this hour."

If the limits of this volume permitted, it might be alike interesting to pause and inquire what it was that gave such intensity and power to sermons such as this on the death of Lord Camelford, which the venerable Christopher Anderson and others remembered with so much feeling. It was not the bewitching influence of human oratory; it was not the capacity of ministering to intellectual enjoyment; it was not by appeals which gratify the imagination or stir the ordinary faculties of the soul. The secret of such preaching has been deeply scanned by the philosopher of Stanford Rivers, in his work intituled "Wesley and Methodism, by Isaac Taylor." It may be thought, perhaps, that he scarcely attaches sufficient weight to the difference of natural gifts possessed by preachers using the same spiritual weapons, and too much confounds such men as Wesley and Whitfield with their disciples. Natural and spiritual gifts both proceed from the Father of lights, and natural gifts are never to be lost sight of, even in the discussion of the effects produced by those which are spiritual. Whether this criticism be correct or not, there is at all events much truth in the following contrast, where the eloquent writer sketches the picture of a congregation listening to Dr. Chalmers, and contrasts it with another picture of a congregation listening to a preacher of the school of Whitfield :—

"We can many of us recal the recollection of those overcrowding times, when a preacher of unmatched power and grace, a perfect orator, used to fix every eye upon himself through his hour of fluent and affluent sublimities. How did all faces gleam with an intensity of intellectual enjoyment, longing to vent itself in loud acclamations at every pause! And when that hour of fascination was over, what looks of gratulation were exchanged among friends from pew to pew! what shaking of hands, and how many smiles and nods passed to and fro, among the delighted people!

"But now all these pleasurable indications must be dismissed, for it is a Methodist of Wesley's or of Whitfield's order that is in this same pulpit. As a preacher he is not more sincere or right-minded than the last; and as an orator he is far less highly gifted. . . . But his words sink into the hearts of those that hear. While he speaks, a suppressed anxiety rules the spirits of the crowd, and this feeling breaks forth into sighs on every side. The preacher's style is not, in itself, oratorically affecting, and yet many weep, and an expression not to be simulated, of anguish and of dread, marks many faces. What is it, then, that has taken place? It is this, that a sense, deep seated in the structure of human nature, but which hitherto has slumbered, has suddenly woke up. There is a tumult in the soul, while a power irresistible is claiming its rights over both body and soul. Instead of that interchange of smiles which lately had pervaded the congregation, while the orator was doing his part, now every man feels himself, for the hour, alone in that crowd. Even the preacher is almost forgotten; for an immortal and guilty spirit has come into the presence of eternal justice. Within the dismayed heart it is as if the moral condition, hitherto unheeded, were spread abroad for strictest scrutiny. Quite gone from the thoughts are all those accessories of religious feeling, which so often, in times past, had been the source of agreeable devout excitement. It is a dread of the supreme rectitude that now holds the mind and heart. . . It is as if a lost rudiment of the moral nature had sprung into activity. It is a sense of the soul's relationship to God,—a relationship which nothing can dissolve, and which demands the immortality of its subject. This awakened sense, at the first, can be painful only; and its activity is an anguish—an agony. The belief, or rather the vivid consciousness, of a future life, results involuntarily from this new perception of the infinite import of good and evil."

---

In the summer of 1801 Mr. James Haldane again visited Buxton, with his wife and eldest daughter. He availed himself of every opportunity of preaching, as on the former occasion, as well as of speaking on the concerns of eternity to those whom he met at the hotel. But he also left Mrs. James Haldane at Buxton for a few weeks, whilst he made an excursion to Dublin, where he frequently preached at the Bethesda Episcopal Chapel, of which the excellent Mr. Mathias and the learned Mr. Walker, of Trinity College, were then ministers, occasionally assisted by the Rev. Thomas Kelly, the well-known Christian Poet, the Rev. George Carr, and the Rev. Dr. Thorpe, whose eminent talents as a popular preacher soon afterwards pointed him out as the fittest associate of Mr. Mathias, when Mr. Walker resigned his fellowship and left the Established Church. At that time religion was at a low ebb in the Church of Ireland, and the Bethesda Chapel was like a beacon-light on the pathless deep. At the time of Mr. James Haldane's visit, there was a little band who had a separate meeting, such as Mr. Simeon held at Cambridge, where they prayed together, receiving the Lord's Supper at an hour when it was not publicly administered.

From Buxton Mr. James Haldane proceeded, with his wife and daughter, to London, preaching at Manchester, Sheffield, and other places on their route. During their stay in London they paid several visits to friends in the neighbourhood, but a great part of their time was spent at Hatcham House, the residence of the late Mr. and Mrs. Hardcastle. At this period Mr. James Haldane was much followed, and preached to great crowds in the Tottenham Court Chapel, Mr. Whitfield's Tabernacle, in the City-road, and in Camden Chapel, Camberwell, afterwards the scene of the Rev. Henry Melvill's great popularity.

He had hoped to have reached London in time to have offered himself to accompany Lord Duncan to Scotland. An alarming paragraph in the newspaper, relative to the Admiral's health, had, however, been contradicted, and prevented his fulfilling his first intention of hastening to town. But scarcely had he arrived in London when he heard of his uncle's death, at the inn at Cornhill on the Tweed, which he reached on the 4th of August, 1804, attended only by a servant. He went to bed in his usual health, but soon afterwards rang his bell, and expired. In his will he showed his unabated confidence in his nephews, by including Mr. Haldane as one of the trustees and guardians of his children, with Viscount Melville and the Lord Chief Baron Dundas. His affection for his sister had been great, and his care over her two sons most exemplary, although his hopes concerning their worldly prospects had been sadly disappointed.

The following is a letter written by Mr. James Haldane, on the death of his uncle :—

"*London, August* 14, 1804.

"MY DEAR AUNT,—On our arrival in town on Saturday last we received the very distressing account of your beloved husband's death. It was at the same time comforting to hear that you were as well as could be expected. But, indeed, the stroke is severe. To be finally separated, as to this world, from one with whom you have long lived in the most intimate and endearing connexion, is truly distressing. The manner of it, too, so sudden and unexpected, renders it still more affecting. What poor creatures we are! How ignorant of what a day may bring forth!

And yet how thoughtless are we apt to be when we enjoy any measure of ease or prosperity! This dispensation of Providence is a loud call to us all, Be ye also ready, for in such an hour as ye think not the Son of Man cometh.' It has been my prayer to God that it might be abundantly sanctified to you and to your family, and to all concerned. I have felt the necessity of looking to God in my own behalf that it may more deeply and powerfully impress my own mind with a sense of the shortness of time and the nearness of eternity. Indeed, the Judge standeth at the door. I should wish constantly to connect every word I speak and every action I perform with the judgment-seat of Jesus, for according to our words and actions we shall stand or fall. The holiness of our lives, our deadness to the world, and all that is in it, our constant pressing forward to win Christ, and to be found in Him; esteeming everything else but loss and dung; sacrificing to this great object every inclination of our corrupt nature, and every consideration which would for a moment divert our attention from Christ, these and these alone will in the great day of God be the proofs of our having been Christians. If we be risen with Christ, let us seek the things that are above. Yes, we shall infallibly do so, for in that case we must have the spirit of Christ, and where the spirit of Christ dwells there will be conformity to him, whose whole heart and affections were constantly fixed on his heavenly Father. How earnestly do I desire, my dear Aunt, that you, in time and in eternity, may have cause to bless God for this dispensation of his providence, that you may indeed say, It was good for me that I was afflicted; the removal of my beloved husband has practically taught me the utter vanity of all below, and now I find in God not only my wants all supplied, and an habitual source of joy and satisfaction which fellowship with Him can alone communicate to the mind. It would, indeed, be very ungrateful in me if I did not look back to my dear uncle's disinterested kindness towards myself. I trust I shall never forget it. I can truly say there were few in whom I was more deeply interested. I hope your family are in good health. They must greatly feel the bereavement they have sustained of so kind and affectionate a parent. It is my prayer to God that they may all prove real comforts to you, and that you may live to see t ʌem walking in the truth.

"My wife joins me in most affectionate regards to you. We shall hear of you often, and, I trust, shall not forget to bear you on our hearts before our gracious God. I remain, my dear Aunt,

"Most sincerely and affectionately yours,

"J. A. HALDANE.

"*To the Right Hon. Viscountess Duncan, George-square, Edinburgh.*"

In the spring of 1805 Mr. J. A. Haldane made another extended tour, accompanied by Mr. John Campbell, who returned from Kingsland for that purpose. They proceeded by Perth and Dunkeld into Breadalbane, where they separated. The people on this occasion came out by thousands to listen to Mr. J. Haldane. At Killin, in 1803, they could not hear of one earnest Christian. Now there were a goodly number of true disciples. Mr. Peter Grant, a pious preacher, who is also styled, amongst his countrymen, the Gaelic poet, gives the following account :—

"The novelty of a field-preacher, especially a gentleman, attracted multitudes. In a short time the whole country was in a stir. Many said, that we were all in a lost condition ; others endeavoured, by arguments and ridicule, to banish all their fears; but the Gospel kindled a flame at that time which I hope is not yet extinguished. May the Lord continue it for ages to come!

"I was young, and had little concern about my own soul when Mr. Haldane visited this place. All that I remember is, having seen himself and John Campbell preach at Granton, on a market-day. They took their station a little out of the village, where a church has been since built. Almost the whole market gathered to hear. At first they thought to drown his voice by laughing and sporting, but, in a short time, his powerful and commanding voice overcame all their uproar, and a solemnity prevailed till the end of his discourse ; some have since acknowledged to me, that they received their first impression there on that occasion.

"But my wife, though as young as myself, was better acquainted with Mr. Haldane. The children not being accustomed to strangers, especially a gentleman, would hide themselves in holes, but my wife somehow saw something in his smiles that encouraged her to come near him ; and often did she show me how, with his hand, he stroked her head, and endeavoured to impress upon her young mind the importance of attending to the concerns of her soul in the days of her youth. He sometimes endeavoured, by signs, to make her understand what she could not otherwise understand, being very deficient in the English. She was not certain whether she was truly converted at this time, but the impression then made never was effaced.

"Another circumstance not to be forgotten is, that he induced my father-in-law to set up a Sabbath-school, especially to teach the people to read the Scriptures in the Gaelic language, for hitherto the children were only taught to read English, of which they did not understand one word. Thus Mr. Haldane was the founder of the first Gaelic Sabbath-school that ever was in our country, and, as far as I have heard, the first in all the north of Scotland. Now there are about ten in this country.

I think Mr. Haldane helped my father-in-law to get up a small meeting-house for the schools and other meetings. This house was set on fire on a Sabbath morning, by parties whom we will not mention. This made a great stir. When the proprietor (Sir James Grant, predecessor of the Earl of Seafield) heard of it, he was much displeased, and showed much favour to my father-in-law as long as he lived, for the family of Grant were always favourable to religion, virtue, and liberty.

" I was told that Mr. Haldane, while here, met with a captain with whom he was acquainted on his sea voyages. This captain invited him to his house, but, in the invitation, made use of a great oath. Mr. Haldane faithfully admonished him, but went for a night to his house, and the captain never again manifested hostility to religion.

" Ever after this Mr. Haldane felt a lively interest in the cause of God and truth in Strathspey. In every letter he sent salutations to the Church, and desired an interest in our prayers. For many years he and his brother supported Mr. Macintosh, as our faithful and beloved pastor, when we could do nothing ourselves to support him ; and without him I fear our prosperity would soon have come to an end. He felt a great interest in our late revival, and gave us many wise counsels regarding the young people who newly professed the truth. We sought his advice in all trying circumstances, and we believe his wise counsels, as a father in Israel, were at least one means of the measure of prosperity, unity, and love, that remained among us when many other Churches divided and separated till they made themselves a by-word and a proverb among the people."

It would be tedious to pursue every step in their tour to Inverness, Dornoch, Tain, to Wick and Thurso. But there are two letters, written in the simplest style and in very short words, to his eldest child, a little girl of ten years old, which may perhaps exhibit some glimpses of his character. The first is dated June, 1805 :—

" MY DEAR ELIZABETH,—I wrote to your mamma, from Dunkeld, and hope she received the letter. I left Dunkeld on Monday, and preached at Logie-rait, where the river Tummel joins the Tay. The Tay is the largest river in Scotland, and runs out of Loch Tay. I rode up the side of the river to Kenmuir, which is situated at the end of the Loch. Taymouth, where Lord Breadalbane has a house, is within a mile of Kenmore. It is a pretty place, and has a large park, with deer. After preaching I walked to the house, but it was very late, and I saw little of it. The old house is now almost taken down, and a new one is building.

" I rode up the south side of the Loch to Killin, which is just at the other end of it. The Loch is sixteen miles long, and is very pretty, but it has no islands. Killin is a very beautiful situation, and might be made a finer place than Taymouth. On the north side of the Loch is Ben Lawers, one of the highest mountains in Scotland. It is above four thousand feet above the level of the sea. But what pleased me more than the beauty of the place was, to see many believers in Christ, where there were hardly any a few years ago. The Gospel has greatly civilized them. They are full of affection to all who love the Lord Jesus. I preached three times, at different places, on Monday, for they are much scattered. The Psalmist says, God maketh the wrath of man to praise him. This is illustrated by what has happened here. A man, who had a small farm, was brought to a knowledge of the truth. He, at the same time, carried on a linen manufactory, and the Highland Society, for encouraging improvements, had given him the use of four looms. When he became acquainted with Christ, false reports were raised of him, as having become idle, and the Society ordered the looms to be taken from him. This was accordingly done, and by this means a large place was emptied, which has served the Church to meet in, in winter, ever since. Is not the Lord excellent in counsel, and wonderful in working? Had it not been for this, they would not have met in winter at all.

" On Tuesday we breakfasted with this man, who lives near Kenmore, and proceeded north to Dalnacardoch; we were obliged to walk a good part of the way, on account of the hills, and dined at a place, where we could hardly get anything but eggs. Dalnacardoch is the next stage to Blair, on the Highland road. It is situated in Athol, and is very high, and cold, and disagreeable. Next day we crossed the Grampian Hills, which run quite across Scotland. They take their rise at Aberdeen. The distance from Blair to Aviemore is fifty miles, but people on foot can go through the mountains, so as to save half the distance. The road runs through an opening in the mountains, or it would be impassable for carriages. It rained on us very much, but with the umbrella we were kept pretty dry. In the middle of the mountains we called at the house of a poor woman, whom God lately brought to a knowledge of the truth, by means of a preacher, who called to get some refreshment, and spoke to her the word of the Lord. She was very glad to see us, and very contented and happy; but told us she was praying to the Lord to open some way for her to remove where she might be nearer the Gospel, and the people of God. Some time after we passed her house, we found we were at the summit, by observing a small stream running north. We dined at Dalwhinnie, and afterwards crossed the Spey, a little below its source. It becomes a considerable river, and is the most rapid in Scotland. We slept at Pitmain, and while supper was getting ready, walked to a small village, where we knew there were some believers. The Duchess of Gordon lately sent for one of them, a blacksmith, and asked him many questions about religion. He told her what the Gospel was, and referred to some passages in his Bible, which he took out of his pocket, which struck her much ; but I must conclude, for my paper is full. I trust you are all well. I hope to get a letter from your mamma, at Forres, to-day. Write to me, as soon as you receive this, to Wick. We intend to be there next Lord's-day. Give my kind love to all, and to your grandmamma, if she is at Portobello, as I suppose."

When they arrived at Wick, Mr. Campbell observes that, before Mr. James Haldane's tour in 1797, only three families "worshipped God," but now they heard the voice of melody in almost every dwelling. Such was the change effected in that destitute country. Both of his former tours were fondly remembered, and some of the people now came twenty miles to hear. His second letter to his youthful daughter is as follows :—

" *Wick, June* 22, 1805.

" MY DEAR ELIZABETH,—As I began to give you an account of our journey, I shall conclude it in this letter, instead of writing your mamma, as I intended. I left off at Pitmain. We preached there in the morning, and proceeded to Aviemore, where we left the Inverness road, and came on to Granton. On our way to Aviemore, we called at the house of one of the converts, who had been in the Artillery, and lost both his hands by the going off of a gun. He was brought to a knowledge of the truth, by a sermon of Mr. Campbell's, the last time we were north. We did not find him at home, but just as we were setting off, after dinner, he came running to see us, and appears to be very happy in waiting for the coming of Jesus. He occasionally exhorts his fellow-sinners, and sometimes holds out his arms, and calls their attention to the goodness of God, in not allowing him to die when he was ignorant of Christ.

" When we arrived at Granton, we found a number of people assembled at a fair, and the town also almost full of volunteers, at that time quartered there. We preached, although it was late. Granton is a village situated on the banks of the Spey. Near it Sir James Grant has a house (Castle Grant), and the whole is his property. Next day we came to Forres, a very pretty place, about four miles from the sea. It is in Morayshire, which is one of the best corn countries in Scotland, and the harvest is, in general, as early as about Edinburgh. If your mamma would have the travelling map brought down to Portobello, you might trace the journey we have taken, and this would help to teach you the geography of Scotland. I left Mr. C. at Forres, and went on the same evening (Saturday) to Elgin, where I spent the Lord's-day. On Monday I returned by Forres to Nairn. Several young people are under much concern about eternal things. May the Lord, my love, manifest His glory to you, as he does not to the world! On Tuesday we preached at Fort

George, which was erected after the Rebellion of '45, for the security of the Highlands. We crossed the Moray Frith, which is there very narrow, and, after crossing another ferry, got to Invergordon, a small village, and from thence to Tain, the capital of Ross-shire. Owing to our being detained and missing our road, it was between twelve and one before we arrived. We found the town quite full, owing to a review of volunteers and a company of players who were there. We could get no beds. At last, the landlady got some blankets spread for us on the floor, where we slept very comfortably. Next day we attempted to cross the Frith of Dornoch, at what is called the Muckle Ferry, but as there was too much wind, we were obliged to return to Tain. By this means we preached there in the evening; perhaps the Lord had some wandering sheep to gather in, and sent us back to proclaim the joyful sound. All His ways are wonderful. Next day we crossed the frith, dined at Dornoch, the capital of Suther- land, which was all bustle about the election of a Member of Par- liament. A few miles from it we crossed the little ferry, and passed Dun Robin Castle, belonging to the Marquis of Stafford. It is a pretty place, and has a good many trees, which are not plentiful in that country. We went along the sea-shore to Helmsdale, where we arrived late. The house was very bad, and their *best* room was occupied. Next morning we entered Caithness, and crossed the Orde, as it is called, which, I am told, signifies hammer. It is a great precipice, almost perpendicular, from the road to the sea, some hundred feet. The roads were so bad, that we were obliged to walk, and lead our gig. We breakfasted at Berriedale, where Sir John Sinclair has built a pretty good inn. It is a very romantic place, surrounded with mountains. We found here, that a part of the ironwork of the gig was broken, and therefore proceeded on foot, and slept at a small house, about twelve miles from this, and arrived here to-day, in good health. Mr. C. is gone to Thurso. Thus we have cause to say, hitherto the Lord has helped us. I am sorry to hear you have been unwell, but hope you are better, and that the Lord will make the illness useful to you. Our life is but a vapour. Let us live for eternity. I received your mamma's letter at Forres, and expect one here from her.—Yours, &c.,

" J. A. HALDANE."

They remained in Caithness for a fortnight, and went by the sea-shore to Dun Robin Castle, where Mr. James Haldane addressed a regiment of volunteers, who, although out on a field-day, were dismissed early, that they might hear him preach. They returned, by Inverness and Huntly, to Aberdeen, and thence to Edinburgh, preaching along the line of road.

This was the last of his prolonged and extensive tours, of

which he had accomplished nine in the course of nine years, exclusive of his many shorter excursions. Before taking leave of Caithness it may be interesting to notice an entry in the first Journal of the tour of 1797, under date of October 9th, where it is said, " Visited a woman ill of fever, and another who had been long confined." The female alluded to as having been long confined was a Miss Campbell, to whom Sir George Sinclair, in a letter, dated Thurso Castle, 13th August, 1852, thus alludes :—

" If any circumstance should prevent you from visiting Montauban this year, I hope you will bend your steps northward in the course of the present autumn, and even during the continuance of our present early harvest glean a few precious memorials of your revered father's labours of love, which are still so highly appreciated throughout this district. Had you come here a few weeks ago you would have still seen one of his earliest converts, a pious and excellent female, to whom he preached at her bed-side during his first sojourn at Thurso, supposing that she had not long to live; but it pleased God that she should remain sixty-nine years confined, without intermission, to her bed."

In a short biographical notice of this remarkable case, published in a Caithness newspaper, it is stated, that after having been confined to bed fourteen years, " the late Mr. J. A. Haldane preached beside her the last sermon she ever heard." She survived his memorable visit fifty-five years, and died at the age of eighty-four.   It is added :—

" Though labouring under complete prostration of body, and during the last few years of her life afflicted with deafness, neither were the faculties of Miss Campbell's mind impaired, her temper soured, nor her sympathies contracted by her lengthy affliction. She looked steadily at ' things unseen and eternal,' and her cheerful resignation to her own trying lot was not more conspicuous than her profound interest in the welfare of her numerous and attached friends. Sustained and cheered by the truths of revelation, and by the sympathies of kindred spirits, and cared for with unwearied affection by her youngest sister, her life glided away in tranquil happiness. Her end like her life was peace. She died from exhaustion of nature. The day previous to her death she was much in her usual way, but her mind was impressed with the idea that her end was near, and having given directions concerning her funeral and some other matters, she quietly waited in religious exercises for her departure. Her spirit passed away without even a sigh. When one thinks of her life as prolonged to such a period, without exercise, or even exposure to the open air, of the changes which have taken place in individuals and nations since she lay down on her bed of weakness; of her peace and happiness in a condition of so much suffering and weariness; it is difficult to say, whether her history, thus briefly indicated, is more interesting to the physiologist, the moralist, or the Christian."

Although the tour of 1805 was the last of Mr. James Haldane's prolonged tours, there was no abatement of his zeal and no intermission of labour. In the following year, and at various other times, Mr. James Haldane made many shorter tours, both in the Highlands and the west and north of Scotland, and in the Isle of Man. But he was never again absent for many weeks together. The number of faithful ministers throughout the country was now greatly increased, and, not to dwell on the great awakening in the Established and other Presbyterian Churches, there were already dispersed through the country, from Mr. Haldane's seminaries, nearly two hundred preachers, exclusive of those who had retired from the service, emigrated to America, died, or become disqualified. That number was still augmenting, for, in 1805, there were sixty-four students in Edinburgh, besides those at Elgin and Armagh. It is also proper to take into account the growing cares of a large Church and congregation, the former probably then consisting of six hundred communicants, irrespective of those belonging to Mr. Aikman's.

The late Dr. Russell, of Dundee, who was one of the chief ornaments of the seminaries formed after their removal from Glasgow, has left on record the following testimony :—

" By means of the movement which took place at that period, there was awakened a spirit of greater zeal in various religious bodies. A more pointed manner of preaching was adopted by many. There came to be more discrimination of character. The empty flourish of the instrument gave place to the well-defined tones and melodies, which awaken all the sympathies of the soul. The unfettered freeness of the Gospel was more fully proclaimed, while its practical influence was more distinctly unfolded. In the course of time, there appeared an increased and increasing number of Evangelical ministers in the Establishment, and a beneficial influence was formed to operate upon other denominations."

When the Haldanes and their early coadjutors entered the field they were almost the only preachers of the Gospel in the destitute parts of Scotland, such as Caithness, Kintyre, Arran, or Breadalbane. They were almost the only promoters of Sabbath-schools, which the General Assembly denounced, and the only distributors of religious tracts. But now, Scotland was placed under a new spiritual agency. The " missionaries," as they were called, were found preaching in every village and Highland glen, and in every locality they had their schools and lay agency. At first, they had all the *prestige* which belonged to Reformers in the Church in which they were educated, but after the institution of Congregationalism they lost this advantage, and became shackled by divisions in their own camp.

Provided Christ was preached, it mattered little to either of the Haldanes what instrumentality was employed. To them Churchmen or Dissenters, Baptists or Independents, were alike welcome, if they proclaimed the Gospel in its purity and power. An extract from a letter of Mr. Simeon, without date, but written in 1805, will show how he too, in the maturity of his judgment, continued to overlook party distinctions :—

" MY VERY DEAR FRIEND AND BROTHER,—I have just received from you a parcel containing some books and tracts, both of your own and others, for which I most sincerely thank you. . . . I suppose that you may have seen my sermon on the Churchman's confession, and apprehended, from the note that is in it, that I am become an Arminian and a Methodist, in the strict sense of the word. I am happy to assure you, if this be your fear, that you may dismiss it utterly. My sentiments are precisely the same as when I had the happiness of travelling with you. . . .

" You, my dear brother, have been stirred up to activity in the service of your God ; and *I rejoice unfeignedly in all the good that you have been enabled to do.* You alone can judge how far your original design (somewhat according with the first intentions of the Methodists) has been kept in view ; but I apprehend that it is almost impossible for such weak creatures as we to execute any new projects in such a manner as not to find, at a future period, that there was some room for improvement.

" You will be glad to hear that, all things considered, we have great reason for thankfulness at Cambridge. The work, on the whole, is going on both in the town and University, and souls are added to the Lord.

" I hope your good lady is prospering, both in soul and body, and that our gracious God will continue both to you and her his richest blessings.

" *Rev. J. Haldane.*" " C. SIMEON.

A A

# CHAPTER XVI.

[1799—1810.]

THE institution of Congregational Churches separate from the
Scottish Establishment was the result of unforeseen circumstances, and not of a preconcerted plan. For a long time after
the formation of the Tabernacle Church, questions of ecclesiastical discipline never seemed to impede the hallowed object
to which its pastor had consecrated his life. To use his own
language, "It was, in fact, no separation from the Establishment. It was merely opening another place of worship for
preaching the Gospel without regard to *forms* of external
arrangement or Church order, and where the pastor and many
of the members showed their catholic spirit by going to the
Sacrament in the Established Church. Add to this, that the
preaching was almost entirely addressed to the people of the
world." It might have been well, had it been possible, that
these views and objects had always remained the same. But in
the very nature of things this was not to be expected, although
years elapsed before attention to the apostolic order of primitive
Churches seriously distracted attention, and necessarily produced
difference of opinion, accompanied by divisions.

Mr. Ewing, as might be anticipated, was foremost in the promotion of a new system of Church order, and to him, no doubt, may be conceded the title which has been claimed for him, as " the Father of modern Congregationalism in Scotland." No one can turn over the early pages of his " Missionary Magazine" without discovering something more than the germ of every progressive change which afterwards took place in trying to approximate to the ideal model of primitive Christianity. His intimacy with his Baptist friend, Dr. Charles Stuart, tended to this result, as well as his early partiality for the works of Glas and Sandeman. In 1801, Mr. James Haldane addressed to him a letter from Dumfries, amongst other things, warning him against their introduction into the Seminary, and complaining of his " enthusiastic manner" of speaking of these frigid and bitter theologians. Mr. Ewing replied, that he had so much approved of this letter as a whole, that he had read it all to the class, excepting that part of it which related to Glas and Sandeman.

In 1808, Mr. Aikman declared, that before the secession from the Establishment, mixed communion in the Lord's Supper,—that is, communion with inconsistent or worldly professors,—had been to him and others an " intolerable burden." It became, therefore, one of the first principles of the new Church, that none should be admitted whose sentiments and consistency of conduct did not, in the judgment of charity, evince the truth of their own vital Christianity. It was asked, with much force, whether this was not a vain and Utopian endeavour after a beautiful ideal purity, which never can be attained until the last day, when the tares and the wheat shall be for ever separated. Such, however, was their leading principle, and it necessarily involved an implied protest, which gradually became more distinct, against an alliance with the State as interfering with pure communion. It was next assumed by the new Church as a principle, that Christians are religiously bound to conform their ecclesiastical usages to the practice or customs of the apostolic Churches. Proceeding on this assumption, Mr. Ewing first introduced at Glasgow the practice of celebrating the Lord's Supper every Lord's-day. This innovation on the Scottish custom of having it only twice a-year was adopted in Edinburgh not long afterwards, and finally in all the new churches in Scotland from the date of Mr. James A. Haldane's treatise, published in 1802, to prove that it was agreeable to the apostolic order and the practice of the primitive Churches. Mr. Ewing, in his published " Rules of Church Government," next added, " Besides the ordinary public worship of the Lord's-day, there shall be a Church-meeting weekly, for the purposes of social worship, discipline, and mutual edification." In social worship, Mr. Ewing intended to include the practice of the pastor's occasionally asking any private member, who appeared to have a gift in prayer, to lead the devotions of the Church. The " mutual edification" was to be carried on by any private member, spontaneously or by appointment, offering an " exhortation," or address to the Church, on a passage of Scripture. This last plan was, no doubt, an innovation calculated to usurp the pastor's office, but it was originally proposed by Mr. Ewing, as his amiable biographer records, " as affording what he had long before wished for, namely, a fellowship meeting on a large scale."

In 1804, Dr. Innes published his " Reasons for separating from the Church of Scotland, in a Series of Letters, chiefly addressed to his Christian Friends in that Establishment." About the same time, Mr. Carson, who had left the General Synod of Ulster in Ireland, and whom Mr. James Haldane first met at Coleraine during his tour in Ireland, published a pamphlet containing his reasons for separation. Mr. James Haldane, in 1805, next produced a volume, which quickly ran through two editions, entitled, " Views of the Social Worship of the first Churches," &c., " a work," says Mr. Orme, " which contained much important truth, in a spirit with which even the adversaries of his system could scarcely be offended."

These publications drew forth replies from the Rev. Mr. Brown, parish minister of Langton, and some other writers, which were answered by Mr. J. Haldane, Mr. Ewing, and Mr. Carson; but it was not till 1807 that there was any open manifestation of division in the new Churches. At length, however, to use the words of Mr. Kinniburgh, in his very candid "Historical Survey,"—"A withering blast came from the north, which was attended with direful consequences. We refer to the circulation of Ballantyne's 'Treatise on the Elders' Office.'" Mr. Ballantyne had been at first placed in Thurso, but afterwards removed to a Tabernacle at Elgin, also built by Mr. Haldane, capable of holding 1,500 people, where, also, a class of missionary students was under his tuition. In 1805 Mr. James Haldane's "Views of Social Worship" had indicated his decided opinion, that, instead of having, what Mr. Ewing termed "fellowship meetings on a large scale," only on the week-days, when many of the Church could not attend, they should be held on the day consecrated to the worship of the Lord. He argued that, if "exhorting one another" were really one of the means positively appointed by Christ for the public edification of the Church, as Mr. Ewing had contended, it was difficult to comprehend why it should be observed in a corner, and not be deemed proper on the Lord's own day. The Rev. John Newton himself, in the third letter of his "Apologia," states, that he considered mutual exhortation to be so clearly an apostolic practice, that the neglect of it was one reason for his not having joined the Dissenters; and he argued, that, if they did not observe this apostolic practice, Dissenters could not blame him for deviating in other respects from the primitive model.

But the views propounded by Mr. James Haldane were never intended by him to have been prematurely forced into practice at the risk of fomenting division. In these matters he felt it his duty honestly to state his own convictions, and then to leave them to work their way, acting on the apostolic model, "Whereunto we have attained, let us walk by the same rule." His brother had similar convictions as to apostolic usages, and was, moreover, less disposed to delay the experiment of carrying them into actual operation. In 1805, accompanied by Mr. Ballantyne, Mr. Robert Haldane made a journey to England, preaching both at Newcastle and in London, where they

remained for some time, practising the views of social worship
which were developed in his brother's book, and which both of
them then thought calculated to call into exercise the gifts of
the private members, and to minister to the edification of the
Church. The late Rev. James Harington Evans appears, at a
much later period, in the maturity of his judgment, to have
entertained the same views which so many years before commended themselves in theory to the two Haldanes. It was
probably well for the Church in John-street, Bedford-row, that
" only occasional addresses were given," although his recently
published letters show that he considered his Church incomplete
in its constitution, because it had not a plurality of elders " to
labour co-ordinately with, or subordinately to him," and did
not enjoy the advantage of mutual exhortation by those of the
deacons and members who were supposed to be peculiarly
gifted. In the midst of these debates the paramount importance of preaching the Gospel was upheld as firmly as ever by
both the brothers, whilst their views of Christian forbearance
remained unshaken to the close of life. Mr. Ballantyne's
pamphlets, which also contended for a presbytery, or plurality
of elders, in every Church, were circulated by Mr. Robert
Haldane, and embodied his own sentiments.

Into a discussion of these topics it is needless to plunge.
Whether the Lord's Supper should be observed twice a year,
once a month, or once a week; whether the mutual exhortation
of the brethren, by means of public speaking, be, or be not,
a binding duty; whether a plurality of elders be, or be not,
imperative in every properly-constituted Church; whether collections should be made at the doors from the public, or only
privately amongst the communicants; — these are questions
which may be weighed and decided in their proper place, but
must be regarded as the tithe of mint, anise, and cummin,
compared with those great and saving doctrines of the Gospel
with which the time, the talents, and labours of the two
brothers were, after all, supremely occupied. It is enough
for the purposes of this work, to give an outline of the facts
faithfully and without partiality.

After these debates had been for some time in agitation, Mr. James Haldane, in a letter, dated February 19th, 1808, informs Mr. Campbell, that at various intervals he had entertained doubts as to the scriptural authority for infant baptism, although he had, again and again, come to the conclusion, that the presumptive evidence in its favour preponderated. Still the recurrence of these doubts led him to suspect that he had not fully fathomed the subject, and, therefore, after his return from England, at the end of 1804, he had determined again to search the Scriptures at his leisure, with prayer for direction and a desire to be led to a right conclusion. He felt that, on former occasions, his examinations had been conducted under the influence of a fear of diminishing his usefulness, if he were obliged to renounce infant baptism, but at last he was "delivered from this snare," and became satisfied that the more simply he followed the Lord, the more useful he should in reality be. In short, he now viewed the conflict of duty and usefulness as one that was absurd. The result was, that, after mature deliberation and reading deeply on the subject, his doubts so much increased that, on an occasion when requested to administer infant baptism, he was obliged to inform the Church, that, although his mind was not made up to become himself a Baptist, yet that, at present, he could not conscientiously baptize children. He concludes his letter:—" If I had not been compelled to baptize, I should never have mentioned my doubts till they were fully satisfied. At the same time, I informed the Church that, although I were baptized, I should be of the same mind as formerly, that the Baptists and Pædo-baptists might have fellowship together."

On the 21st of April he again addresses Mr. Campbell, informing him that the crisis was past, and that he had been baptized, although, with regard to the Church, this was to be a matter of forbearance. He adds, " If we are all acting on conviction and both desiring to know the will of Jesus in this and in all other respects, I have no apprehension of disunion. Of one thing I am sure, that all who love the Lord Jesus should, so far as they agreed, walk by the same rule and mind the same things; and if it be improper for Baptists to be in fellowship in the same Church, it must be equally improper to have occasional fellowship in private."

These letters, and much more that might be produced, indicate Mr. James Haldane's anxiety to prevent disunion on a point upon which Christians differ. But these fond hopes were doomed to disappointment. His views of mutual forbearance, however strongly urged, were not reciprocated, and a rupture took place in the Edinburgh Tabernacle Church, which, to use the words of Mr. Orme, severed " one of the most numerous and respectable Independent Societies that had ever been in Britain."

" Some of the members," says Mr. Robert Haldane, " went back to the Established Church, some to the Church in College-street (Mr. Aikman's), others to that in Niddry-street (Mr. Maclean's), while a considerable number determined to become a separate Church and rent a large room to meet in. The rest remained with my brother, in the Tabernacle. These which were more numerous than any of the other divisions, were of one mind, except on the subject of baptism, which they thought might be made a matter of forbearance."

The division spread, not only in the Edinburgh Churches, but throughout the whole of Scotland. In Edinburgh the excitement was great. Within a year nearly 200 members, including Mr. Robert Haldane, also embraced Baptist sentiments. Still it might be matter of surprise that the separation between the Baptists and Pædo-Baptists in the new connexion should have been so complete. But the numbers who followed their pastor, and the great influence of both the brothers, as well as the proselytizing zeal of some forward and inexperienced students and preachers, probably alarmed Mr. Aikman, and urged him to take a more decided line of opposition than appears consonant with his amiable spirit and the strong personal respect and attachment with which he still regarded his old friends. A letter from Mr. Aikman to Mr. Campbell, dated Edinburgh, 15th April, 1808, will exhibit the views which actuated the leaders of that large and respectable section of the Tabernacle Churches which declined forbearance :—

" MY DEAR BROTHER,—Had ability been afforded me, I would

certainly have written you before this, to communicate to you the very painful situation in which the Churches have been placed for some months past."

After speaking of his own health, and the suffering state of his eyes, he proceeds,—

" I have seen it my duty totally to withdraw from the connexion at the Tabernacle, as well as a number of the most respectable members of the Church, who now assemble at Bernard's-rooms. My stipulated supplies from the Tabernacle are now cut off. *Indeed, I have now completely given them up*, as I perceive it to be of much importance for the general good of the cause *to have no visible* or Church fellowship with brethren who have for years past, at Newcastle and London, been acting upon a system which appears to me to be destructive, both of the pastoral office and of all order in the house of God. This I have fully stated to both our dear brethren and to our Church, who have, after long and painful discussion, decided to continue to act upon their acknowledged principles, and to decline the relation of a sister Church with a Church composed of Baptists and Pædo-Baptists, under a Baptist pastor." He adds, " Our necessity is now very great, and I can no longer reckon on supplies."

The allusion, in the foregoing letter, to the schism at Newcastle, is to Mr. Robert Haldane's proceedings on the journey, in 1805, already noticed, when he first introduced the practice of mutual exhortation, three years before it was commenced in Edinburgh. Mr. J. A. Haldane was, in this matter, rather more cautious than his brother. But, although he gave no countenance to the meetings at Newcastle or London, he never, like his colleague, Mr. Aikman, dreamed of stigmatizing them as " schism, for which Mr. Haldane and Mr. Ballantyne ought to have been excommunicated." " A sinful respect of persons," Mr. Aikman adds, " prevented his brother, as I believe, *and certainly myself*, from making that business a matter of Church discipline." Such were the views of Christian liberty entertained even by so good and holy and amiable a man as Mr. Aikman. Mr. Robert Haldane's own defence of his conduct is contained in a letter to Mr. Campbell, dated December 26, 1807 :—

" Everything," he says, " ought, indeed, to have its proper place in our esteem. But is it reverential to God to suppose that He has enjoined some things which have a tendency to lead us away from heaven, or that everything He has revealed is not in itself directly subservient to his glory and our salvation? Are the things spoken of not a part of his revelation? Then let them not be called *small things* and *non-essentials*. Let them be called *nothing*, and then we ought decidedly to oppose them, as forming no part of our duty. But if they are a part of it, then it is surely both irreverent and unwise to set them aside under any name whatever. This is changing times and laws. It is taking too much upon us."

But, in order to comprehend clearly how it was that the shock arising out of these divisions was so fatal to the progress of Congregationalism in Scotland, it is necessary to observe how much the whole of the recent ecclesiastical movement depended on the two brothers. It was easy for Mr. Ewing to complain, in not very courteous language, that it was improper that a great theological seminary should be dependant on the will of " an individual ; " and it was quite open for him and other leaders to unite in the declaration, that they would have " no visible or Church fellowship " with Mr. Haldane or his brother. But it was not so easy to neutralize their influence, or to get on without it. One important part of this influence is stated by the Rev. Dr. Lindsay Alexander, whose own talents and weight of character have now made himself a chief pillar of the " Scottish Congregational Union."

" In estimating," says Dr. L. Alexander, " the causes which furthered the rapid growth of Congregationalism in Scotland at the first, beyond what the intrinsic energies of the system, left to their own operation, would, in all probability, have effected, something must be assigned to the excitement of the public mind at the time ; something, also, to the novelty of the plans adopted by the founders of that system ; and not a little to the sympathy which was felt for men of high character and talents, who were made the objects of ecclesiastical censure and personal obloquy, simply in consequence of their zeal for the spiritual welfare of their countrymen. *The chief* of these extrinsic causes of prosperity, however, was, *beyond all question*, liberal pecuniary aid afforded to the party by Mr. Robert Haldane.

" The establishment of a new religious sect in such a country as this is always, of necessity, connected with heavy expenses, or a serious weight of pecuniary obligation. Places of worship must be built, and funds for carrying on the cause must be provided ; and where the adherents of the new party are neither numerous nor wealthy, the impediment thus thrown in the way of their progress is often insurmountable. From all such difficulties the first propagators of Congregationalism in Scotland were, in a great measure, exempted, by the liberality with which Mr. Haldane employed his great wealth* in advancing the interests of their cause. By the support of itinerant preachers, by money advanced to erect chapels, and by aid rendered to Churches that were unable of themselves adequately to support their pastors, Mr. Haldane contributed very materially to give Congregationalism a prosperous footing in Scotland. The influence, however, thus exerted was rather from without than within; it was a system rather of forcing than of natural growth; and the consequence was, a show of flower and fruit much greater than the plant, when left to itself and to ordinary influences, could sustain."

All this seems to have been forgotten or overlooked, when the disruption, on account of questions of ecclesiastical polity, was precipitated, in spite of the earnest public and private remonstrances of both the Haldanes. But was it reasonable to suppose that, when the body was thus torn asunder, Mr. Haldane should continue to lavish his fortune upon that section of it whose leaders had thus peremptorily resolved to have " no visible Church fellowship " with him or his brother ? Had he at once withdrawn his support from all the Churches by whom he was practically excommunicated; had he at once shut up all the chapels in the possession of those who came to such a violent conclusion, who could have justly blamed him ? Was it not rather strange that men who, for such trivial reasons, refused all " visible connexion " with him in Church fellowship, should have desired to avail themselves of his property ?

But, unhappily, there was also another " root of bitterness," which had, in fact, secretly tended to precipitate the disruption, connected with a personal misunderstanding between Mr. Robert Haldane and Mr. Ewing. For the first few years of their intercourse, Mr. Haldane had admired the persevering industry of Mr. Ewing, as well as his natural talents and ardent character. But almost from the moment when a pecuniary relation was established between them, conferring on Mr. Haldane the rights incident to the oversight of his own property, and of the

---

* *Great* and small are comparative terms. But the term, *great wealth*, by no means applied to Mr. Haldane's fortune, according to the scale of modern opulence. The amount which he devoted to the cause of the Gospel was, indeed, very large, but it was still more remarkable as contrasted with the comparatively moderate extent of his income.

students whom he supported, almost from that moment Mr. Ewing became jealous of Mr. Haldane's relative position and impatient of his control. The removal of the Seminary from Glasgow was the natural consequence, and ended one fruitful source of mutual discomfort, but the management of the Glasgow Tabernacle still left occasion for painful collision. The details of Mr. Ewing's complaints, for the most part in themselves unimportant, were contained in a pamphlet of 206 pages, which it is impossible to read, at the distance of more than forty years, without something like a feeling of " melancholy mirth " at the jaundiced medium through which a grieved or troubled spirit viewed Mr. Haldane's motives, not only in regard to the Tabernacle and the Seminary, but even as to the disinterested proposal that Mr. Ewing should have a distinguished place in the Indian Mission. Mr. Haldane had already printed letters addressed to Mr. Ewing on the subject of the matter in discussion, but probably the annals of controversy never produced a more complete and detailed refutation than was published by him in the year 1810, in a volume of 406 octavo pages, which was sold for the nominal sum of one shilling, and gives a minute history of every one of his transactions with Mr. Ewing from the beginning of their acquaintance. It would be far more agreeable to allow the whole to sleep in oblivion, and yet it seems needful, as a matter connected with the ecclesiastical history of Scotland, to offer a few words of brief explanation. Happily these are to be found under Mr. Robert Haldane's own hand, written not long before his death, when every spark of irritation against Mr. Ewing had been long extinguished, and he was looking forward to his own departure at no very distant period.

" The unhappy difference which arose between Mr. Ewing and me was not matter of private discussion. Every particular, even the minutest and most ridiculous, was, thirty years ago, brought before the world, and into every single one of his charges I entered fully and particularly, in a volume which was widely circulated, which was never answered, and which, I fearlessly add, was unanswerable.

" With Mr. Ewing I became acquainted in the year 1795, when he was introduced to me by his brother-in-law, then minister of Stirling, as one whose talents and character fitted him to be a coadjutor in a plan, which I at that period entertained, for the promotion of Christianity in Bengal. Mr. Ewing was then the assistant minister of Lady Glenorchy's Church in Edinburgh, with a salary of 120*l.* per annum. In arranging the scheme of the Bengal Mission, I thought it right to secure the temporal interests of those whom I designed to carry with me to India. I therefore agreed to pay to Mr. Ewing, as well as my other coadjutors, 3,500*l.* before leaving England, and also to convey them to Calcutta at my own expense. The design failed, in consequence of the opposition of the East India Company Directors and of the Board of Control. Baffled in my endeavour to be useful in India, I turned my attention to the state of religion in Scotland, and among other plans to which it is unnecessary to advert, I purchased a building at Glasgow, which I converted into a Chapel, or, as it was called, a Tabernacle, and there placed Mr. Ewing. The cost of the building was 3,000*l.*, and I secured it to Mr. Ewing for life, on the condition that he should fulfil certain stipulations connected with the preaching of the Gospel, the celebration of Divine ordinances, and other objects of a similar character.

"For some time the plan answered exceedingly well. Mr. Ewing preached to a large congregation, and formed an Independent Church. He also, in connexion with his other engagements, taught a theological seminary, which was a sort of appendage to the Tabernacle, where a number of young men were educated for the ministry, solely at my expense. By the bond securing the chapel to Mr. Ewing, I made myself responsible that he should receive, at all hazards, 200*l.* a-year from the Church, but that the surplus of the seat-rents, if any, should be devoted to the maintenance of the seminary, for conducting which Mr. Ewing was also to have an annual payment of 200*l.* In the course of time, however, differences arose between us. Mr. Ewing was unwilling that I should exercise that control over the class which I never felt it my duty to abandon, and by degrees he also deviated, in several important particulars, from the views which he had undertaken to support. In the midst of the discussions to which these differences gave rise, Mr. Ewing intimated his opinion, that I should not only leave him in the full control of the seminary, but that I should also resign to others the property which I retained in the Tabernacle. The absurdity of such a proposal is self-evident, more especially when viewed in connexion with the fact, that the Church and congregation being numerous, were well able to defray the expenses of a building in which to meet for divine worship. But while I at once rejected the unreasonable proposal, it immediately occurred to me that it would be in every way preferable that Mr. Ewing's wish as to his independence of me should be carried into effect, although not by the uncalled-for sacrifice of my property. I therefore offered to part with the Tabernacle to his Church; and in order to make the matter easier, I intimated my willingness to sell it for two-thirds of the price which it cost. This might have been enough to satisfy both Mr. Ewing and his supporters, but the offer was rejected, and I was still urged to surrender it into their hands, and without reserve.

" It was at this stage of the business that I began to see the unsatisfactory character of the arrangement we had originally entered into, and, in my turn, I requested Mr. Ewing to resign his interest in the house, and to call upon his Church to provide accommodation for their minister and themselves at their own, and not at my expense. To prompt Mr. Ewing's determination, I assured him that the price which I was willing to accept should not be employed for my own private advantage, but should be devoted to some public object connected with the translation and distribution of the Scriptures.

" Such is the history of this transaction. I never, as Mr. Ewing at one period chose to imagine, intended to deprive him of his life-rent interest in my property by any legal process. My appeal was solely to his sense of justice and his Christian principles, and in the sequel he did resign the chapel, although not till after a painful discussion, in which, as I have already said, I did not leave unanswered one charge, however minute, that was brought against me. Mr. Ewing had departed publicly from the views on which we had agreed to act. He had attacked the seminary which he had engaged to conduct, and which was to have been supported out of the surplus produce of the house. He had attacked the Society for Propagating the Gospel at Home. He had fomented the schism in my brother's Church in Edinburgh, of which I was a member. He was impatient of my retaining my property in the chapel. Was it wonderful, then, that I should seek to put an end to a connexion which was only calculated to occasion pain to both parties? And was not my conduct in desiring the termination of our disputes, by the means there pointed out, at least as reasonable as the conduct of those who were willing to maintain possession of the chapel, and to enjoy, at my expense, that accommodation which they were so well able to procure for themselves, at the same time that they were publicly and violently opposing the principles on the profession of which it was dedicated to their use? It is unnecessary to enter on the particulars of some of the charges then brought against me by Mr. Ewing. My answer to these charges will be found in the history of the thirty years which have passed over me since they were first advanced. But as almost all of them resolved themselves into some form of covetousness, I may add that, at the time when they were advanced, I had in the course of nine years (from 1799 to 1807) expended between 50,000l. and 60,000l. on objects connected with the propagation of the Gospel at home, with which Mr. Ewing was well acquainted."

To the above expenditure must be added that of the other years not included in the co-operation with Mr. Ewing, besides the loss on loans, on which interest ought to have been paid. Reckoning from 1798 to 1810, the years of Mr. Haldane's extraordinary exertions, it appears that, in round figures, he had given away within that period more than seventy thousand pounds.

The difference with Mr. Ewing was one which occasioned pain to Mr. Haldane in proportion to the pleasure of their previous mutual co-operation. The following is an extract from one of Mr. Haldane's letters to Mr. Ewing, before the latter published on the subject :—

" On looking back on the intercourse you and I had, I see many things amiss on both sides, while I trust there is also cause for thanksgiving. But while we should be humbled in the dust on account of all that has been wrong, we should remember with gratitude that the door of mercy and pardon through a Redeemer stands open, and we ought to be ready mutually to explain, to repent, and to intercede for one another. Should the matter for the present unhappily end otherwise, I shall regret it exceedingly, but I thus exonerate myself; and in order to make the return on your part to the path of duty, at any time afterwards, as easy as possible, I declare it is my determination, through grace, that no sinful distance or interruption to the maintenance of peace and love shall in future rest with me."

With reference to the charge, which at this distance of time seems so utterly absurd, that in reclaiming the Glasgow Tabernacle Mr. Haldane was influenced by mercenary motives, the following is an extract from another letter :—" I have informed Mr. Harley and you that pecuniary reimbursement is not my object. If you now purchase the house, or give it up, it is my intention to apply, without delay, what I receive from the property in translating and multiplying copies of the Scriptures." This voluntary pledge was faithfully observed. After some delay, the Glasgow Tabernacle was restored by Mr. Ewing, and a new one built by his congregation. The old one was sold to Mr. Macgavin for 2,090l., which was devoted by Mr. Haldane to the translation and circulation of the Scriptures. Interest was added every year on the capital not expended, and the whole account was settled by two auditors, so scrupulous was he in a matter where, in the heat of passion, his motives had been so unwarrantably aspersed. But one lesson Mr. Haldane was most anxious to enforce. It is this : " I wish solemnly to warn others, who may be afterwards placed in circumstances similar to those in which I stood, never to deviate so far from the line of duty, under the idea of doing a service acceptable to God, as to place their talents by a legal instrument at the disposal of another person, however highly they may esteem him. This is a very different thing from laying down property at the feet of an apostle."

After what has been said, it might seem scarcely needful to allude to another of the charges at one time pertinaciously brought against Mr. Robert Haldane in the heat of controversy, namely, that of distressing the Churches which did not embrace his views, or suddenly withdrawing his support from their preachers. No doubt the cessation of his bounty was, in itself, " distressing," but it was attributable to those who refused to practise mutual forbearance, and was to a considerable extent compensated by the contributions which it prompted from the Congregationalists in England, as well as Scotland. It might be contradiction enough, to state one broad fact, that out of a sum amounting to 26,295*l.* expended upon chapels, excluding the original cost of the one at Edinburgh, Mr. Haldane never received back more than 5,596*l.*, of which he retained none, and, in fact, gave out of it 4,245*l.* within one year. But to the groundless charge of harshness, in recalling his property from those who refused communion with him, he published two conclusive answers, the one in 1810, and the other in 1816. The whole of his pecuniary transactions with the Scottish Congregationalists had been managed by the late excellent and respected William Dymock, Esq., of George-square, Edinburgh, W.S., who himself adhered to Mr. Aikman, and was opposed to Mr. Haldane's sentiments, both on baptism and Church government. Mr. Dymock's testimony was therefore the more important, because it was not only backed by knowledge, but characterized by candour. By desire of Mr. Haldane, his letter-books were opened to full examination, and it was proved by the exhibition of his correspondence and the chapel accounts, that none of the complaints had any just foundation. Never, in any solitary case, had Mr. Haldane resorted to coercion, in order to recover his money. On the contrary, he often remitted a great part of the capital due, and still oftener all the interest. In regard to the chapels, the real grievance was this, that he did not convert into a gift what was only intended as a loan; and so far as the preachers were concerned, he distributed amongst them no less than 700*l.* out of his own purse, in the year following the disruption. Dr. Ryland had heard of subscriptions being called for in England, to repay Mr. Robert Haldane's demands on chapels, and, as if it had been intended that this charge should be published, in order to secure a public refutation, the good Doctor thoughtlessly mentioned the report in his " Life of Andrew Fuller." But when called upon for his authority, he had none ; and, after a full examination of Mr. Dymock's documents, he appended an apology to his volume, saying, "I am now convinced that the report there stated (in the ' Life of Fuller') is *utterly without foundation.*" The part which Dr. Innes, from a high sense of duty, took in satisfying Dr. Ryland, unfortunately gave umbrage to his brother-in-law, Mr. Ewing, and severed their friendship; but Dr. Innes' testimony to Mr. Haldane was all the more valuable, because, without any breach of good feeling or angry disputation, he had voluntarily relinquished a bond, securing to him an income out of the Tabernacle of Dundee, similar to that which his brother-in-law, Mr. Ewing, held at Glasgow. On quitting Dundee, Dr. Innes came to Edinburgh, in the first instance to assume the care of the seceders from the Tabernacle, but shortly afterwards he himself having changed his own sentiments on infant baptism, became the pastor of a Church composed of Christians holding various views on that subject, but not practising exhortation on the Lord's-day forenoon. To that Church he has since ministered, attracting round him the respect and the love which are due to his consistent holiness of life, his devoted zeal, and his great sacrifices for the sake of the Gospel, as well as to his ministerial faithfulness and amiable character.

These aspersions on Mr. Haldane's conduct might at this distance of time have been safely left to be answered by the tenor of his long and honourable career, had they not been partially adopted, or, at least, hinted at in the late Mr. Orme's " Historical Sketch," published in 1819. This Sketch is often referred to as an authority, and it was therefore necessary that they should be glanced at, and repudiated on evidence which is beyond all dispute. The part taken by Mr. Orme was the more to be wondered at and regretted on account of the remarkable circumstances of his early history. Mr. Orme himself acknowledged that he owed his own soul to the preaching of James Haldane, and all his future advancement in life to the patronage of the elder brother. One Lord's-day evening, a young journeyman operative, William Orme, had been strolling about on the sands of Leith, and, on his way home, for want of something to do, followed the crowd into the Tabernacle. He heard Mr. James Haldane preach, and the word was with power. Aroused from his spiritual slumbers, and awakened to the importance of eternity, he sought an interview with the preacher, and finally joined his Church. His talents and industry were soon noticed, and being admitted into Mr. Robert Haldane's seminary, he obtained the elements of that theological education which has given him a name in the literary world. But if Mr. Orme, under the influence of personal disappointment, was unjust to his early patron, a very different spirit has been indicated by the late Mr. Kinniburgh, whose prejudices and interests were, as much as those of Mr. Orme, linked in with that section of the Congregationalists which sided with Mr. Ewing. One instance may be given by reference to the Life of Mr. Dewar, of Nairn, as contained in Mr. Kinniburgh's Biographical Sketches:—

It appears from Mr. Kinniburgh's statement, that Mr. Haldane had advanced 400*l.* on loan for the completion of the chapel at Nairn. This sum was secured to him by bond over the property, and had accumulated with arrears of interest to about 500*l.* There was little or no prospect of raising funds to pay off either this sum or the other debts incurred; and, Mr. Haldane having ineffectually tried to obtain a settlement, the property was ordered to be valued with the ultimate view of being sold. Mr. Dewar, however, succeeded in raising 250*l*. by subscription, and set out with great reluctance to make a personal appeal to Mr. Haldane himself. "On candidly informing Mr. Haldane that only half of the 500*l*. could be paid, that good man (with a generosity seldom to be met with) assured Mr. Dewar that the property should not be sold, and frankly forgave the rest. Mr. Dewar returned home rejoicing."

This is a fair specimen of Mr. Haldane's conduct in all of these vexatious affairs, but even in cases where he frankly forgave a large portion of his claims, there were not wanting persons of less candour and less justice than Mr. Kinniburgh, who blamed him because he compelled others to contribute to the liquidation of the debt, and did not undertake the whole burden. More recently, the Rev. Dr. Struthers, in a "History of the Relief Church," has, from a deficiency of information, in several instances been betrayed into grave errors, one of which is too glaring to be omitted. At page 405, he observes:—

" It is impossible to look at the extent and expensive nature of the apparatus which was set up, without perceiving that Mr. Haldane had involved himself in obligations which he would soon be unable to meet. 'I felt,' says he, 'the calls on me, from different quarters, increasing very fast.' This led him to take measures to diminish the expense of the seminaries, by offering Mr. Ewing 100*l*. annually, instead of 200*l*.; to be more sparing in the sums given from the Home Mission Fund, and to suggest that the Glasgow congregation should relieve him of the purchase money of the Circus, at 1,000*l*. less than it cost him."

Here is a new and striking instance of the little dependance that can be placed on what is often called history. A statement is made apparently supported by extracts from Mr. Haldane's own writings, whereas the historian has omitted to observe dates, and consequently failed to discover that his authorities by no means support the weight of his precipitate conclusions. The quotations from Mr. Haldane's answer to Mr. Ewing refer to a period *before* the commencement of his greatest expenditure, when he was just beginning to discern the vastness of the field on which he had entered, and the necessity of economising his gifts to individuals, in order to have more to bestow upon the masses. He commenced by securing to Mr. Ewing 200*l.* a-year for the Tabernacle, and adding 200*l.* more for the seminary. But, as he increased the number of his seminaries, Mr. Haldane began to think that 300*l.* a-year was enough, and therefore proposed to reduce the allowance for the seminary, more especially as he had just given Mr. Ewing *a further allowance* of 100*l.* a-year for an assistant in the Tabernacle. In like manner the proposal that Mr. Ewing's congregation should take the Glasgow Tabernacle, was not a measure of retrenchment, but an attempt to terminate all occasion of dispute, by a very handsome contribution of 1,000*l.* to a plan, which would have gratified Mr. Ewing's desire, that he, with his large and wealthy congregation, should be independent of the private bounty of an individual.

But, apart from these details, it can be proved to demonstration, that Mr. Haldane never involved himself, as Dr. Struthers gratuitously imagines, " in obligations," either immediate or prospective, which he was not fully able to meet. The Tabernacles were all paid for, and free from debt to any one but himself, and in regard to those chapels on which he lent money, he generally paid off all the other creditors, as in the case of Perth, where he became sole proprietor; and, as in the case of Dumfries, which had been built by himself and his brother, at the joint cost of nearly 2,000*l.* It was the same with regard to the seminary. The " obligations " he undertook were not in perpetuity, but simply for a particular class of students, for one, two, or, at most, three years; and he had, moreover, cautiously guarded himself against any actual or implied promise for the sustentation of the preachers. In fact, it never was and never could have been intended that a man of Mr. Haldane's income should have gone on giving away nearly 7,000*l.* a-year. On the contrary, he only designed to meet a great exigency, and to give the Home Mission a fair start. He always made his prospective calculations with the systematic minuteness of an official budget, and by different wills left to his brother ample funds to carry out every " obligation " into which he had himself ever entered, whether it related to the chapels, the African children, the seminary, or the Propagation Society. The sum varied according to circumstances, but at the period of which Dr. Struthers speaks, Mr. Haldane, in his will, estimated that 12,000*l*. would have amply fulfilled all his engagements.

But although Dr. Struthers is so much mistaken on these points, yet the spirit which characterizes his work is praiseworthy. His observations on the disruption are as follow :—

" Though too many, no doubt, chuckled over this rupture, which, in a great measure, laid in ruins one of the noblest schemes which modern times have witnessed for diffusing religion, and evangelizing the population of the country; yet the good and the liberal of all parties, who rejoiced in the spread of religion, grieved over it, and could have wished it had been obviated."

Happily in very few cases did these divisions interrupt the continuance of the mutual friendship and esteem of the parties concerned. Even in that of Mr. Ewing, although the bitterness of his attacks might have seemed to render any advance on the part of Mr. Haldane impossible, terms of reconciliation were, year after year, proposed by the latter. Mr. Aikman, as a mutual friend, was the mediator, but unhappily without success. Mr. Haldane desired a reconciliation on the ground of burying the past in oblivion, and assuming that there might have been faults on both sides. Mr. Ewing, on the contrary, demanded an acknowledgment of error, and as if to render the acknowledgment impossible, also required the payment of a sum of money, "were it only a shilling," in token that the Glasgow Tabernacle had been unjustly reclaimed. Mr. Haldane's last attempt ought not here to be omitted, were it only as an illustration of his Christian principle, and of the depth of kindly feeling which was sometimes concealed under a manner that to strangers appeared rather stately and reserved. Indeed, when it is remembered how much there was in his composition of a spirit naturally lofty and unbending, the pathos with which he pleads for the restoration of peace, both on the ground of principle and of feeling, will appear all the more remarkable. The following letter was written at Montauban a few months before he left that field of useful labour, in 1819. It is as follows :—

"*Montauban.*

" MY DEAR SIR,—Having had the other night a pleasing dream respecting an interview which I thought I enjoyed with you, and which recalled all that tenderness of affection I once had for you, I cannot let the feeling it excited pass without sending you these lines. Life is too short for such a prolonged contention. A great portion of yours and mine has passed since the unseemly strife began. Peace be with you!

" I would not, however, desire to place so important a matter merely on the foundation of feeling, but it appears to me, considering the complication of circumstances which were, and perhaps still are, viewed by us in different lights, and the long period that has elapsed since we met, that while to each of us there are strong grounds of searching of heart, all real or supposed offences may now be mutually set aside and give place to peace and cordial goodwill. May He who, I trust I may say, has loved us both, and washed us in his blood, subdue all our iniquities and cast our sins behind him into the depths of the sea! Being at such a distance, it is uncertain if we shall ever meet on earth. May we enjoy a blessed eternity in his presence!

" I am, my dear Sir, yours,

" ROBERT HALDANE."

This letter was not sent from Montauban, but carried by himself to Scotland, and delivered in 1821, through Mr. Aikman, to whom Mr. Haldane writes : " The feeling it expresses towards Mr. Ewing has long possessed my mind, and, I trust, will never be effaced." Mr. Ewing replied with courtesy, and even kindness, adhering to his refusal, and yet, with strange inconsistency, concludes : " Aid us with your prayers ! " Mr. Haldane rejoined in an elaborate letter to Mr. Aikman, striving to prove, that although he could not conscientiously comply with the unreasonable demand to acknowledge himself to be in the wrong, whilst he believed himself to be right, yet that reconciliation was surely a duty. " If," he said, " we both expect to meet together in the presence of God and the Lamb, surely we ought to be able to live in peace and love in the presence of men." He begun this letter by noticing, that " it was with no small emotion I once more saw a letter from

Mr. Ewing addressed to me in the style of former affection and reciprocal regard, after so long an interruption of friendship." And he concludes: " The time cannot now be very distant when reconciliation between us in this world will be in our power no more. May we not only enjoy together a blessed eternity in the presence of God, but be once more again united in the presence of men ! " These efforts were in vain so far as concerned a public reconciliation, but it may be charitably concluded, from the tone of Mr. Ewing's reply to the Montauban letter, that all personal bitterness and animosity was on his side also at an end.

There was another circumstance connected with the disruption which is worthy of record. It was the manner in which Mr. James Haldane evinced his unchanging conviction of the infinitely superior importance of the Gospel itself as compared with any point of controversy in regard to its ordinances. The public excitement produced by the announcement of his change of sentiment in regard to baptism, was proportioned to the notoriety of his character and his popularity as a preacher. He announced his intention of stating his reasons on the following Lord's-day, and the Tabernacle was crowded as when he preached with reference to Lord Camelford's duel, or more recently on the death of his venerable friend, John Newton. He observed many persons present, chiefly attracted by motives of curiosity, some of them men of station, others men of literature or science, professors, philosophers, general officers, and magistrates. It was not in his heart to allow a congregation of 4,000 souls to feed on the husks of a barren controversy about the meaning of βαπτω and βαπτιζω, or νιπτω, or even about the proper objects of Christian baptism. Looking round, therefore, on the vast assemblage with a solemn and scrutinizing glance, he pointedly asked, and paused as if for an answer to the question, what were the motives which had drawn them together ? " Was it," he inquired, " to hear a man who had changed his opinion ? Ah ! my friends, there is something of infinitely deeper importance, which concerns the present and eternal welfare of the immortal soul of every one now present." Starting from this point, he powerfully pressed home upon them a sense of their lost and ruined state, and called on them to behold the Lamb of God, who taketh away the sins of the world. He then noticed the differences which existed between believers, and the stumbling-block which these differences proved to the world. It was, in fact, a sermon in which he found no opportunity to speak particularly of the rite of baptism, although he dwelt much on the thing signified, and he postponed his promised statement till the following Lord's-day. The effect was solemnizing, and the sermon might have been sufficient in itself to have stayed the impending disruption.

Such was not the will of God. The two brothers had been raised up as extraordinary instruments to effect an extraordinary work. They were not, however, ambitious to be the founders of a new sect, or the leaders of a new party. Much good service was still reserved for them, both at home and abroad, but it was not to be in reviving apostolic usages or primitive Church order. What would have been the history of Congregationalism in Scotland, had no division taken place, it may be difficult to conjecture. But as its popularity was already on the wane, so it may be fairly surmised that its star had culminated, and that, even if Mr. Robert Haldane's pecuniary support had been continued for some years longer, the results would have been far from realizing the sanguine expectations of those who have spoken of their " flinging away a golden sceptre of Evangelical reform, which the prayerful in Scotland have hailed with rapture, and which both awed and improved the Kirk and the Secession." The work of Evangelical reform was indeed begun, but it did not comport with the will of God, that the new party should rise on the ruins either of the Kirk or the Secession.

In a very able and faithful review of the position and prospects of the Scottish Congregational Union at the end of fifty years, the Rev. W. Swan candidly admits,—

" It is evident, from the history of our Churches, that they have never been popular, and the present aspect of things around them gives no indication of their rising in public favour. It is stated that these Churches numbered, in 1849, less than 100 in all, comprising a membership of between 8,000 and 9,000. During the first years of our history, Churches multiplied rapidly, but then it was because *conversions* were frequent, and the accession to the Churches so planted were numerous."

The disruption not only divided and diminished the Church, but shattered the great congregation in Edinburgh to which Mr. James Haldane was wont to preach, and, excepting the evening services, probably reduced it to one-third of its former average number. This must have been a subject of regret to him, but it was one to which he seldom alluded, and never felt as a personal mortification. "*I am the Lord's servant*," was a frequent expression of his, and whether he preached to thousands or to hundreds, only concerned him so far as it afforded the opportunity of proclaiming the everlasting Gospel. It was the glory of God which he tried steadily to keep in view. To the love of popular applause he seemed insensible, and considered any sacrifice made to this end to be derogatory to the profession of the Gospel and degrading to the character of a minister of Christ.

In October, 1810, Dr. Charles Stuart, always in extremes of joy or depression, thus wrote to Mr. Campbell: "All here is dark indeed. I *once* thought, that if Mr. James Haldane was but convinced that none but disciples should be baptized, *I should see the consummation of my earthly bliss!* But, alas! this conviction has been attended with causes of misery, which have ever since broken my heart." Much pains had Dr. Stuart taken to inculcate his own views on his friend. He had attended his ministry, listened to his preaching with rapt admiration, and called on him two or three times in every week to discuss the topics which were delivered from the pulpit. He had gone so far as to say he would sacrifice half his fortune to see Mr. James Haldane a Baptist. But much as he had contributed to force on the attention of the latter this and other subjects, his cultivated taste was not prepared for what he very justly stigmatized as "useless talk, under the name of exhortation, by persons quite unqualified."

Dr. Stuart was, no doubt, in one of his gloomy frames when he thus wrote, and gravely added, that the changes which he so

much contributed to promote were " bringing some of us to our
graves." It was about this period, and very probably at the
very date of the foregoing letter, that the good Doctor had been
much mortified by an interview with the celebrated Henry
Brougham, whom he met at his son's house in the country.
The great orator and future Lord Chancellor, well knowing
Dr. Stuart's connexion both with Mr. Ewing and the Tabernacle, and probably not at all sorry to dwell on the divisions
which had taken place, could only talk about Mr. Robert
Haldane's controversy with Mr. Ewing. He professed to have
read the pamphlets with great interest, and particularly noticed
the acuteness and argumentative power of Mr. Haldane's reply.
All this was gall and wormwood to Dr. Stuart, but his low
spirits did not long continue, for suddenly Dr. Chalmers shot
like a brilliant meteor across the northern hemisphere, and that
great man,—great in intellect as in Christian attainments,—
together with Dr. Gordon, Dr. M'Crie, and other Presbyterian
ministers, once more aroused and absorbed the sympathies and
admiration which at one time Dr. Stuart seemed to have concentrated on James Haldane. Indeed, it is a circumstance not
without instruction, that Dr. Stuart ended his career where it
began, if not as a communicant, at least as a worshipper within
the pale of the Church of Scotland. Still it will be seen hereafter, that there was another instance of the steadiness of James
Haldane's friendships, in his unabated regard for Dr. Stuart.

There was for some years a lack in the Edinburgh Tabernacle,
according to the views entertained of apostolic times, and that
was a Presbytery, or plurality of elders, " in every Church."
It was not easy to find one whom the Church in Edinburgh
would permanently endure as a colleague for their pastor. At
last the office was, in a manner, forced upon his brother, but
with the express understanding that it should, in his case,
be deemed only temporary and provisional till others were
appointed. Many able discourses, particularly an Exposition of
the Epistles of Peter, were delivered by him during the few
years he thus officiated. After he went to the Continent
another attempt was made to secure a Presbytery for the

Church, but it did not succeed, and furnished one of the grounds of the frank and candid admission made in 1821 by Robert Haldane to his friend Dr. Bogue, that "the system did not work." What were Mr. James Haldane's sentiments on this subject might be seen from a letter written in 1822 to his son on his going to reside in London. The following extracts exhibit the simplicity of his aim, and his earnest desire, like Caleb of old, wholly to follow the Lord. After plainly stating that he had no wish to influence his son to unite himself to the communion of any of the Churches whose order resembled that observed in his own, he proceeds :—

"There is something in the conduct of Divine Providence, in regard to these Churches, which I do not understand. I am sure all the Lord's ways are right, and it is our folly and ignorance which prevents us from seeing His wisdom and goodness in them all. I think it evident that the apostles were most jealous of any deviation from the ordinances delivered by them to the Churches, and that they foretold that this would issue in the establishment of the Man of Sin. . . . I should wish you to be connected with that Church in which most of the religion of Jesus was exemplified, where the deepest impressions of the value of your soul, and the importance of eternity, the riches of the love of God, the freeness of His salvation, and the glory and beauty of holiness should be maintained in your heart, where you would have fewest temptations to conformity to this present evil world, and where the doctrine you heard was most scriptural and impressive. Perhaps you go too far about bigotry and illiberality. These are terms which are bandied about among all sects, and not without reason. There is much party spirit amongst all. The Churchman really thinks the Dissenter a great bigot; the Dissenter conscientiously returns the compliment. The Independent is impatient of the illiberality of the Baptist, and he is at a loss to reconcile the unfairness of the Independent's arguments with a good conscience. The liberality which chiefly prevails, I think, in England is most unscriptural. It is an idea that Scripture has laid down no rules for Church order, and that we are to do what appears to us most calculated for usefulness. If I adopted this sentiment, *I should myself be much disposed to join the Established Church*, for in many respects the field of usefulness there is greatest. But I see plainly that the order of a Church is not unimportant, and that, although at present there are many defects in all parties, we ought to love all who love the Lord Jesus Christ, and that our love to them ought to abound in proportion as we see the great features of the kingdom of God, righteousness and peace and joy in the

Holy Ghost abounding in them, and when these are observed it ought to enable us to throw a mantle of love over their defects. There is much more apology for what is commonly called bigotry in those who think they are obeying the Word of God, than when people are acting under the idea of expediency or usefulness. The former think they are obeying God, the latter are confessedly acting upon their own judgment. The former may think an opposite course hishonouring to God, but if the latter have not much forbearance, it must arise, in a great degree, from self-will and dissatisfaction that others will not agree with them. May the Lord look on His Church on earth! Its state is very low, and He alone can send times of refreshing. . . .

" May the Lord Himself abundantly bless you, and guard you from every danger, and preserve you to His kingdom, is the prayer of yours, most affectionately, " J. A. H."

Other letters of a similar purport might be produced, and in every public prayer he offered up intercession for all the people of God upon earth, " by whatever name they are known amongst men." His brother's views were the same, and are fully expressed in his " Exposition of the Romans."

Mr. J. A. Haldane's efforts to promote union without compromise were not discouraged by their ill-success with Mr. Aikman. Three years later he published, in 1811, a treatise on the duty of *forbearance*. It was answered by Mr. William Jones, the pastor of a Baptist Church, in London, and a writer of considerable talent, but much asperity. Mr. Jones considered it as covertly levelled at the Scotch Baptists; and, almost at the same moment, one of Mr. Haldane's late students, a Scotch Independent pastor, wrote another pamphlet, to show that the real object was to subvert the Congregational preachers. In 1812 Mr. James Haldane replied. Unmoved by the ill-humour of the strict communion Baptist, or the doleful imaginings of the Independent, he, in the first place, mildly remonstrates against the evils of controversial irritation, and the idea that harsh, contemptuous, or sarcastic language, is calculated to promote the cause of Christ. He then alludes to the supposition that he was " haunted by the idea of these preachers day and night; " but pleasantly entreats both of his assailants to be assured that they are mistaken. " I am full satisfied," he says, " that, in so far as either the Pædo-Baptist preachers, or the

Churches to which Mr. Jones refers, oppose the will of God, their system will come to nought; and, in so far as they do his will, I heartily wish the prosperity of both." He adds, that he had referred, not to Churches, or individuals, but to principles, in his previous treatise. " But, if I had any Churches particularly in view, it was those which bear the name of Mr. Glas, because I believe they carry the principle of non-forbearance further than any other." To many of the principles of Glas and Sandeman, and especially to their bitter intolerant spirit, both the brothers were at all times strongly opposed. There were, indeed, some parts of their writings which were regarded as exhibiting noble views of the freeness of the Gospel and the simplicity of faith, but, as a whole, the Glasite, or Sandemanian system, was abhorrent to their principles and feelings. On one occasion Mr. Haldane was speaking on this subject whilst walking by the side of one of his plantations on the undrained moss at Auchingray. He stopped and pointed to the slow and stunted growth of these young trees, as contrasted with the rapid growth of those which had been planted on a prepared soil, and said, with a smile, " There is a picture of Sandemanianism. There is life, but its expansive powers are contracted and dwarfed."

On the subject of faith one of the most useful and valuable of Mr. J. A. Haldane's practical works is a treatise on the " Doctrine and Duty of Self-examination." It contains the substance of two sermons preached in 1806. Another work on the same subject was published in 1830. Both the brothers have remarked, that trust, or confidence, in Christ, seemed substantially to express the meaning of faith. It was the dying declaration of their father,—" I have full confidence in Jesus;" and they both adopted the terms as their own definition of faith. It is at once simple and comprehensive. There may be many degrees of trust or confidence, but some feeling of trust, however feeble and flickering, seems essential, in order to distinguish between the mere act of intellectual assent, and the saving reception of the Gospel concerning Jesus Christ as the Son of God.

# CHAPTER XVII.

MR. HALDANE PURCHASES AUCHINGRAY AS A COUNTRY
RESIDENCE—HIS IMPROVEMENTS—PLANS FOR THE CON-
TINENT—AIRDRIE—EVIDENCES OF CHRISTIANITY—LET-
TERS OF MR. HARDCASTLE AND MR. HILL—" EDINBURGH
CHRISTIAN INSTRUCTOR "—MR. J. A. HALDANE CONTINUES
TO PREACH IN THE VILLAGES ROUND EDINBURGH—
PORTO BELLO—SIR DAVID MILNE—SCENE AT NORTH
BERWICK—VISIT TO HARROWGATE—THE HIGHLANDS
—ANECDOTE—DEATH OF MRS. JOASS—ABERCROMBY
FAMILY — ROMAN CATHOLIC ARCHBISHOP — CAPTAIN
GARDNER—DEATH OF MRS. J. A. HALDANE.

[1810—1819.]

FROM the period when Mr. Robert Haldane first planned his
Mission to India down to the summer of 1810, the variety and
extent of his occupations were such as to render it surprising
that he had been able to devote so much of his time to private
reading and study. After he left Airthrey, in 1798, and
embarked in plans for propagating the Gospel at home, he had
been employed in widely circulating Bibles and tracts, in establishing Sabbath-schools, building chapels, and sending out home
missionaries, as well as in superintending the education of young
men as preachers, catechists, and Scripture-readers. All this
was done under his own superintendence and at his own expense,
so that, in fact, there is hardly an object to which he at first
devoted his individual energies for which there has not since
been established a special Society.

In the midst of all these engagements, many of them involving
a vast amount of secular business and secular discussions, there
was much to distract, and there can be no doubt that an interval

of leisure was desirable for calm repose and quiet meditation.
This interval seemed to be graciously vouchsafed; whilst his
labours on the Continent, as well as his after-writings, indicate
how wisely he spent the comparative leisure which intervened
between the close of his earlier labours and his first visit to
Geneva, in 1816. There were those who regarded his seclusion as an abandonment of the objects to which he had dedicated
his life. His future self-denying course furnished the best
answer to these censorious observers. His usefulness was only
beginning at the time when they predicted its close. Up to the
year 1810, the spiritual portions of the labours of the two
brothers more especially devolved on James Haldane, whilst
his elder brother was to a great extent doing the work of the
Societies which now send forth missionaries, Bibles, and tracts.
But the last thirty years of Robert Haldane's life were to
be honoured by spiritual occupations and spiritual blessings
which will place his name high amongst the chief worthies of
the Church of Christ.

Towards the end of 1809 he bought the estate of Auchingray,
in Lanarkshire, on which he soon afterwards erected a comfortable and spacious residence. Amongst those who watched his
career with an unfriendly eye were some who criticised his
conduct in retiring to the country, as if it were inconsistent
with the motives which influenced him in the sale of Airthrey.
But such critics usually seize upon points that seem open to
their censure, without taking a view of all the circumstances.
There was a great difference between occupying a place like
Auchingray and one like Airthrey. The original cost of
Auchingray amounted to a very inconsiderable portion of the
price of Airthrey. Some farms adjoining Airthrey had been
reserved out of the original contract of sale, but these, too,
were disposed of before the new purchase. The manner in
which he acted, in regard to the last sale, was often mentioned
by Sir Robert Abercromby as stamping his character as a
gentleman. The farms unsold were much more valuable to
Sir Robert, as the owner of Airthrey Castle, than to any one
else. It would, therefore, have been easy to have extracted a

considerably larger price, to prevent annoyance, had such an
element of value been brought into the calculation.    But
Mr. Haldane declined taking advantage of this circumstance,
and, having obtained an estimate from his land-surveyor, Mr.
Morison, he sent the result to Sir Robert, offering the farms at
the price there named, which was 30,000*l.*    A proposal so liberal
was at once gladly accepted, and these lands became reunited
with Airthrey.

It was after the sale of the remainder of Airthrey, and of the
estates of Lochton and Keithock, that Mr. Robert Haldane purchased Auchingray.    Some country residence was necessary for
the purposes of health, retirement, and recreation.    For himself
and Mrs. Haldane the selection proved both agreeable and convenient, although the place was not adapted to persons dependent
on society.    At a comparatively small cost, he obtained a large
tract of land.    Its wildness pleased his taste, as its improvement
furnished an agreeable refreshment to his energetic spirit.    A
great part of Auchingray was then a muir, lying on the bleak
summit level between Edinburgh and Glasgow.    His plans for
draining, and, in some instances, cutting away the moss, were
conducted with equal skill and enterprise.    He covered several
hundreds of acres with larch, firs, birch, ash, and coppice.    As
he had been one of the first to transplant full-grown trees at
Airthrey, so, at Auchingray, he was one of the first to attempt
planting on the moss.    In all that he did the force and originality
of his character appears.    On an estate, consisting of 2,400 acres,
there was but one solitary tree, a weather-battered ash, which
stood beside the door of the farm-house in which the Principal
of the University of Glasgow, Dr. Macfarlane, was born.    Mr.
Haldane found the greater part a barren wilderness.    He left it
a waving forest, studded with slated cottages and new farm-
homesteads, an ornament to the surrounding country, the
improvement of which, by drainage and the application of lime,
had been stimulated by his example.    The grounds and farm-
buildings were laid out and planned chiefly by himself, sometimes aided by his old friend, Mr. Morison, of Alloa, with whom
he had consulted about most of his improvements at Airthrey.

The walks through the plantations were also made with so much skill, that a stranger might lose himself amidst winding foliage, where, formerly, there was nothing to interrupt the sweep of the north-eastern blast from the estuary of the Forth to the estuary of the Clyde.

But these pursuits were merely the pleasant relaxations of a mind at peace with God, and able to enjoy the temporal bounties of his providence, in consistency with far higher objects. His establishment was but little increased, whether he lived at Edinburgh or Auchingray. He kept only one riding-horse, and no carriage. Whenever it was necessary, a post-chaise was ordered from the inn at West Craigs; and, whilst he maintained an abundant hospitality, nothing was sacrificed to ornament or show. To live in this quiet, unostentatious way, at Auchingray, was something very different from occupying Airthrey and keeping up its park, its ornamental woods, and walks, and pleasure-grounds. The following letter will show how little his new occupations at Auchingray diverted his thoughts from the great missionary works he had in view when he parted with Airthrey. It is addressed to Mr. Campbell, and dated 25th December, 1810 :—

" I now trouble you with this, to ask you if there be any translation of the Scriptures which you think would be useful and is not likely to be carried into effect by the societies in London ; or if you have any opportunity of an enlarged distribution of the Scriptures which you are not able at present to embrace ? I should be glad to consider anything of this kind that you should recommend. In giving, perhaps, considerable assistance to such objects, I would wish to do it in such a way as would be an *addition* to what is at present going on. Do you know if anything in this way could be done *on the Continent ?* Can anything more be done for Spain and Portugal, &c. ? I suppose nothing could be attempted as to France,—or would it be possible to send over more copies of the Bible to that country ? When convenient, I shall be happy to hear from you on the subject ; and, as I am writing to other places, I should be glad that it were soon. All your friends here are well."

For two summers after he purchased Auchingray, he occupied the house at Hillend, belonging to the Monkland Canal Company, situated at the eastern extremity of the great reservoir,—

a sheet of water extending along the high road, two miles in length, in front of Auchingray, and said to be the largest artificial lake in the world. The capabilities of ornament connected with this beautiful lake, no doubt, constituted one of Mr. Haldane's chief inducements to select Auchingray as a place of residence. After the house was finished, it was his usual retreat during those months which he spent away from Edinburgh. On the Lord's-day he was for several years in the habit of going to Airdrie, where there was a Church formed on the model of that with which he was connected in Edinburgh. He generally himself delivered an exposition, in the forenoon, of some part of Scripture, which was always carefully studied, and full of useful practical instruction and profound theology. In the offices at a little distance from the house, he had a chapel fitted up, where Mr. James Haldane used to preach two or three times a-week when he visited his brother, and where he himself, after his return from the Continent, usually conducted public worship every Lord's-day. He was also at this time preparing his work on the Evidences and Authority of Divine Revelation, the first edition of which he published in 1816, and contained the fruit of his early and laborious inquiries.

His motive for writing that book was his own dissatisfaction with most of the works which professed to exhibit the evidences of Christianity. Looking along the whole line of the popular defenders of its historical truth, it was too manifest that the most eloquent and argumentative had not always been the most evangelical of its apologists. Warburton, Paley, Lardner, and Watson were great names, but of which of these distinguished writers could it be said with confidence, that he received the Gospel in its native power and simplicity? Bishop Warburton was a giant in learning, but his views of the Mosaic economy were sufficient to indicate his unsoundness. Archdeacon Paley, in his latest days, is said to have been greatly changed for the better; but speaking of him as a writer on Christianity, his principles exhibit a man groping in the dark, whilst his system of morals falls below the standard of a virtuous Pagan. Dr. Lardner was an Arian, disbelieving the Deity and atonement of

Christ; whilst Bishop Watson's own sentiments were as hetero-dox as his characteristic worldliness was inconsistent with his apostolic office. The works of such writers, although admirable in composition, unanswerable in argument, or valuable as a mine of information, betray in every page the absence of vital acquaint-ance with those truths, whose outward strength and glory they profess to establish. It appeared also to Mr. Haldane that these, and such-like books of evidences, were generally addressed to Infidels, and assumed the possibility that Christianity might prove a fable. On the contrary, he believed that the proofs of Christianity could only be properly set forth by those of whom it may be said, that the eyes of their understanding have been enlightened to know the exceeding riches of the grace of God in Jesus Christ; and further, that the evidences of the truth of Revelation ought to be peculiarly studied by disciples, not because they doubt, but because they desire to know more of the certainty of those things, which they most surely believe.

The work was considerably enlarged and improved at a much later period of his life. The first edition, although less complete, contained a body of conclusive evidence in favour of Christianity, written by a powerful reasoner, who had himself doubted, and profoundly fathomed the subject, whilst it was also an admirable exposition of the Gospel of salvation. One of his reviewers justly points out the singular skill and adroitness, with which he involves the antagonists of Christianity in the most awkward entanglement of self-contradiction. Out of the insinuations of Gibbon and the subtleties of David Hume, which he had scanned with an eye that pierced through all their sophistry, he elicits, by a masterly examination, a conclusive answer to their own objections. He strips them of their boasted claims to candour and philosophy, reduces them to that most humiliating of all discomfitures, self-refutation, and shows triumphantly not only the weakness, but the malice of their aggression. From his youth up, he excelled as a reasoner in the Socratic method; and it will be found that at Geneva and Montauban it was by the same process that he was enabled, most successfully to convince inquirers of the hollowness of their anti-scriptural doctrines. The concluding chapter, addressed to the various classes who hear the Gospel, was described by the same reviewer as " an impressive compendium of glorious and awful truths, forcibly, and sometimes eloquently, written."

Before he left this country for the Continent, Mr. Haldane received many tokens of the estimation in which his work was held, and especially from some of those old friends with whom he first set out in his plans for propagating the Gospel. The two following letters are amongst the few which he preserved. The first is from Joseph Hardcastle, Esq., the Treasurer of the London Missionary Society, with whom he had taken so much counsel in connexion with his Mission to India, the education of the African children, and the establishment of a Village Itinerancy Society in London. It was in a suite of rooms connected with Mr. Hardcastle's counting-house, as a Russia merchant, that most of the religious Societies established at the end of the last century were instituted and for several years carried on. There the home management of the London Missionary Society, the Religious Tract Society, the Hibernian Society, and the Village Itinerancy Society, were long carried on at Mr. Hardcastle's expense. There, too, the British and Foreign Bible Society held its first meetings.

" *Hatcham House, October* 2, 1816.

" MY DEAR SIR,—Your important and very valuable publication on the ' Evidence and Authority of Divine Revelation,' was sent to me about a fortnight ago, and I received it with much pleasure, as an acceptable token of regard from a friend whom I have not had the satisfaction of seeing for many years, but for whom I have not ceased to retain an affectionate remembrance.

" But although I felt the obligation due to your kindness, yet I thought it best to delay my acknowledgments till I had perused the work, which I have now done, and I can say, with the greatest sincerity, that it has afforded me very much pleasure, and I hope improvement also. I regard it as a work of great importance, admirably adapted for much usefulness, and I hope the blessing of God will accompany its perusal, and fulfil your wish in rendering it the occasion of promoting his glory, the honour of His word, and of that glorious Messiah, to whose person, offices, and salvation it bears, through all its parts, so full and complete a testimony.

" With what satisfaction and thankfulness must we contemplate the aspect of the times in which we live, and especially the operations and success of our Bible and Missionary Institutions. I have lately read over the last Report of both Societies, and am induced to think that we are witnessing the effects of a remarkable effusion of the influences of the Holy Spirit, and that we are probably discerning the dawn of that bright day which is predicted to shed Divine light on all the nations of the earth.

" An energy seems to pervade the Christian world, unknown for several preceding ages; and a generation appears springing up, who are likely to follow up with increased zeal the measures of their predecessors.

" I consider myself as standing on the verge of the eternal world, and the decays of nature frequently admonish me that the time of my departure cannot be very remote. But I am cheered sometimes with the contrast which the present state of things exhibits, compared with that which existed when I first became acquainted with society; and I am thankful to God for the privilege I have enjoyed of associating with so many excellent friends, who have been made instrumental in producing results so beneficial and so extensive.

" All my family unite in the desire of being kindly remembered by yourself and Mrs. Haldane, and by your brother and sister, whose interviews occasionally at our house afforded the greatest pleasure, the recollection of which is cherished in all our minds.—Believe me, my dear Sir,

" Respectfully and affectionately,

" JOSEPH HARDCASTLE.

" *Robert Haldane, Esq.*"

The second letter is from his venerable friend, Rowland Hill, whose attachment remained unshaken by the changes that had taken place :—

" MY DEAR SIR,—I feel much ashamed that I have not before now sent my very affectionate acknowledgment of your present of your volumes on the Evidences of Revelation ; but I first read them over attentively myself, and then lent them to others, before I ventured to pass my estimate on them; and however feeble my testimony may be, and highly worthy as your work may be of approbation of superior minds, yet a better compilation of the evidences of Christianity, because so perspicuous and so easy to be understood, to the best of my recollection I never read before.

" You have done, dear Sir, not only, I trust, the most essential service to the general cause of Christianity in what you have written, but also to the spirit and temper of the Gospel, by wisely dropping all those inferior differences that are of no essential importance when compared to the cause itself.

" Yes, dear Sir, and the older we get, and the riper we grow in the

Divine life, the less we shall regard matters that are disputatious and non-essential, because not so much the positive subject of Divine revelation, and consequently the cause of minor differences among those who are the happy recipients of the same grace, and partakers of a Divine union with the same spiritual Head. And in this I desire to express my thankfulness before God for the concluding pages of your volumes.

" While some have vindicated Christianity as a mere nominal religion, you have not only pleaded for the Temple of Truth, but shown that God himself is to be the inhabitant of His own temple, and that men are to be unspeakably blessed in Him.

" On a subject similar to this, I cannot express what high satisfaction and delight my mind has received in perusing a recent publication by Dr. Mason, of New York. As it is sold in Edinburgh, I should suppose it has attracted your attention.

" If all the world were of his opinion, what a peaceable, united Church would be exhibited on earth, and what a strong argument against the sacred cause of Christianity would its enemies lose, if all manifested it by being possessed of the same delightful mind which is so evident through the whole of that invaluable publication!—Believe me to be, dear Sir,

" Most faithfully and respectfully yours,

" ROWLAND HILL."

A review of " The Evidences " appeared in the " Edinburgh Christian Instructor," in 1820, from the pen of the celebrated Dr. Andrew Thomson, before Mr. Haldane was personally known to that great champion of the Bible and of the Church of Scotland. The review was written with somewhat of the author's characteristic vivacity, which, for a religious periodical, seemed to border too closely on the flippant gaiety of the early numbers of the " Edinburgh Review." Dr. Thomson bestowed considerable praises on the excellences of the book, but dropped some good-humoured jokes about " lay-preaching," and warned the author that he could not expect to gather many " laurels of triumph," or much of " popular acclaim," on a field which had been already traversed by so many " champions of renown." There was nothing in the review to cause annoyance. It cannot, therefore, be supposed that any feeling of resentment towards his future friend and coadjutor in defence of the integrity of the Bible, dictated the letter which, on this occasion, Mr. Haldane addressed to Dr. Thomson. It rather proceeded from a desire to draw attention to the danger connected with books of evidence, written by men who had not themselves a living belief in the Gospel. The celebrity both of Dr. Andrew Thomson and of his magazine, seemed to present a favourable opportunity for interesting the public mind on the very subject which had induced Mr. Haldane to write a book of evidences. The publication of his pamphlet, entitled, *"A Letter to the Editor of the Christian Instructor,"* was, however, an instance of his fearless nature, for Dr. Thomson was then in the vigour of his colossal faculties, and in the full blaze of his great popularity. It may well be doubted whether it was worth while to reclaim against the judgment of the reviewer with regard to Warburton, Paley, Watson, and Campbell, as people were sure to imagine that the remonstrance was, at least in some measure, dictated by personal dissatisfaction with Dr. Thomson's criticisms. But whether this was the case or not, the Letter was a powerful exposure of the unfitness of the great " champions of renown," in whose hands, for the most part, the defence of Christianity had been left, and it contained a forcible remonstrance against the lawfulness of seeking for "laurels of triumph" in any work connected with the service of God.

The concluding passage is characteristic of Mr. Haldane. He tells Dr. Thomson that he was the more anxious to deliver this warning, because, although " I have not the pleasure of being personally acquainted with the Editor of the 'Christian Instructor,' I have had the satisfaction of hearing what is calculated to produce respect for him." The passage thus concludes,—

" Dismiss, then, your ' champions of renown,' your 'popular acclaim,' your 'laurels of triumph.' Give them back to him who has such base and unworthy considerations ever at hand, to dazzle and seduce his votaries to their ruin. Expressions like these become not so sacred a subject. We are all too prone to pursue ' *lying vanities.*' But shall we for a moment allowedly entertain such ideas ? Shall a Christian Instructor gravely hold them up as objects of ambition, or ends of legitimate pursuit ? If it be not a ' desire to be useful' that prompts us to whatever we do in the service of the Gospel, we had better employ our time and our labour in any other way, than in acting upon principles which debase its nature, and divert from its proper object all its tendencies."

Meanwhile nothing had occurred to damp Mr. James Haldane's zeal for the propagation of the Gospel. In some respects his labours were increased, because he had less assistance at command; but he was no longer able to make wide tours, occupying two, three, or four months in duration. Since 1799, and the formation of the Circus Church, Mr. Aikman had, for the most part, ceased from his labours as an itinerant in the summer months. Mr. Rate was now quietly and usefully settled as minister of a Presbyterian Church at Alnwick. Mr. Innes could seldom absent himself from his own duties at Dundee, or Mr. Ewing from Glasgow. Mr. Campbell was removed to Kingsland, and, although Mr. James Haldane was the last to quit the field, which he was the first to enter, yet he too began to experience the increasing difficulties connected with a prolonged absence from home, and from the Church of which he was the pastor. The necessity, too, had become less urgent, and the Gospel was now flourishing in districts where it had been previously almost unheard of by the existing generation. Under these circumstances, he felt himself less called upon to continue his laborious missionary tours.

During the summers of 1808 and 1809, he was particularly zealous in preaching, sometimes on the Calton Hill, sometimes under a rock, near St. Anthony's Well, in the King's Park; sometimes on Bruntsfield Links, and, at other times, at Newhaven, Leith, Portobello, Musselburgh, Dalkeith, Lasswade, Stobb-hill, Broxbourn, and other places, either in the open air, or under shelter, as the weather, the audience, or convenience dictated.

In 1809 he was also much occupied with the formation of the Edinburgh Bible Society, of which he was always an active member, and afterwards became a Vice-President.

The village of Portobello, to which he was frequently accustomed to resort, with his family, during the summer months, was the scene of many occasional labours, for a period of no less than half a century. The following is a letter, referring to his preaching at Portobello, from the daughter of a well-known magistrate of Edinburgh, the late Baillie Jamieson, whose name is associated with the rise of that favourite and now populous marine appendage to Edinburgh :—

"*Summerfield, March* 22*d*, 1851.

"DEAR MISS HALDANE,—I have read with the deepest interest the little sketch of the life and labours of your venerated father, which you had the goodness to send me, and have been reminded vividly of many circumstances in his history, which, long ago, I had often the happiness to hear from his own lips. Few, comparatively, are now alive, who remember your dear father, in the full force of his early zeal and success, who witnessed the crowds that then attended his preaching, or who had the privilege of enjoying his friendship and conversation. To *me*, who was so favoured, the details of the sketch are peculiarly interesting, and I am glad to understand, that a narrative, still more extended, is in contemplation, which, I have no doubt, will, by the blessing of God, be most useful to many inquirers. Will you allow me to suggest, that, in the event of a more complete memoir being published, some notice should be taken of Mr. Haldane's ardent, affectionate labours at my native village, Portobello, where, for a series of years, his efforts for the spiritual good of the people, by preaching and private ministration, were unwearied and highly appreciated. The more so, perhaps, that, at the outset, he had to contend with certain prejudices, which the enemies of pure, evangelical preaching had created in the minds of some of the friends of the Government, by insinuating that he was inimical to the ' Powers that be,' and that he did not even pray for the King, or the minister of the parish !

" The oldest proprietor at Portobello, on whose lands most of the village was then built, who had many of the common people in his employment, and enjoyed their implicit confidence, had heard these rumours. He was a zealous supporter of the Government, and he was advised by certain parties about Edinburgh, that, in their unsettled state of political feeling, he should use any influence he had, to suppress Mr. Haldane's efforts, as calculated, they said, to set the minds of the people adrift, and to unhinge the institutions of the country. It was reported that Mr. Haldane was, on a certain day, to preach near the high road, and the proprietor referred to appeared on that occasion among the numerous audience collected around him, and of whom many had come from Duddingstone, and other neighbouring districts.

" His purpose (agreeably to the information he had received) was to remonstrate, at least, with the people under his own care, or even, if necessary to exert his authority as a justice of the peace in dispersing them. He had not listened, however, but a few minutes to the fervent discourse which was then being delivered, so suitable to the circumstances of the audience, before he saw that he had been misinformed and mistaken ; and with that contrition which honest minds feel when they perceive they had been about to act unjustly, my father at once confessed his error. Fortunately, the falling of a heavy shower afforded him an opportunity of requesting Mr. Haldane and his congregation to adjourn to a large barn, which had been lately furnished with coarse benches, and where the minister of the parish occasionally met his people. The offer was cheerfully accepted, and the services of the evening were peacefully concluded. Thus began, my dear Miss Haldane, an acquaintance, which I still look back upon, as one of the happiest circumstances of my life. In the same place Mr. Haldane continued his labours on many a winter as well as summer evening for years, sometimes alternating afterwards with Mr. Ewing or Mr. Aikman, and having frequently for his auditor the amiable and pious Mr. Bennett, then minister of Duddingstone, who felt delighted to encourage, by his presence and example, any effort which was likely to arouse, or quicken the piety of his people. Your excellent father resided with his family in the village for several seasons, when, in addition to his exertions in the pulpit, by Christian counsel and advice he was the means of awakening and comforting many an afflicted mind. In my own case, I owe much to Mr. Haldane. He was fully alive, I think, to the gratitude I felt to him, for early leading my attention to those views which he told me, could alone give peace to the conscience, and which, in my declining age, I find now my chief solace. You will forgive me, therefore, for the wish I have expressed, to see in the record of his life some notice of his devoted labours in a sphere to which I once felt much attached. Since the time I speak of, what was a mere village has grown into a sizeable town ; the population, I dare say, more than quadrupled, and a number of churches have been built. I question, how-ever, if more real good is now effected than when Mr. Haldane laboured unostentatiously by himself, in the way of private ministration, or when, on the summer evenings, his warm and thrilling appeals to the heart and conscience were listened to by a deeply-impressed audience, in the old barn at Portobello." . . .

There is a postscript to Mrs. Robertson's letter, which recals Mr. James Haldane's intimacy, when at sea, with one who was in early life a kindred spirit, the late gallant Admiral Sir David Milne, whose achievements in the navy, and especially as second to Lord Exmouth at Algiers, have rendered his name justly renowned. The other gentleman alluded to, sailed in the same ship with Mr. James Haldane :—

" On reading over the above, incidents occur to my mind connected with your dear father, during the time of his valuable labours at Porto-bello. His old friends and shipmates, Admiral Sir David Milne and Mr. Chalmers, had just returned from abroad, and hearing of Mr. Haldane's fame as a preacher of the Gospel, expressed a desire again to meet with him. This they soon did in my father's house, and heard from himself how the change in his views and habits had been brought about. He did not hesitate to state, with his usual firmness, simplicity, and candour, the circumstances which had led to the unlooked-for change. The detail was interesting, and the evening passed most happily, with interchange of kind feelings toward each other; for, although differing, alas! from Mr. Haldane on spiritual subjects, the gallant Admiral and his friend found that the manly worth and affection which had always distinguished their old acquaintance, were in nothing impaired."

Long afterwards, Mr. J. A. Haldane, in a letter dated May 10, 1845, notices the sudden death of Sir David Milne, in the steamer on his way to Scotland, and observes: " Many years ago we were at Bombay. He was second mate of the General Elliot, and I of the Montrose. He was five years older, but we were then rather intimate friends. When we got home, war had broken out, and as he had previously passed as lieutenant, he joined the Boyne under Sir John Jervis."

In connexion with Mr. James Haldane's preaching in the neighbourhood of Edinburgh there is another incident, which belongs to an early date. It relates to an excursion which he made to North Berwick, as it is believed, in 1798. He had announced the intended sermon in the usual manner, and had begun to preach one summer's evening not far from the shore of that beautiful bay, stretching nearly twenty miles along the coast, at one extremity of which the Bass Rock and North Berwick Law rise, as from the ocean, to confront the ancient Castle of Edinburgh and the majestic rocks of Arthur's Seat. At that period the convivial habits of East Lothian were notorious, even in an age when Scottish hospitality had become stained with the vices of riotous excess. There were many of the East Lothian lairds who drank so hard and so habitually, that it is said by those who knew them well, that they never went to bed sober. It happened that the officers of the East Lothian yeomanry, and certain justices of the peace, including a Baronet who long sat in Parliament for the county, were dining with the Provost and magistrates of North Berwick. According to the wretched habits of the times, they were already deep in their

potations, when they were informed that Mr. J. A. Haldane was
preaching in their immediate vicinity to the assembled people of
North Berwick.   The sound of the Gospel had no charms for
them, nor were they willing that others should hear it.   Already
heated with wine, they began to consult in what way they
should put down this missionary invasion of their own territories.   One of them, more reckless than the rest, said that
it would be a capital plan to seize on the preacher, as had been
done in the case of some political lecturers in England during
the suspension of the Habeas Corpus Act, and send him at once
on board a man-of-war.   It was replied, that this would be
rather dangerous, and besides, that it would be awkward, as
the Admiral of the North Seas was Mr. Haldane's uncle by
blood, whilst the Commander of the King's Land Forces was
his uncle by marriage.   But as they drank on, they became
more and more resolved that in some way he should be put
down, and open-air preaching crushed in North Berwick.
Rising from the table, the Provost and magistrates sallied forth,
threatening that if the preacher did not desist, they would make
a law to stop him if they did not find one.   In this infuriated
mood they rushed forward to the spot, a boisterous throng, not
omitting oaths, with horrid imprecations, and other melancholy
proofs of their half-inebriated state.   James Haldane had a
spirit which always rose with the occasion.   He received them
with calm self-possession, and in reply to their demands, intimated that he was infringing no law, and interrupting no
thoroughfare.   He said, at the same time, that if as magistrates
they required him to desist from preaching in that particular
spot, he would certainly obey, but added, that when he heard
men in authority setting such an example of profane swearing—
" What ! " exclaimed the magistrates, eagerly interrupting the
half-finished sentence,—" what do you say of us ?"   " I would
not," he replied, with firmness,—" I would not say what I think
of you."   " Conscience," it has been truly said, " makes cowards
of us all ;" and the same determined composure, which a few
years before had overawed the intoxicated mutineers at the door
of the powder-magazine of the Dutton, seemed now to have

paralyzed the godless throng who had rushed from their revel to seize upon the preacher. In the meantime, great was the indignation that arose amongst the people who witnessed this wanton and indecent interruption, and it is difficult to say what might have been the result, had not a respectable farmer come forward and requested him to adjourn to his field, which was private property, and where the jurisdiction of the Provost ceased. He did so, and drawing a moral from the enmity to the Gospel just witnessed, preached a powerful and impressive sermon, which sent away the people awed and solemnized. It was long remembered at North Berwick and in the neighbourhood. That sermon was not, however, permitted to end without interruption, for such was the rancorous feeling of the Provost and magistrates, that, nettled at the defeat they had sustained, they prevailed upon one of the county gentlemen who commanded the Yeomanry to lend his drum, for the purpose of drowning the preacher's voice. This undignified act of magisterial interference did not, however, succeed, as the drummer was not allowed to enter the field, and the interruption was more vexatious than successful.

There was, however, a melancholy coincidence forming a sequel to the story. Shortly afterwards Mr. James Haldane was returning home, and as he reached his house in Edinburgh, No. 16 (then No. 8), George-street, he observed the unusual spectacle of a great funeral procession with two hearses passing his door. He inquired whose funeral it was, when he was shocked to learn that it was the funeral of the Provost of North Berwick, and his wife, who had both died suddenly, and were about to be buried in the same grave. Another and more pleasing reminiscence has been since associated with this scene of interruption. Twenty years afterwards, when walking one summer evening near Portobello, with some of his children, Mr. J. A. Haldane met a tall, portly gentleman, of commanding presence, who, on seeing him, rather abruptly left the foot-path, and uncovering, made a profound bow. Mr. J. A. Haldane returned the unlooked-for courtesy of the stranger, and next day discovered that it was the officer who lent the drum at North

Berwick. Since that evening he had never met the preacher, but had deeply repented of the part which he had been tempted to take in the affair; it was a recollection that lay heavy on his conscience; and he afterwards charged his sons to do what in them lay to show respect for Mr. James Haldane and kindness to his family. It is still more pleasing to think that this officer was himself a trophy of Divine grace, and that the preacher to whom he had once refused to listen, and whose voice he had tried to drown, spoke to him the words of peace and prayed by his side when laid on the bed of death. Four gallant sons of his had engaged in defence of their country; one of them distinguished himself as the colonel of a Highland regiment, and another received promotion for his zeal and conduct on the field of Waterloo. Both became, what was far better, good soldiers of Jesus Christ. The last time that Mr. James Haldane preached near London, was in the year 1848, when he proclaimed the Gospel to a crowded military audience at Woolwich, in the Scottish Free Church, at the request of Colonel Anderson, who holds an important command in that garrison, and is the eldest surviving son of him who, just fifty years before, had been a party to the interruption at North Berwick.

The occurrence of such incidents naturally grew less common, as Mr. J. A. Haldane's work fell more within the usual routine of an ordinary labourer in the ministry of the Gospel. But seldom has there been a man of whom it might be more truly said, that he was " instant in season and out of season." As the pastor of his own people, and the visitor of all who sought his spiritual aid, he was an example even in old age, down to the close of his lengthened days. Misery or wretchedness only constituted a fresh claim on his sympathy, and the dread of contagion or infection never interrupted his errands of mercy. On one occasion a pestilential fever was raging in a house at Stockbridge, and Dr. Alison, the eminent brother of the distinguished historian, left a person in charge, expressly to stop Mr. J. A. Haldane's entrance into a house where the danger was imminent. But the warning made no impression. He said he was in the path of duty, and ought not to be deterred from it by any personal apprehension. If the desertion of duty would be deemed an act of cowardice on the part of a soldier or sailor, why should there be less of loyalty or boldness in a soldier and servant of Christ?

His gentle and soothing manner in a sick room was the index to the sympathy of his heart, and contrasted finely with the natural energy of his fearless nature. His experimental knowledge of the truth, his wonderful familiarity with Scripture, and his remarkable unction in prayer, rendered his visits peculiarly acceptable to those who sought for and valued spiritual comfort. Often was he invited to attend on those who were not connected with his Church, and it was remarked by many who had seceded from it at the time of the disruption, that in seasons of affliction they still gladly turned to him who had been their pastor in the Circus and the Tabernacle.

The people of Edinburgh always knew him as the friend of the poor, and the confidence which his character inspired was unbounded. It happened that an attached member of his congregation happened to be thrown into the society of Infidels, who were scoffing at the ministers of religion. They turned to the stranger and asked, in a light tone, what ministry she attended On hearing that for nearly fifty years she had attended that of Mr. James Haldane, they immediately dropped their levity, and said, "Well, we cannot deny that he is a consistent good man!" One of the most remarkable instances of the confidence reposed in him was connected with the long-remembered robbery and murder of the porter of the British Linen Banking Company of Edinburgh. The perpetrator of this daring act was never discovered, although the extraordinary sensation produced by "Begbie's murder" was not forgotten for many years after the event. The unfortunate porter was carrying a large sum in bank notes in a leather bag, when he was stabbed about dusk on the staircase leading to the bank, then in the Old Town, and the booty carried off. The murderer hid a large bundle of the notes, amounting to several thousand pounds, in a hedge in Bellevue, not far from the spot on which Drummond-place now stands, but then constituting a

part of the once beautiful pleasure grounds formerly surrounding the villa of the celebrated General Scott, father of the
late Duchess of Portland, at Bellevue.  In that neighbourhood
buildings had been already commenced, and, about a year after
the murder, a journeyman mason discovered the bank notes, and
hardly knowing what they were, put the bundle in his coat
pocket, which he carelessly threw aside whilst engaged in his
work.  At the close of the day he took counsel with some of
his companions as to the course he should pursue.  On the one
hand, it was suggested that the possession of so much money
might bring him into trouble.  On the other, he desired to
secure a reward for its restoration.  None of them were
acquainted with Mr. James Haldane.  But they unanimously
resolved that he was the fittest person to be consulted on the
matter, as one on whose kindness and judgment the poor could
always rely.  Their confidence was not disappointed.  Mr. James
Haldane conducted the man to the late Mr. Sheriff Duff, a
relation of his wife, and after conference with him and some
of the managers of the bank, secured a reward of 100*l.* for the
mason, whose information did not however lead to any further
results, as the murderer, although often reported to be discovered,
was never brought to justice.

Among the many solemn scenes which he was called to
witness in the course of his visitations, there was one peculiarly
striking, which occurred towards the close of his ministry.  He
was urgently requested to visit, without delay, a dying man in
great distress of mind.  He went, and was told by the unhappy
sufferer, that many years before he had gone to the Tabernacle
and heard a sermon which had so alarmed him as to eternity,
that he had returned home in a rage, and uttered a prayer to
God to strike him dead if ever he again entered a place of
worship.  Years elapsed, and he had kept his vow until the
previous Lord's-day evening, when he had thoughtlessly strolled
once more into the Tabernacle and again heard Mr. James
Haldane preach the same solemn truths.  Shortly after he left
the place, he was struck with paralysis.  Mr. James Haldane
declared to him the Gospel, and told him it was not too late to

repent and turn to the Lord. The poor man listened with intense interest, but the result is known only to God, for he shortly afterwards expired.

In the summer of 1810 he visited Harrowgate, on account of his wife's health, and during the weeks he remained there embraced frequent opportunities of preaching in the Assembly-room and in the neighbourhood. In 1811, he took his two eldest boys a short Highland tour, but whilst introducing them to the beauties of Dunkeld, or the wild grandeur of Killiecranky and Blair Athol, and beguiling the journey, as they returned by Perth to Stirling, Carron, and Linlithgow, with tales of other times and reminiscences of his own and his brother's boyish days, he never forgot his one great vocation. At every place where they stopped he endeavoured to be useful, whether by preaching, as at Dunkeld, by distributing tracts, or speaking a word in season as opportunity offered. One day, when halting at a rude country inn in the Ochil Hills, not far from the Rumbling Bridge, there were two gentlemen in the same room, with whom he entered into friendly conversation. At that time French brandy was scarce and costly, unless it happened to be smuggled, and some was brought which one of the gentlemen pronounced to be "excellent upon his salvation." Mr. J. A. Haldane did not notice this profane levity, but continued to converse with him until their carriage was announced. They took leave with politeness, when, following them to the door, he requested the gentleman to accept of a tract of his own, entitled "The Great Salvation." "You were talking, Sir," he said, "of your salvation; perhaps you will permit me to offer something that I have written upon that important subject." The stranger coloured at the implied rebuke thus delicately conveyed, but expressing his sincere acknowledgments, drove off.

In the spring of 1812 he made a journey to Newcastle, where the pastor of a Church, who had been educated at the early class in Glasgow, had apostatized into Socinianism. This was one of the comparatively few amongst all these students who actually denied the faith. Mr. James Haldane preached

with great power " on the Person of Christ," and the notes of
his sermon were afterwards published in a very excellent little
treatise, embodying the testimony of Scripture both to the
Godhead and manhood of the Saviour. His labours at Newcastle and in the neighbouring towns were highly prized, and
were deemed most important on this occasion.

In the following year he made another tour to Carlisle
through the south of Scotland, where he was as indefatigable as
in his earlier years in fulfilling his commission to preach the
Gospel. He also visited the late Rev. John Fawcett, of
Stanwix, an excellent clergyman of the Church of England,
under whose tuition he was desirous of placing his eldest son,
now deceased. Mr. Fawcett's numbers were complete, but he
recommended his friend, the Rev. L. Grainger, of Wintringham,
who had been the much-esteemed curate and usher of Joseph
Milner, the historian, and the tutor of Henry Kirke White.
With him Mr. James Haldane successively placed his two eldest
sons, a circumstance worthy of record as exhibiting, in a practical form, his love for good men and his superiority to mere
sectarian prejudices.

In 1814, he repaired, first to Buxton, and then to Harrowgate, for the health of his beloved wife, taking with them their
eldest daughter, and second son, then on his way to Wintringham. On their journey he stopped at Millbank, near
Warrington, the residence of Robert Spear, Esq., an eminent
merchant, who took a deep interest in objects connected with
the propagation of the Gospel. He had then repeated opportunities of preaching both at Millbank and in the neighbourhood of Warrington, where he once more enjoyed an agreeable
meeting with Rowland Hill, then a septuagenarian, and engaged
on what he intended to be his last tour for the Missionary
Society. On the following Sunday Mr. James Haldane went
by request to preach in the open air, in a village where there was
a large manufacturing population and no Gospel ministry. He
was accompanied by Mr. Thomas Smith, one of his brother's
students, who was then tutor in Mr. Spear's family, and lately
Professor at the Rotherham Academy. On arriving at the

place where the sermon was to have been, on the village-green, the constable, addressing Mr. Smith, told him that he could allow of no preaching. Mr. J. A. Haldane, with great presence of mind, took out his Bible, and uncovering his head, observed, that, at all events, there could be no objection to his reading a portion of the Word of God. The constable seemed perplexed, and was struck, as it was said, with the bearing and appearance of the stranger, who thus quietly assumed his undoubted right to read the Scriptures to the people. The result was, that from reading he began to expound, and by and by to speak, without interruption, directly and forcibly to the assemblage, and concluded with prayer.

At Buxton he constantly officiated on the Lord's-day, and occasionally on week-days, in the chapel at that place, attracting a large number of the visitors, as well as of the ordinary inhabitants. The war had then scarcely ceased, and such watering-places as Buxton were, at that time, much frequented by the gentry and aristocracy. In his old age Mr. James Haldane became more silent in mixed company, or with strangers; but in his earlier years, he had a happy faculty of introducing interesting conversation, and frequently turning it to good account. As he remained at Buxton long enough to rise, according to usual rotation, to the head of the public table, his influence was more and more felt, and although there had been, at first, a dread of his Methodism, he afterwards became a general favourite with the most intelligent portion of the company, which comprised Judges, Members of Parliament, counsellors, clergymen, general officers, and country squires. There was there a rector, from Anglesea, the uncle of a Welsh Baronet and Member of Parliament, who, knowing nothing at the time of Mr. James Haldane, observed that "these *poor devils*, the Calvinists, make their people believe that everything, whether good or evil, is of God." Without taking any umbrage at the worthy and good-humoured rector's unceremonious description of the Calvinists, and, in reality, smiling at his prejudices, Mr. James Haldane quietly replied, "Ah, Sir, that is a grave subject. Do you not remember the vision which the prophet told to King Ahab, how he saw the hosts of heaven standing around the throne of God, on the right hand and on the left; and how the lying spirit received his commission to go forth and persuade Ahab to go up to Ramoth Gilead; and how Ahab went, and fell, although warned of his folly and his danger?" Before Mr. J. Haldane had finished, the portly and well-meaning but not well-instructed divine, colouring red as crimson, professed himself more than convinced, and gladly turned the conversation. Before he left Buxton he received letters of acknowledgment from several of the visitors, thanking him for his tracts, or expressing their gratitude for spiritual instruction they had received. The few weeks he remained at Harrowgate were spent in the same manner, preaching, as opportunity offered, wherever there was an open door, and trying to introduce the Gospel into his conversation, without forcing it on others in such a way as to increase the offence of the cross.

In December, 1814, Mrs. James Haldane lost her mother, who had survived her husband more than twenty years. She was a very superior woman, and had much of the character which belonged to her family. She was in her seventy-seventh year, and died without any illness or previous warning, but leaving behind her a good hope that she had entered into the rest that remains for the people of God. Her father, Mr. Abercromby, of Tulliebody, who was born in 1704, and died in 1800, was distinguished for his strong sagacity, as well as for his longevity. There was something remarkable about this family. He had four sons and four daughters by his wife, Mary Dundas, of Manor, a niece of the celebrated Bishop Burnet. "He lived," says General David Stuart, of Garth, in his "History of the Highland Regiments," "to see all his four sons honoured and respected, and at the head of their several professions. At one time, whilst his eldest son, Sir Ralph, was commanding in chief in the West Indies, his youngest son, Sir Robert, held the same station in the East Indies, each having the red ribbon and star of the Order of the Bath. Another son, Burnet Abercromby, commanded an East Indiaman, and retired with a large fortune; whilst his remaining son, an eminent, learned, and accomplished

Scotch Judge, by the title of Lord Abercromby, was also much distinguished as a writer in the literary circles of Edinburgh." After stating these facts, General Stewart adds, "Three of his (Mr. Abercromby's) daughters were married to gentlemen of family and fortune, who resided so near him that he could dine with either any day he chose; and his fourth daughter, continuing unmarried, devoted her days to the declining years of her father. Latterly he lived with his son." Of these daughters Elizabeth married her cousin, Major Joass, the grandson of General Abercromby, of Glassaugh, and great-grandson and heir of line to George, second Lord Banff, and heir-general of the third and fourth Barons, who died without issue. Two other daughters were married, the one to Colonel Edmonstone, of Newton, and the other to Mr. Bruce, of Kennett, whose family claim the male heirship of the Royal house of Bruce, but who was himself better known by his title of Lord Kennett, as an eminent and much respected Scotch Judge. Had General Stewart lived, he might have added the remarkable fact, that of Mr. Abercromby's grandsons, who had reached manhood before his death, two were destined to sit at the same time as Peers of the realm, after one had been the Speaker of the House of Commons, and another a general officer and Knight of the Bath. General Stewart's account of Sir Ralph's departure on the expedition to Egypt is interesting :—

" I happened," he says, "to be in Edinburgh in May, 1800, and dined with Lady Abercromby on the day Sir Ralph left her to embark on that expedition from which he never returned. A King's messenger had arrived from London the day before, and Sir Ralph, only waiting for a few family arrangements, set out on the following morning. When at dinner with the family, after his departure, I was affected, in a manner which I can never forget, by the respectable old gentleman's anxiety about his son, and his observations and inquiries about his future intentions, and what service was intended for him. His particular destination was not known at that time, but it was suspected that he would be immediately employed. 'They will wear him out,' said he, 'too soon' (the son was then in his sixty-eighth year), 'and make an old man of him before his time, with their expeditions to Holland one year and the West Indies the next; and if he would follow my advice, he would settle at home and take his rest.' And when Lady Abercromby observed that she was afraid that he must go abroad, ' Then,' said he, ' he will never see me more.' The verification of this melancholy prediction was to be expected, from his great age, being then in his ninety-seventh year. He died in the month of July following, eight months before his son, whose absence he regretted so much."

In 1816 Mr. James Haldane spent some weeks at Gilsland, in Cumberland, in the hope of recruiting his wife's drooping health. On that occasion he met a well-known Roman Catholic Archbishop, the late Dr. Everard, titular of Cashel. He was one of the old school of Irish priests, before the well-educated and well-mannered race, trained in France, had been exchanged for the coarser and more turbulent pupils of the College of Maynooth. Dr. Everard was a man of very cultivated mind, who had lived in the families of some of the highest English aristocracy, and had seen much of the world. His character was described in glowing colours by Lord Glenelg, in one of his speeches in favour of what was called Roman Catholic emancipation. At first he appeared at the hotel simply as Mr. Everard; and the only circumstance which created any suspicion, in regard to his rank, was the awe with which he was obviously regarded by a priest, who was also staying at the hotel, and whose reserved conversation and altered habits denoted a restraint, which he had not previously indicated.

On the very first day that they met at table, Dr. Everard singled out Mr. James Haldane from the crowd of visitors, and in the evening made up to him and engaged him in very interesting conversation. Next day his attentions became more marked, and, at dinner, it appeared that the Doctor's servant had received orders to wait on Mr. and Mrs. Haldane as much as on himself. The intimacy increased, and every day hours were spent in the walks or drives around Gilsland, discussing the claims of the Romish Church and the doctrines of the Gospel. Mighty in the Scriptures, and armed in Christian panoply, Mr. James Haldane repelled every argument drawn from the traditions of the Church or the authority of man; and, on the other hand, assured his new acquaintance, that, if Romanists refused an appeal " to the law and to the testimony," it must be because there was no light in them. These friendly discussions were carried on with intense earnestness, and in a spirit that inspired mutual respect. Dr. Everard confidentially disclosed his rank and position in the Romish Church, but solemnly appealed to heaven, that he sought only the truth, and was indifferent to all secular considerations. The conversations became daily more interesting. On the Lord's-day Mr. James Haldane preached in the assembly-room. Before the service, Dr. Everard begged the daughter of his Protestant friend to persuade her father to preach in the drawing-room, and tell him how much he himself desired to listen. After the service was over, Dr. Everard asked why his request had not been complied with, and why the sermon had not been preached in the drawing-room, " where," he said, " I could have remained and listened without any breach of discipline or canonical law, although, of course, it was impossible to follow you to another place." It was explained that many servants and cottagers would have been excluded from hearing, had he conducted the service in the drawing-room, but he offered to go over all the leading topics of his discourse. This he did, and discussed them with his usual candour. A few days before he left Gilsland, Dr. Everard confined himself to his room and did not appear in public. He afterwards sought a parting interview with his Protestant friend; it was at once solemn and affecting. The Archbishop told Mr. James Haldane that the conversations he had enjoyed with him, and particularly his appeals to the Bible, had shaken him more than anything he had ever before heard, and that they had made him very uneasy; that he had, therefore, determined, with fasting and prayer, once more to seek counsel of God, in order that his error, if he were in error, might be shown to him. He added, that his meditations, during his hours of fasting and retirement, had led him to this train of thought: " Here is a man who is certainly mighty in the Scriptures, but who interprets the Bible for himself and depends on his own private judgment. The case is different with myself. If I err, I err with a long line of holy men who have lived and died in the bosom of the Catholic Church." Mr. James Hal-

dane endeavoured to show the danger of trusting to the example
or opinions of fallible men, although some of those named, such
as Pascal and Fenelon, had been themselves persecuted for their
Protestant tendencies; and he contrasted the conclusions based
on the shifting sands of human opinion, with the certainty that
belongs to the written Word of God, read by the light of God's
Holy Spirit shining on its pages. He also said something
about "the traditions of the apostles." "What," said Dr.
Everard, "do you speak of traditions? I had thought you
discarded them entirely." The reply was, "The traditions of
fallible men I reject, but the traditions of the apostles, as
recorded by the finger of inspiration, are to be received as every
other part of the inspired Word of God." Mr. James Haldane
added, "Pardon me, but I must tell you, in faithfulness and
love, that it is my firm conviction, that the Church which you
so much esteem is no other than the woman which the apostle
John beheld in the Apocalypse 'drunken with the blood of the
saints and martyrs of Jesus.'" Again he said, "Do not think
me rude." The Archbishop affectionately pressed his hand, and
said, "No, my dear Sir; I know you too well to think so. I
am persuaded that you only speak for my good." The
necessity of further investigation of the Bible with prayer, was
once more urged on the amiable Prelate. A compliance
with this request was promised, coupled with an urgent entreaty
that his Protestant friend would do the same. Mr. James
Haldane replied that his convictions were based upon a rock too
solid to be shaken, and one which would admit of being again
and again examined with minute attention. But he reminded
Dr. Everard, that all the claims of Popery rested on human
testimony; on principles that would not bear the light of God's
Word, and around which there was, at best, a lurid halo of
doubt and uncertainty. They parted with mutual expressions
of regard, and Dr. Everard died a few years afterwards, at
Cashel, where there were whispers in the neighbourhood, which
intimated that his dying room was carefully watched to prevent
the intrusion of those whose presence was not desired, and that
the mystery which was kept up, as to his illness, arose from

suspicions that he did not continue stedfast in the Romish faith. The death-bed of the celebrated Bishop Doyle, at Carlow, was attended with similar and even darker suspicions, some of which have been since confirmed by the touching narrative published by his amiable wards, who were not suffered to enter his chamber until the lifeless corpse was laid out in state, in his Episcopal robes, attended by monks, with lighted torches, chanting his requiem, amidst all that pompous ceremonial with which Rome strives to make the senses the slaves of the imagination.

In 1817, Mr. James Haldane received an unexpected visit from his old friend, Captain Patrick Gardner, under whose care he had gone to sea, and to whom, as has been already seen, he had so earnestly written, pressing on him the concerns of his immortal soul. The pleasure with which Captain Gardner was welcomed, the interest taken in recalling the names and pursuing the history of their old ship-mates and early friends, seemed to renew the days of their youth. But Captain Gardner's health was broken; and after an absence from Edinburgh of some weeks, on inquiring for him at his hotel, it was found that he had returned dangerously ill. During his illness he was daily watched by his friend, who did everything to promote his comfort, and particularly sought opportunity to call his attention to the Word of God. Captain Gardner at first intimated that he was unable to listen long, and proposed about five verses. This request was punctually attended to, and the parable of the Pharisee and the publican was read, followed by a short prayer, founded on the cry, "God be merciful to me, a sinner." By degrees Captain Gardner came to listen with greater interest, and after he returned to London he wrote to his old friend, thanking him for all his unremitting kindness, and telling him that he tried himself now to pray. He died rather unexpectedly in April, 1818, leaving behind the hope that his visit to Edinburgh had not been in vain. His will had been made many years before, but Mr. James Haldane was the chief executor,—a circumstance which called him to London, where he had the opportunity of renewing his acquaintance with some of his old friends, and particularly at Hatcham House, with the late Mr. Hardcastle, who was then fast approaching the confines of the eternal world. He was also present at some of the principal meetings in May, and particularly took part at the anniversary of the British and Foreign Bible Society, in Free-masons' Hall, where he delivered an effective speech. He preached as usual, whenever there was opportunity, but nowhere with greater interest to himself, or with more acceptance to his audience, than in the Seaman's Floating Chapel, then recently established on the Thames.

On his return from London, it was with deep feeling that he found his beloved wife more than ever suffering from shattered health. Again he conducted her to Harrowgate, in quest of renovation. The change of air and scene, which always cheered her bright spirit, appeared beneficial for a time, and there, too, her husband enjoyed the opportunities in which she delighted, for preaching, or conversing amongst strangers concerning the things which pertain to the salvation of the soul. On this, as on former occasions, he had much pleasure in the society of the Rev. Mr. Hardy, of Thorpe Arch, a clergy-man of the Church of England, with whom he had frequent intercourse during several visits to Harrowgate. In the winter, the chronic ailments of Mrs. James Haldane gradually became more serious, and in February a course of active treatment was proposed by an eminent East Indian physician, and assented to by Dr. Gregory and Dr. Abercrombie, under which her con-stitution rapidly gave way. Nothing could exceed the tender-ness with which her husband watched over her dying couch, and the earnestness of his prayers for her restoration. It was not, however, till within thirty hours of her death that any imme-diate apprehensions were entertained. The moment that the danger became imminent, he gathered all his children together, and kneeling down in the midst of them, offered up a prayer never to be forgotten, in which the most pathetic and intense supplications for her recovery were mingled with expressions of unreserved confidence in the love of God, and submission to the Divine pleasure. In particular, he gave thanks that on a former occasion of dangerous illness, in 1803, the Lord had been pleased in an unlooked-for manner to answer prayer, to rebuke the fever, and to prolong her life during the sixteen years that had intervened. It was a night much to be remembered. It exhibited the struggle and the triumph of faith, contending with the fondest earthly affection, the tenderest and deepest feelings of the husband and the father controlled by the resignation of the believer, enabled to say, " Though he slay me, yet will I trust in him." It was the declaration of a heathen, that a good man struggling with adversity was a sublime spectacle, and so it might be said of him, whose faith in a covenant God enabled him to triumph over the agony of an impending calamity. Prayer was at all times the weapon which he grasped in every hour of need. It was not, however, the will of God on this occasion to listen to his cry to spare the wife of his youth, or to hear the supplications of those whose aid he sought in intercession with their heavenly Father. On Saturday evening, the 27th of February, 1819, in the presence of her husband and eight surviving children, she fell asleep in Jesus. The blow was severe, but her husband knew whence it came, and where to look for comfort. He deeply felt his loss, but he sorrowed not as those who have no hope. In writing shortly afterwards to her only remaining uncle, Sir Robert Abercromby, who had addressed to him a sympathising letter of condolence, he touchingly remarked : " As I closed her eyes, a tear trickled down her cheek, and I thought that it was the last she would shed, for she had gone to Him who wipes away all tears from the eyes of His people." On the very evening of her death, he wrote to the following effect, in answer to the affectionate sympathy of his oldest friend, Lady Duncan, who had watched over him as a boy, and to whom he was tenderly attached.

" My dearest Aunt,—It has pleased Almighty God to remove out of this vale of tears my beloved wife. The stroke is heavy, but she is done with pain and sorrow, and is gone to be present with the Lord. And shall we murmur because another tie to earth is cut away ? Not surely those who have learned to account themselves strangers and pilgrims in this world, who wait for the appearing of their Master, and who declare that they have here no abiding city, but that their hearts and their treasures are in heaven."

It was remarked that at this time it seemed as if he had taken another step within the vail, and as if his communion with the Father and his Son, Jesus Christ, had become closer and more intense. His feelings on the vanity of the world, as contrasted with the solid resting-place which belongs to the citizens of that city which is stable as the mount of God, are well expressed in a letter which, many years afterwards, he wrote on the death of his friend, Mrs. Hardcastle, the mother of his daughter-in-law, Mrs. Alexander Haldane :—

" It is a beautiful remark of Leighton's, that the apostle contrasts the dispersion of believers in this world with their election in heaven. They are spiritually alienated from the world, and interested in the new Jerusalem. Let us, my dearest Alexander, highly prize our privileges. Let us live to God. The night is far spent, and the day is at hand, and the nearer we approach to the full enjoyment of blessedness, the more may we feel the attraction of Him whom our soul loveth! Many years ago, I read in the ' Arabian Nights ' of a mountain of loadstone. Ships at a great distance felt its influence. At first their approach to it was scarcely perceptible. There was a declining from their course hardly to be noticed, and it excited little apprehension. But the attraction gradually became stronger, until the vessel was irresistibly impelled onwards with increased velocity. At last it drew all the nails and ironwork to itself, and so the ship fell to pieces. ' The path of the just is as the shining light.' When first the believer feels the love of Christ, it is like a mustard seed ; but it increases, and he is constrained by its influence to press more earnestly after the full enjoyment. At last the spirit can no more be kept at a distance from Him whom it loves. It flies to His embrace, and the body is dissolved."

# CHAPTER XVIII.

[1816—17.]

TWENTY chequered years of failure and success had not damped
the youthful ardour with which the two brothers had devoted
their lives to the spread of the Gospel. Their zeal was not the
offspring of wild enthusiasm, and its energy was not dependent
on human contingencies. After a brief period of comparative
repose, the termination of the great revolutionary war opened up
to Mr. Haldane a new field of enterprise, which he was not
slow to occupy. In the summer of 1816, he hastened through
the press his work on the Evidences of Christianity, for which
he had been long collecting materials. The reason of his
urgency was not very obvious to his printer, the late excellent
Mr. Ritchie, who, although willing to go to India as the superintendent of a missionary press, was not so prompt to change

the slow-going habits of the olden time.  But the explanation
shortly followed, when Mr. Haldane announced his intention of
making a missionary tour on the Continent of Europe.  The
results of that Mission stretch into eternity, and will for ever
connect the name of Robert Haldane with the revival of the
Gospel in France and Switzerland.  The distinguished historian
of the Reformation, himself a trophy of this work of grace, has
said that a narrative of its origin and progress would form "one
of the most beautiful episodes in the history of the Church."

Apart from the scattered notices of Mr. Haldane's Continental
labours, which are to be found in the history of many faithful
pastors in Switzerland and France, there are several sources
from which something like a connected account of his proceedings may be gathered.  One is contained in his own letter to
the Arian Professor of Divinity at Geneva, published in 1824,
both in French and English, which is replete with massive
theology, as well as with valuable and delightful details connected with the results of his visit to Geneva.  The other is
a friendly letter to the late Rev. Edward Bickersteth, correcting
some mistakes of the Rev. Richard Burgess, of Chelsea, published in a little volume, entitled "A Voice from the Alps."
Previous to that publication, with characteristic aversion to
egotism, Mr. Haldane had resisted all the importunity used to
induce him to furnish a connected narrative of his labours at
Geneva and Montauban.  But when he saw so erroneous
an account of a great work of God, not only as to its extent,
but as to the manner in which it had been carried on, he felt
that some contradiction was necessary, lest silence should be
mistaken for acquiescence.  It was his firm conviction that
the blessing on his labours was designed as an encouragement
to those who should cast away worldly policy, and setting
before them nothing but the glory of God, rest boldly on the
blessing promised, both to the written and spoken word.  Prejudices are not needlessly to be offended.  Opposition is not
needlessly to be encountered.  But neither prejudices nor opposition were, in Mr. Haldane's reckoning, any just apology for
keeping back any part of the whole counsel of God.

"*Auchingray, Sept.* 4, 1839.

" My dear Sir,—Among the valuable books with which you kindly presented me during your late visit to Edinburgh, I turned with interest to the work you have published under the title of ' A Voice from the Alps.' I rejoice to find that, in the midst of your other useful labours in the missionary cause, you have not been unmindful of Continental Europe, and that you are desirous of stimulating the zeal which has of late years been kindled in the breasts of British Christians, in behalf of those countries where the candle of the Lord had been well nigh extinguished.

" In the ' Voice from the Alps,' I found an address to a clerical meeting by the Rev. R. Burgess, of Chelsea, which contains an account of my own proceedings at Geneva altogether erroneous. Mr. Burgess has doubtless been misinformed on the subject; but his mistakes have been shared or adopted by Mr. Meston (of Lille), in his recent ' Observations on the Present State of Religion in France.' To prevent the further currency of these misstatements, which, if uncontradicted, will be repeated by others, I shall first notice the errors into which these gentlemen have fallen, and then briefly relate the leading circumstances connected with my residence on the Continent, in which the hand of the Lord may be clearly seen, to the praise of the glory of His grace.

" The narratives of Mr. Burgess and Mr. Meston alike confound dates and circumstances. It was not in 1818, as stated by both of these gentlemen, but in 1816, that I went to Geneva. Mr. Drummond and I did not labour there together, as it would appear by their accounts. Mr. Drummond did not arrive at Geneva till two days before I left the place. I was not ' armed with religious tracts and addresses,' as Mr. Burgess affirms, but with the Word of God. The distribution of tracts is in general highly to be commended; but in the circumstances in which I was placed at that period in Geneva, I should have considered such weapons but ill-fitted to assault the strongholds of Satan. Far from finding ' but *few* voices to respond to my appeal,' as Mr. Burgess and Mr. Meston both intimate, by the blessing of

God, I found *many.* And instead of not appearing ' to have met with success,' during my stay, according to Mr. Meston, the success with which the Lord was graciously pleased to accompany the testimony borne to his truth was very remarkable ; and perhaps the more so, because it was, so far as I know, the first, after the termination of the war, systematically and publicly borne on the Continent, by any one from Britain, to the grand distinctive doctrines of the Gospel. Dr. Malan ' raised his voice in behalf of the truth,' not, as they assert, ' after,' but before I left Geneva. The following brief narrative of my proceedings on the Continent may illustrate the gracious providence of God, and prove an encouragement to others to speak out boldly and fully, as they may have opportunity of declaring the whole counsel of God.

" For many years I had cherished the idea of going to France, with the view of doing something to promote the knowledge of the Gospel in a country in which I had been three times before as a traveller. Accordingly, when the return of peace rendered my design practicable, I went to the Continent. Being, however, unacquainted with a single individual there, and therefore unable to arrange any particular plan of action, I feared that my object might prove abortive ; and, in consequence, when asked, before I left Scotland, how long I expected to be absent, I replied, ' Possibly only six weeks.' The Lord, however, was pleased to open a wide and effectual door, leading me in a way that I knew not, and my residence abroad continued about three years.

" On arriving at Paris, involved, as it appeared, in Egyptian darkness, I soon perceived that I had no means of furthering the object of my journey in that great metropolis. Unexpectedly, however, I met with Mr. Hillhouse, a gentleman attached to the American Embassy, of whom I had not before heard. He had landed at Bordeaux, and travelling through the south of France, had gone to Geneva, and thence to Paris. Having passed through Montauban, where the French Theological Protestant Faculty was founded by Napoleon, he had there, and in other places, inquired respecting the Protestant ministers, and he communicated to me all his information on the subject. He told me that at Geneva there were only two individuals to whom I could have access, the one (M. Moulinié) a pastor, in advanced years, the other not a pastor (M. Galland), but what is termed a minister, and that nearly the whole of the other pastors were Arians or Socinians.

" Finding no opening at Paris, I immediately set out for Geneva, hoping that something might be done through the two individuals referred to by Mr. Hillhouse. On my arrival I called on the pastor alluded to, the late M. Moulinié, and conversed with him on the Gospel. He was very kind, but appearing to acquiesce in all that I advanced, discussion on any point was out of the question, and no progress was made. Being, therefore, unable to discover means of usefulness at Geneva, and finding on inquiry that the young man also spoken of by Mr. Hillhouse, had some time before removed to Berne, I repaired to that city, where I found he had been ordained a pastor. He was not an Arian or Socinian, but although very ignorant respecting the Gospel, he was willing to inquire and hear concerning the great truths which it reveals. I remained in Berne about eight days, during which he came to me every morning at ten o'clock, and continued till ten at night—in fact, as late as it was possible for him, the gates of the city, beyond which he lodged, being shut at that hour. During the whole day I endeavoured to set before him, as far as I was enabled, everything relating to the Gospel, and have good reason to believe that the word spoken was accompanied with the blessing of the Lord. I was afterwards informed, that subsequently to my departure he conversed with his colleague, the other pastor of the Church, on the subject of our discussions, and that in considering what had been advanced, they arrived at the conclusion that it must be the true doctrine of salvation.

" I hesitated whether I should return to Geneva, but at last resolved to do so, having heard of two Prussian clergymen,* who had recently been in England, and were passing through that town, with whom it was supposed I might have an opportunity

* Professor Sack and his brother.

E E

of conversing on the Gospel,—and also of a pastor at a little distance in the country, who, my new acquaintance at Berne informed me, would listen to my statements, but would ' draw himself up, and not answer a word.' To Geneva I accordingly returned. With the Prussian clergymen I found no satisfaction in conversing, and, although I subsequently did not experience the reserve I anticipated in the pastor just referred to, yet I had not the gratification of meeting him till after the lapse of some time.

" I, however, again visited M. Moulinié, with whom I had before conversed, who, as formerly, was very kind, but with whom I could make no progress. From all I could learn from him, Geneva was involved in the most deplorable darkness. It was, as Mr. Burgess observes, ' an unbroken field of labour,' with a ' fallen Church.' Calvin, once its chiefest boast and ornament, with his doctrines and works, had been set aside and forgotten, while the pastors and professors were in general Arians or Socinians. Some exceptions among them there were, including M. Moulinié, who held the divinity of our Lord Jesus, and, I believe, loved and served him according to their light ; but that light was so obscure—they were on the whole so ignorant, so incapable of rightly dividing the word of truth, that their preaching was without fruit. They preached neither law nor Gospel fully, and their doctrine did not seem to affect the consciences of their hearers. A small prayer-meeting had for some time been held, in consequence, I believe, of a visit of Madame Krudener to Geneva ; and by one belonging to it, I was told, that, sensible of their want of knowledge, they had prayed that an instructor should be sent to them, and that their prayer, they now believed, was answered.

" Being unable to meet with any other person with whom I might converse on the Gospel, I resolved to quit Geneva without delay, and proceed to Montauban. The Lord, however, is often pleased to overrule our purposes, by occurrences which, in themselves, appear trifling, and thus to bring about results that could not have been anticipated. M. Moulinié had politely offered to conduct Mrs. Haldane to see the model of the mountains, a little way out of town, and with this object he promised to call on us the day following. In the morning, however, we received a note from him, saying, that, having suffered from a severe headache during the night, he was himself unable to come, but had sent a young man, a student of divinity, who would be our conductor. On this providential circumstance depended my continuance at Geneva, which I had been on the point of leaving. With this student I immediately entered into conversation respecting the Gospel, of which I found him profoundly ignorant, although in a state of mind that showed he was willing to receive information. He returned with me to the inn, and remained till late at night. Next morning he came with another student, equally in darkness with himself. I questioned them respecting their personal hope of salvation, and the foundation of that hope. Had they been trained in the schools of Socrates or Plato, and enjoyed no other means of instruction, they could scarcely have been more ignorant of the doctrines of the Gospel. They had, in fact, learned much more of the opinions of the heathen philosophers, than of the doctrines of the Saviour and his Apostles. To the Bible and its contents their studies had never been directed. After some conversation, they became convinced of their ignorance of the Scriptures, and of the way of salvation, and exceedingly desirous of information. I therefore postponed my intended departure from Geneva."

During the short interval that elapsed between Mr. Haldane's first visit to Geneva and his return to that city, as noticed in the letter, he had traversed a great part of Switzerland. At Lausanne he met a pious and zealous English lady (the late Miss Greaves), whose enthusiastic importunity was subsequently very instrumental in persuading him to return to Geneva. The eloquent M. Galland was the young pastor, with whom he had so much interesting discussion at Berne, and who was then led to embrace the truth. Thence Mr. Haldane proceeded to Basle, where he met M. Empeytaz, in the household of the celebrated Baroness Krudener, the friend of the Emperor Alexander. "With that lady," says M. Gaussen, "Mr. Haldane had a long conversation.

He found in her, as he said, much of the spirit of charity, but very little knowledge." After considerable hesitation he was induced to abandon his intention of leaving Switzerland and to return to Geneva, partly in the hope of conversing with Professor Sack on the religious state and prospects of Germany, to which country, despairing of Switzerland, he was also turning his attention, but chiefly with the view of seeing M. Gaussen, whom M. Galland has described as a young minister, living six miles from Geneva, "who would listen to his statements, draw himself up, but not answer a word." Soon after his arrival at Geneva the second time, Mr. Haldane inquired for M. Gaussen, who had been licensed, in 1815, as a minister, and ordained on Good Friday, in 1816, as the pastor of Satigny, a delightful little village, five or six miles beyond the walls of Geneva. " I had already," says M. Gaussen, "submitted my faith to the great doctrines of the Word of God, but the gravity of Mr. Haldane, the authority with which he always appealed to the Scriptures, and his profound acquaintance with them, made an impression on me never to be effaced, and that just before the time when the Lord, by a sudden stroke, took from me all the joys of this world. When I paid him my first visit, it was on the invitation of Charles Rieu, and when he said to me, in the middle of our conversation, that he had returned to Geneva purposely to see me, I looked at him with astonishment, and his countenance became so red. I love to recal these little details, because all the *souvenirs* of that excellent man, and of the good which he did amongst us, are dear and precious. His visit to Berne was blessed to M. Galland, and his visit to Geneva was blessed to us all." " I visited him," adds M. Gaussen, " only occasionally, but I make bold to number myself with those who cherish his memory with the fondest and most affectionate gratitude." Such were the providential circumstances under which, at the close of the year 1816, Robert Haldane took up his abode in the city of Calvin, of Farel, and of Beza.

Geneva is a name which symbolizes something far more glorious than the little town, whose ancient battlements were at once the monuments of the defensive skill of Vauban, and of the persecuting tyranny of the house of Savoy. Geneva has been for ages the symbol of all that is antagonistic to Rome. Placed at the extremity of its own placid and beautiful lake, where the blue waters of "the arrowy Rhone" rush onwards to the ocean, this free city, as if designed to be a witness for God against Popery, whether Ultra-montane or Gallican, stood between the Jura and the Alps, themselves the types of beauty and sublimity. Within its hospitable gates were received several of the distinguished French and Italian families, proscribed for favouring the Reformation. It was the city where Knox, with other British exiles, found an asylum, and whence he imported into his own favoured land that form of Church government, to which Scotland has so fondly and firmly adhered. At a later period it welcomed many of those noble confessors, who fled from the bitter persecutions which both preceded and followed the revocation of the Edict of Nantes. Geneva was, indeed, the glory of the Reformation, the battle-field of light and darkness, the Thermopylæ of Protestantism, from whose Alpine heights the light of Gospel truth once streamed forth with brilliant lustre, athwart the blackness of Papal superstition. But Geneva fell from her ancestral faith, and proved how vain are historic names, orthodox creeds, and scriptural formularies, where the spirit ceases to animate the lifeless frame. The younger Turretine, the degenerate son of an illustrious sire, is said, more than a century ago, quietly to have laid aside the doctrine of the Trinity, when he was Professor of Theology. In 1777, Professor Vernet allowed Arian theses to be maintained before him by the students of the University. But the crowning proof of their apostasy is to be found in the fact that, twenty years before that period, the Infidel D'Alembert complimented the Venerable Company,* in the French Encyclopædia, in an article, in which he observes,

---

* In the national Church of Geneva there are about twenty-five pastors, who serve the five churches of the city, according to a system of rotation. These, with the country pastors of the canton, constitute *the Venerable Company*, and with the addition of some lay elders and government

" To say all in one word, many of the pastors of Geneva have no other religion but a perfect Socinianism, rejecting all that they call *mysteries*." The answer of the pastors was unsatisfactory and equivocal, and the questions afterwards put to them received no explicit reply. Their apostasy was indeed clandestine rather than avowed, and provoked the bitter sarcasm of D'Alembert, " I should be extremely concerned to be suspected of having *betrayed* their secret."

But in the writings of the " self-torturing sophist," Jean Jacques Rousseau, there is a still more melancholy picture of the lapsed condition of Geneva. In one of his " Letters from the Mountains," he thus writes :—

" It is asked of the ministers of the Church of Geneva, if Jesus Christ be God? They dare not answer. It is asked, if he were a mere man. They are embarrassed, and will not say they think so. A philosopher, with a glance of the eye, penetrates their character. He sees them to be Arians, Socinians, Deists ; he proclaims it, and thinks he does them honour. They are alarmed, terrified ; they come together, they discuss, they are in agitation, they know not to which of the saints they should turn, and, after earnest consultations, deliberations, conferences, all vanishes in *amphigore;* and they neither say, yes nor no. Oh! Genevans, these gentlemen, your ministers, in truth are very singular people ! They do not know what they believe, or what they do not believe. They do not even know what they would wish to appear to believe. Their only manner of establishing their faith is, to attack the faith of others."

The citizens of Geneva have done homage to Rousseau, and, amidst the modern improvements of their city, have placed his statue by the side of the bridge, which now spans the Rhone at the spot where that river rushes from the lake.

The presence of Voltaire for two years at Ferney, within a pleasant walk from the gates, was not likely to improve either the theology or the morals of the Consistory. Lausanne is little more than twenty miles further up the lake, and the fact that Gibbon selected that place for his residence, may probably deepen the shadows of this picture of surrounding Infidelity. Gibbon

officers, constitute the *Consistory*. Before a student can become a *pastor*, he must be licensed as a *minister*. These distinctions require to be kept in view in speaking of the Genevese Church.

announced to his friends, that the first stroke of a rebel drum should be the signal for his departure from the Canton de Vaud. He himself had been sounding the tocsin of rebellion against the King of kings, and was more intolerant of a true Christian than of a revolutionary leveller.

During the reign of Napoleon, Geneva was incorporated with France, but the Emperor permitted the Consistory to resume its functions, and maintain its lifeless form of Protestantism. At the close of the war, it was annexed to the Helvetic Confederation, but with French intercourse, French manners had crept in. The theatres were opened on the Sunday evenings, and even the pastors, on certain solemn festivals, such as the *Fête du Lac,* dismissed their congregations earlier, in order that they might themselves participate in the festivities of the Lord's-day, which was closed with fireworks and the discharge of cannon.

It was at this period of its history that Robert Haldane entered Geneva, and, as he was passing through its ancient gates, observed to one who travelled in his carriage, and was sanguine as to the anticipated results, that he had been pondering on the strife and divisions which would infallibly ensue, if the Lord should see good to make the Gospel of his grace the power of God unto salvation. But by whatever means the Lord is pleased to work, it is important to observe, how all the glory exclusively belongs to Him, who is the Wonderful, the Counsellor, the Mighty God.

For several years before Mr. Haldane was so unexpectedly conducted to that famous city, through no wisdom or foresight of his own, some smoking embers had been collected, and some sparks of light already kindled amidst the gloom of its spiritual apostasy. Even so early as 1810, MM. Empeytaz, Bost, and a few other youthful but earnest inquirers after truth, had become impatient of the wretched food supplied by their spiritual pastors, and instituted a reunion, called "*La Société des Amis.*" "They knew," says M. Guers, "the way of salvation very imperfectly," but it is impossible to read the close of their First Annual Report, written by M. Empeytaz, without seeing that he, at least, had even then been led to soar far above the chilling mists of Socinianism, and to feel somewhat of the same adoring love, which burned in the heart of the convinced Thomas, when he fell at the feet of Jesus, exclaiming, " My Lord, and my God! " But this little Society was frowned upon by the Arian clergy, and had, in 1814, even ceased to exist. Its more seriously-disposed members, in quest of nourishment, joined themselves to a little Moravian flock, possessing more of spiritual life, if not exacter notions of the truth as it is in Jesus. " Still," continues M. Guers, in his interesting Life of Henri Pyt, " the time of the pure light had not arrived, either for him or many of his friends. It was only for them the twilight of the Gospel day." In 1813, Madame Krudener had induced M. Empeytaz to enter her household as chaplain, but her own views were indistinct, flickering, and, in some respects, visionary. At the beginning of 1816 a pious English or Welsh mechanic *(industriel)*, of the Calvinistic-Methodist persuasion, established himself on the ruins of the ancient convent of Rive, where, for the first time, the Reformation had been proclaimed, in 1534, by William Farel. There a few of the defunct *Société des Amis* met this good man, whose name was Richard Wilcox, and conversed with him about the deep things of God. But, according to M. Guers, Wilcox seems to have insisted chiefly on the eternal love of the Father, and on the certainty of the salvation of the elect, " elevating the building, without taking sufficient care to lay the foundation." In short, he appears to have unwisely directed his preaching exclusively to the elect, instead of adopting the scriptural proclamation of the Gospel, which, leaving secret things to God, is like the fan in the hand of the husbandman, separating the wheat from the chaff, revealing pardon only to faith, which is the gift of God, but declaring even to the vilest of sinners, " Whosoever will, let him take of the water of life freely." M. Guers adds, " whilst he strengthened those who knew the Gospel a little better than their brethren, he did not open to others the gate of salvation."

These earnest inquirers were, however, feeling after truth, and for some time used to hold in concert a sort of *agape*, or love-feast, after the manner of the early Christians, which was termed *Le Repas des Douze* (the repast of the twelve) on account of the number who gathered round the board, and conversed about the things that belonged to their eternal peace.

Thus it was, that by all these means the Lord was opening the way for another of his servants, a deeply experienced and established Christian—a man of vigorous intellect and calm sagacity, strong in faith, mighty in the Scriptures, full of zeal for Christ, well instructed in the relative proportions of the doctrines of the Gospel, and able rightly to divide the Word of truth. Robert Haldane was conducted to the place at the right time. M. Empeytaz, one of the leaders of the little band, had quitted the field of his unequal combat, with a consistory determined to crush him. His colleague, M. Bost, had assumed the post of Suffragan Pastor at Moutiers Grand Val, in the Canton of Berne, so that his genius and piety no longer "electrified" his young friends by "his noble aspirations after God and holiness." Wilcox, the humble artisan, was himself leaving Geneva, no more to encourage these inquirers by raising them to the contemplation of the eternal love of the Father. But the prayers of those who were hungering and thirsting after righteousness were graciously answered, and the instructor for whom they were anxiously supplicating the throne of grace, had been actually brought, "by a way which he knew not," to prove to them a messenger of everlasting peace, and not only to them, but to many others in Geneva.

Mr. and Mrs. Haldane had left Edinburgh on the 9th of October, 1816, and nearly contemporaneous with their arrival at Geneva, there appeared, about the middle of November,* a pamphlet intituled, "Considerations on the Divinity of Jesus Christ," by Henri Empeytaz. Falling amongst the students of theology, to whom it was addressed, it produced

---

* This fact is mentioned in the "Histoire Veritable des Momiers de Genève," an anonymous publication, which in the first edition of this work was erroneously ascribed to M. Empeytaz, by whom it was presented to the biographer. By some it is attributed to the Abbé Lamenais, by others to a Jesuit, formerly Popish Curate of Geneva.

great excitement, and "an impression difficult to describe." The students, siding with the pastors, assembled in the grand hall of the consistory, and choosing for their president one of their own number—himself destined to receive the Gospel from the lips of Mr. Haldane, and to become an illustrious champion of the truth,—addressed to the Venerable Company a letter, in which they solemnly protested against what, in their ignorance, they termed the "odious aggression" of the "calumnious" pamphlet of M. Empeytaz. The state of the students may be judged of from two facts—first, that M. Henri Pyt and M. Guers were the only individuals amongst them who refused to sign this anti-christian protest; and, next, that their chosen president was no other than M. Merle D'Aubigné.

The arrival of Mr. Haldane has been already mentioned in his own simple narrative. The following are the more glowing terms in which it is described by the pious biographer of Henri Pyt:—

"Our English friend departed in January, 1817, leaving his brethren hungering after a better acquaintance with the counsels of God. But at that very moment, the Lord, touched by their prayers, sent them one of his most eminent servants. Richard Wilcox had not quitted our walls before Robert Haldane was within our gates. The chosen instrument in the hands of God to confirm the faith of Pyt and his friends, he was destined to become the source of blessings to *many* others. In a very short time, a striking revival, effected by his means, was manifested in the school (l'auditoire) of theology. Around the venerable Haldane, their true professor, there gathered habitually more than twenty pupils of that auditory, converted (alterés) by the instructions of that blessed Word, which they began immediately to distribute at Geneva, or, at a later period, to carry to neighbouring countries,—and amongst the latter may be named Henri Pyt, Jean Guillaume Gonthier, Charles Rieu, who died pastor at Fredericia, in Denmark. It was on Thursday, the 6th February, 1817, that Mr. Haldane undertook to read and explain to them the Epistle of St. Paul to the Romans.* ' He knew the Scriptures,' says Pyt, ' like a Christian who has had for his Teacher the same Holy Spirit by whom they

---

* It is presumed that this date refers to the time when Mr. Haldane recommenced his expositions for the benefit of those who had not begun to attend with the eight original students.

were dictated.' He spoke in English; first M. Rieu, then M. Fred. Monod, of Paris, or M. James, of Breda, interpreted. Never, we venture to say, since the days of Francis Turretine, and Benedict Pictet, of holy and happy memory,—never had any doctor expounded the whole counsel of God with such purity, force, and fulness—*never since that period had so bright a luminary shone in the city of Calvin.*"

The student of theology who came to Mr. Haldane's hotel, and was the unconscious means of detaining him at Geneva, little thought that he was then employed as the messenger of grace, both for himself and others. It was M. James, now the Evangelical French pastor of Breda. His companion was M. Charles Rieu, whose brief but brilliant career, and triumphant death-bed, are associated with the history of the Church of Christ.

Robert Haldane was, indeed, an instrument chosen of God for the great work of reviving the Gospel on the Continent. The attempt was, however, so arduous, that at first sight it might have seemed Utopian. There were many circumstances calculated to discourage one of feebler faith and less natural force of character. Had human wisdom selected a missionary to assail Socinianism at Geneva, he would probably have been a man of great renown, either as a scholastic theologian or a philosopher. He might have been a Horsley, a Chalmers, or an O'Brien. But even their qualifications would have been deemed insufficient apart from a familiarity with the language, the manners, and the habits of the French. To some of these advantages Robert Haldane made no pretensions. Possessing no European reputation; his theology drawn from the pure fountains of inspired truth rather than from the admired repositories of scholastic lore; incapable of conducting discussions without the aid of an interpreter;* his foreign manners exhibiting none of that brilliant vivacity and external warmth most fitted to captivate his youthful disciples; even his

* To suppose that he was unacquainted with the language is a mistake into which some have fallen. This was not so. Before he went to sea he could read French with ease, and it will be remembered that Sir John Jervis for this reason specially selected him, after the capture of the Pégáse, as the medium of communication with the French captain. At a

powdered hair still retaining the queue universally worn in his younger days, and his somewhat antiquated costume rendering his personal appearance, in the esteem of the gay Frenchmen, dignified and grave, rather than attractive;—everything to the .eye of man conspired against his bold attack on the strongholds of Genevan heresy.

" But," says M. Frederic Monod, in a recent and valuable communication, " on reflection, I have been led to think that these very circumstances, seemingly so adverse, were, in the Lord's hands, the principal means of arresting our attention, and this was one of the first things to be done, and the most difficult." He adds, " I am not sure that this could have been accomplished by another Christian of equal zeal and faith, more or less known to us beforehand, speaking in our native language, with our manners and habits, and moulding his thoughts into the forms to which we were accustomed."

With reference to the state of Geneva, and the character of the students, M. Monod continues :—

" I find, indeed, little or nothing to add to the full and accurate statement contained in the first edition of your work, relative to your sainted uncle's blessed labours at Geneva, and I must confine myself to personal *souvenirs* of thirty-six years' standing, which are still vivid in my mind and heart, although much has, of course, escaped my memory. . . . When that blessed man, whom, under God, I call with a loving and grateful heart my spiritual father, ' for in Christ Jesus he begot me through the Gospel,' came to Geneva, every possible circumstance seemed to militate against the success of his mission of faith and love. If I look to the religious field on which he was entering, it was overgrown with thorns and briars; for too truly have you stated the religious condition of Geneva at that time. If I look to the young men, the special objects of Mr. Haldane's mission, we were most of us thoughtless, deeply tainted with worldly-mindedness, and immersed in gaiety. Though students of theology, true theology was one of the things of which we knew the least. God's holy Word was to us *terra ignota*, whilst Unitarianism, with all its chilling influence, and all its soul-destroying appendages, was the only doctrine taught to us by our Professors. For myself, I may add, as a most astonishing fact, in illustration of these statements, that during

---

later period he made the tour of Europe, trusting to his own acquaintance with French, and although an interval of thirty years had elapsed since he had been accustomed either to speak or to hear French, yet its disuse had not effaced his previous knowledge.

the four years I attended the theological teachers of Geneva, I did not, as part of my studies, read one single chapter of the Word of God, except a few Psalms and chapters, exclusively with a view to learning Hebrew, and that I did not receive one single lesson of exegesis of the Old or New Testaments."

Such is M. F. Monod's description of the field which Robert Haldane was sent to break up, and sow with that incorruptible seed which has since flourished with " the power of an endless life." His first lodgings were at the hotel in the Rue du Rhon, still known as *La Balance*. When he had resolved to winter at Geneva, he removed to the Place Maurice, No. 19, on the Promenade St. Antoine, where he occupied a very agreeable suite of apartments, overlooking the gardens on the Boulevards, to the east of the Palais plain, and with a southern prospect towards Savoy and the Alps. Pointing to these apartments, not many weeks ago, and addressing a French pastor, M. Merle D'Aubigné exclaimed, " Voila le berçeau de la Seconde Reformation de Genève." There the students of Divinity were wont to assemble, despite of their irate Professor, M. Cheneviere, who was accustomed to walk under the shade of the trees on the Promenade at their hour of meeting, chafing with indignation at their disregard of his wishes, frowning on them as they entered Mr. Haldane's door, and noting down their names. In two spacious saloons, communicating by folding-doors, between twenty and thirty students were accustomed to sit on chairs placed on each side of a long table, on which were laid Bibles, in French, English, German, and other modern languages, besides the original Greek and Hebrew. It was as the expositor of the Bible that Mr. Haldane came, and to no other authority whatsoever did he make his appeal.* M. Monod thus continues his narrative :—

" To whatever cause it may be attributed, the fact is certain, that our most serious attention was arrested, and that a large majority amongst the students were soon induced regularly to attend Mr. Haldane's instruc-

---

* The description of these meetings, as made in the General Assembly of 1845, by M. Monod and Dr. Merle D'Aubigné, so kindled the enthusiasm of the celebrated Dr. Chalmers, that he declared, that thus to sit round a table, with the Bible, was his *beau ideal* of the study of theology.

tions, although it was said at first, that not more than six would be so entrapped. What struck me most, and what struck us all, was Mr. Haldane's solemnity of manner. It was evident he was in earnest about our souls, and the souls of those who might be placed under our pastoral care, and such feelings were new to all of us. Then his meekness, the unwearying patience with which he listened to our sophisms, our ignorant objections, our attempts, now and then, to embarrass him by difficulties invented for the purpose, and his answers to each and all of us. But what astonished me, and made me reflect more than anything else, was his ready knowledge of the Word of God and implicit faith in its Divine authority,—that Word of which our Professors were almost as ignorant as ourselves, and which they quoted, less as being the only and infallible source of religious truth, than as a means of puffing off their own teaching. We had never seen anything like this. Even after this lapse of years, I still see presented to my mind's eye his tall and manly figure, surrounded by the students; his English Bible in his hand, wielding as his only weapon that Word which is the sword of the Spirit; satisfying every objection, removing every difficulty, answering every question by a prompt reference to various passages, by which objections, difficulties, and questions were all fairly met and conclusively answered. He never wasted his time in arguing against our so-called reasonings, but at once pointed with his finger to the Bible, adding the simple words, ' *Look here—how readest thou ?* ' 'There it stands written with the finger of God.' He was, in the full sense of the word, a living concordance.

" These introductory meetings prepared us for listening with greater confidence to those more didactic teachings upon which he soon entered, expounding to us the Epistle to the Romans, which several of us had probably never read, and which none of us understood. In going regularly through this Epistle, he had an opportunity of laying before us a complete body of Christian theology and Christian morals, which, by the accompanying Spirit of God, found its way to the conscience and heart of most of his hearers who, like myself, trace to this venerable and faithful servant of God their first knowledge of the way of salvation and of Gospel truth. I reckon it as one of the greatest privileges of my now advancing life, to have been his interpreter, almost through the whole of his expositions of that Epistle, being almost the only one who knew English well enough to be thus honoured and employed. The number of Christian ministers who attended Mr. Haldane's instructions, and who have since been signally blessed as devoted and useful instruments for propagating the good seed sown, you have touched upon in your book. But I cannot forbear again naming, with adoring thanksgiving, Galland, Gaussen, Gonthier, Guers, James, Malan, Merle, Pyt, Rieu, and others who escape my memory. The name of Robert Haldane stands inseparably connected with the dawn of the revival of the Gospel on the Continent of Europe.

The work he began in 1817 has been advancing ever since, and the extent of it will not be known until the day of the revelation of all things. His memory is embalmed in our hearts, and is hallowed amongst us. May it please the Lord to send many such labourers into his harvest!"

This testimony is corroborated by that of M. D'Aubigné, in the following extract from a speech delivered in Edinburgh, in 1845 :—

" When I and M. Monod attended the University of Geneva, there was a Professor of Divinity who confined himself to lecturing on the immortality of the soul, the existence of God, and similar topics. As to the Trinity, he did not believe it. Instead of the Bible, he gave us quotations from Seneca and Plato. St. Seneca and St. Plato were the two saints whose writings he held up to our admiration. But the Lord sent one of his servants to Geneva; and I well remember the visit of Robert Haldane. I heard of him first as an English or Scotch gentleman who spoke much about the Bible, which seemed a very strange thing to me and the other students, to whom it was a shut book. I afterwards met Mr. Haldane at a private house, along with some other friends, and heard him read from an English Bible a chapter from Romans, about the natural corruption of man,—a doctrine of which I had never before heard. In fact, I was quite astonished to hear of men being corrupt by nature. I remembered saying to Mr. Haldane, ' Now I see that doctrine in the Bible.' ' Yes,' replied that good man, ' but do you see it in your heart ?' That was but a simple question, but it came home to my conscience. It was the sword of the Spirit; and from that time I saw that my heart was corrupted, and knew from the Word of God that I can be saved by grace alone ; so that if Geneva gave something to Scotland at the time of the Reformation,—if she communicated light to John Knox, Geneva has received something from Scotland in return, in the blessed exertions of Robert Haldane."

More recently, at the last meeting of the Evangelical Society at Geneva, in June, 1852, its excellent President, the pious Count de St. George, thus spoke :—

" The Church of Christ knows nothing of the political limits of terrestrial kingdoms or republics. Geneva remembers with gratitude that it was France that sent her Farel, Calvin, and Theodore Beza, nor is she ashamed to trace the origin of the present revival to a pious Scotsman, Robert Haldane."

After such testimonies, Mr. Haldane's own account of his

labours will probably be read with greater interest.   His letter
to Mr. Bickersteth proceeds :—

" The two students with whom I first conversed brought six
others in the same state of mind with themselves, with whom
I had many and long conversations.   Their visits became so
frequent, and at such different hours, that I proposed they
should come all together, and it was arranged that they should
do so three times a week, from six to eight o'clock in the
evening.   This gave me time to converse with others, who, from
the report of the students, began to visit me, as well as leisure
to prepare what might be profitable for their instruction.   I
took the Epistle to the Romans as my subject; and this portion
of Scripture I continued to expound to them during the winter,
and to dilate on the great doctrines which it unfolds.

" After having proceeded in this manner about a fortnight
with these eight students, I was earnestly solicited, in the name
of the other students, to begin anew, in which case I was
assured that the rest of them would attend.   I accordingly
complied with this request, and during the whole of the winter
of 1816-17, and until the termination of their studies in the
following summer, almost all the students in theology regularly
attended.   And God was graciously pleased to accompany his
own Word with power.   In addition to the general knowledge
which all of them acquired, a goodly number soon appeared
to be turned to the Lord.   Some of them have now finished
their course with joy, and, like MM. Rieu, Gonthier, and Henri
Pyt, have left behind them the blessed assurance that they are
now in the presence of God and the Lamb; while others have,
in like manner, evidenced the reality of the work of grace by
the stedfastness of their faith, and the abundance of their ministrations.

" Besides those who attended regularly, some who did not
wish to appear with the students came at different hours,
and in conversing with them at those times, or after finishing
the public course at eight o'clock, I was often engaged till
near midnight.   Others of the inhabitants of Geneva, uncon-

nected with the schools of learning, and of both sexes, occasionally visited me in the afternoon to receive instructions respecting
the Gospel.

"The impression produced at Geneva was, by the blessing of
God, so great that discussions became frequent on the grand
truths connected with salvation.   The pastors and professors
in the Faculty heard of the doctrine I was inculcating, and the
manner in which I spoke of their false doctrine.   They began to
preach openly against what I taught, and I as plainly controverted what they taught, collecting their arguments, setting
them before the students and others to whom I had access, comparing them with Scripture, and labouring to refute their
destructive heresies.   They insisted that men were born pure,
and spoke of the Saviour as the first of created beings, and I
opposed and refuted such errors and blasphemies.   They taught
that the Gospel was useful, but not indispensable, to salvation,
and adduced the case of Cornelius, as an example of a man
accepted of God without the knowledge of the Gospel.   I proved
that this was an egregious misrepresentation of the fact, and
that the history of Cornelius formed no exception to the uniform
doctrine of Scripture, that there is no other way of salvation
but by faith in the Saviour.*   It was not, then, by avoiding
controverted subjects, and simply dwelling on truths common
to the professing Christians, as some good men have recommended as the proper course to be pursued on the Continent,
that I laboured to raise up the fallen standard of the Gospel at
Geneva.   It was, on the contrary, by not shunning to declare
the whole counsel of God, so far as I was enabled to do so—
it was by dwelling on every doctrine of the Bible, whether
it was controverted or not, or however repulsive to the carnal
mind, and by confronting and bringing to the test of Scripture

---

* See the case of Cornelius fully discussed in vol. iii., p. 296, of
"Exposition of the Romans," in the chapter on the "State of the
Heathen destitute of the Gospel."   See also "Remarks on Mr. Scott's
View of Cornelius," vol. i., seventh edition of "Exposition," at the fourth
chapter, p. 316.

every argument levelled at my instructions both by pastors and professors.

"In this manner matters proceeded at Geneva till the middle of the summer of 1817, the period which terminated the studies of the theological students. The pastors attempted to instigate the Government to banish me from their canton; and when this proved unsuccessful, it was proposed in the 'Venerable Company' that I should be cited to appear before them, to answer for the doctrines I was inculcating on the students. On this it was observed by one of them, 'Vous ne gagnerez pas grande chose par cela!' (You will not gain much by that!) And the matter dropped. At the same time they did all in their power to prevent the attendance of the students. I have since that period conversed in this country with M. Gaussen, and in answer to my inquiry, How it was that the pastors failed in this attempt, he replied, That this was the first blow that had seriously affected them, and although they were anxious to adopt every means in their power to prevent the students from coming to me, yet they found it impossible, because if strong measures had been resorted to as the penalty of disobeying the prohibition, the students had resolved to leave their professors. The pastors, however, did not cease to labour to counteract the effects of the change that had taken place in the minds of so many of the students, and particularly by framing the 'Reglemens' of May 3, 1817, consisting of certain articles which every student was ordered to sign before he should be 'consecrated,' and which were intended to exclude from the pulpits of Geneva the doctrines which they so violently opposed, and particularly the doctrines of the Godhead of the Saviour—of original sin—of grace and effectual calling—and of predestination. In spite of all their endeavours, the light was diffused to a very remarkable degree in Geneva, which, through the ministration of these Socinian, Arian, and Arminian teachers, had fallen from the glory which once belonged to it, and instead of being the centre of illumination to Protestant Europe, had become a synagogue of Satan and a citadel of ignorance and darkness."

It is no matter of surprise that the Professor of Divinity at Geneva was stung to the quick, by the results produced through the labours of a foreigner, who, with the Bible in his hand, had been enabled in the Lord's strength to trample down the pride of an infidel philosophy, and to recal attention to the written word of God. Some years after Mr. Haldane's departure, M. Cheneviere, in his "Summary of the Theological Controversies which have of late years agitated Geneva," pointedly attacked him, as one of the chief authors of all the agitation. The Professor describes him as a rigid Calvinist, who invited a number of ministers and students to his house, where he occupied their minds with the *mysterious* points in the Christian religion, "inoculated them with his own intolerant spirit," taught them "to despise reason," and to "trample on good works."

To this attack an able reply was written by Dr. Pye Smith, and published both in the "Monthly Repository," a Socinian magazine, and also in a separate form. With reference to the attack on Mr. Haldane, Dr. Pye Smith writes:—

"Mr. Haldane is a man of family, fortune, and talents, who has for many years devoted himself, with a generosity rarely equalled, to the most benevolent purposes that can be entertained by a human mind. There are few persons who are more addicted to *cool reasoning*, or who have more correct views or more consistent practice on the subject, I will not say of *toleration*, but of the entire rights of *religious liberty*. Abundant proof that he does not contemn reason, but employs the processes of induction and argument in a manner highly judicious, scrupulous, and logical, will appear to any one who will read his work on 'The Evidence and Authority of Divine Revelation,' two vols., 8vo. On the first opening of this work, my eye has been caught by a passage, which I transcribe, because it furnishes a fair indication of the author's mental habits. He has been speaking of the unhappy prevalence of unexamined assumptions and conclusions drawn without sufficient evidence in matters of religion." (Dr. Smith then transcribes a striking paragraph from the introduction, and proceeds:) "This passage affords a fair insight of Mr. H.'s intellectual character. I had never the happiness of knowing a *more dispassionate or careful reasoner*, or one whose habits of mind were more distinguished by the demand and scrutiny of sufficient evidence upon every subject. A grosser error could not be committed,

than to impute to such a man the sentiment, that 'in the affairs of
religion, reason ought to be trampled under foot.'"    (P. 22.)

Mr. Haldane's letter in reply to M. Cheneviere, published in
1824 both in French and English, is in itself a manual of solid
and practical divinity. He meets his opponent point by point,
giving an epitome of his exposition of the Romans, and
touching with a master's hand almost every controverted topic
subsisting between the enemies of the truth and its supporters.
With regard to the Professor himself, Mr. Haldane plainly
avowed :—

"I am free to declare, that never in my life did I hear the word of God
so directly contradicted from the pulpit. In your exclamation, 'Ah! are
we not born pure?' profound ignorance of the Word of God was manifested, and the whole train of your reasoning proceeded on this assumed
principle—a principle not more contrary to the express declarations of
Scripture, the conduct of Providence, and the whole plan of redemption,
than to the universal experience of mankind. And yet, Sir, you are
Theological Professor at Geneva."

The venerable Daniel Wilson, now the Bishop of Calcutta,
describes M. Cheneviere as "a harsh, violent, impracticable man,
confessedly a Socinian in principle. He really frightened me
by his fierce attack on spiritual religion."

It may be edifying to dwell for a short time on Mr. Haldane's
mode of teaching, and especially to follow him in his calm and
dignified exposure of the Genevese heresies, as he contrasts them
with the truths contained in the Epistle to the Romans. Beginning with an account of his meetings with the students, he
proceeds, in his reply to the irate Professor :—

"The attention which these interesting young men very soon manifested
to the Word of God was more than I anticipated. The truth is, that anything like Biblical instruction was altogether new to them. The study of
the Word of God had formed no part of their preparation for the ministry.
. . . As far as I was enabled, I endeavoured to lay open to them the
rich stores of religious instruction contained in the Epistle to the Romans,
a portion of the Word of God which, on the Continent, was very generally
considered unintelligible.

"In studying this Epistle, I turned their attention to the great doctrines
of the Gospel, so successfully revived at the Reformation by Luther and

his associates, as well as by Calvin, with whose writings, though the
founder of their Church, they had no acquaintance, and whose theological
sentiments they had been taught to regard as altogether antiquated.   In
discarding the instructions of these Reformers, they had been led to understand that they were following the superior illumination of the present
age.   I did not attempt, however, to make them disciples of Calvin or of
any other man,—to say, 'I am of Paul, and I of Apollos,'—but to bring
them to be followers of Christ, to sit at the foot of His cross, and to learn
of Him 'who spake as never man spake.'   I therefore appealed to no
authority, either ancient or modern, but solely to the law and to the
testimony, always reminding them that, 'if they spake not according to
this word, it was because there was no light in them.'   (Isaiah viii. 20.)

"With doctrinal instruction I connected attention to practical godliness, and constantly inculcated the necessity of their paying regard, in the
first place, to their own salvation.   I showed them that they must have a
light view of God as revealed in Scripture, subsisting in three distinct
persons,—the Father, the Son, and the Holy Ghost,—infinite, eternal,
unchangeable.   I drew their attention to the character of God as holy,
just, good, and merciful,—perfections which, in their combination, are all
of them gloriously displayed in the Gospel.   I warned them against the
loose and erroneous notions so generally entertained concerning the way
in which mercy is exercised.   God is indeed 'merciful and gracious;'
'He delighteth in mercy;' but while justice is an essential attribute,
mercy is solely vouchsafed as He sees good.   Accordingly, to fallen angels
God has displayed only his justice; while to fallen man He has declared
himself merciful. (Psalm ciii. 17.)   This mercy, however, is never exercised
but in strict conformity to justice, and mercy is only to be found where
justice has received full satisfaction.   Here we were led to consider the
state of fallen man, and his personal character as a sinner, as well as to
examine the holy law of God, both in its perfect precepts and awful
sanctions, and to see that it is only in Christ we can be redeemed from
its curse and eternal condemnation, or born again, in order to participate
in the blessings of His redemption.   In introducing and dwelling on these
subjects, we followed the course traced out in the Epistle."

Having exhibited the ruined state of man, and proved that no
human suffering, nor the sufferings of all creatures, could "*finish*
transgression*," or "make an end of sin," Mr. Haldane showed
that Christ fulfilled the law, both in its precept and its penalty.
"None but He who suffered on the cross could say, '*It is
finished.*'   In one word, the righteousness provided for man,
which will place those invested with it nearest the throne, and
first in the song of praise, is the RIGHTEOUSNESS of God."

With reference to this righteousness, which is provided solely by grace, and received solely by faith, Mr. Haldane quotes the following words of Luther: " He who affirms the justification of all men who are justified to be perfectly free and gratuitous, leaves no place for works, merits, or preparations of any kind; no place for works, either of condignity or congruity; and thus at one blow Paul demolishes both the Pelagians with their complete merits, and our sophists (the Arminians of Luther's day) with their petty performances."

The epitome of each chapter, as given in the letter to the Genevese Professor, is striking and comprehensive. Of the ninth chapter he says: " The doctrine of God's sovereignty is here fully treated of, and that very objection which is daily made, ' Why doth he yet find fault ?' is stated and silenced. Instead of national election, the great subject is national rejection, and the personal election of a small remnant, without which the whole nation would have perished. So void of reason is the objection usually made to the doctrine of election as being a cruel doctrine."

Of the eleventh chapter Mr. Haldane says :—

" There was nothing brought under the consideration of the students which appeared to contribute so effectually to overthrow their false system of religion founded on philosophy and vain deceit, as the sublime view of the majesty of God, which is presented in these concluding verses of this part of the Epistle. ' Of Him, and through him, and to Him, are all things.' Here God is described as His own last end in everything that He does. Judging of God as such an one as themselves, they were at first startled at the idea that He must love himself supremely, infinitely more than the whole universe, and consequently must prefer His own glory to everything besides. But when they were reminded that God, in reality, is infinitely more amiable and more valuable than the whole creation, and that consequently if He views things as they really are, He must regard himself as infinitely worthy of being most valued and loved, they said that this truth was incontrovertible. Their attention was at the same time turned to numerous passages of Scripture, which assert that the manifestation of the glory of God is the great end of creation; that He has himself chiefly in view in all his works and dispensations; and that it is a purpose in which He requires that all His intelligent creatures should acquiesce, and seek to promote as their first and paramount duty."

This was a doctrine on which both Robert Haldane and his brother loved to expatiate. It animated them in all their labours, and raised them far above the consideration of merely *visible* success. The glory of God and the advancement of his cause was the object which they set before them, and everything else, how important soever it might be, was regarded as subordinate. In his Essay on Wesley and Methodism, Isaac Taylor has largely entered into this subject, so far as it is a motive of action, and he has very clearly shown, that in the case of the Apostle Paul, as well as in that of Whitfield, the glory of God was more directly the mainspring of all their exertions, than the salvation of men. On the contrary, he points out that in modern missionary efforts, greater stress is laid upon motives which appeal to the claims of philanthropy than to the glory of Christ. Philanthropy ought to be a powerful motive to action, and the worth of immortal souls is incalculable, but there is no doubt that God must be his own chief end, and that His own glory must be inseparably connected with the happiness of all His intelligent and obedient creation, seeing that the contemplation of the Divine perfections is the great source of enjoyment to those who surround the throne. In exhibiting the doctrines of the Gospel at Geneva, the glory of Christ was the object ever present to the mind of Robert Haldane. He sought, first, the kingdom of God, confident of God's blessing. This was, in fact, the secret of his boldness in bringing forward the truth, without compromise. When he first began to instruct the students, some of the statements which M. Frederic Monod had to enunciate as interpreter, made the young inquirer feel "as if his hair would stand on end." But in the sequel it proved that the Lord's blessing rested on this single-hearted boldness and confidence in the power of the incorruptible Word of God, and Mr. Haldane always held it forth as an example to others.

The charge of undervaluing reason and human intellect is met with equal force and precision, and the refutation is masterly. In winding up this part of the argument, Mr. Haldane turns upon the Professor, and with his usual logical skill involves M.

Cheneviere in the entanglement of self-refutation. He exposes the folly of the Arian scheme, in professing to believe that a *creature* was in the beginning with God and was God, that without him nothing was made that was made, and consequently that he made himself.

" I do not," he adds, " instruct them to acknowledge the Bible to be a revelation from God, and at the same time to consider themselves at liberty to sit in judgment on its contents. But I showed them the folly and daring impiety of summoning their Creator to the bar of their reason, and of receiving or rejecting the different parts of His Word, according to its proved decisions. I taught them that being convinced that 'all Scripture is given by inspiration of God' (2 Tim. iii. 16), they ought to search it with diligence, to study it with prayer, that God would open their eyes to behold the wondrous things which it contains, and to use them as rules of obedience, and as motives and encouragements in the exercise of it; and in things evidently mysterious, to bow in humble submission to the Divine teaching, and to receive with adoring faith and love what they could not comprehend. In one word, I reminded them of the declaration of the apostle, which it would be well for you to ponder: 'The weapons of our warfare are not carnal, but mighty through God to the pulling down of strongholds; casting down *reasonings*, and every high thing that exalteth itself against the knowledge of God, and bringing into captivity every thought to the obedience of Christ.' (2 Cor. x. 4.)

Having thus informed the Professor of the doctrine which he taught, Mr. Haldane, referring to the charge of having occupied the minds of the students "with the mysterious points" of Christianity, thus proceeds :—

" Turning the attention of the ministers and students in the above manner to this instructive part of the Word of God, I occupied their minds, as you assert, with 'the mysterious doctrines of the Christian religion.' I did this in the full conviction that they are conducive, in the highest degree, to the interests of holiness, and that in no respect do they interfere with the responsibility of man. It is the doctrine of Divine revelation, rather than its precepts, which furnishes the chief means of advancing holiness. Love to God is not so much excited by the precept, 'Thou shalt love the Lord thy God,' as by the discoveries of the excellences of His character, and of the abundance of His grace.

" When the apostle Paul had, in the first eleven chapters of this Epistle, dwelt at such length on the glorious and mysterious doctrines of Divine revelation, he looked back on the whole with mingled astonishment and delight. Under the impression of these feelings, he exclaims, 'O the depth, both of the wisdom and knowledge of God, how unsearchable are his judgments, and his ways past finding out.' Far from judging as you do, that Christians have nothing to do with 'the mysteries,' he delighted to expatiate on them; he designates them 'the mercies of God;' and all his exhortations to practical duty are constantly founded on them. The distinguishing character which he assumes to himself and his fellow-labourers, is that of '*ministers of Christ, and stewards of the mysteries of God.*' (1 Cor. iv. 1.)"

Another charge advanced by M. Cheneviere was, that Mr. Haldane had inculcated them with his own exclusive, intolerant spirit. On this point he replies:—

" I shall deal with you as frankly as I have done in regard to the mysterious doctrines of religion. On the subject of what you call an *exclusive* spirit, I hold a very decided opinion. While errors in religion are endless, I am convinced that there is but one exclusive system of Divine truth, but one foundation which God has laid in Zion, but one name under heaven given among men by which we can be saved,—the name of Jesus, the great Mediator. Hence a mistake concerning his person as God and man will, if persisted in, prove fatal. This I inculcated on the students to the utmost of my power. But I am also aware that the apostle Paul, in the very place where he affirms that other foundation can no man lay than that is laid, has also declared that on this foundation different materials may be built, so that many errors may exist in the mind of one who holds the fundamental saving truth. You will accordingly find this sentiment fully expressed in my (French) Commentary, vol. i., p. 18, where it is denied that Arians and Trinitarians can both of them be Christians.

" Besides an exclusive spirit, you impute to me an *intolerant spirit.* As to toleration respecting differences of opinion among Christians in articles not fundamental, I taught a system the very opposite to intolerant. To this I was directly led by the consideration of the fourteenth and part of the fifteenth chapters of the Romans. You will find a long article in my Commentary, which carries forbearance towards all Christians, as far as the Christian character can be discerned. The whole of that discussion is summed up in the following rules:—1. To do nothing to preserve communion with our brethren which would mar communion with God. 2. To maintain communion with our brethren as far as we can do it without marring communion with God."

With reference to the charge of trampling on good works, he appeals to his exposition of the twelfth chapter, in which the Roman converts are besought, " by the mercies of God," to present themselves a living sacrifice, holy and acceptable to God. He proceeds :—

" A most beautiful delineation of Christian duty follows. Humility, that distinguished grace, takes the lead here, as in the Lord's sermon on the mount. Then follow exhortations to diligence in the employment of diversified talents,—to love, fervency of spirit, joyful hope of eternal life, patience, prayer; and the whole is summed up in an earnest recommendation of particular duties to brethren, to friends, to enemies. Produce to me, if you can, anything in the writings of all Pagan antiquity that is comparable, in the most distant degree, to this portion of the Word of God, either in the practice which it enjoins, or the motives which it suggests to enforce that practice."

Obedience to civil government was enforced in expounding the thirteenth chapter. In regard to civil liberty, he held it to be a great blessing, so far as it was the companion and support of religion, without which he was wont to speak of it as little better than a dangerous plaything. In connexion with the fourteenth chapter, he took occasion to prove the obligation of the Lord's-day. On the awful desecration of the Sabbath at Geneva, he pointedly remarks,—" A desecration countenanced by pastors, who, instead of spending the evening of the day in retirement, were not afraid to pass the time at balls, in soirées, or frivolous amusements, and at cards. It could not," he said, " be added, that family worship was thus precluded, for family worship on any day was a thing then unknown, both amongst pastors and people of Geneva."

The letter to M. Cheneviere furnishes, in fact, a complete epitome of most of the leading doctrines of the Gospel, expressed in forcible language, and placed in a striking light. With reference to good works, there is an important remark which ought not to be overlooked. Mr. Haldane, having disproved the accusation, and asked the Professor where was his warrant for the charge of warring against good works, thus proceeds :—

" The whole of my writings speak a language directly the reverse. The Scriptures declare that men are not *chosen* (Rom. xi. 6), are not *justified* (Rom. iv. 2, 5), are not *saved* (Ephes. ii. 9), by their works; that they are not *saved according* to their works (2 Tim. i. 9), but they uniformly declare that men shall be *judged* according to their works."— P. 68.

But as a striking instance that good works did flow from the reception of the doctrines he taught at Geneva, he says : " It pleased the Lord in his infinite goodness, to bless his own Word to the conversion of a goodly number of young men, who are now preaching the Gospel in different parts of the Continent where the French language is spoken.  On this subject I have received from several of them the most pleasing accounts, accompanied with every expression of gratitude for having had their minds thus directed to the words of eternal life.  I may mention one, as his spirit is returned to Him that gave it, who is now, I trust, before the throne, beholding Him, whom having not seen he loved; in whom, although he saw Him not, yet believing, he rejoiced with joy unspeakable, and full of glory. I have a letter from M. Charles Rieu, late Pastor of Frederica, in Denmark, dated July 7th, 1819."

Of that remarkable letter the following are only extracts :—

" SIR, AND MUCH HONOURED FATHER IN JESUS CHRIST,—   . . . I have at all times deeply engraven in my heart the instructions which the Lord vouchsafed to me the grace to receive from you, Sir, and which opened my eyes to the fundamental truths of the Gospel.  Now that I am called by a benediction, for which I cannot enough praise the Lord, to teach them, as well as to feed on them continually myself, I feel every day more and more the incalculable importance and the absolute necessity of founding upon these truths all other instructions and exhortations, if we wish that they should penetrate into the heart.  . . .

" To lead a parish of labouring people to Christ is the work that the Lord has confided to me at this time.  Not having heard the truth preached to them for many years, I found them in that state of luke-warmness and alienation which naturally follows the neglect of the Gospel. . . .  I seek to dispense to them the mystery of godliness with the greatest fidelity possible.

" If your engagements permit you to send me a word of friendship, will you impart to me all the counsels, exhortations, and directions, that you believe proper to fortify me in faith and piety in Jesus Christ.  In my situation, insulated from all my brethren, I have greater need than others to be roused by salutary advices.  I desire, above all, to make rapid progress in the knowledge of the Holy Scriptures, since these are our only powerful arms, to convince, to overturn, and to build up.  Following your counsel, I have resumed the reading of the Old Testament, and I have there found what I did not before know was there, when I was less instructed in Divine truth, and when, in many respects, the veil remained upon my eyes, that Christ is everywhere in it, from one end of it to the other.

" All render testimony to Him. The prophecies, in particular, were never presented to me with so much grandeur and. so much beauty. Oh! how admirable is this! What perfection! what agreement! How is this work raised above all the impious attacks of men! . . .

" I recommend myself always to the continuance of your kind regards and to your prayers. It is with a very lively sentiment of gratitude that I shall ever remain, Sir, and much honoured father in Jesus Christ,

" Your very affectionate and devoted servant,

" C. RIEU."

Mr. Haldane, after noticing the way in' which M. Rieu expressed himself respecting the mysterious doctrines of the Christian religion, asks M. Cheneviere,—

" Will you affirm that he neglected good works? Read the account of his faithful and laborious discharge of the trust committed to him, by which he made ' full proof of his ministry,' and of his happy departure from this world. In his death he has furnished an example of the triumph of faith, which nothing in modern times can be found to exceed. A young man in the vigour of life, in the very midst of his usefulness, in the service of his beloved Master, when his last illness commences, can with difficulty bring himself to believe that so great a grace should be vouch-safed to him, when he had but just entered on his work, that the Lord should remove him, and call him away by death."

M. Rieu closed his short but brilliant career within two years from the date of the above letter. He was seized with an epidemic fever, and addressed a solemn charge to his parishioners, telling them that the vaulted roof of their church would bear witness that he had preached to them Jesus Christ, and declaring to them the counsel of God, although with too much weakness and fear of men, assuring them that even to his latest breath he would pray for them, and calling down on them the blessings of the Almighty. His Journal, which he kept almost to the moment when he became delirious, was intended for his family, and indicates what he calls the "unutterable peace and joy" of his soul.

" I know," he says, " in whom I have believed. I advance with a joy, not to be described, into the dark valley, for I advance towards Jesus, towards my God, towards Christ who has conquered for us. All his promises converge in one point to overflow my soul with a joy it never felt before. No, he has not deceived us. Happy those who have believed without having seen. I go to see him as he is. I see him already. I feel his hand supporting every part of my soul; in proportion as this clay falls, the inward man is renewed. I go to be changed into his image, to be like unto him. There, where there is no mourning! How could I wish to make this joy pass into your souls! But it is there where you will enjoy it, and it is he who will now console you; for I am not separated from you; the moment when I fall asleep here, I see with you Christ coming in the clouds. May you all sleep in Him! . . . Resurrection and life—Eternity—Eternity with Jesus."

But whilst contemplating the departure of Charles Rieu, as he appeared to ascend in a blaze of glory to the Master whom he loved, we must not forget the warfare at Geneva, in which he bore his part in the spring and summer of 1817. Day by day, without intermission, for many months did Mr. Haldane, in " his own hired house" on the Promenade St. Antoine, receive all who chose to come to him, and converse about the things that belonged to the kingdom of God. Discussion respecting the Gospel became frequent, but there was no public collision with the pastors or professors. He heard their sermons levelled against himself, or received the report of them from others, and so took occasion, with as little of personality as was possible, to expose their ignorance, rebuke their errors, and refute their sophistry. "As in the presence of God," he says, "I spoke and acted, resolving to know no man after the flesh, and to give place to no one by subjection, no, not for an hour. These duties appear to me not to be peculiar to prophets and apostles, but in such circumstances to be incumbent upon all who know the Lord, and seek to serve him with such talents as He has committed to them. Accordingly I laboured to introduce the knowledge of salvation among that benighted people."

But the flame was not long destined to smoulder within the precincts of the Venerable Company. It suddenly burst out with violence against a young minister, Regent in the College of Geneva, whose genius and accomplishments had promised to conduct him both to emolument and renown. It was to Cæsar Malan that the grace and the glory were given to be the first publicly to raise from the ground the tarnished banner of the Church of Geneva, and from the pulpit of Calvin boldly to proclaim, without reserve and without compromise, that Gospel whose echoes scarcely lingered within his temple. He, too, although not one of the *Société des Amis,* was amongst those who, at the period of Mr. Haldane's arrival, was becoming partially roused from a state of death to some sense of spiritual destitution. But to use his own words, in his letter to Mr. Bickersteth,—

" At the time I was awakened to life everlasting, I was still in darkness and great feebleness in almost all points, and I know how useful, how efficacious, under God's blessing, to my mind, to my soul, to my humbled heart, were the teaching and fatherly guidance of Mr. Haldane, whom, in the bonds of love, I honour as a father sent to me by God, and who, before he left Geneva, had seen, not only in myself but in numerous other instances, that the word of truth, and not ' tracts or addresses,' had been blessed—yes, Sir, wonderfully blessed from above— for the present and the eternal happiness of *many* souls. The glory be to the Lord, but the joy to that servant of Jesus and his spiritual children and brethren in our precious faith."

M. Malan being himself a minister, could not with propriety attend at the meetings appropriated to the students, and being still in great darkness, he was strongly prejudiced against what M. Gaussen told him of the Calvinistic doctrines inculcated. But after spending an evening with the missionary visitor, soon after his arrival, at his apartments in the hotel called *La Balance,* where he at first resided, M. Malan went away more favourably impressed. His satisfaction was increased by an incident which occurred on the evening of the 31st of December, 1816. M. Malan was then the manager of a charitable Society, in which he was deeply interested, and which was much in need of support. Its claims had been mentioned to Mr. Haldane, and when he accompanied his guest to the door of his apartments, and took leave of him, without solicitation he placed in his friend's hand some gold pieces as a contribution to the charity. As soon as the door was closed, M. Malan, by the light of the nearest lamp on the staircase, counted the Napoleons he had received, and found that they amounted to the very sum, 240 francs, which was next day required to pay the baker's bill, and the want of which was, on that very evening, a source of depressing anxiety. This circumstance, which he regarded as an interposition of Providence, contributed, as might be expected, to increase M. Malan's interest in the remarkable stranger, and from that night his visits were repeated, his inquiries became more searching, and their conversations more earnest. The result is told in the words already quoted, and was previously announced by Dr. Malan in one of those delightful tracts which, published in the form of a dialogue, present the truth with a vivacity and point so well adapted to the taste of the French. In his "Conventicule de Rolle," written in the form of a dialogue, in answer to the question, "Were you then (in 1816) entirely converted?" he answers, in the character of a Genevese minister,—

"*The Genevese minister.*—No; not yet. I had been in error. I had then become as far as I remember, orthodox, but my soul had not yet been awakened. I had not seized upon my salvation, such as it is in our Saviour.

"*Third Inquirer.*—And who was it that led you to peace?

"*The Genevese minister.*—It was the honoured Robert Haldane, member of the Presbyterian Church of Scotland. This man, grave, and profoundly skilled in the knowledge of the Holy Scriptures, came to pass some months at Geneva at the same time that the friends of whom I have just spoken were there. I saw him at the house of one of them, and I paid him the first visit, for he was a retiring man, and unostentatious, who neither sought to make himself known or listened to. You cannot form too high (*belle*) an idea of the wonderful sweetness, the staid prudence, which accompanied all the words and actions of this venerated man. His countenance was peaceful and serene. There was, in his expression, a charity so profound, that it was impossible, in his presence, to condemn or judge harshly of any one. Never did he allow me to do so. I was young and animated by first zeal, which is almost always imprudent and bitter. I spoke, with some warmth, of persons opposed to the Gospel. 'Leave persons, my friend,' said my father in the faith, 'they are all under God's judgment, and in no way under your's. Speak to me only of their errors in order to avoid them, both on your own account and that of others.' How many times have I seen him moved with sorrow at the sight of the enmity which already declared itself against the Word of God. He said to me, as had also the Rev. Dr. Mason, of New York,—'Oh! if it were necessary to give my blood to bring over those who raise themselves against the Gospel, I would shed it.' But, added he, ' It is not the blood of man which is necessary, it is that of the Son of God, shed upon the cross.'

" *The first.*—By what method did he teach you the truth? how did he make you receive it?

" *The Genevese minister.*—You know, dear brother, that it was the Spirit of God who implanted it in my heart; but it was thus that the wise Haldane taught me. In general he waited till I put a question to him, and I only went to his house to hear his answers. He often made me repeat the question, in order to assure himself that he had entirely understood me. ' What do you think on that subject?' he would say to me. I gave him my opinion. Then he would ask me to support it by Scripture. It was thus that he convinced me of ignorance or weakness. And when he saw me perplexed by my want of acquaintance with the Bible, he would begin to establish the truth in question by passages so clear, so explicit, that it was impossible but that I should yield to the evidence. If one of these passages did not appear to me conclusive, or if I gave it a false interpretation, he would produce immediately four or five others which supported or explained the other, and put the true sense beyond a doubt. In all this discussion he would only say a few words. It was his index which spake: for, exactly as his Bible, literally worn out from having been read and re-read, opened of itself here or there, his finger rested upon the passage, and, while I read it, his piercing eye looked me through, as if he wished to discern the impression which the sword of the Spirit made upon my soul.

" *The third.*—But was he not a Separatist, as is said?

" *The Genevese minister.*—Never did he produce a single opinion which could have made me suppose so. He manifested, and with justice, a great horror of heresy, but I never saw in him anything which betokened narrow or particular ideas. Moreover, we do not meet with such in the two works which we have of his,—the one a treatise upon the ' Evidences of the Divine Authority of Christianity,' the other, at which he laboured while at Geneva, a ' Commentary upon the Epistle to the Romans.' The last work is an admirable course of the purest theology. One finds there, united with the candour of a soul devoted to Jesus, all the depth of the science of salvation, and the judgment, the common sense, and exquisite tact of a veteran, prudent and accustomed to the wiles of the human heart and to the lies in which it envelops itself. I invite you strongly, my friends, to make a serious study of this commentary. I consider that every minister who shall read it before God, and verify, by the Bible, all the quotations which it contains, will have made the most ample provision of knowledge and of strength against the errors of our day,—against that religion of words and beautiful phrases with which so many people amuse themselves or nourish others."

In the Conventicle of Rolle Dr. Malan distinguishes between his spiritual state, as convinced of orthodoxy, and the awakening of his soul. Before the arrival of Mr. Haldane, he had written, and, as it appears, actually preached in the country an eloquent sermon that was doctrinally correct, although, to use his own words, his soul " was not yet fully awakened," and his orthodoxy more in the head than the heart. But when, through the instrumentality of Robert Haldane, he was " led to peace; " when he was indeed aroused, and these sentiments came to be uttered, before the Arian and Socinian Company, by lips touched with evangelic fire, from a heart burning with love to Christ, all the enmity of the natural man rose up in arms against the faithful witness for a dishonoured Saviour. His eloquent words dropped on the leaden slumbers of his audience, like bolts of fire shot from heaven. Pastors, professors, syndics, and private citizens, were cut to the heart, and almost gnashed on him with their teeth, as Dr. Malan descended from the pulpit and passed through their opening ranks unrecognized, an avoided and rejected man. It was not in his loving nature and tender sensibilities to disregard the insult and derision to which he was thus publicly exposed. His own relatives turned away from him with mingled emotions of disappointment, vexation, and shame. His attached wife, not then, as now, a partaker of the same glorious faith, beheld him with a grieved and wounded heart, and, by her looks, reproached him with the shipwreck of all the cherished dreams of their young ambition. He walked in his robes from the ancient temple of Calvin to his own house, dejected and overwhelmed, about to hide himself in his secret chamber. But, on entering his door, " the majestic form" and benignant countenance of Robert Haldane met his eye, and his sinking spirits were revived, as by a cordial, when his hand was grasped and the words were heard, "Thank God! The Gospel has been once more preached in Geneva!"

Mr. Haldane has himself left on record the impression produced by that celebrated sermon, which forms so memorable an era in the history of Geneva. Addressing M. Cheneviere, he says :—

" But this doctrine of salvation, possessed of such incomparable energy, and, when carried home to the heart by Divine influence, accompanied with such signal effects; this doctrine, which had for so long a period been unknown in the pulpits of Geneva, and which formed such a contrast to what was then held forth in its Arian, Semi-Arian, Pelagian, Arminian, insipid nothingness, could not be borne among you. When it unexpectedly burst on you in one of your temples, 'to the amazement of the hearers,' it was like a clap of thunder. I shall not soon forget the astonished, chagrined, irritated, indignant countenances of some who were present. Many seemed to say, as the Athenians did, when Paul preached to them, 'Thou bringest strange things to our ears.' But far were those, who 'seemed to be pillars,' from adding, 'We would know, therefore, what these things mean, and we will hear thee again of this matter.' An interdict against appearing in the pulpit was soon after laid on the preacher, who, on account of his perseverance in well-doing, has been since divested of all his offices, and driven as far as the apostate Church of Geneva has been able to pursue him. Its language to him, from that day to the present, has been similar to that directed to the prophet of old,—'O thou seer, go, flee away into the land of Judah, and there eat bread, and prophesy there: But prophesy not again any more at Beth-el: for it is the king's chapel, and it is the king's court.' (Amos vii. 12, 13.)"

But Dr. Malan was not the only preacher who was now enabled to "bring strange things" to the ears of the people. M. Gaussen, who had been, in some sense, the occasion of inducing Mr. Haldane to return the second time to Geneva, had also been confirmed in faith and strengthened in knowledge, experience, and courage. He was, indeed, without the walls of the city, but still his learning, his talents, his influence, and high character, were now all consecrated to that glorious Saviour, whose Divine character and Royal priesthood were denied by the Company of Pastors. Others were crowding into the ministry imbued with the doctrines which M. Cheneviere so loudly denounced. Two of the students, M. Henri Pyt and M. Guers, had been already ordered to send in a confession of their faith. With the simplicity of the dove they avowed their faith, but, with the wisdom of the serpent, they clothed it in the language of a confession, venerable from the fact, that it had been sealed with the blood of some of the noblest martyrs of the French Church. The professor declared that such sentiments were enough to make men " brigands ;" and although the youthful confessors were not at the moment excommunicated, yet, in a very short time, they were denied ordination by the Consistory, and compelled to preach the Gospel without its bounds. But the Word had gone with power to the hearts of many. The great body of the pastors looked on with rage and consternation, whilst those who in any degree held the truth, like M. Moulinie, seemed overwhelmed by the opposition which they had not the courage to stem, and did not even, like Obadiah, in the house of Ahab, secretly supply a hiding-place for the prophets of the Lord. Once more let us hear Mr. Haldane :—

" Towards the end of the session, and when the time arrived that the students were to be ordained, it became sufficiently apparent that they knew something else besides the morality recommended by Heathen philosophers and nominal Christians.

" You found they could do more than deliver a smooth harangue, inculcating the observance of a scanty morality, accompanied by the studied attitude of a comedian, to give it stage effect. They had begun to take him for their model, whose speech and preaching were not with enticing words of man's wisdom, but in demonstration of the Spirit and of power. They could address their hearers in a style different from the smooth language of the Geneva pulpit, as if all were Christians—all very good sort of people, who needed only to be reminded to go on as they were doing in the performance of their duties, or who, at most, required some little reformation. They could tell them they were guilty sinners, lying in the ruins of the fall, and as being one with the first Adam, involved in his condemnation. But, at the same time, they could direct them to the Lamb of God, who taketh away the sin of the world. They could declare to them, that whosoever believeth in Him hath eternal life. They could point out to them the necessity of being born again—of being washed in that fountain which is ' opened to the house of David and to the inhabitants of Jerusalem, for sin and for uncleanness.' "

To meet the exigencies of the times, the pastors, who had rejected ancient creeds and formularies, resolved to put down all controversy, and under the pretence of charity, peace, concord, and a good spirit, to banish all discussions on four topics, which to them were peculiarly hateful. The first was on the divinity of our Lord ; the second, on original sin ; the third, on the operation of grace, or effectual calling ; and the fourth, on predestination. By a *Reglement*, dated 3d May, 1817, these articles of a treacherous peace were agreed upon by the Company, and were ordered to be signed by every minister before he should be allowed " to exercise the pastoral functions," and by every student before he should be " set apart for the Gospel ministry in the canton of Geneva." There was a further engagement added, which prevented public opposition to the sentiments of any pastor, and pledged the subscriber not to expatiate on the topics contained in the four articles, if they should, by the words of Scripture, or otherwise, be led to mention them. It is instructive to remark, that M. Cheneviere, whose " fierce attack on spiritual religion " so shocked Bishop Wilson, actually pleaded for these restrictions, as a tribute to what was called a good spirit, as a lover of peace, and as an enemy to controversy.

" The homage of the heart," he exclaims, " charity, the love of peace—these are the key-stone of the arch to the Christian." The words of Madame Roland on her way to the scaffold, may here be parodied, and what she said of liberty might be applied to charity : " O *Charity !* what crimes have been committed in thy name !" In M. Cheneviere and his fellow-Socinians, it was made the apology for denuding M. Malan of his ministerial and academical offices—for driving MM. Guers, Pyt, Gonthier, Bost, Empeytaz, Porchat, and l'Huillier, and others, into secession— for sending M. Merle D'Aubigné away from his native city to finish his studies at Berlin, whence he was called to minister in the Royal Chapel at Brussels, and, finally, in the maturity of his spiritual knowledge, to return to Geneva, uniting with M. Gaussen to build up and adorn the new Evangelical Institution, which has alike proved as a bulwark against Socinianism and Neology.

It may well be supposed, that the persecution begun by the regulations of the 3d May, 1817, produced great excitement. M. Cheneviere himself admits that they were regarded as " an instrument of tyranny," whilst " the clergy of Geneva were reproached with it as a demonstration of their heresy." Many of the young ministers were reduced to great straits by the destruction of their prospects. Some were at first obliged to seek a precarious support by teaching, and others by book-selling. Their sufferings would have been still greater had it not been for another providential circumstance, which will next be mentioned, and in which the finger of God was again visible.

The academic session was concluded. At Geneva there was now a goodly number instructed in the truths of the Gospel, and able to communicate them to others. The names of Gaussen and Malan were of themselves a tower of strength, and they still for a time clung to the ancient Church, although by their own doctrine protesting against its apostacy. MM. Guers, Pyt, Gonthier, and others, held reunions in the place where the young Reformer Froment had in ancient days opened a gratuitous school, and been the first to re-light the lamp of pure Christianity in the city, to which Calvin afterwards imparted the lustre of his name.

"Disciples," says M. Guers, "on the Monday and Thursday" (adding, with affectionate recollection, *Jours Haldane*), "they were themselves teachers on the other week-days. Pyt and his friends expounded the Word with unction. The joy of the Holy Spirit more and more filled their hearts in proportion as the plan of redemption was unrolled before them; watered themselves, as well as watering others, they grew in grace and knowledge of the Lord Jesus Christ, and their assemblies were more and more frequented."

Mr. Haldane considered his own work accomplished at Geneva, and the same impulse which had conducted him to Geneva was about to lead him to Montauban. But there were several reasons, more or less acknowledged, which probably influenced his departure. Many years afterwards, in a letter addressed in January, 1840, to the "Scottish Guardian," he thus writes:—

"During the whole time I was abroad, both at Geneva and Montauban, I confined myself exclusively in all my intercourse with others to the Gospel itself, avoiding, on all occasions, saying anything whatever of its institutions, or concerning different denominations of Christians. In my peculiar circumstances, I considered this to be my duty, and I acted uniformly according to the declaration of the apostle, who says, 'Christ sent me not to baptize, but to preach the Gospel.'" But although this was the rule which Mr. Haldane had laid down for the regulation of his own conduct—although he was silent in regard to all the questions which had agitated and divided the Congregational Churches in Scotland, he could not have maintained this reserve had he continued much longer in Geneva. Into such discussions he did not wish to plunge. His object was to replace the great fundamental doctrines of the Gospel in the French Churches, without reference to rites or ceremonies. On this subject the testimony of MM. Gaussen and Malan is conclusive, but it is corroborated by M. Monod in the valuable letter from which so much has been extracted :—

"One of the remarkable features of Mr. Haldane's teaching was that not a shadow of sectarianism was mixed up with it. He confined himself strictly to the essential truths, believed in common by all Christians, and with which Christianity itself stands or falls. Though he was, if I mistake not, a Baptist in his personal views, none amongst us except those who privately inquired knew any of them. He never said to us, baptize infants or baptize only adults, but he said, and repeated every time we met, and with a great variety of forms and applications, 'Believe in the Lord Jesus Christ, and thou shalt be saved.' 'Neither is there salvation in any other, for there is none other name under heaven given among men whereby we must be saved.' And not only did he teach this in our general meetings with him, but in his daily walks, he used to invite one or another amongst us to accompany him, and many a time have I for one, thus walked by his side in the beautiful environs of Geneva, listening to his earnest teachings and admonitions, whilst he thus incessantly pursued his blessed work."

We shall cite once more the words of the biographer of Pyt, who seems to have preserved the memory of dates and days connected with Robert Haldane with a pious care, which indicates the same feelings which led M. Gaussen to hail him as "the second father of the Geneva Church."

"Mr. Haldane took leave of Pyt and his friends on the 20th June, 1817, to present himself at Montauban, conjuring them, with adieus the most fraternal, in all things to take the Word of God as their rule, and never to apply that rule except with prayer and mature consultations,— recommending them, withal, to shun noise (éclat), not to expose themselves to needless persecution, to be modest, exemplary, in all respects, but also to march forward, animated with a holy courage, and fully assured of succour from above. The dealings of the Lord towards Pyt and his friends had something in them that was remarkable and paternal. The *Société des Amis*, then the Moravian flock, then the Christian Methodist, had brought them to the door of the Sanctuary. But Haldane's was the hand of the Lord to open it to them. He was one of those men who, by their faith, their reverence for the Bible, and their devotion to the Lord, have most plainly stamped upon their character the true disciple of Jesus Christ."

Thus Robert Haldane finished his work at Geneva. "Scarcely," says M. Cheneviere, "Scarcely had this champion left the field, when he was succeeded by another, not so profoundly skilful in his art, but much more impetuous." Mr. Haldane was preparing for his journey, and actually counting the money sent to him from the bankers, when a young Englishman, scarcely thirty years of age was announced as a visitor. His pleasing manners and aristocratic bearing, his finely-chiselled features and intellectual forehead, bespoke his breeding and intelligence, whilst in his acute and penetrating glance, wit, sarcasm, and the love of drollery, seemed to contend with earnestness, benevolence, and an ever-restless Athenian craving after novelty. The stranger introduced himself as a Scotch connexion of Mr. Haldane's, but they had not before met since the time when Henry Drummond, then a little boy, living at Dunira with his grandfather, the first Viscount Melville, used to make his appearance after dinner. The interview was mutually agreeable, and Mr. Haldane heard with delight of the interest with which Mr. Drummond was then inquiring into the deep things of God, and his eagerness, at the same time, to put forth his active and energetic efforts for the support of the Gospel. The occasion of Mr. Drummond's arrival at Geneva had in it also something providential. Early satiated with the empty frivolities of the fashionable world, and pressed by the address of our Lord to the rich young man, he had at first broken up his hunting establishment, and finally sold his magnificent house and beautiful estate of the Grange, in Hampshire. His plans of usefulness were, however, indistinct, and he was going with Lady Harriet to visit the Holy Land. As the nephew of the First Lord of the Admiralty, he had been accommodated with a passage on board the frigate of the present gallant Commander-in-chief of the Mediterranean Fleet, Admiral Deans Dundas, whose pious mother, a sister of the late Lord Amesbury, was a frequent hearer of Mr. J. Haldane, and a member of the Rev. Christopher Anderson's Church, in Edinburgh.

Standing on deck beside the Captain, just as they were going to dinner, Mr. Drummond's quick eye perceived at a distance a ripple on the waters. He remarked it to Captain Dundas, when in an instant orders were given to take in sail, and trim the ship. The ripple indicated the approach of one of those sudden storms for which the Mediterranean has been famed, from the day when the Apostle Paul was caught up in the Euroclydon. In this instance it was the means of sending Mr. Henry Drummond to Geneva. The ship took refuge in the port of Genoa before nightfall, and Lady Harriet begged with tears that they might land. At Genoa, Mr. Drummond accidentally heard of Mr. Haldane's doings, and of the commotion at Geneva. His resolution was taken. He came to Geneva, and introduced himself to Mr. Haldane two days before he left the city. The biographer of Henry Pyt thus speaks :—

" After him (Robert Haldane) Mr. Henry Drummond came to add new benedictions to those we already possessed. He had for the blessed Pyt a particular affection, which he himself reciprocated. In his conversations, Mr. Drummond chiefly insisted on the mystical union of Christ and the Church, and its glorious results. He spoke little of sanctification, although his example was sufficient. He was indefatigable in his zeal for the glory of the Lord. Labours, watchings, fatigues, cost him nothing. His simplicity, his brotherly goodness, and his affability won all hearts. He had not then the peculiar opinions which he has since exhibited."

M. Guers might have added, that Mr. Drummond's great wealth and boundless liberality made him to the persecuted ministers, a wall of defence against the bigoted zeal of the Consistory. Taking up his abode at the beautiful hotel of Sêcheron, beyond the walls of the town, his hospitable apartments were open to all who were interested in the Gospel, and chose to visit him. The Company had hoped that, in getting rid of Mr. Haldane, they were going to enjoy an easy victory, but the gallant zeal, the untiring energy, the chivalrous generosity of Mr. Drummond filled them with despair. They appointed a deputation to go to Sêcheron, and remonstrate. In a recent letter of M. Gaussen, he thus writes :—

" I was the occasion, without intending of it, of that visit to Mr. Drummond. Your uncle was on the point of departing, when, at a sitting of the Venerable Company, they were loudly inveighing against him in very injurious language. ' Sirs,' said I, ' Mr. Haldane is not only a man profoundly versed in the Scriptures, he is also a gentleman. Send to him a deputation. State your complaints, and he will reply to you. He never speaks against you personally to the students ; he only instructs them in the Holy Scriptures, but the language which is here tolerated against him is beneath the dignity of this assembly.' It was this that occasioned the deputation to go to Mr. Drummond, who arrived the same week in which your uncle left, and seemed to have been expressly sent to replace him. The Consistory had intended M. Ferriere, late pastor in London, to be of the deputation, but, without authority, he caused M. Cheneviere to go as his substitute. Your uncle, during his visit, was chiefly occupied with the students. His apartment was filled with them, and the lectures of the professors were deserted. *Inde iræ.*"

The deputation thus despatched, consisting of MM. Pictet and Cheneviere, found Mr. Drummond in the garden of the hotel at Sêcheron, in conversation with a friend. M. Cheneviere, with a manner more resembling that of a dancing-master than a professor of divinity, pompously demanded if he were going to teach the same doctrines as Mr. Haldane, and Mr. Drummond, with consummate address, baffled the impertinent inquirer, by requesting an exposition of Mr. Haldane's doctrines. In the sequel, the deputation returned in a rage. A violent letter of remonstrance was met by a reply which added fuel to the flame. In a Genevese newspaper, of the 5th of September, 1817, it is described as a letter in which Mr. Drummond dared to treat the Venerable Company as heretics and blasphemers of the name of Christ. Mr. Drummond was summoned to appear before the Council of State, and after an interview, which was intended to intimidate, and in which he was required to withdraw his letter, he removed his quarters from Sêcheron into the

French territory at Ferney Voltaire, where, at a villa, called Campagne Pictet, in sight of the irate Company and their supporters, he remained at a time when his countenance and support were of the greatest consequence to the Christians suffering under their Arian persecutors. Of Mr. Drummond's "Letter to the Pastors," M. Gaussen says, "It was very well done," and displayed the same brilliant talent and manly courage which he has since evinced in his exposure of Cardinal Wiseman and the Jesuits, qualities which only deepen our regret that they have not always been guided by equal stability of purpose, consistency of scriptural doctrine, and right judgment in all things pertaining to the kingdom of God. One of Mr. Drummond's first efforts was to restore Martin's ancient version of the Bible, instead of that which the Arian clergy had corrupted by false translations. The Genevese Consistory were filled with alarm, and spread the report that the new sect were about to publish a translation favourable to their own peculiar notions. This misrepresentation Mr. Drummond repelled in the newspaper where it appeared. After intimating how easily he could expose the Arianism of the Consistory, and prove that those who deny the Deity of our Lord are blasphemers, he adds, "I fear all new versions, where there have been others long received, and I abhor that of the Arians of Geneva as well as that of the Socinians of England." "In proportion as the Bible is known, the Church is sound, and the people moral. In proportion as the Bible is concealed, the Church is corrupt, and its members perverted."

If Robert Haldane, after his experience in Scotland, shrunk from new discussions on Church polity at Geneva, the sanguine temperament of Henry Drummond made up for his backwardness. He encouraged the rejected ministers to form themselves into a Church, and seeing that M. Malan was not likely long to hold his place, he was entreated at once and finally to break with the Arian Consistory, and take the oversight of a flock ready to gather round him. At the same time, an annuity, which would have secured the independence of M. Malan and his wife, was declined. The offer was as creditable to the generosity of those who made it, as the refusal to the disinterested integrity of Dr. Malan. He assigned as the reason, that he desired to be dependant on none but God, and to this determination he has adhered. MM. Mejanel, Gonthier, and Pyt, finally accepted the joint office, "and the Gospel made new converts from week to week;"* and, it may be added, on the authority of M. Gaussen, that Geneva now contains more true Christians than any city on the Continent.

On the 21st of September, 1817, just three months after the departure of Mr. Haldane, the Lord's Supper was administered for the first time out of the Arian Church of Geneva:—

"It was at the house of Mr. Drummond," says M. Guers, "and it was Dr. Malan who officiated. It was a meeting of ten, of whom, at least, seven bear distinguished names. Besides the two just mentioned may be named, Pyt, Mejanel, Gonthier, Guers, and Christopher Burchhardt, the missionary, who, in 1818, died at Aleppo, in the bloom of youth, and in the midst of his usefulness. It reminded us," says M. Guers, " of another supper, that which, in 1536, another disciple of Jesus, M. Jean Guerin, distributed to some pious souls, assembled in the garden of Stephen Dadaz, at Pré l'Eveque, and which was the first communion of the Protestants of Geneva."

About the same time another of Mr. Haldane's converts, the excellent M. Du Vivier, preached a sermon in the oratory of Carouge, in which he asserted the divinity of our Lord, the total corruption of human nature, and the doctrine of the atonement. The discourse was denounced as "scandalous" by the Company, and to prevent a "similar disorder," they decided that no student should be allowed to preach, unless his discourse had been submitted to three professors, one of whom was to be the lynx-eyed and violent M. Cheneviere.

Shortly afterwards M. Mejanel was banished as a Frenchman, but M. Empeytaz, about the same time, returned from Germany. It would be out of place to pursue the history of the progress of the revival of true Christianity at Geneva, down to the period when the last ornament of this once glorious Church was

* The Church is now known as La Pelisserie, from the street in which it assembles. It is in communion with the Oratoire, in which MM. Gaussen, Merle, and Pilet minister.

removed, and M. Gaussen being deposed in 1831, became one of the founders of the Evangelical School of Theology, along with Merle D'Aubigné and Galland. Soon after, Dr. Malan obtained a new chapel, although it was, unfortunately, without the walls, and not favourably situated for a permanent congregation. The cost of the building was about 850*l.*, of which a considerable proportion was provided out of the money obtained by M. Malan for his writings and his pupils.* Afterwards the Oratory was provided for the Church, in connexion with the Evangelical School and the Evangelical Society of Geneva, an institution which boasts of ministers and professors whose abilities and faithfulness it will be difficult to overrate. But these matters belong to the history of the Church, and not to the lives of individuals. It was, however, necessary, to prevent the repetition of mistakes that have been made, to show that Mr. Haldane's career was very different from Mr. Drummond's; and that, whilst Mr. Drummond's services in a time of need deserve to be holden in perpetual remembrance, Mr. Haldane's mission was restricted to the preaching of the Gospel, without reference to ecclesiastical polity or rites and ceremonies.

On this matter it is almost superfluous to add the conclusive evidence of M. Gaussen, who thus writes:—" His wisdom at Geneva was indicated by the sobriety of his language, and by the pre-eminence he assigned to all that was essential. He was himself a Baptist, but never did I hear him utter a word on the subject. I have been told that our brother, M. Guers, at that time also a Baptist, wrote to him, 'We have baptized two persons,'

---

* There were those who grieved to think that their persecution had not crushed Dr. Malan, under the weight of poverty, and M. Cheneviere maliciously circulated the report, that the gates of fortune had been opened to him by his Methodism. This report, notwithstanding its origin, at one time obtained belief amongst Christian travellers passing through Geneva. There is no doubt that, to use the words of Dr. Pye Smith, " M. Malan's spotless character, rare talents, distinguished attainments, and amiable manners, were such as to hold out the promise of advancement, in whatever situation he might be placed, and it might be allowable to express the wish, that the report had been as true as it is notoriously the reverse."

and that your uncle replied, ' I should have been much better pleased had you written that you had converted two persons.' "

During the meetings of the Evangelical Alliance in London, in 1851, one speaker was recommending the Foreign-Aid Society, on the ground that it only employed native preachers, when Dr. Merle D'Aubigné rose and said, that he for one could not accept this as a recommendation, for if it had not been for the grace of God in ordering the mission of the venerable Robert Haldane, from Scotland, " I myself, so far as man can see, would not have been here to-day."

Dr. Cheever, a well-known American, after describing the proceedings of Mr. Haldane, in his work, entitled, " Wanderings of a Pilgrim in the Shadow of Mont Blanc," thus writes :—

" This was a most remarkable movement of Divine Providence, one of the most remarkable to be found on record. What renders it more astonishing, is the fact, that Mr. Haldane, at first, was obliged to converse with these students through an interpreter, in part at least, so that he could not then have conveyed to them the full fervour of his feelings, nor the fire of the truth, as it was burning in his own soul. Nevertheless, these singular labours, under circumstances so unpromising, were so blessed by the Divine Spirit, that sixteen out of eighteen young men, who had enjoyed Mr. Haldane's instructions, are said, by Dr. Heugh, to have become subjects of Divine grace. And among the students thus brought beneath the power of the Word of God, was the future historian of the Reformation, young Merle D'Aubigné. . . . Felix Neff, that Alpine missionary of apostolic zeal and fervour, was another of these young converts. Never was the seed of the Gospel sown to better effect than in these hearts."

Dr. Cheever mentions Felix Neff as one of those who received the Gospel from the lips of Robert Haldane. This, however, was not exactly the case. Neff was, like many others, what has been termed his *grandson*, rather than his son in the faith. The Gospel sounded out from Geneva, and its echoes reverberated through the mountains and valleys of Switzerland, till they passed the Jura, and were heard in France, in Belgium, and even in Germany. Mr. Haldane seemed to have on his mind a becoming awe in regard to the work in which he had been only an instrument in the Lord's hand. He seldom spoke of these conversions, and never, but under a solemnized impression, and for some good end.

It does not appear from what source of information the late able and excellent Dr. Heugh, of Glasgow, derived the statement, repeated by Dr. Cheever, that *sixteen* out of *eighteen* students were brought to Christ during Mr. Haldane's residence at Geneva. The number of the students who attended was not, however, eighteen, but "about twenty-five in all," according to M. Guers, who was of the number. But respecting *all*, M. Gaussen thus writes :—

"During the time of your uncle's sojourn, almost all the students in theology attended his expositions *(suivirent ses explications)*. Of the whole of them there was *but one* who did not appear to have been touched, but there were some of them who did not afterwards appear to have been savingly profited. Still it is certain that the greater part *(la plupart)* of those who attended him, have become men *eminent* in the service of God. The Evangelical work at Geneva was the child *(fille)* of Haldane; the work of grace of Vaud the daughter of that at Geneva; and, still later, the work in France, to a great extent, the child of that of Geneva and of Vaud. To Robert Haldane was given the grace to accomplish a work, of which the revelation of the last day will only show the extent. May a benediction from above rest on all his family!"

It is one of the characteristics of his visit to the Continent, that the extent of the good that was then done was but little known for many years. The eminence, and even the literary distinction of the ministers who either enlightened, converted, or confirmed, is one of the remarkable circumstances chiefly meriting the notice of those who love to trace the footsteps of an over-ruling Providence. Several of them were the descendants of French Protestant exiles, and assuredly never since the revocation of the Edict of Nantes, had there shone amongst the pastors of Switzerland and France such a galaxy of talent as appeared in the reunion of such men as Gaussen, Galland, Merle d'Aubigné, Malan, Monod, James, Vivien, Bost, Bonifas, Guers, Du Pasqueil, Du Vivier, Gonthier, and Rieu. The magnitude of the work has become more visible as years have rolled on, and whilst the hand of the Lord is seen directing, controlling, overruling all, it becomes more and more evident, in the words of Dr. Cheever, "it was of God that Robert Haldane should visit Geneva at that time."

# CHAPTER XIX.

MR. HALDANE PASSES THROUGH LYONS—FRENCH COMMEN-
TARY ON THE ROMANS—LETTER TO MR. BICKERSTETH—
MM. PICTET AND PRADEL — MONTAUBAN — SKETCH OF
THE HISTORY OF FRENCH PROTESTANTISM — ITS LOW
STATE IN FRANCE—MM. GACHON, BONNARD, MARZIALS,
CHABRAND — MR HALDANE'S LABOURS — ANECDOTE OF
M. DE VILLELLE AND LORD STUART — CONTINENTAL
SOCIETY—HENRI PYT—COLPORTEURS—CONVERSION OF
A PELAGIAN PASTOR—MR. HALDANE QUITS MONTAUBAN
—M. BONNARD ACCOMPANIES HIM TO PARIS—JOSEPH
WOLFF—LETTERS OF M. MARZIALS.

[1817—1823.]

IT was at the end of June, 1817, that Mr. and Mrs. Haldane
left Geneva, on their route to Montauban. They travelled by
way of Lyons, where they spent the Lord's-day, and attended
the French Protestant worship. There, however, they "heard
not a word of the Gospel." Mr. Haldane sought an interview
with the pastor, but found, as he writes, that "he had not time
to converse with me on the subject of religion, being fully occupied with the fashionable amusements in which those who are
there designated Christians spend the evening of that day."
More than thirty years had elapsed since Mr. Haldane had
visited Lyons, and admired the magnificent site of that illustrious city, where the relics of the palace of the Cæsars, and the
tombs of the early Christian martyrs, alike remind us of the
fading glories of this world, and of the immortal trophies of the
victory of faith. But Mr. Haldane had now but one object in
view; and in quitting Geneva he sought neither relaxation nor
amusement. There were few who more enjoyed the beauties of

nature, or viewed with deeper interest the ancient monuments of Roman grandeur. At Geneva, much as he enjoyed magnificent scenery, he steadily declined joining in any excursions which might divert from the important work which at that time he incessantly pursued. For the most part, it was only in the afternoon that he there walked out with Mrs. Haldane, on the Promenade St. Antoine, on the southern boulevards. "With her," says M. Gaussen, "I knew that he had much secret prayer for a blessing on his labours." But whilst he stuck to his missionary work with such intense earnestness, his frequent allusions to the grandeur of the mountains round Geneva, and to the rich and well-watered landscape, told how greatly in his evening walks he had admired those glorious sunsets, whose varying hues light up the stern and icy sublimities of Mont Blanc, or gild with a softened effulgence the milder beauties of the wooded Jura.

At Montauban they arrived in July, 1817. He had now become comparatively familiar with the language, and could enjoy the conversation of those who spoke only in French. Mrs. Haldane was also able to share in this pleasure, and had the happiness to be regarded as a messenger of grace to Madame Marzials. She translated into English some of the works of Drelincourt, and other French Protestant writers, and she employed herself in copying for her husband, more especially when he had to superintend the publication of his Evidences of Christianity, and his work on the Romans in French. The first was translated by Charles Rieu, the latter by M. Combe Dunous, and was, in fact, the fruit of the expositions at Geneva and Montauban. It may, in fact, be considered as the first edition of that elaborate work, on which he continued, from time to time, to bestow his thoughts and meditations, until it was published in English in 1834. The French Commentary was intended for the Continent, and is much more discursive than the English. In some respects it was better calculated for popular reading; and many persons who had admired the richness and fulness of the French Commentary, with its numerous episodes, have complained of a want of interest in the more exact and critical English Exposition. The former, which appeared in two octavo volumes, was of itself a great undertaking, in a place where the author had little access to books. It was therefore more exclusively elaborated by his own hands, excepting a small portion of it, in which he acknowledges his obligations to the Sermons of Claude. It has not the advantage of elegant French, a circumstance not wholly to be ascribed to the fault of the translator, but partly to the fact, that he, being an unbeliever, was so closely watched by Mr. Haldane, lest he should corrupt the meaning, that it is much too literal as a translation, and is full of English idioms. A large edition of the work was published, and many copies distributed all over France and Switzerland. It is now nearly out of print, but for a long period a copy was given, out of a store left for the purpose, to each student of divinity at Montauban when he quitted the College, and instances of the good it has done are continually occurring.

The conclusion of Mr. Haldane's letter to Mr. Bickersteth contains a brief but interesting sketch of his visit to Montauban :—

"But before I conclude, I may notice the course I was led to adopt at the close of the academical session at Geneva in 1817. After the departure of the students, at the termination of their course, I resumed my design of going to Montauban, in the south of France, where the Faculty for the education of French Protestants is established, and which is considered the centre of all the French Protestant Churches. Through the kindness of the late excellent M. Bonnard, then Professor of Hebrew, but afterwards Dean, or Principal of the Faculty, I was introduced to such of the French pastors as occasionally visited Montauban, and by his means, and in consequence of the extensive correspondence he maintained with all the parties in France, I was enabled to obtain much valuable information, as well as general circulation for the books I published there, in every part of the kingdom. From my valued friend, the present President of the Consistory, M. Marzials, to whom I was also under peculiar obligations for the assistance he afforded me among the students and others, I some time ago received a letter, in which he says: 'Many of our pastors are now proclaiming the Gospel, who, but for your abode among us, would have been preaching Neology.' By another letter from him, recently received, dated July 13, 1839, I am informed that every student, on finishing his studies, and leaving Montauban, is furnished with a copy of my 'Evidences,' which were translated into French, and of the French 'Commentary on the Romans,' which I prepared and published at that place.

"The late M. Pictet, of Geneva, whose name is so well known among the *savans* of Europe, and who had been appointed by Bonaparte one of the Inspectors of the Protestant Churches,—who has asserted in one of his publications that 'the Methodism,' meaning the Christianity, 'of England threatens to conduct the world back to barbarism,'—officially visited Montauban some years after I left it. On that occasion M. Pradel, then Dean of the Faculty, and a man equally opposed to the Gospel as M. Pictet, told him, with tears in his eyes, that 'since the appearance at Montauban of that disastrous meteor (*météore desastreux*), Mr. Haldane, all had been poisoned with his doctrine.' M. Pradel publicly used the same expressions on another occasion in addressing the students, and thus unintentionally bore witness to the blessing with which the Lord was pleased to accompany the declaration of his Gospel.

"I state these things, my dear Sir, because, as I have already intimated, the account which has appeared under the sanction of your name would, if uncontradicted, be henceforth considered authentic, and because it may advance the objects which both of us have at heart for the good of the Continent to publish this short record. Placed before the world as Mr. Burgess's narrative now is, it requires to be rectified; and I also trust that a memorial of the Lord's goodness in prospering an attempt to revive the knowledge of his truth in Continental Europe, may stimulate the zeal of others, and redound to the glory of God, whom you serve in the Gospel of his Son, and to whom, in whatever capacity we are placed, it is our bounden duty to consecrate every talent with which we are intrusted.

"I am, my dear Sir, yours, &c.,

"ROBERT HALDANE."

Montauban is the centre of theological education for the Reformed or Calvinistic Churches in France. Situated on the right bank of the Tarn, in the vast and luxuriant plain of Languedoc, its name is inseparably associated with the vicissitudes of Protestantism, its struggles, its triumphs, and its reverses. If bloodshed and persecution have devastated its streets, it has also been ennobled by many acts of heroism. In 1621 it sustained a memorable siege, when the Royal army, led by Louis XIII., the Constable of France, and the *élite* of the nobility, were repulsed from its gates. For nearly three months various attempts were made to carry it by assault, till at last the King broke up his entrenchments, withdrew his batteries, and retired, shedding burning tears of indignation and shame. The besieged were first cheered with the prospect of deliverance by a Protestant soldier in the Royal army, who, on the previous night, beneath the ramparts, played on his flute a well-known Protestant tune to the words of the 68th Psalm, "Let God arise, and let his enemies be scattered." At a later period, Montauban capitulated to Cardinal Richelieu, but not till Rochelle, "the City of the Waters," and the chief hostage for the observance of the Royal faith, had also fallen before the terrible energy of that Prince of the Romish Church. With Montauban perished the temporal power of Protestantism as an independent commonwealth within the realm. But it was not till 1685 that its defenceless condition tempted Louis XIV. to consummate the treachery of his house by the revocation of the Edict of Nantes. Even before this concession to the bigotry of Louvois, Père la Chaise, and Madame Maintenon, the theological Academy of Montauban had been suppressed in 1661, through the intrigues of the Jesuits. From that period there was no school of theology for the Protestants, until 1730, when one of the most remarkable of the persecuted ministers, the admirable Antoine Court, established a Foreign Seminary at Lausanne, which became the nursery of "the Pastors of the Desert," until it was transported to Geneva, there to continue until restored to Montauban by the policy of Napoleon.

This, then, was the city to which Robert Haldane directed his steps in 1817, under a painful conviction that the Protestantism of France had become little better than a lifeless form. But, in order to appreciate the nature and results of his labours, it will be useful to show how the Churches of the French Reformation had sunk so low as to stand in need of a missionary from Scotland. The history of Protestantism, and, it may be added, the history of Christianity, in France, is traced in characters of blood. It records many bright examples of enduring faith, and of a patience that nothing could subdue, but it is also a melancholy commentary on the words of the holy seer, who beheld in vision the beast which should "wear out the saints of the most High," "making war and prevailing against them." The martyrdoms of the early Christians at

Lyons and Vienne, by the Pagans, were but the prelude to the equally bitter and more relentless persecutions of the Papists. The ruthless crusades against the Albigenses again and again decimated that unoffending people, till, in the thirteenth century, such acts as the slaughter of myriads of men, women, and children, in the streets of Bezieres, exhibited instances of wholesale butchery, more horrible than any ever perpetrated on the banks of the Seine by Catherine de Medicis or Robespierre. The massacre of the Albigenses once more ushered in other scenes of bloody persecution, which attended the dawn of the Reformation in France. During the last years of the chivalrous Francis I., all Europe stood aghast, when the unoffending Vaudois of Provence were nearly exterminated by fire and sword; whilst the King himself gloated on the blazing spectacle of Protestants suffering a lingering death on the Place de Grêve, at Paris. It was the diabolical resolve of the priests to crush heretics, at all costs. They were hunted down like wild beasts, and exposed to the rack, the gibbet, the stake, and other kinds of judicial torture. But all did not avail, and it appears, from the remonstrance of Charles IX. to the Pope, that, in 1565, "one-fourth part of the kingdom was separated from the communion of the Church." With the Protestants were numbered many "gentils-hommes, old soldiers, experienced in war," and "three parts of the men of letters," besides much of the wealth, both of the nobility and the Tiers Etat. It is added, that, over and above those in a state of separation, there were "many others who had a continual struggle of conscience on the worship of images, the administration of the sacraments, and the mass." How melancholy to reflect that France almost embraced Protestantism, and yet stopped short! The wars of the League deluged her fields with the blood of her citizens, and also blunted the etherial weapons by which alone Christianity can effectually triumph. Certain it is, that within seven years from the date of the remonstrance just quoted, the Massacre of St. Bartholomew, in 1572, broke the political power of the party, and became the culminating act of treachery of the Guises and the Medicis.

The prospect does not brighten as we trace the sad history down to modern times, and we still vainly seek for some spot on which to repose amidst the sanguinary deluge with which we are surrounded. It has been truly said, that the story of these persecutions, "so merciless, so unrelenting, and so continuous," is one "which no man would either willingly read, or repeat, or even abbreviate. It pervades every era of the French annals. It assumes every conceivable form of cruelty and injustice, and many forms inconceivable to the darkest imagination unaided by an actual knowledge of those horrible details. If the most terrific act of this prolonged tragedy was the Massacre of St. Bartholomew, the most revolting was the Dragonnades of Louis XIV." * But, in thus glancing at this dark page in the annals of a guilty world, it is well to observe that these crimes did not escape the righteous indignation of Heaven. The persecuting House of Valois speedily perished one by one, through violent or shameful deaths, leaving the brand of St. Bartholomew on their tombs, and verifying the denunciation of the Word of God, that "bloody and deceitful men shall not live out half their days." But the Bourbons did not take warning. Twice did Henry of Navarre deny the faith taught him by his pious mother, Jane D'Albret, but his compliance did not save him from the dagger of Ravaillac, directed as it was by the Jesuits who, seventeen years before, had sent his voluptuous and worthless predecessor to his last account. Even in the reign of Henry IV. some atrocities were committed, with comparative impunity, reviving the memory of Vassy and Toulouse, and his three immediate successors have left their names stained with the infamy of persecution. The fourth perished by the guillotine; the fifth spent the greater part of his life in exile, whilst the sixth and seventh, compelled to abdicate a throne purchased by apostasy, have left their posterity exiles from France.

Justice seemed tardy, but the Revolution at last broke the slumbers of the House of Bourbon; and the sins of the fathers were visited on the children of the oppressors, in a way too striking to be overlooked. The majority of the men of letters

* I. Sir James Stephen's Lectures, 151.

were once Protestant. They were now Infidel. The Romish
Church could once boast of such men as Pascal and Fenelon.
But the Jesuits, who had destroyed Port Royal, and proscribed
the Jansenists, as they had before revoked the Edict of Nantes, and
proscribed the Reformation, had been in their own turn proscribed.
Abandoned to voluptuous security, the clergy had no strength to
resist the tide of Atheism. Infidelity armed itself with the weapons
of a persecuting hierarchy. We read with horror of the Noyades,
the Fusillades, the confiscations, the proscriptions of the Convention and the Triumvirate. But can it be forgotten that the
counterparts of these acts of an Infidel philosophy may all be
found in the history of Popish tyranny ?

In the year 1560 the revolutionary *Noyades* of the Loire were
anticipated, except, says a recent Lecturer at Cambridge, "that
a Prince of the Church, Charles, Cardinal de Lorraine, took
the place of the butcher Cariere, and except that Catherine de
Medicis, and her Ladies of Honour, assumed in this dismal
tragedy characters to which, even in the frenzy of the Reign of
Terror, the vilest of the Poissardes of Paris would scarcely have
descended." But, if the Noyades of Nantes had their counterpart
in the Noyades of Amboise, so too were the Fusillades at Lyons
but the repetition of the Fusillades in the same city, two centuries before. The Glaçiere at Avignon is still gazed at by the
traveller, with the horror inspired by the recollection of those
priests and citizens, with whose blood it was crimsoned during
the outbreak of a godless democracy. But that horrid tower
of the old Papal palace looked down upon another scene
of greater barbarity, when the priests pronounced a public
blessing on the savage murderers who had massacred the
Protestants of Cabrieres, and even burned to death the
women who had sought refuge in a barn. When the clergy
were despoiled of their property, and hunted down by the
Convention ; when the exercise of their religious rites became
a crime, and the attempt to emigrate was enough to send them
to the scaffold, could it be forgotten that through their influence
the Protestants, during the early part of the same century, had
been despoiled of their goods, condemned to the galleys, to

confiscation, and to death, for uniting to read their Bibles, or for trying to escape to a foreign land? When, in the reign of Louis XIV., the Protestant pastors were dragged to the scaffold or the stake, and their voices drowned by the roll of the drums, who would have believed that, before another century had elapsed, one of his own Royal descendants would appear upon a scaffold, and vainly plead to be heard, in front of the gardens of the Tuileries? When Protestant children were torn from their parents, and compelled to deny the faith of their fathers, who could have anticipated the time when the innocent Dauphin of France would be snatched from his mother's side, and taught the blasphemies of the "Age of Reason?" When the dead corpses of the Protestants were drawn through the streets, or exposed to insult, who would have thought that, before long, the Royal vaults of St. Denis would themselves be violated, or the bodies of apostate and persecuting kings and princes dragged from their coffins by the mob, tumbled in the mud, and exposed to every indignity and outrage?

But there is one feature in the history of the French Protestants far more melancholy than the apparent fruitlessness of all their multiplied and prolonged afflictions. It is "the wearing out" of the faith of the saints, and the decay of vital godliness amidst abounding iniquity. Its brightest period is seen before the Wars of the League; before the Condés, the Bourbons, the Montmorencys, and other princes, made Protestantism the tool of their ambition. Many, from a feeling of honour, adhered to the cause of the Reformation, who, like Sully, manifested that they knew nothing of its spirit. The banishment of the leading pastors by Louis XIV., was a blow more fatal than all his dragonnades. From that period true religion seemed to languish, although, for a long time, it was manifest that the lamp of faith still glimmered in the socket. When the mountaineers of the Cevennes, in a paroxysm of despair, made war upon Louis, baffled army after army, led by Maréchals, and shook the throne of the great monarch, it is evident that amidst much that was vain and worldly in their chiefs, and more that was fanatical in their prophets, there was still burning amongst these Camisards, a portion of the holy flame enkindled at the Reformation.

But, after the Revolution, when religious liberty was, for a time, achieved; when the renowned Paul Rabaut was no longer hiding amidst the rocks or preaching in deserts; when his gifted son, Rabaut-Etienne, raised to a fatal eminence, could write to his father, with a swelling heart—" The President of the National Assembly is at your feet "—then it was seen how well oppression had done its work, and how nearly the faith of the Protestant Churches had perished. The spirit that seemed to endure in the attitude of a sublime resistance against the relentless persecution of Popery, yielded to the seductions of an Infidel philosophy. In the destitution of the means of grace; in the want of Bibles; in the absence of faithful pastors, true religion had, in a great measure, evaporated.

At last the Goddess of Reason was enthroned in the chancel of Nôtre Dame, and the bust of Marat substituted for the statues of the saints. The Lord's-day was formally abolished. Decades were substituted for weeks; work on the Lord's-day became compulsory; and every private library was ransacked and pillaged of its religious books. Every Bible that could be found was burned; and any of the works of the old Reformers that escaped destruction were then buried in the ground. "I have often," says Mr. Robert Haldane, "heard pious men in France, who witnessed these scenes, describe them with horror, and with evident marks of the deep impression they had produced upon their minds." But when the storm abated, and when the decree of the 21st of February, 1795, restored liberty of worship, the spectacle presented by French Protestantism was truly melancholy. There were then few pastors to take advantage of the privilege. Some were dead, some had assumed occupations, some had embraced Infidel or Socinian principles, and amongst these were the pastors of Paris, including a son of Paul Rabaut. No religious works were published. The old Protestant writers were not reprinted, and even the want of the Bible created no uneasiness. The cold hand of Infidelity, with a crushing grasp, had seized on Protestantism, fainting under the wearing-out persecutions of Popery, and the inanimate condition of the French Churches continued, with scarcely a symptom of spiritual life, down to the conclusion of the war, and the period when, in July, 1817, Robert Haldane, having quitted Geneva, presented himself at Montauban, the metropolis of French Protestantism.

In his Second Review of the Bible Society, Mr. Haldane has himself sketched a picture of the low state of religion in that once Protestant and Christian city.  The College had been restored by the Emperor Napoleon in 1808-10, but this had been merely an act of diplomacy on the part of one who was too wise a politician to abandon himself entirely to the priests.  In passing through Montauban, on his return from the Spanish campaign, against Sir John Moore, Napoleon was so well received by the Protestants, that, anxious to play them off against the captive Pope, he issued an order, on his return to Paris, for the restoration and support of the Protestant faculty. At the head of this new school of Protestant theology was installed an officer of Engineers, who had distinguished himself in war, but had been originally educated for the ministry at Geneva.  To use the emphatic language of Mr. Haldane, "This engineer of Satan laboured to disseminate the baleful poison of Socinianism amongst the students, most of whom had enrolled themselves to avoid the conscription.  About one hundred withdrew when the conscription ceased, and left the Faculty almost deserted."

Nearly one-half of the city, now comprising more than 24,000 inhabitants, nominally belonged to the Reformed Church, and there were in the Faculty of Theology sixty-four students. Nothing could be worse than the state of the Churches through-out France, but at Montauban itself the darkness was not quite so palpable as that which but a little while before had brooded over Geneva.  Amidst abounding unbelief and enmity to the Gospel, there was a feeble glimmering of light in the South of France.  This was in a great measure attributed to the labours of an amiable Moravian, M. Gachon, pastor, first of St. Hyppo-lite, afterwards of Mazére in Arriège, who devoted a long life to a humble and quiet career of unpretending usefulness.  Of the Moravians, M.Vincent, in his "Views of Protestantism in France," observes, " that they dogmatized little, and placed religion in love, and above all, in the love of Jesus." But although the Gospel was not preached with much power,—and they were timid in their proceedings,—yet a blessing had accompanied the declaration of its simple truths; and amongst those who had caught the heavenly spark were the excellent M. Bonnard, Professor of Hebrew at Montauban, and M. Marzials, one of its ministers.  It is to M. Bonnard that Mr. Haldane alludes, as " one faithful witness to the testimony of Jesus, who, so far as it was in his power, firmly opposed the Socinianism of the other Professors."  This conduct drew upon him the indignation of M. Pictet, whom Napoleon had made Superintendent of the French Protestant Churches.  " M. Pictet wrote letter upon letter on the subject, yet, backed as he was by the authority of the Emperor of France, neither the threats nor the inducements which these letters contained made the smallest impression in the quarter to which they were directed."

M. Marzials, now the venerable President of the Consistory at Montauban, was another witness to the truth, against the cold spirit of Voltairian infidelity, and the more subtle and dangerous influence of that Pantheistic Rationalism which was then in its infancy.  The first Lord's-day after his arrival, Mr. Haldane heard M. Marzials preach in the Protestant Temple, on the text Rom. v. 1, and at the conclusion of the service observed to M. Bonnard, that this was the first occasion on which he had heard the Gospel preached from any pulpit in France.  Both M. Bonnard and M. Marzials felt their need of support in maintaining the life of godliness amidst the sepulchral darkness and enmity of Arianism and unbelief.  M. Bonnard is gone to his rest, but M. Marzials still remains, one of the oldest and firmest friends of the Gospel in France.  To both of them Robert Haldane became a tower of strength, encouraging them to speak out more boldly, and to lay hold of stronger and clearer views of the great doctrines of the Gospel.  Besides these, there was another friend of the truth who still survives, the venerable

M. De Rapin, a private gentleman of fortune, the grandson of the celebrated historian, residing at his chateau at La Garde, five or six miles from Montauban, between whom and Mr. Haldane there grew up a mutual friendship. He had been a faithful confessor of Christ, even in revolutionary times, when it was a crime to possess the Bible, and people sometimes buried it in their gardens, in order to escape the guillotine. Avoiding interference in politics, M. De Rapin steered his steady, quiet, uncompromising course through the storms by which others were overwhelmed. At Toulouse, about thirty miles to the south of Montauban, M. Chabrand, pastor and professor, was also like a light burning in a dark place. He frequently came to see Mr. Haldane, and they had much pleasing intercourse. M. Chabrand pressed his Scottish friend to go to Toulouse, and see that famous city, the seventh, in point of importance, in France, in which the last of the French martyrs died on the scaffold, little more* than half a century before, and which may also be said to have drank up like water the blood of the saints. Mr. Haldane, adhering to his rule as a missionary not to travel for pleasure, observed that he would willingly go sixty leagues to meet another Christian, but that he would not journey six to behold a city. " Since you are here, I see enough of Toulouse." Had Robert Haldane visited France some years later, he would have found the motives which were then wanting to induce him to visit Toulouse. But he lived long enough to rejoice in hearing of the work of the Lord, which has so much prospered at Toulouse, not only under the ministry of M. Chabrand, but through the untiring exertions of three eminently pious brothers, the MM. (Frank, Louis, and Amand) Courtois, the bankers, who have devoted themselves to the circulation of the Scriptures and religious works with a zeal, perseverance, and success, for which their reward will be in heaven.

At the time of Mr. Haldane's arrival at Montauban, the

---

* Amongst the instances of retributive justice might be mentioned the fact, that all the surviving members of the Parliament of Toulouse who condemned the pastor Rochette, the Greniers, and Calas, were sent for to Paris, and perished by the revolutionary guillotine.

Dean of the Faculty was the distinguished M. Daniel Encontre, who, up to the year 1814, had been President of the Faculty of Sciences at Montpelier. M. Encontre held a high place as a man of science, and, next to La Place, was then considered the most distinguished mathematician in France. " I have seen," said the celebrated Fourcroy, " two or three men in France his equals in intellect,—I have never yet seen his superior." In theology, Mr. Haldane found him to be a strong Arminian, and very indistinct in his apprehensions of truth ; but the philosopher soon learned to regard the talents, as well as the piety, of his new acquaintance with profound respect. Confident in his own powers and great attainments, M. Encontre was usually somewhat dogmatic in the assertion of his philosophic views ; and it was remarked, by a surviving pastor, who knew him well, that the only person before whom he ever seemed disposed to bow was Robert Haldane. They had many earnest conversations together on the way of salvation, and there was obviously a great struggle in his mind between the humbling truths of the Gospel and the arrogance of a proud philosophy. " Oh, science ! science !" he would sometimes exclaim, as if he felt the painfulness of the contest. He candidly acknowledged to Mr. Haldane that he was a better mathematician than a theologian. But the victory was not doubtful, and when he finally took leave of his friends to go for change of air to Montpelier, M. Encontre, who was then in a feeble and, as it proved, a dying state, grasped Mr. Haldane's hand and said, with emotion, " Je suis un grand pécheur, mais j'ai un grand Repondant." (I am a great sinner, but I have a great Surety.) This confession alone, made as it was by an admired philosopher, who had himself experienced so much of the pride of intellect, was evidence enough that his lofty spirit had been humbled, that his heart had been renewed, and that he had become as a little child, in order to enter the kingdom of heaven. He had stooped from the heights of dark and vain speculation, in order that he might learn those two simple truths which he so emphatically expressed ; and, approaching as a great sinner to a great Redeemer, there is every reason to conclude that he obtained entrance through that narrow gate from which the rich in their own esteem are sent empty away. The strong public testimony which he latterly bore to Mr. Haldane, and the value he set on his writings, was another token that their intercourse had not been without fruit. After recommending to the students the "Evidences of Christianity," Dr. Bogue's "Essay on the Authority of the New Testament," which had been translated into French, and is said to have been read by Napoleon at St. Helena, and noticing Paley, he added, " Read also, as soon as possible, that admirable work which the learned Robert Haldane, of Edinburgh, now residing at Montauban, is about to publish,—a man who seems to have consecrated his whole time and labour and watchings, and, in a certain sense, all his property, to the Church of the Lord."*

This testimony of one so distinguished in the walks of science and philosophy as M. Encontre, was calculated to make a deep impression on the students. This impression must have been increased when M. Bonnard succeeded to the vacant Presidency of the College. But there is melancholy evidence of the actual state of spiritual death which at that period reigned almost undisturbed in the Protestant Churches of France, whether we appeal to the testimony of such good men as Bonnard or Marzials, or to that of the enemies of the Gospel. In a letter published in a Socinian magazine, in London, by a Mr. Goodier, whom Mr. Haldane himself met at Montauban, this emissary of a destructive heresy observes :—

" I am collecting all the information in my power on the state of the French Protestants, who, in general, are very far from being Calvinists. I have never yet heard a doctrinal sermon ; and, in general, I do not even hear an orthodox expression in the public services, if I except some vague language on the *merits* of Christ. At Bordeaux there are several demi-Unitarians, and their most popular minister would be condemned at once,

---

* The lecture was in Latin, and the words were as follows :—" Legite etiam quam primum poteritis, præstantissimum opus quod mox editurus est in lucem, Robert Haldane, doctus Edinburgensis, nunc Montalbani degens, qui totum tempus suum, et operam et vigilias, et omnia bona videtur quodam modo sacravisse ecclesiæ Domini."

by our English Calvinists, as a Socinian. 'Believing that secret things belong unto God,' the Protestant ministers in France seldom preach upon the mysteries of the Gospel, as they are termed. Election, predestination, justification, and the operation of Divine grace, are subjects almost exploded. If there remain any orthodox doctrine in the pulpit, it is that of satisfaction."

A still more striking proof of the low state of religion in France is connected with one of Mr. Haldane's first and most important acts at Montauban. He saw the lamentable want of Bibles. The Book of God had been proscribed by Popery, and hunted down by Infidelity. In 1802 Mr. Hardcastle, Dr. Bogue, and the other deputies from the London Missionary Society diligently searched the shops of Paris, but in vain, for a single copy of the Scriptures. An edition, called " Stone's Bible," had been printed in consequence of the representations of these gentlemen, but when Mr. Haldane came to Montauban he found neither Bibles nor Testaments. He lost no time in calling attention to this lamentable want, and pointed out that it was a mockery to exhort the people to read a book of which copies could not be obtained. In consequence of his representations, it was agreed, at a meeting with MM. Encontre, Bonnard, Marzials, and Rapin, that M. Bonnard should address a letter to all of the Consistories in France, requesting their co-operation for the printing of the Bible in French. The sum which it was proposed to raise was only 27,000 francs, or 1,080*l.* ; but, to M. Bonnard's circular, *not one Consistory replied!* This fact speaks volumes. The good men at Montauban were discouraged, and disposed to abandon the work in despair. Not so Robert Haldane. Had it been necessary he would have been himself at the whole expense, but securing to M. Bonnard an immediate donation of 100*l.*, and promising as much more as might be necessary, he urged that a second letter should be addressed to the Consistories, and that a subscription should at once be commenced at Montauban. He himself also wrote to England and obtained a grant of 300*l.* for the undertaking, so that it was soon in progress, and an edition of 6,000 copies was followed by another of 10,000 at

Toulouse, in spite of the opposition of some of the ministers, and particularly of the then President of the Consistory, because, although calling himself a Protestant, he disapproved of a Bible without notes.

The coldness with which the Protestant Consistories received the proposal to reprint the French Bible sufficiently indicates the state of deadness and unbelief into which they had lapsed. It has, however, been already noticed that there were a few pastors scattered through the south of France, who in some measure preached the simple truths of the Gospel. But the spark was scarcely sufficient to make the darkness visible, and M. Bonnard, although in official correspondence with all the French Reformed Churches, could only point out about four or five other ministers, besides those at Montauban and Toulouse, of whom it could be said, with any good hope, that they knew or preached the Gospel. From these statements it will be best understood how it was that MM. Bonnard, Marzials, Chabrand, and others, trace the revival in France to Robert Haldane. It was under these circumstances that he began his labours, but the course of opposition to the Divinity Professor adopted at Geneva was not suited to Montauban. M. Encontre, although no longer an unbeliever, was enveloped in much of Pelagian, or semi-Pelagian, darkness, and teaching grievous error, although the truth was struggling in his heart, and Infidelity or Rationalism could no longer claim him for their own. Towards him, therefore, Mr. Haldane assumed a far different manner from the direct front of opposition with which he met M. Cheneviere, of Geneva. As an example, it may be mentioned, that, for the use of the students at Montauban, Mr. Haldane printed Luther's celebrated Letter to Erasmus, on Justification by Faith; but, instead of sending copies directly to the young men, he forwarded them to M. Encontre, with the request that they might be distributed by the Professor. The Professor appreciated the compliment, and was candid enough to inform the students of Mr. Haldane's request, but added, that, being doubtful whether he could approve of the doctrines expressed by Luther, he regretted that he was unable to be the medium of circulating the publication. However, he took the tract to his home, and having read it with attention, consideration, and prayer, he became convinced that Luther was right. Having arrived at this conclusion, he one day requested the students to remain after his lecture, and then, with a candour worthy of all praise, distributed to each, with his own hands, a copy of the tract, telling them he was now able to recommend it to their serious attention.

But whilst the wisdom of this mode of action was thus evinced, there was the same uncompromising boldness at Montauban as at Geneva. Mr. Haldane neither mitigated what M. Encontre reckoned the sternness of his theology, nor failed to point out the errors of those who either compromised or resisted the doctrines of the Gospel. He at first took up his abode in a house which has since been burned down, overlooking the banks of the Tarn, at the end of a fine avenue of trees, about half a mile below the College. The situation, although beautiful, and in clear weather commanding a view of the Pyrenees, proved inconvenient for his work. He therefore removed to a less agreeable situation in the town, and, during the greater part of two years, occupied the upper part of a two-storied house in *La Rue de la Fantaisie*, containing four or five apartments in front of a garden, in which the house of M. Marzials was then situated. There he laboured at his French Commentary; there he prepared many tracts, chiefly containing extracts from the writings of the German and French Reformers; there he received the visits of the students and of ministers, whom he endeavoured to instruct in the doctrines of the Gospel. There was not so much of excitement or *éclat* as at Geneva. He had not to contend with the same opposition or persecuting tendencies, and it may be added, that his converts were not, for the most part, so distinguished by natural ability as those at Geneva. Such men as Gaussen, Galland, Merle d'Aubigné, Malan, Monod, Guers, Pyt, and Rieu, are not to be found every day collected together at the same time and at the same place. But his success was not the less decisive, and Robert Haldane's visit to Montauban became a land-mark in the history of the

Protestant Churches. One after another received the Gospel at his hands; the dry bones were shaken; and those who knew the Lord were strengthened and encouraged to advance in their course.

In a publication of Mr. Haldane's, in 1829, when he was led to contend for the duty of speaking boldly and without compromise, he observes :—

" At Montauban, where I resided more than two years, I proceeded in the same manner as I had done at Geneva, in what appears to me to be the spirit which the Scriptures both inculcate and exemplify. I spoke plainly to the students, and to all with whom I had an opportunity of conversing. With pastors who came from a different part of France I entered into such close conversation as led us at once to discover the points on which we differed, and then discussed them fully. I endeavoured to expose everything false in doctrine that I had heard from the pulpit, and to point out to all to whom I had access whatever appeared to be erroneous.

" The pastor who, at that time, was President of the Consistory, and a Member of the Legion of Honour, who has since left Montauban, was one of the ablest speakers in France. He had a very superficial knowledge of the Scriptures, and opposed the Arian and certain other heresies held by so many of the French pastors, but, after all, he did not preach the truth as it is in Jesus. Of this I had great difficulty to convince some whom I particularly wished to convince, and to show them that, after all, he was a false teacher; nor was I able to do so till he preached from Luke x. 25—28, when, on talking over his discourse, they clearly perceived that if he had understood the Lord's answer as well as the lawyer did to whom it was addressed, which is proved by the reply of the latter, ' he willing to justify himself,' he would have preached a very different sermon.

" He afterwards showed himself to be completely destitute of the knowledge of the truth. At the election of a professor to fill the divinity chair, at Montauban, he gave his casting vote against a servant of God, in favour of an Arian, who had been educated at Geneva.

" The Lord was graciously pleased to give testimony to the word of grace, which I was enabled to declare at Montauban, both among the students and others.

" This I have no reason to believe would have been the case, had ' I avoided all controversy,' and dwelt only on ' truths common to all Churches, and interesting to every soul of man,' and acted in any way to conceal or to keep back any part of the truth respecting the great fundamental doctrines of the Gospel; or had I flattered its enemies, saying,

'Peace, peace,' when I was persuaded there was no peace. A general attention to the Scriptures was soon excited, and much discussion took place.

"Some were turned to the Lord, and the hearts of his servants were encouraged and their hands strengthened. In the letter addressed to me, of December, 1827, by the present President of the Consistory there (M. Bonnard), he writes:—'Believe it, that your abode in the midst of us has been blessed to many, and the word of truth is announced this day in many churches, when they would not, perhaps, have yet heard anything but the teaching of a fatal Rationalism, if we had not had the advantage of knowing you.'"

Testimonies to the same effect are borne in all the letters of the venerable Bonnard, of MM. Marzials Père, Chabrand, and others; and it was not the fault of the Pelagian party that Mr. Haldane's labours at Montauban were not put down by the strong arm of the Government. Happily their opposition was not successful; partly because they were not themselves in favour with the ruling powers, being generally tainted with Republican or Napoleonist principles; and partly because the Government considered any form of religion as better than none. At the time when Professor Pradel regarded him as "a disastrous meteor," Mr. Haldane was denounced to the Minister of the Interior as a fire-brand, who was teaching Calvinism. In consequence of these representations, M. De Villele, then at the head of the French Cabinet, judged it right to make some inquiries of the British Ambassador respecting this remarkable foreigner. Sir Charles Stuart, afterwards Lord Stuart de Rothsay, accordingly took an opportunity of appealing for information to two of his guests who were dining at the Embassy. Whether from accident or design, he pitched upon one who was the cousin of Mr. Haldane, and another who was the brother of his wife. Being told of the excitement their friend was occasioning, taking, perhaps, an exaggerated view of its consequences, and believing that any private remonstrances of theirs would be useless, they both deemed it most convenient to ignore acquaintance with Mr. Haldane's objects, and to leave the French Minister to adopt the course he judged best, whether in expelling their relative, or addressing to him such a representation as the Ambassador suggested might be made by them with a view to his personal safety. But, in truth, Mr. Haldane was in no danger; and it is a fact worthy of note, that M. De Villele, after full inquiry, declared that it mattered not to him whether Mr. Haldane taught Calvinism or any other *ism,* provided it was not *Deism.*

This anecdote very strongly indicates the excitement occasioned by his continuance at Montauban, and effects produced on so many of the students and ministers who were then awakened from the sleep of death. To the careless card-playing and Sabbath-breaking Pastors, Mr. Haldane appeared indeed to be " a disastrous meteor," and the Gospel which he forced on their attention was like the hand-writing on the wall, which disturbed the Babylonish Sultan in the midst of his banquet. But supported as he was by the dying testimony of Daniel Encontre and the living voice of his successor, M. Bonnard, his influence increased among the students. In the Protestant temple at Montauban he was accustomed to take his place in front of the pulpit, in one of the ancient oaken stalls, which had once belonged to the dignitaries of a Romish Church, but was now reserved for the Professors, the Consistory, and other Protestants of note. With MM. Marzials, Bonnard, and a few other Christians, he had been at first accustomed to communicate in private, but afterwards, when the Lord's Supper was administered by M. Marzials, after due warning as to the danger of communicating unworthily, he joined in this ordinance in public—thus showing in France how gladly he could once more unite with his Presbyterian brethren.

His favourite walk was on the Promenade des Carmes, beneath an avenue of acacia trees, the same, it is believed, which was long ago described by the celebrated Arthur Young, with his usual minuteness of observation :—

" The Promenade of Les Terrasses on the borders of the Frescon, and on the highest part of the ramparts, commands that noble plain, one of the richest in Europe, which extends on one side to the sea, and in front to the Pyrenees, whose towering masses, heaped one upon another in a stupendous manner, and covered with snow, offer a variety of lights and shades from their indented forms and the immensity of their projections. This prospect has a sort of oceanic vastness, in which the eye loses itself; an almost boundless scene of cultivation; an animated but confused mass of infinitely varied parts, melting gradually into the distant obscure, from which arises the amazing frame of the Pyrenees, rearing their silvered heads far above the clouds."

"Often," said the venerable M. Marzials, as he lately stood upon that very promenade, and spoke with deep emotion of the visit of Robert Haldane, "often did I walk with him on this very spot during his blessed sojourn amongst us, and, especially, when he went out, as his custom was, to take a walk for an hour before his repast." His time was always occupied, and besides the labour of preparing his publications, his correspondence was very great both with his friends at Geneva, and the students and ministers to whose spiritual revival he had been blessed both there and at Montauban.

His papers also show how much trouble he had taken to obtain information from different quarters as to the best means of instituting the Continental Society, whose operations were signally blessed, and which was, in fact, formed on the model of his own original association in Scotland, for propagating the Gospel at home. But to Mr. Henry Drummond belongs the merit of having actually set the plan in motion. The conduct of the Venerable Company at Geneva, in refusing ordination to those who would not come under fetters as to preaching the divinity of Christ and the doctrines of grace, furnished a supply of well-educated, able preachers, full of zeal and of heavenly unction. Satan may be said in this, as on other occasions, to have been taken in his own snares. Whilst consultations and correspondence were going forward as to the constitution of a new Society, Mr. Drummond finding himself surrounded with rejected ministers, resolved, with characteristic energy, at his own charges, to despatch M. Bost on a mission to Alsace,—a mission which was followed by striking results. It was not, however, till 1819 that the Continental Society was, properly speaking, fully organized. But in consequence of the bigoted measures first adopted at Geneva, and then followed up at Berne and in Lausanne, the preachers, like the early Christians when scattered by the first persecution, "went everywhere preaching the Word," and it may be truly added, " the Lord was with them."

Amongst the first of the Continental missionaries was M. Mejanel, himself one of Mr. Haldane's converts, who was expelled from Geneva at the instigation of the Company, on the 4th of March, 1818. His labours at Paris, in the Department of L'Aisne le Somme, Le Pas de Calais, and the North, were greatly blessed. Another, and with Felix Neff, the most eminent of the Continental missionaries, and one who remained with the Society till his death, was the judicious and heavenly-minded Henri Pyt, who was first employed in the Department of Arriege, at Saverdun, as a Suffragan Pastor. Some passages in his early history at Geneva have been already related.

" Towards the end of 1818," says his biographer, " Pyt repaired to Mr. Haldane's residence at Montauban, where he resided after he left Geneva. The question on which they consulted concerned the best means of propagating the truth in the neighbourhood of Saverdun. The conversations of the blessed Pyt with his venerable friends at Toulouse and Montauban, but chiefly his conferences with Mr. Haldane, exercised a strong influence on his future career. From that time he understood better that his position there was not tenable, and that the only one which became him henceforth, was that of a simple evangelist, unfettered by any ecclesiastical engagement, and preaching free salvation from place to place. It was the only position in which he did not run the risk of compromising his friends of the National Church, and the only one which entirely satisfied his own conscience. From that time he turned towards the Continental Society, which, as a mark of their confidence, left him the choice of the places to which he would be the messenger of peace. ' What joy,' he writes to his friend Gonthier, ' to see the kingdom of the Lord advance with such rapidity! Is it possible to remain idle in the midst of that devouring zeal which burns for the cause of Jesus in so many thousands of our brethren ?' "

The visit of Henry Pyt to Montauban was memorable on another account. " The question on which they consulted " did indeed refer to the best means of propagating the Gospel round Saverdun, but it had a much larger and more extensive bearing.

Mr. Haldane perceived the vast field presented in France for missionary exertions; the eagerness with which the people read or listened to the Bible; and their willingness to hear the Gospel.  But how was this field to be occupied?  The Pastors in France were few and scattered.  In 1807 there were not 200. In 1818 the numbers could not have increased very greatly, for even now there are only about 400.  But amongst the existing Pastors, few as they were, there were, as we have seen, scarcely any who really knew or loved the truth.  On the other hand, at Geneva and other places, there were several converts to the truth in the humbler walks of life, of whom he thought that like the young men whom he had educated in Scotland, they might be usefully employed as Scripture-readers.  In short, he represented to M. Pyt that, in his opinion the restoration of the old system of Colporteurs would be best adapted to the existing state of France.  At the beginning of the Reformation much good had been done by pious travelling hawkers, and the Colporteurs, sometimes also called porte-paniers, basket-carriers, or travelling booksellers, of the times of Francis I. and Henry II. had materially contributed to the spread of those doctrines, which made such rapid progress before they became mixed up with the schemes of political ambition and the wars of religion.  The idea of renewing the use of the Colporteurs belongs to Robert Haldane.  It was on this account, as M. Chabrand relates, that he sent for M. Pyt, but as soon as the plan was presented to that zealous missionary, it was at once grasped at as a bright thought, and one full of promise for the spiritual regeneration of France.  It was immediately put into execution.  Mr. Haldane also supplied at his own expense detached portions of the Bible, printed for distribution by the Colporteurs, in the form of tracts.  Under Henri Pyt were placed several of these pious men, and the benefits of the system being once discovered, it has since been greatly extended.  When, therefore, the blessed effects of the labours of the Bible Colporteurs in France and Switzerland are mentioned, it ought to be remembered that here, too, we behold one of the results of Robert Haldane's mission to the Continent.

In the Life of Henri Pyt, M. Guers testifies to the strong manner in which Mr. Haldane guarded those over whom he had influence against preaching baptism, or any other disputed tenet, not affecting the foundation of the Gospel. From the time when Pyt visited Montauban, that devoted missionary was convinced "that he ought only to preach Jesus Christ and him crucified, and risen for us." In this respect, says his biographer—

"His views harmonized with those of the venerable Haldane, who had, however, been misinformed by a false report to the contrary, and thus wrote to Pyt: 'In always speaking of baptism, preachers forget their own spiritual misery and the love of the Saviour, and, in fact, are seeking to advance their own peculiar opinions, rather than the edification of the Church of God.'"

For many years Henri Pyt was to the Pyrenees and the Bearne, what another Continental missionary, Felix Neff, was to the Alps of Dauphine, and amongst the Vaudois. Neff, as has been noticed, was one of those called to the knowledge of the Lord at the time of the awakening at Geneva, yet not through the direct instrumentality of Mr. Haldane, but indirectly, through Gonthier and Francois Olivier, of Lausanne, who were his instructors in the faith. MM. Guers, Porchat, L'Huilier, Ladam, Caulier, Calderon, and others of the same school, were also amongst the first labourers of the Continental Society. Seldom has there been an institution which could boast of such missionaries. Still more seldom has there been one so signally owned of God, and so little valued by men.

Many instances might be related of the benediction which followed Mr. Haldane's labours at Montauban. There is one which he has himself recorded. It concerned a pastor in the South of France, who came to visit his brother at La Garde, who had first been partially awakened by M. Gachon, and afterwards more fully instructed and confirmed in the truth by Mr. Haldane. His father, too, an old man of ninety years of age, had listened with joy to the Gospel, as preached by Henri Pyt. He himself was opposed to what he reckoned the fanaticism of Mr. Haldane's doctrines, and he had even succeeded in shaking the faith of his aged parent. During a visit to his brother, he was grieved to hear that brother now speak of salvation by faith without works, but on attempting to enter into controversy, was told, that if he wished to argue on the subject, he had a fine opportunity of doing so with Mr. Robert Haldane. Confident in himself, the indignant pastor obtained an introduction, called on Mr. Haldane, entered into discussion with him, and finally was himself enlightened in the knowledge of the truth. The story is told in Mr. Haldane's own words. It is only needful to observe, that before the conversation, which was so signally blessed to this pastor, another had arisen, out of the inquiry, what was to be his text on the next Lord's-day, and in what manner he was to treat his subject. The pastor relates, that Mr. Haldane asked him how he could reconcile his religious sentiments with a text which he pointed out with his finger. "I replied," says the pastor, "that this was an isolated and extraordinary text." Mr. Haldane then showed me another, equally embarrassing, and turning over his Bible, pointed, with the same index, to fifteen or twenty passages, all directly contradictory of what I going to preach. Not only was I confused at not being able to prove my doctrine from the Bible, but I was astonished at the great facility with which Mr. Haldane found the passages he wanted. When I left him I could not help thinking that perhaps my arguments were right, but that, at all events, Mr. Haldane's seemed to be drawn from the Bible, and I felt that I had too little studied the Scriptures, and had a very imperfect knowledge of their contents. This made me lose confidence in myself, but I did not let him know my distrust. When I next conversed with him, he proposed, after a few moments, that we should take a walk into the country." It is the result of this conversation on the banks of the Tarn that is related by Mr. Haldane :—

"During my stay at Montauban, a French pastor from near Marseilles visited that place. Immediately on his arrival, my friends brought him to visit me, as they were in the habit of doing with pastors who came from different parts of France or Switzerland. We entered directly on the subject of the Gospel. I found him strongly fortified in his opposition to the grace of God; and I learned, that on his journey to Montauban, having heard of the discussions that were agitated there respecting the way of acceptance with God, he had, in various meetings, entered keenly and even violently into the subject, thinking it his duty to oppose, with all the energy he possessed, such a doctrine as that of justification by faith without works. That question, among many others, we discussed fully at our first and subsequent interviews; and I had not encountered one who appeared more decidedly hostile to the truth as it is in Jesus, although he was not an Arian or Socinian, but one who professed to believe in the divinity of Christ. I met him one evening, and proposed that we should walk out together. We immediately entered, as usual, into a discussion respecting the Gospel, each of us maintaining his own sentiments on the subject. At length I began to speak to him on that all-important declaration of the Lord on the cross, ' *It is finished,*' and endeavoured to show from that expression, that everything necessary for a sinner's acceptance with God was already accomplished, and that Christ is the end (the ' finishing' or accomplishment) of the law for righteousness to every one that believeth. I had not spoken but a few minutes, when it pleased God, in infinite goodness and compassion, to shine in his heart, to give him the light of the knowledge of God in the face of Jesus Christ. He suddenly stopped, and, with extended arms, vehemently exclaimed, ' C'EST TROP GRAND POUR ETRE VRAI!' (It is too great to be true!) From that moment there was no more difference of opinion betwixt us— no farther opposition on his part—no more objections. In Christ he was a new creature. Old things had in a moment passed away,—behold, all things had become new. It was now all his desire to hear more of the great salvation. We returned to town holding the most delightful communication. He remarked, with earnestness, how differently he would preach when he should return to his flock. He confessed, at the same time, that he had often preached on texts in which there was something he had not fathomed, ' *aprofondi,*' and that he now knew what it was. This is worthy of notice, as it discovers the unsatisfactory state of mind of many, who, professing to preach the Gospel, understand neither what they say, nor whereof they affirm. He said, he wondered that his people should have had patience to listen to such a system as he had been endeavouring for seven years to inculcate upon them—so totally different from the doctrine of the grace of God. When we parted, he, who an hour before hated and opposed the doctrine of salvation, was filled with peace and joy in believing.

" This happened on Friday evening. Next morning he called on me in the same state of mind I had left him in the evening before, rejoicing in the grace of God; but he said, that after we parted, being engaged to preach on the Lord's-day, he read the sermon he had prepared, and found that not one sentence of it could he preach, for it was altogether opposed to what he was now convinced was the truth of the Gospel.  He added, that he did not know what he should do, for that sermon, the only one he had with him, and which he had admired, being, as he thought, so well composed, he would not and could not on any account make use of, and that he was not accustomed to preach extempore.  I replied, that I never knew a case so similar to his as that of the jailor at Philippi, and therefore advised him to preach on his question to the apostle, and the answer he received: ' What must I do to be saved ?   Believe on the Lord Jesus Christ, and thou shalt be saved.'  After pausing a few moments, he said he would do so.  The place where he preached was at some distance in the country; I did not therefore hear him, but was informed that the people who had known him before, listened with astonishment, wondering that he now preached the faith which so lately he destroyed.  He spoke with great feeling and power, and what he said made a deep impression on those who heard him.  I had afterwards, during the short time he remained at Montauban, most agreeable conversations with him, and shall never forget his prayer when we parted.  It was one of the most affecting I ever heard—evidently the warm effusion of his heart—entirely different from those studied and written prayers which many of the French pastors prepare before they deliver them.  He referred in a very striking manner to his conversion, and to his former and present state ; confessed the great sinfulness of the past part of his ministry, and prayed earnestly for himself and his flock.

" On his return home, he passed through a town (Montpelier) where he preached the same sermon as in the neighbourhood of Montauban.  It came closer on the consciences of his hearers than the discourses to which they had been accustomed to listen.  One of the pastors of the Church (M. Lessignol) preached the Gospel, but with less force.  A flame was instantly kindled among them.  The elders of the Consistory remonstrated with their own pastor in the strongest manner, demanding of him how he could have allowed a man bringing such doctrines to preach for him.  He declared that these doctrines were the same that he himself preached.  They denied this most peremptorily ; and the discovery was now made that some of them were Socinians.  They threatened to denounce their pastor to the Government, and, during more than three months, the greatest agitation prevailed in his Church.  I saw several letters which in the course of that time he wrote to his friends at Montauban, declaring his apprehensions that it would terminate in his being expelled from his charge.  At length, however, the storm subsided, and the preaching of the pastor from the neighbourhood of Marseilles appeared to have done good.

" A very different feeling was excited when the account of his conversion was given to his father, a man above eighty years of age.  I afterwards saw another pastor, who happened to be at his house on a visit.  It was truly affecting, he said, to see the old man quite absorbed in the subject, and for several days going about his house clasping his hands, and joyfully exclaiming, ('It is finished,') 'TOUT EST ACCOMPLI.'"

In another letter, M. Audebez, a well-known French minister, who has been since much in England, connected with the Foreign-Aid Society, wrote to Mr. Haldane, in 1825, to tell him how the pastor just mentioned had become, in the hands of God, the means of awakening him out of spiritual death. After describing himself as having been a blind man leading the blind till the year 1822, Mons. A. proceeds :—

" At the above period, I went to visit my former flock at ——, where I saw, after nine years of separation, one of your spiritual children, my old fellow-student." (The pastor above referred to.) " HE BECAME, IN THE HAND OF GOD, THE INSTRUMENT OF MY DELIVERANCE. I then learned the great mystery of godliness, God manifest in the flesh ; and transported out of myself by the joy of my salvation, I returned to my Church, where since then the Lord has given me grace to render testimony to him, and to advance a little, but very little, in the knowledge of him."

There was less of excitement and *éclat* in Robert Haldane's labours at Montauban than there was at Geneva. He did not meet with so much of direct and public opposition, for the wisdom of M. De Villele's government shielded the Protestants from persecution, and himself from expulsion. Still the work of Evangelization went on prosperously, and whilst his Christian friends acquired fresh confidence and courage, many young students were brought to Christ, many ministers were delivered out of error, and the seed was sown of a future and abundant harvest in France.*

* In " The History of the Protestants of France from the Origin of the Reformation down to the present times," compiled by M. G. de Felice, formerly of Yverdun in Switzerland, but now a Professor at Montauban, there is a studied silence with regard to Mr. Haldane's proceedings at Montauban, and to his writings there published. There was a time when M. de Felice would not have thus ignored the remarkable work of God effected by Mr. Haldane's mission to the Protestants. But like M. Scherer, of Geneva, M. de Felice has unhappily erred from the faith, and having fallen into the snares of Rationalism, he exhibits a melancholy proof of his unhappy state of mind by ignoring facts which as an historian of ordinary candour, he was bound in some way to have noticed whether he

But the term of Mr. Haldane's labours on the Continent was
now approaching.    Mrs. Haldane's venerable father, the late
Mr. Oswald, of Scotstown, was at this time drawing near the
end of his mortal career, and she was naturally anxious to see
him once more before his departure.    Her separation from their
beloved daughter had also been painfully prolonged.    In the
hope of again visiting Montauban at a future time, a hope
never to be realized, Mr. Haldane resolved to return home.
Their journey to Paris was rendered doubly pleasing by the
society of the venerable Dean of the Faculty of Theology,
M. Bonnard, the recollection of whose living faith and affectionate simplicity of heart was always fondly cherished.    On
the rumble of Mr. Haldane's carriage there was another
remarkable person, not then known to fame,—a young converted Jew, who had lately escaped from the Propaganda at
Rome and the fangs of the Inquisition.    It was Joseph Wolff,
the celebrated traveller and missionary, who had been recommended to the protection of Mr. Haldane, and it is not one
of the least remarkable of his exploits, that between Montauban
and Calais, he contrived to learn and speak the French
language.

Mr. Haldane was never again to return to the Continent, or
again to meet his friends at Montauban, but their correspondence proves that the friendship which had been founded on

approved of them or not.    Although professing to describe the *internal*
condition of the Protestants under the restoration, he is equally silent as
to the testimony borne to the truth by MM. Gachon, Bonnard, Chabrand,
and Marzials.    He alludes to Felix Neff, but it is only in the spirit of
hero-worship.    With regard to English books translated into French at
that period, he mentions other writers with great minuteness, including
Miss Kennedy, the late amiable authoress of " Father Clement," "Dun-
allan," and other works of fiction, whilst he is profoundly silent as to the
" Evidences of Christianity," which M. Encontre termed Mr. Haldane's
" Prestantissimum opus," and as to his " *Commentaire* sur L'Epitre aux
Romains."    This is all the more melancholy, as M. de Felice once wrote
ably in defence of the Bible, and to his work entitled " La Voix du
Colporteur" was appropriated part of the last donation given by Mr.
Haldane to his friends at Montauban and Toulouse in the cause of the
Bible.

Christian sympathy was enduring. Ten years afterwards the venerable M. Marzials thus writes to Mr. Haldane :—

" *Montauban, 8th July,* 1831.

" . . . Though I have remained silent so long, a day does not pass without your being present to our minds, or without our conversing about you. Yes, my dear brother, M. De Rapin, M. Bonnard, and I, are never together without recalling with thanksgiving the time you passed in this town, and your example is still a continual encouragement to us to speak in season and out of season according to the truth and Gospel of Christ."

Another letter, written in 1842, on hearing of Mr. Haldane's approaching dissolution, conveys the President's matured experience of the results of the visit to Montauban :—

" We have borne him in our heart ever since the moment when the Lord blessed us by bringing him into the midst of us, and the good which he has done to us, and which is extending more and more in our Church, renders, and will render his name and memory for ever dear. When he first appeared in our town, the Gospel of salvation was in little honour, and its vital doctrines entirely unknown except by a very few, who, encouraged by our venerable brother, frankly announced them in spite of the opposition of unbelief. But thanks be to God, now in this Church, as in a great number of others in our France, the truth of God is preached with power, and without ostensible contradiction. The great majority of pastors are approaching nearer and nearer to the orthodoxy of our fathers, and many among them are truly examples of zeal for the house of God. I am often touched even to tears in seeing pastors, at whose ordination I did not wish to take part, preach Christ, and Christ crucified, with liberty of heart, full of force and blessing. I tell you these things, dear Sir, because it is most certainly the fruit of the good seed sown here and elsewhere by your venerable uncle. Would that we could diminish the number of his years, and see him once more in the midst of us, with his honoured partner in life ! Great would be our joy, and his would be great also. But your letter saddens us. Happily his soul is full of the joy of the Lord. For the rest, he is one of those who cannot occasion a doubtful thought to any of his friends. Yes, he is one of those of whom the Spirit says *for certain,* ' Blessed are the dead which die in the Lord, for they rest from their labours, and their works do follow them.' Tell him all the affection of our heart for his dear person. I include M. Rapin amongst those who recommend themselves to his regard : that dear friend always speaks of Mr. Robert Haldane with affection of heart. Amen.—Receive, &c.

" MARZIALS.

" *Alexander Haldane, Esq.*"

# CHAPTER XX.

MR. and Mrs. Haldane left Montauban about the end of
August, 1819, and arrived in Scotland in the month of
September. His father-in-law, Mr. Oswald, of Scotstown,
whose declining health was the immediate cause of their return,
died soon afterwards, at a very advanced age, deeply regretted.
Shortly afterwards, the death of Captain James Oswald, R.N.,
and of his younger brother, Alexander Oswald, Esq., opened
the succession of the entail of Scotstown to the elder sister of
Mrs. Haldane, and that property could not easily have fallen
into the hands of one more desirous of devoting it to the same
objects in which her sister and brother-in-law were so deeply
interested. Whilst the world was disposed to regard Mr. Haldane's projects only as the ebullitions of "eccentric" zeal, she
knew how to appreciate their untold value. For the sake of
Christ she shared in their reproach, and down to the present
time the name of Miss Oswald, of Scotstown, still continues to
be associated with ardent zeal for the glory of God and the
liberal support of Christian Missions.

Very soon after his return, Mr. Haldane made arrangements

for placing ten Home Missionary students under the instruction of Mr. L. Macintosh, at Grantown, with a view to their itinerating as Home Missionaries in the Highlands of Scotland. But whilst he was not overlooking the claims of his native country, for several years Mr. Haldane was chiefly occupied in promoting the furtherance of the Gospel on the Continent, by means of the Continental Society. His personal acquaintance with France and Switzerland, and his correspondence with Germany, rendered his advice and co-operation of great importance. The Continental Society had always to contend with opposition, chiefly fomented by Arian and Neologian influence abroad. But its missionaries were men like Felix Neff, Henri Pyt, and Francois Olivier, who, for the most part, had been confessors of Christ, and felt in their inmost soul that Gospel which, in the midst of dangers, discouragement, and toil, it was their joy to proclaim. Well may M. Guers exclaim, when looking back on the fifteen years of its existence, " The day of Christ will tell what it did for the glory of the Lord."

In Edinburgh, an active Auxiliary was formed, in the spring of 1821, through the influence of Mr. Haldane, and a public Meeting was held at the Waterloo Rooms, where he himself, for the first time after the lapse of many years, addressed a promiscuous assembly. He spoke with great force, and was listened to with the deepest attention. His details respecting the past and existing state of religion on the Continent were highly interesting, and his views as to the necessity for the combined co-operation of Christians, irrespective of denominational differences for ever swept away the false impressions which had been produced during the heat of controversy with regard to the Congregational Churches. His early friend, the Rev. Dr. Campbell, formerly of Kippen, near Stirling, but then of the Tolbooth Church, was present, and made an able speech, in which he furnished out of his own stores of information some lamentable details as to the Infidelity of Geneva. But nothing in that speech was so interesting as the allusions made by this venerable minister of Christ to the interest with which he had marked Mr. Haldane's course, from the happy days spent in his society at Airthrey, when first entering on his Christian career, down to the period of that successful warfare, which single-handed he had waged in a foreign land with Arianism and Infidelity. The crowded assembly went away at once interested and instructed. None seemed more impressed than Mr. Haldane's old friend, Mr. Aikman, who, as he walked along Princes-street with one of the nearest relatives of his former associates, seemed, by his brief exclamations, to express a new pang at the recollection of the disruption, which might have been less complete had he and his friends listened to the united wishes of the two brothers pleading for mutual forbearance.

During the summer of 1821, Mr. Haldane made a journey to London, unaccompanied by Mrs. Haldane, with a view to set in order some matters connected with the establishment of the Continental Society, and particularly to meet two of his students at Geneva, MM. Gonthier and Guers, who had come to London, to receive the ordination which had been denied them at Geneva. With these excellent men he spent much of his time, reading with them, and expounding the Scriptures. M. Guers mentions that he generally selected the whole of an Epistle, or some large portion of Scripture, instead of fragments, for the subject of their mutual conversation. At this period he again met Mr. Wilberforce, who for several years enlivened the Annual Meetings of the Continental Society with the charms of his melodious eloquence. Of that Society, M. Guers writes, many years after its extinction :—

" It was, in 1818, the first to carry the Gospel into the North of France, and then into the South, and then into the centre. Wherever its missionaries went they found nothing but spiritual death, and in the hands of the Lord they became for multitudes the instruments of life and salvation. The Society with courage and success passed through the reign of Jesuitism in France, that period of unhappy memory, during which the Government of Charles X., making a noiseless war against the religious movement, laboured everywhere to plant the banner of Rome. In spite of every difficulty, the Continental Society, which was the only Society engaged in the evangelization of France, humbly proceeded with its work, under the protection of the Lord."

M. Guers proceeds to trace the progress and downfall of the

Continental Society, which he attributes to Irvingism. But he is not quite accurate as to the details so far as concerns Britain. In Paris it was always the object of jealousy—a jealousy natural to the Arian, Pelagian, and Arminian enemies of the Gospel—a jealousy which was also fostered by English influence, seeking a pre-eminence which, in the first ages of Christianity, characterized Diotrephes. It was also attacked by some, who were not ashamed to complain of the banished Swiss as *foreigners*, and therefore not adapted for the office of evangelists in France, from which their ancestors were refugees. But it was chiefly opposed on a ground that artfully appealed to High Church prejudices in England ; namely, that the preachers had no right to go into the parishes of other ministers, even although nothing but Socinianism or Neology was taught. A remonstrance, embodying these complaints, together with some instances of trifling indiscretions, was at one time got up in Paris, and signed by a formidable array of Lutheran and Reformed Pastors, chiefly Arians or Neologians, as well as Peers of France, members of the Chambers, and even agents of the British and Foreign Bible Society. To this document, Mr. Haldane, on the invitation of the London Committee, prepared a powerful and crushing reply, asserting, from the Word of God, the right of the evangelists to preach the Gospel wherever a door was opened, and warning the remonstrants against the criminality of fighting against God, and trying to stop the progress of the truth. There were, no doubt, some who signed that unworthy remonstrance from Paris, who did so under mis-conception, and the influence of more designing men. It failed, however, of its object of destroying the Society, and the counte-nance which men like Henri Pyt and the two Oliviers derived in Paris from the Rev. Lewis Way, the Rev. Mr. Lovett, and other men of God, went far to neutralize the influence which sought to arrest its useful operations in France. But the chief and most formidable opposition to the missionaries sent out by the Continental Society was to be found in the Foreign Bible Societies, which were at that time overrun with Neology and unbelief. There is no doubt that in too many instances these

institutions constituted at that period what has been termed
"an organized hypocrisy," and had no love for the Gospel
revealed in the Scriptures. To these, therefore, the preaching
of the truth was odious, and they did what they could to
prejudice the minds of British Christians against men, of many
of whom it is now known that "the world was not worthy."

It is not necessary to pursue the history of the decline and
fall of the Continental Society. Had it not been enfeebled
through the unmitigated hostility it experienced abroad, it
would not have been left to perish in the distrust inspired
by the errors or ephemeral extravagances of a section of its
supporters—extravagances which did not infect its missionaries
or taint its foreign operations. But it had nobly done its
Master's work, and that work was subsequently carried on,
first by its original Auxiliaries in Scotland,* which under Mr.
Haldane's advice, had wisely assumed independent action; and
finally, by the Sociétés Evangeliques of Geneva and Paris, after
the whirlwind of the Bible Society controversy had cleared the
atmosphere, and by exposing the character of pretended friends
to the cause of the Bible, left the evangelization of the Continent in the hands of men of God, instead of being intrusted to
those who either combined in Bible Societies abroad, for the
sake of fashion, or to attain their own selfish objects.

On Mr. Haldane's journey from London to Scotland, in 1821,
he was induced to stay a few days at Leicester, for the sake of
conversing with the celebrated Robert Hall, and also with the
amiable and accomplished Mr. Vaughan, who had not then
adopted those peculiar opinions, which he is said to have
regretted on his death-bed. Mr. Hall often spoke with deep
interest of this visit. "He is a remarkable man,—a very
remarkable man," was his observation. He also noticed that

* Dr. Struthers, in his History of the Relief Church, imagines that the
institution of provincial Societies in Scotland, separate from the London
Continental Society, was a proof of a design on the part of the Established
Church in Scotland to obtain an ascendancy. The truth was, that the
separation was made in the hope of averting what Mr. Haldane foresaw
as an impending danger, the interference of Irvingism.

before he met Mr. Haldane he had never fully understood the force of the Apostle's argument in Romans ii. 6—10.

After Mr. Haldane's journey to London in 1820, he was prevailed on to visit Ireland in the following year, with the view of exciting an interest on behalf of the Continental Society. He took with him M. Mejanel, who had lately arrived from France. In Dublin he met his old friend, Mr. Kelly, and other Christians of various denominations, both Churchmen and Dissenters, from whom he received every token of affectionate respect. In particular, he had much pleasure in a visit to Powerscourt, in witnessing the ardent zeal for the truth which animated the heart of the noble proprietor, whose brief career of Christian devotedness was soon to terminate. From Powerscourt Mr. Haldane went to Tullamore Park, on the invitation of the Earl and Countess of Roden; and during his residence at that beautiful place, had an opportunity of preaching on the Lord's-day in their domestic chapel, to an overflowing congregation, which blocked up both its doors and windows. In private, every morning after breakfast, for six successive days, he expounded the Epistle to the Romans, to a small circle, who heard with deep interest those edifying and comprehensive views of Divine doctrine which he knew so well how to enunciate. Amongst those who then listened to the truths which dropped from his lips, was the late Lady Anne Jocelyn, the beloved sister of Lord Roden, who was in an eminent degree partaker of the same precious faith which enriches her noble brother, but who was speedily to be removed from amongst the worshippers below, to join in the song of the redeemed before the throne of God and the Lamb. In the next year, Mr. Haldane had the pleasure of receiving Lord Roden at his own house at Auchingray, and a clergyman who accompanied his Lordship preached there on the Lord's-day. It was probably the first sermon from an Episcopalian divine ever heard by that congregation, who were for the most part the descendants of the west country Covenanters.

The following extract of a letter, written in June, 1822,

contains a short but interesting account of Mr. Haldane's visit
to Ireland :—

" I received last night a letter from my friend in Ireland, mentioning
with great delight a visit which Dublin had lately received from Mr.
Robert Haldane.    He was accompanied by a M. Mejanel, a French
minister, with whom —— was also much pleased.    Mr. Haldane has been
wonderfully useful among the clergy on the Continent.    Mr. Kelly told
him, on the authority of M. Mejanel, that it is calculated that more than
sixty ministers had been converted by his means in France and Switzerland.    My friend says, ' He spent one morning with us, and we also met
him twice.    He spoke on the Scriptures with very great power and judgment.    Indeed, he seems to have drank deeply at the fountain of knowledge.    He is not a clergyman, but our clergy were delighted to sit at his
feet, and they gave him the lead wherever he went.' "

Mr. Haldane could not regard what he saw of the lamentable
state of Ireland, without feeling a desire to do something to
promote its regeneration, and he strongly stated his opinion
that this would never be accomplished but by the aggressive
power of the Gospel.    He therefore urged that some combined
effort should be made to send preachers into the Romish
districts, to break up the fallow ground, and to publish those
truths which are mighty through God to the pulling down of
strongholds.    But the Lord's time was not yet come, and his
efforts were in vain, although at first supported by laymen of
great influence.    The idea of proselytizing was treated as chime-
rical, and as likely to be attended with dangerous consequences.
A few years afterwards, Ireland was visited by another champion
of the faith, the well-known Captain J. E. Gordon, who in the
following letter describes in his own case the very arguments
with which Mr. Haldane's previous remonstrances had been
parried.    Mr. Haldane's plan contemplated the mission of
preachers without reference to Episcopacy or Presbytery, just
as the Continental Society was employing agents in France.
Mr. Gordon's plan was to have been carried out in connexion
with the Established Church.    The details are curious, and
worthy of being preserved :—

                              " *Hadlow House, March* 23, 1852.

" The entire period of my connexion with Ireland, extending to not less than two years, was occupied with one continuous and sustained effort to introduce the Reformation into that country, or, in other words, to prompt just such an aggressive effort, upon the part of the Establishment, as she is now exerting with such success in the provinces of Connaught and Munster. As that Church, however, had then discharged herself from all responsibility with respect to the Roman Catholic part of the population, there was not merely the *vis inertiæ* of ignorance and apathy to overcome, but a conventional opposition to such an effort, founded upon the conviction, that any interference with the Roman Catholic population would be a transgression of the limits of pastoral jurisdiction. All, therefore, which I found it possible to accomplish, was the promotion of controversy, through the platform and the pulpit, when practicable, and that movement it was, under God, which gave the initial tendency to the progress of inquiry in the Irish mind. Not satisfied, however, with such random and partial efforts, I conceived the design of a mission, which should act independently of local authority and local obstruction. Being acquainted with Lord Liverpool, then Prime Minister, and in the habit of confidential communication with him upon the religious and moral condition of Ireland, I proposed to him the establishment of a mission, under the Royal authority, upon the same principle as that authorized by Edward VI.,—a mission consisting of a body of evangelical, zealous, energetic clergymen, who should traverse the length and breadth of the country, and occupy either the pulpit or the court-house, as might best suit their purpose.

" His Lordship was much struck with the proposition, but said that it would entirely depend upon the degree of countenance it might receive from the Irish Church, and that it must appear to come from that quarter. I told his Lordship, that I possessed an intimate acquaintance with Dr. Magee, Archbishop of Dublin, and that I had very little doubt of his countenance in the scheme. ' If,' said his Lordship, ' you can secure the sanction of that Prelate, his influence would be sufficient to carry it through the difficulties it would have to encounter from the Church on this side of the water.' I lost no time in putting myself in communication with Dr. Magee, whose capacious intellect and active zeal immediately grasped and adopted the proposition in all its bearings, and he assured me that he would do everything which his situation might enable him to do in favour of the design. Thus stood the matter when, in the mysterious providence of God, Lord Liverpool was removed from office, and became politically defunct, and the Archbishop was soon after summoned from his labours to his rest.

" Believe me, very sincerely yours,

" J. E. GORDON.

" *A. Haldane, Esq.*"

Once more it was seen that the Lord's time was not come; and although this does not excuse the opposition to any aggressive action on the part of the Church, yet the ground was being prepared by the preaching of such admirable home missionaries as the Very Rev. Denis Brown, and by such institutions as the Irish Society. At last, however, after a battle too long conducted on defensive principles, the Rev. A. Dallas was honoured boldly to conduct the onward movement, which God has blessed so as to silence the cavils of objectors, astonish the unbelieving world, provoke the zeal of many, and fill the hearts of Christians with wondering joy, causing them to exclaim, " What hath God wrought !"

In the winter of 1821-2 Mr. Haldane had been engaged for some weeks in a way not accordant with his usual habits. It had been his brother's custom, and one of the proofs of his unwearied zeal, always to seek an interview with prisoners in gaol, when under sentence of death. His labours in the very first case which he attended, in 1799, at the beginning of his career, seemed to have been blessed, and there were several others in which there was reason to hope that the word had not been spoken in vain. In fact, during the time when our criminal code was so sanguinary, its only redeeming feature was to be found in the opportunity which it gave to the unhappy criminal solemnly to consider his state in the sight of God, and ask for mercy through the only appointed channel. In November, 1821, two prisoners, the one a Swede, Peter Heaman, and the other a Frenchman, Francois Gautier, were tried for murder and piracy on the high seas, and convicted. The vessel in which they sailed had on board a quantity of specie, and the captain was the only obstacle in the way of the crew's obtaining the prize. This was sometimes referred to in jest, but at last the foul deed was committed; the captain and one of the crew murdered; and the vessel and cargo seized by Peter Heaman and his comrades. They were afterwards all captured, and two of the ringleaders justly condemned. It was the duty of Dr. Campbell, according to rotation, to attend these convicts, and, being foreigners, he requested of Mr. Robert Haldane, with reference to the language, the aid which he willingly rendered. In regard to the Frenchman, Gautier, there was nothing peculiarly satisfactory, and he was attended to the scaffold by a Romish priest; but in the case of Heaman, there was strong reason to conclude that he received repentance to believe the truth. He was a man of intelligence and some education, and sketch of his life, written by himself, was afterwards published as a tract, "with remarks by J. Campbell, D.D., and an account of him in the gaol, and at his execution, by Robert Haldane, Esq." The narrative of Heaman bears the stamp of sincerity and deep contrition, whilst the prefixed notices of two men so eminent as the editors could not fail to attract attention. It was satisfactory to Mr. Haldane to find that the Judges expressed an opinion that this tract was free from those objections which too often apply to the accounts of converted criminals.

Dr. Campbell's remarks are valuable, as pointing to the power of the devil as a tempter in leading ungodly men into crime. Mr. Haldane's details of the conversion of Heaman are remarkable as a short and comprehensive compendium of the Gospel, exhibiting the lost condition of man and the way of salvation in language at once clear, powerful, and well supported by Scripture :—

" When he began to converse with Heaman he did not dwell on his particular crime, excepting in so far as it was a proof of the depravity of his heart. When Heaman urged his occupation at sea as an apology for the neglect of religion, he was told that the person talking to him practically knew the life of a sailor, and considered that occupation anything rather than an excuse for neglecting the salvation of God. Nowhere was there a better opportunity for reading the Scriptures, for meditating on them, and holding communion with God; and nowhere was there a louder call to exercise habitual dependence on God than on board of ship. There, too, vice often appeared in forms so gross as to render it peculiarly odious, and, consequently, more easily restricted and overcome than when it presented itself in shapes more alluring and seductive, because more refined and disguised.

" The Gospel was then stated to Heaman. The atonement made by Christ is complete. His righteousness is applied to every individual of the human race who is united to Christ by faith. For the great purpose of sanctification, the outpouring of the Spirit is obtained through the mediation of Christ. Heaman was shown, in the words of Luther, that 'if I were to work to eternity on the plan of reformation and self-justification, I could never find rest to my conscience, for I should never be certain that I had done enough.'"

At the end of another conversation to the same effect, Heaman said that he felt "lightened," and that this was "good news, indeed;" and that he had never before met a single person who presented to him such views of the Gospel. It was after this that he made his confession, and, in token of his true penitence, gave up a sum of money which he had the full opportunity of leaving to his wife and family. For eight days before his death his countenance indicated a settled peace, and his composure continued to the last. On the scaffold there was no hardened indifference to death, nor any of that levity and trifling which miscalled philosophers have affected.

"He appeared," says Mr. Haldane, "to be properly sensible of his situation as a criminal justly condemned by the laws of God and man, and as an immortal creature who was about to appear before his final Judge. At the same time there was a dignified composure visible in his deportment, as of one who knew in whom he had believed, and whose feet were placed on a rock that stood immoveable, against which the threatening billows that beat around him dashed in vain.

"Part of the fifty-first Psalm was sung, and a very impressive address delivered by Dr. Campbell. Heaman, after bowing to the spectators, confirmed the Reverend Clergyman's statements. Mr. Haldane remarked to him, that this was a large assembly, but that, in a few minutes, he would see a very different one,—the innumerable company of angels, the general assembly of the spirits of just men made perfect, and Jesus Christ Himself. He expressed his humble conviction that this would be the case. These triumphant words were then suggested,—' O death, where is thy sting? O grave, where is thy victory? The sting of death is sin, and the strength of sin is the law; but thanks be to God, which giveth me the victory through our Lord Jesus Christ.'" Mr. Haldane's narrative proceeds:—"He repeated them aloud, with great earnestness. An ejaculatory petition was put up by one (Mr. Haldane) standing by, that God would receive his departing spirit. He then prostrated himself on his face on the scaffold, and continued for a short time in secret prayer.

"Everything being ready, for the execution, he asked if he should yet be allowed time to pray. He was assured it should be granted, and a handkerchief was given him, as the signal both for himself and his fellow-prisoner, to be dropped when all was ready. A cap was placed on his head to cover his face, and the rope was placed round his neck. With an unfaltering voice, and with great apparent earnestness, he then uttered a very suitable prayer. It consisted chiefly of those parts of the fifty-first Psalm, which had just been sung, that were most applicable to his case, and of the part of the 130th Psalm, beginning, 'Out of the depths have I cried unto thee, O Lord;' then of the twenty-third Psalm, of which he distinctly repeated, 'Yea, though I walk through the valley of the shadow of death, I will fear no evil; for thou art with me.' In that awful moment, on the brink of eternity, with the fatal rope round his neck, it might have been supposed that his thoughts would have been entirely absorbed in his own situation, and that, as soon as he had finished his prayer, he would have made the signal, but even then a proof of self-possession and of feeling consideration for his fellow-sufferer was exhibited, to which it will not be easy to find a parallel. With perfect seeming composure he turned to him his face, covered as it was, and said, 'Francois, do you wish to pray?' Afterwards he himself resumed his supplications. Having expressed his entire confidence in his Redeemer, distinctly repeating these emphatic words, 'I know whom I have believed, and am persuaded that He is able to keep that which I have committed unto Him,' and having resigned himself into His gracious hands, saying, 'Lord Jesus, receive my spirit,' he threw the handkerchief to the side of the scaffold, in a manner which seemed to indicate that he was not only ready, but willing, to depart."

The course of the narrative has of late chiefly concerned the elder brother. Meanwhile James Haldane was enabled to hold on the even tenor of his way, neither elevated by the excitement of popularity, nor depressed by isolation. In 1820, having occasion to visit Liverpool, he availed himself of the opportunity to cross over to the Isle of Man, where he preached to large and attentive congregations. To the last he had many seals to his ministry, and, except at the very commencement of his career, there was no period at which his usefulness was more remarkable, than at that which followed the disruption of the Tabernacle connexion. To his own success he hardly ever alluded, but, in writing to Mr. Campbell, of Kingsland, in 1809, he says, "We were told that 'the world' would leave us, that no good would be done, and that there would be an end of usefulness. But numbers still attend (he, doubtless, meant in the afternoon and evening), and we have received more converts from ' the world ' than for four years previously." But the good of which he was instrumental will not be known till the books shall be opened on the day of the gathering round the great white throne. We are told that, in that day, there shall be a bright diadem for those who have turned many to righteousness ; and that this honour was reserved for James Haldane, long after he ceased to itinerate and preach to wondering thousands, is proved by many authentic testimonies. Amongst others, it is stated on the authority of persons still living, including Mr. Aikman's sister, that Dr. Jones, who had one of the largest districts in Edinburgh, but who had been much prejudiced against the Circus and Tabernacle, candidly acknowledged, that, in examining candidates for admission to his half-yearly communions, he had found a greater number of instances of awakenings attributed to the preaching of Mr. James Haldane than to that of any other preacher in Edinburgh. The same testimony was borne by the celebrated Dr. Andrew Thomson, and it agrees with an anecdote resting on the authority of a venerable minister in England, who states that, in a conversation with Dr. M'Crie, they were discussing the merits of various preachers, when that eminent historian and theologian observed, that, in his opinion, Mr. James Haldane preached the doctrine of free justification through faith more fully and more clearly than any other minister he knew.

At the end of 1819 their mother's last surviving sister died. She was the mother of Admiral Haldane Tait, and of three other sons, one of whom was long numbered amongst the most esteemed ministers in Edinburgh. The third son, who was well known, both in the counties of Perth and Forfar, as the resident manager of the Earl of Camperdown's estates, dated his conversion to his conversations with Mr. James Haldane, and to a tract which he had recommended, intituled, " Three Dialogues between a Clergyman and his Parishioners." Mr. James Haldane's attention to his dying aunt was another illustration of his character. During the last weeks of her life it was unremitting.

Besides his daily morning visits to her house, whatever were his engagements, and how late soever he had been occupied by prayer-meetings, Church meetings, or preaching,—whatever was the hour or weather; both on the week-days and the Lord's-days, he never failed to walk to her house, in order that he might pray beside her bed and comfort her with some of the precious promises of the Gospel.   It was in these things, in his domestic circle, amongst his friends, and in his private as much as in public engagements, that he exhibited one of the brightest examples of that pure and undefiled religion which consists in visiting the widow and the fatherless, and keeping himself unspotted from the world.   He was a man who never acted a part or seemed to be what he was not.   His character, both in public and private, was earnest and truthful.   The more closely his walk was surveyed, the more did it appear that his steps were ordered of the Lord, and that he himself adorned the doctrines which he so fervently believed and faithfully preached.

For five years he conducted the " Scripture Magazine," which contained many valuable elucidations of the Word of God, both critical and expository, of different works that appeared on disputed points.   Its chief object was to establish the grand truths of the Gospel, and it contains, amongst other valuable essays from his own pen, and " notes on Scripture," a series of articles which he once thought of consolidating into a volume, under the title of the " Revelation of Mercy."   They were intended to illustrate the gradual unfolding of the great scheme of redemption, from the garden of Eden to the garden of Gethsemane; to have followed its development through all its successive stages, from the promise made to the first Adam, after his fall, to.the moment when the great work of the second Adam was finished on Mount Calvary.   He particularly intended to show the inseparable union between the Old Testament and the New; how Jesus Christ lives and breathes in every page of the sacred volume; how his righteousness was alike exhibited in the types of the Mosaic ceremonial and the Levitical sacrifices, in the shadowy grandeur of ancient prophecy, and the wonderful history of the Jewish economy.   The design of publishing this volume was never accomplished, but he afterwards printed a valuable little tract, intituled, "The Revelation of God's Righteousness," embodying an epitome of his views. After being out of print for nearly thirty years, a third edition was lately published, on the recommendation of some very competent judges, who have expressed their obligations to that treatise, as having enlarged their views of the wonderful connexion between the Old and New Testaments.*

In 1819 he wrote some very able "Strictures on a Publication upon Primitive Christianity, by Mr. John Walker, formerly Fellow of Dublin College." Mr. Walker had assumed the principle that a mere profession of belief was all that was required to constitute a claim to Christianity, and that, if a brother professed repentance after an offence, he was to be restored, "although they should have the next day to accompany that brother to the gallows;" and that this was to be their duty and their rule, although such a professing brother should commit the same offence seventy times seven. Mr. Walker was a great scholar, and a clergyman from whom much had been expected; but as Mr. James Haldane observes, although he seemed likely "to run well," he had been "hindered," and whilst he grievously mistook our Lord's rules of discipline by applying the law intended solely for personal quarrels between brethren to the case of questions as to the evidences of Christian character, he also took a false view of faith, after the manner of the Sandemanians, leaving out of account the responsibility of man, and admitting the inspired test of faith, which Mr. James Haldane adopts as the motto of his "Strictures:" "Little children, let no man deceive you; he that *doeth* righteousness is righteous, even as he is righteous." The venerable Mr. Jay, of Bath, in writing to the late Mr. Robert Spear, in 1804, says of James Haldane: "I was much pleased to hear his views of faith, although I was obliged to oppose them in order to hear them." Mr. Walker's erroneous views on this subject drew him out in print, and showed the

* "The Revelation of God's Righteousness." By the late J. A. Haldane. London: Nisbet and Co. Edinburgh: Whyte and Co.

consistency with which he continued to hold the sentiments which, fifteen years before, had attracted the notice of Mr. Jay. Like one able rightly to divide the Word of God, and who had drank deep into the Spirit of Christ, Mr. James Haldane exposed those errors which had tempted Glas and Sandeman into others of an opposite and more dangerous kind. Some of the good old writers, in order to guard against self-deception, had so veiled the shield of faith as to have dimmed the brightness of its glory.

" Saving faith," he says, " was defined so as to include every holy disposition, and there was no small danger of men being led to establish their own righteousness under the name of faith. Glas and Sandeman boldly opposed the popular doctrine, and asserted that faith is simply the belief of the truth. But, ' in guarding against self-righteousness ' they ridiculed ' heart religion,' and encouraged, in some respects, a very improper laxity of conduct."

The whole of the discussion is important. The glory and simplicity of faith is, on the one hand, vindicated from the error of those who would interpose something between the sinner and Christ, and, on the other, from the still more dangerous extreme of making the profession of a mere intellectual act, unaccompanied by any change of heart, a title to salvation. The sovereignty of God and the responsibility of man were two doctrines which the Haldanes never tried to reconcile, but both of which they fully and strongly taught :—

" No man who is not warped by a system will hesitate to use the language of Scripture : ' Seek ye the Lord while he may be found; call ye upon him while he is near. Let the wicked forsake his way, and the unrighteous man his thoughts, and let him return unto the Lord, and he will have mercy upon him, and to our God, for he will abundantly pardon.' But Mr. Walker is so apprehensive of self-righteousness that he seems afraid of anything resembling those tender and pathetic expostulations so frequent in the inspired volumes. To inadequate views of human responsibility I attribute, in a great measure, that harshness and severity which characterize the writings of Mr. Walker."

In 1822, Mr. James Haldane was called to sympathize with his friend, Dr. Stuart, on the melancholy occasion so well known to the world, when his son, Mr. James Stuart, was involved in

a political duel, in which he killed Sir Alexander Boswell, the
son of the celebrated biographer of Dr. Johnson.    At that time
party ran high in Edinburgh.    It was the crisis of a long
protracted struggle between the Tories and the Whigs, or
Liberals.    The Tories had for so many years exercised a paramount influence in Scotland, which had been for some time
declining.    Mr. James Stuart, who was one of the earliest and
most intimate friends of Lord Brougham, had taken a leading
part on the side of the Whigs, whose great political organ and
rallying point had been the "Edinburgh Review."    In 1819-20
he had been bitterly lampooned in the "Sentinel," a weekly
political journal set up in Edinburgh about the same time that
the "John Bull" had been established in London.    A quarrel
amongst the publishers induced one of them to betray the
secrets of the contributors, and disclosed Sir Alexander Boswell
as the satirist of Mr. Stuart as a coward.    A duel followed, of
which an account is given in the following letter.    It is needless
to say that Mr. James Stuart had then at least no sympathy
with his venerable parent's religious sentiments :—

"*Edinburgh, April* 6, 1822.
"    .    .    .    Dr. Stuart is pretty well, but much distressed.    Boswell
said, after he received his wound, that Stuart could not have acted
otherwise.    It was a singular coincidence, that after Boswell was
wounded, and carried to Lord Balmuto's, his Lordship showed (Sir)
George Wood, who had gone as his surgeon, different rooms, that he
might choose where he should be laid.    He fixed on one, and that very
day a picture of Lord Auchinleck, Boswell's grandfather, had come from
Edinburgh to Balmuto, and it was removed from the bed on which it had
been laid to make room for the grandson.    When Boswell first got Lord
Rosslyn's message he was a good deal agitated, suspecting what it referred
to, and told his wife.    She sent for Baron Hume, and, in consequence of
his advice, the Sheriff's warrant was obtained.    This, however, only
extended to the county of Edinburgh, and probably rather hastened the
catastrophe.    Douglas (afterwards Marquis of Queensberry), Boswell's
second, called for him at three in the morning, and told him the thing
was blown, and not a moment was to be lost.    They immediately set off
for Fife.    Boswell, it is said, asked Douglas if he ought to fire.    This
question Douglas declined answering ; and it is said he did not mean to
fire, but his pistol went off when he received his wound.    .    .    .    Boswell,
instead of raising his pistol when the signal was given, was holding it up

over his head, and thus exposed himself.  Had not this been the case, he would probably have received the ball in his arm.  George Bell (the surgeon), whom I met at your uncle's last night, told me this.  Into what difficulties do men plunge themselves when they forsake the Divine authority!  As soon as that is lost sight of they think themselves obliged to do what they feel and know to be most improper.  They are shut up to risk their own lives, and, perhaps, to murder their fellow-creatures.  Truly the way of transgressors is hard."

Rather more than three years after the removal of his first wife, Mr. James A. Haldane formed a second union.  On the 23d of April, 1822, he married Margaret Rutherford, a daughter of the late well-known physician and Professor of Botany in the University of Edinburgh, Dr. Daniel Rutherford, the maternal uncle of Sir Walter Scott.  The second Mrs. James Haldane was thus the cousin-german of the celebrated poet.  In all things she was like-minded with her husband, the value of whose exalted excellencies she thoroughly appreciated, whilst her own amiable and valuable qualities contributed to render the union happy and prosperous.  Down to the last hour of his mortal life it was her constant study to minister to his comfort and promote that of his family.

In the summer of 1824, Rowland Hill revisited Scotland for the first time since his tour in 1799.  The Circus no longer existed as a place of worship.  The Tabernacle, although still spacious, was curtailed in its dimensions, but he once more preached for both of his old friends, Mr. James Haldane and Mr. Aikman, to congregations of more than 1,200 persons.  Although no longer able to make his voice heard on the Calton Hill by 20,000 hearers, his spirit was unchanged, as is evinced in the following letter :—

"*London, 29th May,* 1824.

" MY DEAR SIR,—It is with the sincerest gratitude and thankfulness I return my most grateful acknowledgments to you for your affectionate invitation to your hospitable abode.

" There is a gratification in seeing and conversing with old friends peculiar to itself, and arising among living Christians from their union with Christ, whereby all his members are made one with each other, as being one in him, while to love the image of Christ, as we see it upon our fellow-mortals, is one of the brightest evidences that we have been beloved by him.

" While I lament that the Lord has taken from you your late beloved partner, yet I trust you will prove, by your present union, that he has repaired the breach. Little did I think when I was last in Scotland—now, I believe, three-and-twenty years ago—that I should yet live. Within the short space of a few weeks from hence, and I shall enter the eightieth year of my age, and though no wonder that I feel not as I once was, yet I ought to be very thankful that I am as I am.

" Some of my old friends in Scotland, I suppose, are still remaining. To such I beg my most cordial love and respects. Oh! that we may be kept from declining in spirituality in our declining days, blest with an ardent desire to work as long as we can work, and longing for still brighter evidences of that glory that shall be revealed.

" Mrs. Hill returns grateful thanks for Mrs. Haldane's kind invitation, though she does not accept it; and be assured, dear Sir, that I can subscribe myself, yours, very affectionately and sincerely,

" *Rev. James A. Haldane.*"            " ROWLAND HILL."

Nine years later, on the 23d April, 1833, Mr. James Haldane thus writes :—

" Rowland Hill has finished his course. His life has been very long, and he has maintained a most consistent character. Everything here is fleeting and transitory. The vanity to which all things are subjected is modified by circumstances, and assumes various appearances, but still it is but vanity. Creation is travailing in pain for that glorious day when the mystery of God shall be finished, when his children shall be manifested, and his righteous judgment revealed. The cloud now spread over creation by the introduction of sin, will then be dispersed, or rather, it will form the shade which shall give prominence to the picture. It will no longer appear a blot upon the Divine workmanship, but will be seen to have been the occasion of the grandest display of the wisdom, power, and goodness of God, and, consequently, to have in the highest degree advanced the happiness of all his obedient creatures. Satan had established a kingdom whose foundations appeared immoveable. Mankind had come under the curse, and the immutability, as well as the truth and justice of God, seemed to preclude the possibility of its reversal; but Satan was taken in his own snare, his usurpation was overturned, and he himself made the unwilling instrument of exhibiting the manifold wisdom of God. The angels now desire to look into the mystery of the Incarnation, but then the curtain will rise, and the glory of the consummated plan of redemption, in all its unrivalled splendour, will burst upon the universe. May we live under the influence of this animating prospect!"

# CHAPTER XXI.

IMPORTANCE OF THE APOCRYPHA CONTROVERSY AS INVOLV-
ING THE CANON OF SCRIPTURE—ITS ORIGIN IN 1821—
FAILURE OF MR. HALDANE'S PACIFIC ENDEAVOURS—
REV. JOHN OWEN — VIBRATING RESOLUTIONS — FIRST
EDINBURGH STATEMENT — CAMBRIDGE PROTEST — MR.
SIMEON AND MR. GORHAM—DOUBTS AS TO THE SACRED
CANON—MR. HALDANE'S FIRST REVIEW—TOULOUSE AND
MONTAUBAN BIBLES—SECOND EDINBURGH STATEMENT
—CHARACTER OF DR. ANDREW THOMSON — DR. STEIN-
KOPFF'S PAMPHLETS—MR. HALDANE'S SECOND REVIEW
—HAFFNER'S PREFACE—M. BOST—FOREIGN BIBLE SOCIE-
TIES OPPOSE THE PREACHERS OF THE GOSPEL — DR.
GORDON'S TESTIMONY—LETTER OF MR. HALDANE.

[1821—26.]

FROM the year 1816, to the close of the year 1824, Mr.
Haldane's chief efforts had been directed towards the Continent
of Europe, with that intense earnestness and concentration of
purpose which always characterized his plans and operations.
But at the end of 1824, he was called on to gird himself for a
new contest, and one which was far more painful, as it was not
merely with Arians, Socinians, or Neologians, but with some
whom he loved and honoured as fellow-labourers in the Gospel
of Christ.

In approaching the Bible Society controversy, the difficulties
of the subject stand out in strong relief. But truth cannot
suffer from discussion; and nothing is more remote from the
design of this volume than to stir the embers of a smouldering
fire. In a Life of Robert Haldane it would, however, be impossible to omit all reference to what he deemed his most important
work. Even if silence were attempted, it would be rebuked by

recollections too sacred to be forgotten.  Only a few days before his death, after a calm and solemn review of the principal events of his life, he himself, when thus standing on the confines of the eternal world, intimated his wish that at some period, although not till a few years should have elapsed, an account should be written of the Bible Society controversy.  He thought that it would be useful to preserve such a record, that Christians might better understand the immense importance of the subject in debate, involving as it did the Divine authority of the holy Scriptures, and the integrity of the sacred canon, as well as the principles on which it was lawful to associate and act with unbelievers for the circulation of the Bible.  Ten years have passed away since this injunction was given, and in the interval most of those who were implicated in that arduous contest have disappeared from the busy scene of mortal life.  Many of the evils against which Mr. Haldane, Dr. Thomson, and their compeers, warred, have since been entirely removed, and the rest greatly abated.  The British and Foreign Bible Society has been every year approaching nearer and nearer to those principles of Christian simplicity, a departure from which at one time involved its administrators in much that was embarrassing, and not a little that was sinful.  The majesty of the Word of God is no longer insulted by the intermixture or addition of Apocryphal fables, or the writings of lying prophets.  Although some of the Foreign Societies still pursue this unhallowed course, and even now contain in their Committees the enemies of the Gospel, yet the British representatives of the Society abroad are not now, as formerly, in alliance with Infidels, Socinians, or persecutors.  Romish priests, receiving unacknowledged salaries, no longer exhibit the contradictory marvel of Popery enlisted in the cause of Bible distribution.  Translations are no longer intrusted to men such as those who vitiated the sense of Scripture at Lausanne, or, in the Turkish version, exchanged the simple grandeur of the eternal Word for the tawdry bombast of an Oriental paraphrase.  The missionaries and preachers of the Gospel in France and Switzerland,—such as Malan, Bost, Empeytaz, Felix Neff, or Henri Pyt,—are no longer ignored or publicly disclaimed by the agents

of British Christians.   Neologians can no longer evade the laws,
and by dexterous contrivances deface the blessed volume of
inspiration with infidel introductions or heretical notes.   In a
word, the British and Foreign Bible Society, whilst collecting
round its standard the excellent of every Christian denomination,
has been gradually retracing its steps out of that labyrinth of
error in which it was involved at the time when Robert Haldane
first uplifted his warning voice, and recalled its members to a
sense of the guilt and danger of pursuing the unhallowed course
into which some of their leaders had been imperceptibly and
unconsciously betrayed.

When the British and Foreign Bible Society was first instituted, there is no doubt that its rules contemplated the exclusion
of the Apocrypha.   This is sufficiently established by reference
to the written words, but the testimony of the Rev. Josiah Pratt,
one of its founders, is conclusive: "That Society," says Mr.
Pratt, himself a partisan of Earl-street,—"That Society was
formed—we speak advisedly and of our own knowledge—on the
principle of the utter exclusion of the Apocrypha."   And again:
"We have no reason to believe that a single native of the British
islands had any other intention than to disperse the inspired
Word of God, and that only, throughout the world." *   This
rule was strictly adhered to in regard to the English authorized
version, with the exception of one edition, which was admitted
to have been an error, and which became, in 1818, the subject
of a remonstrance from the Edinburgh Society, by whom the
mistake was first detected.

It matters little at what time the laws of their Institution
were first contravened, but Mr. Gorham, with his usual minute
and scholastic accuracy, holds it to be established, that "up
to the month of January, 1812," the Committee considered
themselves debarred from sanctioning the addition of the
Apocrypha, whether appended or interspersed.   From the 7th
June, 1813, the downward course became bolder and more
rapid, until, at last, in 1819, the administrators of the Society,
growing confident in immunity from censure, began themselves

* " Missionary Register," 1827.

to print foreign Bibles with the Apocrypha either appended or intermingled, according as they were designed to gratify the Continental prejudices of Protestants, Romanists, or Greeks. It is scarcely needful to observe, that in the intermingled Bibles intended for the members of the Romish and Greek Churches, there is nothing to distinguish the inspired from the uninspired books; and that although the Council of Trent had not dared to insert the third books of Esdras and of Maccabees, these were printed in the Sclavonian Bible in 1815, and received the public thanks of the Archbishop Vicarius of Moscow. This excessive adulteration of the pure Word of God was sanctioned on grounds of expediency; but the subsequent overthrow of the Bible Societies in Russia, and the exclusion from Russia of the agents who had assisted in the work, only exhibit another instance of the importance of standing upon principle, and not faithlessly yielding up the truth of God, in the vain endeavour thus to promote his glory.

But during all the time that the laws were thus violated, no public intimation of it was made to the Society. The Clerical Secretary, the Rev. John Owen, was a man of fine parts,— brilliant as an orator, a good tactician, energetic in his zeal for Bible distribution, somewhat vain of his diplomacy, and little disposed to be stopped in his ardent career by dry rules or technical difficulties. His influence was paramount in Earl-street. He was, as one of his friends and apologists declared, "the dictator" of the Committee, and it would have been a bold act for any member to have opposed his measures, or questioned his decisions. Much was done in Sub-committees which never came before the general body. Even so late as 1825, active and intelligent members could be named who were still in the dark; and Mr. T. Pell Platt, the friend and admirer of Mr. Owen, as well as Honorary Librarian to the Society, published a letter to Dr. Wardlaw in 1827, where he declared that Mr. Owen designedly suppressed the information. It was publicly admitted to have been a common saying in Earl-street, that "John Bull would never stand an intermingled Apocrypha." These are things which now belong to history;

and whatever irritation the charge of "studied concealment" occasioned at the first, the fact was afterwards admitted, and the plain statement of the truth is due, not only to the assailants of the Apocrypha, but to a large majority of the Committee, who were unconsciously involved in the guilt of adulterating the Word of God.

It was in August, 1821, when Mr. Haldane was in London, that he called with a friend at the offices of the British and Foreign Bible Society, to make some inquiries with reference to an edition of Martin's French Bible, which he had himself originated. That edition had been printed at Toulouse, at the expense of the Society, under the inspection of Professor Chabrand, to whom the office of editor had been committed, on the recommendation of Mr. Haldane, acting through General Macaulay, whom he had met at Montauban. On the occasion of his visit to Earl-street, Mr. Haldane forgot his umbrella, and being much accustomed to observe the leadings of Providence, it was to this *accident* that he was wont reverentially to trace the part he took in originating and carrying on the Apocrypha controversy. He returned on the following day to reclaim his umbrella, and was requested by Mr. Zachary Macaulay to join a Sub-committee, which was then in conference with Dr. Pinkerton in regard to the Toulouse Bible. To his surprise, he discovered not only that the Apocrypha had been appended to this edition, but that the earlier edition, begun in 1817 at Montauban, had undergone the same contamination, although his contributions to its cost had been made under repeated pledges that it should contain nothing but the pure Word of God. These discoveries were as startling to the noble President himself as they were to Mr. Haldane. They led to other inquiries, and the whole truth with reference to the indiscriminate circulation of the Apocrypha was very soon disclosed. Mr. Hughes seemed anxious to abate the evil, and Mr. Owen looked like one who was disconcerted at the discovery, but who felt that further perseverance in the same course would be madness. Had Mr. Owen lived, it is difficult to say how he would have steered the gallant vessel which had so long been his pride and his boast. It is probable that, between two difficulties, he would have chosen that which would have secured peace at home, and renounced the Apocrypha. But he did not long survive, and his successor, Mr. Brandram, was unfortunately wedded to the system into which Mr. Owen had fallen, and he ultimately did battle in defence of the Apocrypha, with an honest zeal and unbending determination worthy of a better cause. During the interval between the day when Mr. Haldane first privately opened the subject in Earl-street, in August, 1821, and the public rupture in 1825, there was much friendly negotiation. On his return home, he addressed a long letter to one of the Secretaries, dated Auchin-gray, 6th October, 1821, which was read in Earl-street, pointing out, in minute detail and with great force of argument, the evil of which the Society was guilty.

Mr. Drummond has published a narrative of what happened in the interval, between 1821 and 1825. It is characterized by his usual clearness and precision, as well as by his terse, graphic, and forcible style. He relates how conversations were held with the Secretaries, how they admitted the violation of the funda-mental principle of the Society, and how they begged for time; how all went on well until, nearly a year afterwards, " we learnt, to our great surprise, that faith had not been kept with us; that the Committee was going on just as it had been doing before." Mr. Drummond proceeds :—

" It was then agreed to be necessary to bring the question to the formal decision of the Committee. A Committee was specially summoned, after a long notice, for August 19, 1822, at which Lord Teignmouth presided. After much debating, it was resolved that the practice should be discon-tinued; but that as the Committee had been going on for a considerable period in their error, it should take time gradually to retrace its steps ; that nothing should be done hastily, but that firmly, perseveringly, and mildly, the distribution of the Apocrypha should be stopped, and a Resolution framed for this purpose was adopted unanimously."

Matters were thus quietly arranged, and everything promised peace, until the month of September, 1824, when, on the appli-cation of a Romish priest,—the same who was subsequently dismissed from their service,—the Committee *unanimously* voted 500*l.* for an intermingled Apocrypha.

" A clergyman," says Mr. Drummond, " who usually attends the Com-mittee, heard of this, and wrote a letter to protest against it. At the following meeting some of the Committee thought the most dignified course to pursue was to take no notice of the protest, but to confirm the vote of the preceding meeting. Upon Lord Teignmouth, however, who was in the chair, asking the Committee, whether in case they confirmed their vote they were prepared for seeing the clergyman's protest in print, they agreed to postpone the further consideration of it to another meeting. Accordingly the subject again came forward at a third meeting, when, without one single word being uttered by any individual for or against it, the vote of 500*l.* was *unanimously* rescinded. Is cool judgment and inflexible principle, or impulse and feeling, the guide of a Board, which is *unanimous* one day upon any given point, and as *unanimous* the following day upon its direct contrary?"

The Anti-Apocryphal resolution of the 19th August, 1822, allowed that the omission of the Apocrypha was necessary, in order "to keep entire good faith with the members of the Society." The vote of Dr. Van Ess, in 1824, was therefore not a sin of omission or carelessness, but a departure from the pledge privately made to Mr. Haldane, Mr. Macaulay, Mr. Drummond, and Dr. Thorpe, in 1821, a pledge which was, in the following year, publicly repeated and recorded in the minute-books. The vote to Van Ess dashed the hopes cherished during three years of patient delay, and now Mr. Haldane felt that the time for compromise was gone, and the moment had at last arrived for action. As his previous conduct had been characterized by moderation and forbearance, so were his future acts to bear witness to his Christian courage and indomitable firmness. On the 21st of September, 1824, a letter of expostulation was, for the first time, addressed to Earl-street, from the Edinburgh Bible Committee. A temporary Resolution, suggested by Lord Teignmouth, passed on the 20th of December, 1824, allowing that to be done indirectly, which could not be done directly. The well-meant effort of the Noble President to please both parties, on a question too grave to admit of compromise, was, in fact, on all hands allowed to be ineffectual for the objects it had in view. It settled nothing, and satisfied no one.

Still the Edinburgh Committee were adverse to an open rupture. In the hopes of obtaining terms of peace, they addressed to Earl-street a further remonstrance, dated the 17th of January, 1825, embodied in a series of Resolutions, chiefly drawn up by the late Rev. Edward Craig, an English Episcopal clergyman, a fact worthy of record, as contradicting the allegation, industriously circulated, that the question was one of geography, interesting to Scotland, but indifferent to England.

But the supporters of Apocryphal circulation were not idle, and a remonstrance of an opposite character was, on the 11th of February, prepared at the lodge of Corpus Christi College, Cambridge, and signed by twenty-six members of the Senate, protesting against that part of Lord Teignmouth's compromise, which denied pecuniary aid to editions of the Bible in which the Apocryphal books were "mixed and interspersed."

To this document the following note was appended:—

"We have no desire whatever that the Apocrypha should be circulated where the canonical Scriptures will be received without it; but we earnestly wish that the circulation of *these* may not be impeded, by any determination which will excite direct opposition from the very Churches that most need to be supplied with them."

The opinion of the Secretaries, as well as that of their most active coadjutors in the Committee, unhappily accorded with the Cambridge Protest, and, on the 7th of March, 1825, the same day on which it was read in Earl-street, it was at once resolved, "That *all* the Resolutions of this Committee relative to the Apocrypha be rescinded." Another unsatisfactory Resolution of the Committee, passed on the 22d April, leaving *money grants* unnoticed, and sanctioning the gift of canonical books in parts, thereby supplying *facilities* for the interspersion of the Apocrypha, indiscriminately mingled with the sacred text, and indirectly favouring the circulation of A FALSE CANON OF SCRIPTURE. It thus appeared, that the Committee was no longer agreed as to the contents of the book which was to be called the Bible; that, at best, they were at variance on the question of what was, and what was not, holy Scripture. The Bible, instead of being associated with the hallowed influence belonging to its character, as only containing the Word of God, was henceforth to be a term meaning anything or nothing, according to the latitudinarian views of Romanists, Neologians, or Pantheists.

So soon as this melancholy conclusion was known to the Edinburgh Bible Society, the Committee met and issued their first " Statement relative to the circulation of the Apocrypha, by the British and Foreign Bible Society." It contained a brief narrative of the discussion which had already taken place, the Resolutions prepared by Mr. Craig, and an Appendix, drawn up by the learned and venerable Professor Paxton, exhibiting the corruptions, false doctrines, and superstitions, sanctioned by the Apocryphal writers. Of this remarkable document five thousand copies were printed, and circulated all over the kingdom. The rival Protest from Cambridge was, at the same time, printed by the opposite party, and from the warehouses of Earl-street it was profusely distributed, accompanied by an Introduction and Notes, written by the Rev. Henry Venn. The Cambridge gentlemen maintained two very rash propositions, which were proved to be equally incorrect and untenable : first, that all the foreign Churches regarded the Apocrypha as an integral part of the Bible ; and next, that it was " *impossible* to circulate among them, to any extent, Bibles which do not contain it." With reference to the first proposition, it was true in regard to the Church of Rome, which finally sealed its apostasy, when, at the Council of Trent, it betrayed its trust by purposely incorporating the Apocrypha with the Sacred Scriptures, and pronouncing its anathema upon those who do not receive these lying fables. It might possibly be also true in regard to the Greek Church, although its decision had not been collectively pronounced, but it was not true in regard to the foreign Protestant Churches. With reference to the second proposition, even had it been certain that it was impossible to circulate the Bible without the Apocrypha, such a fact would not have justified a violation of Christian principle; but the experience of more than a quarter of a century has now happily dissipated the gloomy forebodings of those who signed and issued the Cambridge Protest, and has shown that the God of the Bible has not reduced his people to the humiliating necessity of adulterating his holy Word, in order to secure for it the acceptance of his own guilty creatures.

The Cambridge Protest was followed by a letter from the

Rev. Charles Simeon to Lord Teignmouth, in which it seemed as if the venerable and amiable writer had meant, in his own person, to add another illustration to the precept, " Cease ye from man." In a speech, supposed to be uttered by the Apostle Paul, Mr. Simeon strenuously urged the expediency of intermingling the Apocrypha, if it were necessary to render the pure Word of God more acceptable to the taste of the superstitious, idolatrous, and corrupt Churches of the Romish and Greek persuasion. The duty he strove to inculcate from the principle of becoming all things to all men, and from the circumcision of Timothy, as if it were lawful to do evil that good might come, or as if in the case of one whose mother was a Jew, although his father was a Greek, compliance with an act in such a case lawful, if not actually binding, were parallel to a participation in the corruption of the Word of God.

To the remarks accompanying the Cambridge Protest, Mr. Gorham published a masterly reply, in which, with much scholastic ability and profound research, he demolished every argument adduced in mitigation of the sin of violating the canon of Scripture, and by an appeal to history, antiquity, and actual fact, proved that it was impossible for the Bible Society to intersperse the Apocrypha, without violating its original constitution, going back to the principles of Romanism, and undoing the work of our great Ecclesiastical Reformers.

Meanwhile, the remonstrances of the Edinburgh and other Scotch Societies were followed by protests from several English Auxiliaries, and the aspect of affairs appeared so threatening, that, on the 2d of August, 1825, it was resolved to refer the whole subject to a Special Committee.

Whilst this Committee was deliberating, several incidental circumstances tended to show how much reason there was, that Christians should be called to a sense of the importance of maintaining inviolate the sacred canon. Every argument used in palliation of an intermingled Apocrypha, might evidently be traced to doubts or uncertainty on this momentous question. Nay, so little had Christians been accustomed to observe the bulwarks and mark the battlements which encircle the sacred canon, that Mr. Simeon himself evinced some confusion on the subject, in a second letter, which he printed, but was persuaded to withdraw; whilst, emboldened by such authorities, a clever writer in the "Eclectic Review" published an article in February, 1825, expressing doubts with regard to no less than ten books and one hundred and forty chapters of the Old Testament Scriptures. This article was hailed with delight by the leading Philo-Apocryphists, and acquired a demi-official character from the zeal with which a reprint was sent out, with the aid of the organized machinery of Earl-street, and at the expense of members of the Committee.

On the subject of the Apocrypha the country was now in a blaze, but although Mr. Haldane was the first to lay the matter before the Edinburgh Society, and maintained a constant correspondence with members of the London Committee, and others who attended its meetings, it was not till the close of the year that he himself publicly appeared in the field. It was then that he published his first "Review of the Conduct of the British and Foreign Bible Society relative to the Apocrypha, and to their Administration on the Continent; with an Answer to the Rev. C. Simeon, and Observations on the Cambridge Remarks." His two well-chosen mottoes contain the gist of all his writing and speeches on this subject during a period of nine years: "Add thou not unto his words, lest he reprove thee, and thou be found a liar" (Prov. xxx. 6); and, "Shouldest thou help the ungodly, or love them that hate the Lord?" (2 Chron. xix. 2.) During three years Mr. Robert Haldane had used every effort to adjust the question amicably and privately. During a fourth year he had laboured to obtain the withdrawal of the Apocrypha, through the instrumentality of the Edinburgh Society, of which he was Vice-President. At last, he came forward with his "Review of the Conduct of the British and Foreign Bible Society." It consisted of five chapters, each grave, convincing, and effective. In the first, he asserts the importance of the question, involving, as it did, the authenticity of Scripture, the integrity of the canon, and the sovereignty of the Word of God, against those who talked as if it were a light matter to contaminate the sacred oracles by Apocryphal corruptions, whether added or interspersed. In his second chapter, he encountered Mr. Simeon's arguments, which he not only fully answered, but, in the words of Mr. Zachary Macaulay, "pulverized." In his third chapter, he sifts the testimony adduced in the Cambridge Remarks, drawn from the alleged necessity of the case, and by that process of reasoning, of which he was so great a master, turns against the Cambridge protesters the evidence of all their witnesses, and proves that the foreign letters, on which their case was grounded, had either been mutilated and garbled, or were, from their own internal evidence, unworthy of credit. One of the omissions in the letter, published as that of Van Ess, contained this important statement, which was excluded, without an asterisk to denote the hiatus :—"*It is but candid to say, that, individually, I, like many other enlightened Roman Catholics, feel disposed to take no umbrage whatsoever at such a separation.*"

Professor Kieffer's arguments were still more triumphantly disposed of. His comparison of the Bible and Apocrypha to the parable of the wheat and the tares, was not only shown to be "a licentious misapplication of the Word of God," but an index to the same doubts or indifference as to the sacred canon, which lurked behind every argument in favour of the Apocrypha. Of Mr. Haldane's forcible mode of reasoning, and of the manner also in which he generally turned the defences of Bible adulteration into foolishness, the following is an example :—

"Ought we not, with perfect confidence," says Mr. Kieffer, "to leave to the Almighty the means and the time, which, in His incomprehensible wisdom, he shall consider the most fit and proper for separating those books from the inspired writings?" Mr. Haldane replies, "According to Mr. Kieffer's application of the parable of the tares, the Bible is the wheat, the Apocrypha the tares, the devil is the author of it, and the servants are forbidden to take away what he has indited. Extraordinary as it may appear, that, in pleading the cause of the Apocrypha, he should have laid down such premises, the conclusion which he draws is still more remarkable. In plain language it is as follows :—Let us, then, imitate the conduct of this enemy, and, as long as the servants shall sleep, unite with the devil in sowing tares among the wheat, by continuing to print the Apocrypha. Arguments like these, should arouse the most dormant and inconsiderate, while they prove to what lengths such perversions of Scripture would conduct us."

These references to Mr. Haldane's first Review are given as records of the real state of affairs at the time when he commenced his public exposure of the abuses, which had grown up under the shelter of the British and Foreign Bible Society. That Institution had an object of surpassing glory, but the glory of the object had been too much transferred to the agents, and to the Society. They had, in a certain sense, lost sight of the end in idolatry of the means. The circulation of the Bible is a glorious thing as a means of promoting the knowledge of Christ, but the knowledge of Christ and the salvation of men will not be accomplished by diplomatic craft inconsistent with the holiness of God. The cause of God never can be advanced by swerving from the requirements of his infinite purity.

In the fourth chapter of the Review Mr. Haldane particularly draws attention to that fact, that the Apocryphal writers have blasphemously usurped the prophetic character. "The word of the Lord came unto me, saying," &c. "Thus saith the Lord." The conclusion, then, is inevitable. The Apocrypha is either the Word of God, or an addition of lying prophets. That it is the work of lying prophets is proved both by external and internal evidence, and he therefore winds up his demonstration in the following words :—

"If the man, or angel, who shall preach another Gospel than that which the Bible contains, is by the Holy Ghost pronounced accursed, then does this awful denunciation apply to a book, which, pretending to record the message of an angel from heaven, teaches another Gospel. Under this anathema, then, the Apocrypha lies. By the authority of an apostle, we are bound to hold it accursed."

Professor Kieffer's facts were as conclusively overturned as his reasoning. The case of the Toulouse Bible is an example. It had been unscrupulously asserted in Paris, that this edition had been at first actually published without the Apocrypha, but that, in consequence of a "protest on all sides" against this omission, the Society had been obliged to supply the want.

Far from this being the case, it was proved, first, that the Apocrypha was added before the experiment was made; secondly, that it was inserted to satisfy the old Paris Bible Society, composed, as it was, of Arians, Socinians, and unbelievers; thirdly, that it was done in defiance of the Christian remonstrances of Professor Chabrand, who alleged that by doing so "there was danger of the Protestants confounding the Apocryphal with the Canonical books;" fourthly, that not only was the Apocrypha thus forced into the Toulouse Bible, but, under the pretence of not giving offence to Romanists, David Martin's admirable preface had been omitted, although it contained one of the most luminous views of the history and errors of the Apocryphal books. In opposition to the statement, that there was a protest on all sides against the omission of the Apocrypha, MM. Chabrand, Bonnard, Marzials, Pyt, and others, with one voice testified that there were no such complaints, except it might be from quarters very little entitled to the consideration of true Christians.

The case of Martin's Pocket Bible was equally misrepresented; for it was clearly proved, that, in its unadulterated state, it had sold better, and circulated more freely, than the adulterated Bibles. The Montauban Bible was another striking illustration of the sad state of the foreign agency and Associations of the British and Foreign Bible Society at the commencement of the controversy, and its history furnishes an example of Mr. Haldane's labours in the South of France. Whilst the printing was going forward during Mr. Haldane's residence at Montauban, not a syllable was uttered about adding the Apocrypha, nor was there a word of complaint on the subject of its omission. It was not till *three thousand copies had been disposed of* that the Paris Bible Society, under Socinian or Neologian influence, procured the addition of the Apocrypha, in spite of the remonstrances of the *Christians* at Montauban, who decidedly opposed the measure, and considered it alike improper in itself, uncalled for by the people, a breach of faith towards Mr. Haldane, with whom this edition of the Bible originated.

After citing other convincing proofs to show that the adulte-

ration of the French Bibles was entirely the result of Socinian
influence in France, he exclaims :—

"Here I cannot but exult in the Christian conduct of my good friends
at Montauban. I feel high satisfaction when I compare it with the
worldly policy of many. In all things they have approved themselves to
be clear in this matter. Thus wisdom is justified of her children. The
weight of the opinions of such men on a religious subject is very different,
indeed, from that of some of the correspondents of the British and Foreign
Bible Society." (P. 78.)

Mr. Haldane's Review was in truth unanswerable, both in
arguments and facts, and it may be said to have closed the
first campaign,—for contemporaneous with its publication, the
Special Committee, to whom the whole subject of the Apocrypha
had been referred, gave in their Report, which, although anti-
Apocryphal in substance, was still compromising and unsatisfactory.

---

But a new chapter was about to open in this painful history,
and a new champion was about to enter the lists. The Report
of the Special Committee in Earl-street was adopted on the
21st November, 1825, and a Resolution confirmed on the
28th, which prohibited the circulation of the Apocrypha,
either appended or interspersed, but in the matter of *money*
grants, left, as Dr. Wardlaw expressed it, " *a postern*," by
which its efficacy might again be evaded. Considering the
previous vacillations of the Earl-street Committee, and the fact
that Mr. Brandram had gone so far as to record a formal protest
against its limited restrictions, it is no marvel if the Edinburgh
Society were still dissatisfied with the Resolution. It was indeed
difficult to persuade them to trust to so doubtful a rule, in
the hands of administrators avowing such sentiments, especially
after all the concealments which a mistaken policy had dictated.
If any one interested in the question chooses to read the article
which was reprinted from the " Eclectic Review," of April,
1826, he will see ground enough to justify this distrust, and
vindicate the decided course adopted in Edinburgh. To the

writer in the "Eclectic," who was the chief advocate of the Apocryphists, the praise of zeal, ability, and out-spoken frankness may all be fully conceded. He was well known as the friend of James Montgomery, and as being himself the author of some beautiful gems of sacred poetry, which the Christian world will not willingly let die. But he did not hesitate to avow it as his honest opinion, that "the great error" of Earlstreet consisted in "vacillation and indecision," that they ought not to have compromised the point at issue, and that their attempt to conciliate had "paralyzed their friends, without satisfying their enemies." He boldly argued, that the Committee were entitled to have taken "higher ground," that they had been compelled "to defer to the clamour" in abandoning the Apocrypha, that their "indecision," their "vibrating Resolutions," were attributable to divisions amongst themselves, or to the interference of privileged members. He adds, that, out of deference to public opinion, they had only "given ear too patiently, and given way too timidly."

It was at this crisis that the Rev. Dr. Andrew Thomson, for the first time appeared in the field in a cause worthy of all the energies of his colossal mind. His gigantic intellect, his unflinching courage, his elastic spirits, his buoyant humour, his indomitable industry, his vigorous pen, his powerful eloquence, and his capacity for business, entitled him to rank amongst the first men of his age. As a debater in the General Assembly and Church Courts of Scotland he stood unrivalled. Not one of his opponents had been able to stand before him, and the superiority of his practical talents, his ability to detect a weak point in his adversaries' line of battle, his quickness and self-possession, enabled him to triumph on occasions where even the majesty, the brilliancy, and the thrilling eloquence of Dr. Chalmers were insufficient to secure a majority. His chief appeal was not to the passions, but to the judgment of his auditory. His logic was irresistible, but he could also touch the tender chords of feeling, as in music he was wont to blend the highest and the lowest notes in delightful harmony. He could speak for hours without fatiguing his audience, whilst his

gravest arguments were diversified by bursts of splendid declamation, or by flashes of that playful wit and withering sarcasm,
which could alike captivate a listener or confound an assailant.
Deeply penetrated with a sense of the importance of the Gospel,
he had thrown his mighty ægis over that section of the Scottish
Church, whose courage had too long been paralyzed by the
opposing spirit of moderation. Many battles had he fought in
its defence, and under his guidance the Evangelicals were first
led on to victory, and enabled to roll back the tide of secularity
and Pelagianism by which the ancient doctrines of the Gospel
had been nearly overwhelmed. No wonder, then, that he became
" the foremost and most conspicuous man" in Scotland, and that
all the deepest sympathies of the best portion of the nation were
fondly associated with the name of Andrew Thomson. There
is no doubt that he was one of those stirring spirits that find a
pleasure in the excitement of action. Like the war-horse, that
" smelleth the battle from afar," he heard of the contest in
which Robert Haldane then took the lead,—" the thunder of the
captains, and the shouting." He approached the battle-
field, as he himself avowed, with some feelings of doubt and
jealousy as to the chief of the Anti-Apocryphal forces, whose
rebuke he had not then forgotten. But when he came to fathom
the depths of the subject, and to understand its bearings,—
when he came to see that the supremacy of the Bible was at
stake, that the question involved the canon of Scripture, the
Book of God, the record of saving faith, the charter of our
salvation,—all his doubts and misgivings were flung to the
winds. He generously gave the right hand of fellowship to his
late antagonist, and threw himself into the conflict just at the
moment when Mr. Z. Macaulay and others in England were
deserting Mr. Haldane, and content with a compromise, or
tired of the contest, were leaving him to fight alone the battle
of the purity of God's Word and maintain the protest against
Socinian or Infidel alliances. To the office of Secretary of the
Edinburgh Bible Society Dr. Thomson was appointed, on the
motion of Mr. James Haldane, one of its original founders, as
well as one of its most active and steadiest friends. The Second

Statement of the Edinburgh Bible Society was the first public intimation that Dr. Andrew Thomson was in the field. It is difficult to speak too highly of its ability and force. Comprised in 151 octavo pages, it embodied six distinct propositions, each of which was logically and elaborately proved. To much of the scholastic accuracy of detail which distinguishes the pamphlet of Mr. Gorham, without its minuteness, it added a fuller, more comprehensive, more thorough-going, and more popular survey of all the bearings of the questions at issue, whether they concerned the laws of the Society, the importance of the sacred canon, or the history of the mistakes, the vacillation, and the instability which had marked the policy of the British and Foreign Bible Society's administrators. Viewed as a piece of sustained reasoning, it will endure as a monument of talents which were sufficient to have placed the author in the first rank of debaters in the most august assembly in the world, whilst it also contains occasional bursts of majestic eloquence rising out of the argument, combined with all the native simplicity, which imprinted on his manly brow the stamp of intellectual aristocracy.

This document was welcomed by Mr. Haldane with cordial pleasure. On the 16th January, 1826, he writes :—

" Dr. Thomson has executed it with singular ability. To-day we had our Meeting of the General Committee, which was very fully attended, with Dr. Davidson in the chair. A considerable part of the statement was read, and received with the highest satisfaction and most cordial unanimity. Dr. Peddie (of the Secession Church), in the most candid and open manner, declared himself convinced. Mr. Craig was the only dissentient. We went with it immediately to the printer's, and expect the first part of it on Wednesday. . . . Let me know how many should be sent to England. Expense will not be spared, as we consider it the greatest question that has been agitated since the Reformation. I never saw the religious public here so unanimous on any subject as they have been since the publication of my (first) Review."

The Second Statement was circulated throughout the country, and fell amongst the Philo-Apocryphists like the stroke of a tempest. By the Eclectic Reviewer it is described as having " taken by surprise " the Committee, who " were not prepared " for a " proceeding so invidious and so malignant." The act

of the Edinburgh Committee might have been condemned
without a personal attack on their Honorary Secretary, but from
several quarters Dr. Thomson was bitterly assailed with great
asperity and unwarrantable invective.  Had he been a Melancthon instead of a Luther, he would have been compelled to
answer for himself.  Amongst other unlawful shafts hurled
against him in the pamphlets circulated from the depositories in
Earl-street, he was, at this early stage of the controversy, held
up to reprobation as exhibiting a "violent and intolerant
spirit," and as wielding a pen which had "been compelled
to apologize for its own *libels*."  The writer knew not how little
solid ground there was for this bitter accusation.  It was only
to be found in Dr. Thomson's generous reluctance to betray a
friend, but after his death Dr. M'Crie published the fact, that
in the case alluded to, when he stopped a prosecution by paying
its expenses, and inserting an apology in the "Edinburgh
Christian Instructor," he was "*as innocent as the child unborn.*"
He paid the forfeit rather than give up the name of his friend,
who was morally responsible, thus evincing, as Dr. M'Crie
justly adds, "an example of generous self-devotion which has
few parallels."  Whether he was right in thus submitting to
the obloquy which belonged to the mistake of another is a
separate question, but it exhibits himself as indeed "the hearty,
gallant, and out-and-out trustworthy friend," described by Dr.
Chalmers.

Meanwhile, the Earl-street Committee-room continued, during
the winter of 1826, to be itself the arena of perpetual strife and
acrimonious debate.  The termination of the contest waged
between what were called the Philo-Apocryphists, consisting
chiefly of the elected Committee, headed by the Secretaries, and
the Anti-Apocryphists, consisting chiefly of privileged members,
headed by the Rev. Dr. Thorpe, Mr. Gorham, Mr. Drummond,
Mr. Irving, and others, was, however, still uncertain, when on
the 23d March, 1826, it was resolved that a deputation should
be sent to Edinburgh, with the view of proposing further terms
of compromise.  The deputation consisted of two of the one
party and two of the other, namely, the Rev. Joseph Hughes

and Mr. E. N. Thornton of Southwark, with Dr. Thorpe and Mr. Percival White. It was not to be expected that a divided deputation should prove very successful diplomatists. Their admissions tended to strengthen the cause of pure Bible circulation, and as they set out without any definite propositions of peace, the failure of their mission is not wonderful. The Philo-Apocryphist members themselves appreciated the earnest adhesion to principle which characterized the members of the Edinburgh Committee, and in particular, they acknowledged " the affectionate hospitality " with which they were personally welcomed by Mr. Haldane and his brother, at the same time that they both strenuously opposed the principles of the Apocryphal advocates. At the General Meeting of the British and Foreign Bible Society, on the 3d of May, 1826, Resolutions were adopted which approached still nearer to the original requirements of the Scottish Societies, and closed up that "postern" for Bible contamination which had been first pointed out by Dr. Wardlaw.

A Third Statement explains the grounds on which the Edinburgh Society were still unable to compromise. There were three principal points on which the London deputation and the Edinburgh Committee had been at variance. These were,—

I. As to the propriety of an expression of regret for the past violation of what was now admitted to have been the fundamental law.

II. The necessity of breaking off all connexion with foreign Societies which should continue with their own funds to adulterate the sacred canon.

III. Some change in the membership of the London Committee, so as to ensure an administration in accordance with the laws of the Society.

The first of these requisitions was resisted as derogatory to the dignity of the Committee, whilst the Edinburgh Society, not without reason, argued, that, considering what had happened between 1821 and 1825, it was necessary as a security for the future, and that if an error had been committed, and the same administration were to remain, some acknowledgment was due to the cause of truth, as confession was the first token of repentance. This difficulty would not, however, have been insuperable had the other points been conceded. But Earl-street refused to break with the Apocryphal and Neologian Auxiliaries on the Continent, and far from acknowledging any sense of error, Mr. Brandram, in one of his speeches, asserted, that for himself he " could not cease to reprobate the Resolutions of the Meeting against the circulation of the Apocrypha," and declared his continued adhesion to the Protest, which is dated the 28th November, 1825, and was thus recorded in the minute-book :—

"We protest against the present decision of the Committee on the subject of the Apocrypha, as being, according to our deliberate judgment, in direct opposition to the moral bearing and general spirit of God's Word."

About the same time also, Dr. Steinkopff, the Foreign Secretary, published his " Letter addressed to Robert Haldane, Esq., containing some Remarks on his Strictures relative to the Continent and to Continental Bible Societies." It was written with all the mildness and gentleness of spirit which characterize the venerable author; but he declared that he considered it a duty to yield to the prejudices of foreigners, and, for the sake of the Bible, to aid them in circulating the Apocrypha. It did not disprove the substance of Mr. Haldane's " First Review," and scarcely touched one of its details, but it gave occasion to Mr. Haldane's " Second Review," consisting of more than 200 pages, which, like the first, passed through two large editions, and contained most interesting and valuable, although melancholy details as to the irreligious state of the Continent. The Second Review was, in fact, a fuller development of the fifth chapter of the first, and gave an awful demonstration of the Infidelity which reigned over a large proportion of the Foreign Bible Societies. That this was not a private opinion of Mr. Haldane may be proved by the testimony of one of the favourers of Apocryphal circulation, the learned Dr. Pye Smith, whose own views of the sacred canon were always cloudy. Before the commencement of the controversy, when his opinions

were not coloured by party strife, he thus described the Geneva
Bible Society in his answer to Chenéviere :—

" On the last day of 1814, a Bible Society was formed at Geneva ; but
M. Chenéviere must bear with me, while I bluntly remind him that so
long as it was under a management which he perfectly understands, *it was
little, if at all, better than a blind to the public, a covering for doing nothing,
A ROUGH GARMENT WORN TO DECEIVE.*"

No language employed by Mr. Haldane ever went beyond that
of Dr. Pye Smith. It was, in fact, describing such Neologian
Societies, as being what they really were, " an organized hypocrisy." From personal observation, and the testimony of other
Christians, Mr. Haldane had arrived at the conclusion that Dr.
Pye Smith's opinion was correct, and that the greater part of
the Continental Bible Societies were no better than those of
Paris, Geneva, and Lausanne. What, indeed, could be expected
of Neologists like Professor Paulus, " the most atrocious of them
all," or of persecutors like Levade, Curtat, or Chenéviere?
Such Societies were, to adopt Dr. Pye Smith's words, only
" blinds to the public, a covering for doing nothing," or
rather, " synagogues of Satan," where the enemies of the
Gospel found a rallying point, from which, with the aid of
British money, they could encourage one another, and frown
upon those who attempted to preach a pure Gospel.

It would be tedious and painful in this place to give many
instances in corroboration of these statements. Still it is necessary to furnish some proofs of the awful facts which Mr. Haldane
brought so prominently into view, or it might be argued that he
was justly accused of having needlessly disturbed the peace of
the British and Foreign Bible Society. One of the most flagrant
and melancholy illustrations of the manner in which Foreign
Bible Societies, under pretence of circulating the Scriptures,
prostituted their influence in order to diffuse Socinianism and
Neology, is to be found in the history of what has commonly
been termed " The Strasburg Preface." Professor Haffner was
by no means an avowed Infidel, but he was what is worse,
because more subtle and more dangerous,—he was a strong
Neologist, or Rationalist. The excellent and amiable M.

Empeytaz, of Geneva, who wrote an account of the persecution of M. Bost, thus speaks of Haffner and his Preface:—

" This Neologian, who enjoyed such a reputation that no one dared to contradict him, did indeed praise the sacred books; but this praise is so feeble, so deceitful, that it could not conceal his impious intentions. M. Bost (then a missionary at Strasburg for the Continental Society), believing that it was his duty as a Christian and a minister, took up his pen, and with his characteristic force compared the Preface with the Word of God. He openly unmasked the malice of the Pope of Strasburg, and it created a great public sensation. The friends of Haffner denounced it as *sacrilege*, whilst the cowardly half-Christians, those pests of the Church, actually united with its declared enemies to decry Bost and load him with the vilest calumnies. Bost, in the midst of all this tumult, exhibited a noble magnanimity, exhibiting on all occasions an immoveable calm, which was given to him of the Lord, for, as he himself said, in all this affair he only acted under the dictates of his conscience."

M. Bost was the friend, the instructor, and the biographer of Felix Neff. He has been already noticed in connexion with the dawn of a revival of Christianity at Geneva, and a beautiful sketch of his faithfulness and self-sacrifice has been published by the Rev. Mr. Burgess, of Chelsea, in the " Voice from the Alps." He is also mentioned by Dr. Pye Smith, in his answer to Chenéviere, as " a man of good sense, of research, and capacity for sound reasoning." His attack on the Preface had nearly cost him his life; for the students, filled with hatred of Methodism, and hearing of what had happened, were exasperated to the highest pitch, and with murderous intent assembled under M. Bost's windows, with stones concealed in their cloaks. Knowing that he was passionately fond of music, they sung a German hymn to induce him to come out, whilst they were ready to knock him on the head the moment he appeared. The Professors, however, not being prepared to carry the matter so far as to commit murder in cold blood, having heard of their design, concealed themselves in an adjoining house, and ran in amongst the students at the moment of danger, and succeeded in dispersing them. Haffner and the other Infidel Professors did, however, procure from the mayoralty an order for his banishment; but to the honour of the Government of Louis XVIII., it must be added that its confirmation was refused by

the Prefect.   There is a more pleasing sequel to this melancholy
exhibition of enmity to the Gospel.   In Strasburg, there was an
aged and pious pastor, who had been overawed by the talents
and power of Haffner, and so prevented from faithfully declaring
the Gospel.   One day he went on a parochial visit to call on a
Christian family, who had read M. Bost's pamphlet.   The lady
of the house addressed him as he entered, " Well, Mr. Pastor, a
stranger has done what the Christian pastors ought to have
done."   The rebuke was felt.   M. Bien sought out M. Bost,
and, with tears in his eyes, thanked him for his faithful
testimony, confessed his own shameful fear of the champion
of Neology, and in token of his resolution from that moment
to act a more Christian part, went home and wrote an answer
to Haffner.

Such were the circumstances under which Dr. Haffner's Preface was published.   Information of this daring outrage on the
Word of God, perpetrated by a Bible Society in connexion with
the British and Foreign, reached the Continental Society on the
2d of August, 1819, and on the 9th of the same month was
conveyed to the Secretaries of the Earl-street Committee.   From
that date, the facts may be gathered from the official documents
which were printed.   From these it appears that, in violation of
a solemn pledge, the Strasburg Committee had published, with
their own money, an introduction to a Bible which the London
Committee had enabled them to print.   Ignoring the character
of the preface, of which M. Bost had given copious extracts, the
Secretaries despatched a gentle remonstrance to Strasburg,
assuming that the preface might be " innocent and faultless,"
instead of being, as they were fully informed, a deliberate
attempt to pervert the Scriptures.   They evaded every entreaty
to ascertain with certainty its nature or purport, and thus left
the Strasburg Neologians to imagine that the objection to the
publication was rather formal than substantial.   The Strasburg
Committee replied by assuring Mr. Owen, in the blandest terms,
that they too had, on the same 9th of August, resolved " *that it
should be sold and distributed separately,*" but that they could
not prevent such as wished it from binding up this introduction

with their copy of the Bible, since it is printed in the same size."
And as if to pour profane mockery on the whole affair, by
imitating what they doubtless reckoned the cant of British
Methodists, they add: "May the Lord vouchsafe his blessing
to our labours, and cause *the good seed,* which we shall not
cease to scatter abundantly abroad, to bear fruit!" The rulers
in Earl-street might well have been startled by the answer made
to Mr. Owen, and although they passed a public resolution,
"approving of the measures adopted by the Strasburg Society,"
another private letter was addressed to the offending parties,
intimating that the Strasburg resolution was not sufficiently clear,
and recommending that as a Society they should, both as to
expense and otherwise, "renounce every concern in that publication." "By these means," says the letter, "*the voice of slander*
which has been raised against your Society will be hushed."
Notwithstanding these gentle remonstrances, couched in terms
so flattering to the Neologian wrong-doer, M. Haffner, and so
insulting towards M. Bost, the promises of the Strasburg Society
proved delusive, and by means of what Dr. Thomson and Mr.
Drummond have justly stigmatized as "artful and mendacious
evasions," the Strasburg Neologians still sold and distributed
the Infidel Preface for nearly two years after the time of its first
exposure in August, 1819. During that interval a donation
in money was granted to them to purchase 500 Bibles and 250
Testaments, "without the preface." Meanwhile, the attention
of Earl-street was again called to the scandal, and in March,
1821, a stronger remonstrance was despatched from London.
The Strasburg Secretary, annoyed at the pertinacity of these
remonstrances, replied by complaining that "the same spirit of
hostility and *intolerance* which disturbed our peaceful Association
eighteen months ago, still works in the dark, and pursues us
with false accusations and calumnies." But he frankly admits
that the preface was in their depositories, was sought for, was
sold, was circulated, although not bound up by the Society with
its Bibles. "We cannot," he says, "be responsible for what
*private* persons or *clergymen* may think proper to do." In
short, during the interchange of these complimentary protocols,

no fewer than 5,000 copies of this Infidel Preface had been circulated in Alsace along with Bibles paid for with British money.

At length, after further remonstrances on the part of Sir Thomas Baring, Mr. Drummond, and the Continental Society, Dr. Pinkerton was despatched on an embassy to Strasburg. His narrative furnishes one of the most curious, and, but for the melancholy occasion, amusing examples of the mimic State diplomacy then pursued. He tells how carefully he avoided even reading the preface, in order that he might be enabled to profess his incompetency to pronounce an opinion on its merits. He declined seeing any one before he met the redoubtable Haffner himself, and at last, by much fair speech and the aid of the President, succeeded in inducing the Professor to move for the exclusion of his own preface from the Strasburg depositories, although not from circulation. It was, in fact, purchased by Baron Turkheim, their President; and in permitting it to be no longer issued by the Society, although still patronised and sold or distributed by its members, the Baron declares that "the elevated, though *Christian* humble mind of our venerable Vice-President, Dr. Haffner, appeared in its true light." It is to be regretted that these hollow compliments were re-echoed in the Annual Report of the London Society, where "the generous sacrifices to the principles of our common union" are actually spoken of in "terms of real satisfaction."

In glancing over the melancholy details of this painful history, no one can fail to discern the sad consequences of being, in a religious work, "unequally yoked with unbelievers." The Bibles were furnished by the British and Foreign, but the preface was provided by the Strasburg Society. No one charged a single member of the Earl-street Committee with sanctioning, far less desiring to circulate, such Infidelity. Their fault exclusively lay in continuing to maintain an alliance with such "an organized hypocrisy," with Socinians and Rationalists, who were at the same moment attacking the Scriptures of truth and persecuting the ministers of Christ.

But the Strasburg preface was destined to originate a discussion concerning the integrity of the canon, and the plenary inspiration of Scripture, which issued in sounder and more established views on these important subjects. It was Dr. Pye Smith's inconsiderate defence of the preface that produced these effects. In the exercise of a charity which sometimes conducted him into error, the good doctor made an unwise and ill-judged attempt to palliate the mischiefs of the Infidel Preface. In reply to a correspondent of the "Evangelical Magazine," he strove to represent Dr. Haffner as one of those who had sometimes defended the outworks of Christianity, although he never entered the gates of the temple. Nay, in the warmth of his zeal, he was so inconsiderate as to say, that, although the author was no doubt "a Rationalist," yet in some respects his preface was "an interesting and valuable performance." With reference to this rash proposition, it is right to add, that in a private letter addressed in August, 1837, to his old antagonist in the "Evangelical Magazine," the learned and pious Doctor, with the amiable candour for which he was pre-eminent, refers with regret to the expressions he had used. But these expressions were eagerly laid hold of, and, strange to say, even copied into the "Church Missionary Register," then edited by the Rev. Josiah Pratt. This rendered it necessary for Mr. Haldane, Dr. Thomson, and others, to say much more than would otherwise have been necessary of the worthless production of Dr. Haffner, in which the early history of the Jews is compared to the fables of "the heroic ages" of Rome, the prophets are represented only as "men whom God had furnished with superior mental endowments," "unveiling to them the near future, and permitting them to anticipate the more distant." Daniel had "the art of interpreting dreams." Ezekiel "a very lively imagination," and his prophecies "resemble a poetical picture, the only features of which we find in the Revelation of St. John," who "*modelled*" his vision after those of Ezekiel and Daniel. The Deity of our Lord, the corruption of human nature, the renewing power of the Holy Ghost, were of course doctrines beyond the scope of Professor Haffner's philosophy, and on the subject of prayer he is profoundly silent. Even the character of a prophet was denied to our Lord, and He was said to have had only "a presentiment of his own death." An eminent clerical member of the Earl-street Committee, misled by Dr. Pye Smith's panegyric, on one occasion ventured publicly to express the opinion that, after all, there was nothing very bad in Haffner's preface. A privileged lay member, amazed at the statement, immediately read some of the extracts, when the clergyman started up, and, interrupting him, begged to retract what he had stated, and earnestly " declared to God " that he had not been aware that it contained such shocking impiety. Dr. Pye Smith's defence of Haffner proved the commencement of an important discussion concerning the inspiration of Scripture, in which Mr. Haldane was prominently engaged.

The case of Dr. Haffner's preface was not, however, the only evidence of the character of the foreign auxiliaries of Earl-street, which was brought forward in Mr. Haldane's Second Review. The unfaithful translation, called the Lausanne Bible, with its fifty thousand spoliations and its objectionable notes, the Hanover Preface, the Turkish Testament, and other similar cases, were all examples of the evil of associating in such a work with men who scrupled not to violate the laws of the Society, and some of whom afterwards became bitter persecutors of the ministers of Christ. Amongst the heads of the Lausanne Bible Society was Dean Curtat, who published, what Mr. Haldane says, " I never before met with, in any theological discussion, a laboured apology for spending the evening of the Lord's-day *in playing at cards.*" His arguments, drawn from the *silence* of our Lord and his apostles respecting card-playing, might seem a burlesque on the practice after the manner of Dean Swift. Another of the leading foreign correspondents of the Bible Society, was Professor Levade, of Lausanne, who, in his letters, used to boast of " the good resulting from the establishment of a Bible Society in our Canton." Although a translator of the Scriptures, and President of the Lausanne Bible Society, he was a bitter *persecutor*, and actually procured the banishment of a zealous English lady, already alluded to, whose hand he had previously sought. After Mr. T. P. Platt resigned his office of Honorary Librarian of the British and

Foreign Bible Society, he publicly related, that when, as a very young man, he visited Lausanne, his connexion with the British and Foreign Bible Society did not prevent his being introduced to a party of clergymen, Professors, and play-actors, with whom he was invited to sit down to a rubber at whist on the Lord's-day evening.

But this was not all. The encouragement given to the ungodly was bad enough. This could not, however, be done without also discountenancing the true ministers of Christ, and that at a time of persecution and trial. It would be easy to record facts as startling as they are painful, relative to the conduct and demeanour of the agents of Earl-street, when, in the presence of the persecutors and the persecuted, they were reduced to the necessity of determining whether to endure reproach with the people of God, or enjoy the support of His enemies. It is more agreeable to throw a veil over such occurrences, and only to allude to them as a solemn warning against the exercise of such worldly policy. M. Chenéviere did not, however, fail publicly to make use of these instances of unfaithfulness, as proofs that he had been enabled to "rectify" the notions of the representatives of the British and Foreign Bible Society. The principle on which they then acted was hollow and unsound, but it was a principle which had neither been canvassed nor fully examined. It was the principle of attempting to secure the circulation of the Bible by any means, and especially by the co-operation of the strongest and most influential party, without considering whether it consisted of the friends or the enemies of the Lord. In the Second Review, there is a remarkable letter from an eminent Genevese pastor, which contains the following passage :—

"Mr. Ronéberg (then Assistant Foreign Secretary of the British and Foreign Bible Society), wrote to me that, in passing by Geneva, he could not but laugh at seeing these little ones, who think that the whole world should be occupied about their four articles of controversy, while the Bible Society has many thousand Bibles to send to China, and over the whole world. By this you may judge, dear brother, if the old dragon does not know how to make use of Bible Societies." "The four articles,'

adds Mr. Haldane, " include the divinity of Christ, and the most important doctrines of the Bible."

Mr. Haldane had made good both of his points.  He had
proved that the Apocrypha was not necessary for the circulation
of the Bible, and, on the contrary, that it had been forced upon
those who were averse to the contamination of the Word of
God.  He had further proved, that by forming Associations
composed of Neologians and Socinians, there had been established on the Continent a machinery, by means of which the
preaching of the Gospel had been arrested, and persecution
promoted, by those who continued to enjoy the countenance
and correspondence of the British and Foreign Bible Society.
Time has illustrated both of these positions.

But perhaps the most flagrant proof of the wretched consequences of these unchristian alliances on the Continent, will be
found in the fact, now almost incredible, that the Bible Society
was induced, by the dread of giving offence, to refuse to intrust
Bibles for distribution to such able, holy, and zealous men as
Bost, Henri Pyt, the missionary of the Bearne and the
Pyrenees, or Felix Neff, " the apostle of the Alps."  Their
opportunities, as Continental missionaries, could not be doubted,
and Lord Teignmouth at first assured the late Sir Thomas
Baring, that there would be no difficulty in complying with
this request.  But Lord Teignmouth's desire was overborne,
and the refusal was justified on the ground of the jealousy
entertained in regard to them by the foreign allies of the
Society.  On this subject Sir Thomas Baring addressed an
indignant remonstrance to Lord Teignmouth :—

" If our Society " (the Continental), said its President, Sir Thomas
Baring, " were to publish all that has come to our knowledge respecting
the conduct of the Paris, Geneva, Strasburg, and other Bible Societies on
the Continent, to whom very liberal aid has been given by the London
Bible Society, it would very much weaken the confidence placed in these
Societies, consisting, as I have understood, of a large majority of free-
thinkers, who, having neither the glory of God nor the good of men
at heart, are not fit agents to be employed by the British and Foreign
Bible Society."

Mr. Haldane's Second Review produced a great sensation, and

in some quarters, as may be supposed, excited no little resentment.  In Scotland, it confirmed the impression made by the Edinburgh statements, and was appealed to in every future discussion.  Dr. Andrew Thomson characterized it as "by far the most powerful essay which has yet appeared on the controversy," and declares "that it gives such a view of the Foreign Societies, as should make every man tremble at the thought of employing them as agents."  Its accuracy was peculiarly striking, considering the vast variety of facts it deals with, and the large field over which it travels.  Every effort was made to impugn its statements, whilst vague charges of exaggeration or over-colouring scarcely deserved notice.  In a letter written on the 15th August, 1827, Mr. Haldane observes : "Is it not remarkable, that not a single statement in either of my Reviews has been disproved ? "  Among the many testimonies borne by distinguished men to the value of these publications, one may be selected.  It is that of the Rev. Dr. Gordon, who justly ranks as one of the most highly-gifted and spiritually-minded ministers of the Free Church of Scotland.  It is contained in a letter addressed to Mr. J. A. Haldane's son-in-law, Col. Eckford :—

" I cannot help alluding to the grand question that has for a considerable time agitated the Christian world.  I mean the controversy of the Edinburgh and British and Foreign Bible Society, about the circulation of the Apocrypha.  Our venerable friend, Mr. Robert Haldane, has stood forward in apostolic simplicity and might, the champion of the purity of God's Word.  His knowledge of the Continent gave him an advantage over the sickly, puling advocates of a worldly policy, and in two publications of unrivalled power, he has demolished the fairy and fanciful fabric which the compromising circulators of the Bible have reared, with the view of impressing the Christians of Great Britain that the seat of the beast had already become the garden of the Lord.  The public mind is not so stedfastly and so generally on the side of truth as we could wish, but it will come round.  I hope that among the communications you receive from this country, you will have these publications, as well as the statements of the Edinburgh Committee.  I cannot express to you the veneration I feel for Mr. Haldane's character.  Oh, for something more of his spirit, his simple, uncompromising, stern adherence to the truth!"

An extract from one of Mr. Haldane's own letters will serve

to indicate the temper in which he was so earnestly contending for what he believed to be the faith delivered to the saints. During the heat of the conflict, about the end of the year 1826, when such facts, as have been just related, were producing much excitement, one of the few members of the Elected Committee, who had both in public and in private assisted in putting down the circulation of the Apocrypha, and the employment of Neologian agency, seemed ready to faint, and had expressed himself as disposed to shrink from any longer encountering the pressure of opposition and obloquy to which the opponents of the rulers in Earl-street were exposed. To this Mr. Haldane thus alludes :—

"*25th December*, 1826.

" I trust that Mr. W—— will not faint in this business, and become weary of well-doing. Remind him of the magnitude of the question, which refers to the purity of the Divine Word, and the expulsion of that dreadful abomination, the Apocrypha—a question which now shakes all Europe, and which was never before agitated on its true merits, or to such an extent. Never in his life, it is probable, will he have such another opportunity of glorifying God. So far from sinking under the persecution and evil-speaking which he has to encounter, he should take fresh courage from them, like the Apostle Paul, and like him fight the good fight of faith. Let him by no means give up attending the Committee, but watch more earnestly and sedulously than ever. Let all of us remember the words of God, and not incur the rebuke, ' If thou faint in the day of adversity, thy strength is small.' ' If thou hast run with the footmen, and they have wearied thee, then how canst thou contend with horses ? and if in the land of peace, wherein thou trustedst, they wearied thee, then how wilt thou do in the swelling of Jordan ? ' Most gladly, then, let him rejoice in these tribulations. ' Be not afraid of their faces, for I am with thee to deliver thee, saith Jehovah.' Could the enemy desire anything better than that the servants of God should flee from their post, like Jonah, and succumb in such a struggle ? Let us be followers of them who through faith and patience inherit the promises ; and let us imbibe the sentiments, and imitate the conduct of him, who said, ' None of these things move me ; neither count I my life dear unto myself, so that I might finish my course with joy.' ' *Behold I come quickly !* hold that fast which thou hast, that no man take thy crown.' It is by taking this serious view of the subject, that those engaged and exposed to the heat of the battle will be enabled to stand, looking not to the things which are temporal, but to those which are eternal—to God, and not to man.

" Most affectionately yours, " ROBERT HALDANE."

This message was communicated to the member referred to, and he replied :—

" You have encouraged my heart and strengthened my hands by your kind letter, so full of Christian counsel and consolation.    Pray offer my affectionate respects to your venerable uncle, and tell him that it shall be my prayer, that his holy admonitions may be an effectual means of keeping me stedfast, unmoveable, always abounding in the work of the Lord." . . .

After remarking that those who were contending for the preservation of God's Word might truly say, "the battle is the Lord's," and the victory is his, he adds :—

" But I must stop.    You see that your kind letter has rekindled my smoking flax.    There is to be a meeting on Monday, although it be New Year's-day.    I think it will be anything but a *dies non.*
" With great respect and esteem, your obliged Friend,
" P. W."

Not long afterwards, Dr. Thomson thus writes :—

" It is now more necessary than ever for the friends of truth to speak truth, to uphold truth, to propagate truth, and not to be led away by that flimsy, mawkish, delusive sentiment, which is so prevalent amongst your men of flaming profession, and supersedes all exercise of understanding, and all depth of feeling, and all inflexibility of principle in matters of religion.    The more I know and observe the more am I jealous of its finding its way into Scotland, and impairing that honest, substantial, old-fashioned system, which has so long maintained its place amongst us. We need improvement, but we must not seek it, for we cannot get it, in the South.    The Bible Society controversy has opened my eyes wider to the fact than ever they were before.    The laxity of opinion that obtains among you is frightful.    Mr. Pratt, in his last ' Register,' tells an awful tale of those who prefer an unadulterated to a pure Bible."

Dr. Thomson would have modified his opinion as to "the South" had he been spared to see the improved tone of Christian principle which, at the Annual Meeting of the British and Foreign Bible Society in 1849, gladdened the heart of the late Edward Bickersteth.

# CHAPTER XXII.

THE CANON AND INSPIRATION OF SCRIPTURE — DR. PYE
SMITH'S DEFENCE OF DR. HAFFNER—DR. CARSON'S REPLY
—MR. HALDANE ON INSPIRATION—EXTRACTS FROM DR.
CARSON—PROFESSOR GAUSSEN'S THEOPNEUSTIA—PRO-
GRESS OF RIGHT VIEWS ON INSPIRATION—PROGRESSIVE
REFORMATION OF THE BIBLE SOCIETY — DISMISSAL OF
VAN ESS—ANGLICANUS—MR. HALDANE'S PAMPHLETS—
DR. THOMSON'S SPEECH—HIS VISIT TO PAUL'S CRAY—
DEPLORES THE PREVAILING LAXITY OF CHRISTIAN
PRINCIPLE—MR. HALDANE AT AUCHINGRAY.

[1826—1833.]

BOTH of the brothers always regarded the certainty of the Canon
of Scripture as the grand point at issue in the Apocrypha controversy. It was long, however, before this issue was distinctly
taken, and many vindicated the circulation of contaminated
Bibles, without considering the practice as one calculated to
disparage the majesty of the Word of God. Dr. Pye Smith's
apology for Haffner's preface at last introduced the discussion,
not only as to the canon, but the inspiration of the Bible. His
apology was, no doubt, a rash act of chivalry, partly attributable to his own indistinct views on the subject, and partly
to a desire to throw his shield over the Earl-street Committee.
It has been already noticed, that in a letter, written in 1837, he
himself acknowledged, with his accustomed candour, that, in
regard to Haffner, he "reflected with sorrow on the tone and
manner in which he wrote;" and Dr. Smith was too good and
holy a man to allow his pride long to triumph over his piety.

On Christmas-day, 1826, Mr. Robert Haldane writes:—

"At the end of this week Dr. Thomson's letter to Lord Bexley is to be
published; and in next month's 'Instructor' will be the review of the

Strasburg minutes. That subject demands the greatest attention. Dr. Pye Smith's papers, in vindication of Haffner, are the most dangerous that have yet appeared in the Apocrypha business. Your answer to him is quite triumphant, but the *principles* contained in his first paper require a full investigation. This has been very ably done, at my request, by one who does not wish his name to be affixed to it. Your father has read it, and much approves of it. From its development of general principles, it is calculated to counteract the erroneous sentiments of Dr. Smith, as well as to be very generally useful. The expense, of course, if it does not pay itself, I am answerable for."

The pamphlet alluded to was not, however, published anonymously, but appeared under the title of a "Review of Dr. Pye Smith's Defence of Dr. Haffner's Preface, and of his Denial of the Divine Authority of Part of the Canon, and of the full Inspiration of the Holy Scriptures, by Alexander Carson." Just before it appeared, Mr. Haldane writes :—

" There will," he says, " be about fifty pages respecting Haffner, and as many respecting Dr. Smith's theory of inspiration. The last, on inspiration, is not quite finished. They are both most powerful, especially the latter. Dr. Smith will find himself matched in learning and everything else."

In the same letter he writes :—

" I am also preparing, for separate publication, the two chapters in my first volume of ' Evidences on the Authenticity and on the Inspiration of the Scriptures.' Will you be so good as to read them as soon as you receive this, and send me any suggestions? The question of inspiration is one of the deepest moment, and will excite great attention."

Accordingly, he first re-published his own able treatise on the " Authenticity and Inspiration of the Scriptures," announcing, as its sequel, " Dr. Carson's Review of Dr. Pye Smith." Mighty in the Scriptures and simple in his aim, Robert Haldane never flinched from any contest in which the truth of God was at stake. He drew his arguments from an armoury with which he was perfectly familiar; but, knowing that he was not a match for Dr. Pye Smith in scholastic learning, philology, or minute criticism, he did not himself attempt this warfare. These branches of knowledge he neither overrated nor undervalued. The pastor of Tubbermore, in the north of Ireland, was a man of deep spiritual attainments and noble independence; one whose skill in the refinements of criticism, the subtleties of metaphysics, and the philosophy of language, left him few competitors. But, in his isolated position and with his contracted means, there was danger lest his abilities might be unexercised, like a piece of artillery which has fallen into a ditch or wants a gun-carriage. On various occasions it was, therefore, Mr. Haldane's privilege to be able to bring Dr. Carson's talents into the field by securing to him at least some reward for his literary labours, and always shielding him from loss. For many years a large proportion of Dr. Carson's works were, from time to time, sent over to Edinburgh and published at Mr. Haldane's expense. One of his productions, distinguished for its originality, is an "Essay on Figures of Speech." It was written whilst Mr. Haldane was on the Continent, and was therefore sent to his brother, who could not, however, find a publisher willing to undertake the risk, although the celebrated Dr. Thomas Brown, by whom the manuscript was read, pronounced it to be a master-piece. It was afterwards published in Dublin. Another work was his "Letter to Mr. Richard Carlile," the Atheist, which contains a striking argument, with reference to the character and attributes of God, in refutation of Infidelity. The question of inspiration was, however, most of all congenial to his tastes, his habits, and previous studies.

More than ten years before, Mr. Haldane had himself published a chapter on the plenary inspiration of Scripture, which had already attracted considerable attention and established the faith of several eminent ministers, amongst whom was the Rev. Marcus Dods, author of the valuable work on the Incarnation. It had also met with some opposition from those whose minds had been perverted by the unwarrantable theory of a graduated scale of inspiration, which Doddridge had imported from the German innovators who preceded Semler, the father of modern Neology. Mr. Haldane's was the first systematic treatise asserting the doctrine of plenary, or, what has been less appropriately called verbal, inspiration. But there were subtle objectors, who started puzzling questions, requiring to be discussed by a scholar critically acquainted with the original languages and well versed in all philological science. To some of these difficulties Dr. Carson addressed himself in his "Review of Dr. Smith's Defence of the Strasburg Preface." It was the first of a series of publications, each written at the suggestion of Mr. Haldane, and each published at his risk; so that, during a period of nearly ten years, Dr. Carson was enabled triumphantly to maintain the field against all comers, while he not only defended the Canon, which had been assailed, but, by overthrowing one adverse theory after another, proved to demonstration that the plenary inspiration of the Scriptures can never be successfully assailed, except through the sloth, the ignorance, or the cowardice, of those who choose to surrender without a struggle.*

* The following are some of Dr. Carson's works, relating to the inspiration of Scripture, which passed through Mr. Haldane's hands and were published for the learned author :—

1. "Review of the Rev. Dr. Pye Smith's Defence of Dr. Haffner's Preface to the Bible, and of his Denial of the Divine Authority of Part of the Canon, and of the Full Inspiration of the Holy Scriptures." 8vo., 1827.

2. "The Incompetency of the Rev. Professor Lee, of Cambridge, for Translating or Correcting Translations of Holy Scriptures, proved and illustrated in a Criticism on his Remarks on Dr. Henderson's Appeal to the Bible Society." 8vo., 1829.

3. "An Answer to the Letter of the Rev. Professor Lee, in Reply to the Proof and Illustration of his Incompetency for Translating or Correcting Translations of the Holy Scriptures." 1829.

4. "Theories of Inspiration of the Rev. Daniel Wilson (now Bishop of Calcutta), Rev. Dr. Pye Smith, and the Rev. Dr. Dick, proved to be erroneous; with Remarks on the 'Christian Observer' and 'Eclectic Review.'" 12mo., 1830.

5. "History of Providence, as unfolded in the Book of Esther." 1833. Second Edition, 18mo., 2s., 1836. This went through two editions, and was published in Dublin.

6. "Examination of the Principles of Biblical Interpretation of Ernesti, Ammon, Stuart, and other Philologists." 12mo., 1836. This is a most learned and elaborate specimen of a work which unhappily was never completed.

7. "Refutation of Dr. Henderson's Doctrine in his late Work on Divine Inspiration, with a Critical Discussion on 2 Timothy iii. 16." 1837.

8. "Review of Dr. Brown on the Law of Christ respecting Civil

The value of these works to a student of philology, as well as to the plain Bible reader, can hardly be overrated. Of the " Examination of the Principles of Biblical Interpretation," it is to be regretted that the second part was never completed. In the judgment of a learned Bishop, it proved the author to be " a first-rate scholar." But, away from College libraries, the labour was too great, and the second part never appeared.

Dr. Smith had said, that the book of Esther and the books of Chronicles, though not inspired, are " very properly included in our canon as both authentic and true." Dr. Carson replies, in a passage, exhibiting the logical accuracy as well as the force and the faults of a style which secured its author against plagiarism :—

" Now what canon? The answer is self-evident: canon of Scripture. What other canon is the writer here concerned with? *Included* in the canon of Scripture, while they are not Scripture! Included in a canon to which they do not belong! Included in the canon of inspired books, while they are not inspired! As well may Dr. Smith be included in the peerage, while he is not a peer; or be enrolled among crowned heads, while he is but a subject. Include the writings of men among the writings of God, under one designation! Was ever absurdity more monstrous? I had thought that the Church of Rome had exhausted all the mines of absurdity, but it seems there are some rich veins of unappropriated ore, left to be worked by Protestant divines, for the support of sophistry. The authenticity of a book does not entitle it to be taken into the canon of Scripture. Mathematical demonstrations have no more right to a place in the canon of the holy books, than the most extravagant romance. They are truths, but they are not the truths written by the Spirit of God, for the spiritual instruction of mankind. The Jewish canon was the canon of Scripture, not the canon of authentic books in general. Our canon is the canon of the books acknowledged as inspired, not the canon of all true history; Dr. Smith's canon would include all the authentic history of all ages and countries. Is not a canon a rule? and what rule ought any uninspired book to be in the things of God? . . . I thank thee, great Jesus, that thou hast not left the making of our Bible

Obedience, especially in the Payment of Tribute; with an Appendix relative to Grammatical Accuracy, as it bears on the question of Inspiration of the Scriptures, in reply to the Rev. Mr. Menzies, the translator of Tholuck." 1838.

to the ingenuity of learned doctors.  Much of thy wisdom in it appears to them to be folly.  Their learning is employed in mending thy work, and polishing what thy hand has left unfinished.  Go, Dr. Smith, enrol thy name with that of him, who, in the arrogance of his wisdom, boasted that he could have given a better model for creation, had he been admitted to the Divine counsels.  But let the Bible alone.  It is the very wisdom of wisdom.  The blemishes that the wisdom of this world finds in it, are often its greatest excellences."

After putting his own work to press, Mr. Haldane writes, on the 27th of January, 1827, "I am truly rejoiced that the subjects of the canon and inspiration have now come forward." He entertained no alarm as to the issue of the combat, and felt convinced that it was only from ignorance of their own strength, that Christians, like Dr. Pye Smith, had been tempted to abandon this citadel to the enemies of the Bible.  As an instance of the fearful extent to which a latitudinarian spirit had been spreading, the following extract is taken from one of Dr. Thomson's letters, written at the same time :—

" The battle rages in Newcastle. . . . The friends of your (the Earl-street) Committee are ruining their credit by eulogising the Apocrypha.  I am challenged to disprove its inspiration, and I am dared to prove the inspiration of some parts of the Bible, particularly those parts on which Pye Smith has put his ban !"

Mr. Haldane's treatise on inspiration sold rapidly.  It was published in March, and, on the 18th of May, he writes that his publisher informs him that the demand continued, and only two or three copies remained.  Other editions followed, and their good results have appeared in the wide diffusion of scriptural knowledge on a subject which till then had been little studied.  Dr. Carson's writings, notwithstanding his great qualities, were not generally popular, and although himself simple in his manners, humble and amiable as Dr. Pye Smith himself, the dogmatic power with which he denounced error, and the unsparing sarcasm with which he unmasked every attempt at sophistry, created prejudices which it was difficult to surmount.  For example, in the very first page of his " Review," he characterizes Dr. Pye Smith's defence of Haffner's " Preface," as "one of the most *detestable* productions" he had ever seen from the pen of a Christian. Yet for Dr. Smith's personal character he entertained a high respect. It was not Mr. Haldane's fault if Dr. Carson's writings were not more generally sought after, for he distributed, gratuitously, hundreds of almost every work he published. For example, in a letter, dated the 12th of April, 1827, he writes:—

"By mistake only two hundred of Carson's 'Review' were sent to London. I intended that there should have been three hundred, that you might consider in what way it was best to distribute them. It is so important a publication, containing principles so essential and so ably stated, that it is peculiarly adapted for England, where many view the subject of which it treats in a very loose and superficial manner."

The reader has already seen something of the style of Dr. Carson. It is so clear and epigrammatic; it possesses so much of idiosyncracy and originality, that a paragraph or a sentence of his might be picked out amongst a thousand. His concluding address to Dr. Smith is equally applicable to those who, like Coleridge and his disciples, would deny the inspiration of large portions of the Bible, and still say that it contains the Word of God. It is not thus that either Deists or Pantheists will be convinced:—

"Let not Dr. Smith vainly imagine, that by throwing the objected books overboard, he will be able to keep the ship from sinking, and save the rest. When he offers to surrender these books to the Deist, if he knows his business, the Deist will not take them from him. He may reply, Dr. Smith, these books that you give up to me, are authenticated by him you call your Master, and, by him, you denominate the great Apostle of the Gentiles. You must acknowledge them as yours, or you must surrender at discretion, and give me up all the writings of Paul, and all the authority of Jesus. If the one falls, the other will fall, of course. Who can depend on Jesus, if he has acknowledged the authority of a book, which you and I have found to be the writing of a 'wicked Jew?' What credit can be given to Paul, if he has so egregiously lied about these books? 'Or fight, or yield.' . . . Dr. Smith, you are engaged in a very unholy cause. Your genius and learning are very ill employed. You are labouring to unsettle the canon of Scripture, and to unhinge the mind of simple Christians, by your speculations. You have denied the verbal inspiration of the Word of God, and every kind of inspiration to all the passages that any one may choose to consider not of a religious or moral nature, and you close by rejecting whole books, on principles that will condemn the whole Bible. Your speculations are very crude. Your sentiments are self-contradictory, and your half-formed conceptions show that you have been too hasty in giving your opinions to the world. You must go back or forward. Stationary you cannot remain. Make the best use of your learning, but humble yourself before God, and seek more of the teaching of his Spirit, in the reading of his Word. Without much learning it is impossible to be a Biblical critic; but all the learning of Bentley will be insufficient, without that child-like disposition of the wisdom given from on high, which teaches to cry, 'Speak, Lord, for thy servant heareth.' Mary, the sister of Lazarus, is a better model for a Christian minister than Dr. Haffner, the learned Professor of Strasburg."

Nothing can be named in the history of Robert Haldane's labours, more important than his efforts to establish the doctrine of plenary inspiration. Rather more than two years before his death, he had the satisfaction of welcoming an able defence of that great truth from the pen of his friend, Professor Gaussen, of Geneva. The following is an extract of a letter written to Mr. Haldane by that accomplished and eloquent divine, dated Geneva, the 26th of March, 1840 :—

" I would much like to see your 'Strictures on Tholuck.' I only know Carson from his excellent 'Treatise on Inspiration.' I have prepared for publication on the same subject, a volume, in which I have applied myself to the removal of those objections which are made to plenary inspiration on the Continent. I will send it to you. It was your writings on that subject, which *first* made me feel the importance of being immovable on that doctrine, and the more I advance, the more am I convinced of its truth."

In another letter, at the end of the same year, M. Gaussen, in sending his " Theopneustia," observes :—

" Allow me to address to you this volume. You will read it with the interest you take in the subject, but with that which you have in the author. It was yourself who *first* made him feel the truth and importance of this doctrine, and it was your excellent book, which kindled in him the desire that there might appear in French some work adapted to the wants of our Church; and answering the objections which have the greatest run among us. I shall always take a filial and fraternal interest in hearing tidings of you, and as to your writings, *I consider them as*

*bearing more than any other modern works, the character of an accurate
and profound theology.* I beg you, very particularly, to present to your
brother, Mr. James Haldane, the expression of my respect, and my
remembrance of his fraternal reception. Adieu, my dear Brother, and
receive my true and tender regards.

"Your devoted,

"L. GAUSSEN."

M. Gaussen's "Theopneustia," or "It is written," became
a magazine of sound argument and information, both on the
Continent and at home. It has been translated into English,\* 
both in Great Britain and America, and its popularity has
become deservedly great. Dr. Chalmers, as Professor of Theology, was wont to use as class-books the Treatises both of Mr.
Haldane and Dr. Carson, so that, at home and abroad, the
views on inspiration, which were, at first, scouted by the
"Eclectic," as "*Mr. Haldane's wild dogma,*" are taught by
authority, and very generally received by the soundest divines.
Several instances of learned Professors who had previously
adopted Dr. Doddridge's German theory, abandoned the erroneous and groundless system of gradations, and publicly acknowledged the change. Such was the case with the late
learned Dr. Steadman, the head of the Baptist College at
Bradford, who told his students that, in regard to inspiration,
he had been misleading them, and that Mr. Haldane's work had
convinced him of his mistake. He, therefore, proposed to read
and comment on that gentleman's Treatise, as a substitute for
his own former lectures.

The following extract from a letter of the learned and Rev. Dr.
Gordon, of Edinburgh, is an answer to those, who, through
ignorance of the subject, have imagined that in contending for
plenary verbal inspiration, Mr. Haldane was arguing for ventri-
loquism, as Coleridge imagined, or "for mechanical dictation,"
as others have assumed. Even Dr. Eadie, of Glasgow, in his (on
the whole) excellent treatise, has, from superficial observation,
fallen into this extraordinary mistake. No one who has atten-

---

\* The best translation is that by David Dundas Scott, Esq., published
by Messrs. Johnstone and Hunter, Edinburgh.

tively read Mr. Haldane's book will entertain such a prepos-
terous notion :—

"I really have nothing to suggest on your chapter on Inspiration. *I
have perused it again, and it appears to me complete.* I see that at
page 138 you have the *substance* of what I hinted the other day about
the varieties to be found in parallel accounts of the same transactions.
At the same time I think it might be useful to enlarge a little upon it, as
I have reason to believe that it is one of the strongest points in the estimation of the supporters of degrees of inspiration. It is evident that the
variety militates no more against plenary inspiration than against the
inspiration of superintendence, if the Holy Spirit sanctioned variety, and
it might be shown that such variety is of essential importance in the
Gospel narratives, in bringing out very interesting views which could not
be exhibited in a single narrative. What would you think of offering
something in the way of a definition of what you mean by plenary inspiration? For one of the arguments of opponents will be to attach a meaning
to the expression which you do not attach to it. *For example, they will
assume that it made the inspired writers mere mechanical utterers of
sounds.* I am aware that you have met this fully at page 138, in the
paragraph beginning, 'Neither does the difference,' &c. But, perhaps,
to enunciate it as a proposition might bring it more clearly out."

Another of Dr. Gordon's suggestions which Mr. Haldane so
justly valued, not only on account of his piety, but of his
mathematical and logical turn of mind, relates to the sophism
so often used during the Apocrypha controversy, to the effect
that the question of the canon was only a matter of erudition :—

"It occurred to me that a sentence might be inserted, at part marked
with the cross ✕, somewhat to this effect : 'That the integrity of the
canon is no more a point of erudition than the question whether there be
a revelation at all. If it be a question whether the books contained in
the Bible be those which the Jews possessed, and if this question be
determined by examining the unbroken chain of evidence which has
come down from the time of the Jews till the present day, so it may be a
question whether the Jews ever received any such books; and if it be
lawful to doubt the former question, because it may involve what is called
a matter of erudition, in the same way the second may be doubted
without blame, or, in other words, we are at liberty to take as much or as
little of the Bible as we please.'

" I don't know if you will perceive the drift of my remark, nor am I sure that it would at all add to the strength of your argument.

" Yours, ever truly,

" Robert Gordon."

There is a passage in Paul's last Epistle to Timothy which has often been referred to as beneath the dignity of inspiration, that passage, namely, in which Paul, whilst incarcerated in the dungeons of the Mammertine prison, and awaiting his martyrdom, sends for the cloak which he left at Troas. Mr. Haldane's exposure of the futility of this objection is an example of his simple, yet forcible style, and of the power of contrast in which he excelled. After some prefatory remarks, he proceeds :—

" On the approach of winter, in a cold prison, and at the termination of his course, the Apostle Paul appears here to be a follower indeed of Him who had not where to lay his head. He is presented to our view as actually enduring those hardships which elsewhere he describes in a manner so affecting,—' in prisons, in cold, in nakedness.' He had abandoned, as he elsewhere informs us, all the fair prospects that once opened to him of worldly advantages, for the excellency of the knowledge of Christ, and had suffered the loss of all things; and in this Epistle we see all that he has said on the subject embodied and verified. He is about to suffer death for the testimony of Jesus ; and now he requests one of the few friends that still adhered to him (all the others, as he tells us, having forsaken him) to do his diligence to come before winter, and to bring to him his *cloak*. Here, in his solemn farewell address, of which the verse before us forms a part, the last of his writings, and which contains a passage of unrivalled grandeur, the Apostle of the Gentiles is exhibited in a situation deeply calculated to affect us. We behold him standing on the confines of the two worlds,—in this world about to be beheaded, as guilty, by the Emperor of Rome,—in the other world to be crowned, as righteous, by the King of kings,—here deserted by men, there to be welcomed by angels,—here in want of a cloak to cover him, there to be clothed upon with his house from heaven."

To assert and defend the authenticity of the canon and the plenary inspiration of Scripture, was one of the great objects for which Robert Haldane lived. To him it mattered not by whom the truth was assailed. In the judgment of Dr. Pye Smith, and of all competent observers, he was addicted to " cool reasoning" beyond most men, and after the calm study of the

Word of God, and a careful examination of the subject, he had arrived at the deliberate conviction that the Bible was in all its parts,—in thought, in meaning, in style, in expression, in every part, and in the strictest sense,—the work and the Word of God. Persuaded of this great truth, he felt its power in his heart, and laboured with a zeal worthy of all admiration to beat down the assaults of error and clear away the mists of prejudice, doubt, or unbelief. It was this that roused him to contend as he did against the contamination of the holy Scriptures by the foreign agents and Continental Auxiliaries of the Bible Society. "The grandeur of the cause" sustained him, and that grandeur will be fully appreciated when it is seen in the light of eternity.*

---

\* There is an interesting anecdote, which was related by the late Rev. Dr. Walter Buchanan, with reference to one of the means which seems to have been provided in order to secure the New Testament either from interpolation or corruption:—

"I was dining," said Dr. Buchanan, "some time ago with a literary party at old Mr. Abercromby's, of Tullibody (the father of Sir Ralph Abercromby, who was slain in Egypt), and we spent the evening together. A gentleman present put a question which puzzled the whole company. It was this: Supposing all the New Testaments in the world had been destroyed at the end of the third century, could their contents have been recovered from the writings of the three first centuries? The question was novel to all, and no one even hazarded a guess in answer to the inquiry.

"About two months after this meeting I received an invitation to breakfast with Lord Hailes (Sir David Dalrymple) next morning. He had been of the party. During breakfast he asked me if I recollected the curious question about the possibility of recovering the contents of the New Testament from the writings of the three first centuries? 'I remember it well, and have thought of it often without being able to form any opinion or conjecture on the subject.'

"'Well,' said Lord Hailes, 'that question quite accorded with the turn or taste of my antiquarian mind. On returning home, as I knew I had all the writers of those centuries, I began immediately to collect them, that I might set to work on the arduous task as soon as possible.' Pointing to a table covered with papers, he said, 'There have I been busy for those two months, searching for chapters, half chapters, and sentences of

The Annual Meeting of 1826 commenced a new era in the British and Foreign Bible Society, and one of gradual reform. But the change was not at first clearly discerned. On the contrary, apart from the requisition to acknowledge past errors, to renounce Apocryphal connexions abroad, and to effect some changes in the personal administration of the Society, there were repeated instances of what at least appeared to be a disposition to revert to the circulation of adulterated Bibles, and, at all events, to permit of an agency whose functions were divided between pure and impure Bible distribution. This arose partly from the fact that the Society had still on hand, in foreign depôts, a large number of adulterated Bibles; that, at first, there was also a considerable stock of stereotype plates, from which more copies might be taken at pleasure of the intermingled Apocrypha, and that some of the foreigners in whose custody they were, openly disapproved of the Anti-Apocryphal Resolutions, and regarded them as, at best, only prospective in their operations. Many a warm discussion arose in the Committee out of this state of things, and for several years the warfare was in Earl-street carried on by the Anti-Apocryphists with more or less success, obtained through the aid of privileged members, who occasionally outvoted the elected, and once even carried a Resolution amounting to a vote of censure on the Secretary.

The majority of the Committee still placed unbounded reliance on Leander Van Ess, although many things had occurred which ought to have shaken their confidence in that Romish priest. The fact that he was a priest and a Romanist threw an air of romance over his zeal for the book which is " mighty through

the New Testament, and have marked down what I found, and where I have found it, so that any person may examine and see for himself. I have actually discovered the whole New Testament except seven or eleven verses (I forget which), which satisfies me that I could discover them also. Now,' said he, ' here was a way in which God concealed or hid, the treasures of his Word, that Julian, the apostate Emperor, and other enemies of Christ who wished to extirpate the Gospel from the world, never would have thought of; and though they had, they never could have effected their destruction.' "

God to the pulling down of the strongholds" of Popery. It would, however, in those days have sounded like bigotry had any one ventured to throw doubt on his sincerity. " I would gladly sit at the feet of such a man as Leander Van Ess ! " exclaimed an eloquent clergyman at a Meeting of the Hibernian Society, where the Marquis of Lansdowne presided ; and no doubt the Noble Marquis was induced to believe that the warfare of opposing sects was wearing out, and that Rome and Geneva were about to fraternize. After a protracted struggle, the Philo-Apocryphists succeeded in gaining permission for Van Ess to receive grants of Bibles *unbound*, on the plea that the restrictive Resolutions applied to Societies, and not to individual agents. But the delusion in regard to this remarkable priest was not destined long to survive. It was at length clearly shown, that besides a salary of 300*l*. a-year, and other allowances, to which there was no objection but their concealment, Van Ess had received in money grants 20,000*l*. in nine years, and that all the while he had in his own person united the characters of printer, bookbinder, and bookseller. It was therefore clear, to say the least, that he was not the man represented as seeking no earthly " treasures where moth and rust corrupt." But, in addition to all this, the attention of the Committee was pointedly called by one of its elected members to the startling fact, for more than three years known to Mr. Haldane, Dr. Thomson, and others, which seemed to indicate that his practical morality was, at all events, no higher than that of some of his order. When asked for an explanation as to the lady whom hitherto he had introduced as his sister, he pleaded the seal of the confessional as an apology for a continued mystery. It is needless to add, that he ceased to be an agent of Earl-street, and thus, but not before the year 1829, one flagrant occasion of contention was removed. Happy would it have been for the Society had this course been taken in 1824, when Van Ess adjured the Committee, by that name which is above every name, to continue an adulterated Bible, and, if necessary, to do so in a manner that would have been an evasion.

The melancholy case of Leander Van Ess has been very lightly touched, and it would not have been here touched at all, except as another historical fact illustrating the danger of alliances with Rome, and proving with how little reason the opposition to such an agent had been denounced as an example of a bad spirit. Well might Mr. Haldane exclaim, " What must be thought of the principles of those foreign coadjutors who did not deem it necessary to communicate what they *knew* of Van Ess !" Many of the most esteemed friends of the Bible Society were deceived into a veneration of that Romish priest amounting almost to idolatry, so that to have " sat in his chair," to have " seen his study," or to have passed a day in his presence, was published as an honour worthy of record. Other facts might be mentioned of a similar purport, but for the desire to avoid painful reminiscences. For this reason, the greater part of the discussions occasioned by the letters of Anglicanus, the debate about the Septuagint* and the canon of Scripture introduced by Mr. Gorham, together with other matters of the same kind, may be left, with this passing notice, to sleep in oblivion. In regard to Anglicanus, a few words will suffice. His pamphlet was published at the end of 1827, under a delusive *nomme de guerre*. The discovery of the editor was made by one of those singular occurrences which illustrate the adage, that truth is stranger than fiction. The proof sheets of a pamphlet, in which Dr. Thomson was the chief butt for ridicule and vituperation, were carried, by the mistake of a printer's boy, to Dr. Thomson himself, and so divulged the editor. It might possibly have been better had the secret never transpired, and had both the editor and author been able to preserve their mask. The publication of Anglicanus indicated the partial division which had taken place in Scotland. The unanimity previously subsisting was broken, and a few of the original Anti-Apocryphists seceded from the Edinburgh Committee, and formed first a Corresponding Board, and then an Auxiliary, in connexion with the London

---

* The chief facts of this discussion which concerned the question of the canon are to be found in the " Edinburgh Christian Instructor," and in Mr. Henry Drummond's " Letter to Alexander Haldane, Esq., respecting the Septuagint," with a preface, by Dr. Thomson, 1829.

Society. Amongst the chief leaders were the Rev. Henry Grey, the Rev. Dr. John Brown, and the Rev. Edward Craig. In Glasgow there was also a partial secession, headed by the distinguished names of Dr. Wardlaw, Mr. Ewing, and Dr. Dick. To the publications of Mr. Grey, Dr. Wardlaw, and Dr. Dick, as well as to the statements of the Edinburgh Corresponding Board and the new Glasgow Auxiliary, answers were successively written by Mr. Haldane, in no less than six distinct pamphlets, each exhibiting his usual uncompromising steadiness of purpose. To Mr. Ewing he, with great good taste, avoided all allusion. Scotland, upon the whole, remained firm in its opposition to Earl-street, and Dr. Thomson's efforts to put down everything that threatened the integrity of the sacred canon were unwearied and astounding. In February, 1829, after noticing a meeting at Dunfermline, where he spoke for four hours and a-half to a crowded assembly, who did not separate till past midnight, he writes :—

"I have no fear of conquering, if I have time and strength. But really I am obliged to neglect some professional duties, and my bodily frame begins to feel weariness. I sometimes wonder that I hold out. The grandeur of the cause animates me, and I look to Him whose Word it is that we are defending for the strength that is necessary."

The establishment of the Edinburgh Corresponding Board, and the singular discovery of the authorship of "Anglicanus," produced a great sensation. The Annual Meeting of the Edinburgh Bible Society, in July, 1828, was looked for with intense interest. The following is an account from Dr. Thomson's own pen :—

"Our Annual Meeting on Tuesday went off amazingly well. I requested your father or your brother to write you a full account of it, as I was too much engaged to get that accomplished so early as you wished to hear of the affair. Your uncle and Lockhart gave us excellent speeches. The crowd was immense. The interest seemed to be deeper than ever, and there was every conceivable symptom of our principles and our cause being now triumphant. I opened a battery on the Corresponding Board, and fired for three hours and ten minutes. I repudiated their laxity of sentiment. . . . The complete sympathy of the audience followed. In short, we never had such a glorious Meeting. Your uncle was so much impressed, that though in the course of his own speech he rather condemned the practice of ruffing (violent applause, beating with the feet, &c.), and is, you know, very much against it, I detected him more than once using his umbrella most vigorously on the platform. This is a capital joke I have got against him. He was truly delighted with the whole affair. The speeches were taken in short-hand, and are to be published by Whyte. Of course, whenever they and the Report appear, I will send you copies for yourself and our good friends."

In the earlier part of the same summer, Dr. Thomson visited London, and for six Sundays preached in the Scotch Church, Regent-square. He also held a public Meeting, at which he gave an account of the reasons for the continued rupture between the Northern and Southern Bible Societies. During this visit many prejudices against him vanished, and those who had pictured to themselves a son of the desert, stern and bigoted in his zeal, were agreeably surprised to find him bland and engaging in his manners, full of the milk of human kindness, with all the generosity superadded to the boldness of the lion. Amongst others, he was welcomed by the venerable John Simons, of Paul's-cray. It was Mr. Simons to whom Mr. Haldane, in his first review, alludes as a much-respected Rector, who said he had " come to town on purpose to bear his testimony against the horrible idea of man's attempting to bolster up the Word of the living God by a lie. Granted, that Romanists will not receive the Bible without this false book being appended to it; and let all the priests array themselves to oppose it; let there be a pitched battle, and see whether God or man will prevail. Can He who gave that Word not open a door for its reception? Or has the Society the presumption to imagine that God will go forth to battle with such miserable aid to secure his victory?"

When Mr. Simons, therefore, heard of Dr. Thomson's being in London, he invited him to pay a visit at his Rectory, and welcomed him as the champion of the pure Bible, and the assailant of Neologian alliances. The venerable old man came out of his Rectory to the lawn to meet him and his friends, as soon as their carriage stopped, and after a fashion peculiar to himself, bringing with him bread and wine, he blessed them in the name of the Lord. The blessing Dr. Thomson gladly accepted, but he declined the offer of the bread and wine, thinking that it betokened a reference too sacred and sacramental. In the evening the great Presbyter, who was passionately fond of music, accompanied a relative of Lord Bexley's on the organ, whilst he himself sung and chanted some of the Psalms to the fine old Scottish tunes, which are endeared to Scotland by the memory of the sufferings of their ancestors, from Hamilton, the first, to Renwick, the last of the martyrs. It was one of those sunny days, leaving behind bright recollections always to be fondly cherished. Shortly afterwards, in one of his letters, as usual full of life and vivacity, Dr. Thomson thus recals his visit to Paul's-cray :—

" So Captain Atchison is to be married to Miss Simons. Give my best Christian wishes to both. How is the old gentleman? I remember him with a sort of romantic affection. He is like no other human being I ever met with. The perpetual outpouring of his thoughts and feelings, the giving of the sacrament on the circular plot of grass, the innocent peculiarities of the dinner table, the marvelling that I should not speak when he would not listen, the approbation of the organ and the Scotch Psalms, &c., I have more than once recalled to my recollection, with *melancholy mirth*. Good old man! I love him. Give my filial reverence when you see him. I beg my very best remembrances to my demi-semi Apocryphal friend, Mrs. Haldane, who must have been greatly shocked at the affair of Scio's Bible and the attempted concealments of June 2."

There were those who predicted that it would be found impossible for two such uncompromising chiefs as Dr. Thomson and Mr. Haldane to persevere in harmony. Their opponents watched for their halting, and tried to separate them. But they were disappointed; for the secret of their union consisted in this, that they were not acting a part, or courting personal renown, but were both thoroughly in earnest in the same cause. In particular, Aliquis reprinted Mr. Haldane's rebuke to the editor of the " Edinburgh Instructor," published in 1820, and jocosely foretold another chastisement for the editor's more recent misdemeanours in the way of levity in the Bible Society controversy. Dr. Thomson noticed this, and observed, with equal magnanimity and good sense, that the attempt to sow strife between brethren would not succeed; that Mr. Haldane had given the "Instructor" some very sound advice, from which he trusted he had profited. In fact, his affection and admiration both for Mr. Haldane and his brother, "for the truth's sake," increased as they went on harmoniously together. He would sometimes use the homely Scotticism, which betokened his own humility and his panting after greater conformity to the mind that was in Christ, that they had "got further ben" than himself; meaning that they had penetrated further into the interior of the heavenly mansion. Often would he relate with pleasure little traits exhibited by Mr. Haldane of that social hilarity in which he himself so much delighted, and would tell how welcome were some of the unlooked-for evening visits to his house of his venerable friend, and how the hearts of his children had been won by little acts of kindness and atten- tion. In a letter written in 1829, he says: "Your uncle has been ailing, but is now getting better, and the doctor assures me he is in no danger. May his valuable life long be spared!"

The excitement occasioned by the disclosure of such facts as those related in this chapter could not fail to produce much hot discussion. But, in the midst of it all, Robert Haldane was enabled steadily to keep in view the great and glorious object for which alone he contended. The following is an extract of a letter, dated 17th September, 1827, shortly after the publication of "Anglicanus:"—

"At Auchingray I much enjoyed his spiritual conversation. Truly 'his communion is with the Father and his Son Jesus Christ.' His prayers are of a character altogether heavenly. There is such an absence of excitation, and yet such a soaring to the presence of God himself. Ah! my dear ——, let those who speak so lightly of the Apocrypha contro- versy, whilst they are themselves busy with the world, go and see him in his own house, and then say if his is the spirit of the mere controversialist. On this question he is indeed as resolute as ever, and speaks of the good already accomplished with gratitude to God. He encouraged me much as to the issue of the contest. 'Look back,' he said, 'if you live twenty, or even twelve years, and then, when prejudices have died away and angry passions are lulled, remember what I told you, and observe the results of the battle which now rages so fiercely. All of human infirmity that now obscures this great work will pass away like smoke, but the flame will continue to burn and prove a beacon to distant posterity.'"

# CHAPTER XXIII.

RISE OF IRVINGISM—REV. EDWARD IRVING—MR. J. A. HAL-
DANE'S REFUTATION—DISCUSSION WITH MR. DRUMMOND
—GIFT OF TONGUES—MR. J. E. GORDON—DEATH OF DR.
THOMSON—HIS CHARACTER—DR. THOMSON'S FAREWELL
SPEECH—CAPTAIN J. E. GORDON—ANNUAL MEETING OF
THE BRITISH AND FOREIGN BIBLE SOCIETY, 1831—
INSTITUTION AND FAILURE OF THE TRINITARIAN BIBLE
SOCIETY—PAMPHLETS OF MR. SCOTT, MR. J. J. GURNEY,
AND OTHERS, ANSWERED BY MR. HALDANE—MR. WILKS'
ATTACK—MR. HALDANE'S ANSWER—CHARACTER OF MR.
HALDANE'S PAMPHLETS—PROGRESSIVE PURIFICATION
OF THE BIBLE SOCIETY—MR. BICKERSTETH'S MOTION—
GOOD EFFECTS OF THE CONTROVERSY.

[1820—1833.]

In the midst of the debates relative to the certainty of the
canon and the plenary inspiration of the Bible, there arose a
more ephemeral but still an important discussion, in which
James Haldane took a prominent part. It related to the pretensions to miraculous powers, and the gift of tongues, assumed
by the followers of Edward Irving. These assumptions were
connected with metaphysical speculations on the humanity of
our Lord, which Mr. Irving and his followers were not disposed
to regard as that "holy thing" spoken of in Scripture. They
described our Lord's humanity not merely as fallen, but actually
sinful. With many of the Irvingites, there is, however, no
doubt that there was more of metaphysical confusion than of
wilful heresy mixed up with these unprofitable and dangerous
speculations. Almost from the beginning Mr. J. A. Haldane

descried the peril, and sounded the alarm.  The following is an extract from a letter dated 11th August, 1827 :—

" I have always been afraid of the system of the prophets, from the moment I first heard of it.  It has always struck me as being a snare of Satan to lead believers away from the fundamental doctrine of Christ, to what is at best but a speculation.  I remember when I was a child asking Lord Duncan, who was, as I saw, much taller and stouter than other men, and of whose great strength I had formed a high opinion, whether he thought he was as strong as the devil?  And I asked the question in all seriousness.  He told me he was not, and I believed him. Now, if I thought myself as strong as the devil, I should be less afraid of quitting the plain ground of Scripture, and embarking in speculative inquiries, but as I do not think so, I am like one who will not venture into a dark wood with a person whom he distrusts.  I believe the prophets to be excellent men, but I dread the subtlety of Satan, and am much afraid he will in some way get an advantage over them, although he may be transformed into an angel of light.  We all require to watch and pray, and then we need not fear him."

But the first development of the error respecting the sinful humanity, is thus alluded to in the following letter, written nearly a year later :—

" *Edinburgh, 19th June,* 1828.
" Captain Tait will tell you of the dreadful accident at the church of Kirkaldy, where Mr. Irving was to have preached, of which, however, you have probably already heard.  Every one here complains of the want of the Gospel, in Mr. Irving's lectures, and even of a want of practical application of the doctrine of the coming of the Lord. . . . No one will question the importance of the belief of the personal reign, if it be true, but Mr. Irving has told us it was a subject of which the apostles were ignorant, and I am less afraid of erring in company with apostles than with Mr. Irving.  It is quite different from election, for the know-ledge of election is essential to just views of the Gospel of man's lost estate, and the riches of the grace of God.  The apostles could not have been ignorant of election.  Doubtless, a man may depend on Christ for salvation, while election is to him a bugbear, but *every one who holds that all good is from God, and all evil from ourselves, virtually holds election,* and this is the case with all Christians, however they may express them-selves.  Mr. Irving lately brought forward a very pernicious sentiment, that the flesh of Christ was, like ours, disposed to sin, although he was preserved from sin by the power of the Holy Ghost.  This was inserted in the newspapers, in the account of his lecture.  I preached in consequence on Luke i. 35, not, of course, referring to him.  I after-

wards dined with him at a large party at your uncle's, and the subject was introduced, not by your uncle or me, for we were both against its being spoken of. Mr. Irving became rather warm,—at least, seemed hurt. I was sorry for it, as he has had a great deal of labour. I liked his conversation on the whole, although he feels himself too much like an oracle. But perhaps the discussion may be useful to him, for it is a most pernicious error. He rested on the words, ' being tempted in all things as a man.' This, like many other declarations, is true in one sense, and not in another. For every man is tempted when he is drawn away of his own lust, and enticed. This was not the case with Christ, for the prince of this world found nothing in him, no lust on which his temptation could operate. Objects of temptation were presented, but like a thing perfectly incombustible, on which the fire makes no impression, so was the holy mind of Jesus. Considering Christ's human nature as having no personal subsistence, but subsisting in the person of the Son of God, two distinct natures in *one* person, the idea of anything verging to unholiness in Christ's human nature is absurd."

This, however, was only the beginning of the evil, and when Mr. Irving afterwards employed language which was subversive of the doctrine of imputed righteousness, and of the foundations of the Gospel, Mr. J. A. Haldane published a " Refutation of the heretical Doctrine promulgated by the Rev. Edward Irving, respecting the Person and Atonement of the Lord Jesus Christ." Rejecting the metaphysical speculations of the Irvingites, and bringing their bold but contradictory statements into the light of God's revealed Word, he writes in a spirit altogether becoming the disciple of his Master: but as the danger has passed over, it is unnecessary minutely to enter into the question. The name of Edward Irving will remain to all time a monument of the folly of a proud reliance upon self, and of the danger of popular applause. His genius, his talents, his eloquence, and his eccentricities, were a snare to him, and but for the grace of God, must assuredly have proved his ruin. He borrowed his doctrine of the sinful humanity from Mr. Vaughan, of Leicester, whose metaphysical subtlety procured him the title of the modern Aquinas. Mr. Vaughan's delicacy of perception prevented his going to the same length as his less discriminating disciple, but whilst the language used by Mr. Irving was awful, and on some occasions bordering even upon blasphemy, it is

only charitable to hope that his heresies consisted in the unad-
vised words of his lips, not in the actual rebellion of his heart.
Many were led by him to deny the imputation of Christ's
righteousness, and finally to stumble for ever on the dark
mountains. But although a cloud rests upon the closing scenes
of Edward Irving's life, there is ground to believe that amidst
the flickering light of bewildered reason he was discovering his
errors, and at last found resting on that rock which is Christ.
Mr. James Haldane's Refutation was the first decided blow
struck at these novelties. It was followed by some able
reviews in the "Edinburgh Christian Instructor," and afterwards by the masterly work of the Rev. Marcus Dods, on the
"Incarnation of the Eternal Word." Mr. H. Drummond,
without adopting all of Mr. Irving's heretical language, came
to his rescue in what he rather facetiously termed, "A *Candid*
Examination of the Controversy between Messrs. Irving, Andrew
Thomson, and James Haldane." Mr. Drummond's acuteness
of intellect, acquaintance with literature, and smartness of
repartee, were enough to render his apology both clever and
specious. It was, to say the least, a diversion in favour of his
friend, and a carrying of the war into the enemies' camp, by
splitting hairs in metaphysics, detecting the inconsistencies,
real or supposed, of his opponents, and wringing from their
language a meaning which they never entertained. But the
character of his mind was not adapted for the details of that
patient investigation which the great subject in debate demanded.
He was too daring in his flights, and too eager to exercise himself with things too high for finite man. He knew much of
theology, but although his perceptions were quick, and his
reading varied, he had not studied it as a science, in its comprehensive principles, its consistent proportions, or its historical
illustrations. Hence, it is no matter of surprise that, like some
other able men, he did not always distinguish between essential
truth and the errors grafted on it by human fancy, between
"the deep things of God" and the false and deceitful lights
which emanate from "the depths of Satan." Hence the
inconsistency of his extraordinary career, during which he has

been at one time claimed by Geneva, and at another almost welcomed by Rome.   Hence his support of those wild vagaries which made Edward Irving pass away like a blazing meteor, instead of shining as a fixed star of the first magnitude.

Mr. James Haldane's answer to the Candid Examination, published by Mr. Drummond in a volume of two hundred and seventy-seven pages, was, as Dr. Thomson said, not only able, acute, and well-timed, but for ever settled the question between the two combatants.   The collision was to be regretted, but Mr. Drummond was the assailant.

" I wrote," says Mr. James Haldane, " to Mr. Drummond with kindness, privately, according to the feeling of my heart, but I will not mince matters in regard to any man when I think the truth of God is concerned.   I am sorry for it, but the truth will prevail.   It is my prayer that both he and Irving may find mercy of the Lord in that day.   I am not called on to judge of their state as believers, or otherwise, nor do I intend to do so. I shall endeavour to reply to his charges, and I trust the Lord will enable me to do it as I ought."   Again : "I am not puzzled in replying to any of Mr. Drummond's arguments, and this is a guarantee against personal irritation.   He is a clever man, but his position in life, especially connected with his peculiar cast of mind, is a great snare.   May the Lord grant that he may find mercy in that day!"

Mr. Drummond's " Supplement to the Candid Examination " displayed more of mortified feeling than it was wise to exhibit, and drew forth another rebuke from Mr. J. A. Haldane, against whom the weapons of misplaced ridicule were all pointed in vain. The painful discussion died a natural death, with the dangerous novelties in which it originated.   At this period he writes :—

" I think Mr. Drummond has acted improperly, and he has given me just cause of offence; but, so far as I know myself, I can say, forgive my trespasses, as I *fully and freely* forgive this. . . .   Were I to meet him to-morrow I should do so with as perfect goodwill as formerly, and could laugh with him over all the smart things he has said of me personally.   But I think, with grief, that he has forsaken the right way, and it is my prayer that God may give him repentance."

At the distance of ten years from that time, Mr. James Haldane, in travelling near Albury, unexpectedly met Mr. Drummond, then supposed to be absent on the Continent.

They stopped and shook hands with mutual and hearty good-will, like Christians and gentlemen, as if nothing had occurred to interrupt their cordiality; and, although this brief meeting was to be their last in this world, it was to both a source of gratification that they had again met and parted with the expression of friendly feeling.

The Irving Controversy scarcely interrupted the progress of the discussions respecting the certainty of the Canon of Scripture, and the foreign agencies of the Bible Society. But, just at the time when the confusion occasioned by the doctrinal errors and miraculous pretensions seemed to render hopeless the prospect of forming a pure Bible Society, a gallant effort was made, and ultimately crowned with success, although not in the establishment of a new Institution. The visit of Captain J. E. Gordon to Scotland, in April, 1830, stirred his spirit to make this attempt, in the face of all opposition. His appearance in Edinburgh, on that occasion, is noticed in the following extract from a letter of Dr. Thomson :—

" You have heard, I suppose, of the doings in the west of Scotland. Mary Campbell (afterwards Mrs. Caird), &c., have got the gift of tongues. Mary speaks and writes in foreign languages, which nobody can interpret. I have seen a specimen of one of them. It looks like the Chinese character, but it is arrant nonsense. The folks are actually mad. In this marvellous thing many believe,—a writer to the signet, an advocate, Thomas Erskine himself, Rev. Mr. Campbell, of Row, it is said, and foolish girls and old women innumerable. Is not all this most melancholy? The tumour has not come to a head (as they say), and must be laid open and discussed. We have formed an auxiliary here to the Reformation Society. And what is more, we had discussion for three nights in St. George's Church. The scene was somewhat ludicrous. There was a solicitor-at-law, with a brown surtout, standing in my pulpit, and preaching the infallibility of the Pope of Rome!!! But Captain Gordon demolished him nobly. He reasoned very powerfully and successfully, and altogether managed his argument so skilfully, and was so much an overmatch for his antagonist,—and twenty such,—that none of us ministers had any the least reason for interfering. The crowds were immense, and I hope good is done. Our Society will now take active measures against Popery."

The ability of Captain Gordon, which so much attracted the

admiration both of Dr. Thomson and his friends, before it was displayed in Parliament, induced them to urge that gallant champion of Protestantism to appear at the next meeting of the British and Foreign Bible Society, in May, 1831, as the advocate of a purer system of management, which should exclude from membership Socinians at home and Neologians or Infidels abroad. But, in the interval, and before Captain Gordon's protest could be made, a sudden arrest was laid upon Dr. Thomson, and he who was ever foremost in the battle-field, instinct with buoyant life and vigour, the asserter of truth and righteousness, was, in the words of Dr. Chalmers, suddenly "locked in the insensibility of death."

Dr. Thomson's character has been pourtrayed by two illustrious writers. The sketch by Dr. Chalmers is one of the happiest exhibitions of his own eloquence. That by Dr. M'Crie is worthy of the historian of Knox and Melville. Both agree that "truth and piety and ardent philanthropy" formed the basis of the moral constitution of the departed Presbyter. Both agree in their estimate of the colossal grandeur of his intellect, the simplicity of his nature, the tenderness of his domestic affections, and what Dr. Chalmers terms the "dauntless and direct and right-forward honesty that needed no disguise for itself, and was impatient of aught like dissimulation or disguise in other men." Hence, in the Apocrypha controversy, allowance should be made for the righteous indignation that kindled at the diplomacy which could fraternize with Paulus, Chenéviere, Curtat, or Levade, look coldly upon Malan and Empeytaz, and refuse Bibles to Henri Pyt or Felix Neff; which could pay court to the haughty Neologian of Strasburg, and frown upon the humble and persecuted Bost. There are some who think only of the vehemence with which, in his stormy moods, he, Luther-like, assailed even good men, when he found them in the paths of error. But it is right, as Dr. Chalmers says, to discriminate between the vehemence of passion and the vehemence of sentiment. "His was mainly the vehemence of sentiment, which, hurrying him, where it did, into what he afterwards felt to be excesses, was immediately followed up by the relentings of a noble nature."

His power over the public mind was great. His sermons on the immorality of the stage, for a time almost ruined the Edinburgh theatre; and his discourses on Infidelity alike prostrated the pride of the sceptic and gave confidence to the timid believer.

Dr. Chalmers' description of his energy in public life is striking :—

" And when one thinks of the vital energy by which every deed and every utterance were pervaded,—of that prodigious strength which but gambolled with the difficulties that would have depressed and overborne other men,—of that prowess in conflict and that promptitude in counsel with his fellows,—of that elastic buoyancy which ever rose with the occasion, and bore him onward and upward to the successful termination of his career,—of the weight and multiplicity of his engagements, and yet, as if nothing could overwork that colossal mind and that robust framework, the perfect lightness and facility wherewith all was executed, —when one thinks, in the midst of these powers and these performances, how intensely he laboured, I had almost said, how intensely he lived, in the midst of us, we cannot but acknowledge that death, in seizing upon him, hath made full proof of a mastery that sets all the might and all the prowess of humanity at defiance."

His last great speech, at the Meeting of the Edinburgh Bible Society, in 1830, had in it something both striking and prophetic. It might have been intended as a farewell to the controversy. He had spoken for nearly three hours and a half to a crowded and listening audience, when he closed by claiming the indulgence of the Meeting whilst he alluded to himself :—

" For the part I have taken in this great and honourable cause, in which we are all deeply concerned, and to which I profess myself cordially and unalterably devoted, I need not tell you I have suffered much reproach. . . . But I have been comforted under the pressure of that evil by many considerations, and I trust that, through the grace of God, I shall be able to sustain and triumph over it all. (Cheers.) I am quite aware that I have sometimes spoken unadvisedly with my lips, and been provoked to say things which I sincerely wish that I had never uttered. I have been tempted to print animadversions and expressions which I earnestly wish could now be wholly and for ever obliterated. But let justice be done even here, and let me not be made the victim of idle and iniquitous clamour.  Let it be remembered, that while the things I have alluded to as the subject of my unfeigned and perpetual regret, are altogether distinct, immeasurably separate, from the real merits of the momentous question that we have been agitating, the original assailants were on the other side; this is a matter of historical, undeniable fact. Before I had penned a single sentence on the topics of dispute, with the exception of the 'Second Statement,' which I was earnestly requested to draw up by the Edinburgh Committee, which was adopted by that Committee as their own, after a careful revisal, . . . I was dragged before the public, individually and by name, and loaded with vituperations of the grossest and most vulgar kind.  . . .  I say, Sir, that I was subjected to persecutions that would have irritated the temper and called forth the retaliations of better and wiser men than I can pretend to be.  And, though I confess the error and deeply bewail it, I cannot admit that my severity of style, which has been so sincerely regretted by some and so malignantly denounced by others, has the aggravation of being either wanton or undeserved.  Sir, I have fought for myself; I have been called to do so; having withstood to the face and sharply rebuked and relentlessly exposed the desecrators of God's Holy Word.  . . .  I have fought for my brethren, and, verily, from such I have had my reward.  But, Sir, I have fought for the Bible, the book of God, the record of saving faith, the foundation on which rest all our hopes for eternity.  I have fought for the Bible, and there is a reward for that; there is a reward for it here (pointing to his breast); there is a reward for it yonder (pointing to heaven); and that is a reward which, be he friend or be he foe, no man taketh from me." (Immense cheering.)

His death created a profound and universal feeling of pungent regret.  Men of all parties combined to do honour to his memory.  For his family a pension was granted by the Crown, and a subscription was raised by the public.

At the next Annual Meeting of the Edinburgh Bible Society, Mr. Haldane bore a strong testimony to the Christian worth of his departed friend.  In simple, strong words, he described the many rare and valuable qualities of Dr. Thomson, and, whilst glancing at those faults which had been so much exaggerated, he observed that, looking to the whole tenor of his course, it might still be said, that he had "adorned the profession of Christianity by a life and conversation becoming the Gospel." Of his great services in defence of the canon of Scripture, he remarks :—

" From the midst of the contest, which he thus maintained for the purity of the Divine word, he was not removed till he saw the great cause so far triumphant, the eyes of a large body of Christians in this country opened, the delusion dispelled under which they had so long laboured, and their hearts animated as to the primary objects of Bible Societies, to circulate the Scriptures in their original purity."    *    *

" And there is no reason to doubt that in the moment when he was suddenly called away, and his spirit returned to Him who gave it, he was admitted to appear among the spirits of just men made perfect; and that as he had before enjoyed on earth the testimony of his conscience, he then received the anticipated reward of grace."

The fall of his illustrious coadjutor was like that of a standard-bearer in the field of battle, but it did not, for a moment, shake the calm determination of Robert Haldane. He felt the loss, but remarked, " The cause for which he contended will not be lost. It is the cause of truth, the success of which depends not on any man, or body of men, but on God."

The event did not interfere with Captain Gordon's determination to bring the matters in discussion before the Annual Meeting of the British and Foreign Bible Society in May, 1831. But dropping all reference to the Apocrypha and other topics, which had been so fiercely controverted, he determined to propose a resolution on general Christian principles, which should exclude Socinians from the management of the Bible Society. That Meeting became famous, for what has been justly termed his " noble and intrepid stand," and an interesting and graphic account of it was given by Robert Paul, Esq., of Edinburgh, and afterwards published. At first Captain Gordon was heard with attention, and the cheering indicated that he had in his favour the sympathy and support of a large body of the subscribers. But when he came to talk of Socinianism, and to make references to Scripture, he was assailed, from various quarters, by a storm of hissing and confusion. At last the Noble Chairman, Lord Bexley, ruled that, as the Society was instituted for the purpose of giving the Bible without note or comment, so he could not permit any one to expound or preach from the Bible, on the platform of the Meeting. Mr. Paul then states, that Captain Gordon having " entered his solemn protest against the doctrine, that in a Bible Society, the Bible was not to be appealed to, was forced to conclude amidst a scene of tumult and disorder, which might almost baffle belief, and defies description." His seconder, the Hon. and Rev. Baptist Noel, was not much more successful. Afterwards, the Rev. Rowland Hill, although opposed to Mr. Gordon's motion, and approving of the Society's acting with men of all opinions, while they confined themselves to the diffusion of the authorized version of the Scriptures, rebuked the disorderly conduct of the interrupters, " which he characterized as being more suitable to a bear-garden than a Bible Society," and then quoting the text, " Lift up holy hands without wrath and doubting," he added something to this effect :—

" I have seen many hands held up here this day, but can I think that they are holy hands ? without *wrath*? I greatly fear that this cannot be said—far less without doubting, for that means without disputing. So! as I consider the Society to be, by its conduct this day, virtually dissolved, I shall take French leave of you, and be off."

It would be tedious to pursue the history of the attempt to form another Society, with which neither Mr. Haldane nor his brother took part, or to detail the very obvious causes of its failure. It is enough to say, that without due deliberation, the helm was seized by parties who had known little of the previous contest, and were very little qualified for the part they had assumed. It would have been wiser had Captain Gordon and his associates declined to act with them, until the basis of union had been more firmly laid. Still the new Society was launched under a name which many, and amongst others both the Haldanes, deemed objectionable, and the *Trinitarian* held a successful, and rather a brilliant Meeting in Exeter Hall. The Rev. Henry Melvill, the Rev. Mr. Brown, Captain Gordon, and others, spoke in a manner that produced a considerable impression. But when one member after another, holding views approximating, more or less, to those professed by Mr. Irving, was proposed to the Committee, and it was discovered that the Rev. Washington Phillips, the Clerical Secretary, was himself bewildered in doubtful speculations about the miraculous gifts,

and fallen humanity, divisions followed, and it seemed needful
to adopt some measure to stay the mischief.    Thus it was that,
on the question of Irvingism, the Trinitarian Bible Society
made shipwreck before it reached the ocean.    The vessel was
subsequently refitted, and with the Rev. A. S. Thelwall as its
Clerical Secretary, and several able and distinguished laymen
and clergymen amongst its Directors, it has done some good
service, more particularly by calling attention to the importance
of correct translations.    But it never regained the confidence of
the public, and has moved in a comparatively limited sphere.

All this was, no doubt, wisely ordered for the purification of
the old Society, without its destruction.    The Rev. Charles
Bridges, the Rev. Edward Bickersteth, Rev. J. Haldane Stewart,
and others, combined in a protest against the absence of prayer,
and the alliance with Socinians.    The excitement produced by
Captain Gordon's effort in 1831, and the statements made at
the Meetings of the Trinitarian Bible Society's early meetings,
brought into the field several new defenders of Earl-street.
Amongst these were the Rev. John Scott, of Hull, who had all
along favoured Apocryphal circulation, and the celebrated Mr.
John Joseph Gurney, of Norwich, whose learning, talent, and
Christian devotedness, rendered him the ornament of the Society
of Friends.    Finally, the Rev. Samuel Wilks, editor of the
" Christian Observer," devoted nearly two entire numbers of
that magazine to a cause which would have been better served
by a frank confession of the evil consequences of an alliance
with Neologians and persecutors, than by acrimonious person-
alities, and the clever evasions of charges that could not be
openly encountered.    To each of these writers Mr. Haldane
fully replied in distinct pamphlets, and if, at the distance of so
many years, any candid inquirer may think it worth while to
refer to them, he will at least be struck with the fairness, the
truthfulness, and the fulness of the statements, as well as the
high standard of Christian principle, to which Mr. Haldane
uniformly appeals.    In the answer to Mr. Scott, he powerfully
demonstrates that the errors of the Bible Society might be
traced to their regarding the circulation of the Scriptures as

an *end* instead of a *means*. If ever any justification could have been made for Coleridge, when he tried to fasten on the Evangelicals of Great Britain the nickname which he borrowed from the Infidel writings of the German Lessing, it might have been justifiable to charge as *bibliolatry* the sin of separating the distribution of the Bible from its proper object.

"In all efforts," says Mr. Haldane, "to distribute the Bible, it ought to be kept in view, that the Bible itself cannot bless the world without the immediate energy of the Spirit of God, and therefore our chief reliance ought to be placed on the presence of God accompanying the Bible. When the contrary course is pursued, the people of God will be under temptation to keep silence with respect to the end of the Bible Society to save sinners." . . . "If God is to be overlooked, if Christ is to be forgotten, then let us fraternize with Papists and Socinians. But if all hope rests on the blessing of God, then let us look to the Lord Jesus, and trust in his declaration, 'All power is given unto me, in heaven and in earth.' "

Mr. Scott had rather, in the old style of exultation, spoken of the success of the British and Foreign Bible Society, as something exceeding what had " ever been seen since the cessation of miracles." Mr. Haldane quietly recommends Mr. Scott, when indulging in such flights of fancy, to reflect on what Bishop Wilson had said, " I am sure we have little idea in England of the state of things abroad. *We amazingly overrate* the comparative amount of good effected by our Societies." But turning to actual fact, he calls attention to the revival of religion in Switzerland, which had, beyond all doubt, been effected not only without the aid of the Bible Society, but in spite of the leading members of its " kindred institutions," such as Pictet, Chenéviere, Curtat, and Levade. He contrasts the state of Switzerland as it was when the Secretary visited that country, and its appearance when, eight years afterwards, the Rev. Francis Cunningham was filled with admiration at " the advancement in piety," which was then so conspicuous.

"And what," exclaims Mr. Haldane,—" what have been the means by which this happy change has been effected? Has it been produced by those to court whose favour and alliance the agent of the British and Foreign Bible Society 'broke through a hedge,' and was guilty of so great an outrage on Christian principles? No! God, in producing it, has wrought it, exclusively, by means of his despised followers.  He has done more, he has not only wrought it *exclusively* by means of his own people, and *without the co-operation* of the Auxiliaries of the Earl-street Committee in Geneva, but absolutely *in spite of them*—in spite of their efforts to the contrary, seconded, too, by the malignant enmity to his cause, of the 'kindred institutions' at Neufchatel and Lausanne, and its Bible translators there ! ! !   'My thoughts are not your thoughts, neither are your ways my ways, saith the Lord.'   'Where is the wise ?   Where is the scribe ?   Where is the disputer of this world ?   Hath not God made foolish the wisdom of this world ?'   Such, reader, and for thine instruction mark it well, has been the sequel of one of the greatest sacrifices of Christian principles, that is to be found in Christian records."

It was with reference to these solemn facts, that the late Rev. William Howels, of Long-acre Chapel, himself an early and ardent supporter of the Bible Society, beautifully spoke, at a Meeting, at Exeter Hall, on the 20th of December, 1831. After stating that the acknowledgment of God in prayer would have been the most effective test of membership, he proceeds :—

" The British and Foreign Bible Society would then have breathed the atmosphere of heaven.   Jehovah himself, with all the shields of truth, would have surrounded it, and Socinians never would have had sufficient temerity to force themselves into it.   But, having forgot God, when they begun the work, mark the consequence !   He has, in judgment, left them to commit an act of suicide, unparalleled in the history of the universe. The army of the Lord God of Hosts has opened its bosom, and invited traitors into it !   There is nothing, I repeat it, parallel to this suicidal act. .  .  .   All this the penetrating eye of truth ought to have foreseen, and the British and Foreign Bible Society would have been at this moment one happy band—the orthodox of every name and denomination, marching hand in hand towards the heavenly Canaan, treading the path of life themselves, and inviting others to follow therein; placing the Word of God in the hands of their fellow-sinners, as they passed them by; bequeathing to them the gracious inheritance of the saints in light."

The answer to Mr. Wilks was the last of Mr. Haldane's Bible Society pamphlets.  It was addressed to the Bishop of Salisbury (Dr. Burgess), to whom Mr. Wilks had dedicated his letters, and it is written with all the respect due to his Lordship's position, and, in fact, in a tone which drew out the grave remonstrance of some of the Covenanting Presbyterians in the vicinity of Auchingray, to whom the idea of owning Lordship in a Prelate seemed a dereliction of principle. Mr. Wilks had been bold enough to defend some of the worst acts of the agents of the Society, particularly in connexion with the persecuted Christians at Geneva; and whilst he intimates his pity for " the victims, some of the now sainted victims of ecclesiastical persecution," he intimates that much allowance was to be made for the feelings of the Swiss authorities, " irritated by the spirit displayed by certain British travellers and agents, and which certainly was not according to the meekness that is in Christ."

Mr. Wilks, in the same reckless spirit, also observed, that " in the recent revival of religion in Switzerland, there are those who are far removed from the excesses *either of Mr. Haldane's party* or the Genevese Pastor's party. Such men, for instance, as M. Gaussen, of Satigny, are truly the salt of the earth in that country."

This allusion to one of Mr. Haldane's dearest and most devoted friends, as a contrast to " Mr. Haldane's party," was indeed an instance of the recklessness of controversy. In the same month, M. Gaussen thus wrote to Mr. James Haldane :— " We are going, in a few days, to lay the foundation of a temple consecrated to the preaching of the truth. It is not far from where your honoured brother expounded the Scriptures. It was he, in fact, who, under God, laid the first stone." The slightest inquiry would have satisfied Mr. Wilks that no man had more strongly approved than M. Gaussen of the singular prudence and judgment with which Mr. Haldane had conducted himself. He would have also found that M. Gaussen, viewing Mr. Haldane as the instrument by whom the Lord, according to his sovereign good pleasure, had been pleased once more to introduce the light of the truth into that benighted place, had been affectionately accustomed to denominate him the second father of the Church of Geneva,—" *Le second Père de l'Eglise de Genève.*"

In noticing Mr. Wilks's charge of fomenting " a furious theological war," Mr. Haldane calmly replies :—

" A short time since I had the pleasure of seeing M. Gaussen at my house in the country, where, during his short stay in Scotland, he came twice to visit me. Respecting the cause of the irritation, he replied, that my proceedings at Geneva gave the first blow to the pastors that they had received, and that, as to preventing the attendance of the students, they found it was beyond their power, unless they had dismissed the whole of them. Such was the commencement of that 'furious theological war' which Mr. Wilks speaks of as 'raging' in Switzerland, evidently intending, by the phraseology he employs, to place it in an odious light, 'which,' says he, 'Mr. Haldane was one of the chief instruments in promoting.' This war has gone on and increased to the present hour, and for the part in it that the Lord graciously honoured me to take I humbly bless his name, and to Him be all the glory!"

In November, 1830, Dr. Thomson, in one of the last of his writings, thus described Mr. Haldane's labours :—

"During the whole course of the Bible Society controversy, Mr. Haldane has shown himself an able and indefatigable contender for the faith. And in the pamphlet which is now before us, he exhibits the same zeal for the purity of Scripture, the same accurate and comprehensive power of stating the facts that enter into the history of this question, the same acuteness in detecting the sophistry and disingenuousness of his opponents, the same talent for expounding and arguing every position that he undertakes to establish against them, and the same high-toned principles respecting the sacredness of God's Word, and the character of its professed circulators, which he has all along displayed in his anti-Apocryphal career."

It was, indeed, a struggle, before which most men would have quailed, and although he did not contend for triumph, he looked back upon its fruits with deep thankfulness. If, as he said, Dr. Thomson was not removed from the scene of combat until he saw the cause for which he laboured in some measure triumphant, he saw himself privileged to witness that triumph still more decidedly marked. One by one the Strasburg, the Paris, the Lausanne, the Geneva, and other Socinian or Neologian Auxiliaries, dropped off, and left the Parent Society more and more disencumbered of enemies of the Gospel. A well-known clergyman, who acted as a deputy from the British and Foreign Bible Society on the Continent in 1826, reported on his return that the mischief was incurable, that "Neologists had been placed on a vantage-ground," and "our connexion with them was a matter of necessity more than of choice." M. Blumhardt, the head of the Missionary Institution at Basle, himself a strong Arminian, declared that "the

Socinian party, which continues very strong, was particularly interested " in maintaining the Apocrypha for the sake of " *enveloping in obscurity, and lowering the idea attached to inspiration.*" But when the means of thus contaminating the Word of God were curtailed, and their own services superseded by the employment of a more Christian agency, the Neologians found their influence weakened and their own treachery practically rebuked.

Still more, in 1850, a Resolution was passed, on the instigation of the loyal-hearted and lamented Edward Bickersteth, that the meetings should begin with prayer; and although the method of carrying out that Resolution was clogged by Mr. Brandram's steady and consistent opposition, still the principle has been admitted.    The true character of the Bible Society is becoming known not as a mere bookselling Institution, but as one seeking the blessing and glory of Christ—a rallying point for "the orthodox of every name and denomination."

Whatever, then, may be said of the evils of that controversy, it had, as Dr. M'Crie remarks, the effect of " purifying the moral atmosphere, and freeing it from much of the selfishness and duplicity and time-serving with which it was overcharged." In this view, the language with which Dr. Thomson closed his last speech against slavery may be quoted, not only for its eloquence, but its truth:—

" Give me the hurricane rather than the pestilence. Give me the hurricane, with its thunder and its lightning and its tempest. Give me the hurricane, with its partial and temporary devastations, awful though they be. Give me the hurricane, with its purifying, healthful, salutary effects. Give me that hurricane infinitely rather than the noisome pestilence, whose path is never crossed, whose silence is never disturbed, whose progress is never arrested by one sweeping blast from the heavens,—which walks peacefully and sullenly through the length and breadth of the land, breathing poison into every heart, and carrying havoc into every home, enervating all that is strong, defacing all that is beautiful, and casting its blight over the fairest and happiest scenes of human life, and which from day to day and from year to year, with intolerant and interminable malignity, sends its thousands of hapless victims into the ever yawning and never satisfied grave."

# CHAPTER XXIV.

MR. HALDANE'S PRIVATE LIFE—SKETCH BY SIR GEORGE
SINCLAIR—THEOLOGICAL SEMINARY IN PARIS—PUBLICA-
TION ADDRESSED TO THE REV. DANIEL WILSON—PREPA-
RATION OF HIS EXPOSITION OF ROMANS—MR. JAMES
HALDANE'S ENGAGEMENTS—HIS LETTERS—REV. EBENE-
ZER BROWN'S SERMON BEFORE LORDS BROUGHAM AND
DENMAN—DR. COLQUHOUN AND MINISTERIAL POPU-
LARITY—DR. STUART'S DEATH—THE ROW DOCTRINE OF
UNIVERSAL PARDON—MR. JAMES HALDANE'S PREACHING
TOURS IN 1829-30—DEATH OF HIS ELDEST SON, JAMES—
DR. M'CRIE'S APPROVAL OF MR. JAMES HALDANE'S DOC-
TRINE OF PERSONAL ASSURANCE—MR. HOWELS' DEATH—
MR. AIKMAN'S DEATH, AND ROWLAND HILL'S.

[1824—1833.]

THE Bible Society controversy, reckoning from its origin in
1821, may be said to have extended over twelve years. During
that period, including his letter to M. Chenéviere, and his
volume on Inspiration, Mr. Haldane published no less than
fifteen elaborate pamphlets, in all of which there is matter of
deep and lasting importance, worthy to be rescued from the
oblivion of passing time.

Meanwhile, the winters and summers were very equally divided
between his town house, No. 10, Duke-street, Edinburgh, and
his country residence at Auchingray. When in Edinburgh, he
never allowed any matter connected with the management of his
estate to absorb his attention, if it could be avoided or postponed. When at Auchingray, his mornings were devoted to
prayer, the study of the Scriptures, and the preparation of his
work; but the latter part of the day was occupied, both before and
after dinner, which was at five o'clock, with such matters as

might require consideration in regard to his tenants, his plantations, or other country business.  His evenings, after eight
o'clock, were spent in the drawing-room, where he usually sat in
a large chair near the fire-place, with a little table by his side,
and a newspaper or book in his hand, so that he could either
read, listen, or converse at pleasure.  There were few more agreeable, or even fascinating, when he found himself in congenial
society.  The urbanity of his manners gave little indication of the
sternness with which he confronted error; and when in the
company of those whose knowledge or information he valued,
his flow of conversation was at once easy, graceful, interesting, and instructive.  It was never idle or frivolous.  He could
for a time talk of the ordinary topics of the day,—its politics,
its remarkable occurrences, its prospects.  He had a good
memory, and a great fund of anecdote connected with his own
times, the eminent persons he had known, the scenes which he
had witnessed, and the generation that had passed or was passing
away.  But it was on the great truths of the Gospel, and
the things pertaining to the progress of the kingdom of God,
that both the brothers chiefly delighted to dwell.  On those
matters their conversation was at once cheerful, animated, and
full of edification.  There was no constraint, no conventional
talk about religion, no merely sanctimonious phraseology.  It
was the utterance of the heart, the expression of real feeling,
never indicating any approach to that Pharisaic style of communication which equally chills the doubting heart of the humble
Christian and repels the man of the world.

Many eminent Christians who visited Edinburgh during the
latter years of the two brothers, have since expressed regret that
they did not make the acquaintance of men so highly honoured
of God.  The truth is, that neither of them went much into
company, and were not to be generally found in places to which
they were not obviously called by their Master's service.  On
the contrary, from the time when they turned their back on the
gay world, they seemed rather to shun the danger of being
entangled with another world of religious excitement.  Yet
both were eminently social in their tastes and habits, and those

who were induced to seek their society had often abundant reason to recal the pleasure and profit it afforded. An illustration of this remark may be found in the following extract of a letter from a distinguished and very accomplished Baronet, for whom Mr. Haldane entertained a high esteem. In a letter dated Thurso Castle, August 3d, 1852, Sir George Sinclair observes with characteristic felicity of expression, that the delight and edification experienced in recalling the memory of both the brothers, was such, that " he would rather have read a narrative of their lives than seen the pyramids of Egypt," adding, that " the characters of two such eminent Christians are far more valuable and interesting than those gigantic brick and mortar repositories where forgotten tyrants lie entombed." Sir George then proceeds,—

" I had not the privilege of being so well known to your venerated father (though I occasionally enjoyed the satisfaction of hearing him preach and pray at the Tabernacle), as to your enlightened and excellent uncle, of whose majestic form, earnest manners, playful urbanity, gentlemanlike bearing, and heavenly-minded conversation I can never cease to cherish a hallowed and grateful recollection. He honoured Lady Camilla and myself with a share of his regard, which we both highly prized. I remember his calling on us one day in Edinburgh, about half-an-hour before dinner, and we pressed him very much to remain (there being no company), which he declined; but the conversation between my wife and him became animated, and when dinner was announced, he changed his mind, and favoured us with much spiritual and intellectual converse (besides conducting family worship), until eleven o'clock. The Christian *Agape*, of which from time to time I partook under his hospitable roof, were always so conducted, that it must have been my own fault, and that of every other guest, if we did not leave his house both wiser and better men than when we entered it.

" I offer no apology for allowing my heart to dictate these few hurried and unpremeditated lines.—Believe me to remain, with much esteem and regard, my dear Mr. Haldane, very faithfully yours,

" GEORGE SINCLAIR."

The Apocrypha controversy and the defence of the inspiration of Scripture for many years occupied much of Mr. Haldane's time, but not to the exclusion of other subjects. When MM. Olivier, Chavannes, Rochat, Juvet, and other pious ministers, became the victims of persecution, and were banished from the

Canton de Vaud, he placed at Paris, under the care of the two MM. Olivier, twelve young men, whom he educated for the ministry in France. The superintendence of their studies, although carried on by correspondence, engrossed much of his attention; whilst he was accustomed to observe opportunities where letters or presents of books might be useful in enlightening the views or encouraging the hearts of his old pupils, or other foreign preachers, whether in France or Germany.

In 1829, partly as connected with the Bible Society controversy, and partly with the hidden evils it disclosed, he published a little volume, addressed to an eminent clergyman, justly respected for his talents and piety, who is now also the Metropolitan of India. It was as a public man, and a standard-bearer in the Church, that the Rev. Daniel Wilson was singled out. Mr. Wilson was a leader in the Bible Society, and although not personally implicated in many of the transactions which originated the painful controversy, yet he was one of its most zealous advocates, and became mixed up with the defence of its most questionable proceedings. He was also an influential member of the Church Missionary Society, and Mr. Haldane longed for an opportunity of publicly calling attention to the evil of selecting missionaries out of a German Swiss Institution at Basle, where from personal observation he knew that the theology there taught was then deeply tainted with Arminianism, and by no means free from the poison of Infidel Rationalism. Mr. Wilson had just published two volumes of "Letters from the Continent," which seemed to present a very superficial and mitigated view of the Neology and anti-Christian spirit that prevailed in places with which Mr. Haldane was himself intimately acquainted. The Letters were the result of a hasty summer's ramble, and should never have been published with the weight of Mr. Wilson's name. It was against the system of worldly policy and false expediency which had grown up in the Church, that Mr. Haldane wrote,—a system which never in his eyes appeared so monstrous or so dangerous as when it sanctioned the desecration of the Bible for the purpose of promoting the glory of its Almighty Author.

The views which he now published were not hastily adopted. In fact, he had long been persuaded that the temporizing spirit fostered by some of the most illustrious Evangelical laymen had far exceeded the limits of Christian simplicity. He conceived that Mr. Wilberforce himself, and what has been termed "the Clapham sect," had associated too much with Socinians and ungodly men, as well as with mere worldly politicians, for the purpose of promoting the abolition of slavery and other objects of philanthropy. When, therefore, Mr. Haldane saw the same spirit of compromise pervading plans designed to promote the Gospel of Christ; when he saw those of whom the world was not worthy either disowned, or their persecutions unjustly palliated by the convenient charge of imprudence on the part of their defenceless victims; when in the same pages he saw their ungodly persecutors held up to public esteem, his spirit was roused within him publicly to expose the evil, and to call the attention of the Lord's people to what he considered to be the unfaithfulness of which they were unconsciously guilty. These were his views, and it was not against individuals that his pungent remonstrances were pointed. Throughout the whole volume there is, as might be expected, much valuable matter, both as it regarded the state of the Continent, the duty of exposing error, and the necessity of bringing forward all the doctrines of revelation in their proper place, regardless of the offence which they may occasion. The signal and continued blessing that had accompanied his own labours entitled him to speak with some authority as to the advantage of dealing faithfully and without compromise.

The character of the Tracts circulated by the Society for promoting Christian Knowledge was another topic which he urged on the attention of the Evangelical Clergy of the Church of England. His language is strong, sometimes even severe; but it is the language of a man of God, who had in view the judgment-seat of Christ rather than the opinion of the world,— of one who loved the praise of God more than the praise of men,—of one who was in earnest, and wrote not to wound but to correct, not to gratify personal feeling, but to vindicate that truth to which he himself adhered with the simplicity of a child and the courage of a veteran.

There is a reminiscence indicating the spirit in which he conceived and executed this publication. It was late on a Saturday night at Auchingray, in the winter of 1829, that he finished it. Just before he retired to rest, he found himself suddenly attacked by an internal hemorrhage, which at his time of life he conceived to be an indication of approaching dissolution. In the morning he informed Mrs. Haldane that he wished a messenger to be sent to West Craigs for post-horses to take him to Edinburgh. Surprised at the announcement, she observed that she supposed he had forgot that it was the Lord's-day. He replied that he was unwell, and required medical advice, and believed that his work was done. He added, that he had not slept during the night, but had been meditating on the prospect of closing his earthly labours, and entering on the rest of an eternal Sabbath. Under these impressions, he committed to her care the manuscript just finished, with a solemn charge to publish it in the event of his death, as he was firmly persuaded that the matters there discussed were of deep importance to the Church of Christ. He said, that, although he had not prophesied smooth things, he had written in no bad spirit, as had often been alleged, but in the earnest desire to recal the Lord's people to the wisdom of depending more simply on their Master's strength, and to the folly of trying to help on the cause of an almighty and holy God by the feeble and faithless aids of a sinful and worldly policy. Happily his illness, although the first premonition of the taking down of his earthly tabernacle, passed away, and the result proved that his "work was not done," but that much good service was still reserved for him on earth.

Connected with Mr. Haldane's strictures on Mr. Wilson's proceedings in the three great Societies, an anecdote has been preserved, beautifully characteristic of the late Edward Bickersteth. That admirable and simple-hearted clergyman was dining with the Bishop of Calcutta, at the house of John Bridges, Esq., when some one jocularly alluded to the public admonition Mr. Wilson had received from Mr. Haldane. It was remarked that its severity must defeat its own aim, when Mr. Bickersteth exclaimed, " Ah, brother, that rebuke will do you and me far more good than all the pleasant compliments we are accustomed to receive." Five years afterwards, Mr. Haldane publicly expressed his satisfaction that Bishop Wilson had been called to a station of so much usefulness in India, and he listened with pleasure to every instance which he heard of that distinguished Prelate's zeal to banish error and defend the truth. One extract from this treatise shall be given. Mr. Wilson had said, that in order to do good abroad " all controversy about Churches, I had *almost* said about different *doctrines,* must be avoided." To this Mr. Haldane replies, "I do not wonder that Mr. Wilson faltered in his recommendation."

" If," he adds, " all controversy about different doctrines, and on the way of salvation, ought either ' almost' or altogether to be avoided, then the apostles were firebrands, instead of heralds of the Gospel of peace. Their whole ministry, as well as that of the Lord himself, was one continued discussion. The Lord Jesus, instead of concealing his disapprobation of the corruption of the truth by the Pharisees, exposed all their errors, and declared that every plant which his heavenly Father had not planted must be rooted up. The apostles never spared the false teachers, nor shunned to declare the whole counsel of God, lest the blood of sinners should be on their heads. Instead of enjoining on those who proclaim the Gospel to avoid all controversy, they make it an essential qualification in pastors to be able to convince the gainsayers. If another and more effective method of spreading and defending the truth is now discovered, it must establish itself on the ruin of the character of the apostles."

Mr. James A. Haldane fully sympathized in the same objects which occupied his brother's energies, although he was not usually so much engaged in the heat of controversy, but was, for the most part, patiently labouring with equal zeal in the vineyard of the same Master, to whom they had both devoted themselves in early manhood. In one of his letters, he remarks : " I see many evils, both at home and abroad, which I hope the Lord will correct ; but I do not see anything which I can do, unless it be to live near to God, and to preach His Gospel where I am placed in the course of His providence." He had supreme confidence in the declaration, " My word shall not return unto me void." Instant in season and out of season, he was always at his post, and without ever dreaming of rest on this side of the grave, continued as much as ever to delight in sounding abroad the proclamation of the Gospel. He was not often absent from his own church, but occasionally he was enabled to preach to the sailors in the floating chapel at Leith, where his sermons, as coming from an old seaman, were always welcomed by his hearers. At an earlier period, and before the introduction of steam navigation, he was on one occasion crossing from Kirkaldy to Leith, and, according to his manner, entered into religious conversation with some of the boat's crew. He observed that seamen were very apt to neglect the concerns of eternity. One of them objected to this assertion, and boldly challenged his unknown monitor to produce an instance of a better Christian than Captain Haldane. In a letter, he observes, " We dined yesterday at ——. Lord Decies was there, and he told me that as I am to preach next Lord's-day at the floating chapel, his relative, the Admiral on the station (Sir John Beresford) is coming to hear me as an old sailor." The elder brother of Lord Decies had been a school-fellow of both the Haldanes, and lived with them at Dr. Adam's. His Lordship was himself frequently a hearer of Mr. J. Haldane during the winter he resided in Edinburgh.

His correspondence with his absent children was always delightful, and a collection of his letters would form another interesting cardiphonia of experimental, doctrinal, and practical religion. The following contains an interesting account of a sermon preached by the venerable Ebenezer Brown, before the future Lord Chancellor and Lord Chief Justice of England. The letter is dated October, 1823, and was written soon after his return from a little tour which he made, through Normandy to Paris and Brussels, with one of his sons and the late Mr. Alfred Hardcastle :—

" You saw, in the newspapers, that Brougham and Denman heard Ebenezer Brown preach at Inverkeithing. It was not, as we supposed, owing to any quarrel of James Stuart's (of Dunearn) with the established minister. They asked him if he could give them a specimen of the old Presbyterians. He carried them to Mr. Brown's, who knew nothing of their coming, but was told, as he went into the pulpit, that two gentlemen of high rank were to be his hearers. As usual, he spoke from the psalm which was to be sung, and lectured (*expounded*), and then preached. The subject of the lecture was Acts xvi. 20—34. The service was long, but they did not tire ; and, I understand, were highly gratified by his simplicity and earnestness. Dr. Stuart wrote to him for an account of the lecture, and read to me his reply, in which its substance was given. It consisted of observations drawn from the passage, such as, that in every situation God's people have access to Him; that the presence of scoffers and ungodly men should not prevent them from expressing their dependance on God in the ways of his appointment; that He is able to deliver them in every situation; and that they may be assured that He will do so at the proper time. This, you will see, is a different doctrine from that taught by our friend whom we heard (at the Ambassador's chapel) in Brussels. From what I heard of the discourse, I should think it more calculated to be useful to them than Mr. Irving's *orations*. Mr. Brown writes, that when he heard who had been present, he had been led to earnest prayer that they might obtain a blessing."

When the Bible Society controversy arose, his supreme reverence for the Word of God induced him, like his brother, warmly to espouse the cause of those who were contending for the integrity of the canon and the full inspiration of Scripture. Except as an active member of the Committee, he did not, however, deem it necessary to take any very prominent part in the public discussion, and he was, consequently, saved from the pain of all personal warfare. At the General Meetings his unction in prayer frequently pointed him out as one to be asked either to open or to close the proceedings. But in the progress of the controversy he took a deep interest, and more especially after it came more decidedly to turn upon the integrity of the canon and the plenary inspiration of Scripture. On the 17th of October, 1826, he writes :—

" Dr. Thomson mentioned, yesterday, at the Committee, that Mr. E——, of Glasgow, had publicly said that the canon of Scripture was not yet settled. Dr. Stewart, of Liverpool, asked him, among what denomination of Christians the canon was not yet settled. I trust that He who ultimately rules all for his own glory will bring much good out of this controversy, and that many will be led to entertain juster views of the glory and excellency of the Scriptures. I preached yesterday on Rev. ii. 17; and gave as one reason for the expression, *hidden* manna, that it was covered with the dew, and only found when the dew was gone up. The manna was a figure of Christ, the true bread; and as the manna in the wilderness was given with the dew in which it was enveloped (Ex. xvi. 14; Num. xi. 9), so is Christ, the true bread, given to his people in the Word of God (Rom. x. 17; Gal. iii. 2, 5, 6), to which the dew is compared (Deut. xxxii. 2; Ps. lxxii. 6; Isa. lv. 10, 11). The hidden manna promised in the text is the manifestation of the glory of Christ bestowed on his people in the path of duty (Acts ix. 31), as well as the full enjoyment of Him in glory (1 John iii. 2). The white stone refers to the justification of believers. Stones are said to have been used in judgment as black and white balls still are. On the stone a new name was written. This is an allusion to God's changing the names of his people on certain occasions. Abraham was the first who got a new name (Gen. vii. 5), so did Sarah and Jacob. Isaac did not, because his name was given him by God, before his birth, and as the child of promise (Gal. iv. 28); he was a remarkable type of Him who is the same, yesterday, to-day, and for ever. (Heb. xiii. 8.) A new name was always connected with special privileges, of which it was descriptive; and here it is said to be written on the white stone, denoting the acceptance of the people of God, through faith, with which is inseparably the sanctification of their natures, or their being created anew. (Tit. iii. 5; Eph. ii. 10.) This new name, which all believers receive (Isa. lxii. 2; and lvi. 5), is the name of Christ written upon them. (Rev. iii. 12.) They are united to him in body and spirit (Eph. v. 30; 1 Cor. vi. 17); and, in virtue of this union, stand in a new relation to God, and have a new character and new feelings. This privilege is hidden from the world. (1 John iii. 7; and 1 Cor. ii. 14.) The change of character is ascribed to hypocrisy or delusion, but the spirit of adoption, in consequence of their union with Christ, is felt only by themselves. (Rom. viii. 15, 16; Gal. iv. 4.) The promise of the white stone with name is parallel with Eph. i. 13; 2 Cor. i. 22. These were some of the ideas which occurred to me on this passage. It is my prayer that you may enjoy much nearness to God, and have much experience of the power of his grace on your heart."

In another letter, written a fortnight later, he alludes to a dissension which had taken place in the Church of his venerable friend, Dr. Colquhoun, of Leith, the author of the valuable work on spiritual comfort, whom both he and his brother were accustomed to regard with much esteem and took much delight in visiting :—

" It is a pity that, in the Doctor's old age, such a dispute should have arisen, but I hardly ever saw it fail, when people looked up in an extra-ordinary degree to a minister (as I believe his congregation did to him), that something did not arise to sweep away their idolatrous attachment. I have frequently seen the same thing in individual members of our Church; so much so, that now I never see any person who appears peculiarly ardent in expressions of admiration, but I lay my account that a complete revolution will ere long take place. It is the purpose of God to stain the pride of human glory, and his purpose shall stand. The nearer we live to Him the more we are engaged in contemplating his glory, his love, and his grace to us, the more willing shall we be that He *alone* should be exalted ; and, as He is infinitely exalted above all created conception, so the happiness of the whole obedient and intelligent creation will arise and continue through eternity in beholding his glory. Did we perceive more of it, it would hide pride from our eyes ; but, as when the sun is withdrawn the stars are bright, so, when our minds are turned away from God, we hold ourselves and the persons of our fellow-creatures in admiration, because of some real or supposed advantage over others."

This extract exhibits the habitual frame of his mind; and his observation on the mutability of ministerial admiration naturally calls up the recollections of his old friend, Dr. Stuart, of Dunearn. He had, at one time, entertained an almost overweening admiration of the preaching and character of Mr. James Haldane. He had written, that to see him a Baptist would be " the consummation of his earthly felicity." His wish had been granted, and with it had come disappointment and change. He was one of those who had thus taught Mr. J. Haldane the lesson which he says he had learned. Still, nothing had ever occurred to interrupt their mutual friendship, and Dr. Stuart continued to the last to express a deep sense of gratitude for the spiritual obligations received from his former pastor, whose attentions were as great as if Dr. Stuart had still been one of his ardently-attached congregation :—

" *Edinburgh*, 30*th May*, 1826.

"Dr. Stuart died last Lord's-day, very suddenly. I saw him on Friday, and had some very pleasant conversation with him. While I was there his son John was announced. He had just been telling me how very kind John had been since his illness. I got up to go away, that he might see his son. He said, he wished there had been time for me to have prayed. I said there would be time, and without any intention or suspicion that it would be the last, I thanked God for his kindness to him, in having kept him in the truth, and expressed confidence that he would perfect that which concerned him, and then went away. On Saturday I asked at the door how he was, and heard that he was better, but, as Robert was with me, did not go in. After the evening sermon, your aunt told me that he had died that day. I went over to George's-square, and found that he had taken his breakfast better than usual. Mr. White, the surgeon, called, to whom he said, he was sorry he had come that day, as he was so much better that it was unnecessary. He was so well that his daughter only kept one servant at home, sending the others to church. About half-past three he came down stairs, and took a turn in the drawing-room, then walked up stairs again, and having sat down, asked for his dinner. His daughter went down to hasten it, and returned to tell him it was ready in the next room. He got up from his chair, and gave a kind of sigh and fell back into her arms. She prevented his head falling on the floor, but could not support him. A medical man was soon obtained, but he was gone, I have no doubt, to be with Christ. I never had before said anything in prayer with him about his being kept in the truth, but it has often been in my mind, considering Dr. Stuart's temper, his love of novelty, and his constant study of commentators, many of them German Socinians, &c. I have often admired the Lord's goodness to him, that he was never suffered in any measure to swerve from the truth; and it was remarkable that, on that day, I expressed, in his hearing, my feelings on that subject for the first and last time. No one took a deeper interest in all that was going on for the promotion of the Gospel than he did. He had strong prejudices, but he was truly a lover of good men, and deeply under the influence of the truth. May we be followers of those who, through faith and patience, inherit the promises."

Mr. James Haldane had been, as we have seen (p. 346), the first founder of Gaelic Schools in 1805, and, along with Dr. Stuart, Dr. M'Crie, and Mr. Christopher Anderson, had originated that useful institution called the Gaelic School Society. After Dr. Stuart's death, at its next public meeting, Dr. M'Crie pronounced a beautiful oration with reference to their departed friend, which is now published in the appendix to " Dr. M'Crie's Life," written by his son, who inherits much of the talent of his father. One sentence must suffice. " In Dr. Stuart I always found the honourable feelings of the gentleman, the refined and liberal thinking of the scholar, and the unaffected and humble piety of the Christian."

In the summers of 1829-30, Mr. James Haldane made two short preaching tours, the first in Ayrshire, and the second in the North of Scotland.

In a letter to his eldest daughter, dated Elgin, 5th July, 1830, he says :—

" I have made out my journey remarkably well, and have had many opportunities of preaching, and the people have come out to hear very well indeed. There is a great desire to hear in all the parts of the country through which we have passed."

His voice continued clear and powerful beyond the limits of fourscore, but it appears from one of his letters, that even as a sexagenarian he found it no longer equal to the prodigious exertions which distinguished the first twelve years of his active career. He mentions that he had not preached in the open air, fearing that he might lose his voice, as he had done the year before in another preaching tour. The last time that he was known to speak in the open air seems to have been in Ayrshire, in 1829. Two years before, he delivered a very striking and solemn address in the new Calton-hill cemetery, over the grave of Mr. John Stirling, one of his most attached people, and long a deacon of his Church. Mr. Stirling was well known as a public officer under the Town Council, and was much respected. He was "an Israelite indeed, in whom was no guile;" and when Mr. James Haldane saw the crowd that had assembled to do honour to the departed, he felt an impulse which induced him, without premeditation, to address them. He began, "My friends, you are standing around the grave of a man of God!" and, after dwelling on the meaning of that lofty title, he said, "I will not pronounce any panegyric on the dead, but I am anxious, in the presence of my fellow-creatures, to say something to the praise and glory of Jesus, who has enabled his aged servant to descend into the dark valley with so firm a confidence in His love, witnessing a good confession to all around." He then spoke of the power of the Gospel with an energy and a feeling that imposed the deepest silence. This address so extemporized amidst such a scene and in the presence of such an audience, produced a visible impression. "It seemed," writes one who was present, "to draw aside the curtain which shrouds the invisible world. The sun was shining on his face, and it was lighted up with a smile of heavenly joy, which reminded me of the countenance of Stephen, when he saw heaven open and Jesus standing at the right hand of God."

The beginning of the year 1831 was saddened by the death of his eldest son, James, whose vigorous constitution but a little while before promised a long continuance of life and health. After a short but severe illness, and in spite of the efforts of his skilful physician, Dr. Abercrombie, he died on the 24th January. His end was peace; and although unable to speak much, he told his father that he had full confidence in Jesus, and entertained no fear of death. In a letter dated five years before, his father expresses the gratitude with which he had first discerned a work of grace in the heart of him whom in 1831 he followed to the grave:—

> "*Edinburgh, 23d August,* 1826.
>
> "I have had great pleasure in seeing James. He seems to be under the influence of the truth. It is an unspeakable cause of thanksgiving that so many of you have been brought to the Lord. Pray that ——— may be made to taste that He is gracious, so that the whole may be enabled to look forward to a blessed meeting with your dear mother, and with each other in the mansions of bliss. The first, Catherine, is, I have no doubt, there already; and, oh! what an unspeakable blessing would it be, should we all, without one being left, be brought with joyful hearts to the presence of Christ, and dwell with him for ever! Such, I trust in his love and power and goodness, will be the case. It is my daily prayer for you all, that you may walk worthy of God, rejoicing in his salvation; nor do I forget to mention your dear Emma, and little Anne. May all be bound up in the bundle of life with the Lord."

Within a few weeks after the death of his eldest son, he lost an infant boy, George-Oswald. Shortly afterwards, his fifteenth and youngest child was born, whom he named James, in memory of him whom he had lost. About this period he wrote his " Observations on Universal Pardon, the Extent of the Atonement, and Personal Assurance of Salvation." It is like all his writings, full, as it has been said, " of the marrow of the Gospel;" and the ability with which the subject is handled received the approving testimony of some of the ablest divines. Dr. M'Crie had received from Mr. Robert Haldane, a copy of his brother's " Observations on Universal Pardon," and wrote on the evening of the same day his " unqualified approbation of the last part, respecting the assurance of personal salvation." The Doctor observes, that he " turned it up first, and could not stop till he had finished it." He adds, " The point is of *vast importance,* both in relation to the doctrine of grace and practical religion, and I am sorry to say it is ill understood by many of the opponents of universal pardon, both within and out of the Establishment." Dr. M'Crie concludes by requesting Mr. Robert Haldane to express to his brother without delay his "acknowledgments for having so much refreshed his spirit," and to tell him, that from the summing up of the argument in the conclusion, he has "no doubt I shall be equally gratified with the discussion of the other topics."

In October, 1832, Mr. J. A. Haldane thus alludes to the death of Rev. William Howels, of Long-acre, in London :—

"Mr. Howels' death will make a great blank, but the Lord liveth, and is carrying on his eternal purpose, and everything, little or great, is subservient to its accomplishment. Humanly speaking, however, the death of an influential man, who opposed the heresies and errors of the day so steadily, is a great loss."

In 1833, he visited his eldest surviving son in London, and as usual availed himself of every opportunity that offered of preaching the Gospel, both in the great Metropolis and the neighbourhood, as well as on board the steamer. In particular he enjoyed some pleasant intercourse with his old associate, Mr. John Campbell, of Kingsland, and preached in his pulpit to crowded congregations, as well as in those of the Rev. Dr. Burder, at Hackney, and of the Rev. James H. Evans, in John-street Chapel.

On the 6th of February, 1834, the following letter to Mr. Campbell, announces the death of Mr. Aikman :—

"MY DEAR FRIEND,—I embrace the opportunity of my son Robert going to London with his sister Catherine, on her way to India, to write you a few lines, and to thank you, in Mrs. Haldane's name, for your little book, which she received with much pleasure, both as coming from you, and on account of its intrinsic value. I have also to communicate to you what you will have heard probably before this reaches you, that our old friend John Aikman fell asleep in Jesus last night at seven o'clock. You know he was very ill when he was in England, and his health did not improve after his return. About three weeks or a month ago he was seized with breathlessness, which he never had had before. I saw him after it came on, and he considered it to proceed from asthma. However, it rapidly grew worse, and his nights were very painful. Having heard that he had become much worse, I called, and saw him on a sofa in the dining-room, where his bed had been removed. He was very weak, and spoke with difficulty. The last time I saw him was two days afterwards, when he was in bed and very feeble. I said, I hoped the Lord was with him. He replied, he had every reason to trust him, and repeated Ps. cxix. 92: 'Unless thy law had been my delights, I should then have perished in mine affliction.' He was very weak, and it was a great exertion to speak. I never saw him again. His mind afterwards wandered a good deal. I understand he sent for Mrs. Aikman yesterday morning and took leave of her, and prayed. He has been a very consistent character and will be much missed. But his work is done, and he is now, I doubt not, with the Lord. It is a very long time since we used to meet together in Mr. Black's; but if the night is far spent, and the day is at hand, we have no reason to sorrow for the lapse of time. Mrs. Haldane unites in kind love to you and Mrs. Campbell. All my family join with us. Catherine is just going to her sister, Mrs. Eckford, in India. Pray for her."

Mr. Kinniburgh, in his "Historical Survey," thus notices Mr. Aikman's departure:—

"Mr. Aikman died on the 6th of February, 1834, in the sixty-fourth year of his age, and thirty-seventh of his ministry. On the 13th he was buried under the communion-table of the chapel, which he had built. Mr. James Haldane, at the request of the Church and the relatives of the deceased, delivered on the occasion, from 1 Thess. iv. 13—18, an able, solemn, and scriptural address to the large company and congregation of mourners, in the course of which he bore a just and honourable testimony to the faithful companion of his early labours, and which was heard with the deepest attention by all present."

Mr. James Haldane had not been invited to preach in that chapel since the period of the disruption of the original Churches. But it was honourable both to him and Mr. Aikman, that nothing had occurred to interrupt the harmony of their Christian friendship. The substance of the address delivered at the funeral was published in the "Quarterly Christian Magazine," which, during the three years of its existence, was conducted by him, and contained many interesting and valuable papers, chiefly bearing on the grand doctrines of the Gospel.

# CHAPTER XXV.

MR. HALDANE PUBLISHES AN ENLARGED EDITION OF HIS "EVIDENCES"—ANECDOTE OF DAVID HUME'S DEATH-BED —ANECDOTE OF ADAM SMITH—PUBLICATION OF "EXPO-SITION OF ROMANS"—DR. CHALMERS' OPINION OF THE WORK—LETTERS TO DR. JOHN BROWN ON THE ANNUITY-TAX—LETTER TO MR. MACAULAY ON HIS SPEECH ON THE BALLOT—LETTER TO THE "EDINBURGH CHRISTIAN INSTRUCTOR"—COMMENCES HIS LAST LABOUR.

[1834—1840.]

IT was characteristic of Robert Haldane that he seldom did anything in haste, and never attempted to effect two objects at the same time. This was the more remarkable on account of the energy with which he pushed forward any design upon which he had fully and finally decided. His plans were seldom formed without much deliberation, but, when once resolved, nothing stopped him. He "spared no arrows," and it might be said, that whatever his hand was put unto, "he did it with all his might." His work on the Evidences of Christianity was first published in 1816. Soon after his return from the Continent a second edition was called for, but "other engage-ments," as mentioned in his preface, interfered. These engage-ments were the discussions connected with the Bible Society, and the defence of the canon, so that it was not till 1834 that the second edition appeared. The enlargements were truly valuable. Several new chapters were added.* The introduc-

---

* The following contains the table of contents of the Third Edition :—
" The Evidence and Authority of Divine Revelation." By Robert Haldane, Esq. In two vols. Pages 1026. Third Edition, price 12s.
" Heads of Chapters :—
" Vol. I.—1. Necessity of a Divine Revelation. 2. Persecuting Spirit

tion was remodelled, and "the conclusion" expanded into three chapters, entitled "the Gospel," "the various Effects of the Gospel," and "the State of the Heathen World without the Gospel." If the new addition had contained nothing besides these full and striking views of the doctrines of grace, it would have been more than worth all his labour. This work was placed in the hands of the Duke of Wellington, and there is reason to believe that its manly, unpretending style commended it to the attention of the illustrious chief, by whom it was carefully read.

One chapter embraces a branch of evidence which had been almost entirely overlooked. It relates to the harmonies of times and the coincidence of events, many of which, as collected by the celebrated French Protestant, Jean Despagne, are certainly remarkable. But it is a subject requiring to be handled with caution, and it is not surprising that one so little disposed as Mr. Haldane to indulge in what is fanciful, should, on mature consideration, have excluded from his third edition some which he inserted in his second.

When he first sat down to write on the Evidences, he carefully reperused several of the most eminent Infidel works, particularly David Hume's "Moral Essays," and Gibbon's Infidel chapters. The self-contradictions which he brings home to these writers are striking. He singles out David Hume as an example of the folly of pushing reason beyond its legitimate

of Paganism. 3. Credibility of Miracles. 4. Canon of the Scriptures, 5. Their Genuineness and Authenticity. 6. Their Inspiration. 7. History of the Old Testament. 8. Miracles. 9. Types. 10. Prophecies.

" Vol. II.—1. Review of the Evidence from History, Miracles, Types, and Prophecies of the Old Testament. 2. Expectation of the Messiah. 3. Appearance of the Messiah. 4. Testimony of the Apostles. 5. Testimony of the first Christians. 6. No Contradictory Testimony. 7. Admissions of Opposers. 8. Testimony of Jewish and Heathen Historians, and Public Edicts of Roman Government. 9. From Tradition. 10. From Success of the Gospel. 11. From the Opposition it has encountered. 12. Prophecies at present Fulfilling. 13. Evidence from Chronological Harmonies, and remarkable Coincidences in Scripture. 14. Gospel. 15. Various Effects produced by the Gospel. 16. Internal Evidence of Scriptures. Conclusion."

province, and preferring the dubious glimmer of its darkened
ray to the pure and steady light of Divine revelation.  "The
whole," says Hume, " is a riddle, an enigma, an inexplicable
mystery.   Doubt, uncertainty, suspense of judgment, appear
the only result of our most accurate scrutiny concerning this
subject."  It is a melancholy confession, and enough to cloud
the joy of any rational or thinking mind.   But Hume's friends
delighted to represent their philosopher as "treading the
common road into the great darkness," not only without fear,
but actually with gaiety.   This was the testimony of Adam
Smith, the author of the " Theory of Moral Sentiments," who
also considered Hume "as approaching as nearly to the idea of
a perfectly wise and virtuous man, as, perhaps, the nature of
human frailty will permit."   When Adam Smith thus wrote,
he knew that Hume had in his lifetime published an essay
vindicating suicide, whilst in the correspondence, published
since his death, he not only justifies, but even commends
adultery.   Had the picture drawn of the last days of the dying
philosopher been a true one, it would still have been unspeakably melancholy, and it matters little to the faith of the true
Christian how an unbeliever dies.   Mr. Haldane has, however,
stated enough to throw some doubt upon these representations.
He does not name his authority, but it was his neighbour in
the country, Mr. Abercromby, of Tullibody.   The details are
curious and worth preserving.   It happened in the autumn of
1776, very shortly after Mr. Hume's death, that Mr. Abercromby was travelling to Haddington with two other friends,
in one of those old-fashioned stage-coaches which Sir Walter
Scott has so graphically described at the commencement of the
"Antiquary."   The conversation during the tedious journey
turned on the death-bed of the great philosopher, and as Mr.
Abercromby's son-in-law, Colonel Edmonstone, of Newton, was
one of Hume's intimate friends, he had heard from him much
of the buoyant cheerfulness which had enlivened the sick-room
of the dying man.   Whilst the conversation was running on in
this strain, a respectable-looking female dressed in black, who
made a fourth in the coach, begged permission to offer a remark.

"Gentlemen," she said, "I attended Mr. Hume on his death-bed, but I can assure you I hope never again to attend the death-bed of a *philosopher*." They then cross-examined her as to her meaning, and she told them, that when his friends were with him, Mr. Hume was cheerful even to frivolity, but that when alone he was often overwhelmed with "unutterable gloom," and had, in his hours of depression, declared that he had been in search of light all his life, but was now in greater darkness than ever.

Other testimonies indicate that the philosopher's own friends did not themselves possess the confidence attributed to their hero on his death-bed. One of the anecdotes which rendered Mr. Haldane's conversation so interesting, and which generally depended on original and authentic information, related to Adam Smith. It was one fully believed by those who knew the political economist. Speculating as to "the great darkness," the philosopher, at the request of Adam Smith—a request quite in the spirit of Mr. Strachan's published letter—promised, if it were in his power, to meet his friend in the shady avenue of "the Meadows," behind George-square, and "tell the secrets of the world unknown." Probably the promise was made and received during the last days of David Hume, with the same levity as the conversation which Adam Smith has actually recorded about Charon and his boat. But such was its effect on the author of the "Theory of Moral Sentiments" and the "Wealth of Nations," that no persuasion would induce him to walk in the meadows after sunset.

No sooner had Mr. Haldane published the second edition of his "Evidences," than he bent all his energies to the completion of his great work, "The Exposition of the Epistle to the Romans." Upon this he had been more or less engaged for nearly thirty years. That portion of the Word of God had taught him the sovereignty of God, the corruption of man, and the perfection of that righteousness, which is provided and appointed for the salvation of believers. When Mr. Haldane went to Geneva, he had selected the Romans as furnishing the most systematic view of Christian doctrine, in opposition to

the Pelagian, Arian, and Neologian heresies of the Venerable
Company.  In the narrative of Mr.  Haldane's proceedings at
Geneva and Montauban some account has been given of the
manner in which he there laboured in its exposition.  But the
more he sounded the depths of that portion of the Word of
God, the more he discovered of its unfathomable riches : and,
before publishing his Commentary in English, he determined to
obtain all the additional light in his power, for the elucidation
of the general purport and minutest words of this remarkable
Epistle.  With this view he read and weighed every Commentary,
ancient and modern, whether in Latin, French, or English,
which threw light upon the subject, comparing one with another,
and pondering all with much of meditation and prayer for the
illuminating influences of the Holy Spirit.  In the next place,
he made the Romans the subject of a succession of Lord's-day
evening lectures in the Tabernacle, and continued them, at
intervals, for two or three years.  They were listened to with
great interest, and were frequently attended by some of the
most eminent ministers, and literary or metaphysical professors.
Each lecture or exposition was the fruit of intense study, and
when he went to the country, the same portions of Scripture
were frequently again selected for a different congregation.  His
friends eagerly pressed him to publish an exposition, which
seemed to them so fully matured, but he still sought new light
on every passage that was either dark or doubtful.  With reference to what, in the jargon of German pedantry, is termed the
Hermaneutics and exegesis, or what, in plain English, may be
called the critical interpretation of the language and meaning of
the Epistle, he knew his own deficiency in the higher branches
of Greek scholarship, and he rejoiced to find, in Dr. Carson, a
philologist and critic of the highest character, whose views of
doctrine were truly scriptural.  He, therefore, invited Dr.
Carson's counsel on those points where his philology and critical
skill were calculated to throw light on the Epistle, and he found
his assistance very useful.  There was no man who ever had a
happier art of laying under tribute, for objects which he deemed
important, the talents and learning of other men.  Never

sparing himself, he was as little careful about sparing trouble to his friends. None who enjoyed his intimacy were allowed to leave any talent they possessed unemployed. He was either pointing out fields which they might occupy themselves, or matters in which they might co-operate with himself. He lived as the servant of Christ, and he frequently warned others of the danger of hiding their Lord's money. But in regard to any aid which he sought or obtained in the elaboration of his writings, such was his discrimination and independence of thought, such the force of his master mind, that whatever aid he thus borrowed, he was enabled to assimilate so as to make it substantially his own. " Not used," " to be considered," " to be returned," " partly used," or " adopted," were endorsements on papers, which were furnished, at his request, by Dr. Carson, and a few other learned divines. But those with whom he conversed and corresponded on every part of the work in all its stages, first when in manuscript, and then when going through the press, can best tell how independent he really was of all foreign aid. In regard to his counsellors he consulted them as he would a dictionary or a commentator, and adopted, modified, or rejected their suggestions, with the confidence of one who was at home in his subject, and knew the Word of God to be its own best interpreter.

His object was not fame, but usefulness. Hence, notwithstanding the value he attached to minute criticisms, they were for the most part laid aside in his publications, where there is little of critical or philological learning, except the results. These results were, however, most valuable, whilst he himself sticks close to the text, and makes it his business, by means of all the aids within his reach, and by the exercise of his own judgment, to bring out the meaning of the Apostle with fulness and precision. In him, as it has been said of Calvin, there was found " the exemplary union of a severe masculine understanding, with a profound insight into the spiritual depths of the Scriptures." Hence his writings are particularly calculated to be useful in counteracting the erroneous tendencies of an age, in which, on the one hand, we are threatened with an inundation of Romanizing and Patristic mysticism ; and, on the other, by the still more dangerous Rationalism, which seeks to erect a tower by which men shall scale the heavens, without being compelled to enter the kingdom of God as little children.

The " Exposition of the Romans " was published in three volumes. The first, containing five chapters, appeared in 1835, and its venerable author lived, within seven years, to see it in a sixth edition. The second volume appeared in 1837, and the third in 1839. Each edition of this and every succeeding volume underwent a careful and laborious revision, until the sixth, which was published in 1842, shortly before his death, and contains much new matter.

The " Presbyterian Review," in an able article, in 1840, observes :—

" It is a remarkable fact, that one of the most satisfactory and useful expositions of one of the most difficult portions of Scripture, has Mr. R. Haldane, a layman, for its author—and that one of the most copious and *not* least satisfactory treatises on the Evidences of Christianity proceeded from the same able hand."

The Rev. Mr. Halley, whose early death closed a brief career of bright promise to the Church of Scotland, was the author of another and elaborate review of the first volume of the Exposition in the same journal. The following is an extract :—

" We took up this volume with no ordinary expectations. Its author's works on the Evidences of Christianity and the Inspiration of the Scriptures, have proved him to be so able a maintainer and defender of the truth, and have been so distinguished for comprehensive and vigorous thinking, that an announcement of a comment on Romans from his pen was identified in our mind with the promise of a bold and successful vindication of the leading doctrines of the Gospel. Our anticipations have been more than realized. There is, in this Exposition, all his usual simplicity and terseness of statement, and all his usual firmness and faithfulness of adherence to Evangelical doctrine, with even more than his usual grasp and compass of thought. Occasioned principally by the republication in this country, under high auspices, of Professor Stuart's work on the Epistle to the Romans, it has especial reference to the errors of that calm and unimpassioned, but inaccurate and dangerous writer : while it contains many most just and useful animadversions on the subdued Neology of Tholuck, and the frigid criticism and strange perversions of Macknight.

On all the topics of great and fundamental moment, which meet us in the first five chapters of the Epistle, it presents us with the largest and loftiest views.  It holds forth the genuine doctrines of grace in their due prominence, and unfolds, with singular beauty and effect, the way in which every part of the Divine dealings with man contributes to their illustration. And although, being chiefly intended as a counteractive to doctrinal errors, and being founded on a purely doctrinal part of the Epistle, its main character is that of a work in dogmatic theology,—still Mr. Haldane has never fallen into the too common mistake that, in order to be rational, we must be cold—that, in order rightly to investigate, we must cease to feel—that, in order to ascertain what the mystery of Christ imports we must set aside, for a time, its warm and living influence on the active principles of the inner man.  On the contrary, amid much of clear and sound statement, of acute analysis, and of strong and energetic controversial writing, we meet, not unfrequently, with profound practical remarks, with glowing and ardent descriptions of Gospel blessings, with those gentle breathings of sweetness, which show how fragrant to the mind of the writer is the message of mercy which is engaging his meditations. . . .  Although we love philology in its own place, we can imagine nothing more refreshing than, after being engaged for a time on the dry discussions of Tholuck, or the still more sterile pages of Stuart, to turn to the rich and fertile veins of thought which are opened up in the volumes of Calvin and Haldane. . . .  Of the learning which appears in Stuart and Tholuck, it (Mr. Haldane's work) embodies the results, while it wants the ostentation.  In ingenuity, it is equal to Turretine; in theological accuracy, superior.  Equally sound with Brown of Wamphray, it has none of its wearisomeness.  It is at least as judicious as Scott; and more terse, pointed, and discursive.  The only Commentary of Romans that we have read which it does not excel, is that of Calvin.  Had Melancthon been less scholastic, and on some points more decided, his comment, with its noble prolegomena, might have held as high a place as any.  But as the case is, Calvin and Haldane stand alone—the possessors, as expositors of this Epistle, of nearly equal honours. . . .  The two, taken together, will come near our conception of a perfect commentary; and the reader, who wishes completely to master the doctrine of justification as developed by Paul, we strongly recommend to study them both."

Soon after the publication of the first volume, in December, 1835, Dr. Chalmers thus writes :—

" MY DEAR SIR,—I return you my best thanks for the much-valued present of your works, which I very highly esteem, *and for nothing more than the noble stand you have made at all times for the purity and fulness of Divine truth.*  Ever believe me, my dear Sir, &c.,

" *Robt. Haldane, Esq."*                                        " THOMAS CHALMERS.

Dr. Chalmers styled it " a well-built commentary," and strongly recommended it to the students of theology. In his " Sabbath Readings," for 1836, under date June 12, he writes : " I am reading Haldane's ' Exposition of the Epistle to the Romans,' and find it solid and congenial food." He also specially acknowledged the light he had himself obtained from the exposition of the fifth chapter, with reference to " the two Adams," who are there contrasted, and intimated that he intended, when opportunity occurred, to give publicity to the fact. Other testimonies to the value of the " Exposition" were borne by some of the ablest divines, such as the Rev. Dr. Gordon, the Rev. Dr. Cooke, of Belfast, and the Rev. Dr. Duff. In England, the Rev. J. Harington Evans characterized it as " a rich legacy to the Church of Christ ;" and the late venerable Mr. Biddulph, of Bristol, " blessed God that he had lived to see so faithful a development of Christian doctrine." The Rev. Dr. Duff, before leaving Britain for the scene of his noble warfare in India, thus closes a letter to Mr. Haldane :—

" It has long been an ardent wish on my part, that I might be privileged with the pleasure and the profit of an interview with one whom I sincerely admire and esteem and love as a father in Christ; and if the Lord will, I trust that privilege and profit is yet in store for me before I finally quit these shores.—Yours, most sincerely and gratefully,

" ALEXANDER DUFF."

In the course of the " Exposition" Mr. Haldane specially called attention to the grievous errors of three other commentators, namely, Macknight, Moses Stuart, and Tholuck ; the first a Scotch Presbyterian, the second an American Independent, and the third a German Lutheran. With reference to Macknight, he was an able critic, but evidently neither intellectually knew, nor experimentally felt, the truths about which he was occupied. It is not, then, wonderful that " audacious heterodoxy," as has been justly said, should pervade his works. Professor Moses Stuart, in his " Commentary on the Romans," disclaimed " a sermonizing commentary;" but Mr. Haldane observes,—" There is no complaint with respect to the propriety of confining himself to the work of a critic and translator.

The complaint is, that, by false criticism, he has misrepresented the Divine testimony in some of the most momentous points in the scheme of Christianity." In an appendix to his third volume, Mr. Haldane points out consecutively the great and fundamental errors of this Professor, and yet there was a time when even evangelical divines, attracted by the appearance of critical research, had been induced to recommend his writings. A late admirable clergyman, the Rev. Francis Goode, acknowledged his obligations to Mr. Haldane, for having called his attention to the dangers of a commentary which he had himself been induced to recommend, in consequence of the manner in which it had been reviewed.

Next to Moses Stuart comes Professor Tholuck, of Halle, who at one time obtained considerable credit by his exposure of the Pantheism of Strauss and other German Infidels. But his own views, as to the supreme authority of the Scriptures, were lamentably deficient; and the want of reverence for the written Word totally unfitted him for the office of its interpreter. In fact, his writings abound with false doctrine and startling Neology, as may be seen by reference to another appendix to Mr. Haldane's "Exposition."

With regard to Tholuck, he was induced to publish two successive and elaborate pamphlets, the one "For the Consideration of the Church of Scotland," and the other, "Further Considerations," &c. The first of these pamphlets was occasioned by the translation into English of Tholuck's commentary, by the Rev. W. Menzies, a minister of the Scottish Church. The second was a rejoinder to that gentleman's reply. Independently of false doctrine, Professor Tholuck is chargeable with a revolting levity in his treatment of holy Scripture. He unscrupulously charges the Apostle Paul with various errors, arising from "forgetfulness;" with "making a false construction;" and apologizes for supposed blunders by "imagining that Paul was here called away, and that, upon resuming his pen, he supposed that he had begun a new sentence." Still more flagrant examples are given, as in the case of the apostle and evangelist Matthew, whose writings he does not fear to blaspheme, by applying to them several opprobrious names, such as " so contemptible a Gospel." " Thus," says Mr. Haldane, " every idea of the inspiration of Scripture is exploded by Mr. Tholuck. Here is Neology in its very root. No words can express the abhorrence that ought to be felt at such liberties taken with the Word of God."

Yet deep and burning as is the indignation with which Mr. Haldane repelled these profane attacks upon the Scriptures, for Mr. Tholuck, personally, he showed much kind feeling, making allowance for the awful school of Infidelity in which he had been educated; and willing to encourage the hope that, amidst deep spiritual blindness, and in spite of his partial Infidelity, he might still be numbered amongst those who " see men as trees walking."

At the end of 1837, Mr. Robert Haldane was engaged in a discussion on the duty of paying tribute, which attracted great public interest. The question at issue was one in which he was enabled to appear with much effect, as he could not be suspected of interested motives, when, in opposition to an eminent seceder, he enforced the scriptural duty of paying, without a murmur, the tax by which the ministers of the Established Church in Edinburgh were supported.

This tax, commonly called the annuity-tax, had subsisted for 200 years, and had been arranged at a period when there was no Church tolerated except that which the law had established. But, for modern times, the annuity-tax, like the English Church-rates, has become an ill-arranged and obnoxious impost, only calculated to foster a spirit of sectarian bitterness, and make the support of the clergy an occasion for strife and division. To endeavour by every legal and constitutional means to alter, modify, or abolish such a tax, would have been a proper exercise of the privileges of every British subject, whether Churchman or Dissenter. But the attempt to overbear the law, by adopting the system of anti-tithe-rate agitation, introduced into Ireland by O'Connell and the Popish demagogues, was one to which both of the Haldanes strongly objected. It was, therefore, with regret that they beheld men, " of whom better things might have been expected," joining in the passive resistance agitation, until, in October, 1837, the Rev. Dr. John Brown himself stood forward at a Public Meeting, and read a formal declaration, pledging himself to suffer any penalty, even to the extent of bonds and imprisonment, rather than pay a tax which contributed to the support of a State Church. Such was the extent of the agitation, that the clergy were threatened with the total loss of their incomes, and warrants of distress were said to have been issued against no less than 1,961 recusants in Edinburgh.

It was under these circumstances that Mr. Robert Haldane addressed, through one of the Edinburgh newspapers, a short but pointed letter to Dr. Brown, not entering into any elaborate argument, but citing the first seven verses of the thirteenth chapter of Romans, as conclusive evidence that to refuse tribute of any kind, when lawfully demanded, was a violation of a plain and unqualified commandment, and, therefore, rebellion against Christ.

The sensation produced in Edinburgh by this letter was the greater on account of the quarter from which it emanated. No less than 14,000 copies were printed by the clergy, and circulated from home to home. One venerable minister, now belonging to the Free Church, observed, that before its appearance he had seen for himself and his brethren nothing but such a prospect as that of which the Irish clergy were then experiencing the reality. Dr. Brown was naturally very indignant at a charge of rebellion against Christ, and in the heat of the moment was disposed to treat Mr. Haldane's letter only as a *railing* accusation, to which he said that he should not again reply. But the impression produced by his antagonist's clear and intelligible appeal to the Divine law, was producing too strong and general an impression to be safely left unnoticed. Dr. Brown, therefore, published two elaborate discourses on " Civil Obedience, and the Duty of Paying Tribute," which were at first printed with notes, in the form of a pamphlet, and afterwards, chiefly by means of quotations from a variety of authors, were swelled from about two hundred to nearly six hundred pages. Dr. Brown justly argued, that the duty of civil obedience was limited by the primary duty of fulfilling the obligation to "obey God rather than man." But Mr. Haldane asked in vain for any scriptural warrant to support the allegation, that in the matter of tribute any limit had been set to the payment of money lawfully imposed and lawfully demanded. If no such limit appeared in the whole Bible, it was impossible to allege the command of God as interfering with the claims of Cæsar. In regard to ordinary acts of civil obedience, there is obviously a boundary beyond which the rights of Cæsar must bow before the paramount rights of God. But in regard to money, it is the creature of society; it bears the image of Cæsar, and when demanded by Cæsar, according to the laws of the community which he governs, to Cæsar it must go. It is a debt, the payment of which, according to the plain letter of God's law, is to be made, irrespective of the uses to which it may be applied. This was the argument of both the Haldanes, and Dr. Brown's mode of attempting to reconcile the refusal of tribute with obedience to the ordinance of Christ, seemed to them to be not only unsound, but actually subversive of the authority of Scripture. Dr. Brown, on the contrary, argued—and, no doubt, conscientiously—that when the magistrate "leaves his proper province, or interferes with matters with which he has nothing to do," his authority is not binding, even when he requires no personal act of obedience, but only exacts money. It is needless to say that this principle, if adopted, would lead to endless collisions with the executive, and even to civil war. It would authorize, if not compel, every conscientious Romanist in Ireland, and every *Voluntary* in Britain, to refuse all payments, directly or indirectly, required for the support of an Established Church. It would also authorize the refusal of war taxes on the part of those who deem war to be unlawful. In Romish States it would prove an occasion of persecution against those who protest against Romish idolatry. In Heathen lands and amongst Mahommedans it would increase the difficulties of Christians striving to keep a good conscience, and yet to lead quiet and peaceable lives. In short, the consequences of such a principle are calculated to tear asunder the bonds of society, and to make each man's private judgment the arbiter of every tax imposed either by a constitutional or despotic Government.

There were other principles which Mr. Robert Haldane believed to be involved in the line of argument adopted by his antagonist, which that Reverend Gentleman peremptorily disclaims; and assuredly nothing is further from the object of these pages than to renew angry controversy, or to impute to him inferential deductions which he himself denies. But it is only due to Mr. Haldane to state, that he did not stand alone in the opinion, that the Doctor's mode of contrasting the condition of the Roman Christians with that of Britons living under a constitutional Government, tended to introduce a principle of interpretation, which, if followed out, would limit or explain away Scripture in such a manner as to involve consequences which Dr. Brown would at once reject with indignation. He would himself gladly admit that the attempt to qualify the Old Testament Scriptures by the theory of a double code of morality, one for Jews and one for Christians, has been attended with very evil consequences, and it is satisfactory to be informed that he equally repudiates the principle of limiting the New Testament precepts to primitive times and circumstances. But surely he seemed to give too much countenance to a modified application of the apostolic precepts when he directed attention to the fact, that the Christians in Rome were, as he expressed it, "a small body—chiefly of the lower orders—many of them foreigners—under a Heathen Government, essentially absolute, over which they had and could have no control."

Such extraneous considerations were, in Mr. Haldane's opinion, wholly at variance with the doctrines of a "self-interpreting Bible," to which he always adhered, and there was no part of his reply to Dr. Brown which experienced more general acceptance, than his attack on the principle involved in Dr. Brown's unintentional approach to so dangerous a method of interpreting Scripture. In particular, this part of Mr. Haldane's pamphlet was specially singled out for approval in the address of acknowledgment presented to him by Dr. Chalmers' Divinity students of the fourth year, signed, as it was, by the Rev. James Dodds, now the excellent minister of the Free Church at Belhaven, and the Rev. Dr. James Hamilton, of Regent's-square Church, London, whose high ministerial character and popular writings are so well known and justly esteemed. It is, however, a pleasing duty to repeat, that Dr. Brown indignantly disclaims the idea of having ever intended to represent any portion of the apostolic injunction as only local and temporary, and had Mr. Haldane lived, he would have been one of the first to welcome this disclaimer, even had he been unable to retract his own opinion as to the inferences naturally deducible from Dr. Brown's original method of handling the subject.

The Rev. Dr. Cunningham and the late Professor Welsh both supported Mr. Haldane's views, more particularly by lending the aid of their erudition in opposition to the quotations from various authors, which constitutes so large a portion of Dr. Brown's volume.

In a very powerful article in the "Presbyterian Review," for February, 1839, Dr. Cunningham thus writes :—

"Mr. Haldane's letters (collected into a pamphlet) form a very remarkable production, and are an important addition to the many valuable services which their esteemed author has rendered to the cause of truth and righteousness. They are characterized by great vigour of intellect, great force of argument, a thorough knowledge of the subject, and a high and uncompromising love of truth. . . .

"With the main argument of Dr. Brown's work, in regard to the payment of tribute, which was the original and only proper subject of this controversy, Mr. Haldane has, beyond all question, fairly grappled, *and, in the opinion of most men, has utterly overthrown it.* The charge of misrepresentation is one which, in so far as Mr. Haldane is concerned, is quite unfounded. His letters are pervaded by a spirit of uncompromising love of truth, and an entire superiority to selfish and personal considerations. His mind is evidently filled with a deep sense of the importance of the principles involved in this controversy, and of his obligation to contend earnestly for the faith."

The unanswerable force of Mr. Haldane's letters, as well as what was termed his "high and magnanimous disregard of everything but the establishment of truth and the exposure of error," were noticed in Scotland, and repeated in the daily

London papers. Nearly two years afterwards they were thus alluded to in a leading article in the " Morning Herald : "—

" When Dr. Brown publicly declared his resolution not to pay the Annuity-tax, there were warrants against 1,961 persons for refusing. Immediately after the publication of the letters, the number was reduced to less than twenty—namely, fifteen; and such was the revolution caused in the public mind, that the tax was afterwards collected without difficulty."—*Morning Herald, Dec.* 3, 1840.

That the " Morning Herald" went rather too far in alleging that the tax was afterwards "collected without difficulty," is a concession demanded alike by truth and candour. But it is decidedly proved by cotemporary testimony and the evidence of Parliamentary statistics, that after the publication of Mr. Haldane's letters there was a lull in the tempest of agitation that ushered in the winter of 1837-8 in Edinburgh. Early in the following summer, Dr. Brown, under a conscientious but mistaken sense of duty, allowed his own property to be seized and sold to discharge his share of the Annuity-tax; but the fact that he shortly afterwards removed his residence beyond the Royalty of Edinburgh, so as to escape this impost, seems in itself conclusive evidence that the battle was over, and that it was, in his own opinion, of no avail any longer to encourage by his example a fruitless resistance to the Civil power.

No doubt the agitation was again renewed, but not in Mr. Haldane's lifetime, and not until after the fatal disruption in 1843 had introduced a new element of discontent, and changed the aspect of ecclesiastical affairs in Scotland.

In this controversy Mr. J. Haldane was very needlessly dragged into the field, in consequence of Dr. Brown in his notes having attempted to connect the sentiments of Mr. Robert Haldane with those contained in a pamphlet first published by his brother in 1817. There was no doubt a striking accordance of sentiment and co-operation between the two brothers during the whole of their remarkable career, but their mutual independence of thought and action had been sufficiently marked, on several public occasions, to prevent even a controversialist from attempting to make the one responsible for the views of the other. Mr. James A.

Haldane adhered to the opinions alluded to by Dr. Brown, and yet never ceased to deprecate the conduct of those who endeavoured to forward a spiritual object by the use of carnal weapons. Opposition to the payment of the annuity-tax, of church-rates, of tribute of any kind, when lawfully imposed, he deemed to be rebellion, and a refusal to render unto Cæsar the things that are Cæsar's. The title of his pamphlet, " The Voluntary Question, political not religious," was intended to mark his opinion of the agitation which then prevailed, and he always gave it as his deliberate judgment, that those who strove by any other than spiritual weapons to assail the political establishment of the Church, did not understand the nature of the kingdom of Christ.*

* The author wishes to express his regret that anything contained in his very brief and guarded account of the annuity-tax controversy should have given pain to Dr. Brown, or rendered it needful for him to publish his complaint. The narrative in the first edition of this work was chiefly given in the language of the preface to Mr. Robert Haldane's letters. In the statement now inserted in the text, it is hoped that everything calculated needlessly to wound has been carefully removed, and it would have been far more agreeable to have omitted all reference to what is personal or disagreeable. Truth, however, required that the views of the two brothers on an important subject should be fairly set forth, although it is unfortunate that this cannot be done without introducing their antagonist. With regard to the conclusions alleged to have been erroneously deduced by Mr. Haldane and others from Dr. Brown's principles, the Reverend Gentleman's own disclaimer is now prominently stated, and it is far more agreeable to be able to claim him as a friend than to regard him as a foe. As to the result of the controversy, the author regrets that he cannot adopt Dr. Brown's conclusions. His statistics, instead of contradicting, actually confirm the fact, that the discussion greatly tended to discredit the system of passive agitation, and enforce the scriptural duty of paying tribute. One fact is enough. In 1837, it appears from the appendix to Mr. John Shaw Lefevre's Report, that the Whitsunday arrears of the annuity-tax amounted to 713*l*. 10*s*. 2*d*.; and in the following year, notwithstanding the great efforts by public meeting and otherwise to stimulate resistance, and notwithstanding the influence of Dr. Brown's own example, these arrears were only increased by the sum of 311*l*. 13*s*. 11*d*. In fact, the total arrears, from all causes, in 1838-9 did not exceed 1,025*l*. 4*s*. 1*d*.! Even after the disruption, the arrears only amounted to 4,000*l*., but in 1850, when the

The grateful sense entertained of the vigorous and triumphant diversion effected by Mr. Robert Haldane in favour of the Edinburgh clergy, had at one time suggested the idea of some public testimony of respect. But, on more mature consideration, it was felt that such a measure would neither be dignified on the part of the clergy, nor agreeable to the simplicity of Mr. Haldane's character. He could not, however, fail to be gratified with many of the private expressions of gratitude he received. The following is from the pen of Dr. Chalmers :—

" MY DEAR SIR,—I have ordered my publisher to send you the volumes of my lectures on the Romans as they come out. There have no copies come to myself yet, else I should have forwarded one of them to you directly.

" The publication is as distinct in its object from yours, as if it had related to another portion of Scripture altogether—not critical and expository, but pulpit and practical compositions,—a desire for the publication of which had been long expressed by many in Glasgow, and which, now at the end of fifteen years, I set forth in a separate form, for the sake of individual purchasers who might desire to have them, as parts of that series which I am now publishing.

" I am ashamed to mention this forthcoming work of mine along with yours, or, indeed, along with any work whatever of well-weighed preparation on that important part of Scripture, but mine is of entirely a different species, written chiefly on plain points, for Sabbath discourses, and sent out to the world with hardly any change on the first composition of them.

" I cannot close this letter without congratulating both myself and the Christian public on your timely and effective interposition in the

---

resistance had once more come into full operation, the arrears amounted to 27,812*l*. 4*s*. 4*d*. If we only contrast these last figures with the arrears of the year in which Mr. Haldane's letters had been published, the reader will have *data* enough to enable him to draw his own conclusions, as to the revolution produced in public opinion, even after allowing that the statement contained in the leading article of the " Morning Herald" was too strong, when it alleged that the revolution was such that the tax was afterwards collected " without difficulty." The sophism which runs through the whole of Dr. Brown's statistics is to be found in his not discriminating between the abandonment of the agitation in 1838, and its revival after the disruption of 1843.

question of the annuity-tax, and by which you have laid both the Church
and the country under a deep and lasting obligation of a very high order.

"I ever am, my dear Sir,

"Yours, with the utmost respect and affection,

"THOMAS CHALMERS."*

Shortly afterwards, Mr. Haldane made arrangements for the
translation of the "Exposition" into German, so that an edition
of two thousand copies was printed, and is now in circulation.

In the summer of 1839, he was much gratified by a very
friendly visit from the Rev. Edward Bickersteth, who told him
that he had called chiefly to thank him for his works, and
particularly for his treatise on Inspiration, from which he had
derived so much light, that it had induced him to call in one of
his own works, for the purpose of making alterations in it on
this subject, so as to take higher ground than he had previously
judged it safe or prudent to occupy.

At the close of 1839, he published a letter to the Right
Honourable Thomas B. Macaulay, then M.P. for Edinburgh.
It was not on a political question, but one affecting morals and
religion. It related to a speech in Parliament on the Ballot, in
which Mr. Macaulay, in the opinion of his colleague, Lord John
Russell, was considered to have been betrayed into an argument
which tended to "palliate dissimulation." From the moment
when Mr. Haldane read this ingenious piece of sophistry, he
saw its mischievous and demoralizing tendencies. The orator
was distinguished for his genius and eloquence, and he bore a
name which, with the religious portion of the community, was
still encircled with the halo of hereditary fame. Mr. Macaulay
was Member for Edinburgh, and as such, the representative of
a great constituency, of whom Mr. Haldane was one. Mr.

---

* Since the publication of the first edition of this work an able
minister of the Free Church of Scotland has informed the author that
the principles established by Mr. Haldane in the discussion with Dr.
Brown greatly tended to the peaceable solution of the question at
issue between the majority of the Church of Scotland and the Government. The conduct of the Government drove that majority to break off
its connexion with the State; but the disruption might not have been so
peaceably accomplished had the rights of Cæsar not been admitted.

Haldane's letter produced a striking effect. It was copied into the "Times," of the 25th December, and commented on with much approbation in a powerful leading article, in which the author is described as "a man of great talent and respectability." The subject is alike curious and important, but the limits will not allow of more than a few extracts.

" It was very lately said in Parliament, by a noble and learned Lord with whom you are well acquainted, that 'a regard for truth is the first foundation of all honour, comfort, and morals.' Far different is the lesson taught in your speech on the Ballot. Others have perceived that the interests of truth are placed in jeopardy by secret voting; but so far as I know, you are the first who has boldly undertaken to set aside as not ' sound and well-considered ' what you rightly admit to be ' the moral objection ' to its adoption. May I not also add, that you have been the first to represent as venial the systematic practice of deception, if necessary to protect a voter against the effects of the interference of another ? Well might Lord J. Russell, in his speech which followed yours, accuse you, as he did, of ' palliating dissimulation.'

" The value of truth is incalculable ; but when you publicly teach that in forming political arrangements it may be subordinated to their advance-ment; and when, in support of your argument, you sneeringly talk of a ' zeal for truth,' your conduct exposes you to no ordinary censure. After such avowals on your part, can you complain if your own assertions shall be regarded with distrust, and your political pledges with suspicion ? Others, through the force of temptation, may falsify regarding their votes, while they suffer under a strong sense of their degradation, and feel deep contrition on account of their dishonourable conduct. But with you no blush of shame can testify the internal struggle, on the part of high principle, to assert its empire over the man. The principles you have adopted and publicly proclaimed are calculated to silence the voice of conscience, to prevent the perception of evil, and to steel the mind against the visitings of compunctious feeling. Better will it be, far better, if professing your repentance as loudly as your shame has been avowed, you shall retreat without delay from the dishonourable ground you have chosen to occupy, and do all in your power to make amends for the mischief you have perpetrated in promulgating opinions calculated to corrupt the principles of your countrymen, and fraught with the most disastrous consequences to the interests of morality and virtue.

" Till then, Sir, you cannot count upon the support of those to whom principle is dearer than partisanship, and truth more precious than victory. The solid greatness and lasting prosperity of empires must depend, under the blessing of God, on the tone of public morals; and what must be thought of the pretensions of a statesman who in politics would import into Scotland the deceitful habits of Hindoo idolaters as a substitute for that stern integrity and unbending virtue which has raised this country so high in the scale of nations?

" I am, Sir, your obedient servant,<br>" ROBERT HALDANE.

" *Randolph-crescent, Edinburgh, Dec.* 16, 1839."

Mr. Macaulay was soon afterwards called to a seat in the Cabinet, and required to defend his conduct before his constituents.   It was impossible to leave Mr. Haldane's letter unanswered, but it had made too deep and general an impression on the religious portion of his constituency to render silence politic or explanation easy.   His speech proved unsatisfactory. Whilst denying that he intended to advocate falsehood, he still substantially repeated his former arguments, which were all based on the hollowness of worldly morality, and on the license conceded with regard to truth, not only in the world of fashion, but to politicians and men of letters.   On January 23, 1840, Mr. Haldane thus writes :—

" In reading again Mr. Macaulay's apology, it appears that there is now presented a very remarkable opportunity of glorifying God in the vindication of the truth, and of doing good to others, for you will see by their cheers how little the moral import of the question weighs with those who heard him.   He adheres in effect to his former declarations.   The authority of God he puts out of the question, balancing one sin against another, resting all on the opinion and practice of men with regard to character, and the propriety of extending to the poor the indulgence which he affirms is conceded to gentlemen."

The discussion with Mr. Macaulay was but an episode in the progress of his greater works.   But scarcely had he concluded his letters to that celebrated essayist, historian, and orator, when he was called on to defend the doctrines of the " Exposition of the Romans " from an attack made in a friendly quarter.   After the lamented death of Dr. Thomson, the Edinburgh " Christian Instructor " was under the editorial management of the Rev. Dr. Burns, of Paisley, and between that excellent clergyman and Mr. Haldane there subsisted coincidence of sentiment on most subjects.   But in the April number of the " Instructor " of 1840, there appeared an elaborate review, which, in the midst of high eulogiums on Mr. Haldane's talents, munificence, and career of usefulness, disclosed opinions at variance with the standards of the Church of Scotland. These opinions related to original sin, the extent of the atonement, and the sovereignty of God. It had not even been read by the Editor, whose private letters, as well as his public testimonies, show how highly he appreciated the value of Mr. Haldane's theology. It is unnecessary to give a detail of the letter to the " Christian Instructor," because its most important points were interwoven with the last edition which he published of the "Exposition of Romans." Mr. Haldane always considered the term "righteousness" as the "key-note " of the Epistle to the Romans, just as he regarded the term " perfection," or the finishing, to be the key-note of the Epistle to the Hebrews.

With respect to the imputation of Adam's sin to every one of his descendants, as the righteousness of Christ is imputed to all believers, the reviewer had termed Mr. Haldane's doctrine " a startling proposition." His reply is characteristic :—

" Whether it be a startling proposition or not matters little to the humble student of Scripture, who sits at the feet of Jesus, to be taught of Him, and to receive the things that pertain to the kingdom of God as a little child."

Mr. Haldane was himself of opinion that this might be one of the most useful of his publications, "for," he adds in a letter, " at present there is a great departure from sound scriptural doctrine." He was amused with the description of a writer in a Tractarian Review, who said that his works might lead to the supposition that the author was one of the old Westminster Assembly of Divines, who had just risen from the council table. There was some truth in the picture, for he stood upon the ancient foundations, rejected modern novelties, and delighted in the ancient scriptural writings of the Reformers and the Puritans.

This was the last of his controversial publications. It had been suggested that the ancient doctrine, with reference to the sovereignty of God, was disliked by many, and that some modification of the plainness of his language might conciliate prejudice without compromising truth. In reply he writes :—

"I have read it (the pamphlet) over again, and am now of opinion that it is not right in such matters to give way to prejudices, but openly and fully to declare and circulate, so far as possible, sound doctrine, which is the only way through which, by the blessing of God, however much it may be opposed, it will ultimately prevail."

Shortly afterwards he began to prepare for a complete revision of his " Exposition," with a view to final corrections. It is alluded to in the following letter :—

"I hope Mrs. Haldane and you and any of your children will, if possible, come and see us here in the course of the summer. Do consider this, and let me have the pleasure of knowing that I may with some certainty expect it. In a few days,—as soon as I can get a multiplicity of country matters which are on hand settled,—I intend to begin to prepare for a new edition of the three volumes of the " Exposition," that they may be ready for printing when, if spared, we return to Edinburgh in winter. Although I do not need this additional motive for being desirous to see you here, yet were you here for a little, especially if no other company were with us at the time, it would be a very great advantage, so that we might consult as to any final corrections that might be necessary before their going to press."

He was now in his seventy-seventh year, and this was the commencement of the last of his many labours, excepting only two little tracts,—the one on the " Sanctification of the Lord's-day," and the other on " Railway Sabbath-breaking," which, at the request of Sir Andrew Agnew and other friends of the Sabbath, he prepared and printed whilst his greater work was in preparation.

A few years before, in announcing his change of residence in Edinburgh from the house which he had occupied between thirty and forty years, he begins by dating from his new abode in Randolph-crescent, No. 6, June 8, 1836, and proceeds : " You will observe we have changed our quarters. You will have no more occasion to direct to 10, Duke-street. All things earthly come to an end." He, too, was drawing near the termination of his long and arduous career.

# CHAPTER XXVI.

[1840—1842.]

ON visiting Auchingray, in August, 1840, about two months
after the date of the letter which closes the last chapter, it
appeared that Mr. Haldane had made some progress in his
final revision of the "Exposition." It was interesting to
observe the pains which he took in order to arrive at a satisfactory conclusion on the minutest point, a circumstance the
more remarkable on account of the decision he evinced when
his judgment was fully and finally made up.

His health was obviously declining, and yet the vigour of his
mind was not abated, nor did his sight, his hearing, or the
elasticity of his spirits, evince any symptoms of the common
infirmities of old age. The routine of his occupations went on
as in former years, except that he was no longer allowed to
preach on the Lord's-day. In the morning, when the family
assembled, he read a chapter and prayed. When his brother
was with him, as on this occasion, the one usually prayed in the
morning and the other in the evening. At breakfast he was
cheerful and full of animation. No longer able to encounter
the same amount of fatigue as formerly, the time which he
spent in his own room was now prolonged till three o'clock, or

even later. Much of that interval was, at this time, devoted to conversation with the author on the great doctrines of the Gospel, more especially with reference to the final revision of his "Commentary." He never himself appeared at luncheon or required any refreshment between breakfast and dinner. About three o'clock he generally took a walk, when he talked freely on the various topics which arose. But at this time, and in the previous year, it seemed as if he felt that time was passing away, and his communications were full of more than their wonted interest, touching as they did on the workings of his own mind, the history of his religious experience, and the eventful career both of himself and his brother. This was the more remarkable considering how little of egotism and how much of reserve were included in the elements of his character. At dinner he was affable, and even playful. At all times rather abstemious, he now seldom took more than one, or at most, two glasses of wine, and never sat long at table. Before tea he would very generally walk out again, and enliven his conversation with anecdotes of past times, and of the various characters with whom, from his boyhood, he had come into contact. At an earlier period, when in vigorous health, and even so late as 1839, he would often take long walks with his grandchildren and his younger nephews and nieces, or encourage them in their games by his playfulness and good-humour. He was at all times fond of children, and with them would still exhibit his early love of practical jokes. At eight o'clock the tea-table was spread in the drawing-room, and after this very social repast the servants assembled for evening prayers. When this solemn but simple service was over, Mr. Haldane, at the period to which this sketch refers, would retire into his own room, in order that his conversation on the subjects which chiefly occupied his thoughts might not be interrupted by desultory talk. These conversations, often prolonged beyond midnight, were intensely interesting, and the rather because it was impossible not to feel that they were fast drawing to an end. They were, at the last, concluded by a prayer, simple, affectionate, and earnest, breathing the spirit of adoption, and calling down the Divine blessing upon his relative, for whom he asked that the Lord might gird him to fight the good fight of faith and enable him to endure to the end. Those who regarded Mr. Haldane merely as a controversialist little knew the depth of his benevolence, his comprehensive charity, and, above all, the settled peace and joy which he derived from the personal and unclouded appropriation of those doctrines of which he was so earnest and powerful a champion.

The summer of 1840 passed away, and amidst the interruptions that occurred connected with the affairs of his grandsons' and his own estate, he still found the corrections and additions to his " Commentary " incomplete. He therefore determined to remain at Auchingray during the winter, where, in solitary retirement, he persevered undisturbed in his work. His correspondence announces its progress, and how he had adopted the advice to work up in the " Exposition " the substance of the valuable doctrinal arguments contained in the recent letter to the " Christian Instructor." In 1841 it was completed, and before leaving the country, as if feeling that he was not again to return, he was much employed in examining old letters and papers, many of which he committed to the flames.

During the years when he was accustomed on the Lord's-day to preach at Auchingray, for the convenience of the people he followed the Scottish practice, prevalent in the country, of running two services into one. The whole lasted from twelve o'clock to three, and the two sermons were only divided by the interval of a psalm, a prayer, and a second psalm. This was necessarily fatiguing, but the avidity with which the country people flocked to hear, and the tokens of their blessed effects, rendered him unwilling to leave them off. Every Saturday evening, at family worship, he had been wont to pray that many might come to hear, and that a blessing might attend the preaching of the Word. Seldom, probably, have such sermons been preached in such a place, but they were appreciated, and many actually travelled twenty miles or more for the purpose of attending. For most country congregations in England they would have been too doctrinal and elaborate. They cost much preparation, and even the scanty notes which remain would in themselves be sufficient to indicate that they were worthy of the author of the "Exposition of the Romans." In notes made of one of these sermons, the following striking remark occurs : "The first great difficulty is to convince a man that he is a sinner; but the second difficulty is to persuade a believer that he is for ever safe in Christ." It was a beautiful sight at Auchingray on a Sunday to see the country people flocking to the place where he preached, across the hills in the direction of Shotts, or through the moorland and plantations towards Slamannan, most of them on foot, but some in their covered carts or on horseback, the women with red cloaks, and the men with blue bonnets. There was a gravity and a respectability in their appearance that called back the recollection of the old Covenanters of the west of Scotland, of whom they were, in fact, the descendants. Relics of the times of "the Bloody Clavers" might still be seen in their houses, such as the gun which an ancestor had carried to Bothwell Bridge, or some other treasured token of their attachment to the cause which persecution had both endeared and consecrated.

There was no church near the House of Auchingray. The post-town of Airdrie was more than six miles distant; the parish church of Slamannan was not much nearer ; nor the Kirk of Shotts, so famed for the extraordinary revival, recorded in Gillies' "Collections," and following the remarkable sermon of the celebrated Mr. Livingston, nearly two hundred years ago. Several of the neighbouring ministers were far from regarding these services as an intrusion, but an anecdote is told of a very moderate minister, some miles off, who asked one of his parishioners, in a complaining tone, what it was that Mr. Haldane preached, that took away so many people to hear him. With greater frankness and honesty than regard for his minister's feelings, the worthy cottager sturdily replied, "'Deed, Sir, I'm thinking it's just the contrary to your preaching." Mr. Haldane's object was not to attempt the formation of a separate Church, but only to preach the Gospel to those who would not otherwise hear it. The Lord's Supper was, therefore, not administered; and, with respect to baptism, at the close of one of his most striking sermons, he addressed all present with great solemnity, telling them that the grand question was not whether they had been baptized in infancy or maturity, but whether they had been baptized with the Holy Spirit. He also steadily refused the applications made to him to aid the Baptist Bible Society in America, with a view to more correct translations of the disputed words, alleging, in a letter, dated 25th September, 1840, that he altogether disapproved of any external ordinance being made a bond of union instead of faith in Christ and sound doctrine. He stated, that he regarded the term, Baptist, as prefixed to the Society's name, to be quite inappropriate. His correspondence, in 1840, with his old and esteemed friend, the Rev. Mr. Maclay, of New York, is, on this subject, remarkable; and more particularly with reference to doctrinal errors, which were at that time sanctioned by some leading Baptists in England.

At the end of December, 1841, Mr. Haldane left Auchingray, and, for the last time, arrived in Edinburgh. The printing of his "Exposition" was commenced, but, during its progress through the press, his assistance was wanted in the great battle then going on with reference to the desecration of the Lord's-day by the railway companies. To his third volume was added an argument with reference to the sanctification of the Lord's-day, consisting of sixty-two pages, which he also published separately. It takes up the strong scriptural ground which had been, ten years before, occupied by his brother, in an able treatise on the same subject; showing that it was not a Jewish statute, but an ordinance of God from the beginning, necessary for man in Paradise, and still more for man doomed to eat his bread by the sweat of his brow. He also wrote a separate tract in reference to the Glasgow Railway, with all his accustomed force and acuteness, and alluded with striking effect to the dreadful catastrophe which happened on the Versailles Railway on a Lord's-day in that summer, when so many of the passengers were burned to death.

The "Exposition" was printed in June, with his last corrections, and he left it as an injunction that no alterations might be permitted. He also added a separate treatise, of great importance, on the "Testimony of the Word of God, with regard to the State of the Heathen destitute of the Gospel." The conclusion contains a summary of the whole Epistle.

His last labour was a fit termination to the long, active, and arduous career of Robert Haldane. His health had been declining for some time, and in his seventy-ninth year, he could not well expect a revival. He was therefore compelled to abandon the idea of some other Expositions, which he had long contemplated, and for which he had collected materials.*

The Report of the Edinburgh Bible Society, in 1842, so far as it related to the Apocrypha question and the union with Socinians or Neologians, was written by Mr. James Haldane; so that, although the one brother was disabled, the other occupied his post. On the 14th July, Mr. J. A. Haldane writes:—

" This is my birth-day, on which I enter my seventy-fifth year. I have much cause of gratitude for the health I enjoy, as well as for many other blessings. But your uncle has been very feeble for some time. I do not know whether he will go to Auchingray. Your aunt seems to think that he would be the better for the country air. He has been very little out of the house since he has come to Edinburgh."

In August he was evidently sinking in bodily strength, although the clear light of his masculine intellect was as

* Mr. Haldane was also partial to the circulation of the Scriptures in portions, or in the form of tracts. In this way he had, on the Continent, by means of Colporteurs, circulated the Gospel by St. John and other extracts complete in themselves, including the book of Genesis to the end of the first twenty chapters of Exodus, omitting the last verse. In order to induce the Trinitarian to adopt this plan in Portugal, he gave to Mr. Thelwall, when in Edinburgh, in 1842, a special donation of 100*l.* for the distribution of the historical portion of the Old Testament just mentioned, being one which he deemed very important and had been found most acceptable. At that time, however, objections were, strangely enough, taken by the Trinitarian Committee to such extracts, and Mr. Haldane having therefore reclaimed his donation, it was appropriated to the diffusion of the Scriptures in France. Since that period it appears that Mr. Haldane's plan has been adopted in Ireland, and selected portions of the Bible widely circulated by the same Society, in the Irish language, in the form of tracts.

unclouded, and his mental energies as active, as ever. He
discussed matters of business relating to the affairs of his
family with all his usual shrewdness and perspicuity, but
kindled into animation in speaking of the integrity of the
Bible, its plenary inspiration, or the importance of maintaining
the purity of its doctrines. On Saturday evening, the 27th of
August, being very unwell, the doctor was sent for. Shortly
afterwards, in a private interview with his physician, it was
ascertained that Mr. Haldane had asked him to say plainly
what he thought of the prospects of recovery. The doctor
replied, "Mr. Haldane, you are a man of firm mind and not
afraid of death. I have, therefore, no fear of alarming you
when I say that it looks like a last illness." On visiting him
next day, he was in bed, with his old Bible beside him, the
same which he had used at Geneva, and which Dr. Malan
described as then literally worn out by frequent reference.
He had told no one of the doctor's announcement, and he
did not notice it now; but his manner was grave and his
countenance evinced the intensity of his self-searching meditations. He began at once,—"I have been thinking of our
Lord's words to his disciples, in his last discourse, John xiv.
21—23," which he repeated: "'He that hath my commandments and *keepeth* them, he it is that loveth me,' &c., and
the parallel passage, Rev. iii. 20;" which he also repeated.
"Now," he said, "I have been asking myself, what must my
answer be, if tried by this test? Have I kept his commandments,—have I kept his sayings?" And, with emphasis and
an earnest expression, he exclaimed, as his dark penetrating
eye was lighted up with animation, "I bless the Lord that,
through his grace, I can say, Yes; that I *have* his commandments, and have *kept* them." He explained that the commandment is to believe in Jesus Christ, and the Lord had been
pleased to give him grace to believe. "I do believe," he said,
"and I do love Him; and in spite of much sin and weakness
and great unworthiness, it has been my endeavour, ever since
I knew the Lord and received his sayings, to serve Him in
simplicity and with a godly sincerity, and to have a conscience

void of offence." " No doubt," he added, " there have been much alloy and many errors, for I have no righteousness of my own. There is no merit in any of my works, but my trust has been, and is, in the righteousness of Christ. I therefore can say, the Lord being my helper, that I have his commandments, and that I have kept them."

He then spoke of his course as a Christian generally, and of the remarkable unity of thought and action which had always subsisted between himself and his brother, both in doctrine and in practice. He spoke of the divisions amongst Christians, and said, that after all " it was his conviction that the Spirit was given as the Lord saw good to all Churches—that it was the preaching of sound doctrine which the Lord blessed, and not particular systems of Church government. Great good," he said, was done by itinerating, but we were permitted for a time to attach too much importance to some things connected with Church order ; and whether it was that we were not worthy, or whatever was the cause, our efforts to restore apostolic Churches and primitive Christianity were unsuccessful." " The truth," he added, " seems to be, that the Church is in the wilderness, and until the Lord choose in his own good time to bring her out of it, I believe the attempt will be in vain." It had long been obvious that he no longer laid much stress as formerly on Church order. He then added, that although his theoretic views were not changed, and he had detected no flaw in his principles, yet he could not forget that the ministers of the Church of Scotland—such as Dr. Gordon, Dr. Thomson, Dr. Chalmers, and the rest—had been his fellow-labourers in the cause of the Bible and the promulgation of the doctrines of the Gospel, much more than some who might seem from their Voluntary principles to approach nearer to him in sentiment with regard to Church polity. On the Bible Society question, on plenary inspiration, on the Sabbath question, and in regard to the doctrines exhibited in his " Exposition," he had found far greater concurrence of sentiment between himself and the ministers of the Church of Scotland, and such men as Dr. M'Crie, Professor Paxton, &c., than with the Voluntaries, who had, as he thought, been too much ensnared by politics, and some of them too much disposed to follow the German and American theology. In regard to his "Exposition," he felt thankful that it had been welcomed by some of the best men, both in Scotland and England; and for the success that had accompanied it he desired to give all the glory to God. He then conversed about other matters, which have been touched on in this volume, relating to the period when the disruption took place in the Tabernacle connexion. He considered that that had been a time when his motives had been called in question by some who should have known better, and said, that although he had no doubt there was much of worldly excitement unconsciously mingled with the whole of the Congregational system in its first beginnings, and with his own zeal when chapels were built so rapidly, and involved so much of secular business, yet he could now, at the close of the day, and in the calm retrospect of his busy career, appeal to the Great Searcher of hearts as a witness to the purity of his motives, and his simple desire to promote the kingdom of Christ.

Although his physician had truly expressed the opinion that it was a last illness, yet it was chiefly indicated by a failure of strength, and tendency to exhaustion. It was the wearing out of the over-laboured framework of his vigorous and indomitable spirit. During the course of the week, he conversed for many hours almost every day, on matters partly connected with his grandchildren, but chiefly with reference to the great spiritual objects in which he was interested. There were very few of his friends admitted to see him, and, besides his brother, the only exception that occurred during the visits alluded to, was in favour of Mr. George Ross, for whom he entertained a particular esteem and regard, not only as a family connexion, but as one who had in his youth sacrificed much for Christ, and in his mature years always firmly and consistently stood forward as a supporter of the great truths of the Gospel.

These prolonged daily visits were always made by appointment at a particular hour, soon after he got up, which was then not till about eleven or twelve o'clock, or sometimes later. He occupied the drawing-room adjoining which he slept, and he generally sat or reclined in his dressing-gown on a sofa fronting the fire-place. There was no depression in his spirits. On the contrary, there was a good deal of vivacity in his conversation, which was, even on the last of these much-remembered days, enlivened by cheerful and amusing anecdotes.

But most frequently he was solemn and serious. Again and again, but particularly during the last visit, he urged the importance of the ninth chapter of Romans, and of the view it gives of the sovereignty of God. He said he could not express the comfort which he had derived from it at all times, and especially in a recent season of trial. We were thus taught to see God in everything, and to trace everything to God— to see his Almighty hand even in our own mistakes, as well as our successes : in our adversity, as well as prosperity. It was wisdom, therefore, to endeavour to commit ourselves and our concerns to His supreme guidance, to seek to do His will, and to be conformed to it. He earnestly recommended the study of his exposition of that chapter, as exhibiting the only solid ground on which right views of the Gospel can rest, and as calculated to afford the greatest practical comfort to all, who, as little children, will cast themselves in conscious helplessness on the almighty sovereign power of God. In speaking of a special providence, he said he rather objected to the term special, as it seemed to overlook the fact that everything is ordered of God, great as well as small.

On another day he spoke of several of his friends at Geneva and at Montauban, and also mentioned Dr. Gordon, of Edinburgh, with much regard, and spoke with pleasure of that eminent clergyman's having told him that he had derived light from the exposition of the 6th chapter of the Romans, on which Mr. Haldane had bestowed much labour, and conceived that by the blessing of God he had been enabled to present the truth in some new and important aspects.

In the same month, his relative, the Rev. James O'Hara, of Coleraine, was permitted to enjoy an interview, of which he gives the following account :—

" But I believe I was the last person, not of his own immediate family, who had the privilege of spending an evening with your uncle; it was towards the end of September, 1842. He spoke for more than an hour, chiefly on the doctrine of regeneration by the Word as totally distinct from the office of baptism, and I was much struck with the clearness and arrangement with which he handled the subject, more as if he was reading from something he had studied, and committed to paper, than giving expression to passing thoughts. I had often read of the bright views of Christians when on the eve of their departure, but never before had seen an instance such as was the case with him; and I left the house with reverence in my mind, and Balaam's prayer on my lips, as he evidently had but few days to pass on earth. It was a scene which has often recurred to me, and one which I never could forget."

His natural strength of constitution sustained him for more than two months after this period, and he never lost his elasticity of mind. As he became feebler, he more and more preferred being alone, and seldom conversed even with his own family. In a letter, dated Friday, the 25th of November, his brother writes :—

" Your uncle is very ill, and on Monday night he appeared to be gone ; but he has rallied a little. Robert saw him to-day, and mentioned what you said about the money for Geneva and Montauban, and all was arranged. The doctors say, there is no hope of his rallying much. Dr. Davidson said, it was evidently a breaking-up, and this was the expression used to me by Dr. Abercrombie."

On Saturday, the 26th, he sent for his nephew, Robert, and conversed with him for an hour, settled all his worldly affairs, and gave directions as to his funeral. A letter of the same date gives some brief details of this interview, and adds :—

" He sent his kind love to you, and thanks for all your kind attention to him, and interest in all his matters. He exhorted you to hold fast the faith, and sent you his blessing."

In another letter, dated the Monday following, his brother again writes :—

" The message this morning is, that your uncle has had a very bad night. Elizabeth has been there, and brings word that he is more uneasy. Robert will see him, and then we shall hear more particulars. I am not sure that I mentioned before, that he converses more freely with yourself and Robert than with any one besides. He suffers much from weakness, but his mind is perfectly sound. He spoke to Robert for a

good while on Saturday evening. Whilst he was speaking Robert began
to tell him something, but he wished not to be interrupted. Yesterday,
Robert saw him again, when he inquired, with perfect self-recollection,
' What was it you were going to say on Saturday ? ' "

An account of the interview just alluded to, so far as it did
not relate to private matters, was printed after Mr. Haldane's
death :—

" It was now obvious to those around him that the last scene was fast
approaching. His medical attendants had given it as their opinion that
he could not survive many days. On feeling that the hand of death was
upon him, he sent for me to come to him, as he wished particularly to see
me ; and he fixed an hour when he was not likely to be interrupted by the
visits of his physician. So anxious was he for this interview, that he was
the first to hear me ring the bell, and he desired his head to be raised on
his pillow, in order that he might converse the more easily. He then
expressed a wish that all should leave the room ; and he told me to sit as
near him as I could. I shall never, so long as I live, forget our conversation, which lasted for above an hour. Although I had known him
intimately from my infancy, I was never so much struck as on this occasion with the masculine vigour and indomitable firmness of his character.
He told me that the event he had long expected was now at hand, and that
in a few hours he would probably be summoned before the tribunal of God,
the Judge of all. He was as composed as I ever recollect him, and did
not display the slightest emotion. He told me that he viewed the approach
of the last enemy without dismay,—that he died in the faith, possessing
the peace of God, and in the full assurance of understanding. He added,
' You cannot conceive the comfort I possess, and I trust that, when placed
in the same situation, you will enjoy the like blessed hope.' He exclaimed,
' I have fought a good fight,' &c. ; and in the most deliberate manner
repeated the whole passage, laying particular emphasis on the words,
' Not for *me* only, but for *all* who love his appearing.' He remarked,
that, however praiseworthy in the eyes of the world anything he had done
might appear, he in no way rested on it as a ground of acceptance in the
sight of God ; that, on the contrary, he renounced his good works as
much as his bad ones, and desired only to be wrapt in the robe of his
Redeemer's righteousness. He added, that he reposed securely on the
atonement of his Saviour, and that the words which he uttered on the
cross, ' It is finished,' gave him solid peace and comfort. He told me that
he died in peace with all mankind, and he sent affectionate messages to
those connected with him. In particular, he expressed the great comfort
and benefit he had derived from the ministry of his brother, and felt
thankful that they had gone on together hand in hand for so many years

in all their labours, and had differed in nothing. He declared that he firmly adhered to all the blessed doctrines which he had attempted to illustrate in his writings, more particularly in the last edition of his Exposition of the Romans. He survived sixteen days longer, during which time I saw him frequently, and so long as he was able to articulate, he expressed the same firm confidence in the finished work of his Redeemer."

In another conversation, on Sunday evening, the 4th of December, with her who had been for nearly fifty-seven years his faithful partner, he again went over the ground of his hope, which he declared to be fully able to support him. He spoke of the atonement as a reconciliation, which, in the nature of things, could only be for the sheep of Christ; and added, that how much soever a contrary view might, at first, tend to remove difficulties, it was only an apparent and not a real removal, for the same difficulties, although displaced, remained in full force, and never could be solved to one who believed in the electing love of the Father, except by referring all to the sovereign will of God, who, as the Judge of all the earth, must do right. He once more repeated, that he had derived more light on this and other subjects from his brother's preaching than from any one besides, and added that he had always found his brother's writings full of edification and solid comfort. With regard to the atonement, he was understood to refer particularly to a long conversation with his brother, at Auchingray, in 1841. He seemed to have pleasure in dwelling on the harmony and oneness of mind and purpose which had subsisted between them, and alluded to a saying of his friend, Mr. Murray, of George-square, who, on seeing them together, had, on one occasion, exclaimed, "There they are! the two brothers, they have always dwelt together in unity." He spoke also of some of the principal events of his own life, both before and since he knew the Lord. He felt that he had been kept in the grasp of Almighty love, or he must have perished. He touched on the different controversies in which he had been engaged, and said that it would yet appear that the Bible Society discussion, involving, as it did, the integrity of the canon and the plenary inspiration of Scripture, was one of the most important that had occurred since the days of the apostles. It was then that he expressed the wish that an account of it should at some time be published, although it might possibly not be expedient to do so for a few years. He again sent special messages of love to his relations, and of kind remembrance to friends.

After this he seemed to prefer being entirely alone, and scarcely spoke to any one. On the night of the 11th of December, he addressed some kind, pointed exhortations to his attendant, as to the importance of storing her memory with Scripture, and he was also overheard speaking to himself, as if in prayer. The last words he was heard to utter were several times repeated at intervals :—" For ever with the Lord "—" for ever "—" for ever."

On Monday, the 12th of December, he peacefully departed. He was buried within one of the aisles of the Old Cathedral at Glasgow, not far from the spot where, forty-four years before, he stood beside his friend, Mr. Rowland Hill, whilst the latter preached to so many thousands of the citizens of Glasgow.

There were many public testimonials to the estimation in which he was held, and his death was noticed in the prayers and in the sermons of Dr. Gordon, Dr. Candlish, and most of those who are now the Free Church ministers in Edinburgh. The "Witness" contained the first sketch of his character, from which one or two sentences may be extracted :—

" Mr. Haldane was one of those eminent men who leave the impress of their character on the age in which they live; and devoted, as his whole energies from an early period were, to the cause of the Redeemer, and with an efficacy rarely in any age equalled, his is a name which will be remembered among the worthies of the Church when mere worldly fame is gone. . . . At a period when moderation in the Church of Scotland was at its meridian, or rather at its midnight, he arose, and imagined the gigantic enterprise of evangelizing India, with a view to which it was that his estate of Airthrey was sold. . . . It must be unnecessary to refer to the labours of Mr. Haldane, and his still surviving brother, Mr. J. A. Haldane, in this fertile field of usefulness. From the Shetland Islands to the southernmost part of our land, the influence of the Messrs. Haldane was largely and blessedly felt, and numbers date their awakening to the missionary labours of these great and devoted men."

After alluding to the events of his "invaluable life," and

describing his tall figure and impressive bearing, the "Witness" proceeds :—

"His eye was little, black, and signally penetrating. The general expression of his countenance was thoughtful, but bland, good-humoured, and not unfrequently humorous; for he was not only a profound and most acute man, but was a kind-hearted man, and could both make and relish a joke. Of his liberality it is needless to speak."

He never allowed his picture to be taken, and consequently no likeness of him remains, excepting two or three sketches done from memory, or as caricatures, which may recal his appearance to those who knew him, but by no means embody the representation of his venerable and commanding presence. Several attempts were made to induce him to sit for a portrait, and in 1839, a kind note from his daughter, addressed to Mrs. A. Haldane, refers with pleasure to an expectation which then seemed on the verge of accomplishment. But his apparent yielding was not followed up, or perhaps turned out to be only the blandness of his manner and the pleasant appreciation of the affection which urged the request.

His daughter used herself to say that few pictures gave a better idea of the original than his brother's picture did of her father. There was, however, a considerable difference, as well as a resemblance.

Mr. Haldane's death was noticed by the Edinburgh Bible Society in becoming terms, as one whose name must ever be held in remembrance in connexion with the cause of Bible circulation, as one who "ceased not his labours till he had vindicated the plenary inspiration of God's Word, and checked the evils complained of, not in Scotland only, but in England, and to a considerable extent on the Continent of Europe." It is added—

"Till the conclusion of a long and active life, his prayers, his counsels, and his contributions animated and directed the efforts of the Edinburgh Bible Society; and now that he has been called from the scene of his labours on earth, the Committee feel that to him the language of Scripture may truly be applied, ' And I heard a voice from heaven saying unto me, write, Blessed are the dead which die in the Lord, from henceforth, yea, saith the Spirit, that they may rest from their labours, and their works do follow them.' "

On the 19th of June, 1843, exactly six months from the day of her husband's burial, the mortal remains of his companion for fifty-seven years were laid in the same vault in which his dust reposes in the Old Cathedral of Glasgow. She had been in drooping health, but was preparing to go to Leamington with her daughter, who, at the beginning of April, had lost her second son, Robert, after protracted illness. She herself thought that change of air and scene would revive her, and on the 10th of June Mr. James Haldane writes, that "he had that day called to see her, and was much struck with her appearance. I knew she was confined to bed with a cold, but previously felt no alarm about her. I have seen her since every day, and consider her to be in a most precarious state. She has no apprehension of danger herself, but her mind appears stayed upon the Lord." Her sister, Miss Oswald, of Scotstown, has presented the following memorandum with reference to that visit:—" My dear sister this day talking with me after Mr. James Haldane's visit, observed that he had asked what would be her feelings in the event of any sudden change. She did not exactly mention her reply, but very distinctly added, that ever since she knew herself to be a sinner, she had no hope but in the atonement, and could at all times say that she was in the state of the Apostle John, who, when he saw Jesus, fell at his feet as dead, when Jesus laid his right hand upon him and said, 'Fear not, I am the first and the last.' On the afternoon of the day before her death, she said to her youngest granddaughter, 'Don't seek parade, but a close adherence to the doctrines of the Bible. Remember your grandpapa's last words to you, his wish that you might all take your places with him at the last, the place that had been appointed before the foundations of the world. I trust you may take your station there.'" With these blessed hopes in her heart and such aspirations on her lips, she peacefully passed to her rest on the 14th of June, in her 75th year.

On receiving an account of Mr. Haldane's death, the Rev. Edward Bickersteth wrote as follows:—

" *To Alexander Haldane, Esq.*

" MY DEAR HALDANE,—I must thank you for your truly delightful account of your venerable uncle. Such men, indeed, are precious; and now his works will follow him. May we, too, tread in his steps till we meet in our dear Master's presence and glory. To discern, stand by, and maintain God's own truth, in the midst of a world neglecting or opposing it, is our present privilege; and to be acknowledged by our Lord, be with Him and like Him, and for ever, our future glory. Surely God is weaning all his servants in all his Churches from every earthly stay that they may lean on Him alone. In our one Lord,

" Very truly yours,<br>" E. BICKERSTETH.

" *Watton Rectory, Ware, Dec.* 26, 1842."

One of the most recent public testimonies borne to the memory of Robert Haldane is contained in a speech delivered by the Rev. Mr. Ferguson, the Free Church minister of Stirling, at a public meeting held in the month of October, 1852, at the Bridge of Allan. It concludes as follows :—

" I cannot conclude, Sir, while speaking of the landed proprietors of this country, without noticing that if I were called upon to point out the man of this class who, above all I ever heard of, was a very model of excellence to his fellows, I would name an individual who long resided within a mile of the place where we are now assembled, and who went from Airthrey's fair scenes about half a century ago, to scatter more manifold blessings among thousands and tens of thousands, in this and other lands, than perhaps any of his class in Scotland, was ever called to dispense. I allude, Sir, to the well-known and ever-to-be-honoured Robert Haldane, with whose remembrance, too, will ever be associated that of his truly noble brother, James Haldane. Fifty years ago, Sir, Robert Haldane sold that splendid property, in order to establish a Church Mission in the far East. The world looked on and smiled, and pitied the infatuation, and even friends could scarce excuse the folly. But did God ever more signally mark his approval of the course of the rich man, or did a man of his rank ever rise in Scotland, who so benefitted his fellow-men as did Robert Haldane ? (Applause.) Scotland, throughout her length and breadth, has from that day to this present hour, derived richest blessings from Robert Haldane's labours. Nor were they confined to these shores. Europe felt, and feels their marvellous effects. Baffled in his scheme of missionary enterprise in India, Robert Haldane was led, in God's wondrous providence, to the city of Geneva, and there his labours, immediately connected with the conversion of D'Aubigné and many others, led to that general awakening in the south of Europe, which may yet be the salvation of these unhappy lands. (Immense cheering.) Let us bless God that such men are raised up in their rank of society, and let us be found ever giving to them, in this our privileged country, the honour which is their due."

# CHAPTER XXVII.

MR. J. A. HALDANE OPPOSES ERRORS RESPECTING THE ATONEMENT — MR. HINTON, DR. JENKYN, DR. PAYNE, AND DR. WARDLAW — LETTER TO THE EVANGELICAL MAGAZINE—LABOURS AS AN OCTOGENARIAN — LETTER ON THE DEATH OF MR. CLEGHORN—VISIT TO LONDON AND BUXTON — DEATH OF HIS ELDEST DAUGHTER— LETTER ON MISS HARDCASTLE'S DEATH — DEATH OF DR. ABERCROMBIE—TREATISE ON CHRISTIAN UNION— PUBLISHES EXPOSITION OF GALATIANS—HIS LETTERS.

[1842—1848.]

ROBERT HALDANE had now finished his course, whilst more than eight years of active usefulness still separated his brother from the haven of rest. For some time the attention of both had been specially drawn to the doctrine of the atonement, and to certain speculative errors as to the moral capabilities of fallen man, which were unhappily prevalent in America, and had in England found an advocate amongst the Baptists in one of their ablest preachers. To avert the mischief, Mr. J. A. Haldane had, in 1842, published a treatise under the title : " Man's Responsibility : the Nature and Extent of the Atonement, and the Work of the Holy Spirit ; in reply to Mr. Howard Hinton and the Baptist Midland Association." Mr. Hinton, in his zeal to remove the cavils of unbelievers, had maintained a kind of semi-Pelagian view of our innate ability to receive the Gospel ; whilst at the same time, with scriptural orthodoxy, he fully admitted the proposition, that no man " who could live or shall live has received or will receive the truth without the aid of the Holy Spirit." His errors were, therefore, rather metaphysical than substantial, although numbers of younger and less enlightened men eagerly embraced his views, and carried them to an extent which, in subverting the doctrines of the Divine sovereignty, and of Christ's vicarious substitution, also subverted the Gospel. Mr. J. A. Haldane's book sets forth our moral responsibility as a fact alike revealed in Scripture and obvious to the perception of every man's conscience. But holding fast this truth, and maintaining that the rejection of the Gospel is always the result of sin or moral guilt, and not of misfortune only, he equally asserts the scriptural doctrine of the sovereignty of God, as displayed in the history of nations and the lives of individuals.

" If," he says, " we are content to be guided by the Scriptures, we shall not perplex ourselves with vainly attempting to reconcile the sovereignty of God with human responsibility. It is a matter too high for us ; we cannot attain to it. The death of Christ was foreordained, yet this did not interfere with the responsibility of those who through their wickedness fulfilled the Divine purpose. (Acts ii. 23.)"

Mr. D'Israeli, in his " Political Biography of Lord George Bentinck," has lately endeavoured, if we rightly understand him, to screen the Jewish nation from the guilt of the crucifixion, by pleading the mysterious purposes of God which they fulfilled. Thus it is that " parts and parcels of truth " are, as Mr. Howels once said, " the most envenomed shafts which fly from the bow of Satan." Mr. J. A. Haldane counted it the path of wisdom to receive the Word as he found it written, and neither to overlook the controlling, ruling, directing sovereignty of God, nor the equally obvious and revealed responsibility of man. The whole of his treatise is rich in scriptural views of the glory of God, as exhibited in the scheme of redemption. He shows that in order to understand the Gospel of salvation, we must rightly understand our fall in Adam. In Adam all were created. In Adam all sinned. In Adam all came " under the curse of a broken law," and died.

" The occasion," says Dr. Owen, " of all the mistakes or errors that have been about regeneration, has been a misunderstanding about the true state of men in their lapsed condition of nature as depraved."

Mr. Haldane continues :—

" That the unnumbered millions of the human race should have been created in a single individual, would appear incredible, but the birth of children solves the difficulty. Many hold, most inconsistently, that we partake of the *consequences*, but not of the guilt of Adam's sin. But ' by one man's sin many were *made* sinners,' and by the righteousness of one shall many be made righteous."

He thus shows the unity of Adam with every child of man by natural generation down to the end of time, and the unity of Christ with every child of God by the regeneration of the Holy Spirit to all eternity. He shows that Adam's sin was the sin of all mankind, and that Christ's righteousness is the righteousness of all his saved and blood-bought flock. "There is," he says, " a transmission of mind as well as of body. The whole is a mystery. We cannot fathom it."

In his writings, Mr. J. Haldane often enforces his arguments by that happy faculty of apposite illustration from anecdote which availed so much to his popularity as a preacher. With reference to the folly of endeavouring to divest the Gospel of mystery, and bring down heavenly things to the level of our limited capacities, he alludes to the embassy sent by Louis XIV. to the King of Siam. The ambassador told the King, that in France the cold was so intense that men could walk upon the water, and the thing appeared so absurd, that the King imagined it was intended as an insult, and threatened the narrator of the marvel with instant death. Another well-authenticated anecdote to the same effect is told of a poor North American Indian, who returned to the back woods of his distant tribe to recount the wonders he had witnessed at Washington. They were listened to with doubt and incredulity, until he declared that he had seen the white people attach a great ball to a canoe, and so rise into the clouds and travel through the heavens. This was instantly pronounced to be an impossibility; and a young warrior, in a paroxysm of anger, levelled a rifle at his head, and shot him dead on the spot, as too great a liar to be permitted to live.

" If, then," exclaims Mr. J. Haldane, " what takes place in another climate, or in a different state of society, appears absurd because contrary to experience, shall we greatly wonder that the things of the Spirit of

God—those heavenly and eternal things which eye hath not seen, nor ear heard, neither hath it entered into the heart of man to conceive—should be foolishness to all who have not the Spirit, and are consequently alienated from the life of God?"

It would be out of place to go at large into a discussion with regard to the nature, and still more, as to the extent, of the atonement. But the great importance which both of the brothers attached to right views of these doctrines, forbids that a statement of their sentiments should be altogether omitted. To Socinians and Neologians the idea of a Vicarious Sacrifice, by virtue of which God and man are reconciled, appears nothing better than the dream of enthusiasm. It was to the Jews a scandal, to the Greeks foolishness. The first-born of Adam after the fall, spurned at the institution of a typical sacrifice of blood. In his eyes, no doubt, it was contrary to reason and revolting to humanity. In the pride of his self-righteousness the haughty will-worshipper approached his Maker with what he deemed the guiltless offering "of the fruit of the ground." His younger brother, Abel, discerned by faith a righteousness to be finished upon Mount Calvary, and meekly obedient to the heavenly call, poured out the blood of the firstlings of his flock upon the altar of God. From that hour down to the present, the question of an atonement has been one that has divided the two families into which the children of Adam were from the first divided. The seed of the serpent rejects the idea that a merciful and benevolent God requires to be propitiated by blood ; while the seed of the woman, with child-like simplicity, receives the Gospel, that " God *so* loved the world that he gave his only begotten Son, that *whosoever* believeth on him should not perish, but have everlasting life." The Scripture declares, that " without shedding of blood there is no remission of sins." The blood, we are told, is the life ; and as death was the penalty of sin, so Christ poured out his life-blood, and rendered himself up as a ransom for many. Taking upon him the nature of man, after man had incurred the curse of a broken law, he stood in the breach between the offended majesty of the Divine law, and the devoted race of Adam. The curse of the broken

T T

covenant fell upon the man Jesus Christ, but in the impregnable strength of his eternal Godhead, the penalty was not only endured, but exhausted. The curse, which would have sunk a sinful world to the bottomless pit, was sustained and rolled away by the Holy One of God. The infinite and everlasting Jehovah, tabernacled in flesh, under the conditions of a broken law, and having satisfied all its requirements, its precepts, and penalties, he burst the portals of the grave, rose from the dead, and ascended in majesty to his Father's throne, whilst angels, and the spirits of just men not till then made perfect, chanted the triumphant song, " Lift up your heads, O ye gates ; lift them up, ye everlasting doors, and the King of Glory shall come in."

But this doctrine of an imputed righteousness is foolishness to the natural man, and has been assailed by many plausible objections, drawn by inferential reasoners from false and insufficient premises. In all matters concerning the truth of God, it is in a finite creature nothing better than an act of folly to try to overleap the bounds of revelation. It is vain for the finite to grasp the infinite, or for human reason to sound the unfathomable depths of Divine wisdom. The Scriptures have told us that Christ "bore our sins on his own body on the tree," that he was " made a curse for us in order to redeem us from the curse of the law," that " the Lord laid upon him the iniquity of us all." Here the substitution, the suretyship, the vicarious sacrifice, " the Just for the unjust," are clearly declared, and on this foundation the whole fabric of man's salvation rests.

In attempting to meet the cavils of objectors, or to smoothe away difficulties at which unbelief stumbles, many true Christians have been seduced to leave the beaten path of Scripture, and enter on the fields of abstract reasoning. The consequences might easily be foretold by those who remember the warnings of our Lord and his apostles. It is venturing on the wings of speculation into the realms of infinite space, where there is nothing to guide, to support, or to direct. All is darkness, uncertainty, and gloom. The attempt to blend the conclusions of metaphysical theories with the authoritative declarations of the Bible, have uniformly ended in confusion. Against such a method of dealing with Christianity both of the Haldanes earnestly contended from the beginning to the end of their career. "How readest thou?" and not "what thinkest thou?" was the shibboleth of their child-like spirit and scriptural theology.

With regard to the nature of the atonement, there is, as they used to say, less of *real* difference between true Christians who receive the Bible as the book of God, than at first sight appears. Where there is true faith or confidence in Jesus, that confidence must rest on the finished work of an Almighty Saviour, by whom an everlasting reconciliation is made between God and the believing sinner. No true Christian imagines that he is saved by his own acts or merits, and when he believes that his salvation is of God, and not of himself, he in effect believes in the electing love of the Father, in the atoning work of the Son, and in the sanctifying influence of the Holy Spirit. Thus it is that disputes about election and predestination, or the nature of the atonement, are, amongst true disciples, generally little more than strifes of words, arising out of the partial restoration of spiritual eye-sight.

Still, as all errors are dangerous, and we are commanded to hold fast "the form" as well as the substance of sound doctrine, Mr. J. A. Haldane devoted much time and attention to the refutation of the novel and metaphysical views which were successively supported by Mr. Hinton, Dr. Jenkyn, Dr. Payne, and the still more venerable authority of Dr. Wardlaw. He himself stood by the old doctrine, which he had learned as a child out of the Westminster Assembly's Catechism—that doctrine in which he had been confirmed by the study of the Scriptures during more than fifty years—that doctrine which was taught not merely by the old Scottish and Puritan Divines, but by many of the brightest ornaments of the English and Foreign Churches.

In 1843, he published an excellent little tract on the atonement, and in 1845 a more elaborate but still condensed work on the same subject, entitled, "The Doctrine of the Atonement, with Strictures on the recent Publications of Drs. Wardlaw and

Jenkyn." Dr. Wardlaw not only maintained the universality of the atonement, but, like Mr. Hinton, that men have "power to believe and turn to God." Some students in Dr. Wardlaw's class, and also in the Associate Synod, taking advantage of these incautious concessions, proceeded to deny the doctrine of election, the necessity of the work of the Spirit, and the fact of the Substitution, and thus adopted heresies, which, as Mr. J. A. Haldane remarked, accord better with the wisdom of this world, and "promise to modify, if not to remove, the hitherto insuperable difficulty of God's absolute sovereignty in the bestowal of salvation." The system against which he contended teaches that the atonement was an exhibition or a *display*, a *make-believe*, a show or shadow of justice, whilst the Scripture declares it to be a substantial reality.

"In all that is done by the Almighty," he observes, "there is a substance, a reality, which repels the notion of a mere public *display* being the end of his proceedings. Those, therefore, have greatly erred, who would resolve the whole mystery of the wisdom, power, and love of God, comprised in the atonement, into a design of making an impression on his creatures, as if it were 'public justice' only that demanded the death of Christ. The atonement is indeed a wonderful manifestation of the righteousness, holiness, mercy, and truth of God; but the necessity of the atonement did not result from the existence of any creature excepting the transgressor. The eternal justice and truth of God imperatively demanded the punishment of the guilty; and had Adam stood alone, the solitary creature of the Almighty, the essential attributes and character of God, his holiness, justice, and truth would have rendered his doom inevitable, had not wisdom and mercy combined to devise a remedy, by which the claims of justice and truth are satisfied in all their boundless extent. . . . Far be it, then, from those who love the Lord, to represent the atonement as an expedient for the *exhibition* of *public* justice, instead of being an actual satisfaction to the *justice* of God. . . . The wisdom of God, even the hidden wisdom, consists in this, that the 'debt of *obedience*' is paid actually, not figuratively, by our great Surety; that our guilt is as effectually covered with the robe of Christ's righteousness as if it had never existed; and that believers have fulfilled the law in all its length and breadth, so that, with adoring admiration of Him who loved them and washed them from their sins in his own blood, they dare challenge the universe to lay anything to their charge. Is this the language of those who 'have been and ever must continue guilty?'"

He then shows that the mystery of the absolution of the guilty is explained by the unity of Christ, as the head of his Church, with his members.

"It was not," he says, "another who appeared as their surety. It was the head of the body of which they are the members, and the unity of the head and the members of the natural body is not more real than that of Christ and his people. This is the mystery of faith. It may elude the grasp of human intelligence; it may be one of those things into which the angels desire to look. But the fact is certain. HE HATH SAID IT, and instead of perplexing ourselves about the properties of 'commutative or distributive justice,' it will be our wisdom to bow with adoring humility to the unfathomable wisdom of God, and receiving, as little children, the truth as it is in Jesus, to learn the meaning of Christ's words, 'I thank thee, O Father, Lord of heaven and earth, that thou hast hid these things from the wise and prudent, and hast revealed them unto babes. Even so, Father, for so it seemed good in thy sight.'"

In 1847, a second edition of this work being called for, Mr. J. A. Haldane added an Appendix of Strictures on Dr. Payne's Lectures on the same subject. These Lectures he considered as a practical illustration of the danger of "blending metaphysics with Scripture."

"Dr. Payne," he says, "seems to court the title of a Philosophical Divine. It is a dangerous eminence. The man who aspires to it trespasses on forbidden ground. 'Stop, traveller!' is inscribed on the entrance gate. Paul, the ambassador of Jesus Christ, with all the authority of his apostolic character, and under the infallible guidance of inspiration, warns us of the danger of blending our philosophy with the doctrine of Jesus. (Col. ii. 8.) It is impossible to neglect the warning without becoming the dupes of our own subtleties."

Mr. J. A. Haldane's object was to exhibit the simple truth of Scripture, and at the same time expose the futility of every attempt to explain or remove difficulties by philosophical specu- lations. In one word, he held the doctrine of the substitution and vicarious sacrifice of Christ to be a reality instead of a fiction, and as to difficulties, "what we know not now, we shall know hereafter."

But connected with the discussion as to the nature of the atonement, there is another more subtle question with reference to the extent of its operation, which has unhappily divided some

Churches and many Christians, who hold the doctrines of election and of free sovereign grace, in a way which ought to cut off all ground for serious difference of opinion. There is a mysterious sense in which Jesus Christ as man redeemed the world, including all animate and inanimate creation, from the usurpation of Satan; and in this life there is also a sense in which, " for the elect's sake," every creature that breathes on this earth participates in the temporal benefits of redemption. There is also a sense in which all mankind are brought under the purchased dominion of the Son, to whom as man all judgment is committed by the Father. But to affirm that reconciliation has been made for those who die in their sins, and either reject the Gospel or never hear it, is a doctrine which disparages the value of the atonement, and stamps the impress of imperfection on the greatest work of God. If the atonement import reconciliation provided indiscriminately for the lost and saved, is not the work of Christ dishonoured, for, in this case, *through Christ's sacrifice,* there is complete salvation for none? There is, according to that system, full and finished salvation only for those in whom the work of Christ is, to use the words of a profound divine, *" supplemented by something wrought by them or in them."* Is this a doctrine calculated to give rest to the weary? or is it not, in the words of Dr. Candlish, " a revelation after all consistent with the blackness of darkness in hell?" In opposition to contingent salvation through Christ, Mr. James Haldane urged that a full and perfect reconciliation was made by Christ for those, and for those alone, who had been from eternity the objects of the Father's unchanging love; that this atonement was not *applied,* but *revealed,* by the Holy Spirit, whose influence and power upon the heart are the *results,* and not the *causes,* of reconciliation. If a contrary doctrine were to prevail, he argued that Christ could not " see of the travail of his soul and be satisfied;" and that the declaration of an eloquent Arminian clergyman would be justified, when, in one of his flights of fancy, he spoke of every soul that perished as a gem that had dropped from the diadem of Jesus!

The question as to the bearing of the atonement on the

finally impenitent is surely, after all, merely a speculation. If it were at once admitted that Christ's precious blood was, in his Divine purpose, shed equally for the lost as for the saved, for Judas as well as Paul, for the millions and millions to whom the Gospel is never sent, as for the countless multitude who hear and believe, would it remove one of those difficulties which are now an offence to the enemies of the Gospel? If Christ's sacrifice were offered for the world, and not for those whom the Father has " given him out of the world," and if the term, world, is to be understood in an unrestrained sense, without the limitations which the context again and again requires, may it not be asked, Why is not the Gospel carried to every quarter of the globe, and why do millions, every hour, die in ignorance and blindness, without the knowledge of the costly salvation, prepared and planned for their salvation? Does this resemble the designs of the Almighty? Does such a scheme commend itself even to reason, as one issuing out of " the depths both of the wisdom and knowledge of God," or does it not rather resemble one of the abortive imaginations of man, striving to fathom a mystery for which his faculties are insufficient? Is there not after all as much of the supposed mockery in the idea of a reconciliation hidden from a large proportion of the adult world, who die unreconciled, as in speaking of an atonement only for those who were chosen by the Father's love before the foundation of the world, and are spoken of as the sheep given to Christ, in order that they might be washed in his blood? (John x. 17.) In either case there are difficulties, unless it be said, that the Gospel comes to those who reject it, to condemn rather than to save. We are taught, in the Seventeenth Article of the Church of England equally as by the Church of Scotland, that " God hath constantly decreed by his counsel, secret to us, to deliver from curse and damnation *those whom he hath chosen in Christ out of mankind.*" To suppose that Christ shed his blood purposely for the lost as well as the saved, may disparage the value of his work for those who are saved, but it cannot avail the lost, except it be to their deeper condemnation. The sinner, coming weary and heavy laden unto Christ, in search of the promised rest, will find but cold comfort in a vague and general redemption, equally belonging to those who are saved and to those who are lost. It is redemption enduring for ever that he seeks, a redemption which takes away the curse, a redemption that secures the favour of God, a redemption that is a substantial reality, and not a mere illusive phantom. Why fallen angels were passed by, whilst man became the object of compassion, why some were "chosen in Christ out of mankind," and the rest were left out of Christ, are questions which it is presumptuous to ask, and impossible to answer.

To all cavils there is but one reply, and it is that by which the apostle stated and silenced the objection to the sovereignty of God. (Rom. ix. 20.) If it had been the will of God, the Gospel of salvation through Jesus Christ might have passed with the lightning speed of electricity to every corner of the globe on the day of Pentecost. Had it been the will of God, the Gospel might have been preached to every creature under heaven without exception, and the same irresistible power which arrested Saul, the blasphemer, on his road to Damascus could have unlocked every heart to receive the truth. But this did not seem good to Him who ordereth all things according to His sovereign pleasure in the armies of heaven and amongst the inhabitants of the earth, and we know who has said, "No man cometh unto me except the Father draw him." But why are not all drawn? "Ask not the reason," says Benedict Pictet; "it is secret, but not unjust." It is enough to know that the command is plain, "Preach the Gospel to every creature," and that the promise of salvation is secure to "whosoever believe." For "whosoever" will believe, there is an ample provision; for all who will enter in, the door stands open; for all who will drink, the fountain flows. But at best it is surely nothing better than presumption to inquire whether there be the same provision for those who reject as for those who receive the Gospel,—for those who turn away from the water of life as from those who drink, for those who spurn at the door of mercy as for those who meekly enter in. Vague and general statements of Christ's mediation and work are not necessary to justify the freest proclamation of pardon to every sinner who comes to Christ. The Gospel does not consist in declaring such abstract propositions, as that all are pardoned, or that Christ's precious blood was shed not merely for the sheep of which he is the Shepherd, but for those who have "no part or lot" in the mansions he has gone to prepare. The Gospel declares to all who hear it, a Saviour in whom God is well pleased; with the blessed assurance that he is *able* to save unto the uttermost all that come unto God by Him; and not only able but *willing* to save all that come, for "whosoever cometh unto him he will in no wise cast out." These views for which Mr. James Haldane so earnestly contended, have been substantially urged, with much force and eloquence, by Dr. Candlish. In one of his sermons, intituled "Christ's Call to the Weary," Dr. Candlish places the practical bearing of this confessedly mysterious subject in a striking light :—

" We tell you not of salvation contained in a proposition, but of salvation treasured up in a person. We proclaim no general amnesty or indiscriminate jail delivery, purchased for men at large by Christ; but we set before you Christ himself, and we assure all that come to him of pardon, peace, and eternal life. We do not merely tell you of the infinite amount of merit and atoning virtue which there is in the obedience and death of Jesus. But we tell you of Jesus himself, who will clothe you—any of you —all of you—who will only come unto Him, with a robe of perfect righteousness, and wash you in a fountain that will make you all clean. *And we tell you further, that with any questions as to what there may be in Christ—for you or for any—while not coming unto Him you have no concern. It is presumption to ask such questions: it would be vain and useless to have them answered.* Come ye unto Christ; come and see; taste, and see that the Lord is good. This is his present call; this is your present duty; admitting of no evasion and of no delay. Come ye to Christ, and he will make all clear to you. Come unto him, and he will give you rest." *

This was exactly Mr. James Haldane's practical mode of inviting sinners to come as babes to Christ, to believe and be saved; without assuming the proud character of "the wise and prudent," puzzling themselves with abstract questions about the reconcilement of God's sovereignty and man's responsibility,

* Candlish's "Scripture Characters," p. 490.

or the bearings of Christ's work on the impenitent.   But in his work on the Atonement he forcibly observes, that

" If it be admitted that the work of the Spirit is as essential to salvation as the work of Christ, an atonement for all brings no one nearer to the kingdom of God, for without the sovereign, efficacious work of the Spirit, there is an absolute impossibility of a sinner's salvation, so that your opening a door of hope for all is only uncovering a grave that the dead may come forth; it is lighting a candle that the blind may see; it is opening a door for a man without legs to walk out of prison."

These remarks are made not in a polemical spirit, but for the purpose of explaining the discussion concerning the nature of the atonement and its extent, in which Mr. J. A. Haldane took so prominent a part.   He was in his seventy-seventh year when his last treatise on the atonement appeared, and he was verging on fourscore when he published the second and enlarged edition, with an appendix in reply to Dr. Payne.   By a very distinguished Presbyterian divine, who has also used it as a class-book, it was pronounced to be, in his opinion, not only the most vigorous, acute, and logical of all Mr. James Haldane's works, but the best and the soundest work on the atonement he had ever met with, having regard to its condensation of solid truth as well as to its sound, scriptural theology.   Mr. J. A. Haldane had proclaimed the Gospel in all its freeness with a fervour and a success seldom exceeded.   His own views are the reflection of those contained in the Confession of the Church of Scotland, and in the seventeenth article of the Church of England.   No man could charge him with occupying himself with curious points, preaching only to the elect, or by reference to the secret counsels of God, fettering the proclamation of pardon to repenting sinners.   His works, therefore, on the atonement had the double advantage of being the mature opinions of a man mighty in the Scriptures, and of one whose gift seemed especially designed for awakening the careless and persuading sinners to the knowledge of the truth.   Both of the brothers distinctly held that but for his chosen sheep, Christ never would have shed his precious blood, and that no sacrifice could avail without the prayer or intercession of the Priest.   (Heb. vii. 25; Rom.

viii. 24.) They further held that there must be perfect unity, both of design and of execution, in the Godhead. The unity of the Godhead required, that as the extent of the Father's gift, and the extent of the sanctifying work of the Holy Ghost, such also must be the extent of the atonement or reconciliation effected by the Son. To suppose that Christ died for those who were not given to him of the Father, and whom the Holy Ghost does not sanctify, and for whom Christ himself would not intercede (John xvii. 9), was to impute not only disunion but inconsistency, to the operation of the three persons of the blessed Trinity.

But holding these decided views, no man preached the Gospel more freely and fully than Mr. J. A. Haldane, and no man more disapproved than he did of that harsh and unwarrantable method which, overlooking the responsibility of man, only addresses the invitation to the elect, whose names are in the book of life. He rested his appeals on a firm conviction that every human being is bound to believe the testimony of the Father, that Christ is his beloved Son; that the rejection of this testimony is the result of moral depravity and not of natural inability; that whosoever believes this testimony as a little child shall have eternal life, whilst the wise and prudent who reject because they cannot understand it are justly condemned, because, by their unbelief, they exhibit their enmity to truth, and make God a liar. But he never called upon each and every sinner to believe that Christ died or offered up a sacrifice for him in particular, because he was convinced that Christ, in his priestly character, never offered a sacrifice for those on whose behalf he did not pray, and never presented to the Father an atonement which was not for ever complete. Mr. James Haldane was firmly persuaded that if good men were only agreed as to the *nature* of the atonement, there would be far less confusion and no disagreement with reference to its *extent*.

The secession which at this time took place from the Congregational Union in Scotland gave rise to some discussion in the "Evangelical Magazine" for 1844 (p. 670), and for 1845 (p. 142). In these articles a Scotch Congregationalist, willing to justify his own denomination, at the expence of others, and transfer the origin of the new heresies to a remote cause, with more of ingenuity than of truth or logic, traced the mischiefs which had recently sprung up to what had occurred nearly fifty years before in connexion with Mr. Haldane's seminaries. Mr. J. A. Haldane was seldom careful to correct such misrepresentations, and it was with some difficulty that he was prevailed on to place on record a contradiction of the mis-statement. His letter to the editor appeared in the "Evangelical Magazine" for 1846 (p. 549), and is important partly as a memorial of the doctrinal consistency and sobriety of both the brothers, partly as an evidence of their uniform aversion to the frigid system of Sandemanianism, and partly as a testimony to the character of most of the students who were educated in the seminaries of Glasgow, Dundee, and Edinburgh. In the letter he alludes to his first preaching tour, undertaken in 1797, with the view of calling attention to the Gospel, but adds, "whilst I hope I have learned something by studying the Scriptures for almost fifty years, if I were asked in what respect my present views of any great doctrine of the Gospel differ from my sentiments in 1797, I could not specify on one particular." He adds :—

"It may be a reproach, in the opinion of your correspondent, that I hold ' the doctrines of the Westminster Confession,' but I am still willing to bear it, and to this day I prefer it to the improvements made upon it by writers, either in America, Scotland, or England. And I am confirmed in this preference when I witness the fruits of a deviation from some of these doctrines, both in the Secession and Congregational Churches of Scotland."

He then relates what has been already stated in an early part of this volume, with reference to his own and his brother's protest in 1801 against the use of Sandeman's works in the seminary at Glasgow, and his continued and uniform disapproval of them since that period. He adds :—

"Sandeman may be said to set aside the work of the Spirit, for he discourages all concern about salvation in the unconverted ; but he carries the doctrine of Divine sovereignty so high, that it would appear the sinner has nothing to do but to wait till God reveal His Son in him."

A quotation had been made by the writer in the "Evangelical Magazine" from a work on "Errors in Religion," by Mr. Douglas, of Cavers, from which it appeared that the author had rather thoughtlessly associated the leaders of "the Haldane movement" with some Judaizing opinions relating to the preparation of food, entertained by that gentleman's early friend and relative, Dr. Stuart. On this point Mr. J. A. Haldane replies :—

"For my own part, I have always understood the precept, Acts xv. 28, 29, as being parallel to Rom. xiv. 15, and that it was given from regard to the Jews, in whose synagogues Moses was read every Sabbath-day. I never at any time held this prohibition as perpetual, and that my brother's sentiments were similar is proved by the fact, that when Mr. Ewing was about to publish his lecture on Acts xv. 28, 29, my brother intimated his intention of taking a number of copies, till he heard that Mr. Ewing insisted on the obligation under which believers are laid to abstain from blood, when he told him that in that case he could not encourage the sale."

Mr. J. A. Haldane's strength long enabled him to triumph over age, yet frequent attacks of gout reminded him, as he himself wrote, that "the clouds returned after the rain." In a letter written when he was seventy-five, he says :—

"As to exertion and fatigue, you greatly overrate my labours, and I do not feel more fatigued on the Lord's-day evening than on other days. If ever I find, as is likely should I live a little longer, that my work is too great, I will give up the Lord's-day evening service. At present this is not necessary."

Thus, until verging on fourscore years, did he himself conduct three services every Lord's-day, preaching twice, besides administering the Lord's Supper in the morning and delivering two addresses, equal in length to one full sermon.

In the spring of 1843 he had a severe attack of gout, to which he alludes in the following letter to Mrs. M'Neil, which indicates the perfect peace that possessed his soul :—

"*Edinburgh, April* 9, 1843.

"The account which you give of the state of your mind when you received relief from the Gospel is very affecting. The Lord leads the blind in a way they know not, and in paths that they have not known. You went to Thurso for your health in 1797, and the Lord was pleased to meet you there, and to guide your feet into the way of peace. I shall

You went to Thurso for your health in 1797, and the Lord was pleased to meet you there, and to guide your feet into the way of peace. I shall never forget the kindness I received from your worthy father, and, indeed, from all the family. I spent some very happy hours at Staxigo, the recollection of which is still grateful, although most of those in whose company they were passed have gone the way of all the earth. Well! we shall go to them, but they will not return to us. We can anticipate uniting with them in the new song of praise to him who loved us, and hath washed us from our sins in his own blood. I am sorry to hear that you have been so unwell, but I join with you in giving thanks to the God of our life for your restoration. I have also had an attack of gout, to which I am subject. I was laid aside for three Lord's-days, but was able to preach last Lord's-day. I heard lately of a woman in the High-lands, who had been very ill. A friend visited her, to whom she said, ' I thought our next meeting would have been before the throne, but either I am not meet for that blessed place, or my Father has something more for me to do.' Well, which, think you, is the true reason? Why, to tell you the truth, I believe it is the last; for when I think of the glory of my Redeemer's righteousness, in which I shall stand before God, it seems so complete that I have no fear of my acceptance. 'I went,' continued she, ' to my neighbours on my recovery, and told them I was sent back to them from the dead, and some were much affected, and I have reason to believe that one is seeking the way to Zion.' I used to call frequently on Mr. Cleghorn; although his weakness prevented him from speaking in public, I thought it a great privilege to converse with him. He was constantly employed in searching the Scriptures, and was delighted to speak of the wondrous things which he had discovered in God's holy law. I saw him not long before his death; indeed, the first intimation I got of it was in a letter asking me to his funeral. I was unwell, and unable to go. And now I commend you to God and to the word of His grace. May He support and comfort you, and sanctify you wholly! May you be enabled to look stedfastly within the veil, and beholding in the unveiled face of Jesus, as in a glass, the glory of the Lord, may you be changed into the same image, from glory to glory, as by the Spirit of the Lord."

In the summer of 1843, he was induced, on account of his gout, to repair to Buxton with Mrs. Haldane. He went by sea to London, and remained at Hatcham for some time. During his visit, he was able to take long walks with as little fatigue as ever, and, accompanied by his grandchildren, almost daily made some little excursion. Greenwich Hospital was a very favourite object, and he took particular pleasure in visiting the old sailors in their magnificent asylum, dropping a word in season as to their souls' welfare, and in watching the shipping on their still more majestic river. The following letter was at this time written by that venerable and devoted man, the late Rev. George Collison, so well known in connexion with the Theological Seminary of the Village Itinerant Society :—

" There are," he says, " few things of the kind that would afford me more gratification than to meet your venerable father for a few hours at Hatcham House." After stating his engagements, and proposing a particular day, Mr. Collison adds : " Should this be inconvenient, I can only request my affectionate regards to the venerable minister of the grace of God, with sincere prayer for his abundant comfort in the last stage of his important ministry. The names of ' Robert Haldane' and ' James Haldane' are so blended with all my mental associations respecting the kingdom of Christ forty years ago, that I must almost forget myself before I can forget them."

From London Mr. Haldane proceeded to Buxton, where, as usual, he took long walks on the week-days, and preached twice every Lord's-day with great power to good congregations. From the baths and change of scene he appeared to derive great benefit, and returned home about the middle of October. On his arrival, he writes :—

" On reviewing our journey we see much cause for gratitude to God, and there is no part of it on which I look back with so much pleasure as to the time I spent with you at Hatcham and at Buxton, and all your kindness, as well as that of dear Emma and her sister Selina, to both of whom I shall write as soon as I can get my hands free of matters which have accumulated in my absence. It is my daily prayer that the Lord's blessing may rest on you and all your family. You will be surprised to learn that Dr. Malan is here. He was at Aberdeen yesterday, and goes to the Assembly of the Free Church to-morrow at Glasgow. He speaks of being with you. Here I hope he will be with us, and preach for me next Lord's-day."

Scarcely had he arrived in Edinburgh, when the illness of his eldest and beloved daughter Elizabeth, who had remained at her brother's, recalled him to London. She had for many years been in bad health, but without any immediate apprehensions of a fatal issue. Her father was most anxious to take her home, as it was impossible for him, without the neglect of his public

duties, to remain away from Edinburgh. A land journey would
have been too fatiguing for her, but it was arranged that she
should go by sea, and her cousin, Mrs. Haldane Gordon, who
was then staying at Hatcham, kindly accompanied her on the
voyage. She survived, without much suffering, till the 20th
of December. On the evening preceding her death, her father
writes :—

" If you come this week I hope you will see her alive. I had never
spoken to her about my thoughts of her danger till yesterday. I had no
doubt of her union with Christ, and confidently expected that He would
lead her to speak on the subject. When alone with her, she asked me
whether I thought the disease advancing rapidly. I told her I did, and
that she must have seen from the beginning that I had no hope of her
recovery. She said, she knew this, and was looking to Jesus as her only
hope; that she had long known the Lord, and felt secure in his love."

In the same letter he proceeds, at a later hour :—

" Dear Elizabeth is very weak. Whether she will rally is at present
doubtful, but she expressed the hope that she might live to see you once
more, but was afraid that she would not be able to speak to you when
you came. Her mind is quite comfortable. She said to me, when I was
speaking to her a little while ago, that she had got the wish for which
she had prayed on the evening of her mother's death, that she might go
before me, and not see me die. I reminded her of Jordan being dried
up, when the feet of the priests touched the water, so that Israel passed
through dry-shod, and so the empty grave of Jesus stands at the entrance
of the dark valley, the pledge of death being swallowed up in victory."

Nearly two years afterwards the following letter was written
on the occasion of the death of Miss Hardcastle, the early
friend of his departed daughter, and the only surviving sister of
his daughter-in-law :—

" *Edinburgh, November 6th,* 1845.

" My dearest Emma,—I have just received Alexander's letter informing us of the removal of dear Selina. It was very unexpected, although
the state of her health for so long a time rendered it an event which might
reasonably be looked for. I wrote to her on Monday, and my letter
would arrive a few hours after her departure. Many years ago Selina
and Elizabeth were together at Hatcham, and I did not then anticipate,
that, although so much older, I should survive them both. But the path
of death is to be trodden by all, and it is to believers the porch of eternal
life. It has been called by a heathen the birthday of eternity. The life

of all his posterity was committed to Adam, and he forfeited it; but the life of the believer is hid with Christ in God, and the second Adam has said, Because I live ye shall live also.   In him, their glorious head, they suffered the penalty of their guilt.   The triumphant shout, 'It is finished,' was re-echoed from the everlasting hills, when Jesus was raised from the dead by the glory of the Father, and Justice and Mercy united in rolling away the stone, that the Prince of Life, the head of the new creation, might come forth from the sepulchre in which he was laid, when he bore the sins of his people in his own body on the tree.   We are not called to sorrow for dear Selina, as those who have no hope.   She has, I doubt not, slept in Jesus, and joined the spirits of the just made perfect, and we must all shortly follow.   The more we are freed from self-righteousness, the more we look to the righteousness of Christ, the more comfort shall we enjoy.   Some have called faith and repentance the *conditions* of the new covenant.   Both are essentially necessary, they accompany salvation, but we may as well term holiness the condition, for without holiness no man shall see the Lord.   Faith terminates in its great object; the source of our comfort therefore is out of ourselves, and hence it is that salvation is by faith, not by love, or any disposition, or Christian grace, wrought in ourselves; he that glorieth must glory in the Lord.

" The dispensation will be peculiarly trying to you, but I trust you will experience that the Lord's grace is sufficient for you, or, in the language of the Old Testament, in which spiritual things are set forth by those which are earthly and typical, that your shoes shall be iron and brass, and that as your day is so shall your strength be.   The great promise of the Old Testament was the incarnation of Christ.   Its accomplishment has vindicated the faithfulness of God.   The great promise of the New Testament is the second appearing of the Son of God, and he hath said, 'Behold, I come quickly.'   May we all respond, 'Even so, come, Lord Jesus.'   It is a great satisfaction to Mrs. Haldane and myself that we saw Selina once more before her removal.   She sometimes spoke of being able to visit Edinburgh, when the railway was completed.   Hereafter the people of God will not be separated from each other by distance."

Mr. Haldane's public engagements were still discharged without intermission, and the time and labour which he devoted to correspondence with the Highland preachers itinerating for the Baptist Home Missionary Society, indicated that the spirit which animated his early labours was unquenched.   That institution was somewhat similar to the original Society for Propagating the Gospel at Home, and employed about forty itinerants, to carry the Gospel through the Highlands.   For many years the preachers were accustomed to consult him in every difficulty, and receive from him directions as to their spheres of duty. To the energetic vigilance with which he watched over their appointment, to the prayerful wisdom with which he directed their movements, to the combined firmness and gentleness with which he counselled, admonished, or, if needful, rebuked, may, be traced, under God, much of the good fruit that crowned their exertions.

In a letter, dated November 14th, 1844, Mr. Haldane details the incidents connected with the death of the celebrated Dr. Abercrombie, which was very sudden, and somewhat similar in its circumstances to that of Dr. Chalmers. He concludes :—

" He lately sent me a little book, the first of a series intended for the young, on the discipline of the mind, not anticipating that it was to be his last. But I have no doubt that he is gone to Jesus."

Dr. Abercrombie, whose reputation, both as a physician and a philosopher, is European, had been, during the first years of his residence in Edinburgh, a member of Mr. Haldane's Church, and although a pastoral relation had long ceased to exist between him and Mr. Haldane, yet they both felt towards each other a mutual esteem and regard.

In 1845 he announced, with much satisfaction, the success of his eldest son, by his second marriage, Daniel Rutherford, who was pursuing the study of Medicine at the Edinburgh University. "I believe," he writes, "it is unprecedented to gain, at the same time, both the junior and senior prizes. The Professor was much surprised. He also gained the first prize in Physiology, and perhaps would have had that in Anatomy too, had he not lost all last summer by his illness."

In a letter, dated June 4th, 1845, he thus writes :—

" I went, last night, to a Meeting to promote unity. Sir Andrew Agnew was in the chair. Mr. Winslow, from Leamington, spoke ; also D'Aubigné and Monod ; Guthrie, of the Free Church; Drummond and Crowther, Episcopalian; and Candlish concluded. I came away before Dr. Candlish spoke, which I regretted, for I understand it was the best speech of the evening. He disclaimed presuming to judge between essentials and non-essentials, and said in regard to what God had revealed and commanded we were bound to obey in all things, but still to exercise forbearance to each other. On every question on which I have heard him, he always takes high ground. He is decidedly the leader of the Free Church. A man's gift maketh room for him."

These were always his views on Christian union, and he shortly afterwards published a little treatise on the subject, in which he cites, as embodying his mature opinions, what he had written more than forty years before, in his book on Social Worship. In a letter, dated January 5th, 1846, he says, " I do not expect it to be popular. The first part will probably be most so. Mr. Whyte (the publisher) on reading it ordered two hundred and fifty additional copies to be thrown off. He should have waited until he saw the whole." In another letter he writes, " I am not surprised that you do not agree with the second part of the pamphlet " (relative to the duty of following what he deemed the apostolic usages), " but I am fully convinced it is right. The disunion of Christians will continue whilst Moses and Elias remain upon the mount. There are many good men in the Church of England, but I greatly fear, and I say it with grief, that a great part of the clergy of the Church of England will go into Popery. I do not make these remarks to introduce any controversy with you. You are living, I trust, by the faith of Jesus, and have received that anointing which teacheth all things, although, in some points belonging to the kingdom of Christ, I consider you to be in error, and I pray the Lord to guide you in all things, and to preserve you to his heavenly kingdom."

In 1848 he published an Exposition of the Epistle to the Galatians, a volume in which, as in all his writings, there are many delightful and edifying views of Divine truth, and many valuable illustrations of the connexion between the Old and New Testaments. But the third chapter unavoidably led him to discuss the question of baptism, and this necessarily rendered the book less acceptable to those who hold the importance of infant baptism. It is to this objection he alludes in the following letter. The firmness with which he adheres to what he believed to be the will of God, blended with so much charity

towards those with whom he differed, must command the
respect of all who admire the union of manliness, fidelity, and
candour :—

"I am fully sensible that anything I write would be more generally
acceptable were I to omit bringing forward my views respecting Christian
ordinances. My doing so does not arise from party spirit, or a desire
to exalt any one denomination. I see much evil in all, and am convinced
of the obligation under which believers are laid to forbear with each other.
I am convinced that the corruption of the doctrine of Christ originated in
the corruption of the ordinances. The doctrine is embodied in the ordinances. . . . . To represent the ordinances as of little consequence,
provided we hold by the great doctrines, is like a man saying of a geo-
graphical work, that, provided the text be correct, the maps are of little
consequence. The description in the text ought to be exhibited in the
maps, and where they correspond, we have a much clearer conception of
the relative position of the places, than we could otherwise have. If they
do not correspond, it only confuses and perplexes us. I am perfectly
aware that the power of religion does not always correspond with the
apparent accuracy of our views of the ordinances, and that many members
of unscriptural Churches are far superior in point of devotedness to God
to those in a communion guided by the example of the Apostolic
Churches, and not only so, but I see some who have lax and unscriptural
views of some of the great doctrines of the Gospel superior to others who
appear better instructed, but still I do not feel myself at liberty to deviate
from the custom of the Apostolic Churches when I find the apostles so
anxious that there should be no deviation from their practice. (1 Cor.
xi. 2.) Those who think it their duty to separate from the world, may be
viewed as narrow-minded bigots, placing religion in external observances.
But the coming of the Lord draweth nigh. I heartily rejoice in the
number of faithful ministers of any denomination being increased. I see
many, in what I am *fully* convinced to be most unscriptural situations, far
better than myself; *but I am Christ's servant,*—I observe his ordinances in
faith, and I cannot be satisfied that I am right without an equal conviction
that those who are otherwise minded are wrong. For my part, I durst no
more have published an Exposition of the Galatians, and have slurred
over chapter iii. 27, than have put my hand in the fire. The object I had
in view was to show that the great body of Christians are in the situation
of those who were under the influence of the Judaizing teachers. When
I was baptized, nearly fifty years ago, I was convinced that it was the will
of God, but I see its *importance* far more now than I did then. It is not
with me a party matter. I would prefer associating with a Church of
England man, or a Presbyterian who was spiritual and humble, than with
a Baptist who was lifted up with a conceit that he was something. I

would not give up the benefit I have received from right views of baptism in regard to the Gospel for any consideration. May the Lord be with you; draw near to him, and he will never leave you nor forsake you.

"Yours, ever most affectionately,

"J. A. H."

This chapter has conducted us over six years of the life of the surviving brother. It exhibits him bringing forth fruit in old age, and up to the age of fourscore labouring with undiminished zeal for the glory of God, and the salvation of sinners. Were it possible to withdraw the curtain which, to a certain extent, conceals his domestic and private life, to exhibit the closeness of his walk with God, and the calm sunshine of spiritual peace which possessed his soul, it would also be possible to exhibit something of the practical and sanctifying influence of those doctrines for which he so long and earnestly contended. His letters are, perhaps, the best memorials of that steadfast faith, that deep experience, that settled peace and assurance, which cheered and irradiated the sunset of his long and arduous career. The limits of this volume forbid the insertion of much of his correspondence, and some occasional fragments must, of necessity, suffice. The following are parts of letters written on the death of the two brothers of his daughter-in-law in London, the sons of his own and his brother's friend, Mr. Hardcastle, whose name was, at the outset of their career, so much associated with the promotion of all the great missionary objects which distinguished the close of the last century. The second of Mr. Hardcastle's three sons especially resembled his father both in features and in character, and with him Mr. J. A. Haldane had enjoyed much intercourse. It was whilst absent on a journey which they made together into Scotland, that Mr. Alfred Hardcastle wrote of him to his sister, "I cannot express the increasing reverence I feel for that good man's character." On hearing of his death, produced by a sudden inflammatory attack in his fifty-first year, Mr. J. A. Haldane wrote as follows :—

"*Edinburgh, March* 11*th*, 1842.

"MY DEAREST ALEXANDER,—When I saw the outside of your letter, I too surely anticipated the melancholy tidings it contained. But why

should I say melancholy? An heir of God and a joint heir of Christ
has finished his appointed course of trial and disappointment, and has
entered into the joy of his Lord. Since he was called by grace he has
had fellowship with Jesus in the troubles of life, and now the last scene
of his fellowship with his suffering Saviour is safely ended, and he has
departed to be with Christ, which is far better. With what different eyes
does he now regard all that is in the world, and with what gratitude to
Him who bought him with his blood, does he look forward to an exceeding and eternal weight of glory! His lot in this world was smooth and
prosperous, but he now looks back upon all external circumstances as less
than nothing and vanity, except as they bore on that unchanging state
into which he has entered. And yet his happiness is still incomplete;
Satan is not yet bruised under his feet, for he still retains the mortal
body in the prison of the grave; but the resurrection of Jesus is the
assured pledge of the reunion of soul and body,—not in dishonour, as
being doomed to separation; not in weakness, as being subject to pain
and dissolution; not a natural body, as being derived from the first man,
who was of the earth earthy; but a glorious, a spiritual body, of which
the glorious body of the second Man, the Lord from heaven, is the
pattern. The Lord said to his apostles, ' Ye are they which have continued with me in my temptations, and I appoint unto you a kingdom
as my Father hath appointed unto me.' In this there was something
peculiar to them, as the chosen ambassadors of Christ; the twelve
foundations of his Church, as resting upon Him, the chief corner-stone.
They were (as they now do) to sit upon twelve thrones, judging the
twelve tribes of Israel; but all the ransomed of the Lord are made kings
and priests unto God, and they shall reign for ever and ever. And shall
we say, when one of them has entered the haven of rest, that it is
melancholy? It is so, indeed, in reference to survivors; it is the parting
of the closest and most endearing ties which God Himself hath appointed.
He Himself calls us by such a dispensation to weeping and mourning,
but we are not to sorrow as those who have no hope. It is one of those
scenes of tribulation which is calculated to bring sin to remembrance, to
tell us what an evil and bitter thing sin is; to show us that, though the
sinner was the signet on Jehovah's right hand, He would pluck it off.
He adopts a child of Adam into his family; He loved him with an everlasting love; but there was about him that bitter thing which God's soul
hateth, and He changed his countenance and sent him away, apparently
in anger, although He was pacified towards him for all that he had done.
God's Word took hold of him : ' Dust thou art, and unto dust shalt thou
return.' This is very wonderful, but it is the consequence of something
still more inconceivable and stupendous. The only-begotten Son, who
was holy as God is holy, appeared in the likeness of sinful flesh, as the
Head of his body, the Church. He had undertaken to restore what He

took not away.  After living years, as a Man of sorrows, in the world which He had called into existence, without having where to lay his head, justice, in the person of the officers sent to apprehend Him, demanded its victim.  He at once responded to the call, adding, ' If ye seek me, let these go away;' and then He underwent that bitter trial which wrung from Him these awful words: ' My God, my God, why hast thou forsaken me?'  The sword had awaked against Him who was the fellow of the Almighty,—against Him who thought it not robbery to be equal with God, and who, at this time, was at once yielding the most humble obedience to his Father's will, and exercising one of the special prerogatives of the eternal God.  He had received a commandment from his Father to lay down his life, and He did it voluntarily.  No man took it from Him.  Well may we say, ' O the depth of the riches, both of the wisdom and knowledge of God!  How unsearchable are his judgments, and his ways past finding out.'  In God's dealings with his Church, the principalities and powers in heavenly places, see God's manifold wisdom. It is a passage in the history of the universe, which they will never tire of perusing; it is a depth which they shall never be able fully to comprehend." . . .

The death of Mr. Alfred Hardcastle accelerated that of his elder brother, and it was on this double loss that the next letter was addressed to his daughter-in-law :—

*" Edinburgh, March* 21, 1842.

" MY DEAREST EMMA,—Most sincerely do I sympathize with you on the removal of your two very amiable and affectionate brothers.  We were in hopes that the crisis in regard to Joseph was over, but this morning we received the melancholy account of his having followed Alfred.  It is exceedingly affecting; but we must say, ' I was dumb; I opened not my mouth, because thou didst it.'  Shall we receive good at the hands of God, and not evil?  Yet it is not evil.  Both your brothers have been removed from this vale of tears, and both departed in the faith of Jesus.  They had hope in their death, and could look beyond the darkness of the tomb into that world of light which is illuminated by the beams of the Sun of Righteousness. . . .

" Then, in how different a light shall we regard the sorrows of life! We shall look back upon all the way in which the Lord hath led us, and shall see that goodness and mercy have followed us all the days of our life; that all things are ours; that every dispensation of Providence, however afflictive, was a stream from the inexhaustible fountain of everlasting love; and that everything which befel us in the days of our pilgrimage was the development of that wondrous plan for raising us from the unfathomable depth of sin and misery to an exceeding and eternal weight of glory.  These are the true sayings of God: ' Heaven and earth shall pass away, but Christ's words shall not pass away. In the world ye shall have tribulation; but be of good cheer, I have overcome the world.' And so complete is his victory, that the troubles of life and the mouldering of our mortal bodies in the dust are the means employed by Him who is wonderful in counsel and excellent in working, to introduce us to the enjoyment of eternal happiness. . . .

" I received Annie's beautiful letter, giving an account of her uncle Alfred's death. It was, at the same time, indeed, very triumphant and perfectly calm. There may be, and often is, a great deal of excitement in the last scene, but in his removal everything appeared in keeping—solemn, and perfectly placid.* . . . I sometimes think there is more resignation among the poor than the rich. It is a common expression with them, ' It was to be.' No doubt this may be abused; but when the will of God is declared by the event, it is our wisdom to acquiesce and to say: ' Thou, O Lord, hast done as it pleased thee.'"

The next was addressed to his grand-daughter, Mrs. John Corsbie :—

" MY DEAREST ANNIE,— . . The scene you witnessed, in your uncle Alfred's departure, was, indeed, very striking and much calculated to confirm your faith. The Lord there showed you the extent of the triumph which He has achieved in behalf of his people, not by averting the stroke of death,—not by preventing the return of the spirit to Him who gave it, but by transforming the last enemy into a messenger of peace and making the grave the portal of immortality. When Jesus had finished the work which He had undertaken, He dismissed his spirit. He died, was buried, and rose again, and He in this, as in other things, is the pattern of his people. . . . It is a beautiful passage in the book of Job, where he inquires, ' If a man die, shall he live again?' Certainly. And hence he adds, ' All the days of my appointed time will I wait till my change come.' This is not the change produced by the separation of the soul and body; it is the change of this mortal body for the spiritual and incorruptible body. This is evident from what follows: ' Thou wilt call, and I will answer thee; thou wilt have respect to the work of thine hands; thou turnest man to destruction and sayest, Come again, ye children of men.' Our bodies, so fearfully and so wonderfully made, are broken in pieces like a potter's vessel; but in that day God will have respect to the work of his hands. He had reduced it to his original dust, but it had been redeemed by the blood of Jesus; it had been the habitation of God through the spirit, and shall therefore be re-constructed in a

---

* A very striking sermon on the death of these two brothers was published by the Rev. Dr. Collyer, whose ministry they and their Father had long esteemed.

form from which every seed of weakness, corruption, and mortality, shall be removed. And how is it calculated to confirm our faith, to witness one of Christ's blood-bought sheep amidst the swellings of Jordan, delivering himself up with calmness and composure into the hands of the king of terrors, and confidently anticipating the day when Satan shall be bruised under his feet, when death shall be swallowed up in victory. Such was the scene you were so lately called to witness, and I trust you have derived much benefit from it. . . May the Lord himself bless you!"

It was not long after these mournful letters were written that the birth of a grandson, uniting his own and his brother's names, drew from Mr. J. A. Haldane the expressions of congratulation and thankfulness. Every event, whether clouded by sorrow or brightened with joy, was, in his mind, always associated with the better country :—

" MY DEAREST ALEXANDER,—Most sincerely do I congratulate you and unite with you in giving thanks to the Lord for his great kindness to Emma and yourself in the birth of your son. It is my prayer that he may be spared for a blessing to you both; that his name may be found written among the living in Jerusalem; that the Lord may guide him by his counsel, and afterwards receive him to his glory!" . . .

The following letter was written from Dollar, in the Ochill Hills, where he spent two months, in the autumn of 1846, frequently preaching in the neighbourhood :—

" MY DEAREST EMMA,— . . . I do not wonder that you should have felt much in the prospect of leaving Hatcham, with which every circumstance of your past life is so closely interwoven; but, through the kindness of God, you have learnt you are a stranger and pilgrim here, and that your citizenship is in heaven, whither our Lord is gone to prepare mansions for his people. But, although absent and invisible to eyes of flesh, He is not far from us ; and, although we have not literally the cloud and fire to guide us by day and night, He keeps the feet of his saints, leading them in the right way, and will bring us to the city of habitation, when all tears will be wiped from our eyes and we shall enjoy the fulness of that rest which remains for the people of God. This is calculated to support the mind in every situation; but it is delightful to observe how the Lord smooths the road by which He is leading us, thus encouraging us to place the most unlimited confidence in his comparative guidance. You do well to notice the goodness of the Lord, even in the smallest matters, and to receive every proof of his tenderness as a pledge that in every situation his eye will be upon you and his grace sufficient for you. It is my daily prayer that the Lord may be with you and yours; and, although you never can forget Hatcham, yet, considering the changes that have taken place, and the still greater changes that are in contemplation so far as the locality is concerned, I doubt not you will see that the Lord in fixing the bounds of your new habitation, has been providing for your comfort. The house in which I lived at Dundee with my mother, and where I continued after her death till I was nine years of age, has been pulled down many years ago, but I perfectly recollect every corner of it; and I may say the same of the house in whose place the splendid mansion of Camperdown has arisen.

"The cloud which so long stood over Hatcham is now taken up, and you are called to follow it in faith that it is good for you to remove. Many dear friends have finished their course there, but your consolation is, that all the ransomed of the Lord shall return and come to Zion, with everlasting joy upon their heads; they shall obtain joy and gladness, and sorrow and sighing shall flee away. We had a very short, but very pleasant visit from Alexina, with Mrs. N. Hardcastle and her son and daughter. Edmund spent two or three days with us here, and seemed to enjoy the mountain scenery. I suppose he is now on his way to India. May the Lord meet him there, and manifest Himself to him as he does not to the world! Mrs. Haldane and all here unite in kindest love to you and yours. I am happy to hear that your son is so well and promising. May God be his portion!

"Most affectionately yours,

"J. A. HALDANE."

Another letter written on the death of a very amiable Christian lady, the late Mrs. Bruce, of Kennett, may furnish another example of his Christian sympathy, and of his earnest desire that all his relations or connexions might participate in the same spiritual privileges in which he rejoiced:—

"*Edinburgh, May* 20*th*, 1846.

"MY DEAR SIR,—Most sincerely do I sympathise with you under the heavy bereavement with which God has been pleased to visit you. However severely and however keenly you must feel it, I trust it is a token of love. It is indeed a message from God to you, reminding you that this is not your rest; that all our most fondly cherished enjoyments are fleeting and transitory, and that amidst all the comforts and blessings of life, fallen man must eat his bread in sorrow.

"There is but one remedy for the ills of life. Jesus came to deliver his people from this present evil world, not to prevent their receiving with gratitude the bounties of his Providence, but to lead their minds to those exceeding great and precious promises which are all yea and amen in

Christ. He came into this world in the likeness of sinful flesh, that by enduring the curse of all who will hearken to his voice, he might put him in possession of the blessing of eternal life and glory. Adam is the spring and fountain-head of our natural life, but the fountain is dried up, and the streams must fail. But the life of believers is hid with Christ in God, and that eternal life to which he is risen, is the security that they shall never die; because I live, Jesus says, ye shall live also. He has entered into his glory as the forerunner of his people, their elder brother; he is gone to prepare a place for them in that land the inhabitants of which shall no more say, I am sick, and where God shall wipe away all tears from the eyes of his people.

" This affliction is eminently calculated to lead you to listen to the Lord's gracious invitation, Come unto me, all ye that labour and are heavy laden, and I will give you rest. He speaks of his yoke and his burden, but he assures us, his yoke is easy and his burden is light.

" The Psalmist says, ' It was good for me that I was afflicted.' Thousands since that day have had reason to adopt his language, and I trust and pray such may be your experience.

" To her who has left you, death was deprived of its sting. She had heard the voice of Jesus saying, in accents of tenderest love, fear not to go down to the narrow house, for I will be with you, and will surely bring you up again. By Christ's resurrection she had been begotten to a lively hope of an inheritance incorruptible, undefiled, and that fadeth not away. She had been made partaker of that precious faith which overcometh the world. Habitually contemplating the empty grave of Jesus, the king of terrors put on to her a new aspect. She saw his stroke as the last token of her fellowship with her suffering and dying Lord, and in the last contest when flesh and heart fainted and failed, he was the strength of her heart and will be her portion for ever.

" That he may bless and support you is my earnest prayer, and I trust that, severe and overwhelming as the trial is, you will hereafter be enabled to look back on it with gratitude. You long enjoyed the benefit of her example. You have now seen her bid adieu to this world. May you be enabled by faith to follow her within the vail and to behold her joining the spirits of just men made perfect. Mrs. Haldane and all my family unite in kindest condolence.

" Believe me, my dear Sir, to be yours, most truly,

" J. A. HALDANE.

" To Robert Bruce, Esq., of Kennett."

# CHAPTER XXVIII.

MR. J. HALDANE AS AN OCTOGENARIAN—PUBLIC FASTS—
LA MANCHA—MR. BURDON SANDERSON—VISIT TO THE
MANOR HOUSE, EAST HAM—SERMONS AT WOOLWICH—
DEATH OF MAJOR GORDON AND OF HIS MOTHER, MRS.
HALDANE GORDON—JUBILEE—MR. CLEGHORN'S TESTI-
MONY — ILLNESS, 1849 — WINTERFIELD — LETTER TO
COLONEL ANDERSON—ROMAINE'S LETTERS—EXPOSITION
OF HEBREWS — LETTER TO LADY STAIR — PERSONAL
REIGN — PAPAL AGGRESSION—CLOSE OF 1850 — ILLNESS
AND DEATH — HIS FUNERAL — TESTIMONIES TO HIS
CHARACTER AND USEFULNESS—CONCLUSION.

[1848—1851.]

It is not given to many to climb the heights of fourscore years.
To still fewer is reserved the privilege to attain that altitude
with an eye undimmed and an intellect unclouded. To the
very last Mr. J. A. Haldane was enabled to persevere in the
cause to which he had dedicated his strength, and the cessation
of his evening sermons on the Lord's-day was the only token
that he felt his natural force at all abated. Even that was
owing to prudential motives and the intreaties of his family
not to expose himself, especially when heated by speaking, to
the night air. In a letter written with reference to this subject,
when in his eightieth year, he says:—

" *December* 9, 1847.

" MY DEAREST ALEXANDER,—I received your very kind letter, but
could not help smiling at part of it. Had a stranger seen it he would
have concluded that I was so reckless and so much disposed to go out at
night that I had brought on some very uncommon disease, whereas, in
fact, I have had rather a slight attack of influenza, which few have

escaped, and on account of which several classes of the College and the High School and other public schools have been shut up. The good health which I enjoy is an evidence that the plan I pursue is not an unwise one. Your uncle and I acted in an entirely different way in regard to our health, and both acted on principle. He was, in some respects, as I judged, over careful of himself, avoiding every draft of air so much as to render himself more susceptible of cold; while avoiding unnecessary exposure, I have been satisfied to let things take their course, by which I believe I have been a gainer. I have not yet been out, but I am quite well, with the exception of a cough, to which I am not subject, but which I hope and think will soon be removed. I have by no means put myself upon the lowering system, for I was afraid it might have brought on gout."

A few months afterwards he again wrote as follows :—

"*Edinburgh, July* 17, 1848.

" MY DEAREST EMMA,—Many thanks for your very kind letter, written on my birth-day, when I entered my eighty-first year. I have great cause of gratitude to the Lord for the enjoyment of so good health at such an advanced age. I cannot adopt the language of Caleb, Joshua xiv. 11, and still less that of Barzillai, 2 Sam. xix. 35. In regard to preaching, I do not feel any perceptible difference, but the earthly tabernacle must be dissolved. We must have fellowship with Christ in his death, that we may attain to the resurrection of the dead. . . .

" Give my kindest love to all your children by name. I daily make mention of your name and theirs to the Lord, and we know he is the hearer of prayer."

His observations with reference to the Fast-day which was observed in the previous month of March, are worthy of note. Whilst his principles led him to disapprove of the union between the Church and the State, he greatly deprecated those opinions which led certain of the Voluntaries to act and speak as if rulers in their political capacity ought to ignore the worship of the Most High God :—

" The fast-day was kept yesterday. We met twice, and I preached in the afternoon. In reference to those who object to the proclamation of a fast by Royal authority, I showed that had the Ninevites acted on the same principle, Nineveh would have been destroyed. Again, there was the case of Jonah, when the master of the ship called him, and desired him to cry unto his God, he might have replied, ' Am I, the prophet Jonah, to be schooled by an idolater, and is he to dictate to me as to my prayers?' He was hardened through the deceitfulness of sin, but not to so great an extent as to utter such language. He had declined carrying the Lord's message to Nineveh, and now he was compelled to deliver one against himself, and perhaps his doing so was an evidence of his repentance for his previous conduct. I stated that I had little doubt that the manner in which the day was observed through the country would decide whether the judgment in the nation should be alleviated or increased. Some of the sects here did not meet, but I suppose in general it was externally pretty well observed."—" Dr. Alexander's Church met, and I understand that the Provost (Mr. Adam Black), who is one of his deacons, prayed."

Fasting was a duty to which he attended, not merely on public, but on private occasions. He was habitually a man of prayer, and as fasting is in Scripture associated with prayer, so when there was any subject on which he peculiarly desired to seek counsel of the Lord, he was accustomed to set apart a day for the special purpose of humbling himself, and making known his requests on behalf of himself, his family, or the Church. In the summer of 1847, he took the house of La Mancha, in Peeblesshire, about sixteen miles from Edinburgh. It was situated in a thinly-peopled and wild, but healthful, part of the country, having somewhat of the character of Auchingray, to which he had been accustomed to pay an annual visit with his family during his brother's lifetime. La Mancha was four miles from any place of worship; he therefore preached twice every Lord's-day, as well as on other occasions, to good congregations. His labours were highly prized by the country people; his visit to their neighbourhood was most acceptable, and he received very gratifying tokens of personal regard.

The beginning of 1848 was gladdened by the marriage of Isabella, the eldest of his three daughters by his second wife, to Richard Burdon Sanderson, Esq., the younger, of West Jesmond, near Newcastle. His father was the only surviving son of the late Sir Thomas Burdon, by Jane Scott, the youngest sister of Lords Eldon and Stowell. Mr. Burdon afterwards assumed the name of Sanderson, in compliance with the will of his wife's father, Sir J. Sanderson, Bart. Having been a Fellow of Oriel, it is scarcely needful to say that he ran a distinguished course at Oxford. As an undergraduate he was the successful competitor for the Newdigate in 1811, whilst in the list of annual prizes given for English composition, he stands, as in the year 1814, between Mr. Justice Coleridge and the late Dr. Arnold, of Rugby.  He was designed for the bar, and his uncles confidently anticipated that so brilliant a commencement was to be followed up by a career worthy of their own great legal renown. The ferment of religious excitement which then began at Oxford was the commencement of two very different schools of theology, the one rather tending to German, and the other to Romish error.  At the head of the former may be placed Archbishop Whately, Bishop Hampden, and Dr. Arnold; and at the head of the latter, Messrs. Keble, Pusey, and John Newman.  It was at this period of spiritual agitation that Mr. Burdon was led to discern the excellence of the knowledge of Christ, and to distinguish between the dry formalities of the old High Church system, and the living energy of spiritual religion.  It may be permitted to some of his friends to regret that he did not persevere in the profession in which Lord Eldon predicted his eminence, or adopt the resolution of taking orders in the Church, but the post to which he was immediately appointed, as Secretary of Presentations to the Lord Chancellor, gave him such a view of the abuse of patronage in the Establishment for political objects, as unhappily led to the resignation of his office, his prospects, and his churchmanship.  Retiring to the country, he adopted a life of comparative isolation, but one which enabled him to carry out his own ideas of the spiritual nature of the kingdom of Christ.  These views may not unfairly be traced to the lessons derived partly from his tutor, Archbishop Whately, and partly from the still more defined anti-State Church notions of the embryo Tractarians of Oriel.  A visit made by Mr. and Mrs. Burdon Sanderson to Edinburgh, at the close of 1847, issued in the marriage of their eldest son, to whom Mr. J. A. Haldane became much attached, and of whose " sterling worth" and true godliness he entertained a high estimate.

Immediately after his return home from a visit to West Jesmond, Mr. J. A. Haldane was attacked by gout, which was partly attributed to over-exertion in preaching in Newcastle and the neighbourhood. But at Easter he was well enough to pay a visit to his eldest son, near London, accompanied by Mrs. Haldane and their youngest boy. His last journey to the great Metropolis, and the interest with which he visited the places associated with the recollections of his youth, or observed the changes produced by time and modern improvements, indicated the freshness of his feelings. It was also a proof of his remaining physical vigour and self-reliance, that on the first day after his arrival, he walked alone, by a road before unknown to him, nearly five miles to the river side, and having hired a small boat, crossed over to Woolwich. He proceeded up the Thames by a steamer, enjoying, with his usual vivacity of spirit, the sight of Greenwich Hospital, with its beautiful park in the background, and the shipping in the docks and in the pool. From London Bridge he walked through the crowded streets to the Shoreditch terminus of the railway, but finding himself too late for the train, proceeded to one of the cab-stands at the outskirts of the city, and reached home after the usual dinner-hour. He had left the house without any specific design whilst the family were at luncheon, and although as the hours passed on many anxious looks had been directed towards the entrance-gate, and an inquiring welcome greeted his arrival, his own manly, yet not unconscious glance seemed at once to admit that there might have been some cause for solicitude, although he playfully disclaimed its necessity on his account.

During this visit, on two successive Lord's-days, he preached in the Scotch Church at Woolwich. A sergeant who heard him on the first Lord's-day, was, during the week, marched to a distance, but such was his anxiety once more to listen to the same blessed truth, that, on being relieved from guard, very early on the next Lord's-day morning, he obtained leave to return to Woolwich, where he arrived after a wet and fatiguing walk. Mr. J. A. Haldane was himself both interested and roused by his audience, and we have heard that the "word was with power." It was a striking spectacle to witness such a congregation of soldiers and marines, of all uniforms, each listening with fixed attention, as the octogenarian preacher earnestly and impressively urged on them the promises of a free Gospel, with all the fire and energy of his youth, only mellowed by the pathos and gentleness of age.

During the summer of 1848, Mr. J. Haldane took a house in the parish of Tranent, not far from the field which has acquired so much historical renown as the scene of the victory of the Pretender, in 1742, and the spot on which the gallant Colonel Gardiner fell, near his own home, rallying the Royal forces, and died like a Christian hero, refusing to retreat with his panic-stricken dragoons. It had been proposed to erect a monument to his memory, and Mr. James Haldane was one of the first subscribers.

The Indian mail, of February, 1849, conveyed the melancholy intelligence of the death of his grand-nephew, Major John Gordon, eldest son of Mrs. Haldane Gordon, who fell on the 27th of the previous month of December, at the storming of Mooltan. When the siege of that great fortress first commenced, Major Gordon was with his regiment, the 60th Rifles, near Bombay, and before it was ordered to move he volunteered, with another officer, to ascend the Indus, to reconnoitre the line of march and obtain personal information as to the best method of moving the troops. His mission was discharged with equal zeal and judgment, and in September he assisted at the operations before Mooltan, which were attended with so much loss, and were ultimately suspended in consequence of the defection of Shere Singh. He rejoined his regiment, and assisted in the successful march to Mooltan. The arrival of the Bombay troops, at the end of December, was the signal for the assault, and two days before he fell, an entry in his journal, made after attending Divine service with his men, indicates the solemnized feeling with which he thought of the possible nearness of the eternal world. His death was almost instantaneous. He was at the head of the Rifles, conducting them over some broken ground, under the fire of the enemy's marksmen, and being mounted on a white Arab charger, his dark uniform rendered his danger imminent. The Adjutant advanced towards him, and kindly begged him to dismount, but he declined, observing, with characteristic calmness, " I am in my place." Scarcely had he spoken when a bullet pierced his sword-belt, and he fell into the arms of his friend.  It was a crushing blow to his afflicted mother, although the event was not without its consolations, as will appear from the following letter, written by her, in a spirit of Christian resignation, not long after the sad intelligence arrived :—

" *Cadlington, Feb.* 20, 1849.

" MY DEAR COUSIN,—I feel deeply sensible of your great kindness and sympathy in our great affliction.  You knew my beloved John, and could estimate him, and the irreparable loss we have sustained : but, in endeavouring to view it in the prospect of eternity, there is light, even in this dark cloud.  I feel assured confidence that, in that sudden and awful moment, his spirit was received by the blessed Saviour—that the many prayers of those beloved parents, who are now inheriting the promises of God, were answered ; and that there had been a preparation of heart and mind, that led him to acknowledge the sovereignty of God in every event ; and constrained him to seek for happiness in that source where alone it can be truly found.

" Latterly these sentiments have been again and again expressed.  In his last letter, of the 18th of October, before reaching Mooltan, he says, . . .  These few lines will be interesting to you, I feel sure.  I believe that the change has been infinite gain to him, but as yet I can hardly realize more than our great, great loss.  May this trial be indeed sanctified to me, and to his brothers and sisters, and be made to answer the end for which it has been sent.

" Accept my sincere and warmest thanks for all your kindness to him in the days that are past, which was not forgotten by him, nor can it be so by me.  I had a most kind letter from my dear uncle this morning.  There have been many alleviating circumstances, and it is soothing to know that he was esteemed and beloved in his regiment and by his friends ; that it was in the discharge of his duty he fell, and though no human aid could help, he was cared for by his brother officers, and his memory beloved and valued.  I feel thankful for these.  My affectionate remembrances to Mrs. Haldane, and each one of your family.  Accept the same, and believe me to be, your affectionate cousin,

" M. HALDANE GORDON.

" *Alexander Haldane, Esq.*"

The bereaved mother did not long survive the shock.  Her health had been drooping for some time, and she died somewhat suddenly, on the 29th day of September, 1849.  Her remains repose in the beautiful churchyard of Blendworth, in Hampshire, and her ransomed spirit having escaped all " the waves of this troublesome life," has, doubtless, joined the general assembly of the spirits of the just before the throne, joyfully awaiting the resurrection of the body, and the second appearing of the Lord from Heaven.

Not long afterwards a visit of her only surviving son, the Rev. James Gordon, himself a partaker of like precious faith, and a clergyman in the Church of England, is mentioned with much satisfaction in the letters of his grand-uncle. Of this meeting Mr. Gordon himself thus writes :—

" I was very glad to see your father, and quite as well, or better, than I expected. Independent of relationship and association, there is something peculiarly interesting, I may say affecting, in looking upon one who has so nearly fought the good fight, so nearly finished the course, and hearing the sound of a voice, which will so soon be tuned for the harmony of heaven. Christian maturity is very beautiful; softening and mellowing humanity. I felt all this, and much more, in talking to your father; and the interest he took in all I could tell of poor John, and my dear mother, was most gratifying. I rejoiced to have the pleasure of shaking hands once more, and in feeling that another tie than formerly bound us to each other,—the aged servant of Christ to the young disciple."

Mr. J. A. Haldane had many family ties in India. Two of his daughters were residing with their husbands in that eastern province of the British Empire. The death of Major Gordon was calculated to increase anxiety for those who were exposed to the same dangers, and many were the prayers which were offered up on behalf of the husband of his daughter Mary, and their eldest son, who had also entered on the same career as his father. Since the period of his marriage in 1824, Colonel Eckford had been engaged at the storming of Bhurtpore, and served with distinction as brigadier in the successive campaigns for the rescue of the prisoners in Affghanistan, for the repulse of the invasion of the Sikhs, and, finally, for the subjugation of the revolt in the Punjaub. After the passage of the Ravee, and the battles of Ramnuggar and Sowdawallah, in the latter of which he was much exposed, he had very reluctantly gone to take the command of Lahore, menaced as it was by the Sikhs, but it was thus that he escaped being present at the fruitless slaughter of Chillianwallah. Of this occurrence Mr. J. A. Haldane writes :—

"It is indeed a great cause of thankfulness that Eckford was at Lahore. I am glad to hear the testimony of Lord Gough, as well as of Lord Hardinge, to his services. His medals and the Companionship of the Bath are, in themselves, of no great importance; but they may be an advantage to his children, and therefore I would not undervalue them. He held very responsible commands, both in the last Sikh war and the present. The charge of the battering-train and the treasure, which he brought up from Delhi to Sobraon, was very important, and he executed it most satisfactorily. He was nominally under Sir John Littler, at Lahore, but I suppose the charge chiefly devolved on him, for the General was a considerable time absent, and he seems to have acted with great gallantry and judgment in the late campaign. I trust the Lord will hear our prayers in his behalf, and bring him safely home, and spare him for the sake of his children."

These prayers were heard, and Colonel Eckford and his wife both returned home in time to receive the blessing and the welcome of their venerable parent. Mr. J. A. Haldane was always pleased to learn that any one in whom he was interested discharged his duty, but in Colonel Eckford he had the double gratification of hearing of his manly and consistent walk as a soldier of Christ. Wherever he was in authority, Divine service was publicly performed, and a sermon read on the Lord's-day, whether at Jellalabad, at Lahore, at Bareilly, or at Ferozepore; and where there was no chaplain, he himself read the prayers and a sermon, a duty for the performance of which he received the personal sanction of his friend, the Bishop of Calcutta.

On the 3d of February, 1849, Mr. Haldane completed the fiftieth year of his pastoral office, and a wish generally prevailed that the event should be celebrated in such a way as to indicate the respect in which he was held, not only by his own Church, but by other denominations. This was very gratifying to him, although he pointedly declined to countenance another meeting, of a more exclusive and sectarian character, which had been proposed by some who very little appreciated his large and enlightened spirit. The Jubilee Meeting was held on the 12th of April. His old and valued friend, the Rev. Dr. Innes, whom he had first known as minister of Stirling, presided, and opened the meeting by a reference to the labours and services, both of Mr. James Haldane and his departed brother. Of the latter he said,—

"When I look to the extensive scale on which Mr. Haldane carried on his plans of usefulness, the number of preachers he educated, the important situations in which some of these have been placed, while others have been equally devoted in a more limited sphere; . . . when to these I add the numerous places of worship built by him in different parts of the country, I say, putting all these things together, if I were asked to name the individual who has, during the last half-century (nay, I might go further back), done most for the cause of the Gospel, I would without hesitation pronounce the name of Robert Haldane."

The Rev. Christopher Anderson, who has but lately entered into rest, gave a most striking account of the spirit which pervaded the great movement at the end of the last century and the beginning of the present, and which issued in a religious revival in Scotland, so striking and enduring. The Rev. Mr. Kinniburgh, who has also since departed, spoke of the remarkable awakening in the north of Scotland, and alluded to the late Rev. Mr. Cleghorn's account of the preaching in Caithness, as contained in the "Missionary Magazine" for 1803. Mr. Cleghorn says:—"Mr. Haldane's congregations on week-days, though in the time of harvest, were numerous, but on the Lord's-day such congregations were never seen in this place. Many have spoken to me of the effects of the Word on this occasion, but they have always wanted words to express their views of them. Some have compared its operation to that of an electric shock. A solemn silence pervaded the multitude. Many were seen to shed tears, and when some truths were expressed, sighs were heard throughout the congregation. Some have told me there was an astonishing authority, and a sort of indescribable evidence attending the Word, which they could not resist. The Word of God on this occasion was truly quick and powerful. I have been informed by others that they heard Mr. James Haldane as if he had been a messenger sent immediately from God, and thought that what they heard was addressed to them individually, and that they were sometimes afraid lest their very names should be mentioned. In short, the attention of almost every one was drawn to what they called *this Gospel.* It was indeed new to most who heard it, both as to the matter and the manner of delivering it. So generally was the attention of people drawn to it that you could hardly find two conversing together but religion was the subject."

Amongst other anecdotes recorded as to his early preaching, was one indicating the low state of religion and morality amongst the Moderates when Mr. James Haldane first engaged in the work of a home missionary. One evening, as a Highland Baronet was sitting with his lady and some company in his castle, between Taymouth and Dunkeld, his steward entered, for the purpose of making the announcement, that two gentlemen had arrived in the village and intimated their intention of preaching. The chief, feeling it to be an invasion of his territory, declared that this must not be, but he at last gave way to the intercession of his lady, who reminded him that the parish minister was drunken and worthless, and added, " Who knows but that these preachers may be sent for good ?" Mr. James Haldane did preach repeatedly in the village, and a great revival took place in consequence of his labours and those of others who were sent to the neighbourhood.

Mr. Watson also gave an interesting detail of his reminiscences of the preaching in Ayrshire, and Mr. J. A. Haldane himself spoke with the manly simplicity by which he was characterized, and in a manner which evinced the spirit of faith and love and zeal which animated his exertions. The Rev. Dr. Lindsay Alexander's speech was delivered with his usual eloquence, whilst the clergyman of the parish in which the Tabernacle was situated, and other ministers, took part in the proceedings. It was a pleasant sight to witness a kind of Evangelical Union of Christians of all denominations assembled to give thanks to God for that Christian devotedness with which Mr. J. A. Haldane had been through grace enabled, for nearly fifty-two years, to labour with consistent zeal in the service of their Lord and Master. The place was crowded to the door, and hundreds went away for want of room. One sentiment which Mr. J. A. Haldane expressed at the meeting has been in substance already alluded to :—

" I feel much satisfaction in the consideration, that although I began to preach shortly after being brought to Christ, I do not know one point in which my views of the doctrines of the Gospel have varied. They are, of course, more matured and more distinct, but I could not point out an instance of a change in doctrine since I first began to preach."

Several of those present at this memorable Jubilee could recal instances of sermons listened to at particular places. One had heard him for the first time at Alloa, another upon the Calton Hill of Edinburgh, a third upon the links at St. Andrew, a fourth in the Orkney Islands, a fifth in Shetland, a sixth in the churchyard of Kelso in 1798, and a seventh in Bute or Arran. The aggressive movement made at the beginning by James Haldane and his coadjutors upon the darkness of prevailing Moderatism was crowned with a blessing which indicated the power of the Lord, as much as the results that afterwards followed the labours of Robert Haldane at Geneva and Montauban. The conquests of the Gospel in Scotland seemed, at the commencement of the century, to centre round the movement of the Haldanes. It afterwards became more conspicuous in the resuscitated Church of Scotland. But the missionary zeal of James Haldane, as a preacher, never flagged, and his singleness of heart and self-devotion became more conspicuous, even from the absence of that excitement and astonishing success which imparted a character of moral grandeur to his earlier efforts. In the quieter and more self-denying sphere of usefulness which he afterwards so nobly occupied, the true elements of his renewed character might be seen, divested of the halo derived from the admiration of listening thousands and the gratitude of almost daily converts. At both periods he was, as he said, but the servant of the Lord, and at all times, down almost to his last sermon, the success which followed his preaching stamped it with the Lord's approval. After the disruption in the Congregational body, the extraordinary impulse which attended its early movement died away. The Congregational Union itself became stationary, if not retrograde, after their separation from the Haldanes, although they could still boast of the intellectual powers of such men as Dr. Wardlaw, Mr. Ewing, and Dr. Payne, besides Mr. Orme, Dr. Russell, Dr. Paterson, and others of Mr. Robert Haldane's seminary.

Not many months after the Jubilee Meeting he had another attack of gout, which was at one time very threatening. The following letter was written when he began to recover:—

"*Edinburgh, August* 4, 1849.

"MY DEAREST ALEXANDER,—I am much better, but very weak. I never had so bad an attack of gout, but am better. It was attended with a considerable degree of fever. We have taken Winterfield House, near Dunbar, for two months, and intend going out on Tuesday. I received Emma's kind letter, but at present am unable to answer it. We heard that you were going to Tunbridge for change of air. Your sister Henrietta is gone to Cavers, and Margaret to Naughton. I am weak and not able to write more. I have not preached for several weeks. The Lord may be pleased to bless the change of air for my recovery; but with long life has He satisfied me, and I am ready to depart when He sees fit. Kindest love, in which my wife unites, to Emma and all at the Manor. May the Lord's blessing rest upon you!

"Ever most affectionately yours,
"J. A. HALDANE."

Winterfield was the paternal mansion of the family of his friend Colonel Anderson, to whom the following letter is addressed:—

"*Winterfield, Sept.* 1, 1849.

"MY DEAR SIR,—I do not know if you are aware that we are at present occupying your paternal halls. We came here at the beginning of last month, and intend to remain till the end of September. I need not tell you it is a very pleasant habitation, and it is very convenient from being so near Edinburgh, say an hour by rail.

"I often think of the two Lord's-days we spent with you at Woolwich, and the very interesting congregations of your soldiers. . . . The more we understand the Gospel, the more clearly do we see its adaptation to our circumstances, at once excluding boasting, and enabling us to joy in God through Jesus Christ, by whom we have also received the atonement. We are exalted in Christ's righteousness. We are dead. Not only did sentence pass upon us in Adam, but the children of the second Adam endured the penalty in their glorious Head. The constitution which God gave to the human race had a reference to the plan of salvation. We were not created separately, but in Adam, who was the figure of Him that was to come. The life of all his posterity was committed to him and he forfeited it; but Christ came that in Him his people might have life, and have it more abundantly. As the death of Adam was the death-knell of all his posterity, so the resurrection of Christ is the assured pledge of the resurrection to eternal life of all His people. We look to Him who exclaimed upon the cross, 'My God, my God, why hast thou forsaken me?' thus proclaiming that He was for us enduring the curse of the law; and shortly we hear him say, 'I ascend unto my Father and your Father, to my God and your God.' We are commanded to comfort one another with these words. Considered in ourselves, we are alienated from the life of God, through the darkness and ignorance that is in us; but in Christ we are washed, and sanctified, and justified in the name of the Lord Jesus, and by the Spirit of our God. We were at first created in the image of God, but by the disobedience of our first father we lost that image; but it is restored in Christ, and His appearance for us at the right hand of God gives us the assurance of the enjoyment of every spiritual and heavenly blessing. May you continue to enjoy much of the consolation that is in Christ, and continue to be eminently useful in the important sphere in which the Lord has placed you! My wife unites in kindest love to Mrs. Anderson and all your family. May you and she dwell in the secret place of the Most High, under the shadow of the wings of the Almighty! Let us pray for each other, and believe me ever, my dear Sir, yours affectionately in Jesus Christ,

" J. A. HALDANE."

During the time of his residence at Winterfield he had an attack of faintness after walking, which he evidently deemed threatening, and he calmly said to his wife and children, as they gathered round him, " It is all well." He revived, however, in a few minutes, and had no serious attack of illness till the last, nearly eighteen months afterwards.

His vigour was to a considerable extent restored, and, after returning to Edinburgh, he resumed his ministerial duties with all his accustomed energy. At the beginning of 1850 he sent to his daughter-in-law near London a copy of " Romaine's Letters," as a new-year's gift. He valued them much, and during the last year of his life used frequently in the evening, and especially on the Lord's-day, to recline by the fire-side after preaching, and listen with pleasure as they were read aloud by his daughter Margaret, whilst his eldest surviving daughter

Henrietta was visiting the Greenside School, which she has so long and successfully superintended. Of "Romaine's Letters" he thus writes :—

"The fulness and freeness of the great salvation are there very beautifully set forth. Probably you know the same author's 'Life, Walk, and Triumph of Faith.' But the best and simplest book on religion is the Bible. I believe I read more of it than of any other book. The truth it contains is always new. I trust you say, with the prophet, 'Thy word was found of me, and I did eat it, and it was the joy and rejoicing of my heart.'

"I mentioned that I was lecturing on the Hebrews. I have got to the seventh chapter, and have written out my exposition nearly to the end of chapter ix. When I have finished I intend to begin again, and re-write my exposition of the epistle, and, if it then appears desirable, to print it. This is pretty well at the age of eighty-two. Most probably, like your uncle, I may never finish it. You are aware he began the Epistle. There is one word in it on which I have tried to recal what I heard him say, but I cannot. It is the word *perfected*, which frequently occurs. I heard a sermon at Brighton on Heb. v. 9. I thought it a very indifferent one, but I still remember with pleasure one from the Rector of Bath, from Col. ii. 10, 'Ye are complete in him,' which I enjoyed exceedingly."

The sermon, the remembrance of which at the distance of nearly ten years he twice recalled with so much pleasure, was preached at St. Mary's, Brighton, whither, during his visit in 1840, he had gone in the expectation of hearing the Rev. H. V. Elliott. It happened that the Hon. and Rev. Wm. Brodrick preached, and it was his sermon to which he listened with much delight. Mr. Brodrick's conclusion was to this effect :—

"To the established Christian the comfort which the text contains is not new, but as the name of Jesus is as ointment poured out, ever fragrant and refreshing to the believer, so the very renewal of this assurance, as to his being complete in Christ, is like a fresh spring of comfort to his soul. To be complete in Christ in righteousness, in the abolishing of sin, in freedom from guilt, in deliverance from condemnation, in reconciliation, in love,—to be thus complete fully realizes the apostle's declaration concerning Christ, 'To you that believe he is precious.' But oh! what motives to holiness, to self-denial, to devotion, to separation from the world, to active zeal, to passive resignation! What more can you desire? Nothing for your own comfort, but much for the glory of God. I cannot for one conceive anything which makes me so earnestly long and strive and pray to glorify our God, as the belief of being complete in Christ. It calls forth the most influential motives which can impel the soul,—the motives of gratitude and love. 'What can I render to the Lord?' is the soul's expressive language. The soul bears testimony to the full force of that language which the spouse uses in speaking of the Saviour, 'Yea, he is altogether lovely.' It says, with all its energy, and from its deepest feelings, 'This is my Beloved, and this is my Friend. Thou art mine ;—*my* Saviour,—*my* Redeemer,— *my* guide in life,—*my* hope in death. I am complete in Thee now, and yet this is not all Thy goodness towards me. I shall be complete in Thee even in eternity, for I shall behold Thy presence in righteousness.' "

Mr. J. A. Haldane lived to complete his " Exposition of the Hebrews " in his public ministration, and he had even written it out, but it was his design still further to have elaborated it before going to the press. His correspondence indicates how much his mind was interested in the work, and how clear and acute were his perceptions of difficulties. There was a subject on which he had occasion to touch, in expounding Heb. xii. 26, and on which some division of opinion has subsisted amongst Christians. The hope of the second appearing of our Lord in glory and majesty was one which ever occupied his thoughts, but he rejected the idea of a personal reign in this sinful world *before* the destruction of all that is wicked and unholy, and the regeneration of the heavens and the earth. His views are expressed in a letter of earlier date addressed to his second surviving son, Robert :—

" The great promise of the Old Testament was the coming of Christ in the flesh. The promise of the New Testament is his second coming. This will be to judge the world, and to bruise Satan under the feet of his saints, who shall be raised, spiritual and incorruptible. When God separated Israel from the nations at Sinai the earth was shaken, and there was to be another and greater shaking. (Heb. xii. 26.) This was to consist in the removing of the things which were shaken, that the things which cannot be shaken might remain. (Ver. 27.) This took place upon the kingdom being taken from Israel and given to the righteous nation (the children of the new covenant). This took place at Pentecost, and there is to be no other change. The Gospel dispensation remains unchanged. (2 Cor. iii. 2.) Those who maintain that Christ shall come to reign on the earth (*as it now is*), represent a much greater change as taking place than the transition from the Law to the Gospel dispensation, and this is contrary to the word *once more*. At all events, your uncle did not hold the personal reign of Christ in this world in its present state. Christ will reign in the new heaven and new earth, and the earth that now is will flee away when he appears. It once did not afford him a place to lay his head, and in shame and confusion it will vanish from the presence of his glory."

In May, 1850, the somewhat sudden death of his cousin, Lady Henrietta Fergusson, occasioned the following letter to her sister, the Countess of Stair :—

"*Edinburgh, May* 31*st*, 1850.

" MY DEAR LADY STAIR,—I sincerely sympathize with you on this afflicting occasion. The suddenness of the stroke renders it more affecting. It is my prayer that it may be greatly sanctified to you. It is, indeed, a voice from the tomb, loudly saying to us, ' Be ye also ready.' You and your sister have been but little separated during your lifetime, and looking back to the happy days you spent together is calculated to render parting more distressing. But it is frequently better for us to go to the house of mourning than to the house of feasting. It reminds us that we must shortly follow, but dark as is the tomb the believer in Jesus sees beyond it a light too strong for our feeble vision. It is an exceeding, even an eternal, weight of glory reserved for him in heaven, where God will wipe away all tears from his eyes and put him in full possession of the inheritance which his Elder Brother has made sure to him for an everlasting possession, where sorrow and sighing shall for ever flee away, and there shall be no more pain nor separation from those we love.

" That the Lord by the power of his Spirit, may enable you to look stedfastly within the vail, and behold much of the glory of the great Captain of salvation, is my earnest prayer! May you experience at this season that the consolations of God are neither few nor small! One after another of those we loved have been laid in the narrow house, but Jesus says, ' I am the resurrection and the life ; he that believeth in me, though he be dead, yet shall he live, and he that liveth and believeth in me shall never die.'

" To the Christian, what we call death is but its shadow. Christ has abolished death. He has brought life and immortality to light, and his own eternal life is the pledge that his people shall die no more. By death he has destroyed him that had the power of death, that is, the devil. He has put his foot on the neck of Satan, and as Joshua caused his officers to trample on the kings of Canaan, so will the Lord bruise Satan under the feet of his people shortly.

"Believe me, my dear Lady Stair, yours most truly,

"J. A. HALDANE."

The following letter, addressed to one of his grand-daughters, refers to an account of a tour through France and Switzerland and down the Rhine, in the autumn of 1850 :—

"*Edinburgh, October* 3*d*, 1850.

"MY DEAREST EMMA,—I this morning received your excellent letter. Your tour must have been very delightful, and, I trust, will be beneficial to you through life. You have seen some of the grandest natural scenes, and the more of these stupendous works we behold the more should our views be exalted of the power of Him who made them all. But although the eternal power and Godhead of the great Creator is so manifest in his works, it has not prevented mankind from bowing down to the works of their own hands, or changing the image of the incorruptible God into an image of corruptible man and of birds and four-footed beasts. That wisdom, under the influence of which the believer worships God in spirit and in truth, can only be learned by the revelation of the Son of God. He that hath seen Him hath seen the Father, for he is the brightness of the Father's glory and the express image of his person, and under the new dispensation, believers, beholding in an unveiled face the glory of the Lord, are changed into the same image as by the Spirit of the Lord. . . . Your letter contains an excellent account of your tour, which both you and your brother must have enjoyed very much, and I hope your papa and mamma and all will derive great benefit from it. How distressing it is to think that so great a part of Europe is still under the power of the Man of Sin; but they have forsaken the Word of God, and what wisdom is in them! The Antichristian idolatry was introduced precisely in the same way as the Pagan idolatry, by men not being satisfied with the instructions which God gave them in regard to his worship. They added and omitted according to the dictates of their own folly, until they buried true religion under a mass of idle ceremonies. But the Lord will arise, and have mercy upon Zion; the time to favour her shall come. May the Lord hasten it in his time! With kindest love to your papa and mamma, your sisters and brother, in which your grand-mamma unites, as well as Henrietta, Margaret, and Ellen. Adamina is staying with Isabella.

"Ever most affectionately, &c.,

"J. A. HALDANE."

In another letter, a few days later, he notices the sudden death of the Rev. G. F. Dawson, Vicar of Orpington, whose manly and Christian character he had always admired, and in whom he had felt warm interest from the period when his faithful ,remonstrance against being compelled to assist in Romish idolatry, at Malta, had occasioned his dismissal from the artillery, in which he had been an officer. "I am sorry," he says, "to hear of Dawson's sudden death; but the death of a believer is no subject of lamentation. 'Blessed are the dead that die in the Lord.'"

The Papal aggression at this time greatly interested his mind and was frequently referred to in his correspondence, as well as the progress of the Irish Missions.

"Popery," he observes, "is not simply a religion; it claims power over all baptized, and a right, founded on this usurpation, to punish heretics. On the whole, I would not consider them as entitled to the same privileges as those who renounce carnal weapons. Those who consider it to be a part of their religion to use the sword, ought not to complain if the civil power be employed to keep them within proper bounds."

In another letter, alluding to Lady Olivia B. Sparrow, who was then in Edinburgh, and whose zeal for the cause of Christian Protestantism he repeatedly mentions, particularly with reference to her early and munificent support of the Irish Church Missions, he thus writes :—

"*Edinburgh, Nov.* 15, 1850.

"I saw Lady Olivia yesterday; she is very kind and uncommonly agreeable. Her whole heart appears to be fixed on the promotion of the Gospel of Christ. . . .

"The outcry raised about the Pope, in which I fully sympathize, will, I trust, do good. I hope one effect of it will be to lead ministers to put the Irish Government schools on a different footing, so as not to exclude from them the Evangelical clergy. Let schools remain for Roman Catholics, but do not exclude from the benefit of Government education those who will not banish the Scriptures from their teaching. We were with Lady Olivia when your letter arrived, stating what the Queen is reported to have said to Lord John Russell. She was greatly delighted by the information. The Lord reigns, and He is doing all his pleasure. *We may tremble for the ark, but it is as safe in the land of the Philistines as at Shiloh.* This is no reason for inactivity, but it is for calmness."

For some months he had enjoyed excellent health. He looked well, and had been able to preach with much vigour, both at home, and in the neighbourhood of Newcastle, during the summer and autumn of 1850. He continued to visit the sick, and on the Saturdays he was still able to take his favourite walk to Granton pier, to see the London and other steamers preparing to sail. But the time of his departure was drawing near, and the tone of his correspondence, as well as of his preaching, indicated that he was more and more impressed with a sense of the littleness of time, and the magnitude of eternity. With reference to a proposal made for his son, Dr. D. Rutherford Haldane, to travel for a year on the Continent, as physician to a relative, he thus wrote :—

" I trust the Lord will direct in this. His mother and I have made it a subject of prayer, and I doubt not the Lord has heard us, and will take the matter into his own management. It is much that the High and Lofty One who inhabiteth eternity should vouchsafe to interfere in our behalf on any subject, but when we read of the condescension of Jesus, in whom all the fulness of the Godhead dwelleth bodily, we are emboldened to ask much, and to expect much, trusting in Omnipotence."

Such was the spirit which animated his cheerful and active piety. No gloomy foreboding as to a dark and unknown future—no dread of the King of Terrors—no doubts as to his acceptance in Christ, obscured the radiance of his setting sun. In the same letter, written within six weeks of his departure, being then in good health, he thus affectionately addresses his eldest son in London, as if anticipating that his years were numbered :—

" This is the last day of the year, and the last letter I shall write this year. My life has been wonderfully preserved, much beyond the usual course of nature. Goodness and mercy have followed me all the days of my life, and, without the shadow of boasting, I can add, I shall dwell in the house of the Lord for ever. May the blessing of God Almighty rest on you and yours !

" Ever most affectionately yours,

" J. A. HALDANE."

It was the gracious will of his heavenly Father that he should be spared the pain of a protracted illness. There were many things which combined to make his last days and weeks and months a testimony to the strength of that assured faith which bore him onwards and upwards to the heavenly mansions. The following words, as uttered by him in one of his sermons in Northumberland, taken down by his daughter, Mrs. R. Burdon Sanderson, indicate the practical and personal feeling by which many of his closing addresses seemed to be inspired.

" 'I am crucified with Christ.' I died in his death. I rise in His resurrection. I live, yet not I; Christ liveth in me. Not I, a poor wretched rebel, whose foundation is in the dust, who dwell in a cottage of clay. It is I, the disciple of Christ, the member of Christ's body, who look forward to the glorious inheritance, incorruptible and undefiled, and which fadeth not away, when this vile body shall be fashioned like unto Christ's glorious body, when I shall have done with sin, when I shall have done with sorrow, when I shall have done with everything that could interrupt my communion with Christ, and when beyond the utmost bounds of the everlasting hills, I shall lay my crown at His feet, singing the song of Moses and the Lamb, 'Unto him that loved me, and washed me from my sins in his own blood, unto him be glory both now and for ever. Amen.' "

Another letter to his daughter-in-law, in London, was written on the 16th of January, of which the following is an extract:—

" I received your very kind letter. Through the Lord's kindness, we are all well, with the exception of Helen, who has been confined to bed with a slow fever for ten days. I trust there is no danger, yet it is an anxious time; but we are taught to be anxious for nothing, but in everything, by prayer and supplication with thanksgiving, to make our requests known to Him, who, while wielding all power in heaven and in earth, is not ashamed to call his people brethren."

After some other remarks, full of the maturity of Christian experience, he says:—

" I hope we shall also see you during the summer. Perhaps you will think I forget that I am in my eighty-third year, but I wish all future plans to be with this proviso, if the Lord will, we shall live, and do this or that. My wife and all here unite in kindest love to you and all at the Manor. Ever yours, most affectionately,

"J. A. HALDANE."

In a letter to his eldest son, written but a few days before his illness, he again observes that, although remarkably well, he does not forget that he is upon that part of Addison's Bridge of Mirza, where there are many pitfalls. Dr. Macaulay, of

Edinburgh, has addressed to Miss Haldane a graphic sketch of
"Captain James Haldane," in the year 1798, when, in the bloom
of manhood, he stood on the Calton Hill of Edinburgh, in coloured
clothes, "with his hair powdered and tied behind," preaching
with affectionate earnestness, and pressing home the truths of
the Gospel on listening thousands. He concludes his interesting reminiscences, by relating, how fifty-three years afterwards,
"on the 16th of January, 1851, I saw him for the last time at the
Committee of the Edinburgh Bible Society." "I happened,"
he adds, "to be in the chair, and he sat beside me. He closed
the meeting with a prayer, distinguished by that fervour and
propriety which always characterized his addresses to the throne
of grace. When the meeting was over, I saw him returning to
his home, leaning on the arm of your brother Robert, and this
was my last sight of the long-remembered and honoured Mr.
Haldane."

Another attack of his old enemy the gout, which was the only
complaint to which he was ever subject, became slightly perceptible on the 30th of January, when two of the grand-daughters
of his late brother dined at his house, with some other relatives.
It rather increased, so that, on the Lord's-day of the 2d of
February, he was, for the first time, after a short interval, unable
to leave the house. On that day he was to have concluded his
exposition of our Lord's farewell prayer, which had occupied him
for several weeks, and was spoken of as singularly edifying and
impressive. On Tuesday, the 4th, he became worse, but although
suffering much pain, he was wheeled into the drawing-room,
and in the evening prayed as usual with his family. The
twenty-first chapter of the Apocalypse was read in course by
his youngest son, and his whole prayer had reference to the
bright and glorious city, with its streets of gold, its walls of
jasper, and its gates of pearl. He seemed about to close, when,
as if unable to let go his hold, he once more began and prayed
most fervently that all his family, his children and his children's
children, might meet together in the new Jerusalem, and unite
in the song of Moses and the Lamb. It was not then imagined
that he had himself really entered the dark flowing river, and was

about to enter into the joy of his Lord. But his prayers were "ended." It was the last of those supplications, rich in spiritual grace and unction, which always so eminently marked the closeness of his communion with God. From the footstool of the throne of mercy he was removed to his bed, from which he was not again to rise. He survived till the 8th, but after this spoke but little. He had gout all over, and partly owing to the sedatives administered, seemed usually to slumber. But even the feverish visions of his sleep were associated with ideas of the necessity of rising to visit the sick, and with the impression of the priestly character which he sustained in his household. In his wanderings he supposed that family worship was going on in the adjoining room, and often inquired whether those around him waited for a blessing. Occasionally he listened to a few verses of the Scriptures, and intimated a brief assent to the comfort they breathed. On Friday, a passage of Scripture being repeated to him, at a time when it was uncertain whether he was able to listen, he raised himself a little, and distinctly repeated, " When Christ, who is our life, shall appear, then we shall appear with him in glory." He was then asked if he thought he was soon going home. He answered, " Perhaps not quite yet." Mrs. Haldane affectionately said, " Then you will not leave us so soon." He replied, with a smile, " To depart and be with Christ is far better." On being asked if he felt much peace and happiness, he twice repeated, " Exceeding great and precious promises." He then said, " But I must rise." Mrs. Haldane said, " You are not able to get up." He smiled and answered, " I shall be satisfied when I awake with his likeness." She said, " Is that what you meant by *rising?*" He answered, " Yes." On Saturday morning, the 8th, Dr. Alison remarked how forcibly his pulse beat, although his strength was fast sinking, and Professor Miller added, " but he is quickly passing away, like a shock of corn, fully ripe, and you have cause to be thankful that he suffers so little." During his waking intervals, he was in possession of every faculty, even to the last day. About an hour before his departure his devoted wife said, " You are going to Jesus. How

happy you will be soon." A vivid smile lighted up his countenance with the expression of ineffable joy, as he emphatically
said, "Oh! yes." After this, Dr. Innes called, and prayed by
his bedside. But it was doubtful if he heard. For about a
quarter of an hour his breathing was rather difficult. He then
became quite calm. His pulse beat almost to the last minute,
and his face was suffused with colour. Then, in the presence
of his family, he drew the last soft breath, and, in an instant,
the shadow of death passed over his face, and his ransomed
spirit entered into the joy of his Lord.

The close of such a life required no death-bed testimony, to
the sustaining power of that Gospel which had been the delight of
his heart. No man had more fully preached the freeness of the
Gospel message. No man had more strongly proclaimed, that
the oldest and most favoured Christian never entered heaven,
but upon the same self-abasing terms as the thief on the cross.
But none had, at the same time, more plainly declared his belief,
founded on much personal experience, that for the most part
men die as they have lived. His own life had been for fifty-
seven years a bright example of a life of faith; and it was truly
said of him, by his venerable friend and fellow-labourer, the
Rev. Dr. Innes, in his funeral sermon, "To him to live was
Christ, but to die was gain."

He was to have preached on the following day in Dr. Chalmers's Free Church, in the Westport, for the Rev. Mr. Tasker.
That valuable minister, on being unexpectedly informed of the
transition which had taken place, thus expressed his feelings in
writing to Mr. Haldane's son Robert:—

"*February* 8, 1851.

"I cannot give expression to the conflicting flood of emotion stirred in
my breast by the most unexpected tidings of your father's departure to
his home, especially in the circumstances in which he and I were brought
together, with the purpose he so cordially entertained of preaching to us
to-morrow. But his work is done. He is gone. He is gone to the
mountains of myrtle and of myrrh and the hill of frankincense, and the
voice says most distinctly here, 'Write, Blessed are the dead which die in
the Lord from henceforth. Yea, saith the Spirit, that they may rest
from their labours, and their works do follow them.' I am prompted

to follow him and Dr. Chalmers, whither they are met; by different, yet concurring, converging paths; both led by what each believed the Master's will, they warred a good warfare. While here even they saw but in part and prophesied but in part, but now to them that which is perfect is come, and they are, in all respects, one. How striking to us! The Lord sanctify it to our Westport congregation, and to *me!* How fitted is the thought to solemnize, that I shall stand, if spared, to-morrow, in the place that he had willingly engaged to occupy. Surely the Lord has said, ' It was well that it was in thy heart, but come thou up hither, thy son shall build me an house.' And what a memoir will your father's be! He has died in harness, speaking and writing and preaching to the last. Called away to-day, and only in the beginning of this week entertaining the prospect of preaching in the Westport on to-morrow. But his reward is on high! Sustained in the field till the age of " eighty-three !"

It was remarked in the Edinburgh newspapers, that his funeral, which took place on the 14th of February, " although intended to be strictly private, drew together a large concourse of the citizens of Edinburgh, anxious to do homage to his public character and private worth. No man was less disposed to court the applause of men, or indulge the semblance of ostentation ; but the respect shown to his memory by the ministers and members of different religious communities in this city, is a noble demonstration of Christian sympathy with all that is exemplary in a long and consistent career of Christian devotedness." It is stated in another journal, that, besides the mourning coaches, containing the members of his family and private friends, there were no less than 600 ministers, elders, and private members of the different religious communities in Edinburgh. The Presbytery of the Free Church, in a body, headed by the Rev. Dr. Candlish, with their students, joined the procession in George-street. The windows of the houses through which the procession passed were thronged with spectators. From the gate of the West Churchyard to the Church rows of clergymen lined each side of the principal avenue, and uncovered as the coffin passed. There were ministers both of the Established, Free, and Secession Pres-byterian Churches, as well as Episcopalians, Baptists, and Independents, who thus united to pay a voluntary tribute of respect to the public services of a man, who, with his brother, had been honoured to do so much for the revival of religion in Scotland. The "Scotsman," an exclusively political journal, remarks, that such a spontaneous tribute of respect "has rarely been paid to any private individual;" and another, that, excepting the funerals of Dr. Chalmers and Dr. Thomson, "there has not been such an unsolicited demonstration of public feeling on any like occasion."

Many little incidents indicated the reverence and love in which he was held. One aged member of his own Church, since deceased, had placed himself, with the rest of the members, in advance of the hearse, but on account of his age was urged to take a seat in one of the mourning coaches. He declined, alleging that "his proper place was at the feet of his pastor."* Mr. Haldane had been the means of leading

* A remarkable anecdote was lately communicated, on the authority of one personally acquainted with the parties and circumstances. It relates to a dream, and is, therefore, only mentioned as a pleasing instance of the indelible impression which Mr. James Haldane has left on the hearts of many to whom as a preacher he was the messenger of grace. The communication runs thus:—"Perhaps you may remember Mrs. Crystal, of Edinburgh, who was, many years ago, a member of the Tabernacle Church, and to whom the ministry of its faithful pastor had been blessed when she was only twelve years of age. Having lately a slight cold, she was advised to remain for a day in bed, but was in very good spirits, and not in a state to occasion any anxiety. In the night she awoke her daughter, who slept in the same room, and said, 'I am sorry to disturb you, but I have had a delightful dream. I have before dreamed of seeing those who were in heaven, but never before heard one speak.' She then related how she had dreamed that Mr. James Haldane, through whom she first received the Gospel, appeared to her, and said, 'I am sent to desire you to come to a more genial clime. My message to you is, "Come up hither!"' With a smile, he added, 'You will not regret leaving this world, when you enter upon the glory about to be revealed to you.' Mrs. Crystal then said it was a delightful interview, and one never to be forgotten. She went to sleep again, and next day was well and in good spirits, but on the morning following she died in an instant, without suffering. It had been her daily prayer, that when she died it might be without a struggle, and her request was granted." It would be an act of ill-judged enthusiasm to attempt to build an argument on any dream, but the facts being well authenticated, they are, at all events, both curious and interesting.

him to Christ, when, more than fifty years before, he had wandered into the Circus. There were others who gathered round the grave, not connected with his congregation, who bore the same testimony to the blessed effects of his faithful preaching. On the Lord's-day succeeding his departure, honourable reference was made to his removal in many of the pulpits of Edinburgh by clergymen of almost every religious denomination, Presbyterian, Episcopalian, Baptist, and Independent. The character of Caleb, who "followed the Lord fully," was the subject chosen by the Rev. Christopher Anderson, whose early recollections of his departed friend enabled him to supply many interesting anecdotes of his power as a preacher. The Rev. Dr. Paterson, long so much distinguished as the agent of the British and Foreign Bible Society in Russia, who had originally studied with Dr. Ebenezer Henderson at Mr. Haldane's seminary, and been sent out together as missionaries by the Tabernacle Church, thus wrote :—

. . . "I lament that I should have necessarily, from these circumstances, been absent, as my absence must have been noticed by all present who knew the connexion which had formerly subsisted between your dear father and myself. It is true, our intercourse has rather been interrupted for some time past, by our taking different sides about the British and Foreign Bible Society; but my high regard and esteem for your dear father was never interrupted. I can never forget his eminent services in the Gospel of Christ, and his kindness to myself. I shall cherish a kind recollection of his memory till death, and then I hope, through grace, to join him in glory, where uninterrupted harmony and love will ever reign among all the inhabitants of that blessed place. My prayer is, that a double portion of his spirit may rest on all his dear family, and that they all may be followers of him as he was of Christ, and join him never to be more separated."

Nor were such testimonies confined to Edinburgh, or to those only who knew him in Scotland. An eloquent tribute from the pen of the Rev. Dr. Campbell was published in the "British Banner." The following, by the Rev. Dr. Henry Burder, the son of the founder of the Tract Society, and the author of the "Village Sermons," appeared in the "Evangelical Magazine :"—

"But few men, and but few ministers, whom I have known, have attained such a grade of Christian character, or commanded from all classes such a tribute of the homage of the heart. His matured pro-

ficiency in the knowledge of the Scriptures, his enlightened conscientious-
ness, his Christian dignity and decision, his unsullied consistency of
character, and his persevering energy in doing good, will not soon be
forgotten, and ought to have the force of an attractive example. The
mellowed excellencies of the Christian character appeared to great advantage in the autumn of his peaceful and useful life. He seemed exempted
beyond the ordinary lot of the aged from the infirmities and sufferings of
protracted life; and as to him ' to live was Christ,' we are well assured
that ' to die has proved ineffable gain.' "

Another tribute of affection, addressed to his second son,
from Colonel Anderson, Commandant of the Field Batteries
at Woolwich, is the more interesting as contrasting with the
recollections of the scene at North Berwick, related in a former
part of these Memoirs :—

" The first impulse on hearing of the translation of your honoured
father, was to start for the north, and have the privilege of following the
earthly remains of the man of God to the tomb. . . . I cannot well
define the reverence with which I regarded your beloved father. Few
men have been as useful in their generation, and his name will be held in
grateful remembrance by very many. It was a great privilege to be even
known to such a man, and how great was the honour to be the son of
such a man ! The grace of God was surely seen in the departed saint.
A long and eminently consistent life put to silence the foolishness of the
adversary, and I believe many ransomed spirits are now around the throne,
who have welcomed him to the heavenly mansion as the blessed instrument
of turning them from darkness to light, and leading them to a knowledge
of saving truth as exhibited in the Gospel. I have long been persuaded
that your father and uncle were specially raised up to be the means of
reviving the Church in their native land."

Mr. Haldane's relative, the Rev. James O'Hara, of Coleraine,
says of him : " His views on the believer's union with Christ
have shown me more of the HOLINESS necessarily connected
with FAITH than any Commentary that has ever come in my
way." Another eminent clergyman, the Rev. Alexander Irwin,
Rector of Armagh, and Secretary to the Primate of Ireland,
thus wrote, after reading a sketch of his life copied from the
Scotch newspaper into the " Record : "—

" *February* 28, 1851.

" MY DEAR FRIEND,—The 'Record' brought me the account of your
venerated father's removal from earth to heaven. I have read with deep

interest the sketch of his early labours, and the great blessing which attended them.

"It brought vividly to my mind the long and pleasant walk I had with him and dear Dawson and yourself one summer's night, returning from dining at Mr. Hamilton's at Streatham, when he gave me an account of his visiting Donaghadee many years, it seemed almost ages, ago, and his efforts at that time to make known the Gospel in that dead part of Ireland. I cannot but consider it amongst the many advantages which I derived from Dawson's friendship, that it was the means of bringing me acquainted with so eminent a servant of God,—one of the worthies of that ' time of refreshing from the Lord' with which this part of the world was visited, and which the new generation now growing up will look at with wonder and great interest. And now when trials of a different kind, arising from Puseyism and Neology, are gathering round us, the example of that boldness for the truth and persevering energy in its behalf, and cleaving to first principles, and caring nought for the revilings and contempt of men, which were so conspicuous in his character, are a valuable help to those who come after him in the war which is not to cease ' until He come whose right it is to reign over the world.' " *

---

* The following extracts from the Edinburgh "Witness" are important, as a testimony to the character and effects of the labours of the two brothers, free from the bias of denominational prejudice :—

" Till the appearance of these Memoirs, the younger reading public, we believe, were not aware of the *greatness* of James Haldane, nor of the influence and extent of those Evangelistic labours which he extended to almost every corner of Scotland, and to the farthest Orkneys. He was raised up to do a great work, just before the revival of Evangelical religion dawned in the Establishment; and this work he prosecuted with an indomitable will, an intrepid meekness, an energy not to be broken by labour, and with a success for which Scotland will not fail to hold him in everlasting remembrance. The public, from his powerful writings, have been more familiar with the name of Robert Haldane, who was more prominent as the theologian, while James was more prominent as the successful preacher. Robert comes before us from the moment of his conversion, as a memorable instance of devotedness to God. Having determined to sell his beautiful estate of Airthrey with a view to devote his money, his time, and his life to the missionary cause in India, and being compelled to forego his purpose by the opposition of the East India Company, he, along with the intended partners of his enterprise, concentrated on his native land those efforts which he had meant for India. The effect on Scotland was astonishing. There can be no doubt that during the eight years when the party moved on as an unbroken phalanx,

Another letter refers to the remarkable faith in the resurrection which was exhibited by the dying saint amidst all the weakness and wandering incident to approaching dissolution.

" Mr. Haldane's last words were remarkable, and showed strong faith in the resurrection,—a subject exceedingly difficult to realize, doubtless, in the article of death. It is easy to believe anything, while it is not a question, but to believe that we shall rise again assuredly, when we are just going down into the grave, requires a faith like Abraham's, who, against hope, believed in hope,—a faith of His working, who is indeed almighty to save,—in a word, a faith of omnipotence. It is promised, however, that in the hour of need we shall know the exceeding greatness of His power toward *us who believe*, according to the working of that mighty power which He wrought in Christ when he raised him from the

multiplying their tabernacles, and pouring out their reinforcements of ardent Evangelists, they stirred to its depths the quiescent mind of Scotland. Long before this period the Seceders had turned their arms upon themselves. And in 1818 a similar disruption in the party of the Haldanes enfeebled, if it did not terminate, their aggressive progress. In attempting the reproduction of apostolic usages, they lost themselves in that Serbonian bog where armies whole have sunk, and were divided in twain. But they had done their work, and reached their culminating point. And now, within the pale of the Establishment, the sovereign Spirit, who bloweth where He listeth, was fostering that revival which afterwards took such rapid strides towards ascendancy.

" Viewed in his capacity of theologian, we have long regarded Robert Haldane, with all the disadvantages of non-professional education, as one of the GREATEST THEOLOGIANS of whom Scotland can boast, and in one important point of view,—in his uncompromising advocacy of sound doctrine,—the very type of the man of the age. Beyond all question, his Commentary on the Epistle to the Romans is the ablest work and the soundest exposition of that central book of Scripture which has yet appeared abroad or at home during the present century. In solid worth, —even though we should admit that a few isolated passages are strained, —and in the force with which he establishes the great doctrines of imputed righteousness, and its connexion with sanctification and the sovereignty of God, it immeasurably outweighs all that Germany, with its high pretensions, has yet produced. But if there be one service more important than another that Robert Haldane has performed, we should name his labours in the great cause of plenary inspiration, the magnitude of which is every day more fully coming into view."

dead. The faith of Christ's resurrection is the life of our spirit, and the death of unbelief. It strikes a blow at our incredulity which no other weapon can inflict."

In the letter last inserted, the writer expresses his admiration of the faith which enabled the dying saint, even in the hour of dissolution, to look with assured confidence to a glorious resurrection. It was an assurance granted to both of these brothers, and one which gilded the sunset of their career with a hope full of immortality. Was this, then, a mere passing feeling, dependent upon impulse or excitement? Is it to be numbered amongst those transient "fantasies" at which modern unbelievers have sneered? Was it a faith such as that which, according to Gibbon, enables "enthusiasts" to dream of "hallelujahs beyond the clouds?" Both were men of strong intellect, of manly independence, of calm judgment, and, as Dr. Pye Smith said of the elder, addicted beyond most to "cool reasoning." Their zeal was steady rather than impulsive, and their faith established, not on the shifting sands of a dubious sentimentalism, but on the enduring basis of the Rock of Ages. In early manhood, a great moral change passed over both nearly at the same time, but without any communication with each other. It had in it nothing that was sudden, nothing that was imaginative, nothing even that was extraordinary. It was a change produced by the calm and candid investigation of the lofty claims of that holy book, which previously they had called the Word of God, "from prejudice of education rather than from any rational conviction."

But when the great truth found entrance to their hearts; when by the teaching of the Holy Spirit, promised to all who ask, they received the Bible as being, what it assumes to be, the Word and work of God; when they came to discern the grandeur of that Gospel which shines in all its pages, and beheld Him to whom the Law, the prophets, the evangelists, and the apostles, all bear witness; then faith in Christ became a living and energizing principle. In Him they were a new creation; old things had passed away; Christianity was now a reality, exalting and hallowing all their faculties and all their affections; the world no longer maintained its empire over their affections; and they devoted their lives to the service of God with a zeal which can be stigmatized as enthusiasm only by those who have neither felt the constraining power of Divine forgiveness, nor, like them, examined and ascertained the deep and solid foundations of the Christian faith. Upon their principles and with their convictions, it was "a reasonable service," to surrender themselves to Him who had "washed them in his blood;" and as these principles became more firmly settled, and these convictions strengthened by communion with God and the study of his Word, the first impulses of youthful earnestness were approved of and sanctioned by the sober gravity of maturer age. They held fast the beginning of their confidence stedfast to the end, and discerned with joy the glorious light, of Him who is the resurrection and the life, streaming athwart the dark valley of the shadow of death. This was the secret of their triumph over the king of terrors, and of the calm satisfaction with which they regarded the termination of their course. When Gibbon was contemplating the approach of death, he candidly admitted that "the prospect of futurity was dark and doubtful," and that "the abbreviation of time, and the failure of hope, must always tinge with a browner shade the evening of life." He therefore tried to draw some comfort from the thought of his position in the world, which he regarded as "the lucky chance of an unit against thousands." He might, indeed, as he says, have been condemned to poverty, and born a savage, or a slave. But of this he was "willingly ignorant," that the privileges of which he boasts were not the result of accident, but of God's sovereignty, which, if properly improved, should have led him to repent and believe in that gracious revelation, against which he had so long levelled his melancholy sarcasms. It is no marvel that, to him, the objects of the dying Christian's hope appeared only as the dreams of enthusiasm. For him, alas! the palm, the harp, and the crown, or the harmonies of heaven's hallelujahs, possessed no charms. It was otherwise with those who regarded as their Saviour, the Judge who is to sit upon the great white throne, and around whom the swelling anthems of everlasting praise shall be for ever new.

Considering the end, as well as the beginning of their faith, it is not surprising that both of the Haldanes clung to the Bible with a fidelity that could never be shaken. To assert its Divine origin, to uphold its full inspiration, to protect it against those who would either add to the words of God or profanely take them away, was one great object for which they lived and laboured. To defend its doctrines against every blast of heresy and every taint of error was another grand aim which they steadily pursued with consistency and courage, from the outset to the termination of their career. Against the withering spirit of Romanistic formalism and the infidel tendencies of German Neology they uplifted the banner of Divine truth. But, earnestly as they contended for the faith once delivered to the saints, their exertions for the diffusion of the Gospel at home and abroad, were still more remarkable. They taught, as well as vindicated, the great truths of Christianity, and the results of their efforts stretch into eternity.

The attention which at one time they directed to the revival of a primitive form of Church polity in Scotland, is the only part of the career of the Haldanes in regard to which success was not proportioned to their efforts. Perhaps it was necessary that there should be something practically and visibly to remind those who chiefly revered their character, and marked their self-devotion, that they were but feeble and fallible men, able to do nothing of themselves, and owing all their might to God. But even in these matters they were enabled by grace to exhibit their desire with singleness of heart, to cleave to the Lord, to sur-mount the temptations of sectarian aggrandisement, and to renounce their own wisdom. Too many Christians look to the opinions of men to guide their course. They looked only to God. It was his praise they desired to gain; and the praise of men, whether in the Church or in the world, as a motive of action, they resolutely cast behind their backs.

But it is not intended to write a panegyric. Their character will be found stamped on their acts; and whether we regard the labours of the elder brother for the revival of Christianity on the Continent of Europe, or the labours of both in their native land, it has been said with truth that they have left the impress of their name on the age in which they lived. Robert Haldane's success at Geneva and at Montauban, is a landmark in the history of Continental Protestantism. It would be difficult to name one, since the days of Whitfield, whose preaching was more signally blessed to the conversion of sinners than that of James Haldane. Their example and success, both at home and abroad, is an encouragement to all who are willing and able, with equal boldness, zeal, and perseverance, in reliance upon the Divine blessing, to maintain the great truths of salvation, and make known, without compromise, the free Gospel of the grace of God. Both were content for a time to be sneered at by the world, and accounted madmen for the sake of Christ. Both dedicated intellectual talents of no common order to the same cause—the one by his preaching, but still more by his writings; the other, by his writings, but far more by his preaching, taught and vindicated the same great truths. In all their undertakings for the promotion of religion they advanced with united zeal and strength. Although each was distinguished for a determined will, a strict adherence to his own views of duty, strong individuality, and uncompromising independence, there subsisted between both a harmony of design and oneness of spirit, so remarkable, that never during their long and honourable course of mutual co-operation, was there one jarring feeling to disturb their efforts for the common object they so consistently pursued. That object was the glory of Christ and the salvation of their fellow-men; and now that the career of both is closed, and death has affixed his seal on the record of their earthly labours, the simplicity of their holy aim, the depth of their hallowed benevolence, and the stedfastness of their lofty principle, stand more plainly revealed. From the moment they undertook to devote their lives to labour in the Gospel, there was no looking back to scenes of past enjoyment. Wealth, honour, worldly renown, and reputation, were all counted but loss; nor did the seducing hope of earning a name and a place in the Christian world, ever tempt their ambition. Their single desire was WHOLLY TO FOLLOW THE LORD.

# INDEX.

# LIST OF PUBLICATIONS BY THE LATE ROBERT HALDANE.

# LIST OF PUBLICATIONS BY THE LATE

## J. A. HALDANE.

Many widely-circulated religious tracts are not included in the above list, such as " The Great Salvation," " Salvation to the Guilty," " On the Atonement," " Address from a Stranger." Mr. J. A. Haldane also conducted the " Scripture Magazine" from 1809-13, and the " Christian Quarterly Magazine" from 1832-7, in both of which are many valuable contributions from his pen, and particularly many important Notes on difficult passages of Scripture.

## ERRATA.

Page 94, for "Suffer to take," read "Suffer *him*."

  ,, 343, for "1801," read "1804."

  ,, 462, for "Du Pasquei*l*," read "Du Pasquie*r*."

  ,, 506, for "1819," read "1818."

  ,, 609, seventh line, dele the words "producing," and "an impression."

  ,, 602, for "Herm*a*neutics," read "Herm*e*neutics."

  ,, 584, for "agap*e*," read "agap*æ*."

  ,, 637, for "Rev. Mr. Ferguson, the Free Church minister of *Stirling*," read "of the Bridge of Allan."

MACINTOSH, PRINTER,
GREAT NEW-STREET, LONDON.